Rethinking Economic Development, Growth, and Institutions

Rethinking Economic Development, Growth, and Institutions

Jaime Ros

OXFORD
UNIVERSITY PRESS

OXFORD
UNIVERSITY PRESS

Great Clarendon Street, Oxford, OX2 6DP,
United Kingdom

Oxford University Press is a department of the University of Oxford.
It furthers the University's objective of excellence in research, scholarship,
and education by publishing worldwide. Oxford is a registered trade mark of
Oxford University Press in the UK and in certain other countries

First Edition published in 2013
Impression: 1

Published in the United States of America by Oxford University Press
198 Madison Avenue, New York, NY 10016, United States of America

British Library Cataloguing in Publication Data
Data available

ISBN 978-0-19-968480-9 (Hbk.)
      978-0-19-968481-6 (Pbk.)

As printed and bound by
CPI Group (UK) Ltd, Croydon, CR0 4YY

To Adriana, my companion, and to our children,
Alejandra, Diego, and Pablo

Preface

This book is a sequel to *Development Theory and the Economics of Growth*, published in 2000 with the aim to vindicate the theoretical insights and accumulated empirical knowledge of classical development economics and to integrate them into the mainstream of modern growth economics. The growth and development field has expanded in the last twelve years in welcome directions that aim to deepen our understanding of the fundamental determinants of comparative development. This new book evaluates these new directions, including developments in endogenous growth theory and economic geography as well as the rise and challenge of the new institutional economics, in the light of the earlier, classical contributions to development theory.

As with the previous book, the professional economist and researcher will find in the present one original theses on the contributions that early development theory can make to the research program of the economics of growth and comparative development. Graduate and advanced undergraduate students in economics will find a balanced theoretical treatment and an assessment of the empirical evidence provided by new and earlier approaches to economic growth and development.

The elaboration of this book has drawn very heavily on my teaching activity over the past two decades at both the University of Notre Dame and the Universidad Nacional Autónoma de México (UNAM), my research over the years on the growth performance of developing countries, especially in Latin America, in the postwar period, and a long-time interest in classical development economics. While the book has had a very long gestation period, it is only over the past two years, with the generous support of the Faculty of Economics at UNAM, that it has taken its present shape.

I am grateful to the many students that provided feedback on my courses. Very special thanks are due to three students, Santiago Capraro, David Maldonado, and Luis Monroy Gómez Franco, who in addition to their feedback on many aspects of the book provided excellent and enthusiastic research assistance.

I am indebted to many colleagues who commented on all or parts of the manuscript. Yilmaz Akyuz, Luiz Carlos Bresser-Pereira, Ha-Joon Chang,

Amitava Dutt, Carlos Ibarra, Jorge Katz, Alejandro Montoya, Juan Carlos Moreno-Brid, Emilio Ocampo, José Antonio Ocampo, Carlo Panico, Ignacio Perrotini, Gabriel Porcile, Martín Rapetti, and Claudia Schatán provided comments and many suggestions for improvements. The book also benefited from comments by participants in seminars at UNAM and lectures at El Colegio Mexiquense, Facultad Latinoamericana de Ciencias Sociales (FLACSO), Instituto Politécnico Nacional, and the Banco Nacional de Desarrollo Económico y Social (BNDES) in Brazil. I am grateful to Leonardo Lomelí, director of the Faculty of Economics at UNAM for his encouragement and support in this project. My thanks go also to Adam Swallow, Daniel Bourner, and their team at OUP, for an excellent job in converting a manuscript into a finished book and continuous support and patience throughout the process.

Table of Contents

List of Figures

List of Tables

Introduction

In the introduction to *Development Theory and the Economics of Growth* published in 2000, I described this book as a collection of essays in "trespassing" between two disciplines: development economics and growth theory. I saw the need for it given the lack of interactions between these two fields of economics that should have been one and the same. They were not. Growth theory and development economics continued to be distant cousins, and occasionally even hostile to one another.

A lot has happened in the two fields since 1999 when *Development Theory and the Economics of Growth* went to press. With Hall and Jones's 1999 paper on the role of "social infrastructure" in economic development, a big push was given to an expanding literature on institutionalist explanations of cross country differences in income per capita. At about the same time, there was also a remarkable revival of interest in the role of geographical advantages and disadvantages in economic development. Jeffrey Sachs and associates, in particular, asserted a powerful role for geography in the explanation of modern development and underdevelopment (see Gallup, Sachs, and Mellinger, 1999; Sachs 2000 and 2003). Soon after, an institutionalist counterattack followed, led by Acemoglu, Johnson, and Robinson (2001 and 2002), Easterly and Levine (2003) and Rodrik, Subramanian, and Trebbi (2004). More generally, the new institutional economics made enormous progress. In 2012, Acemoglu and Robinson published *Why Nations Fail?*, a book drawing on growth theory, economic history and political science that is bound to profoundly influence the field of comparative development. At the same time, "institutionalist growth empirics" came under attack from different perspectives (see, in particular, Chang 2011).

Alongside developments in the new institutionalist economics and the geography versus institutions controversy, attention also focused on other "deep determinants" of income levels and growth rates. The previous consensus in the endogenous growth literature on the adverse effects of inequality on economic growth was shaken by contributions by Forbes (2000), Barro (2000), and Banerjee and Duflo (2003). Engerman and Sokoloff (2002), providing a historical comparative perspective on the topic, and Easterly (2007) tended, in contrast, to reassert the previous conclusions. The sacred role of trade openness was also put into question. Rodriguez and Rodrik (2001) scrutinized the research on the role of trade policies in growth and shook the field by demonstrating that conventional wisdom on the effects of trade openness lacked solid empirical foundations. New evidence on the developmental effects of natural resource abundance by Lederman and Maloney (2007, 2008) also questioned previous results in Gelb (1988), Auty (1990, 2001), and Sachs and Warner (1995, 2001) that viewed the "natural resource curse" as a major factor explaining differences in growth performance across countries.

In general, all these contributions generated stronger interactions between growth theory and development economics as the two fields moved in parallel in the direction of searching for the fundamental determinants of comparative development. Other developments that contributed to bring the two fields closer to each other include the expanding theoretical literature on multiple equilibria and poverty traps models (see Azariadis and Stachurski, 2005, for a survey) and related policy debates on the kind of poverty traps prevailing in less developed countries. In particular, Easterly's 2006 criticism of Sachs's 2005 call for a massive increase in international aid to poor countries, reviewed in Chapter 3, is reminiscent of controversies in early development economics on the role of low savings and increasing returns to capital versus that of institutional weaknesses in keeping low-income countries in poverty and stagnation.

Developments in endogenous growth theory, with contributions such as Aghion and Howitt (1998 and subsequent writing), clarified the ultimate sources of technological progress and vindicated Schumpeter's approach and his notion of "creative destruction" as discussed in Chapter 5. The role of effective demand in economic growth has also been clarified in various papers; see, in particular, Bhaduri (2006), Dutt (2006), Dutt and Ros (2007), Rada (2007), and Ocampo, Rada, and Taylor (2009, ch. 8). Although unfortunately the contributions in this field have had so far a very limited impact on mainstream growth theory, recent developments in growth empirics, as we shall see in Chapter 11, increasingly recognize the role of demand in long-term growth. These two developments, in Schumpeterian and Keynesian growth theory respectively, have much in common, in particular in the attempt to endogeneize technological progress, but give a very different emphasis to supply side and demand side influences on productivity growth (as we shall see in Chapter 11). Other, more empirically oriented works over the past decade, include important books by Amsden (2001), Chang (2002), Reinert (2007), and Ocampo, Rada and Taylor (2009) that draw on economic history and a theoretical approach in the tradition of classical development economics.

As a result of these developments, it is possible today to go beyond a collection of essays in "trespassing" and give a much more unified account of the two disciplines than twelve years ago. Yet, despite this welcome trend, a major thesis of my 2000 book still holds: classical development theory, as I referred there to the early contributions to development economics, continues to be neglected by the mainstream. This is a puzzle. This approach had a lot to say about why poor countries are poor and what they need to do in order to escape underdevelopment. It is indeed puzzling why, in attempting to address the same issues, modern growth theory and, just as much, the new institutional economics, have largely ignored classical development theory and more recent contributions in this tradition.[1]

Most of this introduction is about why this is so. The rest of the book is an effort to show why the contributions of the pioneers of development economics had many insights that are not only very valuable but can be made perfectly intelligible to researchers working on the economics of growth. After explaining what I mean by modern growth theory and classical development economics, I give an overview of the book's main themes.

Since the mid 1980s, after two decades of quasi-inactivity in the field, the economics of growth became again the subject of intense theoretical and empirical research. This renewed effort took initially two different directions. Some adapted and extended the neoclassical growth model as formalized by Robert Solow and Trevor Swan in the mid fifties, while retaining the assumptions of constant returns to scale and exogenous technical progress. Others have taken more radical departures from the neoclassical approach by bringing in increasing returns to scale and attempting to model technological change. This last is endogenous growth theory. In both cases, and this is perhaps the most novel feature of the reawakened field, these efforts try to explain the process of economic growth in developed and developing countries alike within a unified analytical framework. Important questions such as: Why are some nations poorer than others and why the economies of some countries grow so much faster than others, were put at the center of the research agenda of mainstream growth theory.

This revival of growth economics, or at least most of it until the recent ascent of the new institutional economics, proceeded on the rather astonishing premise that before the mid-1980s the only answers to those questions

---

[1] An example is the influential book by Barro and Sala-i-Martin (1995) which synthesizes contributions to old and new growth theory. The only reference there to early development theory is to Lewis' (1954) classic article which, strangely, is regarded as a big push model. There are, no doubt, exceptions and the contributions of that early period have been the object of a renewed interest with the revival of growth economics. I have already referred to the literature on poverty traps and multiple equilibria (see, in particular, Murphy, Shleifer and Vishny, 1989; Krugman, 1992, 1995; Rodrik, 1994; Ciccone and Matsuyama, 1996; Rodriguez-Clare, 1996; Skott and Ros, 1997; Ros, 2000; Azariadis and Stachurski, 2005).

were to be found in the neoclassical growth model. The premise is astonishing for at least two reasons. First, because some fifty years ago a then new field of economic theory emerged aiming to answer similar questions, to address issues about the persistence of underdevelopment and to search for remedies to overcome poverty. The nature of the issues addressed by the pioneers of development economics—Rosenstein-Rodan, Nurkse, Prebisch, Hirschman, and Leibenstein among others—forced the new field to rely on a paradigm built upon notions of imperfect competition, increasing returns and labor surpluses, which today are used extensively but were then poorly integrated, or altogether alien, to the established body of economic theory.

Second, and somewhat ironically given its central position in the economics of growth today, the Solow model was not meant primarily to answer those questions but rather to provide a solution to some perceived difficulties in growth theory at the time (Harrod's knife edge instability and the adjustment of the warranted to the natural rate of growth in the Harrod-Domar model). Having the neoclassical growth model explain differences in income levels and growth rates across countries requires a number of additional assumptions that Solow himself probably did not have in mind: in a nutshell, that economies differ among themselves only in their initial capital-labor ratios, savings rates and population growth rates.

This inadequacy of traditional neoclassical economics is perhaps one reason why development economics had already taken a distinctive approach a decade before the rise to dominance of neoclassical growth theory. Whether one could make fruitful empirical generalizations about the economic experience of developing countries or not, it was clear that the stylized facts on which traditional growth theory focused—with its emphasis on the stability of the capital-output ratio, savings rates and income shares—had little relevance to the experience of developing countries. Lewis (1954), for example, had tried to account for the trend increase, rather than the stability, of saving and investment rates in the course of economic development. Given its purposes, growth theory tended to adopt a very high level of aggregation, often an economy with one sector producing one good. The striking and persistent presence of dualism (technological and organizational) in underdeveloped countries, led development economics to operate at a lower level of aggregation, with at least two sectors using different technologies.

In addition, growth theory soon became concentrated on the analysis of steady states in which the main economic variables expand at the same rate. Because this analysis did not fit well the experience of developing countries, development theory had to focus instead on disequilibrium states and the process of transition from one steady state to another. As Rosenstein-Rodan (1984, pp. 207–8) argued: "...an analysis of the disequilibrium growth process is what is essential for understanding economic development problems. The

Economic Journal article of 1943 attempted to study the dynamic path towards equilibrium, not merely the conditions which must be satisfied at the point of equilibrium."

This does not mean that development theory was uninterested in steady states. It became concerned, however, with a particular kind of steady state quite alien to conventional growth theory: low level equilibrium traps which are, as the name suggests, equilibria that are locally stable (small departures from it generate forces that bring the economy back to the equilibrium state) but globally unstable, so that large shocks can cause a cumulative departure from the original equilibrium. Leibenstein (1957, p. 187), for example, stated: "The crucial aspect of our theory has to do with an explanation of why the subsistence equilibrium state should possess stability in the small but not in the large."

This leads us to a very important aspect. To the pioneers of development theory, underdevelopment appeared as a situation characterized by a lack of capital—which was consistent with labor receiving lower wages than in developed countries—but also, and this was the puzzle, by a low rate of return to capital. For Nurkse, for example, the scarcity of capital was "at the very centre of the problem of development in economically backward countries. The so-called "underdeveloped" areas, as compared with the advanced, are underequipped with capital in relation to their population and natural resources" (Nurkse, 1953, p. 1). This lack of capital resulted from a low capacity to save, given the low level of real income, but also from the "weakness of investment incentives" that had its source in a low rate of return to capital (Nurkse, 1953, ch. 1). The paradox of both capital and labor receiving lower returns, and the surprising conclusion that the lack of capital may have to be attributed to a low profit rate, understandably led to the search for a novel analytical framework, as anyone familiar with the modern controversies over neoclassical growth theory would probably agree.

This approach generated a model, or rather a set of economic growth models, that departs in two ways from the early neoclassical approach to growth theory.[2] The first difference refers to increasing returns to scale and the associated technological and pecuniary externalities. In his 1943 article on the problems of industrialization in Eastern and South-Eastern Europe, and in later contributions, Rosenstein-Rodan was probably the economist that most radically departed from traditional theory in this respect. Nurkse, drawing on Adam Smith and Allyn Young, stressed also the effects associated with increasing returns.

---

[2] "Avant la lettre", one might add, since most of these writings preceded the neoclassical model of growth at least as formalized by Solow in the mid-fifties.

The second departure refers to an elastic labor supply arising from the presence of labor surplus. Early views on underdevelopment as a situation characterized by a small capital endowment in relation to available labor supplies led to the conclusion that the elasticity of the labor supply in these conditions was likely to be higher than in developed economies that have much higher capital endowments per worker. With a low aggregate capital-labor ratio, the marginal product of labor at full employment in the capital-using sector would be so low that a fraction of the labor force would remain employed in a non-capitalist or subsistence sector, using technologies with negligible capital intensity. Lewis was the economist that developed and emphasized the labor surplus assumption.

These two ingredients—increasing returns and labor surplus—were present from the "beginning" in Rosenstein-Rodan (1943), as Rodan rightly claimed in his 1984 contribution (Rosenstein-Rodan, 1984).[3] A moderate dose of increasing returns and an elastic labor supply can together generate multiple equilibria so that depending on initial conditions the economy can get stuck in a development trap. This was not the only development trap model in the early literature but it is, as this book argues, the most interesting and relevant one for the present state of growth theory.

1. Five Themes

Modern growth theory and classical development economics

The book develops five major themes. The first is the relation between modern growth theory and classical development economics. Just as in macroeconomic theory the neoclassical orthodoxy and its Keynesian critics differ among themselves in relation to the existence or strength of a spontaneous tendency to a full employment equilibrium in a laissez faire economy, in modern growth theory, the neoclassical orthodoxy and its non-neoclassical critics can be said to differ among themselves with respect to a tendency to convergence in income per capita levels across countries in a laissez faire, globalized world economy. The non-neoclassical criticisms come from recent endogenous growth theory, the other major brand of modern growth economics that has departed from old neoclassical theory in various directions. Classical development theorists, well before the convergence properties of the Solow-Swan model were fully explored, were also in the non-neoclassical camp. While neoclassical growth theory and empirics emphasize the conditional tendency to convergence to a unique steady state as rates of return to

---

[3] I believe it fair to say that only Rosenstein-Rodan fully perceived the general equilibrium implications of these two assumptions taken together.

capital would tend to be higher in low-income, capital-scarce countries, classical development theory took as its starting point the "paradox of underdevelopment", the fact that returns to *all* factors of production tended to be lower in low-income countries, a fact that can trap poor countries in a low level equilibrium and prevent convergence to a high level equilibrium.

Yet, despite the relevance of the analysis and implications of classical development theory, the recent wave of theoretical and empirical research on economic growth has generally ignored, as already indicated, these earlier contributions by development theory. I shall argue that this neglect is one reason why the lively controversies on convergence, technical progress and increasing returns, between followers of the Solow model and endogenous growth theorists, appear at times to be in a dead end, confused by an all or nothing situation: between the assumptions of constant returns to scale and the dramatically increasing returns to scale involved in the assumption of constant (or increasing) returns to capital.

This debate appears to have missed a simple implication of early development theory: that a moderate dose of increasing returns to scale combined with the presence of labor surplus can make a dramatic difference to the neoclassical model, a difference that modifies its transitional dynamics in a way that can overcome the long recognized empirical shortcomings of the Solow model[4] while, at the same time, being free from some of the theoretical and empirical objections that have been raised against the new brand of endogenous growth models. As a result, we shall argue, the key contributions of classical development economics provide an approach to the problem of economic development that is more general and more promising empirically than those adopted in either old or new growth theory. The corollary of this argument is that it may be essential to draw much more heavily on the very rich past of development theory if the ongoing research effort is to tackle satisfactorily the formidable task that it has set for itself.

The scope of classical development theory, openness, and the big push argument

A second theme refers to the scope of early writing on development theory. We shall argue that this analytical framework can help us think about a much wider variety of development problems than those to which it was originally applied. Development traps can arise under a broad set of circumstances

---

[4] Chapter 2 addresses the empirical shortcomings of the Solow model. Mankiw (1995) summarizes them well by saying that the predictions of Solow model: 1) understate differences in incomes per capita across countries; 2) overstate the rate of convergence to the steady state; 3) overstate differences in the rates of return on capital among capital-rich and capital-poor countries.

involving increasing returns, demand elasticities and factor supply elasticities. These circumstances are not confined to low levels of economic development. Because the slow rate of accumulation in the trap is due to a low rate of return to capital, the approach has greater generality than other poverty trap models which rely, for example, on vicious circles between income and savings or population growth. The framework can be fruitfully applied to any situation in which a combination of demand and factor supply elasticities together with a dose of increasing returns in new industries interact to hold back the "inducement to invest".

Moreover, those circumstances are not confined to a closed system. Although sometimes formulated or illustrated with a closed economy, the argument survives the extension to the case of an open economy. Interestingly, opening the economy to trade and capital movements introduces important differences and modifies the policy implications but does not make the underlying coordination problems less important. Coordination failures are likely to emerge, in particular, in the transition from old to new patterns of production and trade specialization. Arguably, this situation is characteristic of a number of semi-industrial "sandwich economies" in which old comparative advantages in labor intensive industries are being eroded and the new ones in capital and technology intensive activities are only slowly emerging. Thus, in contrast to the counter-revolution in development economics[5] which denied the usefulness of the approach for the small open economy of a "typical" developing country, I shall argue that it can be fruitfully applied to the development problems of open economies (Chapters 9 and 14).[6]

In fact, I would argue that it is when applied to the interpretation of post-war development experience that the approach taken by early development theory shows its strengths and most useful insights. From this perspective, we can view the staggering success stories of East Asia's industrialization (and, to a lesser extent, of a few Latin American countries for some time before the 1980s) as a succession of policy interventions that accelerated the transition between different patterns of production and trade specialization. It is difficult to see how a primarily market-driven development model, that inspires many of today's policy recommendations to developing countries, could have

---

[5] I use the term "counter-revolution" in development theory or, in other places, "neoclassical resurgence" to indicate the partial abandonment in the 1960s of the labor surplus-increasing returns paradigm in development economics. Both of these terms are, however, somewhat misleading, as there was no neoclassical development economics before the 1940s.

[6] The view that the scope of classical development economics is limited to a closed economy has different sources. One of them, perhaps the most popular, is a confusion between a savings trap (low income leading to low savings and investment) and a profitability trap (a low profit rate limiting investment opportunities). While the first poverty trap is easily overcome through international capital mobility, the second is not and, in fact, may be exacerbated by capital mobility. For a discussion of the topic, see Chapters 3 and 7).

"traversed" those transitions so successfully. This is not because market based successes have been entirely absent (this is very debatable). It is hard to see simply because sound theory suggests exactly the contrary: that market forces are unlikely to address effectively (or, at least, efficiently) the coordination problems of the transition. Chapters 9 and 14 provide the theoretical basis as well as empirical support for this assertion. The extension of the analysis to open economy issues addresses also the role of some neglected factors in cross country growth analysis, such as the pattern of trade specialization, as determined by industrial policies and natural resource endowments.

Keynesian growth theory and classical development economics

A third theme is the relationship of early development theory to Keynesian economics. Growth theory was "born macro" in the sense that in the early years of growth theory, in the writings of Harrod (1939) and later Keynesians, aggregate demand had an important role in the growth process. Development economics was also "born macro", as Taylor and Arida (1988) phrased it in their survey of development theories; but it was not born Keynesian or structuralist. In Lewis's view: "from the point of view of countries with surplus labor, Keynesianism is only a footnote to neo-classicism—albeit a long, important and fascinating footnote" (Lewis, 1954, p. 140). Nurkse was blunter:

> We are here in the classical world of Say's law. In underdeveloped areas there is generally no 'deflationary gap' through excessive savings. Production creates its own demand, and the size of the market depends on the volume of production. In the last analysis, the market can be enlarged only through an all-round increase in productivity. Capacity to buy means capacity to produce. (Nurkse, 1953, pp. 8–9).

We need not take these warnings against the "Keynesian temptation" of development economics too literally to recognize that, no matter how valid Keynes's insights and later contributions to development macroeconomics based on them, the development problems on which Rosenstein-Rodan, Nurkse, and Lewis focused would remain even if Keynesian problems were successfully overcome. Increasing returns to scale are essential to the development problem, and irrelevant to the Keynesian argument. Despite some similarities—such as the presence of an elastic labor supply, which, however, need not arise as in Keynes from a low level of resource utilization—we should not confuse these development problems with the effective demand problems on which Keynes focused. Not much is lost, for example, by assuming Say's law when looking at income differences across countries: as briefly discussed in Chapter 1, differences in resource utilization account for a very small fraction of the large gaps in income per capita across the world.

In the case of differences in growth performance, which approach to take depends on the particular questions one is seeking to answer. Keynesian growth economics seems insufficient to understand why Europe and Japan grew faster than the United States in the post-war period or why the East Asian newly industrializing countries grew faster than the Latin American countries during the 1960s and 1970s. In turn, full employment models may be a good first approximation to explain growth under the post war conditions up to the early 1970s when governments were able to follow high employment policies that effectively removed recurrent effective demand problems, except for rather short periods of time. Yet, economies depart from the full employment path, sometimes for prolonged periods of time, and Keynesian problems and structural constraints on effective demand are not always successfully overcome even when in Trevor Swan's words "the authorities have read the *General Theory*" (Swan, 1963, p. 205, in Sen, 1970). Abandoning Say's law seems then essential. This is the case, we shall argue, for understanding why Latin America grew so little in the 1980s as compared to its long-run performance, just as it is essential to understand the poor performance of Great Britain and the United States economies during the inter-war period, the Japanese economy in the 1990s, and the current growth slowdown following the Great Recession in the United States and Western Europe.

There are thus a number of situations (in developing and developed countries alike) in which medium or even long-term growth performance cannot be properly explained if one remains strictly within the framework of full employment models. This was well recognized by the later structuralist contributions to development economics. The neglect of effective demand failures and structural constraints, while in the spirit of early development theory, can therefore be an important limitation under some circumstances. Chapters 10 through 13 examine the interactions between effective demand, technical change and factor accumulation. These chapters include an analysis of Keynesian growth theory, Kalecki's dual economy model and the contributions of two gap models, and the foreign exchange and fiscal constraints on growth emphasized by later structuralist growth models.

The ascent and challenge of the new institutional economics

A fourth theme has to do with the recent ascent of the new institutional economics and its relation to classical development theory. The relationship between institutions and development was a central theme for Adam Smith in the *Wealth of Nations*. This theme has reflourished in recent times in the contributions of the new institutional economics by Douglass North and his collaborators and has, even more recently, come to occupy a central place in the economics of growth given that, in the view of the neo-institutionalists, differences among countries in the levels of economic development are fundamentally explained by institutional differences. This thesis is expressed in the recent book by Daron Acemoglu and James Robinson (2012) with particular force, clarity and erudition.

Are Adam Smith, Douglass North and lately Daron Acemoglu and James Robinson correct in believing that institutions are the fundamental determinants of the wealth and poverty of nations? Are the political and economic institutions adopted by countries all that matters for development, as asserted by the strong version of the institutionalist thesis? Do the enforcement of the rule of law and the operation of the invisible hand in a laissez faire economy really provide the keys to the kingdom that will allow poor countries access to the first world? More precisely, are "the openness of a society, its willingness to permit creative destruction and the rule of law", to use the words in Kenneth Arrow's blurb of *Why Nations Fail?*, the decisive factors in economic development? Or is it the case, as Keynes would remind us, that policies and the ideas and ideologies shaping those policies are equally or more important? And, if institutions are most important, are those on which the new institutionalism focuses the truly important ones or is it the case, as Pranab Bardhan has argued, that "the new institutionalism got its institutions wrong"? These questions, which were completely absent in the 2000 book, are addressed in the third part of the book, especially in Chapter 17 on institutions and development, Chapter 18 on geography and colonialism, and Chapter 19 on successes and failures in economic development.

Structural change, factor accumulation, and economic growth

A final theme runs through the whole book and refers to the links between resource reallocation, factor accumulation and technological change. The traditional division between the "static" analysis of resource allocation and the "dynamic" analysis of growth as well as the analysis of growth as the outcome of two separate forces, factor accumulation and technical progress, become too artificial in the presence of increasing returns. A reallocation of resources (towards or away the activities affected by increasing returns) may then have long lasting effects on growth and growth itself has to be seen as a process of structural change rather than of mere factor accumulation cum technical change.

It is on this basis that Kaldor, in some of his late writings, built his radical critique of mainstream economics. After stressing the relevance of increasing returns, Kaldor examined the consequences for economic theory. He noted that the concept of equilibrium interpreted as an optimal allocation of given resources, is seriously undermined:

[t]he whole issue, as Young said, is whether an 'equilibrium of costs and advantages' is a meaningful notion in the presence of increasing returns. When every change in the use of resources—every reorganization of productive activities—creates the opportunity for a further change which would not have existed otherwise, the notion of an 'optimum' allocation of resources—when every particular resource makes a great or greater contribution to output in its actual use as in any alternative use—becomes a meaningless and contradictory notion: the pattern of the use of resources at any one time can be no more than a link in the chain of an unending sequence and the very distinction, vital to equilibrium economics, between resource-creation and resource-allocation loses its validity.

In the same passage, Kaldor then concludes: "[t]here can be no such thing as an equilibrium state with optimum resource allocation where no further advantageous reorganization is possible, since every such reorganization may create a fresh opportunity for a further reorganization" (Kaldor 1975, p. 355).

Moreover, as Kaldor and others used to emphasize, the distinction between movements along a production function and technical progress (shifts of the production function) becomes blurred under increasing returns to scale. With the expansion of output, more capital-intensive (or "roundabout") methods of production become profitable and are adopted. This is so whether these techniques were already known, and not used because they were unprofitable at a lower scale of output, or truly new and become part of the stock of knowledge as the incentives for its invention appear with the expansion of the market. In developing economies, unlike those of developed countries, these technical changes mostly result from the adoption of technologies that were known elsewhere. From this perspective, they constitute a movement along a production function. Yet, their adoption, unlike the typical movement along a production function, is not the consequence of a change in factor prices leading to the substitution of capital for labor, but rather the result of these more capital-intensive techniques becoming profitable as the scale of output increases.

The links among resource reallocation, factor accumulation and technological change are evident in the process of economic growth over the last two centuries. This process has been marked by industrialization, understood as the expansion of the range of goods produced under increasing returns, and by the simultaneous sharp increase in the capital-labor ratio. These two aspects, which Chapter 1 highlights in the context of the experience of the last 4 decades, are intimately connected. Paraphrasing Allyn Young (1928), the division of a group of complex processes into a succession of simpler processes, that is made economical by the presence of increasing returns, lends itself to the use of "roundabout" methods of production which imply the use of more capital in relation to labor.

This approach to growth as resource reallocation and structural change was present in classical development economics.[7] The approach faded away, at least in the more theoretically oriented literature, with the triumph of the counter-revolution in development economics that started to dominate the field in the mid-1960s. The neoclassical resurgence brought back the assumptions of constant returns to scale and perfect competition, and restored the traditional distinction between resource allocation and factor accumulation. The move coincided with, and perhaps contributed to, a declining interest in the analysis of growth during the seventies. Endogenous growth theory has revived the interest in growth and has even brought back increasing returns to scale into the analysis. But, for the most part, it has remained largely within the framework of one sector or quasi-one sector models thus missing the links between growth and structural change.

Interacting with the development of these themes is an empirical analysis of a number of questions raised by the post war development experience as well as by the theoretical explanations: How extensively can savings rates and demographic factors account for the vast differences in incomes across the world? How much of these differences should instead be attributed to human capital gaps or to differences in technologies? Or are those differences perhaps the path-dependent outcome of vicious and virtuous circles of development and underdevelopment in otherwise structurally similar economies? The empirical evidence on these and other issues is presented in such a way as to justify the need for relaxing restrictive assumptions and to motivate extensions of, or departures from, simpler theoretical models. Almost every chapter refers to relevant empirical findings in the literature. Most chapters either present original findings or make new use of past research results—for instance, the literature on the Verdoorn law or research on cross-country growth regressions—to illuminate current debates.

Overall, a case for the approach of classical development economics emerges from this empirical analysis. This case is based largely on its consistency with the cross-country pattern of growth rates at low, middle and high income levels (Chapters 7 and 8) and its ability to accommodate the role of often neglected factors such as industrial policy and natural resources in explaining the links between growth and international trade (Chapters 14 and 15). At the same time, remaining within the original limits and motivations of this approach would imply taking too narrow a view of the development process. This view

---

[7] It is also present and certainly fully explicit, in a rather pure state, in Kaldor's later writing on economic development. For Kaldor (1967, pp. 27–8), growth is "the result of a complex process of interaction between demand increases which have been induced by increases in supply, and increases in supply caused by increases in demand....The speed of the chain reaction will be greater, the truer it is that consumers choose to buy more of those goods with a large supply response and the larger the response on the demand side caused by increases in production."

of "underdevelopment" and its implications for the process of economic growth needs to be broadened to cover a fuller range of development traps that can arise as a result of interactions between capital accumulation and skill acquisition or between growth and economic inequality.

Is this theoretical and empirical vindication of development theory also a policy rehabilitation? The answer is not clear-cut. Classical development economics focused on the coordination problems that would remain in an otherwise well functioning market economy. One may criticize the associated policy prescriptions for having neglected other sources of malfunctioning and for an overoptimistic attitude towards government policy interventions. Yet these criticisms do not make those problems disappear. The aim of economic reforms in developing countries over the past 30 years has been to alleviate the malfunctioning of the market economy arising from policy distortions. Rather than reducing it, these reform processes may have enhanced the relevance of classical development economics: precisely because these other (policy) sources of malfunctioning are being removed, the focus may now have to shift again to the kind of market failures with which early development theory was concerned.

In any case, the scope of the book is largely confined to the positive, rather than the normative, implications of the approach taken by early development theory. In this sense, it is closer to Kaldor's later writing on economic development, with its concern on why do growth rates differ among countries (Kaldor, 1966, 1967), than to the normative concerns that inspired the pioneers of development economics.

2. A Brief Overview

After reviewing the main stylized facts of economic development in Chapter 1, the book contains four parts. The first reviews different approaches to growth theory in the neoclassical and endogenous growth traditions. These approaches focus on the supply side of the economy in the sense that the level of output and its growth rate are constrained by either factor accumulation and exogenous technological progress (neoclassical models), the productivity effects of capital accumulation in the presence of increasing returns to scale (some endogenous growth models), or the supply side factors affecting innovation and technological progress (new growth theory). These approaches make a variety of assumptions about key growth factors such as saving behavior, technology and the nature of technological innovation, or the role of human capital in the growth process, from which follow different predictions about convergence and divergence in incomes per capita across countries.

The second part of the book is devoted to classical development theory. As indicated earlier, the nature of the big questions of development theory addressed by the pioneers of development economics, forced these authors to rely on a paradigm built upon notions of imperfect competition, increasing returns and labor surpluses. The presence of increasing returns to scale, a feature that these early contributions have in common with recent endogenous growth models, and a high elasticity of labor supplies, derived from the existence of labor surpluses at low levels of the economy wide capital labor ratio, are the basis of growth models with substantially different convergence properties than those of either neoclassical growth models and some endogenous growth models.

The focus on the supply side, which classical development theory has in common with neoclassical and endogenous growth models, may be a good way of approaching the growth process for most countries during the post-war period up to the mid or late 1970s, a period when governments were able to follow high employment policies that effectively removed recurrent effective demand problems, except for rather short periods of time. Its applicability is, however far from universal. This is why the third part of the book reviews growth theory in the Keynesian tradition in which effective demand can constrain the level and/or rate of growth of output for prolonged periods of time. This is the case, as already alluded to, of such episodes as the interwar period in the United States and several European countries or various situations, ranging from Latin American lost decade of the 1980s to Japan's stagnation of the 1990s or today's European slump, when macroeconomic policies were not able (or leaders were not willing) to remove those demand constraints.

The fourth part of the book focuses on the so-called deep determinants of income levels and growth rates following a distinction, going back to Abramovitz (1952) and Lewis (1955) and by now widely adopted in the modern economics of growth, between the "immediate" or "proximate" determinants and the "deep" or "fundamental" determinants of income levels or growth rates. Given the wide use of this distinction, we should recall Lewis warning in *The Theory of Economic Growth* that the "proximate" determinants, such as factor accumulation and productivity growth, can affect the "fundamental" determinants, such as institutions, so that what we really have is a multiplicity of causes interacting among themselves that are separated only for analytical purposes (see Lewis, 1955, p. 20).

The diagram below, adapted from Rodrik et al. (2004), helps to elaborate on Lewis's point. It presents the main direct and indirect effects of the "proximate" and "deep" determinants of income levels as well as the feedback effects of income on these determinants. The proximate determinants, physical and human capital accumulation as well as technical progress, are the variables on which modern growth theory focuses. Growth theory, and especially classical development theory, also considers the feed back effects of income levels on the rates of factor accumulation, such as, for example, the dependence of the capacity to save on the level of income or those of technical efficiency on income in the presence of increasing returns to scale. The deep or fundamental determinants, shown in the lower part of the diagram, include institutions (political and economic), openness to foreign trade and capital, and geography. Inequality and natural resource endowment can also be regarded, as we do in this book, as fundamental determinants but they are closely related to institutions in the first case and to geography in the second.

The arrows show the main effects and interactions. There are, first, interactions between income and the "proximate determinants": factor accumulation and technical progress affect income directly but income in turn affects investments in physical and human capital and, in the presence of increasing returns to scale, technical progress itself as, for example, when the expansion of markets makes profitable the introduction of new and more "roundabout" methods of production. These proximate determinants and their interactions are examined by the great variety of growth models in the first, second and third parts of the book.

There are also interactions between income and the "fundamental determinants", often mediated (although this is not shown in the figure) by the effects on the proximate determinants. This is the subject of the fourth part of the book which examines the controversies over the deep determinants of economic growth and development levels, i.e., on whether openness, geography, institutions, or other fundamental factors has primacy over the others. The direct effects of geography on income per capita emphasized by geographical determinists and operating through, for example, the level of agricultural productivity or the health environment, are captured by arrow (1). Arrow (2) refers to the effects of geography on institutions (and indirectly on income) through the health environment faced by colonizers and the type of colonization undertaken by Europeans. Arrow (3) makes reference to the effects of geography on openness and its indirect effects on income through the impact of geography on distance from markets or the extent of international integration. Chapter 18 reviews all these direct and indirect effects of geography, including the geography versus institutions debate on the relative importance of the direct as opposed to the indirect effects of geography operating through institutions. Arrow (4) refers to the institutionalist view, discussed in Chapter 17, on the importance of the rule of law and "inclusive" economic and political institutions on income while arrow (5) reminds us that institutions are endogenous given the presence of feedback effects of income on institutions (as claimed, for example, by modernization theory). The subject of Chapter 14, the effects of international integration on income per capita

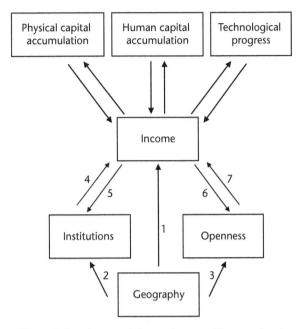

Figure 1 Fundamental determinants of income levels

resulting from the static and dynamic gains from trade and technology transfers are considered by arrow (7) while arrow (6) refers to the feedback effects of
incomes on openness through, for example, the adoption of restrictive trade
policies at low-income levels in order to raise government revenue.

Finally, I stress again that the separation between proximate and deep
determinants of income levels is to some extent artificial given the importance
of feedback effects of income on its determinants and the fact that the various
causes are interrelated. Not even geography is fully exogenous in the sense
that the strength of the direct effects of geography on, say, the low productivity of tropical agriculture is mediated by the fact that tropical countries are
generally poor and most agricultural research in the world has concentrated
on temperate agriculture where the rich countries are located.

1

Some Stylized Facts of Economic Development

Why are some countries richer than others? Why do some economies grow faster than others? Following a distinction discussed at the end of the introduction, in this chapter I present some information on the "immediate determinants" of output levels and growth rates and on characteristics that relate to the deeper determinants. Much of this book is about how the factors highlighted here are determined and how they interact with each other. The main purpose of this chapter is simply to present some stylized facts in the form of robust statistical relationships. Explanations thereof begin in the next chapter.

1. International Differences in Incomes Per Capita

Let's look at differences in per capita incomes within a simple and widely used framework.[1] Income per capita is equal to income per worker times the ratio of workers to the total population (the activity rate). Higher incomes per capita may thus result from either a higher level of output per worker or from a higher ratio of workers to the total population. Demographic and social factors largely explain differences in activity rates. Output per worker can be related, in turn, to the amount of resources, human and nonhuman, per worker and to the efficiency with which these resources are used and allocated. Resources include the stock of capital, the skills, knowledge and energy level of the labor force, and the natural resources available. A higher efficiency may result from a better allocation of given resources, through, for example, specialization in international trade, technological advances arising from the expansion of the scale of economic activity or movements towards the production frontier (adoption of best practice techniques, reductions in X-inefficiencies).

---

[1] See, in particular, Maddison (1982, 1991, 1993).

Table 1.1 Comparative economic characteristics around 2010

	Averages for country groups				
	1	2	3	4	5
GDP per capita[a, b]	100	46.1	18.5	7.0	2.4
Activity rate (%)[b]	52	46	42	41	46
GDP per worker[a]	100	50.7	22.6	8.6	2.7
Capital per worker[a]	100	53.1	21.2	7.2	2.3
Education[c]	11.0	9.2	7.5	6.1	4.4
Arable land (hectares per worker)[b]	0.8	0.4	0.4	0.6	0.4
Trade share[c]	128	74	86	81	67
Market size[a, b]	100	48.3	17.7	54.5	1.9
Industrial employment share (%)[b]	22.2	24.5	21.0[e]	18.2[f]	4.6[g]
Rate of growth (%), 1970–2010[d]	2.4	2.3	1.5	1.1	0.3
Number of countries	17	17	17	18	18

Note: See the appendix to this chapter for countries in each group, definitions, and data sources.
[a] As percentage of group 1 average. GDP in international dollars at PPP constant prices of 2005. [b] 2009 or the latest available year. [c] 2010. [d] Trend growth rate of GDP per capita at constant prices (LCU). See Table 1.4 and appendix for more details. [e] Average excludes Tunisia. [f] Average excludes Zambia, Cameroon, Mauritania, and Cote d'Ivoire. [g] Average excludes The Gambia, Lesotho, Bangladesh, Benin, Nepal, Rwanda, Guinea, Malawi, Burundi, and Zimbabwe.

Table 1.1 presents information on 87 countries, aggregated into five groups according to their 2008 GDP per worker adjusted for differences across countries in purchasing power.[2] The first group includes, broadly speaking, high-income OECD economies, i.e., Western European countries and Western offshoots (United States, Australia, and Canada) plus 2 high income East Asian countries (Hong Kong and Singapore). Group 2 is a diverse collection of high and upper middle-income countries in Latin America (6 countries), Southern Europe (3), Middle East (3), East Asia (3) plus Botswana in sub-Saharan Africa and New Zealand in Oceania. Group 3 includes 9 countries from Latin America and the Caribbean, 4 in the Middle East and North Africa, 3 in sub-Saharan Africa and 1 in East Asia. Group 4 comprises mostly lower middle and low-income countries in sub-Saharan Africa (8), South Asia (India and Pakistan), East Asia (3, including China), Latin America (3), plus Morocco in North Africa. Group 5 refers to the poorest countries in the world, all (with the exception of Nepal and Bangladesh) in sub-Saharan Africa. The information in the table refers to different variables reflecting or influencing the availability of resources and the efficiency in its use. The Appendix gives a full definition of these variables together with data sources and a detailed account of the composition of each country group.

---

[2] These 87 countries are the countries included in both the Penn World Table (PWT or Summers and Heston data set) and the World Bank World Development Indicators (WDI) excluding those countries for which: (a) oil extraction is the dominant activity, (b) central planning was dominant during most of the period since 1970; (c) data is not available going back to 1970; (d) population is less than 1 million. See Appendix for further discussion.

Table 1.1 reproduces a well-known feature of the world economy: its vast heterogeneity in terms of incomes per capita and per worker. Income gaps between rich and poor countries are enormous, over 40:1 when we compare groups 1 and 5. Lower activity rates in middle and low-income countries— determined by socio-demographic factors such as lower participation of women in the labor force and higher dependency ratios than those found in rich countries—account for part of the differences in income per capita. This is especially the case in groups 3 and 4.

On the whole, however, per capita income differences are clearly related to wide labor productivity gaps. What accounts for these large differences in output per worker? Perhaps the most salient feature of Table 1.1 is how closely output per worker correlates with both the stock of capital per worker and the educational level of the labor force. This last is measured by the mean number of years of schooling of the population aged 25 years and above, arguably the best indicator of the stock of human capital per worker that is available for current production.[3] Figures 1.1 and 1.2 show these relationships for our sample of countries and Table 1.2 shows log linear regressions of GDP per worker and each of these two variables.

No aggregate measures of natural resources are available. A crude proxy is a country's arable land. Figure 1.3 shows the absence of any discernible relationship between arable land per worker and output per worker. High-income countries can be resource rich (Australia, Canada, and the United States) or resource poor (Japan, Hong Kong, and the Netherlands). Similarly, some

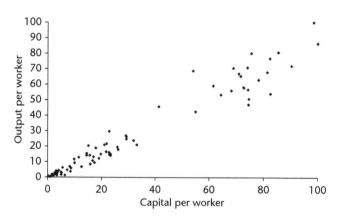

Figure 1.1 Output per worker and capital per worker

Expressed as percentages of maximum value.
See the appendix to this chapter for sources and definitions.

---

[3] Other measures such as school enrollment ratios reflect current flows of education and adult literacy rates do not capture skills obtained beyond elementary education. For a discussion, see Barro and Lee (1993).

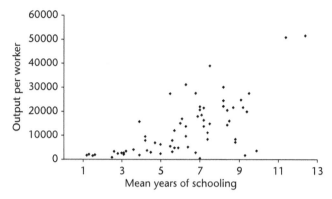

Figure 1.2 Output per worker and education

GDP is measured at PPP in constant international dollars.
See the appendix to this chapter for sources and definitions.

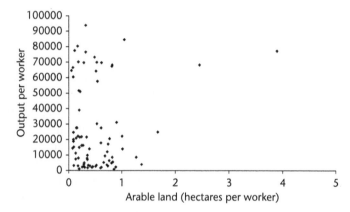

Figure 1.3 Output per worker and arable land per worker

GDP per worker in 2008, measured at PPP in constant international dollars. See the appendix to this chapter for sources and definitions.

Table 1.2 Cross-country regressions

Regression Independent variable	1	2	3
Constant	0.79	5.79	0.84
	(3.64)	(16.39)	(3.49)
Log of capital per worker (K/L)	0.87	–	0.86
	(40.30)		(23.95)
Log of Education (EDU)	–	1.97 (10.89)	0.06 (0.66)
Log of arable land per capita (LAND)	–	–	0.03
			(0.70)
Number of countries	87	87	85
Adjusted R^2	0.95	0.58	0.95

Note: See the appendix to this chapter for definitions and data sources. t-statistics in parentheses. Dependent variable: logarithm (log) of GDP per worker in 2008 (Y/L).

Table 1.3 Cross-country correlations

	Y/L	K/L	EDU	LAND	OPEN	SIZE	IND
Y/L	1.00	–	–	–	–	–	–
K/L	0.98**	1.00	–	–	–	–	–
EDU	0.76**	0.77**	1.00	–	–	–	–
LAND	−0.10	−0.12*	−0.06	1.00	–	–	–
OPEN	0.23*	0.28**	0.23*	−0.17	1.00	–	–
SIZE	0.71**	0.67**	0.51**	−0.10	−0.13	1.00	–
IND	0.73**	0.72**	0.65**	−0.15	0.17	0.50**	1.00

Note: See the appendix to this chapter for definitions and data sources.
*, ** Statistically significant at 5% and 1% level, respectively.

low-income countries in the sample are land poor (Bangladesh and Nepal) while others are land rich (Mali and Paraguay). The negative and insignificant correlation coefficient between arable land per capita and output per worker in Table 1.3 confirms the weakness of the relationship. Regression 3 in Table 1.2 indicates that, given other factor endowments, output per worker is positively correlated with arable land per capita, but the coefficient of this variable is very small and statistically insignificant at usual confidence levels. This suggests that—unlike what may have happened in the pre-industrial stages when the world economy was much more homogeneous in terms of capital and skills per worker than it is today—the natural resource endowment plays a very minor role as a determinant of income differences compared to other factor endowments (human and capital resources). Even then, before the industrial revolution, differences in natural resource endowment may have led to differences in population more than in per capita incomes. According to Kaldor (1967, p. 3): "If we go back a few hundred years for example, to 1700 or 1750, we do not find, as far as we can tell, such large differences in real income per capita between different countries or regions. The populations of most countries lived at about a subsistence level—they all had the appearance of underdeveloped countries, by present-day standards. Differences in natural endowment in climate or the fertility of the soil were fairly well balanced by differences in the density of the population; and the great majority of the population of *all* countries derived their living from primary production, that is, from agriculture."

I consider three efficiency variables: (1) the employment share of industrial activities, for gains from resource allocation towards sectors with increasing returns; (2) the trade share (exports plus imports over GDP) for allocative and technical efficiency gains resulting from specialization in international trade; (3) the economy's size as measured by total GDP, to capture efficiency gains resulting from pure scale effects. As shown in Table 1.1 and the cross-country correlations in Table 1.3, the industrial employment share is closely correlated with output per worker, especially among groups 2 to 5 since group 1, with the highest incomes, shows a diversification away from industry characteristic of "post-industrial" societies. Both market size and trade share have the expected positive influence in the cross-country correlations presented in Table 1.3. The role of the economy's size is also apparent in Table 1.1. Its close correlation with income per capita becomes spoiled only when group 4 (which includes China and India) is brought in. That the influence of the trade share is less apparent in Table 1.1 (or in the simple correlations) may be due to the negative correlation between market size and trade shares (see Table 1.3). This is consistent with the observation that small economies (such as Hong Kong, Singapore, and Switzerland in our sample) have to be very open to achieve high levels of income while large economies, such as the United States or Japan, need not.

2. International Differences in Growth Rates

We now turn to growth performance during the period 1970–2008. Table 1.4 aggregates countries into five groups, according to the growth rate of GDP per worker. The table presents, for these five groups, the average growth rates of per capita and per worker GDP along with a number of other performance indicators.

Table 1.4 Growth performance, 1970–2008

	Averages for country groups				
Growth rates (%per year)	1	2	3	4	5
GDP per capita[a]	3.9	2.1	1.4	0.6	−0.3
GDP per worker[a]	3.4	1.7	0.9	0.2	−0.8
Capital per worker[a]	3.8	1.7	1.6	0.5	−1.8
Industrial Employment Share	0.9[c]	−0.9[d]	−0.0[e]	0.7[f]	−0.0[g]
Education	2.8	1.7	2.8[h]	2.7[i]	2.8[j]
Education 1970	3.6	5.7	3.7[h]	3.0[i]	2.4[i]
GDP per worker[b]	109.3	203.7	98.6	60.2	47.7
Arable land (hectares per worker)	0.2	0.3	0.2	0.2	0.2
Industrial Employment Share 1970 (%)	20.8	33.9	16.9	14.1	15.1
Number of countries	17	17	17	18	18

Note: See the appendix to this chapter for countries in each group, definitions, and data sources.
[a] LCU, constant prices of 2005. Average of growth rate calculated as a trend over the period. [b] Average over the period. Mean value = 100. [c] Average excludes Lesotho. [d] Average excludes Tunisia. [e] Average excludes Nepal and The Gambia. [f] Average excludes Cameroon, Burundi, Guinea, Rwanda, and Malawi. [g] Average excludes Mauritania, Ghana, Cote d'Ivoire, Zimbabwe, and Zambia. [h] Average excludes Burkina Faso. [i] Average excludes Ethiopia and Guinea. [j] Average excludes Nigeria and Madagascar.

Growth and its proximate determinants

A first well-known observation refers to the wide dispersion of growth rates. Whether measured in per capita or per worker terms, the differences between the extremes of the distribution (groups 1 and 5) are staggering. They are such that while these two groups had similar average per capita income levels in 1970 (a 10 percent difference), by 2008, less than 40 years later, incomes in the fast growing economies were almost four times higher than in the stagnant or declining economies of group 5.

Growth rates of GDP per capita and per worker are closely associated. That is, in accounting for differences in the growth of per capita income, changes in activity rates—i.e. changes in labor input per capita, given by the difference between the two growth rates—play a secondary role compared to that of labor productivity growth. Activity rates in all five groups show a rising trend at a rate of 0.5–0.4 percent per year.

The accumulation of capital per worker appears as a major systematic influence on the growth of per capita and per worker GDP, showing a close positive correlation with these two indicators across country groups. Indeed, the very fast growth of capital per worker appears as the most distinctive characteristic of the rapidly growing economies in groups 1 and 2. This is not, however, their only attribute. They also feature, more than a rapid progress in education, an *initial* level of education well above those of the mostly developing economies in groups 4 and 5. At the other extreme, the stagnant economies of group 5 feature both a negative pace of capital accumulation per worker and the lowest initial levels of education. Regression (1) in Table 1.5 summarizes these

Table 1.5 Cross-country regressions

	1	2	3
Constant	−0.17	0.2	−0.53
	(−0.43)	(1.20)	(−0.94)
Growth rate of capital per worker	0.58	0.73	
	(14.09)	(15.04)	
Rate of progress in education	0.09	−	
	(1.00)		
Initial level of education (1970)	0.10	0.05	
	(1.69)	(1.43)	
Rate of industrialization			0.71
			(3.46)
Initial level of industrialization (1970)			0.07
			(3.20)
N	82	82	73
Adjusted R^2	0.72	0.72	0.12

Dependent variable: trend growth rate of GDP per worker 1970–2008.
t-statistics in parentheses.
See the appendix to this chapter for definitions and data sources.

observations by showing the growth rate of labor productivity positively correlated with the growth of the capital-labor ratio and (although not significantly) with both the initial level and the rate of progress of education.

The relationship between the initial level of education and subsequent growth deserves further attention. A common finding has been that countries that grow at fast rates tend to have exceptionally well qualified labor forces *given* their starting level of per capita income and that there seems to be a threshold level of education necessary for growth to take off. Azariadis and Drazen (1990), for example, observed in a data set of 29 countries that no country with a low ratio of literacy to GDP was able to grow fast in the period 1960–1980. More recently, Benhabib and Spiegel (2005), further discussed in Chapter 4, found that there is a critical level of education (around 1.8 years of schooling in 1960) necessary to guarantee convergence to the growth rate of the United States.

Figure 1.4 shows the relationship between the rate of growth of per capita GDP in 1970–2008 and the initial level of education measured by mean years of schooling of the population 25 years and over in 1970, for 82 countries for which information on education was available. The figure suggests a similar, albeit less definitive observation to those of Azariadis and Drazen or Benhabib and Spiegel. With the exception of 10 countries, no country with less than 3 years of schooling in 1970 (the median value being 3.1 years) was able to grow at rates above the median per capita growth rate. Among these countries, only

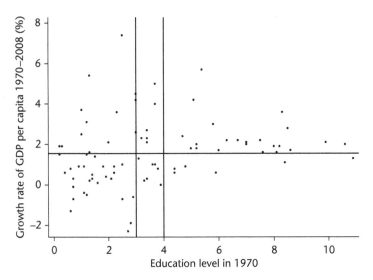

Figure 1.4 Initial level of education (1970) and per capita GDP growth, 1970–2008
See the appendix to this chapter for sources and definitions.

two (Botswana and China) were able to achieve per capita GDP growth rates above 4 percent per year.[4]

Figure 1.4 also illustrates that high initial levels of education are not a sufficient condition for the achievement of high growth rates. Countries with more than 4 years of schooling in 1970 and a per capita GDP growth rate below the median (1.6 percent per year) include Argentina, Jamaica, Philippines, New Zealand, South Africa, and Switzerland. The most remarkable of all countries in this category is probably Argentina, a middle-income country with 5.9 years of schooling in 1970 and a growth rate of 0.6.

It is worth noting the contrast between the significance of the *level* of education in *growth* performance (illustrated by Figure 1.4) and the insignificance of the *level* of education in the output *level* regression (once capital worker is taken into account, see regression 3 in Table 1.2) as well as of the rate of progress of education in the growth regression (see regression 1 in Table 1.5). In Chapter 4, when we discuss Nelson and Phelps's hypothesis on the role of human capital in the growth process, we shall come back to this puzzle.

3. Income Levels, Growth Performance, and the Deep Determinants of Development

As mentioned in the introduction, it is common in modern growth economics to distinguish between the "proximate" and the "fundamental" determinants of economic development. The former have been analyzed in previous sections. The latter include a variety of geographic, institutional, income distribution, and policy characteristics that affect income levels and growth rates (for a given income level) through various channels that we shall discuss in detail in later chapters.

Let's take a preliminary look at these characteristics. Table 1.6 presents the average value around 2008 of a number of indicators for each of the 5 income groups of our 87-country sample. Some striking features are apparent. First, there is a close positive correlation between income level and the value of a rule of law index based on perceptions of the extent to which agents have confidence in and abide by the rules of society, and in particular the quality of contract enforcement, property rights, the police, and the courts, as well as the likelihood of crime and violence.

---

[4] On the development experience of Botswana, see Griffin (1989), Acemoglu, Johnson, and Robinson (2003), and Acemoglu and Robinson (2012). Stable institutional and macroeconomic frameworks and a high savings and investment rates made possible by large natural resource rents (mining) appear to be the key to the fast rate of economic growth in Botswana.

Table 1.6 Main institutional, geographical, and political characteristics

Characteristic	Averages for country groups[a]				
	1	2	3	4	5
Rule of Law[b]	92.9	64.9	41.6	27.4	31.8
Population in non-democratic countries (%)[c]	1.1	11.9	20.3	47.4	30.3
Population in tropical countries (%)[c]	1.9	26.0	71.1	53.6	64.3
Population in landlocked countries (%)[c]	2.5	0.3	0	1.9	35.1
Net-exports of primary goods (%)[d]	0.4	−1.0[f]	−0.6	4.6[g]	−3.2[h]
Gini coefficient of income concentration (%)[b]	32.0	41.6	47.7	43.3	42.3
GDP per capita[e]	38,840.9	17,890.7	7,171.9	2,705.1	932.9

Notes: Characteristics refer to 2008 unless otherwise indicated.
[a] Countries classified by their income per worker. [b] 2008 or latest available data. [c] Percentage of the total group population. [d] Primary goods exports as percentage of GDP. [e] GDP per capita in constant prices of 2005. [f] Average excludes Iran. [g] Average excludes Republic of Congo. [h] Average excludes Benin, Nepal and Sierra Leona.
Sources: See the appendix to this chapter.

There is also a close correlation between level of economic development and political regime. The percentage of the population living in authoritarian regimes tends to increase as income per capita falls, a fit that is only disrupted by the presence, in group 4, of authoritarian China. Geographic determinists would emphasize the relationship in the third row. The level of income per worker tends to increase as we move away from the Equator: while only 1.9 percent of the population of the highest income group lives in the tropics (these are the populations of Singapore and Hong Kong), as much as 64.3 percent of the population of the poorest countries in group 5 lives in the tropics (the minority here are Bangladesh, Lesotho and Nepal). There is also a striking contrast in the percentage of the total group population living in landlocked countries between group 1 (2.5 percent) and group 5 (35.1 percent). Finally, the values of the Gini coefficient of income concentration show that more developed societies tend to be less inegalitarian than underdeveloped ones and there is some indication of a Kuznets curve, i.e. an inverted U-pattern with group 3 showing the highest Gini coefficient well above those of group 5 and, especially, of group 1.

Table 1.7 aggregates countries according to the rate of growth of GDP per worker in 1970–2008. A positive correlation is again visible between growth rate and a rule of law index but now the previously close correlation between income per worker and political regime disappears when we look at growth rates rather than levels of per capita incomes. The relationship is substantially altered now with more than a third of the population in the fastest growing countries living under authoritarian regimes. In fact, from groups 2 to 5 there is now a positive relationship between growth rates and the percentage of

Table 1.7 Growth and main geographical, political, and institutional characteristics

Characteristic	Averages for country groups[a]				
	1	2	3	4	5
Rule of Law[b]	70.2	76.4	48.3	33.6	29.9
Population in non-democratic countries (%)[c]	36.0	81.2	34.3	10.1	3.8
Population in tropical countries (%)[c]	49.7	1.0	45.7	83.4	81.4
Population in landlocked countries (%)[c]	0.6	0.9	10.2	36.3	5.1
Net-exports of primary goods (%)[d]	−3.0	−2.4	−3.3 [f]	0.9	8.3[g]
Gini income concentration coefficient (%)[b]	39.3	34.5	40.6	44.3	47.7
Growth rate of GDP per worker (%)[e]	3.4	1.7	0.9	0.2	−0.8

Notes: Characteristics refer to 2008 unless otherwise indicated.
[a] Countries classified by their growth rate of GDP per worker in 1970–2008. [b] 2008 or latest available data. [c] Percentage of the total group population; for political regimes it refers to 1970. [d] Primary goods exports as GDP percentage. [e] Trend growth rate of GDP per worker 1970–2008. [f] Average excludes Nepal, Republic of Congo, and Benin. [g] Average excludes Sierra Leone and Iran.
Sources: See the appendix to this chapter.

the population living under non-democratic regimes in 1970. At the same time, there is no apparent relationship between the percentage of population in the tropics and the growth rate of income per capita, although there is a high incidence of tropical countries in the slowest growth groups (as well as a high incidence of landlocked countries in group 4). Finally, and interestingly, there is a tendency for the Gini coefficient of income concentration to increase as we move down the growth table. In other words, there is a hint that more egalitarian countries tend to grow faster than inegalitarian ones. We shall come back in later chapters to these relationships and try to make sense of them.

4. The Evolution of the World's Distribution of Income

The international dispersion of per capita incomes has been on the rise since the industrial revolution began in Great Britain and spread to other European countries and Western offshoots in a process that the historian Kenneth Pomeranz (2000) has called the "Great Divergence". This process continued over the last century and a half: the high-income economies today have six to nine times the GDP per capita of the high-income economies in 1870 and the composition of this group has remained largely unaltered;[5] in contrast, the low-income countries today barely increased their income per capita over the

[5] See Maddison (1995) and De Long (1997). There were, however, significant changes in the rankings within this group. For example, the highest level of per capita income in 1870 was Australia's, which was ahead of the United Kingdom, in second place, by a large margin. Today, the United States, but not Australia and the United Kingdom, are among the five richest countries.

period and continue to be largely the same as the poor countries in 1870. In between, the median economy has around four times the income of 1870. This picture implies that the richest countries in 1870, with some exceptions such as Argentina, have been those that grew at the highest rates since 1870, even though they were not the only ones to grow fast. The poorest countries in 1870 have been those that clearly lagged behind. Thus, according to Pritchett (1997), the ratio of GDP per capita of the richest to the poorest country rose from 8.7 in 1870 to 51.6 in 1985, in a process that he calls "divergence, big-time". In 2008, in our sample of 87 countries, the income per worker ratio of the richest (Norway) to the poorest (Zimbabwe) country rose to 274:1.

The data for our 87 countries over a shorter and more recent period of time (1970–2008) shows, however, a more complex picture than simple divergence. Table 1.1 suggests a tendency to absolute divergence with growth rates falling as we move down the income scale. Table 1.4, which aggregates countries according to growth rates, suggests, however, that the relative high income countries of group 2 grow at a smaller pace than the middle-income countries of group 1 and, at the same time, at a faster rate than the lower income countries of groups 3, 4 and 5. In other words, there are definitely not tendencies to convergence since 1970[6] and, at the same time, there are weak and inconsistent tendencies to divergence. The lack of "absolute convergence" should not be confused with the absence of "conditional convergence"—the existence of an inverse relationship between the initial level of per capita incomes and its subsequent growth, once the determinants of the steady state level of income have been controlled for. The absence of absolute convergence can theoretically go together with conditional convergence; this, in fact, is the claim of the extensions of the neoclassical growth model discussed in Chapters 2, 3 and 4.

Great divergence and club convergence: the hump-shaped pattern of growth rates

A closer look at Table 1.4 reveals an interesting pattern. Consider groups 1 and 2 in Table 1.4 with above average incomes per worker. These two groups together include fast growing countries mostly in Asia, Western Europe, United States and Latin America. Within this set of countries there is a tendency to convergence of productivity levels; group 2 with the higher incomes has the lowest growth rate. There is thus an inverse relationship between growth and income level across the set of countries with above average levels of GDP per

---

[6] Or even before that in the post war period. This was recognized early on in the recent literature (see, for example, Barro, 1991). Chapter 3, section 4, reviews the evidence and recent debates on convergence.

worker, a similar phenomenon to the repeatedly noted "convergence club" of OECD countries (see in particular, Abramovitz, 1986; Baumol, 1986, and Baumol and Wolff, 1988). Consider now the rest of the groups comprising developing countries with average or below average incomes per worker. The fastest growing countries (group 1) have the highest incomes, and rates of growth fall as we move down the income table. There is a positive relationship between growth rates and income levels across country groups and, thus, a tendency of per capita incomes to diverge. Evidence of the growing dispersion of incomes among developing countries has been noted in other studies; UNCTAD (1997) has estimated a near doubling of the income ratio between the richest and poorest developing countries over the four decades following 1960.

The lack of strong tendencies towards convergence or divergence for the whole sample is the result of the fact that growth acceleration tends to occur at middle-income levels, as has been noted several times and for other time periods.[7] The consequence is a tendency towards divergence among middle and low-income countries (and to some extent among high and low-income countries) and a tendency towards convergence among middle and high-income countries. Figure 1.5, which shows growth rates and average levels of GDP per capita (for 1970–2008) for the whole sample, illustrates the hump-shaped pattern of growth rates that features the largest incidence of high growth rates occurring at middle-income levels. This pattern would probably emerge more clearly if the 1980s were excluded from the period of analysis, since a number of previously fast growing middle-income countries in Latin

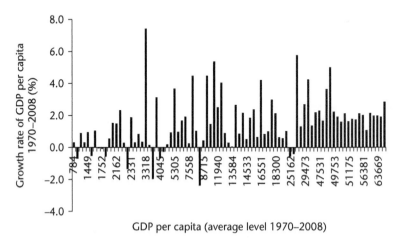

Figure 1.5 Growth rates and levels of GDP per capita
See the appendix to this chapter for sources and definitions.

---

[7] See Kristensen (1974), Chenery and Syrquin (1975), Syrquin (1986), Baumol (1986), Abramovitz (1986), Baumol and Wolff (1988), Lucas (1988).

America then plunged into economic stagnation following the debt crisis of the early 1980s.

The acceleration of growth rates at middle-income levels has been given different explanations. These will be examined in later chapters. At this stage, it is worth pointing out that there is some support in the data for the view that the high growth rates at middle-income levels are characteristic of the transition towards an industrialized economy, with growth being rather slow before and slowing down after the process of industrialization. As Kaldor (1967, p.7) argued: "...fast rates of economic growth are almost invariably associated with the fast rate of growth of the secondary sector, mainly, manufacturing, and...this is an attribute of an intermediate stage of development; it is a characteristic of the transition from 'immaturity' to 'maturity'". Group 1 in Table 1.4 with the highest rates of growth of output per worker recorded the fastest rate of industrialization during the period. Growth is slower in both the more industrialized economies of group 2, which de-industrialized during the period, as well as in the industrializing (but from a much smaller initial base) economies of groups 3, 4, and 5. Regression 3 in Table 1.5 relates overall productivity growth to the pace of industrialization, measured by the difference in the growth rates of industrial and overall employment. This is one of so-called Kaldor's laws, qualified only insofar as it holds for a given initial level of industrialization. That is, given the initial industrial employment share, the faster the rate of industrialization the higher the rate of productivity growth in the economy as a whole.[8] Similarly, given the rate of industrialization, the higher the level of industrialization the faster the overall rate of growth of productivity.

Middle-income traps and the "twin-peaked" distribution

The fact that the largest incidence of high growth rates tends to occur in middle-income groups is not the same as all middle-income economies being the fastest growing. The "transition from immaturity to maturity" is much less smooth than a superficial reading of Figure 1.5 could suggest and some of the major setbacks also appear to take place at middle-income levels. A number of economic and institutional upheavals, to be discussed in later chapters, can throw rapidly growing economies off the path of economic transformation that leads to high-income levels. In our sample and time period, we have already referred to the stagnation of highly indebted countries during the 1980s. The current crisis in Western Europe may be

---

[8] On Kaldor's laws, see Cripps and Tarling (1973), Thirlwall (1983), and Kaldor (1966 and 1967). Chapters 7 and 8 review the mechanisms involved and the evidence on the Verdoorn Law, relating the growth of productivity and output in manufacturing.

the beginning of a similar prolonged stagnation period. In a longer time span, the relative decline of Argentina, once among the richest countries in the world, is another remarkable example.

Growth acceleration at middle-income levels, coupled with occasional set-backs, probably constitutes a major reason why the world's distribution of per capita incomes has evolved towards a persistent bimodal or "twin-peaked" distribution. Using data for 1962–1984, Quah (1993) calculated the probability that a country in one income group will move into another group in the following year. The resulting "transition matrix" with countries divided into five income groups, depending on their per capita income relative to the global average, can then be used to simulate the evolving dispersion of per capita incomes. Holding these probabilities constant over time, Quah shows that the distribution of incomes eventually stabilizes in a "twin-peak" distribution similar to that observed in the world economy today, with many poor and many rich countries and relatively few countries in between. As an illustration, using Quah's transition probabilities to simulate the distribution of per capita incomes, starting from an egalitarian distribution with a zero standard deviation in the log of per capita incomes, income dispersion increases within the first 70 years and then stabilizes with a standard deviation of around 1.5. The key feature of the transition matrix explaining this result is that, unlike middle-income countries in groups 2, 3, and 4, the highest (group 1) and lowest (group 5) income countries have very high probabilities of remaining within the same group from one year to the next.

The twin-peaked distribution has been taken as evidence supporting the existence of development traps and multiple "club convergence". As Feyrer (2008) says: "The most dramatic feature of Quah's distribution is the down-ward movement of a group of countries away from the world mean. Instead of converging to the income of the wealthy countries, these countries are diverging away from it" (p. 27). This is perhaps the stylized fact most difficult to explain by modern growth economics. To the extent that it is concerned by it, this book is partly an attempt to find the origins of Quah's twin-peaked distribution of per capita incomes.

Having said that, Quah's estimated transition matrix implies, with probability one, that any less developed country will eventually move up through all the stages to become a high-income country and conversely that any developed economy will eventually move down to become underdeveloped. This two-way movement produces the long-run stable distribution. Rowthorn and Kozul-Wright (1998) have observed that the experience of the past 150 years suggests that countries do move downwards but only to a limited extent. There is no recorded case, for example, of a country in the high income or even moderately developed category moving all the way down to the lowest income level. This suggests the presence of ratchet effects that limit downward mobility. By allowing a ratchet effect—so that a country in group N can fall back into group N + 1, but having done so cannot fall back further into group N + 2—while assuming all other probabilities to be as in Quah, Rowthorn and Kozul-Wright show this limited downward mobility to have a dramatic impact on the evolution of income dispersion. The ratchet effect implies that the initial polarization of incomes is more rapid and acute than with Quah's probabilities, since the limited downward mobility must initially have unequalizing effects. At the same time, the gap between rich and poor countries eventually narrows as more countries move into the upper income groups. The process of convergence, however, is very slow and it takes 330 years from the initial starting point to reach the stage where 95 percent of countries are in the first two groups.

The bimodal income distribution implied by the transition matrices calculated over recent decades, plus the ratchet effects suggested by historical experience seem thus quite consistent with the hump-shaped pattern of growth rates. Both suggest no rapid tendency for low-income countries, as a group, to converge to high-income levels with, at the same time, some lower middle-income and upper middle-income countries occasionally changing places between the two modes of the distribution. Both suggest that at some stage and for a prolonged period, one should observe the ample and recognizable valley that separates the developed and most of the developing countries and is characteristic of today's world.

This chapter has provided empirical evidence, rather than explanations of income levels and growth rates. It gives background information on what will be explained in subsequent chapters.

Appendix

1. *Country Groupings According to Income Per Capita and Growth Performance*

Indicators in this and other chapters refer to 87 countries. These countries are the countries included in the Penn World Table (PWT or Summers and Heston data set) and the World Bank World Development Indicators (WDI) excluding those where: (a) Oil extraction is the dominant activity (where fuel exports were over 35 percent of GDP in 2008), (b) Central planning was dominant during most of the period since 1970; (c) Data is not available going back to 1970; (d) Population was less than 1 million in 2008.

These 87 countries were classified according to their GDP per worker in 2008 and aggregated into five income groups in Table 1.A1. Within each group, countries are listed according to GDP per worker, and figures are in U.S. dollars at 2005 international prices. The 87 countries were also classified into five groups according to their trend

Table 1.A1 Groupings according to real GDP per worker in 2008
(PPP, international and constant dollars, 2005)

	Group				
	1	2	3	4	5
Average income	$75,180	$38,104	$17,003	$6,434	$2,043
Countries	Norway	Japan	Panama	China	Gambia, The
	Singapore	Greece	Venezuela	Honduras	Lesotho
	United States	Israel	Mauritius	Morocco	Bangladesh
	Belgium	Spain	South Africa	Paraguay	Ghana
	Netherlands	New Zealand	Jamaica	Bolivia	Benin
	Australia	Korea, Republic of	Colombia	India	Kenya
	Austria	Portugal	Brazil	Indonesia	Nepal
	Ireland	Turkey	Tunisia	Philippines	Tanzania
	Hong Kong	Mexico	El Salvador	Pakistan	Sierra Leone
	Sweden	Iran	Peru	Nigeria	Rwanda
	United Kingdom	Chile	Guatemala	Nicaragua	Burkina Faso
	France	Malaysia	Egypt	Zambia	Guinea
	Italy	Argentina	Ecuador	Cameroon	Madagascar
	Finland	Costa Rica	Jordan	Congo, Republic of	Mozambique
	Canada	Uruguay	Namibia	Mauritania	Malawi
	Denmark	Dominican Republic	Thailand	Senegal	Ethiopia
	Switzerland	Botswana	Syria	Mali	Burundi
				Cote d`Ivoire	Zimbabwe
Number of countries	17	17	17	18	18

growth rate of GDP per worker from 1970 to 2008. Table 1.A.2 shows the composition of each of the five groups.

2. Definitions and Data Sources

Data sources are the Penn World Table (PWT) (Version 7.0; see Heston, Summers and Aten, 2011); World Bank World Development Indicators (WDI) (<http://data.worldbank.org/data-catalog/world-development-indicators>); the United Nations Development Program (UNDP) Human Development Report (various issues); Barro and Lee (2010); UNESCO; International Labor Organization (ILO); and the Worldwide Governance Indicators (WGI) project (Kaufmann, Kraay, and Mastruzzi, 2010).

A full description of definitions and data sources for the variables used in this and other chapters is given in what follows:

Activity rate: Labor force as percentage of population in 2009 or the last available year. Source: Penn World Table 7.0. For labor force, own calculations based on Penn World Table. 7.0.
Arable land per worker: Total arable land (hectares) per worker. Source: World Development Indicators (arable land) and Penn World Table. 7.0 (labor force).

Table 1.A2 Groupings according to growth rates

	Group				
	1	2	3	4	5
	Fast growth	Medium-high growth	Medium growth	Slow or no growth	No growth
Growth rate	$g \geq 2.44\%$	$2.44\% > g \geq 1.40\%$	$1.40\% > g \geq 0.47\%$	$0.47\% > g \geq -0.07\%$	$-0.07\% > g$
Countries	China	Chile	Panama	Syria	Kenya
	Botswana	Portugal	Nepal	Jamaica	Brazil
	Korea, Rep. of	Japan	Burkina Faso	New Zealand	Mauritania
	Singapore	United Kingdom	Greece	Paraguay	Bolivia
	Thailand	Dominican Rep.	Morocco	El Salvador	Namibia
	Hong Kong	Italy	Canada	Guatemala	Nigeria
	Egypt	Belgium	Bangladesh	Senegal	Ghana
	Malaysia	Denmark	Israel	Ethiopia	Jordan
	Mauritius	Australia	Mozambique	Burundi	South Africa
	India	Tunisia	Colombia	Argentina	Madagascar
	Ireland	Sweden	Tanzania	Cameroon	Cote d`Ivoire
	Indonesia	Uruguay	Benin	Ecuador	Peru
	Turkey	Spain	Congo, Rep. of	Mexico	Zimbabwe
	Norway	France	Netherlands	Costa Rica	Sierra Leone
	Lesotho	United States	Gambia, The	Honduras	Iran
	Finland	Austria	Philippines	Guinea	Venezuela
	Mali	Pakistan	Switzerland	Malawi	Zambia
				Rwanda	Nicaragua
Number of Countries	17	17	17	18	18

Capital per worker (K/L): Net fixed standardized capital stock per worker in 2005 purchasing power parity. Average for group 1 = 100. Source: Extended Penn World Table 7.0.

Capital per worker growth rate: Trend growth rate of capital per worker from 1970 to 2008. Calculated by regressing the logarithm of capital per worker on a constant and time (2005 international prices). Source: Extended Penn World Table 7.0.

Education (EDU): Mean years of schooling of population aged 25 years and above. Human Development Report Office (HDRO), updates by Barro and Lee (2010) based on UNESCO Institute for Statistics data on education attainment (2011) and Barro and Lee (2010) methodology.

Education growth rate (1970–2008): Trend growth rate of education from 1970 to 2008.

GDP per capita: PPP Converted GDP per capita (Chain index) at 2005 constant prices. Average for group 1 = 100. Source: Penn World Table 7.0.

GDP per capita growth rate: Trend growth rate of GDP per capita from 1970 to 2008 (or 2010 in Table 1.1) at 2005 constant prices in local currency units (LCU). Calculated by regressing the logarithm of GDP per capita on a constant and time. Source: Penn World Table. 7.0.

GDP per worker (Y/L): PPP Converted GDP per worker (Chain index) at 2005 constant prices. Average for group 1 = 100. Source: Penn World Table 7.0.

GDP per worker growth rate: Trend growth rate of GDP per Worker from 1970 to 2008 at 2005 constant prices in LCU. Calculated by regressing logarithm of real GDP per worker on a constant and time. Source: Penn World Table. 7.0.

Gini income concentration coefficient: World Development Indicators and United Nations University World Institute for Development Economics Research (UNU-WIDER)

Industrial employment share: Percent of labor force in industry. Source: International Labor Organization (ILO) and World Development Indicators.

Industrial employment share growth rate: Trend growth rate of industrial employment share from 1970 to 2008.

Market size: PPP Converted GDP (Chain Series) at 2005 constant prices. Source: Penn World Table 7.0

Net-Exports of primary goods: Primary goods exports minus primary goods imports as percentage of GDP in 2008. Primary goods are ores and metals, food, fuels, and agriculture raw materials. Source: WDI.

Population in non-democratic countries: Percentage of the total group population in 2008 that live in non-democratic countries according to Przeworski's (2004) criteria.

Population in tropical countries: Percentage of the total group population in 2008 that live in tropical countries defined as those whose land mass lies mostly between the Tropic of Cancer (latitude 23.5 degrees north) and the Tropic of Capricorn (latitude 23.5 degrees south).

Rule of law index: Reflects perceptions of the extent to which agents have confidence in and abide by the rules of society, and in particular the quality of contract enforcement, property rights, the police, and the courts, as well as the likelihood of crime and violence. Range 0–100; close to zero means low confidence. Source: Kaufmann, Kraay and Mastruzzi (2010), Worldwide Governance Indicators.

Trade share: Exports plus imports/GDP at constant prices (2008). Source: Penn World Table 7.0.

Part I
Neoclassical and Endogenous Growth Models

2

Basic Neoclassical and Endogenous Growth Models

We now embark on the search for analytical accounts of the differences in income levels and growth performances described in Chapter 1. Just as some chess books begin with a basic understanding of "end games", i.e., when the battle is almost over and only a few pieces of the original puzzle remain, we start with a model of a "mature economy"—a picture of how the economy looks like after the transition to a developed state has been completed. This starting point serves two purposes. First, just as in chess books, the understanding of end games facilitates a discussion of openings and intermediate situations. In addition, it will help us to introduce a simple analytical framework and a number of concepts that will be used in later chapters.

We begin with the neoclassical paradigm in growth theory which, in its simplest version, is captured by the standard Solow-Swan model. The chapter contrasts the implications of the model, including its behavior off its steady state, with the observed international differences in per capita incomes and growth rates. In this version of the neoclassical model, all countries have access to the same technologies, there are only two factors of production (physical capital and labor), and the savings rate is constant. This crude version does not stand well to the evidence. We will enquire then whether the key assumption of diminishing returns to capital is the source of the problem and discuss some basic endogenous growth models that abandon that assumption. These include Romer's 1986 model with aggregate increasing returns to capital, which marks the beginning of the revival of growth theory in recent times, the so-called AK model with constant returns to capital, and a hybrid neoclassical-endogenous growth model. The chapter concludes with an empirical assessment of these models.

1. The Solow-Swan Model: Constant Returns to Scale and Exogenous Technical Progress

The Solow-Swan model is the most parsimonious of models. It provides a theory of how the economy converges to a steady state and of the configuration of this steady state. It includes an explanation of why the steady state value of the capital-labor endowment is what it is, and of the determination of the economy's rate of growth in and outside the steady state.[1] There are several ways of presenting this theory. Appendix 1 provides, for the unfamiliar reader, the standard presentation using a diagram that shows the steady state capital-labor ratio at the intersection of gross investment and effective depreciation. Here, I present the model in (real wage, capital per worker) space. The resulting diagram will prove useful in this and later chapters by facilitating the comparison with alternative growth theories.

The real wage diagram

The economy considered produces one good, which can either be consumed or invested. Technology displays constant returns to scale and diminishing returns to variable proportions. We assume a Cobb-Douglas production function: $Y = K^a (AL)^{1-a}$, with $a < 1$, where Y is output; K, the capital stock; L, labor input in natural units; A reflects the state of technology and AL is labor input in effective units. Dividing total output by effective labor (AL), output per effective worker is:

$$y^A = (k^A)^a \quad y^A = Y/(AL) \quad k^A = K/(AL) \tag{1}$$

Investment is the same as saving (Say's law prevails) and there are no effective demand problems. This is because, strictly speaking, this is a one good, non-monetary economy; in an alternative interpretation, "the authorities have read the General Theory", as Swan (1963, p. 205 in Sen, 1970) explicitly assumed, and through aggregate demand policy are able to solve any effective demand problems that may arise.

The labor market clears at full employment through changes in the real wage.[2] Consider the determination of the real wage in this economy. From the

---

[1] The theory is also about the conditions for the existence and uniqueness of the steady state. These conditions were specified by Inada (1963; see on the subject, Wan, 1971). The endogenous growth models discussed later in this chapter illustrate situations in which some of these conditions (either for existence or uniqueness) are not fulfilled.

[2] The properties of the model would remain the same if there were a constant rate of unemployment (with a real wage above the market clearing level).

first order conditions for profit maximization, taking as given the capital stock and technology and assuming atomistic competition, we get the labor demand function (in effective units): $(AL)^d = [(1 - a)/w^A]^{1/a} K$, where w^A is the real wage per effective worker. This yields a downward sloping labor demand curve in (real wage, employment) space. Given the exogenous labor supply, the real wage adjusts to clear the labor market. Setting labor demand equal to the exogenous labor supply (AL), and then solving for w, we obtain the short-run equilibrium wage (w^A):

$$w^A = (1 - a)(k^A)^a \tag{2}$$

In $(\ln w^A, \ln k^A)$ space (where ln refers to the natural logarithm), eq. (2) is the equation of an upward sloping line with slope equal to "a", the capital share in the production function. Indeed, the market-clearing wage increases as the capital-labor ratio rises. A higher capital stock increases the demand for labor and the real wage required to keep labor demand equal to a given labor supply must increase. Alternatively, a higher capital stock (given the labor supply) increases the marginal product of labor at full employment and, since in competitive equilibrium the real wage is equal to the marginal product of labor at full employment, the real wage must increase with the capital stock.

The locus of $(\ln w^A, \ln k^A)$ combinations along which the labor market clears is shown as the w line in Figure 2.1. This w line is a schedule of *short-run equilibria* showing the market clearing value of the real wage at each level of the capital-labor ratio. Note that the slope of the w line is less than unity under diminishing returns to capital (a < 1) and thus the rate at which the real wage increases with the capital-labor ratio is decreasing. It is also worth noting that

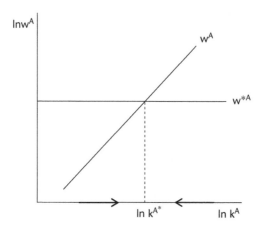

Figure 2.1 The Solow model in (w^A, k^A) space

41

the real wage is a scale-independent function of the capital intensity only under the present assumption of constant returns to scale.[3]

The w^* line in Figure 2.1 is a schedule of *long-run equilibria* along which the capital-labor ratio (k^A) remains constant over time. Therefore, it shows the value of the real wage required to generate the steady state rate of capital accumulation, at each given level of the capital-labor ratio. This required real wage is obtained as follows. Consider the rate of capital accumulation ($g_K = I/K$) expressed as:

$$g_K = (s/a)r - \delta \tag{3}$$

where I is net investment; r, the profit rate on capital; a, the profit share in competitive equilibrium; and s and δ, as before, are the saving and the depreciation rates.[4] The profit rate can, in turn, be expressed as a function of the real wage. Since, in competitive equilibrium, we have $r = a\ Y/K = a\ y^A/k^A$, using (1) and (2) we obtain:

$$r = a[(1 - a)/w^A]^{(1-a)/a} = r(w^A) \qquad r' < 0 \tag{4}$$

In a steady state, the rates of profit and accumulation must be such that the capital stock per effective worker remains constant over time. The effective labor force (AL) grows at a rate given by the sum of the rate of technical progress and the growth of the labor force. Technical progress is exogenous, independent of the economic system, and labor-augmenting (or Harrod-neutral), i.e., it increases output per worker without changing the capital-output ratio. It proceeds at a constant rate $g_A = (dA/dt)1/A$, where A is the level of technology. The labor force also grows at an exogenous and constant rate equal to n. The effective labor force thus grows at an exogenous rate given by $g_A + n$. Substituting from (4) into (3) we can solve for the value of the real wage (w^{*A}) required to generate the steady state rate of accumulation by setting the rate of capital accumulation equal to the exogenous growth rate of the effective labor supply ($n + g_A$). The required real wage is:

$$w^{*A} = (1 - a)[s/(n + g_A + \delta)]^{a/(1-a)} \tag{5}$$

Given that the wage share in total income is (1—a), the steady state value of output per worker is:

$$y^{*A} = [s/(n + g_A + \delta)]^{a/(1-a)} \tag{5'}$$

[3] Setting A = 1, for simplicity, the equilibrium wage can be written as $w = b\ L^{a+b-1} k^a$, where b is the output elasticity of labor in the production function. The wage does not depend on L only if b is equal to (1–a), which implies constant returns to scale (a + b = 1).

[4] Let s = S/Y, a = P/Y and r = P/K, where S is gross saving and P is total profits. Then, (s/a) r is equal to gross savings divided by the capital stock.

Eq. (5) defines the schedule of long-run equilibria or of stationary capital-effective labor ratios. Under our present assumptions, this is a horizontal line in $(\ln w^A, \ln k^A)$ space (see Figure 2.1). Given s, n, g_A, and δ, there is a unique real wage yielding a profit rate such that the capital stock grows at the rate of effective labor supply growth. Clearly, if there is a steady state, the steady state value of the real wage must be given by (5): values off this locus imply that the capital-labor ratio is changing over time and, from (2), the real wage must be changing as well.[5]

2. Transitional Dynamics and Empirical Shortcomings of the Neoclassical Model

Two well-known results follow from this set-up. The first is that the economy described converges to a steady state in which output and the capital stock grow at the same rate, equal to Harrod's natural rate. This growth rate is the sum of the rate of growth of the labor force (n) and the rate of technical progress (g_A), and is thus independent of the savings rate. In the steady state, the real wage (w) and output per worker (y) grow at the same rate as the rate of labor-augmenting technical progress (since $w = w^A A$, $y = y^A A$, and w^A and y^A are constant in the steady state).

The second result refers to what happens when the economy is off the equilibrium path. Suppose, for example, that the capital-labor ratio is below its steady state value. Due to the relative abundance of labor, the market-clearing wage is below the wage required to generate the steady state rate of capital accumulation. In this situation, the profit rate is relatively high and the capital stock will be growing faster than the effective labor force (see eq. 3). With a rising capital stock per effective worker, labor productivity and per capita incomes will be growing at a faster rate than technical progress. Will the capital-labor ratio (k^A) and income per effective worker keep growing for ever? No, because the increasing capital-labor ratio pulls with it the real wage, driving the profit rate down and reducing the rate of capital accumulation. The latter will thus gradually converge towards its steady state value and, when the adjustment is completed, the wage per effective worker (w^A) and the profit rate both remain stationary. During the adjustment, the economy's growth rate is higher than in the steady state, and growth is so much faster the lower the initial value of the capital endowment per worker. Thus, and this is

---

[5] We can also look at the schedules of short-run and long-run equilibria in $(\ln y^A, \ln k^A)$ space. The corresponding equations are (1) and (5'). As the reader can verify, a comparison with (2) and (5) shows that the y and y* lines look exactly like the w and w* lines except that their position is shifted upwards by the term $\ln [1/(1-a)]$, which is positive (since $a < 1$).

the result that we want to emphasize, starting from a relatively low capital-labor ratio, the economy converges to the equilibrium path at a diminishing rate of growth.

In terms of Figure 2.1, this property implies that the excess of the growth rate over its steady state value is a positive function of the gap between the w^A and w^{*A} lines. Indeed, using (3), the profit rate in the steady state must be such that:

$$n + g_A = (s/a)r^* - \delta \qquad (6)$$

where r^* is the steady state value of the profit rate, derived from (4) under $w^A = w^{*A}$. Subtracting (6) from (3), and using $\hat{y}^A = a\,\hat{K}^A$, where $\hat{y}^A = (dy^A/dt)\,(1/y^A)$ and $\hat{K}^A = (dk^A/dt)\,(1/k^A)$, we can express the growth of output per worker as a function of the gap between r and r^*:

$$\hat{y}^A = \Omega(\ln w^{*A} - \ln w^A) = \Omega(\ln y^{*A} - \ln y^A) \qquad (7)$$

Using (4), (5) and (7), as shown in the Appendix, we have as an approximation:

$$\hat{y}^A = \Omega(\ln w^{*A} - \ln w^{*A}) = \Omega(\ln y^{*A} - \ln y^{*A}) \qquad (7')$$

where $\Omega = (1 - a)\,(n + g_A + \delta)$ is the rate of convergence, the fraction of the gap between the actual and the steady state level of income that is eliminated per unit of time. Eq. (7') shows the growth of output per effective worker as an increasing function of the gap between the actual level of income and its steady state value.

The presence of diminishing returns to capital is critical to these properties of the model. To better understand this role, it will be useful to consider for a moment an economy with a constant population and no technical progress. In such an economy, output will eventually stagnate since its equilibrium path is a stationary state in which the economy generates a gross investment just equal to the depreciation of the capital stock. If, starting from this equilibrium, net investment became positive, the larger capital stock would have two consequences. First, output per worker would increase since each worker has a greater capital stock to his or her disposal. Second, at the initial real wage, labor demand would be greater; in the face of an inelastic labor supply, the real wage has to increase to clear the labor market. To say that there are diminishing returns to capital is the same as saying that the positive effect of the larger capital stock on labor productivity is not strong enough to offset the negative effect of the higher equilibrium real wage on the rate of profit. As a result, the market equilibrium wage rises above the required wage (w^*). The rate of return on capital falls below its stationary state value and the positive level of net investment cannot be sustained. The capital stock contracts and eventually returns to the initial equilibrium value. In this equilibrium state there is not, there cannot be, an endogenous process of capital accumulation. This helps us understand the crucial role played by technological progress and growth of the labor force in this theory; steady state growth is the outcome of these forces simply because there are no other forces capable of neutralizing the influence of diminishing returns to capital.

All this is so, of course, on the equilibrium path. If the capital stock per worker is smaller than in the steady state, there is an additional force that drives growth: the fact that the rate of return on capital is higher than in the steady state (the market equilibrium wage is lower than the required wage). With diminishing returns to capital, this driving force is strongest the smaller the capital-labor ratio is, since the lower real wages more than offset the low labor productivity associated with the small capital-labor ratio. Hence, the second result of the model: off the steady state, the economy's growth rate is higher the lower the capital-labor ratio is compared to its steady state value.

The Solow model thus has clear answers to the questions: why are some countries richer than others? Why do some economies grow faster than others? Regarding the first question, there are two sources of income differences across countries. First, they may be due to different steady state values of output per worker. Assuming access to the same technology, we know from (5') that they arise from differences in savings behavior, population growth and depreciation rates. The second source refers to disequilibrium differences in capital-labor ratios, i.e., to gaps across countries in their position vis-à-vis their steady state. Thus, a large difference in output per worker between two countries, for example the United States and India, may be the result of the United States having a higher steady state level of income than India, and/or of India being much further away from its steady state than the United States. Let us then look at the question of how large are the differences in the steady state levels of income implied by the Solow model.

Empirical shortcomings: actual and steady state values
of output per worker

Table 2.1 shows the actual levels of output per worker in 2008, along with other indicators, in our five groups of countries. The first few rows of the table reveal a well-known result: income levels tend to be positively correlated with investment shares in GDP and negatively correlated with population growth rates. That is, countries with relatively high incomes tend to have higher investment ratios and lower population growth rates than countries with lower incomes. This is why when using eq. (5') to regress incomes against investment ratios and a measure of $(n + g_A + \delta)$, we obtain coefficients that have the signs expected by the Solow model. The estimates for our sample are:

Table 2.1 Actual and steady state income gaps in the Solow model

	1	2	3	4	5
GDP per worker (2008)[a]	75,179.7	38,104.5	17,003.5	6,433.6	2,042.9
Investment share (%)[b]	23.5	24.5	22.6	22.5[d]	18.0[e]
Growth of the labor force %[c]	1.2	2.2	2.9	2.8	2.7
Income as a percentage of group 1 (2008)	100	50.7	22.6	8.6	2.7
Steady state income as a percentage of group 1	100	94.7	86.9	87.2	78.5
Number of countries	17	17	17	18	18

[a] International dollars 2005.
[b] Average share (1970–2008) of gross investment in GDP (current prices).
[c] Trend growth rate of the labor force (1970–2008) (percentage per year).
[d] Average excludes Nigeria.
[e] Average excludes Tanzania and Guinea.
See the appendix to Chapter 1 for data sources.

$$\ln y_{08} = 9.82 + 2.85\ln (I/Y) - 4.57\ln(n + g_A + \delta) \quad \text{Adj.}R^2 = 0.46$$
$$\quad (4.62) \ (6.17) \qquad\qquad (-5.85) \qquad\qquad N = 84$$

t statistics are in parentheses. $(g_A + \delta)$ is assumed to be .05 ($g_A = .02$ and $\delta = .03$) following Mankiw, Romer, and Weil (1992). I/Y is the investment share (average for the period 1970–2008).

Is it possible to say more? Yes, if we make some additional assumptions. To begin with, let us use a version of the Solow model that leaves aside differences in technology. Assume therefore the same initial levels of technology (A_0) and uniform rates of technical progress across countries. Eq. (5') then allows us to estimate the steady state values of output per worker in any given group as a fraction of that in group 1. More precisely, letting subscript i refer to groups 2 to 5, eq. (5') implies:

$$\ln(y^*_i/y^*_1) = a/(1 - a)\{[\ln(s_i/s_1)] - \ln[(n_i + g_A + \delta)/(n_1 + g_A + \delta)]\} \quad (5'')$$

Further, assume with Mankiw, Romer, and Weil that $(g_A + \delta)$ is 0.05, a profit share ("a") equal to 1/3, and measure s as the investment share (I/Y). Then, using the data in Table 2.1 and plugging it into (5''), we can obtain the predicted steady state levels of income for groups 2 to 5 (relative to group 1) and compare them with the actual differences in output per worker. We can thus address the question of how much of the income gaps across countries can be explained by differences in their steady state income levels.

The results are shown in rows 4 and 5 of Table 2.1. Differences in the steady state income levels turn out to be rather small compared to the actual income gaps. Consider, for example, the richest and poorest countries: while the actual income gap between them is in the range of 37 to 1, the steady state income of group 5 is only in the order of 20 percent lower than that of group 1.[6]

Empirical shortcomings: Differences in growth rates

The answer of the Solow model to the second question—why do some economies grow faster than others?—is that differences in growth rates of output per worker should reflect differences in the exogenous rate of labor productivity growth and in the position relative to the steady state (the component of growth due to transitional dynamics). Formally, using $\hat{y} = g_A + \hat{y}^A$, eq. (7') implies:

$$\hat{y} = g_A + \Omega(\ln y^{*A} - \ln y^A) \tag{8}$$

where Ω, equal to $(1-a)(n + g_A + \delta)$, is the rate of convergence, as already indicated. Eq. (8) shows the growth of output per worker as the sum of two components: 1) an exogenous one given by the rate of technical progress (g_A); 2) a transitional one, due to capital deepening, which is proportional to the gap between the initial and the steady state values of output per effective worker.

As shown by (8), the Solow model does not imply that poor countries should systematically grow faster than rich countries, even if one neglects differences in exogenous rates of technical progress across countries (and assumes equal g_As). Convergence is conditional on the determinants of the steady state and the implications of the model are consistent with a poor country (close to its steady state) growing more slowly than a richer country that is further away from the steady state.

For this to happen, however, the implied differences in the steady state levels of income must be very large (similar, or even larger in the example above, than the observed differences in actual levels of output per worker). Yet, the picture that emerges from the analysis is that the income gaps implied by the Solow model are largely the result of international differences in the position relative to the steady state, rather than of differences in steady state values of output per worker. Poor countries would appear to be poorer than others largely because they are much further away from the steady state than

---

[6] It is worth noting that the assumed value of the profit share ("a") of one third is far from being uniform across countries. The capital share varies significantly, tending to be higher than one third in many developing countries for which information is available. It is apparent from eq. (5'') that had we assumed a profit share for groups 2 to 5 higher than the value of one third that seems appropriate for group 1, the predicted income gaps would have been even narrower. This is because a higher profit share tends to increase the steady state income level in groups 2 to 5. Strictly, this is so if $s/(n + g_A + \delta) > 1$. Since $s/(n + g_A + \delta$ is the steady state value of the capital-output ratio, the lack of fulfillment of this condition would imply implausibly low values of the capital-output ratio in the steady state and, even more so, below the steady state.

Table 2.2 Actual and predicted GDP growth rates (1970–2008) in the Solow model

Growth rates per year	Averages for country groups				
	1	2	3	4	5
GDP per worker (actual)	1.9	1.6	0.7	0.7	0.3
GDP per worker (predicted)	1.9	3.4	4.8	7.1	9.7
GDP (actual)	3.1	3.9	3.6	3.5	3.0
GDP (predicted)	3.1	5.7	7.7	9.9	12.3
Number of countries	17	17	17	18	18

See the appendix to Chapter 1 for data sources.

wealthier countries. As we know, such a view has clear implications for differences in growth rates across countries: poor economies should grow faster than rich economies.

The evidence presented in Chapter 1 already indicated that this implication finds no empirical support. Much of the "convergence controversy" revolves precisely around the fact that the Solow model appears to overstate a tendency to convergence in the world economy. We can confirm this implication by using eq. (8) to estimate the growth rates predicted by the model. The appendix explains in detail the procedure followed.

Table 2.2 shows the predicted growth rates (with a capital share equal to 1/3 in all groups) together with actual growth rates. Given that differences in the steady state levels of income only explain a small part of actual income gaps, the predicted growth rates increase, as expected, as we move down along the income scale. This is not, however, what happens with actual growth performances. Instead of narrowing over time, the evidence on growth rates of GDP per worker suggests widening income gaps across broad groups of countries (in particular, between groups 1 and 2 on one side and groups 3, 4 and 5 on the other). The results in Table 2.2 add something to this well-known picture. For not only there is no tendency to absolute convergence, there are no strong tendencies either to conditional convergence. This is evident in the case of group 5. Its growth performance suggests that this group was moving *away* rather than *towards* its steady state level of income, given that its growth rate of 0.3 percent growth in GDP per worker was below the rate of technical progress, which is of the order of 2 percent per year.

3. The Nature of Technology

In the Solow-Swan model, technology displays constant returns to scale and advances at an exogenous pace ultimately given, one can reasonably think, by the rate of scientific progress. Since technology is introduced from outside the economic system, one can think of it as a public good freely available to firms. How plausible is this view of technology? To understand the answers to this question in endogenous growth theory, we have to discuss the nature of technology as a non-rival good with limited excludability.

Goods can be classified according to two fundamental attributes: the degree to which a good is rival and the degree to which it is excludable (Cornes and Sandler, 1986). Whether a good is rival or not depends on whether the use of the good by one person precludes its use by another or not. Most economic goods as well as conventional factors of production are rival: if one person uses a piece of physical capital such as a hammer another person cannot use it. Goods can also be classified according to the degree of excludability. The degree to which a good is excludable is the degree to which the owner of the good can charge a fee for its use. A hammer, a CD player, or the services of a dentist are highly excludable (see Figure 2.2).

Rival goods may or may not be highly excludable. Most economic goods or factors are rival and excludable. But rival goods may show low excludability. Goods that are rival but with low excludability suffer from the "tragedy of the commons". A traditional example of such goods is the overgrazing of common land shared by English peasants during the middle ages. A modern example is the over-fishing of international waters. Because fish in the sea is rival but with low excludability, the cost of one fisherman's choosing to catch an additional fish is shared by all of the fishermen, but solely only one fisherman captures the benefit. As a result there are negative externalities that, in the absence of regulation, can generate a tendency to an inefficiently high level of fishing that can potentially destroy "the commons".

Non-rival goods also may or may not be highly excludable. Jones (2002) gives the example of an encoded satellite TV transmission as a non-rival good (the transmission can be seen by many at the same time) with high excludability: the digital signals of an encoded satellite transmission are scrambled so as to be useful only to someone with a decoder. Other non-rival goods are non excludable. National defense, the results of basic research and development (R&D), calculus or a mathematical theorem are examples of non-rival goods that are essentially non-excludable. They are called public goods. They generate positive externalities and tend to be under-produced by markets, providing a classic opportunity for government intervention to improve welfare.

Technology is typically non-rival with partial excludability (Romer, 1990). In contrast with a piece of physical capital, technology, or the set of ideas that we call technology, is non-rival. Just as scientific ideas are non rival (my use of a calculus theorem does not preclude its use by other persons at the same time) just in time inventory methods are non-rival: its use by Toyota does not preclude Ford from taking advantage of the same technique. The other

		Rival goods	Non-rival goods
Excludability	High	CD player	Encoded satellite TV transmission
		Services of a dentist	
		Hammer	Computer code for a software application
			Operations manual for Wal-Mart stores
		Fish in the sea	
		Sterile insects for pest control	National defense
			Basic R&D
			Calculus
	Low		

Figure 2.2 Economic attributes of various goods
Source: Based on Romer (1993)

characteristic of technology is that it is only partially excludable. Its very nature makes it hard to prevent someone else from using them. Computer software is an example: anyone with a disk drive can copy software to give it to someone else. Software companies take advantage of this aspect of ideas in manufacturing software (it lowers the cost of manufacturing) but can also find it to be a problem because of software pirating. Similar considerations apply to the operating manual of a big store or the accounting practices and inventory methods of a large company. These are in principle known only to the company's employees but can be copied by observers of business behavior.

The nature of technology as non-rival good has a number of consequences. First, while goods that are rival must be produced each time they are sold, goods that are non-rival need be produced only once. That is, non-rival goods such as ideas involve a fixed cost of production and zero marginal cost. As Romer (1990, p. S72) puts it: "Once the cost of creating a new set of instructions has been incurred, the instructions can be used over and over again at no additional cost. For example, it costs a great deal to produce the first unit of the latest word processor or spreadsheet, but simply copying the software from the first unit produces subsequent units". Notice that the only reason for a non zero marginal cost is that the non-rival good, the idea, is embodied in a rival good, the CD. More precisely, as Romer (1990) puts it, a design is such that the cost of replicating it with a drafter, a photocopier, or a disk drive is trivial compared to the cost of creating the design in the first place. This means that the economics of ideas is intimately tied to the presence of increasing returns to scale and imperfect competition. The link to increasing returns to scale is due to the fact that ideas are associated with fixed costs. The link to imperfect competition is that price cannot equal then marginal cost because selling at marginal cost would imply a loss since, due to the high fixed cost, average cost is higher than marginal cost. A second consequence of the non-rival nature of technology is that technology transfers across countries differ substantially from transfers of capital. Taking capital from a rich country and moving it to a poor country would make the poor country better off but the rich country worse off. By contrast, if a country is poor because it lacks technologies, then technologies can be transferred from elsewhere without making the country from which they were taken any worse off.

The relatively low degree of excludability of technology also has consequences. Goods that are excludable allow their producers to capture the benefits they produce. Goods that are not excludable involve substantial spillovers of benefits that are not captured by producers, i.e. they involve externalities. In other words, because of lack of excludability often the person who has created a new technology will not reap most of the benefits from its creation. This fact diminishes the incentives for creating technology and is the main justification for protecting intellectual property rights through a patent system.

Before turning to endogenous growth models it is worth noting that the Solow model is consistent with the fact that technological change drives growth, and also with the fact that technology is a non-rival good, but it is inconsistent with the fact that technology is partially excludable and that private, maximizing behavior plays a role in generating technological change. It treats technology as non-rival and non-excludable, that is, as a public and publicly provided good. Technology in neoclassical theory is like calculus, a public good resulting from scientific progress, rather than a piece of computer software, a technological innovation that is non-rival and partially excludable.

4. Increasing Returns and Endogenous Growth

From the perspective of recent developments in endogenous growth theory, the basic properties of the Solow model are unsatisfactory. First, in this view, the convergence properties of the neoclassical model have a number of counterfactual implications: 1) capital-scarce countries do not grow faster than capital-abundant countries; 2) international differences in rates of return on capital are much less than one would expect given the disparities across countries in capital-labor endowments; and 3) capital does not flow internationally towards the poorest countries (see, for example, Lucas, 1988; Romer, 1991). Second, endogenous growth theory objects to the fact that steady state growth in the neoclassical model is the result of exogenous forces—labor force growth and technical progress—which are left unexplained by the theory. Moreover, it objects to the associated steady state properties that have the implication that two different economies investing different shares of their total income will grow at the same rate in the long-run, provided that they have access to the same technology.

The objections to the neoclassical growth model in the recent literature have generated the perception that the shortcomings of traditional theory have a common source: a specification of the technology that gives a too prominent role to diminishing returns to capital. If technology could be re-specified in such a way as to counteract the influence of diminishing returns, this could in principle overcome the perceived weaknesses of the neoclassical framework. It could generate endogenous growth in the steady state without having to rely on the assumptions of exogenous technical progress and population growth, thus enhancing the explanatory power of the theory. At the same time, such endogenous growth would weaken the strong convergence properties of the traditional model, making theory more consistent with the observed historical experience. How should technology be re-specified to meet those two objectives? In this chapter, I focus on the brand of endogenous growth theory that re-specifies the technology assumed by the basic neoclassical growth model without attempting to model technological progress as the endogenous outcome of economic incentives to create or adopt new technologies, a task undertaken by the product variety and Schumpeterian brands of new growth theory reviewed in Chapter 5.

Increasing returns to capital

In the recent literature on endogenous growth, the first approach taken, that initially appeared as most promising, was to abandon the assumption of constant returns to scale. Increasing returns to scale strengthen the positive effects of capital accumulation on labor productivity, as the effect of a higher capital-labor ratio on output per worker is now enhanced by the positive effect of a larger capital stock and scale of production. This opens up the possibility that the positive productivity effects of capital accumulation offset the negative effects of higher real wages on the profit rate. If, as a result, returns to capital do not diminish, capital accumulation can persist indefinitely even without exogenous technical progress or labor supply growth.

Paul Romer in the 1986 article that sparked the recent literature on endogenous growth adopted the assumption of increasing returns to capital.[7] For Romer, the private rate of return on knowledge-intensive investments in research and development can be well below their social rate of return, because the returns on private investments in new technologies are only partially appropriable given the nature of technology as a partially excludable good. As firms develop new technologies, they may make discoveries that many other firms can use at the same time, i.e., the information generated is non rival unlike ordinary inputs which are rival (their use by one firm prevents others from using them simultaneously, see Romer, 1990a, 1994). As a result, these investments need not be subject to diminishing social returns. While returns to capital may be diminishing for the individual firm, they may be increasing for the economy as a whole when account is taken of the spillovers from these investments in research and development. These spillovers generate externalities which in turn lead to suboptimal levels of investment and growth. They are due to inappropriability and are here the source of *aggregate* increasing returns *to capital*. Capital accumulation then feeds itself, and generates a self-sustained expansion at an increasing growth rate over time.

We can use our real wage diagram to more formally present the basic result of the Romer model (see Figure 2.3). Consider a production function with

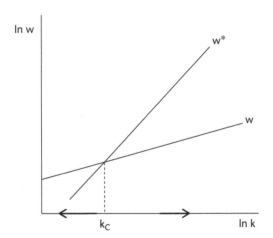

Figure 2.3 A Romer-type model

[7] In Romer's and other endogenous growth models, the non-neoclassical assumptions on technology are combined with that of intertemporal optimization on the part of households. In the presentation of these models, I will continue to assume a fixed saving rate, as Solow and Swan did, in order to facilitate comparison with the neoclassical model in this chapter. I will turn to intertemporal optimization in Chapter 3.

technological externalities in which the multiplicative constant (A) is a positive function of the aggregate capital stock per worker:

$$Y = AK^a L^{1-a} \quad A = (\tilde{K}/L)^\mu \tag{9}$$

where Y is production at the firm level, K and L the inputs of capital and labor, and (K~/L) is the average stock of capital per worker in the economy. Capital here has to be given a broad interpretation which includes the stock of knowledge generated by past investment in research and development. If the external effects generated by the average stock of capital per worker are strong enough, so that $a + \mu \geq 1$, the aggregate production function will exhibit non-diminishing returns to capital.

It is easily shown that the equations of the w and w* curves now are:

$$w = (1 - a)k^{a+\mu} \tag{10}$$

$$w^* = (1 - a)[s/(n + \delta)]^{a/(1-a)} \, k^{\mu/(1-a)} \tag{11}$$

where s is the savings rate, n is the rate of growth of the labor force, and k is the overall capital-labor ratio (K/L).

Compared to the Solow model, the presence of technological externalities modifies the shape of the two curves in the diagram. In particular, the w* line is no longer horizontal but positively sloped. This is due to the (external) productivity effects of increases in the capital stock. Since the profit rate depends on the real wage and productivity, which in turn depends on the capital stock, the same rate of profit and, thus, the same rate of capital accumulation can now be generated at low levels of wages and capital stock and at higher levels of wages and capital stock. That is, with technological externalities there is no longer a unique real wage but rather a locus of real wage and capital per worker combinations that generate the same rate of return on capital: as capital per worker increases, the negative effect of the real wage on the rate of return is offset along the locus by the (now larger) positive effects of the capital-labor ratio on productivity. Moreover, if external effects are large enough to generate increasing returns to capital in the economy as a whole, it is readily verified from (10) and (11) that the w* line will be steeper than the w line, making the equilibrium at the intersection of the two curves unstable.[8] An economy with a capital-labor endowment greater than kc in the figure will generate a growth path of self-sustained expansion with real wages increasing along the w line and rates of return and capital accumulation (a function of the gap between the two schedules) increasing as well. For this to happen, returns to capital, and not only to scale, must indeed increase.

---

[8] With $a + \mu > 1$, the slope of the w* line (given by $\mu/(1-a)$) is greater than the slope of the w line (given by $a + \mu$).

Otherwise, the w* line will be flatter than the w line and the properties of the model will not be radically different from those of the neoclassical model.[9]

The AK model

A particular case is the AK model in which the production function is linear in the aggregate capital stock.[10] In this case, $a + \mu = 1$ in eq. (9), and thus technology displays constant returns to capital. As is readily verified, with $a + \mu = 1$, the w and w* lines have the same slope (see Figure 2.4). Provided that the savings rate is higher than $(n + \delta)$, the w* line is above the w line and perpetual growth takes place at a constant rate of capital accumulation equal to $(s - \delta)$ (given the production function assumed in (9)).[11,12]

The distinction between transitional and steady state dynamics vanishes. The traditional steady state condition, $I/K = n + \delta$, is never fulfilled since the condition for w* to be greater than w is $s > n + \delta$, which implies that the rate of capital accumulation forever will remain larger than the rate of labor force growth. Depending on how one wishes to define the steady state, we can say that the economy remains perpetually in transition or, because it grows at a constant rate, that there is no transition period, the path along the w line being the steady state growth path.

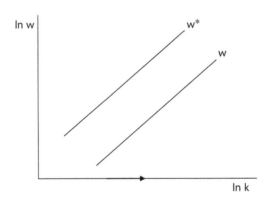

Figure 2.4 An AK model

[9] The point that the neoclassical model can accommodate increasing returns to scale, provided that these do not generate constant or increasing returns to capital, is made by Solow (1988, 1994).

[10] The AK model has become a workhorse in the growth theory literature. The initial versions include Barro (1990) and Rebelo (1991).

[11] For ln w* to be greater than ln w, we must have the term $a/(1-a) \ln [s/(n + d)]$ to be positive. This in turn requires $s > n + \delta$.

[12] The profit rate can be expressed as: $r = a\, k^{\mu/a} [(1-a)/w]^{1-a/a}$. Substituting from (10) and setting $a + \mu = 1$, we obtain $r = a$. The rate of accumulation: $I/K = g = s\,(r/a)-\delta$ is thus equal in this case to $(s-\delta)$. More generally, with a production function: $Y = A\,K$, the rate of accumulation is $s\,A-\delta$.

Unlike what happens in the Solow model, a change in the investment rate now has a permanent effect on the rate of growth of the economy. A higher investment rate shifts the w* line upwards and permanently increases the rate of capital accumulation of the economy. More generally, the parameters affecting the steady state level of income in the Solow model (s, n, and δ) now affect the growth rate of per capita income. With the production function in (9), the growth rate of output per worker is now given by: $g_y = s - (n + \delta)$.[13] This key difference radically alters the convergence properties, compared to the Solow model. For example, two AK economies that are identical except for their initial capital-labor ratios will have identical growth rates and therefore will never converge to similar levels of output per worker. Two economies with different savings rates and population growth rates will have permanently different growth rates, rather than permanently different income levels as in the Solow model.

The AK model illustrates very clearly in what sense growth is endogenous. Further comparison with old growth theory will be helpful to clarify the distinctive features of the newer approach. In neo-Keynesian and neoclassical growth theory, Harrod's warranted growth rate is the savings rate, s, times the output-capital ratio, v. This warranted growth rate (s v) adjusts to the exogenously given natural growth rate (n + g_A) through changes in either the savings rate (caused by income redistribution as in Kaldor, 1956) or in the capital-output ratio as a result of changes in factor prices (as in Solow, 1956). In the AK model, in contrast, the natural rate is no longer independent of the warranted rate: an increase in the investment rate brings about a higher rate of endogenous productivity growth. Provided that returns to capital are constant, this increases the natural rate by exactly the extent necessary to keep it constant at a higher level of growth, equal to the new value of the warranted rate. The endogeneity of the natural rate was anticipated by Kaldor when he introduced the technical progress function into the neo-Keynesian model of growth and distribution (Kaldor, 1957; Kaldor and Mirrlees, 1962). We shall return to Keynesian growth theory in Chapters 10 to 13.

A hybrid neoclassical-endogenous growth model

The comparison between the neoclassical and the AK model can be further clarified if we imagine an endogenous growth model with diminishing returns to capital. This will be the case if the technology features a sufficiently high elasticity of factor substitution that counteracts the role of diminishing

---

[13] In intensive form, and assuming a + μ = 1, the production function is: Y/L = K/L. The growth rate of output per worker is thus equal to the rate of capital accumulation (s–δ) minus the growth rate of the labor force (n).

returns to capital and generates sustained growth over time. In this case, the real wage effects on the profit rate are offset, not by the productivity gains resulting from the presence of increasing returns, but rather by a high elasticity of substitution that tends to reduce the demand for labor more than proportionately. This reduces the share of wages in total output. It is then possible that, even under constant returns to scale, a high elasticity of factor substitution will make persistent growth possible.[14]

Consider a CES production function of the form:

$$Y = A[a\,K^\varphi + (1-a)L^\varphi]^{1/\varphi} \tag{12}$$

which features a constant elasticity of factor substitution given by $\sigma = 1/(1-\varphi)$. If φ lies in the (0, 1) range, the elasticity of substitution is greater than one. Using (12), setting the marginal product of labor equal to the wage, and labor demand equal to the exogenous labor supply, yields the equation of the w curve:

$$w = A(1-a)[ak^{(\sigma-1)/\sigma} + (1-a)]^{1/(\sigma-1)} \tag{13}$$

where k is the capital-labor ratio. This can also be written as: $w = (1-a)\,A^{(\sigma-1)/\sigma}\,y^{1/\sigma}$, where y is output per worker, an increasing function of k, as can be seen in eq. (12). The slope of the w curve depends on the extent to which gains in output per worker accrue to wage earners and the extent to which increases in capital per worker raise productivity.[15]

Consider the schedule w*. The equation of the w* curve is obtained by substituting the steady state value of the profit rate into the wage-profit relationship. Expressing the profit rate ($= \pi\,Y/K$, where π is the profit share in output) as a function of k and using (13), we can derive the wage-profit relationship:[16]

$$w = \left[(1-a)/a\right]^{\sigma/(\sigma-1)}[(A^{1-\sigma}/a^\sigma) - r^{1-\sigma}]^{1/(1-\sigma)} \tag{14}$$

Assuming, for simplicity, that investment is financed exclusively out of profits, the rate of capital accumulation in the steady state must be such

---

[14] On the subject, see Solow (1956, pp.70–1) as well as the contributions of Jones and Manuelli (1990) and King and Rebelo (1990).

[15] Differentiating with respect to k, we obtain the slope of the w curve:

$$dw/dk = [(1-a)/\sigma](ak^{(\sigma-1)/\sigma} + (1-a))^{-1}a\,A[a + (1-a)k^{(1-\sigma)/\sigma}]^{1/(\sigma-1)}$$

It will be useful to look at this expression as the product of two terms: 1) $dw/dy = [(1-a)/\sigma]$ $[ak^{(\sigma-1)/\sigma} + (1-a)]^{(1-\sigma)/\sigma} = [(1-a)/\sigma]\,(A/y)^{(\sigma-1)/\sigma}$, which reflects the extent to which gains in output per worker accrue to wage earners; 2) $dy/dk = a\,A\,[a + (1-a)\,k^{(1-\sigma)/\sigma}]^{1/\sigma-1)}$, which reflects the extent to which increases in capital per worker raise productivity.

[16] As can be readily verified, this wage-profit relationship becomes linear in the case of a fixed coefficients technology: with $k^{(1-\sigma)/\sigma} = 0$, we obtain: $w = A - r$. With a unit elasticity of substitution ($\sigma = 1$) the curve is log linear with a slope such that $d\ln w/d\ln r = -a/(1-a)$, just as in the Cobb-Douglas case. More generally, the slope of the wage profit curve can be expressed as: $dw/dr = -[a/(1-a)]^\sigma\,(w/r)^\sigma$

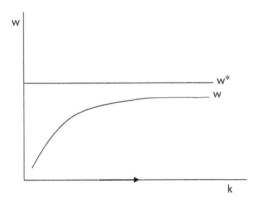

Figure 2.5 A hybrid neoclassical-endogenous growth model

that: $s_\pi \, r = n + \delta$, where s_π is the propensity to save out of profits. With a constant rate of savings out of profits, there is a unique value of the required profit rate, $r^* = (n + \delta)/s_\pi$, which is independent of the capital-labor ratio. Substituting this value into (14) yields the equation of the w^* curve. This is a horizontal line in (w, k) space, since r^* and thus w^* are independent of k (see Figure 2.5).[17]

Consider the case of a high elasticity of substitution $(\sigma > 1)$. As is readily verified, the slope of the w curve now falls as k increases. Moreover, the term dw/dy tends to zero when k goes to infinity so that the w curve approaches the same slope as the w^* line. As illustrated in Figure 2.5, if w^* is greater than w when k tends to infinity, the two curves will not intersect and growth will proceed at a diminishing rate, converging to a constant rate as k tends to infinity. The rate of accumulation does not converge to Harrod's natural rate, as in the Solow model, because with a more than unit elasticity of substitution, the profit share increases as k rises, and tends to unity when k tends to infinity. Then, just as in the AK model, returns to capital become constant since, with $dw/dy = 0$, the negative effect of a higher equilibrium wage on the profit rate no longer counteracts the effect of the larger capital stock on labor productivity.[18] The profit rate remains constant and

---

[17] This shape of the w^* curve depends on the assumption about the savings rate. Otherwise, the steady state condition would imply: $(s/\pi) \, r = n + \delta$, where s is the overall savings rate. Since the profit share (π) varies with the capital-labor ratio, whenever the elasticity of factor substitution is different from unity, the required value of r will also vary with k and w^* will thus not be independent of the capital-labor ratio. Although this formulation would appear to be more general, the assumption that the overall savings rate (s) remains constant in the face of changes in factor shares is, in fact, rather implausible.

[18] As can be seen by manipulating (12), as k goes to infinity, F approaches a function that is linear in K: $Y = A \, a^{1/\varphi} K$. The marginal product of capital falls as k increases but, unlike the Solow model, does not converge to zero. The key difference is that the high elasticity of substitution makes neither capital nor labor essential for production, in the sense that $F(K, L) = 0$ when $L = 0$ or $K = 0$.

equal to $a^{\sigma/(\sigma-1)}$ A.[19] Provided that $s_\pi\, a^{\sigma/(\sigma-1)}$ A > n + δ, the rate of accumulation approaches a constant value, $s_\pi\, a^{\sigma/(\sigma-1)}$ A – δ, which is greater than the natural rate (n).

This model thus blends features of the AK model and the Solow model. Two economies with identical technology and savings rates that differ in their initial capital-labor ratios will not converge to identical levels of output per worker. They tend to converge to the same rate of growth and, for this reason, the initial income gap will not fully disappear. In this aspect, as in the AK model, the strength of convergence is weakened compared to the Solow model. At the same time, the transitional dynamics remain similar to the neoclassical model since the economy with the lower capital-labor ratio grows at a faster rate.

Empirical assessment

It is striking that most of the recent empirical research has focused on testing the neoclassical growth model, with revisions and extensions, rather than on testing the empirical implications of endogenous growth models. This is the case even though, paradoxically, it is the theoretical research on endogenous growth that in part spurred the research that focuses on testing the neoclassical growth model.[20] Part of the explanation, suggested by Mankiw (1995), may be that by emphasizing unmeasurable variables such as knowledge these models have appealed to the more theoretically inclined economists with the result that few attempts have been made to evaluate them. Another reason arises from the intrinsic difficulties in evaluating models based on large technological externalities in an open economy setting. Indeed, a crucial question, as we shall see below, is whether these large external effects of the capital stock are internal to national economies or not.[21]

As we have seen, growth models that rely on externalities of capital stock to generate continuous growth, are led to assume that the external effects of capital accumulation are so large that they generate non-diminishing returns to capital in the aggregate production function. Taking a very long-term perspective, Romer (1986, 1991) finds this assumption attractive because it is consistent with the rising productivity growth rates of the technological leaders over the centuries. Indeed, according to Maddison (1982, quoted by

---

[19] The profit rate can be written as: $r = \pi\, Y/K = \pi\, A\, [a + (1-a)\, k^{(1-\sigma)/\sigma}]^{\sigma/(\sigma-1)}$. When k goes to infinity, π tends to 1 and r approaches $a^{\sigma/(\sigma-1)}$ A.

[20] I say "in part", because empirical research by Baumol (1986), followed by criticisms by Abramovitz (1986) and De Long (1988), was at the origin of the recent work on convergence and also motivated the initial theoretical research on endogenous growth.

[21] In what follows, we restrict our discussion to models with non diminishing returns to capital. As already noted, the transitional dynamics of models relying on a high elasticity of factor substitution are similar to those of the Solow model.

Romer, 1986), the annual growth rate of labor productivity went from zero in the Netherlands for 1700–1785, to 0.5 percent in the United Kingdom for 1785–1820, to 1.4 percent in the UK for 1820–1890, and to 2.3 percent in the United States 1890–1979. It is worth noting that while Romer's observation is interesting and accurate, it is not fully consistent with a model with increasing returns to capital. Why, in such a model, should the technological leadership switch from the Netherlands to the United Kingdom in the 18th century and then from the United Kingdom to the United States in the 20th century?

If we apply this analytical framework to explain cross-country differences in growth rates, we immediately face more severe difficulties. If externalities do not cross borders, then—just as diminishing returns to capital in the neoclassical model tend to generate too much convergence—the assumption of increasing returns to capital tends to generate too much divergence. For not only should the gaps in income per capita widen over time, the differences in growth rates themselves should also become larger. Nobody, to my knowledge, has suggested that this is what we observe. The two pieces of evidence— time series for the productivity leaders and cross-sections of countries—can be reconciled if external effects do cross borders so that the state of technology in, say, Mexico depends on the economy-wide capital-labor ratio in the United States. However, the transitional dynamics of such a model would not be much different from the Solow model. Technical progress, while endogenous in the United States, would still be exogenous in Mexico—a result of shifts in the technology variable in the production function and independent of its own investment rate.[22]

The excessive degree of divergence, in models with local externalities, seems to have its roots in a difficulty repeatedly pointed out by Solow (1988, 1994). A model with a technology exhibiting increasing returns to capital has a mind-boggling implication: it generates infinite output in finite time. In the example provided by Solow (1994), if we assume an investment rate of 10 percent of GDP and a very small dose of increasing returns to capital, this would happen in 200 hundred years, starting from the current per capita incomes of France or Germany. Even though this observation is not a decisive objection, it seems to set the burden of proof on those who believe in the existence of such dramatically increasing returns.

This particular difficulty is avoided in endogenous growth models that restrict the coefficient on capital in the aggregate production function to unity (the AK model) and thus generate persistent growth at a constant rather

---

[22] This observation does not apply (potentially) to the neo-Schumpeterian brand of endogenous growth theory where the extent to which a developing country may internalize the external effects of technological innovations in the productivity leaders may depend on investment rates. However, the focus on explaining technological advances makes these Schumpeterian models, discussed in Chapter 5, mostly relevant, so far, to highly advanced industrial countries.

than an increasing rate. The properties of these models—persistent growth that depends on the investment rate—may help understand the increasing gaps between low and high-income countries. At the same time, replacing the Solow model with a model without transitional dynamics makes it harder to explain the trend towards convergence that has taken place among today's high and middle-income countries. Just as predicted by the Solow model, this process has featured catching up processes with a significant amount of capital deepening (see the evidence presented in Chapter 1 and, on the period 1950–1987, Maddison, 1991). Moreover, the distinctive properties of these models depend critically on returns to capital being exactly constant. This further restricts the assumptions on technology without empirical support. The evidence to be reviewed in Chapter 7 on increasing returns to scale and Verdoorn's law, and research on the external effects of capital accumulation, suggest the presence of increasing returns to scale *and* diminishing returns to capital, especially in the case of the *aggregate* production function.[23]

Appendix

1. The Standard Presentation of the Solow Model

Technology displays constant returns to scale and diminishing returns to variable proportions. We assume a Cobb-Douglas production function: $Y = K^a (AL)^{1-a}$ with $a < 1$, where Y is output; K, the capital stock; L, labor input in natural units; and AL, labor input in effective units. Dividing total output by effective labor (AL), output per effective worker is:

$$y^A = (k^A)^a \qquad y^A = Y/(AL) \quad k^A = k/(AL) \tag{A.1}$$

Figure 2.A.1 shows the graph of eq. (A.1) as a curve that starts at the origin and has a positive and diminishing slope as k increases. In the short run, with given factor endowments (K and L) and a given state of technology (A), the ratio k^A is thus given. The value of y^A along the curve shows then the full employment level of output per worker corresponding to each given value of the k^A ratio.

Over time, technology and factor endowments change. Technical progress proceeds at an exogenous rate (g_A) and the labor force grows at an exogenous rate (n). The savings rate (s) is fixed and, thus, a constant fraction of total income is devoted to the replacement and expansion of the capital stock period after period. The capital-effective labor ratio (k^A) will thus be changing at a rate equal to the difference between gross investment per effective worker (sy^A) and the effective depreciation for the capital-labor ratio determined by the depreciation rate δ and the growth rate of the effective labor supply $(n + g_A)$:

---

[23] For evidence on East Asia strongly suggesting diminishing returns to capital, see Young (1992, 1995).

$$dk^A/dt = sy^A - (n + g_A + \delta)k^A \qquad (A.2)$$

The first term in the RHS of (A.2) is gross investment per effective worker. This term, proportional to output per effective worker, is a function of k^A, and is shown in Figure 2. A.1 as the sy^A curve that has, like the y^A curve, a positive and diminishing slope. The term $(n + g_A + \delta)$ is the sum of the growth rate of the effective labor supply and the depreciation rate. When multiplied by a given value of k^A, it shows the amount of investment required to keep k^A constant at that given value. In Figure 2.A.1, this is a line from the origin with positive and constant slope, given our assumptions of positive and constant values for n, g_A, and δ.

If initially dk^A/dt is positive, will the capital-labor ratio (k^A) keep growing for ever, or will it converge to a constant value? Substituting from (A.1) into (A.2) and dividing both sides of the equation by k^A, the proportionate rate of growth of k^A is given by:

$$\hat{K}^A = s/(k^A)^{1-a} - (n + g_A + \delta) \text{ where } \hat{K}^A = (dk^A/dt)(1/k^A)$$

which shows that the growth rate of k^A is a decreasing function of its level, provided that a < 1 (diminishing returns to capital). In the Cobb-Douglas specification adopted, the growth rate then converges to zero for the value of k^A given by:

$$k^{*A} = [s/(n + g_A + \delta)]^{1/(1-a)} \qquad (A.3)$$

This is the steady state level of the capital-effective labor ratio. The steady state value of output per effective worker is obtained by substituting from (A.3) into (A.1):

$$y^{*A} = [s/(n + g_A + \delta)]^{a/(1-a)} \qquad (A.4)$$

Figure 2.A.1 illustrates the determination of k^{A*} at the intersection of the gross investment curve and the line of effective depreciation. Indeed, k^{A*} is the solution to (A.2) for $dk^A/dt = 0$ and, therefore, to the equation $s\,y^A = (n + g_A + \delta)\,k^A$. The steady state value of output per effective worker is the value on the y^A curve corresponding to k^{A*}. The figure also illustrates the stability of this steady state. For values of k^A below k^{A*}, the gross investment curve is above the depreciation line and, thus, actual investment is larger than the amount required to keep k^A constant at that given value. The capital-labor

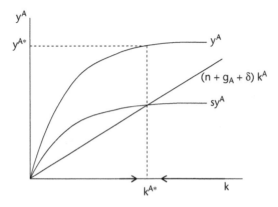

Figure 2.A.1 The Solow model

ratio increases towards k^{A*}. Analogous reasoning applies to the case of values where k^A is higher than the steady state level.

2. Derivation of the Rate of Convergence (Eq. 10')

Eq. (7) implies: $\hat{y}^A = s\,(r - r^*) = s\,(r/r^* - 1)\,r^*$. From (4) and (5), r^* is given by:

$$r^* = (a/s)(n + g_A + \delta) \tag{A.5}$$

Substituting from (A.5) into (7), we get:

$$\hat{y}^A = a(r/r^* - 1)(n + g_A + \delta) \tag{A.6}$$

Taking logs in (4), and using this equation to solve for $\ln w^{*A}$—$\ln w^A$, we have:

$$\ln w^{*A} - \ln w^A = [a/(1 - a)](\ln r - \ln r^*) \tag{A.7}$$

Using now the approximation $r/r^* - 1 = \ln (r/r^*)$, and substituting from (A.7) into (A.6), we get:

$$\hat{y}^A = (1 - a)(n + g_A + d)(\ln w^{*A} - \ln w^A) \tag{A.8}$$

3. Predicted Growth Rates in the Solow Model

The form of eq. (8) used is (see Mankiw, Romer and Weil, 1992):

$$g_y = (\ln y^A t - \ln y^A 0)/t = g_A + (1 - e^{-\Omega t})(\ln y^{*A} - \ln y^A 0)/t$$

where 0 refers to the initial year and t to the final year. The main difficulty involved in using eq. (8) to estimate the growth rates predicted by the Solow model is that we do not have estimates of the initial gap relative to the steady state (y^{*A}/y^{Ao}). However, we can decompose this term, for each group of countries, as follows: $y_i^{*A}/y_i^{Ao} = (y_i^{*A}/y^*{}_1{}^A)\,(y_1^{*A}/y_1^{Ao})\,(y_1^{Ao}/y_i^{Ao})$. The first term in the RHS is the gap in steady state incomes between each country group and group 1. This is the gap estimated in Table 2.2 (since according to the assumption of identical technologies the ratios of output per effective worker are the same as the ratios of output per worker). The third term is the initial 1970 gap in actual incomes that can be obtained from Table 2.1. The second term is the gap, within group 1, between the initial level of income and the steady state level of income in 2008. We can have an estimate of this term, conditional upon the assumption that the model correctly predicts the growth rate of group 1,[24] by using eq. (8) to solve for the value of (y_1^{*A}/y_1^{Ao}) implied by the model.

---

[24] This assumption does not seem controversial given that the consistency of the Solow model with the post-war growth trends in OECD economies is generally accepted.

3

Endogenous Savings and International Capital Mobility in the Neoclassical Model

In the Solow-Swan model the investment/savings rate is exogenous and remains constant throughout the lengthy transition to the steady state. It can be argued that consumers and wealth holders are behaving according to a rule which is not necessarily consistent with utility maximization. Would the relaxation of the assumption of a fixed savings rate improve the fit of the Solow-Swan model?

This chapter extends the neoclassical model of Chapter 2 by removing the assumption of a fixed and exogenous savings rate. The investment rate can vary for two reasons when the economy is off the steady state. In the absence of international capital mobility, the investment rate can change along with the domestic savings rate as a result of an increasing level of income and a diminishing marginal product of capital (and thus a falling real interest rate). With international capital mobility, the investment share will also respond to differences in international rates of return, and will thus be partially or completely de-linked from the domestic savings rate. While this tends to accentuate the tendency to convergence in a model with diminishing returns to capital, the presence of international capital mobility can also make investment more responsive to international differences in political risk with novel implications for the determinants of the steady state.

We look in this chapter at the implications of these different possible ways of extending the neoclassical growth model. We begin by considering a Ramsey model in which households determine how much to save by intertemporally optimizing discounted utility and look at how the steady state properties and transitional dynamics of the neoclassical model are modified as a result. Then, we turn to a model with a subsistence level of consumption in the utility function and examine how multiple steady states arise from this assumption and how the transitional dynamics are modified. We then turn to look at the implications of international capital mobility and conclude with a first approximation to the empirical debates on convergence.

1. The Ramsey Model: Savings and Growth Under Intertemporal Optimization

Consider an economy that produces a good that can be invested or consumed according to a technology featuring constant returns to scale and diminishing marginal returns to labor and capital. In intensive form, the production function is: $y = f(k)$ with $f'(k) > 0$ and $f''(k) < 0$, where y (= Y/L) and k (= K/L) are respectively output and capital per worker.

In the Ramsey model, households with an infinite time horizon and perfect foresight decide how much to consume and save on the basis of intertemporal optimization. Preferences are described by a utility function which depends on present and future levels of consumption and we assume that it features a constant intertemporal elasticity of substitution in consumption. The instantaneous utility function [u (.)] has the form: $u(C_t) = C_t^{1-\theta}/(1-\theta)$, where $1/\theta$ is the intertemporal elasticity of substitution in consumption (showing, as we shall see later, the response of consumption and savings to the interest rate). Population (equal to the labor force) grows at a rate n and I assume away, for simplicity, technical progress.

With perfect foresight, the representative agent maximizes discounted utility subject to the technology constraint, an arbitrarily given initial capital stock, and a dynamic equation for the capital stock which states, as in the Solow model, that in each period the end value of capital stock is equal to its initial value plus the flow of savings and investment net of the depreciation of the capital stock. Consider the maximization problem of the representative consumer and let's derive intuitively the Euler equation governing the behavior of consumption. Suppose that the consumer reduces consumption per worker (c) at time t in a small (formally infinitesimal) amount Δc, and invests this amount for a short (infinitesimally) period of time Δt and consumes the proceeds of the investment at time $t + \Delta t$. In doing so, consumption and capital holdings remain the same at all other times. If the consumer is optimizing, the marginal impact of this change should be zero (otherwise the consumer was not maximizing). The utility cost of this change is the marginal utility of c_t (du/dc) multiplied by Δc. With discrete time and no technical progress, the unit reduction in consumption has then a cost: $[1/(1 + \rho)^t] c_t^{-\theta}$, where ρ is the discount rate. The marginal utility of consumption one period later is: $[1/(1 + \rho)^{t + 1}] c_{t + 1}^{-\theta}$.

The marginal benefit is: $(1 + r) [1/(1 + \rho)^{t + 1}] c_{t + 1}^{-\theta}$, where r is the interest rate (equal to the marginal product of capital). Optimization requires: $[1/(1 + \rho)^t] c_t^{-\theta} = (1 + r) [1/(1 + \rho)^{t + 1}] c_{t + 1}^{-\theta}$. This implies: $c_{t + 1}/c_t = [(1 + r) / (1 + \rho)]^{1/\theta}$. Taking natural logarithms on both sides of the equation, in continuous time this condition yields the Euler equation:

$$(dc_t/dt)(1/c_t) = (r - \rho)/\theta \quad \text{where } r = f'(k) \quad \text{(assuming no depreciaton)} \quad (1)$$

This equation states that the rate of growth of consumption depends on the difference between the interest rate and the discount rate, the response being stronger the higher the intertemporal elasticity of substitution in consumption. What is the intuition behind the Euler equation? Given discount rate, a higher interest rate induces households to sacrifice consumption today in order to consume more in the future. The rate of growth of consumption will thus be higher the higher is the interest rate. Eq. (1) gives us the dynamics of consumption as a function of capital per worker (since the interest rate is a function of capital per worker, $r = f'(k)$).

The dynamics of capital per worker is given as in the Solow model by the difference between gross investment and the investment necessary to keep the capital-labor ratio constant:

$$dk_t/dt = f(k_t) - c_t - n\,k_t \quad (2)$$

where, to simplify, I assume zero depreciation. Note that the only difference with the Solow model is that we do not have a fixed savings rate. Savings, and consumption, are now the result of an intertemporal choice between consumption at different dates together with the dynamics of the capital stock.

Eqs (1) and (2) are a system of two differential equations. The corresponding phase diagram is shown in Figure 3.1. The locus $dc/dt = 0$ is a locus along which the condition $f'(k) = \rho$ is fulfilled, i.e. the marginal product of capital is equal to the discount rate. Since c doesn't enter into this condition, the locus $dc/dt = 0$ is a vertical line at that unique value of the capital stock (k^*) which fulfills the condition $dc/dt = 0$.

The locus $dk/dt = 0$ is a locus along which $c = f(k) - nk$. The slope of this locus, $dc/dk = f'(k) - n$, is positive for low values of k such that $f'(k) > n$, is

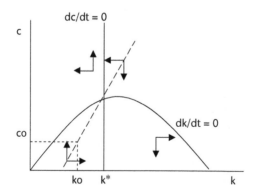

Figure 3.1 Phase diagram of the Ramsey model

equal to 0 for f' (k) = n (the value of k corresponding to the golden rule),[1] and negative for high values of k such that f' (k) < n. The value of c consistent with dk/dt = 0 is thus increasing up to f' (k) = n and decreasing afterwards.

Consider now what happens when the economy is off the loci. To the left of the dc/dt = 0 locus, the marginal product of capital, and thus the interest rate, is higher than the discount rate. Consumption per worker is thus increasing. A similar reasoning shows that to the right of the locus consumption must be decreasing. Above the locus dk/dt = 0, consumption is higher and thus investment is less than necessary to keep k constant. Capital per worker is thus decreasing above the locus and increasing below the locus dk/dt = 0.

As can be seen in the phase diagram, there is a saddle path on which the economy converges to a steady state in which consumption per worker and capital per worker are constant. This steady state path, in which output per worker is also constant, corresponds to the intersection of the two loci. In this steady state, the savings rate is constant as in the Solow model (since both y and c are constant). The steady state is thus a saddle point that can only be reached when the economy moves along the saddle path which determines the value of consumption (co) corresponding to an initial value (ko) of the capital stock per worker. In other words, given an initial value ko of the capital per worker, intertemporal optimization with perfect foresight implies that consumers will decide to consume the amount co corresponding to the initial value of k on the saddle path. From then on, c and k move along the saddle path towards the long-run equilibrium.

What conditions, besides perfect foresight, are necessary to discard other paths than the saddle path? Note first that any of these paths satisfies the dynamic equations of consumption and the capital stock. However, paths above the saddle path and k < k* are characterized by eventually having a capital stock that continuously decreases and violates the restriction that the capital stock cannot be negative. Paths that are below the saddle path are characterized by having a present value of capital holdings that continually increases and by a level of consumption that eventually diminishes. As a result the present value of lifetime income is higher (infinitely higher) than the present value of lifetime consumption. This implies that the households' intertemporal budget constraint, or more precisely the restriction that households satisfy the budget constraint with equality, is being violated.

---

[1] The golden rule level is the value of k at which consumption per capita is at its maximum. In the Ramsey model the equilibrium value of k is less than the golden rule due to the fact that households value present consumption more than future consumption.

The steady state: a comparison with the Solow model

The steady state of the Ramsey model has a number of features that are identical to those of the steady state in the Solow model. First, capital per worker, output per worker, and consumption per worker are all constant and, in the case with technical progress, all grow at the rate of technical progress (g_A) while total capital, output and consumption grow at Harrod's natural rate ($n + g_A$). Second, the savings rate, $s = (y - c)/y$, where c and y refer to the per worker levels of consumption and output, is constant as in the Solow model (but not exogenous). Note also that the role of the savings rate is replaced here by the discount rate. A lower discount rate (ρ) implies a shift to the right of the vertical $dc/dt = 0$ locus: the capital stock consistent with the equality $f'(k) = \rho$ increases to the extent that $f'(k)$ is a decreasing function of k. In the new steady state the growth rates of y, k and c do not change (as in Solow) but the economy achieves a higher capital stock and output per worker as well as a higher level of consumption per worker.

Before turning to the transitional dynamics of the model, note that the model's explanatory power of long-run growth and the differences across countries in income levels is no greater than that of the Solow model and, therefore, the model is vulnerable to the same criticisms from endogenous growth theory. First, even though savings is now endogenous, technical progress is the only source of long-term growth in output per worker. With diminishing returns to capital in the production function as in Solow, the model has a hard time in accounting for international differences in output per worker on the basis of differences in capital per worker. For example, consider 2 countries with a 10 to 1 gap in output per worker. To explain this difference with a Cobb-Douglas production function with a capital-output elasticity of 1/3 one would have to observe differences in the order of 1000 to 1 in capital per worker.[2] We do not observe such differences in capital per worker. The implications for the differences in rates of return to capital also face the same shortcomings. A gap of 10 to 1 in output per worker between two countries should be accompanied by rates of return on capital that are 100 times higher in the lower income country.[3] Again, we simply do not observe this.

Savings and growth in the transition to the steady state

What difference does it make then to assume intertemporal optimization? The difference is in the behavior of the savings rate off the steady state, which

---

[2] Indeed, if $y_1/y_2 = (k_1/k_2)^{1/3}$ then $k_1/k_2 = (y_1/y_2)^3$

[3] With a Cobb-Douglas production function, we have $f'(k) = ak^{a-1} = a\, y^{(a-1)/a}$. With a = 1/3 and $y_1/y_2 = 10$, we get $f'(k_1)/f'(k_2) = (y_1/y_2)^{-2} = (y_2/y_1)^2 = (1/10)^2 = 1/100$.

implies a different transitional dynamics. This is so because saving and consumption are now the result of intertemporal choices between consumption levels at different dates, together with the dynamics of the capital stock, so that in the Ramsey model the savings rate need not be constant when the economy is off the steady state.[4]

Optimization implies that the savings rate is subject to two forces. The first is a tendency to smooth out the time pattern of consumption. As can be seen from the Euler equation if the interest rate and the discount rate were equal to each other, households would consume the same amount period after period, independently of current income level. This is, incidentally, the conclusion of the life cycle theory of savings or of the permanent income hypothesis explanation of the behavior of consumption over time, both of which emphasize the adaptation of current consumption to long-run income levels. This tendency to smooth out consumption implies that in the transition from low to high income levels, the savings rate will tend to increase.

There is, however, a second force which refers to the tendency to substitute present for future consumption in response to the interest rate (or, more precisely to the difference between the interest rate and the discount rate). A higher interest rate (in relation to the discount rate) induces households to sacrifice current consumption so as to consume more in the future. How much they do so depends, as can be seen in the Euler equation, on the value of the elasticity of intertemporal substitution in consumption. Indeed, the willingness of households to substitute present and future consumption is crucial to the response of the savings rate to the interest rate: the higher is the elasticity of substitution $(1/\theta)$ the more are households willing to reduce current consumption (and therefore to increase $\Delta c/c$) in response to the interest rate.

King and Rebelo (1993) addressed the issue of how the savings rate behaves during the transition to the steady state by experimenting with alternative specifications of the households' utility function. In one set of experiments, King and Rebelo use a utility function with a constant elasticity of intertemporal substitution. This case leaves the basic convergence properties of the Solow model unchanged, although the pace of convergence turns to depend on the exact value of elasticity of substitution.

In the case of a relatively high elasticity (equal to one), the simulations show rapid convergence with falling savings rates and output growth rates during

---

[4] Another important difference is that while in the Solow model there is nothing to prevent the capital stock from being higher than the level corresponding to the golden rule, this cannot happen in the Ramsey model. The reason is intertemporal optimization: a steady state with a capital stock higher than the golden rule level implies that reducing the capital stock households can achieve a higher level of consumption each period. In such a path, households can reduce their savings and increase consumption and utility. Thus while over-accumulation (or dynamic inefficiency) is possible in the Solow model, it is not possible in the Ramsey model.

the transition. The fact that the real interest rate is initially very high and falls during the transition, together with the assumption of a relatively high elasticity of intertemporal substitution, accounts for the behavior of the savings rate over time. The strong response of savings to the interest rate and the high marginal product of capital (and thus the high interest rate) at low levels of the capital-labor ratio explain why the savings rate is high at low-income levels and falls as we approach the higher incomes associated with the steady state. The tendency to substitute consumption at different dates dominates the tendency to smooth out the time profile of consumption. Because savings are high initially, the rate of convergence is very high (with a half-life of only five years).[5] The relevant conclusion for our purposes here is that with a relatively high elasticity of substitution, the endogeneity of the savings rate actually exacerbates the counterfactual implications of the neoclassical model. It implies an even faster rate of convergence than that of the neoclassical growth model with a fixed savings rate. In addition, to the extent that poor countries can be assumed to be further away from the steady state, it has the implication that savings rates in poor countries should tend to be higher than in rich countries, rather than lower as observed in the data.

Smaller elasticities of intertemporal substitution have the effect of slowing down the pace of convergence. With an elasticity equal to 0.1 (an estimate obtained by Hall, 1988), the savings rate increases during the transition period and the growth of output is considerably smaller: instead of 5 years in the case of a unit elasticity, the half-life is now 18 years. With less intertemporal substitution in preferences, the savings rate is less elastic and the high interest rates in the initial stages do not offset the tendency to smooth the consumption profile. This is why the savings rate now increases over time. However, because the interest rate is very high in the initial stages, due to low capital-labor ratios, and falls throughout the process, the basic property of a diminishing output growth rate during the transition remains.

The case of a high elasticity of intertemporal substitution can be illustrated in the real wage diagram with a downward sloping w* curve: the high savings rate at low levels of k implies a relatively high required wage (w*) which falls as k increases. The gap between w* and w, and thus the rate of capital accumulation and growth, are even higher than in the Solow model at low levels of k. The case of a low elasticity of intertemporal substitution can be illustrated with an upward sloping w* curve: the savings rate and the required wage now increase as k rises. Provided that the slope of the w* curve is less than the slope of the w curve, the convergence properties of the Solow model are preserved.

---

[5] Compare with the 2 percent convergence rate, claimed by Mankiw, Romer, and Weil (1992) and other empirical studies (Barro, 1991, 1997), which implies that each country moves halfway towards its steady state in thirty-five years.

2. Endogenous Savings and Poverty Traps

In another experiment, King and Rebelo use a utility function of the Stone-Geary form in which there is a subsistence level of per capita consumption and the elasticity of intertemporal substitution then varies over time. The model features, along with a Solow-type steady state, an unstable steady state at the level of the capital stock compatible with subsistence consumption. The savings rate shows a hump-shaped path. This is because the elasticity of substitution rises as output increases. At low output levels, the model behaves like the one with a low elasticity of substitution and savings rates rise with output. In the later stages of the transition, the elasticity of substitution is much higher, tending towards its steady state value of 1, and thus as output increases the savings rate declines. Interestingly, even though the profit rate falls as output increases, now the growth rate of output does not diminish throughout the transition but has a hump-shaped path similar to that of the savings rate.

The basic insight of this case goes back to the older development literature on poverty traps (Nelson, 1956; Leibenstein, 1957). We can illustrate it by modifying the Solow-Swan model of Chapter 2 with a consumption function of the following form: $c = (\psi - \delta \kappa) + \phi (y - \psi)$, where c is consumption per worker, ψ is subsistence income per worker, κ is the capital-labor ratio consistent with a subsistence level of income, and ϕ is the propensity to consume out of non-subsistence income. This consumption function has the property that when income per worker is at the subsistence level, savings are just equal to the depreciation of the capital stock (since then $y - c = \delta k$).

The corresponding savings function is:

$$s = \delta k / y + (1 - \phi)(1 - \psi / y) \qquad (3)$$

which shows the savings rate as a nonlinear function of the level of income per worker and, thus, of the capital-labor ratio. The savings rate rises with income per worker on the condition that the marginal propensity to consume out of non-subsistence income (ϕ) is less than the average propensity to consume out of subsistence income (i.e., than the ratio of subsistence consumption to subsistence income, $(\psi - \delta \kappa)/\psi$).[6] Otherwise, the savings rate would tend to fall as income rises above the subsistence level.

Substituting from (3) and the Cobb-Douglas production function of the Solow-Swan model into the expression for $y^{A}*$ (eq. 5′ in Chapter 2) and

---

[6] This is equivalent to the condition that the marginal propensity to save $(1 - \phi)$ should be higher than the product of the depreciation rate and the capital-output ratio compatible with a subsistence level of income, $\delta \kappa / \psi$). From (3), the derivative of s with respect to y is: $ds/dy = y^{-2} [(1 - \phi) \psi - \delta \kappa]$, which is positive if: $(1 - \phi) > \delta \kappa / \phi$.

using (5) in Chapter 2—leaving aside technical progress and population growth and setting A, for simplicity, equal to 1—yields the following equation for the w* schedule:

$$w^* = (1 - a) \ [(k/k^a) + (1 - \phi)(1 - \psi/k^a)/\delta]^{a/(1-a)} \qquad (4)$$

Unlike the Solow model—where there is a unique value of w*, independent of the capital-labor ratio—the required value of the real wage (w*) is now a function of the capital-labor ratio. Taking natural logs in (4), and differentiating, yields the slope of the w* locus: dln w*/dln k = D / {κ + [(1 – ϕ)/δ] (k^a – ψ)}, where: D = (1 – ϕ) ψ / (δ – a κ) [a/(1–a)]

The slope of the w* schedule is positive and falls as k increases, provided that savings are positive and that the savings rate rises with income per worker.[7] The reason for this upward sloping w* schedule is that as the capital-labor ratio (and, thus, income per capita) increases so does the savings rate. The required wage rises, since to maintain a given rate of capital accumulation a lower profit rate is required.

As shown in Figure 3.2, there is now the possibility of multiple equilibria. One of them, at the high k intersection, is similar to the steady state in the Solow model. The other one is a low k intersection at the subsistence level of income.[8] This intersection is unstable and below it there is a poverty trap. This trap arises because at low levels of k, income per capita is scarcely sufficient for subsistence and savings fall below depreciation. It is only when the economy has a capital-labor ratio larger than κ, the level consistent with subsistence income, that investment rates can become larger than depreciation and a virtuous circle develops between the expansion of income and a rising saving rate. Eventually, however, the falling profit and interest rates will cause a reduction in the investment rate and thus the hump-shaped pattern of the growth rate.

This hump-shaped path of output growth rates was encountered in Chapter 1 (Figure 1.5). There is also some evidence of a hump-shaped pattern

[7] Two conditions affect the sign of the slope of the w* schedule. First, D in the slope of the w* locus is positive if: (1 – ϕ) > a δ κ /ϕ. Since a is less than one, the condition for the savings rate to be an increasing function of income guarantees this inequality. The other condition involves the denominator in the slope of the w*. For it to be positive requires: (1 – ϕ) (y – ψ) + δ κ > 0. This condition states, as is readily verified from (3), that income per worker must not be so low that savings per worker are negative.

[8] The slope of the w schedule of short-run equilibria remains equal to "a", the capital share. The slope conditions for multiple equilibria are guaranteed by the specification in eq. (3), together with the fulfillment of the condition that the savings rate increases with income per worker. Indeed, as k tends to infinity the slope of w* tends to zero and the w* locus is flatter than the w schedule. When k tends to κ, the w* locus is steeper than the w curve. The slope of w* then tends to D/κ which as is readily verified is greater than "a" provided that (1 – ϕ) ψ / δ κ > 1, which is the condition for the savings rate to increase with income per worker. The w* locus is thus steeper than the w schedule at low values of k and flatter at high values of k.

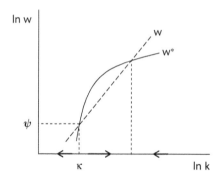

Figure 3.2 A poverty trap model with endogenous savings

of investment rates (see Table 2.1 in Chapter 2). The present model then suggests that the very low growth rates of the poorer countries arise from their economies being so close to a subsistence level of consumption that their savings rates, and as a result their growth rates, are much lower than those of middle-income countries that have moved further away from the savings trap. This is so although their capital-labor ratios are lower and their profit rates much higher than in those middle-income countries. As King and Rebelo put it: "despite the good investment opportunities, the country does not invest because production is barely enough to attend subsistence consumption and to the replacement of the depreciated capital stock" (King and Rebelo, 1993, p. 918).

Sachs' (2005) call for a massive increase in international aid to lift the less developed countries out of their poverty trap seems to be based in such a "savings trap" model. As he puts it: "When people are . . . utterly destitute, they need their entire income, or more, just to survive. There is no margin of income above survival that can be invested for the future. This is the main reason why the poorest of the poor are most prone to becoming trapped with low or negative economic growth rates. They are too poor to save for the future and thereby accumulate the capital that could pull them out of their current misery" (Sachs, 2005, pp. 56–7).[9] Sachs then calls for a substantial increase in the investment rate in these countries, a call that has been wrongly perceived, as we shall in later chapters, as a "big push" strategy (see Easterly, 2006).

This interpretation of the growth performance of the poorer countries, even though at first sight appealing, has a problem. The savings trap argument has a strong counterfactual implication, pointed out by King and Rebelo. As their simulations of this case show, the marginal product of capital is very high in

---

[9] This is not the only reason why, in Sachs' argument, less developed countries can get trapped in a low level equilibrium. Sachs mentions explicitly that at low-income levels, there may be increasing returns to capital. These increasing returns may keep returns to capital very low at low-income levels (Sachs, 2005, p. 250). We shall return to this "profitability trap", to be distinguished from a savings trap, in Chapters 7 and 8.

the initial stages of development and falls during the transition, just as in the Solow model and the other simulations. Even with a small amount of international capital mobility, capital should be rapidly flowing to the poor countries with low domestic savings and take care of the poverty trap problem, making the hump-shaped pattern disappear. In fact, capital does not flow towards the poorest countries. When it flows from developed to developing countries it tends to do so towards middle-income developing countries rather than the poorest countries where the domestic savings rate is lowest.

3. International Capital Mobility and Political Risk: An Introduction to the Role of Institutional Factors

Consider now more fully the implications of international capital mobility. The presence of a large degree of international capital mobility implies that post-tax risk-adjusted rates on return on capital will tend to be equal across countries. This strengthens the process of convergence to the steady state. Moreover, it modifies the nature of the steady state for equilibrium output per worker becomes unrelated to savings rates and population growth rates. Adjusted for taxes and risk factors, capital-labor ratios, output per worker, and factor prices tend to absolute convergence, even though in the steady state incomes per capita will be higher in countries with high savings rates that will be receiving interest payments from countries with low savings rates. With access to the same technology using physical capital and labor, differences in the steady states values of the capital-labor ratio and the marginal product of capital will fully reflect differences in tax rates and political risk. With immobile human capital in the production function, differences in the stock of capital per worker will also depend on the steady state value of human capital per worker, to the extent that returns on human capital are not equalized.

All this suggests that extending the neoclassical growth model to explicitly allow for international capital mobility and political risk, can modify considerably the convergence and steady state properties of the model.[10] The closed economy determinants of the steady state, the investment rate in physical capital and population growth, lose importance while political risk becomes an overwhelming influence. More formally, leave aside technical progress and suppose that the rate of capital accumulation is a function of the difference between the current profit rate and a risk-adjusted, international profit rate (r^*), given a propensity to invest (ψ):

---

[10] Barro, Mankiw and Sala-i-Marti (1995) argue, however, that with immobile human capital and the inability to finance human capital accumulation by borrowing in world markets, the rate of convergence is only slightly altered compared to the closed economy case.

$$I/K = \psi(r - r^*) \qquad \psi > 0 \qquad \psi(0) = 0$$

Setting $I/K - \delta = n$ equal to zero and using the profit-wage function (eq. 4 in Chapter 2), the schedule of long-run equilibria is now determined by:

$$w^* = w^*(A, \psi, r^*, n, \delta) \qquad w^*_1, w^*_2 > 0, w^*_3, w^*_4, w^*_5 < 0$$

Unlike the required wage in the Solow model (see eq. 5 in Chapter 2), w^* is here independent of the savings rate and depends, besides technological parameters, the depreciation rate and population growth, on the propensity to invest and the risk-adjusted profit rate. An increase in political risk, which raises r^* and reduces capital accumulation, has the effect of reducing the steady state value of the real wage. In terms of the real wage diagram, the increase in risk implies a downward shift of the w^* schedule.

Our focus here will be on whether the fact that many low and lower middle-income countries are not converging to the high-income levels of the rich countries is attributable to the role of political risk factors. It is worth noting that there is a debate here. On one hand, Barro (1991, 1997) can largely be seen as precisely an extension of the Solow model that, in addition to the role of human capital, controls for the role of political risk among the determinants of the steady state. The main finding is a positive, although slow, rate of conditional convergence of the order of 2 percent per year that vindicates the neoclassical growth model when extended to include these determinants.

On the other side, a number of authors have expressed serious doubts about political risk being able to offset the vast differences in rates of return between poor and rich countries implied by the Solow model. Referring to the role of political risk in the failure of capital movements to equalize factor prices, Lucas asks: "Indeed, why did these capital movements not take place during the colonial age, under political and military arrangements that eliminated (or long postponed) the 'political risk' that is so frequently cited as a factor working against capital mobility?" (Lucas, 1988, pp. 16–17).

Table 3.1 shows for our five groups of countries classified by GDP per worker, the growth rates and a rule of law index used as an indicator of political risk. The rule of law index (RLI), described in the appendix to Chapter 1, is available for the years 1996 to 2008 so that this is the period for which we can conduct international comparisons. The average values for the RLI in the first row suggest a positive correlation between this index and income level as we have already seen in Chapter 1. Together with the average growth rates in the second row, they indicate a moderately positive influence of the RLI on growth rates. The last few rows in the table present estimates of the RLI and growth rates separately for the fast growing and slow growing countries in each of the five groups—i.e., for countries with growth rates above and below the median growth rate respectively. The exercise can be seen as a "regression"

Table 3.1 Income, growth, and rule of law index (1996–2008)

	Averages for country groups				
	1	2	3	4	5
Rule of law index (RLI)	93.0	66.2	42.9	29.7	30.0
Growth rate	2.3	2.6	2.2	2.5	1.5
RLI in:					
Fast-growing countries[1]	93.8	62.1	49.9	38.4	34.3
	(2.8%)	(3.2%)	(2.9%)	(4.0%)	(3.6%)
Slow-growing countries[2]	92.1	72.2	35	21.7	28.5
	(1.8%)	(1.9%)	(1.5%)	(0.8%)	(−0.4)

[1] Countries with the fastest growth in the group. Average rate of growth of the subgroup in parenthesis
[2] Countries with the slowest growth in the group. Average rate of growth of the subgroup in parenthesis
Sources: See appendix to Chapter 1.

of growth rates on the RLI that controls for the likely two-way influence between income levels and political risk factors (as measured by the RLI).

Differences in RLI values appear to have a significant impact on growth rates except for group 2 in which the slowly growing countries have a higher RLI values than fast growing countries at similar income levels. At low-income levels (groups 4 and 5) growth rates appear to be positively correlated with the RLI values. Yet, differences in RLI values seem too small to account for the large differences in growth rates between the fast and slow growing countries in these groups. Given the similarities in RLIs, the risk-adjusted rates of return on capital should also be rather similar in these two types of countries. If the low RLIs in the slow growing countries of groups 4 and 5 are the major factor explaining the slow growth of low-income countries, why is it that the same low RLIs did not prevent the fast growing economies in these groups from growing at faster rates than, say, the slow growing economies of groups 1 and 2 with much higher RLIs? Chapters 16, 17, and 18 will address more fully the role of institutional factors in development.

4. The Debate on Convergence: A First Approximation

A strand in the empirical growth literature, associated with and inspired by the neoclassical model and its extensions, refers to the analysis of so-called β-convergence. This type of convergence happens when the coefficient of initial income in a growth regression is negative, that is when initial income is negatively correlated with subsequent growth.[11] In turn β-convergence can

[11] By contrast σ-convergence occurs when the standard deviation of the cross section of incomes per capita falls over time.

be absolute or conditional. Absolute convergence occurs when, in a regression of the growth rate on initial income as the only right hand side variable, the coefficient of initial income is negative and significant. Conditional convergence occurs when the coefficient of initial income is negative and significant and other right hand variables in the regression equation control for the determinants of the steady state (such as the savings rate and population growth in the basic neoclassical model). In other words, absolute convergence occurs when poor and rich countries tend to converge to the same income level (and thus poor countries tend to grow faster than rich countries) independently of differences in savings rates and population growth rates. Conditional convergence happens when poor countries grow faster than rich countries but only when their savings rates and population growth rates are the same.

There is a general agreement in the literature about the absence of absolute convergence. As expressed by Barro long time ago: "The hypothesis that poor countries tend to grow faster than rich countries seems to be inconsistent with the cross country evidence, which indicates that per capita growth rates have little correlation with the starting level of per capita product." (Barro, 1991, pp. 407–8). The existence of conditional convergence is more controversial. Barro and Sala-i-Martin have been the main proponents of the existence of conditional convergence with a rate of convergence of 2 percent per year, which implies that it takes 35 years to reduce to half the distance with respect to the steady state. They argue that such a rate of convergence is obtained uniformly in a broad range of samples, including not only samples of countries but also states and prefectures in the United States and Japan.

There are, however, at least two problems with this result. Recall from Chapter 2 that the rate of convergence (Ω) is equal to $(1-a)(n + g_A + \delta)$ and varies therefore inversely with the capital share (a). The problem with a 2 percent convergence rate is that this low rate of convergence implies a coefficient of capital in the production function of 0.9 which is much higher than the value of 0.3 to 0.4 implied by information on income shares in the national accounts. In the next chapter we shall see how the extension of the Solow model by Mankiw, Romer, and Weil (1992) addressed this problem.

The second problem is that the negative coefficient on initial income does not appear to be as robust as Barro and Sala-i-Martin claim. Levine and Renelt (1992) examine how robust are the links between growth and a variety of economic, political, and institutional indicators. They find that the conditional convergence result, while robust for the period 1960–1989, is not robust in the period 1974–1989 or when the OECD countries are excluded from the sample. This suggests that the well-known tendency of the OECD economies to converge in the post war period is responsible for the negative sign of the coefficient on initial income in growth regressions. Given this result it is difficult to conclude that, controlling for the determinants of the steady state, poor countries tend to grow faster than rich countries. There is no tendency to convergence among middle-income and low-income countries, as we saw in Chapter 1. In support of this proposition is the evidence on the positive and significant coefficients of the initial income term (yo) in quadratic growth equations of the form $g = a_0 + a_1 yo + a_2 yo^2$. We shall return to this evidence in Chapter 8.

Technology gaps: a satisfactory solution?

Another empirical approach in the literature on convergence postulates that country and time specific effects affect the productivity variable A. In this approach, the cross country and time series information on growth and its determinants is pooled together and the average growth rates refer to relatively short periods of 5 or 10 years. This permits the estimation of time specific and country specific values of variable A. In comparison with the previous regression approach, this approach is equivalent to augment the neoclassical model with idiosyncratic factors (specific to each country and time period). The typical result is a rate of convergence much higher than the 2 percent rate of Barro and Sala i Martin. This rate rises to 3.8 to 9.1 percent in Islam (1995), 10 percent in Caselli, Esquivel, and Leffort (1996) and up to 30 percent in Lee, Pesaran and Smith (1997). These much higher rates of convergence are not surprising: since the approach allows that A varies across countries, each country is closer to its steady state than in the simple version of the Solow model with a universal value of A. The same growth rate now implies a higher rate of convergence (since each economy is closer to the steady state).

It is not clear what interpretation should be given to the estimates of A associated with country specific effects. In a broad interpretation, the variable A in the production function captures any factors affecting the efficiency with which different countries use their capital and labor inputs, including resource endowments, institutions and access to best practice techniques. Inspired by a large number of empirical studies that conclude that income gaps are related to productivity differences across countries rather than to differences in factor endowments,[12] technology gap explanations reject the assumption of an internationally accessible production function and consider it the major source of the empirical shortcomings of the Solow model.

What if different economies, in particular those of developing and developed countries, operated on different production functions? The low productivity of the technologies in use in underdeveloped countries can then generate low

---

[12] See for example Islam (1995), Caselli et al. (1996), Klenow and Rodriguez-Clare (1997), Prescott (1998), Hall and Jones (1999), and Easterly and Levine (2001).

incomes independently of differences in savings rates, population growth or factor endowment. Moreover, the low productivity of the technologies can be the source of both the low incomes and slow growth of the poorer countries. Formally, we can write the growth rate of output per worker as:[13]

$$g_y = g_A + a[(sA^{1-a}/k^{1-a}) - (n + g_A + \delta)] \tag{5}$$

Consider now two economies with identical saving rates, population growth rates and capital-labor ratios but different production functions reflected in different values of A. The economy using the inferior technology necessarily has a lower output per worker (since the production function implies that $y = A^{1-a} k^a$, and k is by assumption the same in the two economies). From (5), it also has a lower growth rate, since its profit rate (equal to a A^{1-a}/k^{1-a}) is smaller as a result of the lower productivity of its technology. Clearly, if differences in A are sufficiently large, there is nothing to prevent countries with low incomes and less productive technologies from having relatively low growth rates.

Islam (1995) followed a panel data approach to estimate an extended version of the Solow model that allows for "country specific effects". Then, from these estimates he constructed country specific indices of the initial levels of A. Using them to adjust the steady state income gaps implied by the Solow model has a number of shortcomings, including that country specific effects were estimated on the assumption that the exogenous rate of technical progress (g_A) is uniform across countries. Nevertheless, these estimates will prove helpful to illustrate the potential and limitations of interpreting these differences as a result of technical efficiency gaps.

Table 3.2 reproduces the results of an exercise in Ros (2000, ch. 2). It shows Islam's estimates of A (as a fraction of group 1) for five groups of countries classified according to income level. Multiplying these estimates of A by the steady state income gaps implied by the Solow model yields the steady state income gaps adjusted for country specific effects. These are shown in the third row of the table. We can then use eq. (8) in Chapter 2 $[\hat{y} = g_A + \Omega (\ln y^{*A} - \ln y^A)]$ to estimate the predicted growth rates implied by these new values. These estimates assume a capital share of one third.

As the table reveals, adjusting the Solow model for country specific differences in A has the effect of dramatically enlarging the predicted steady state income gaps and thus of bringing them closer to the actual income gaps. The picture that emerges is almost the exact opposite to that of the simple

---

[13] From eqs (2) and (4) in Chapter 2, the profit rate can be expressed as: $r = a (A/k)^{(1-a)/a}$. Substituting this expression into (3) in Chapter 2 and then using $\hat{y}^A = a k^{A\wedge}$ and $g_y = g_A + \hat{y}^A$, yields eq. (5).

Table 3.2 Steady state income gaps and growth rates in a Solow model adjusted for "country specific effects"

	Averages for country groups				
	1	2	3	4	5
Country specific value of A (as % of group 1)	100	57.5	35.4	18.4	9.9
Income as % of group 1 (1997)	100	56.7	25.2	10.7	4.3
Steady state income (pred.) (1985)	100	52.6	32.8	16.1	8.4
GDP growth (actual) (1965–97)	3.5	3.4	4.5	3.1	2.6
GDP growth (predicted)	3.5	3.4	5.2	4.4	4.5
Number of countries	18	14	13	15	13

Source: Ros (2000), ch. 2.

Solow model. Economies are now very close to their steady states and this reduces considerably the differences in growth rates.

That the adjusted model fits the evidence much better than the original should not be surprising: the estimates of A are those that make the adjusted Solow model best fit the data. The question then is whether a technology gap interpretation of differences in A provides a satisfactory account of income levels and growth rates.

There are a number of difficulties that arise when adopting this perspective. First, differences in A appear to be simply too large to be interpreted as technology gaps. It is hard to see why some countries should persistently use technologies that are 10 times less productive than others (as implied by the differences in A between groups 1 and 5).[14] Even a technology gap of 5 to 1 implies, as Mankiw (1995, p. 283) observes, that poor countries are using technologies that are about eighty years out of date (assuming that technological change enhances productivity by 2 percent per year). If their profit rates are so low as a result of the use of inferior technologies, why haven't the large opportunities for technology transfer, in the presence of international capital mobility, narrowed the technology gaps that account for these low profit rates?

The gaps in A are so large that the transitional component of growth rates in the poorer countries (groups 4 and 5) turns out to be negative. In other words, these countries appear to have been initially above their steady states and to be converging from above by reducing their capital stocks per effective worker. This raises a troubling question: how did they get, which such extremely low incomes, above their steady state? These observations suggest that the good fit of the model is to a large extent illusory. The low-income levels and the slow

---

[14] It may be worth recalling that we are still assuming constant returns to scale. Under this assumption, there are no obstacles, strictly speaking, to the adoption of the superior technologies no matter how small the amount of capital that is available to an individual investor.

growth performance of poor countries have to be attributed to poorer countries operating with very inferior technologies, while the key question of why they do so seems hard to answer.

Even if we were to accept the possibility of such large technology gaps, and assume that countries operated on vastly different production functions, rates of technological progress should now also be different. Explaining these differences should be an essential part of a technology gap explanation of why growth rates differ. The natural hypothesis, which goes back to Gerschenkron (1962), is that the larger the technological gap, the faster will be the rate of technical progress since the profit opportunities and potential technological jumps are larger.[15] In terms of eq. (8) in Chapter 2, $\hat{y} = g_A + \Omega$ (ln y^{*A} − ln y^A), this view amounts to reducing the transitory component of the growth in output per worker (due to capital deepening) (ln y^{*A} − ln y^A) while, at the same time, increasing the exogenous component due to technological progress (g_A). While reasonable at first sight, this view has implications that are hard to reconcile with the evidence. Depending on the function relating the rate of technical progress to the technology gap, the resulting model may fit the data better or worse than the simple Solow model. However, insofar as technology gaps are proportional to actual income gaps, the model will share with the Solow model the feature that, for countries with similar characteristics (similar steady state income levels), growth rates should increase as we move down along the income scale. To the extent that large technology gaps should lead to high growth rates as a result of fast technical progress, convergence is seen as a process of technological catch-up, instead of being the result of capital deepening along a production function. But the transitional dynamics remain largely unaffected and, as we have seen, this feature is the major empirical shortcoming of the Solow model.

The determinants of the steady state level of income need not be, however, the same as in the Solow model (savings rate and population growth). Suppose that the country specific rate of technological progress is a function of the gap with respect to best practice technique and of an index of the country's ability to adopt more advanced technologies (for a simple formulation of this function, see Bernard and Jones, 1996). With different abilities to adopt technology (or "social capabilities" according to Ohkawa and Rosovsky's (1973) expression),[16] otherwise similar countries will not converge to the same

---

[15] As Abramovitz puts it: "The hypothesis asserts that being backward in level of productivity carries a potential for rapid advance. Stated more definitely the proposition is that in comparisons across countries the growth rates of productivity in any long period tend to be inversely related to the initial levels of productivity" (Abramovitz 1986, p. 386).

[16] Abramovitz (1986), who also uses the expression, includes as important elements of social capability a society's educational level and its political and economic institutions (including industrial and financial institutions).

level of technology, and thus to the same steady state level of income, even though their rates of technological progress will converge. Technology gaps will persist in the steady state, these equilibrium gaps being determined by differences across countries in their ability to adopt technological advances. The next chapter addresses these issues more fully by looking at the effects of the stock of human capital on the ability to adopt technology.

4

Human Capital in Neoclassical and Endogenous Growth Models

How does human capital affect the level and the rate of growth of output in an economy? There are two ways in which human capital is modeled in growth theory. The standard approach, followed in growth theory by Mankiw, Romer, and Weil's extension of the basic neoclassical model and by Lucas in his 1988 endogenous growth model, is to include human capital, along with physical capital and labor, as a factor in the production function. Then, output per worker depends on physical capital per worker and human capital per worker. Another way to model human capital is to argue that it is not the level of labor productivity but rather its rate of growth which is affected by the level of human capital per worker. In this view, which goes back to Nelson and Phelps (1966), the ability of a country to adopt and implement new technologies depends on its stock of human capital. More educated farmers, for example, will introduce new agricultural techniques faster than less educated ones and thus the diffusion of new technologies will proceed at a faster pace. In the first case, the rate of growth of human capital affects the output growth rate. In the second, the level of human capital (or its level relative to the technological leader) influences the rate of growth of the economy.

In this chapter, I discuss whether extending neoclassical and endogenous growth models to incorporate human capital can help in overcoming the model's shortcomings discussed in Chapter 2. The first two sections examine the extension of the Solow model by Mankiw, Romer, and Weil (1992) and the Lucas 1988 model of endogenous growth with human capital. Both of these models assume that the level of human capital per worker affects the level of output per worker. The third section then turns to the Nelson and Phelps model in which the level of human capital affects the rate of growth of output per worker.

1. Human Capital in the Neoclassical Model: The Extension by Mankiw, Romer, and Weil

The model

Mankiw, Romer, and Weil (MRW; 1992) set out for themselves the task of addressing three problems with the basic neoclassical growth model that Mankiw (1995) expressed as follows: (1) the model does not predict the large differences in income observed in the real world. Actual differences in savings and population growth rates indicate that the model can explain incomes that vary by a multiple of slightly more than two; (2) the model does not predict the rate of convergence that convergence studies estimate; it predicts convergence at about twice the rate that actually occurs; (3) the return to capital differentials predicted by the model are vastly larger than are observed in the world, unless one assumes very high elasticities of factor substitution.[1]

To overcome these defects, MRW extended the Solow model by adding human capital accumulation. In their view, human capital is the key omitted factor in the simple version of the neoclassical model. Suppose, then, that technology is described by:

$$Y = K^a H^b (AL)^{1-a-b} \qquad\qquad a+b<1$$

where H is human capital. As in the Solow-Swan model, the production function exhibits constant returns to scale and the inequality $a + b < 1$ ensures the presence of diminishing returns to all capital. Normalizing by effective labor:

$$y^A = (k^A)^a (h^A)^b \tag{1}$$

or:

$$y = A^{1-a-b} k^a h^b \qquad\qquad \text{where } h^A = H/(AL) \text{ and } h = H/L$$

which shows that output per worker (y) depends now on skills per worker (h) in addition to capital per worker (k) and technology (A).

MRW treat physical and human capital symmetrically. They assume that both types of capital depreciate at the same rate (δ) and that society invests a fraction s_H of its total income in human capital (in addition to a fraction s in physical capital). The accumulation equations for physical and human capital (in terms of their ratios to effective labor) are then:

---

[1] With a high elasticity of factor substitution, the wage share rises less than otherwise in the face of an increase in the capital-labor ratio, thus moderating the reduction in the rate of return to capital. Predicted differences across countries in returns to capital will then be less than otherwise.

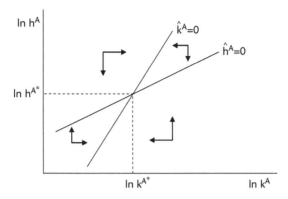

Figure 4.1 The MRW extension of the Solow model

$$\hat{k}^A = s\ y^A/k^A - (n + g_A + \delta) \tag{2}$$

$$\hat{h}^A = s_H\ y^A/h^A - (n + g_A + \delta) \tag{3}$$

where, as in previous chapters, n is the rate of labor force growth and g_A the rate of technical progress. From eqs (1), (2), and (3), setting $\hat{k}^A = \hat{h}^A = 0$, we obtain the steady state values of k^A and h^A:

$$k^{*A} = [s^{1-b}\ s_H{}^b/(n + g_A + \delta)]^{1/(1-a-b)} \tag{4}$$

$$h^{*A} = [s^a\ s_H{}^{1-a}/(n + g_A + \delta)]^{1/(1-a-b)} \tag{5}$$

Figure 4.1 illustrates in $(\ln h^A, \ln k^A)$ space the determination of k^{*A} and h^{*A} at the intersection of two schedules, $\hat{k}^A = 0$ and $\hat{h}^A = 0$, along which one of the two capital stocks per effective worker (physical and human, respectively) remains stationary. These two schedules—derived from (1) and (2) and from (1) and (3), setting $\hat{k}^A = 0$ and $\hat{h}^A = 0$ respectively—are upward sloping due to the positive productivity effects of physical and human capital. For instance, a higher endowment of human capital per worker raises productivity (eq. 1) and stimulates the accumulation of physical capital (eq. 2); to keep k^A constant requires a higher physical capital-labor ratio. Thus the positive slope of the $\hat{k}^A = 0$ locus. We can follow a similar reasoning to derive the dynamics of the economy off the two loci. To the left of the $\hat{h}^A = 0$ locus, for example, k^A is relatively low at each level of h^A. Output per worker, and thus the accumulation of human capital, must then be less than required to keep h^A stationary and the stock of human capital per effective worker must then be falling.

Provided that returns to physical and human capital combined diminish ($a + b < 1$), the two loci intersect at a stable equilibrium.[2] On this equilibrium path both capital-effective labor ratios are stationary and the economy, as in the Solow model, grows at Harrod's natural growth rate. Off the steady state, adjustments will take place in k^A and h^A and thus the growth rate will be above or below the natural rate. As shown in Figure 4.1, the two schedules divide the ($\ln h^A$, $\ln k^A$) space into four regions. Two of them yield respectively (and unambiguously) a growth rate above and below the natural rate. In the first case, growth is accompanied by physical and human capital deepening while, in the second, a reduction of both physical and human capital per effective worker takes place. The other two regions feature respectively physical capital deepening with a reduction of human capital per effective worker (and thus an unambiguously rising k/h ratio) and human capital accumulation with a reduction in the stock of physical capital per effective worker (and therefore a declining k/h ratio).

Substituting now (4) and (5) into (1), we can solve for the steady state value of output per worker:

$$y^* = A[s^a \ s_H^b/(n + g_A + \delta)(a + b)]^{1/(1-a-b)} \tag{6}$$

Eq. (6) shows that, besides A, s, and ($n + g_A + \delta$), the rate of human capital accumulation (s_H) also affects the steady state value of output per worker. In Figure 4.1, a higher s_H shifts the schedule $\hat{h}^A = 0$ upwards and increases the steady state values of h^A and k^A (and thus of output per worker). An alternative way in which MRW express the role of human capital is by combining (5) and (6) to derive an equation showing y^* as the product of two terms: 1) the steady state value of output per worker in the Solow-Swan model ($A [s/(n + g_A + \delta)]^{a/(1-a)}$), 2) a term that is proportional to the steady state level of human capital per effective worker ($(h^{*A})^{b/(1-a)}$):

$$y^* = A [s/(n + g_A + \delta)]^{a/(1-a)} (h^{*A})^{b/(1-a)} \tag{7}$$

Empirical implications and criticisms

We can use eq. (7) to estimate the steady state income gaps implied by this modification of the Solow-Swan model. For this, we need estimates of h^{*A}, and thus of s_H and b which affect the value of h^{*A}. MRW use the percentage of the

---

[2] As is readily verified, the slopes of the schedules $\hat{k}^A = 0$ and $\hat{h}^A = 0$ are respectively $(1-a)/b$ and $a/(1-b)$. Stability requires the schedule $\hat{k}^A = 0$ to be steeper than the schedule $\hat{h}^A = 0$. This in turn implies $a + b < 1$. With constant returns to all capital ($a + b = 1$), by contrast, the slopes of the schedules would both be equal to unity, and the economy would undergo a self-sustaining process of expansion or decline depending on whether the schedule $\hat{h}^A = 0$ lies above or below the schedule $\hat{k}^A = 0$.

Table 4.1 Steady state income gaps and growth rates implied by the MRW model

	Averages for country groups				
	1	2	3	4	5
MRW proxy for $s_H{}^a$	7.5	8.3	9.3	5.8	3.9
Steady state value of h^A	8.2	6.4	5.4	1.9	0.6
Steady state value of h^A (% of group 1)	100	77.9	66.6	23.2	7.1
Education (years)^b	9.1	6.8	5.0	4.0	2.6
Education (years) (% of group 1)	100	74.8	55.5	43.6	28.8
Income as % of group 1 (2008)	100	50.7	22.6	8.6	2.7
Steady state income (pred.)	100	81.8	68.1	37.8	17.1
Actual GDP growth rate (1970–2008)	3.1	3.9	3.6	3.5	3.0
Predicted GDP growth rate	3.1	4.8	6.0	6.5	6.7
Number of countries	17	17	17	18	18

^{a} Percentage of the working age population in secondary school; average 1970, 1980, 1990, 2000, 2008.
^{b} Average years of schooling in the total population over age 25 (average of 1970 and 2008)
Source: World Development Indicators, UNESCO.

working age population in secondary school as a proxy for s_H. Table 4.1 shows this variable for our five groups of countries. We also use the estimate of b (= 0.23) obtained by MRW in their tests of conditional convergence. Using eq. (5), we can then estimate the values of h^{*A} implied by the model. The results, presented in Table 4.1, yield very large differences across countries in the steady state values of human capital, of the order of 14 to 1 between groups 1 and 5. It is worth noting, by looking at the third and fifth rows of the table, that the human capital gaps implied by the model are indeed much larger than the actual ones (of the order of 3.5 to 1 between groups 1 and 5), as measured by the differences in average years of schooling in the population over age 25, a more comprehensive measure than the one used by MRW since it includes schooling at all levels (primary, secondary and higher), complete and incomplete. Multiplying steady state income gaps in Table 2.1 by the factor $(h^{*A})^{b/(1-a)}$, given the estimate of h^{*A} in Table 4.1, yields the steady state income levels implied by the model. As Table 4.1 shows, adding human capital to the Solow model, in the way MRW do it, has the effect of enlarging the steady state income gaps, bringing them closer to the actual income gaps. The large equilibrium differences in human capital implied by the model explain this feature. As in the technology gap explanation discussed in Chapter 3, the picture that emerges is almost the exact opposite to that in the simple Solow model. Differences in actual income levels are largely the outcome of differences in the determinants of the steady state that now include the rate of human capital accumulation, along with savings behavior and population growth.

These implications are also illustrated by the regression estimate of eq. (6) for our sample of countries:

$$\ln y_{2008} = -2.64 + 1.25 \ln(s) + 1.34(s_H) - 4.72 \ln (n_{70-8} + g_A + \delta)(adj)R^2 = 0.67.$$
$$\quad\;\; (1.74)\;(0.43) \qquad (0.19) \qquad (0.62)$$

Standard errors are in parentheses. $(g_A + \delta)$ is assumed to be 0.05 ($g_A = .02$ and $\delta = .03$).

s is the investment share (average for the period 1970–2008). s_H is the percentage of the working age population in secondary school (average of 1970, 1980, 1990, 2000, and 2008 levels).

In contrast to the Solow-Swan model, where low incomes are the result of a scarcity of physical capital relative to labor, with poor economies being well below their steady state, the vision of underdevelopment that emerges from MRW is one of a dearth of human capital, in turn, the result of low rates of investment in education.

This solution to the shortcomings of the Solow model has been criticized on various grounds. A first objection, which applies to MRW as well as to Lucas' endogenous growth model discussed in the next section, concerns the importance that MRW attribute to differences in schooling both as a source of differences in output per worker and as a measure of human capital gaps. The basic point is that it is far from obvious that human capital, as measured by educational attainment, has such an important role as a factor of production. Indeed, if raising the educational level of the labor force was the only way of increasing human capital (as assumed in many *applications* of this view), then this way of introducing human capital in a growth model is saying that a steel worker with 6 years of education will for that reason produce more steel ingots per day than a steel worker with only 3 years of education. This is what the production function in eq. (1) asserts when h is measured by the educational level of the labor force. Taking the other view of human capital mentioned in the introduction to this chapter, that of human capital as a vehicle for technology diffusion, Phelps makes the point in his comment to Mankiw (1995) that "all or most persons in the labor force could forget everything they learned beyond the ninth grade, say, without putting much of a dent in today's output" (Phelps, 1995, p. 312). His argument is that most schooling is learning how to learn, which facilitates the adoption and dissemination of technological advances, and involves precautionary and thus seemingly redundant knowledge. The implication is that international differences in human capital, as understood by MRW, are of little importance to explain actual differences in productivity levels. This implication is quite consistent with the empirical finding by Benhabib and Spiegel (1994) that the change in the stock in human capital contributes insignificantly (and often with a negative sign) to a country's output growth while at the same time the level of human capital affects positively the rate of growth of productivity.[3] Benhabib and Spiegel illustrate these results with the experience of several poor countries in Sub-Saharan Africa that have recorded large proportional changes in the stock of human capital, partly because they started from very low levels, combined with a poor growth performance. The insignificance of the change in human capital also emerges for our sample of countries for the period 1970–2008 in the following growth regression (see also regression 3 in Table 1.2 and regression 1 in Table 1.5 of Chapter 1):

$$g_Y = 0.83 + 0.58g_K + 0.02g_H + 0.75g_L \qquad N = 82 \quad (\text{adj})R^2 = 0.72$$
$$(3.10) \quad (13.66) \quad (0.37) \quad (5.41)$$

where g refers to growth rate (log difference) and Y, K, H and L to GDP, capital, education (H/L times the size of the labor force) and labor force, respectively. t statistics are in parentheses. See Appendix to Chapter 1 for sources and definitions.

A second criticism refers to the fact that if differences in human capital are really so large as to explain much of *actual* income gaps, then the wages of skilled labor and the returns to education in poor countries should be much higher than what we observe. Indeed, allowing for free mobility of physical capital and assuming that the wage for unskilled labor in the poorest countries is one tenth the wage for unskilled labor in the United States, Romer (1995) shows that the baseline MRW model with exponents of one third on each the three factors (K, H, L)—i.e., with a = b = 1/3—has a number of counterfactual implications: 1) the wage for skilled labor should be ten times larger in the poorest countries than in the United States; 2) the ratio of the wage for skilled labor to the wage for unskilled labor in the poor country should be two hundred (given that this ratio is two in the United States); 3) the implied rate of return to education in poor countries should be one hundred times larger than that in the United States, rather than by the factor of two or three suggested by the empirical evidence. These implications are not what we observe; in particular, the wage for skilled labor is lower in poor countries than in rich countries. Rather than a dearth of human capital, underdevelopment seems to be a paradoxical situation in which the returns to *all* factors of production tend to be low. The MRW model is inconsistent with this feature.

The MRW extension of the Solow model has also been criticized on the basis of the large number of empirical studies that, rather than attributing per capita income levels and growth differences to the differences in schooling and capital accumulation invoked by neoclassical growth theory, show a supposedly primary role of productivity levels and growth rates in explaining

---

[3] See also Pritchett (2001). Krueger and Lindahl (2001) disagree, however, and argue that measurement error accounts for the lack of a relationship between growth in income per capita and human capital accumulation.

income gaps and differences in per capita GDP growth rates (see the papers cited in section 4 of Chapter 3). While, as discussed later in Chapter 8, the distinction between these sources of growth falls apart in the presence of increasing returns to scale and/or interactions between factor accumulation and technological innovation, the assumptions of constant returns to scale and exogenous technological progress in the MRW model make it vulnerable to the criticism.

Consider now the implications of the augmented Solow model for international differences in growth rates. We can derive an equation, as we did in Chapter 2, to estimate the growth rates predicted by the model. The equation turns out to be the same as eq. (8) in Chapter 2 except that the rate of convergence (Ω) is now equal to $(1 - a - b) (n + g_A + \delta)$. Using this equation, together with the information in Table 2.1 in Chapter 2 and Table 4.1 above, we obtain the predicted growth rates shown in Table 4.1. It is immediately apparent that differences in growth rates are smaller than those reported for the Solow model in Chapter 2, and thus closer to actual growth rates, especially in the case of groups 4 and 5. The predicted growth rates are lower since developing country groups are now seen as being much closer to their respective steady states. Moreover, by broadening the notion of capital, the MRW model features a larger capital share (twice that in the Solow model) and this slows down the pace of conditional convergence. For these two reasons, the transitional component of growth rates in the developing country groups is now much smaller than in the Solow model.

Although the MRW extension fits the observed differences in growth rates better than the original Solow model, it still overstates the transitional component of growth in developing countries. As shown in Table 4.1, this overestimation becomes larger as we move down along the income scale. This suggests that the very slow growth of the poorest countries (groups 4 and 5) does not seem to reflect a slow rate of conditional convergence. For no matter how slow this pace is assumed to be, the growth of output per worker should have been at least 2 percent per year (with corresponding GDP growth rates of over 4 or 5 percent per year), as long as these countries are seen to be below their steady state. Thus, the only way in which the model, without further extensions, can generate growth rates below 2 percent for the poorest countries is by enlarging even more their human capital gaps so that initially these countries were *above* their steady state.[4] This interpretation would imply that over the period the countries in groups 4 and 5 had been moving to the steady state from above, i.e., that they had been reducing their stocks of human and physical capital per effective worker.

---

[4] The same point is made by Temple (1999, p. 135).

2. Human Capital Accumulation in Lucas' Endogenous Growth Model

Robert Lucas, in a 1988 article, presents a model in which growth of income per capita is endogenous due to the presence of constant returns to human capital accumulation. The following example illustrates the mechanics of economic growth under these conditions.

Consider an economy with two sectors (Y and H). In sector Y, goods and services are produced with physical and human capital under constant returns to scale:

$$Y = K^a(\phi H)^{1-a} \tag{8}$$

where H is the total stock of human capital, ϕ is the fraction of it devoted to the production of goods, and (ϕ H) is then the input of human capital in sector Y.

Sector H produces human capital. The outcome of its activity is to increase the quantity of human capital that can be used in each of the two sectors. Assuming that total human capital (H) grows in proportion to the amount of human capital employed in this sector, $(1 - \phi)$ H, we obtain:

$$dH/dt = \lambda(1 - \phi)H \tag{9}$$

where λ is the effectiveness of the sector producing human capital. If a constant fraction of human capital $(1 - \phi)$ is devoted to sector H,[5] human capital grows at a constant exponential rate:

$$\hat{H} = (dH/dt)(1/H) = \lambda(1 - \phi)$$

The model generates a steady state path in which the rate of accumulation of physical capital is equal to, and determined by, the rate of human capital accumulation. The latter is proportional to society's investment in the sector producing human capital. In this equilibrium path, the rate of return to human capital is constant and income per capita increases continuously, despite the absence of exogenous technological change, as a result of the ever-increasing endowment of human capital per capita. Physical capital accumulation is endogenous but not as a result of the productivity effects of increasing returns as in Romer's 1986 model, the other initial contribution to the endogenous growth literature reviewed in Chapter 2. It is now the continuous accumulation of human capital that increases the productivity of physical capital and neutralizes the influence of diminishing returns.

---

[5] This fraction is derived endogenously by Lucas, under the condition of equality between the rates of return on human and physical capital, and in his model it is constant only in the steady state.

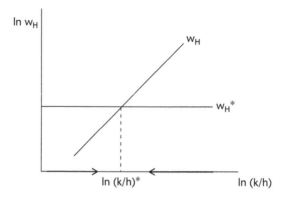

Figure 4.2 A Lucas-type of model

In terms of our real wage diagram, this simple account of the Lucas model results in a representation similar to that of the Solow-Swan model (see Figure 4.2). The w_H curve shows the return to human capital as an increasing function of the ratio of physical to human capital (K/H). The w^*_H curve is horizontal given the technology assumed in (8). On the steady state path, the return to human capital and the ratio of physical to human capital remain constant, but because human capital is growing, so is physical capital (at the same rate). Using the accumulation equation for K (assuming a given savings rate, s) and the steady state condition ($\hat{K} = \hat{H}$), we can derive the steady state value of the ratio of physical to human capital in sector Y, [K/(ϕ H)]. In the steady state, the value of this ratio is: $[K/(\phi H)]^* = \{s/[\lambda(1 - \phi) + \delta]\}^{1/(1-a)}$. This expression is identical to the steady state value of capital per effective worker in the Solow-Swan model (k^{A*}, see equation A.3 in Chapter 2) except that the rate of human capital accumulation, $\lambda (1 - \phi)$, replaces Harrod's natural rate (n + g_A). Thus, the two steady state growth rates are identical if the rate of labor-augmenting technical progress (g_A) is equal to the growth rate of human capital per capita, $\lambda (1 - \phi) - n$. The accumulation of physical capital and output growth are *driven by* the accumulation of human capital, analogous to how in the Solow model, capital accumulation in the steady state is driven by technical progress and the growth of the labor force.

Other analogies to the Solow model, although more remote, can be noted regarding the transitional dynamics. Off the steady state, if the relative endow-ment of human capital is high (i.e., K/H is low) the economy will converge to the steady state with a growth rate that is initially above the long-run equilib-rium rate, and vice versa. If initial conditions are such that the ratio of physical to human capital is relatively high, the economy will converge to the steady state with an initially low growth rate. After a war or an earthquake that has destroyed mostly physical capital, the economy will recover faster than after an epidemic that has destroyed mainly human capital. Another implication, which has brought considerable attention, is the following: an economy with a relatively low ratio of physical to human capital—e.g., a developing country well endowed with human capital—will grow at a relatively high rate compared to the equilibrium path or to other developing economies less well endowed with human capital.

A key question is what assumptions in the model generate constant returns to the accumulation of human capital and, as a result, endogenous growth. In one interpretation (Rebelo, 1991), the critical assumption made by Lucas is that the production of human capital only uses reproducible factors. This assumption is obvious in the particular specification used by in eq. (9) above: human capital alone enters into the accumulation equation. As shown by Rebelo, the model's properties would remain intact as long as only reproducible factors enter directly or indirectly into the accumulation equation for human capital. To illustrate, consider the following accumulation equation: $dH/dt = s_H Y - \delta_H H$, where δ_H is the depreciation rate of human capital and Y is produced under conditions described by (8) so that K, along with H, enters into the production of new human capital. Substituting from (8) and using the steady state condition $\hat{H} = \hat{K}$, the rate of human capital accumulation in the steady state is still a linear function of H: $dH/dt = (sa \, s_H^{1-a} - \delta_H) H$. The reason is that only reproducible factors, under constant returns to scale, enter into the production of Y (see eq. 8). The model then behaves as the limiting case of the MRW extension of the Solow model in which output elasticities with respect to K and H add up to unity. Interpreted in this way, there is an interesting analogy, pointed out by Srinivasan (1994), to the two-sector model of Mahalanobis (1955) and Feldman (1928, as described in Domar, 1957). There, the sector producing physical capital goods uses only reproducible factors (physical capital goods). The model then generates endogenous growth without having to rely on increasing returns to scale. The equilibrium growth rate is determined by the share of investment devoted to capital accumulation in the sector producing capital goods.

In Rebelo's view, the distinctive feature of the model, in terms of the specification of technology, is thus the existence of a "core" reproducible factor that can be produced without the use of non-reproducible factors. This interpretation suggests that the specification in eq. (9) is more restrictive than it needs to be. Yet, in another way this is not the case. Eq. (9) postulates constant returns to human capital accumulation whether or not fixed factors enter into its production—one can imagine, for example, fixed factors entering into the multiplicative constant (λ). The justification for the linearity of the human capital accumulation equation has to do, in Lucas' verbal discussion, with the *external effects* of human capital. Lucas discusses two types of external effects of human capital. One is the external effect of human capital in the aggregate production function. This is like adding a TFP term in the production function and making it a function of aggregate human capital. In the presentation of the model, I have neglected this external effect in eq. (8) because, indeed, it plays no role in generating constant returns to human capital accumulation.

Lucas sees the other external effect as crucial to justify the specification in eq. (9). For as Lucas explains, it is the fact that "human capital accumulation is a *social* activity, involving *groups* of people in a way that has no counterpart in the accumulation of physical capital" that would justify why the initial level of human capital of the younger generations is proportional to the level already achieved by the older generations (Lucas, 1988, p. 19, italics in original). This external effect is assumed to be internalized through non-market mechanisms within small groups, such as firms or families, and, in this way creates no gap between social and private returns. But it is nevertheless an external effect that is viewed by Lucas as critical to the linearity assumption in the accumulation equation, when applied to infinitely lived families rather than finite lived individuals.

It is unclear, however, why these external effects should be large enough to generate constant returns to the accumulation of human capital. If sector H largely transmits already existing knowledge, in schools or within families, returns will eventually diminish in the absence of the production of *new knowledge*. This is why Romer's (1991) interpretation of that sector as a know-ledge-producing sector is perhaps the most coherent, assuming that the production of knowledge is not subject to diminishing returns. However, if this is so, the Lucas model does not go much further than replacing the exogenous rate of technical progress in the Solow model with a rate of human capital accumulation which, along with preferences and technology parameters, is critically determined by the exogenous value of λ, the effectiveness of investment in human capital.

Empirical assessment

Models in which growth is driven by human capital accumulation have been found promising for explaining differences in growth rates across developing countries and especially the extraordinary high growth rates recorded in the East Asian miracles (see, for example, Lucas, 1993). There is support, in particular, for the model's implication that, below the steady state, two developing countries identical in all respects except for the endowment of human capital will grow at different rates, the country with the highest H/K ratio being the fastest growing.

As noted by Pack (1994) and Rodrik (1994), the comparative growth performance of East Asia is not, in fact, easy to reconcile with a human capital based explanation of economic growth. Consider the initial conditions in the early 1960s, when growth in Korea and Taiwan took off at vertiginous rates. The human capital endowment in these countries was rather favorable to growth. Their peoples had levels of education higher than expected, given their per capita incomes. This is likely to have played a role in their subsequent expansion. But how decisive a role? Rodrik (1994) lists four countries (Dominican Republic, Philippines, Paraguay, and Sri Lanka) that had the same kind of educational advantage as Korea and Taiwan in 1960 and were unable to grow at rates anywhere near those of these two countries. And what if the initial conditions had not been so favorable? Would there have been East Asian miracles? A simulation by Birdsall, Ross and Sabot (1995), using a cross country regression framework, concludes that, if South Korea's initial level of education had been similar to the developing country average, its per capita growth would have been less (close to 5 percent per year instead of close to 6 percent), but still much higher than the developing country average. We would still have had a Korean growth miracle.

In addition to their initial educational advantage, during their process of rapid economic growth East Asian countries made substantial investments in education. Yet the same can be said of many other countries that were unable to grow fast. The commitment to improving educational standards was almost universal across the developing world. The results of these human capital investments were often very different, but differences in growth rates may have played a major part in these results. This endogeneity problem can be illustrated by a comparison between Korea and Mexico (see Birdsall, Ross, and Sabot 1995). In 1970, Korea's public expenditure on basic education per eligible child was only slightly higher than in Mexico. Two decades later, Mexico's expenditure on education was only 25 percent the Korean level, secondary enrollment rates were twice as high in Korea compared to Mexico, and the gap in tertiary enrollment rates had become even higher (39 percent versus 15 percent). Public expenditure policy does not explain this divergence: in fact, by the mid 1970s, after an expansion during the first half of that decade, expenditure in basic education *as percentage of GDP* reached temporarily higher levels in Mexico than in Korea. The explanation of these increasing gaps has to be attributed to the fact that Korea's GDP grew at annual rates of 9.6 percent, compared to Mexico's rate of 3.5 percent per year. This difference in growth rates meant that, with the same percentage of GDP invested in education, the resources that Korea was able to invest in this sector expanded at a vastly higher rate.[6]

---

[6] The demographic transition that started earlier in Korea than in Mexico also played a role. This explains why in these two decades, the number of school age children increased by 60 percent in Mexico but fell by 2 percent in Korea.

According to Pack (1994), investments in research and development, unlike today, were of little significance before the mid-1980s in the East Asian developing economies. However, by then, these countries had been able to sustain extraordinarily high growth rates for almost three decades. Gustav Ranis (1995) tells an interesting and significant story. In the 1960s (from 1960 to 1967), around 15 percent of Taiwan's college graduates went to the United States to undertake post-graduate studies, two thirds of them in science and engineering. This suggests a very high rate of human capital formation, especially for a country with Taiwan's income in the 1960s. The most revealing part of the story, however, is that only 4.5 percent of those students returned to Taiwan each year. By contrast, in the second half of the 1980s, when Taiwan's industrialization was no longer based on labor intensive manufactures and was becoming increasingly intensive in science and technology, more than 90 percent of these highly trained graduates were returning to their country. The moral of the story seems to be that those reserves of human capital created over the years were a necessary condition for this technology-intensive industrialization to take off, but did not by themselves represent a sufficient condition for it.

Moreover, just as models with increasing returns to capital a la Romer (1986), human capital driven growth models appear to imply an excessive degree of divergence across countries. Differences in growth rates tend to persist indefinitely and thus to generate increasing gaps in per capita income levels. If the share of resources invested in human capital increases with per capita incomes—for example, as a result of the existence of a minimum (subsistence) level of consumption per capita—it will further accentuate the gaps, even though growth rates need not diverge (as in models with increasing returns to capital) if the differences in the shares of resources devoted to human capital accumulation decrease over time.

These observations seem difficult to reconcile with the notion that differences across countries in the rate of economic growth are to be explained *primarily* by differences in the levels and rates of human capital formation. More generally, it is hard to reconcile them with a view of the development process in which physical capital accumulation and output growth are essentially driven by human capital accumulation.

3. Growth and the Level of Human Capital: The Insight of Nelson and Phelps

Nelson and Phelps (1966) introduced human capital in a growth model in a different form than the traditional one. Rather than viewing the role of education as a factor of production, they viewed it as a factor that facilitates technological diffusion. More precisely, the basic contribution of Nelson and Phelps was to combine two ideas. The first is that the rate at which productivity grows in an economy positively depends, just as in Gerschenkron (1962), on the gap between the current level of productivity and the one corresponding to the technological frontier (or what Nelson and Phelps called the "theoretical level of technology" defined as the level that would prevail only if technological diffusion was instantaneous). The second idea is that the rate at which the gap is closed depends on the level of human capital. Nelson and Phelps find support for this idea in the empirical finding showing that the greater the level of education (of farmers, for example) the faster is the adoption of more advanced techniques. Thus, for them, the true importance of education is based not so much in its direct contribution to production but, precisely, in its contribution to technological diffusion.

In its original version in Nelson and Phelps (1966), these ideas were formalized by making the proportionate rate of growth of the technology variable in the production function (A) a function of the technology gap—the difference between T, the "theoretical level of technology" and A, the current level of technology—and the level of human capital (h).

$$g_A = \Phi(h)\{(T - A)/A\} \qquad \Phi(0) = 0, \Phi'(h) > 0 \qquad (10)$$

This formulation has two implications that are illustrated in Figure 4.3. First, in the long run, provided that h is positive, the rate of growth of productivity (g_A) converges and stabilizes in a value g^*, equal to the growth of T, which is independent of the level of human capital. This is simply because when g_A is below g^*, the technology gap increases and this, according to eq. (10), accelerates the growth of A thus raising g_A to the value g^*. The opposite happens when g_A is above g^*.

The second implication is that the equilibrium (asymptotic) gap is a decreasing function of human capital (h). A higher educational level raises the trajectory *level* of "technology in practice" in the long run. Indeed, it is easy to show that the equilibrium gap is equal to g^*/Φ (h). In terms of Figure 4.3, an increase in human capital (h) makes the g_A line steeper (see eq. 10) and reduces the equilibrium technology gap without long-run *growth* effects on productivity.

Note that the model has features in common with the MRW model and the Lucas model. With the MRW model it shares the feature that the steady state income gap (as determined by technology) is a function of human capital. With the Lucas model, it shares the transitional dynamics, since if we compare the off the steady state behavior of two economies with different stocks of human capital per worker, but otherwise identical, the economy with the greater stock of human capital per worker will grow a faster rate. These similarities are interesting given that the view of human capital and the way

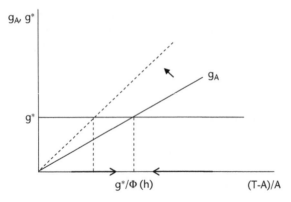

Figure 4.3 The Nelson and Phelps model

in which human capital is modeled in Nelson and Phelps is completely different from MRW and Lucas.

The extension by Benhabib and Spiegel and the "Gerschenkron-Abramovitz hypothesis"

Nelson and Phelps left the path of the "theoretical level of technology" unexplained, i.e. the rate of growth (g*) of the technological frontier is exogenous. Benhabib and Spiegel (1994) adopted the Nelson and Phelps formulation and combined it with Romer (1990) contribution that postulates that human capital can directly influence productivity by affecting a country's capacity to generate new technologies (and not only, as in Nelson and Phelps, the capacity to adopt already existing technologies). In the formulation of Benhabib and Spiegel, we have then:

$$g_A = \Gamma(h) + \Phi(h)\{(T - A)/A\} \qquad \Phi(0) = 0, \Gamma'(h), \Phi'(h) > 0 \qquad (11)$$

The combination of the two forces, domestic innovation and technological catch up, generates various results. First, under certain conditions (in particular when the parameters of the innovation function, $\Gamma(h)$, predominate), growth rates can differ across countries for long periods of time due to differences in the stocks of human capital. Second, a country that is behind the technology leader, but possesses a greater human capital, will catch up and eventually surpass the technological leader. Third, the country with the greater stock of human capital will always emerge as the technological leader and maintain its technological superiority as long as it preserves its human capital advantage.

The more recent and comprehensive analysis using this approach is Benhabib and Spiegel (2005). In this contribution, the authors consider two variants of the original hypotheses of Nelson and Phelps and submit them to empirical enquiry. The first variant corresponds to the 1994 formulation just presented. The second variant consists in adding the term (A/T) to the equation that governs the growth of A as follows:

$$g_A = \Gamma(h) + \Phi(h)\{A/T\}\{(T - A)/A\}, \qquad \Phi(0) = 0, \Gamma'(h), \Phi'(h) > 0 \quad (12)$$

This additional term (A/T) makes the rate of technological diffusion slow down when the distance with respect to the technological leader increases. This is a result of the difficulty of adopting very distant technologies which arises, as argued by Basu and Weil (1998), from the fact that the technological frontier may not be appropriate for follower countries in the presence of very large differences in factor proportions between leader and follower countries. This second variant is related to what one may call the Gerschenkron-Abramovitz view according to which technological backwardness conveys a growth advantage by opening up the relatively easy path of adoption and imitation (the Gerschenkron, 1962, component), but that "social back-wardness" creates an offsetting disadvantage (the Abramovitz, 1986, component). Indeed, as Abramovitz argued: "Countries that are technologically backward have a potentiality for generating growth more rapid than that of more advanced countries, provided their social capabilities are sufficiently developed to permit successful exploitation of technologies already employed by the technological leaders" (Abramovitz, 1986, p. 225).

The second variant of Benhabib and Spiegel takes human capital as the central social capability to which Abramovitz refers in the above quote.[7] The key difference in the predictions of the two variants (i.e., the predictions of eqs 11 and 12) is the following. In the first variant (eq. 11), despite educational differences, all countries converge in the long run to the same rate of productivity growth (just as in the original formulation by Nelson and Phelps). Moreover, in the transition, the greater is the level of productivity the smaller is the technology gap and the lower is the productivity growth rate (in a similar way to the tendency to convergence in the neoclassical model). The convergence in growth rates is the result of the forces of technological diffusion in the model and, as a result, of the tendency to technological catching up.

In the second variant (eq. 12), there is a threshold value of human capital, a critical level below which the rate of growth of the followers with low educational level diverges and the equilibrium relationship between the productivity of the follower and that of the leader (A/T) tends to zero. In other

---

[7] Another related model, besides Basu and Weil (1998), is Howitt and Mayer-Foulkes (2005). Verspagen (1991) discusses another non-linear model in which catching up and falling behind are both possible.

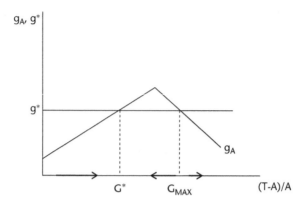

Figure 4.4 The Benhabib and Spiegel model

words, in this variant the process of technological catching up can be slow both when the follower country is very near the technological frontier (because then the technology gap is very small) and when the follower is very far from the leader (because of the difficulties of adopting the technologies of the frontier). It also follows that when the technology gap is in an intermediate range, the growth of productivity is fastest.

Figure 4.4 illustrates the second variant by assuming that g_A is an increasing function of the technological gap only for values of the gap which are below a critical value. For simplicity, as in Nelson and Phelps, the growth of the frontier (g^*) is assumed exogenous. As shown by Figure 4.4, there are now two intersections between g^* and g_A. The first is at low levels of the technological gap when the g_A line is positively sloped. The gap corresponding to this intersection (G^*) is a stable, but only locally stable, long-run equilibrium. The other intersection occurs at high levels of the technological gap when the g_A line is negatively sloped. This intersection corresponds to that value of the technology gap (G_{MAX}) beyond which the gap tends to increase indefinitely and thus (A/T) tends to zero. In this process the rate of productivity growth increasingly diverges from g^*, the growth rate of the technological frontier.

Benhabib and Spiegel (2005) investigate empirically these two variants and find support for the second variant, associated to the "Gerschenkron-Abramovitz hypothesis". In a sample of 84 countries for the period 1960–1995, they find that the critical level of education in 1960 necessary to guarantee convergence to the growth rate of the United States (the technology leader) was 1.78 years of schooling. They identify 27 countries in the sample for which the model predicts a growth of total factor productivity less than that of the United States and find that 22 of these 27 countries effectively diverged. Of these 22 countries, 13 are in Sub-Saharan Africa, 3 in Central America, 3 in the Middle East and North Africa, 2 in South Asia, and the remaining one is Papua New Guinea. The five countries that tended to converge despite having less than the critical level of human capital are Botswana, Indonesia, Pakistan, India and Syria.

While the explanatory power of the model appears striking, it should be noted that there are also 27 countries that despite having more than the critical level of human capital did not have a productivity growth rate higher than the United States as predicted by the model. These 27 countries include a group of 8 highly developed economies with a small initial technology gap with the United States,[8] and a large group of 19 developing countries with low and middle incomes per capita, 14 of them in Latin America and the Caribbean, 2 in Sub-Saharan Africa, plus the Philippines, Fiji and Turkey. Why didn't the laggards converge, in particular those developing countries with a large technology gap and therefore great scope for catching up, despite having enough human capital to do so? In the next chapter, we shall see how the Schumpeterian approach to endogenous growth theory addresses these issues and, in part II of the book, we shall turn to older approaches in development economics that were inspired by questions similar to this one.

---

[8] These countries are (in ascending order according to productivity growth) New Zealand, Switzerland, Sweden, United Kingdom, Canada, Australia, Denmark, and the Netherlands.

5

Industrial Differentiation and Creative Destruction in New Growth Theory

Neoclassical growth models and all their extensions typically assume constant returns to scale and treat technology as a public good (i.e., non rival and non excludable), leaving unexplained the advance over time of the technological frontier. The endogenous growth models reviewed in Chapter 2 partly endogeneize productivity growth by assuming increasing returns to scale as a property of the production function but otherwise leave technical change unexplained. Besides the notion that the accumulation of capital generates technological externalities that may sustain long-term growth, technical progress is absent. The AK model, for example, explains persistent growth as a result of capital accumulation through technological externalities derived from the expansion of the stock of experience. This leaves the question open of whether these technological externalities are in fact the main mechanism that explains the growth of per capita incomes. If this is not the case, we have to endogeneize technical progress in a different way to that adopted by the models with non diminishing returns to capital.

This chapter presents a brand of endogenous growth theory that attempts to model the economic determinants of technical progress and to elucidate the factors that affect the path of the technological frontier, going beyond the suggestion by Romer (1990) and Benhabib and Spiegel (2005) in Chapter 4 that the level of human capital is likely to be an important factor. After a brief review of the contributions of Adam Smith and Allyn Young, section 2 is devoted to the product variety model which attempts to formalize some of Young's insights. Here, innovation takes the form of an expansion in the number of available intermediate products which in turn raises productivity in the final goods sectors. This section also reviews open economy versions of the product variety model in which access through trade to a wider variety of intermediate goods can bring dynamic gains from trade. Sections 3 and 4 then turn to Schumpeterian models in which, unlike the product variety model where new goods do not displace existing ones, innovation is modeled as quality improvements on a given array of products ("vertical innovation"), so that technical progress, in a process of "creative destruction", makes existing products obsolete. Section 3 presents a model without physical capital and discusses the ambiguous and paradoxical relationship between innovation and product market competition highlighted by Schumpeter while section 4 presents a model with physical capital accumulation that clarifies the interactions between capital accumulation and innovation in the growth process, together with an overall empirical assessment of Schumpeterian growth theory.

1. Industrial Differentiation and the Extent of the Market: Smith, Young, and Kaldor[1]

In the first chapter of *The Wealth of Nations*, Adam Smith states that the income level of developed countries depends on the high degree of division of labor they attained. Division of labor increases labor productivity, which in Smith's view is the principal factor affecting per capita income. Smith identifies three positive effects of the division of labor on workers' productivity. When workers specialize, they: (1) increase their skill (dexterity); (2) save the time necessary to switch among different activities; and (3) have the possibility of inventing machines to facilitate their job. In modern terms, we see how Smith had in mind the concepts of: (1) learning by doing; (2) set-up costs; and (3) endogenous technological progress.

In Smith, economic growth is associated with an increase in the complexity of economic activity, brought about by the division of labor: 'It is the great multiplication of the production of all the different arts, in consequence of the division of labor, which occasions, in a well-governed society, that universal opulence which extends itself to the lowest ranks of people' (Smith, 1976, p. 9). In Smith's opinion, profit-seeking capitalists are continuously trying to exploit the possibilities offered by both the division of labor within and among firms.

The analysis of economic growth by Allyn Young (1928) starts from Adam Smith, explores the implications of some of Smith's insights and adds novel elements to his theory. Young considers the division of labor mainly as the process leading to the introduction of (highly productive) capital goods (i.e. the use of indirect instead of direct labor), and to the increase of a network of interdependent productive units. He discusses the economies deriving from

---

[1] For an analysis of the views of Smith and Young together with those of Marshall and Kaldor, see Lavezzi (2001) on which I rely in this section.

the use of specialized machines in production. He emphasizes one aspect of the simplification of some phases of the production process, also treated by Marshall: the possibility and incentive to introduce machines.[2] The main question is to understand when the firm decides to face the (fixed) cost of a new, specialized machine, either by building it or by purchasing it or, to put it in other words, when the firm decides to use indirect rather than direct labor. Young analyzes the economies deriving from the use of specialized machines in production. In his discussion of Smith's idea that a specialized worker is likely to invent new tools or machines, Young stresses that what matters is that the simplification of some phases of the production process allows for the introduction of machines. This is a key difference with Adam Smith's notion that the division of labor is limited by the extent of the market. For Young, productivity increases with the extent of the market because the high fixed costs of increasing returns technologies can only be recovered in large markets rather than because workers can specialize in more specific tasks. It is in this sense that Young says that Smith "missed the main point" (Young, 1928, p. 530): the productivity gains from economies of specialization are of second order compared to the productivity increases arising from more 'roundabout' methods of production becoming profitable. As he puts it:

> It is generally agreed that Adam Smith, when he suggested that the division of labor leads to inventions because workmen engaged in specialized routine operations come to see better ways of accomplishing the same results, missed the main point. The important thing, of course, is that with the division of labor a group of complex processes is transformed into a succession of simpler processes, some of which, at least, lend themselves to the use of machinery.

He also writes:

> [i]n the use of machinery and the adoption of indirect processes there is a further division of labor, the economies of which are again limited by the extent of the market. It would be wasteful to make a hammer to drive a single nail, ... It would be wasteful to furnish a factory with an elaborate equipment of specially constructed [machines] to build a hundred automobiles. (Young, 1928, p. 530)

Young then discusses the process of division of labor among industries, remarking the association between industrial differentiation and growth of production. As Young puts it in his discussion of the process of division of labor among industries:

---

[2] According to Marshall (1910), large-scale production allows economies of machinery resulting from the ability to recoup the fixed cost to be born when a new machine is adopted. A large output allows a firm to keep the machine steadily employed, and gives the firm more resources to spend, easier access to credit and so on. A similar reasoning applies in the case of economies of skill: a large output allows a greater division of labor to be established.

industrial differentiation has been and remains the type of change characteristic-ally associated with the growth of production. Notable as has been the increase in the complexity of the apparatus of living, as shown by the increase in the variety of goods offered in consumers' markets, the increase in the diversification of intermediate products and of industries manufacturing special products or groups of products has gone even further. (Young, 1928, p. 537).

These economies result from an increased division of labor associated with a larger number of goods being produced—or, as Kaldor put it, "from increased differentiation, new processes and new subsidiary industries", so that as a result "economies of scale are derived not only from the expansion of any single industry but from a general industrial expansion" (Kaldor, 1967, p. 14). They are external to the firm, although they arise because, in the presence of internal economies of scale (and indivisibilities in the production of goods), the size of the market limits the number of goods that can be produced without loss. This is what led Young (1928) and Kaldor (1967, p. 14) to view increasing returns and productivity growth as a "macro phenomenon".

Most important is the observation that 'the largest advantage secured by the division of labor among industries is the fuller realizing of the economies of capitalistic or 'roundabout methods of production' (Young, 1928, p. 539). In fact, in the process of division of labor among industries, whenever a new industry is created following an increase in the extent of the overall market for the good it produces, the firms in such industry benefit from the large overall industry output, in the sense that they may adopt specialized machines, i.e. roundabout methods of production.

2. Economies of Specialization and Industrial Differentiation Models

Romer (1987, 1990) formalizes the idea that growth is sustained by the increasing specialization of labor across an increasing variety of activities: as the economy grows, the larger market makes it worth paying the fixed (or sunk) costs of a larger and larger number of intermediate inputs. This in turn raises the productivity of labor, thereby maintaining growth.

The model with economies of specialization[3]

The economy considered has two goods-producing sectors. One sector pro-duces a final good that can be used for consumption or investment and

---

[3] This section and the next rely on Gancia and Zilibotti (2005) and Aghion and Howitt (2009).

operates under perfect competition. Investment must be thought as investment in the production of blueprints. The other sector produces intermediate inputs (for the final goods sector) under imperfect competition. There is also a research and development sector that produces blueprints (for the production of the intermediate goods) and operates under perfect competition, and thus free entry, making zero profits in equilibrium so that the price of blueprints is equal to the costs associated to their development.

Production in the final goods sector (Y) uses labor (L in fixed supply) and a variety of intermediate inputs whose number A varies over time:

$$Y = \left(\sum I_i^a\right) L^{1-a} \qquad 0 < a < 1 \qquad (1)$$

where I_i is the amount of intermediate good i. We can interpret each of these intermediate goods as a step in the production process. An increase in the number of intermediates or components implies a finer division of labor. Due to economies of specialization, this greater division makes labor more productive.

Each unit of intermediate good i produced requires the input of one unit of final good (a one for one technology). Despite the simple one to one technology, imperfect competition arises from the presence of product differentiation. Let X be the total amount of final good used in producing intermediates. According to the one for one technology X equals total intermediate output: $X = \Sigma\, I_i$

Now suppose that each intermediate product is produced in the same amount I (as it will in equilibrium). This implies $I = X/A$, where A is the number of intermediate products, a measure of product variety. Substituting into (1), we get:

$$Y = \sum (X/A)^a\, L^{1-a} = A\,(X/A)^a\, L^{1-a} = A^{1-a}\, X^a\, L^{1-a} \qquad (2)$$

with $dY/dA = (1-a)\, Y/A > 0$ which shows that final goods production is increasing in A. Thus, according to the production function, product variety enhances the productivity of the economy: the greater the degree of specialization and differentiation within the economy the higher the productivity of labor.

Each intermediate product is produced by a monopolist who seeks to maximize profits equal to:

$$\Pi = p_i\, I_i - I_i \qquad (3)$$

where p_i is the price of intermediate good i and the second I_i is the cost according to the one for one technology.

How is the price determined? Since the final goods sector operates under perfect competition, p_i will be the value of the input's marginal product: $p_i = dY/dI_i = a\, I_i^{a-1}\, L^{1-a}$. Using (3) and the expression for p_i, the monopolist profit is then: $\Pi = a\, I_i^a\, L^{1-a} - I_i$. What will be the quantity produced I_i? Profit maximization implies the first order condition: $d\Pi i/dIi = a^2\,I^{i\,a-1}\,L^{1-a} - 1 = 0$, which means that the equilibrium quantity will be the same constant in every sector i: $I = [a^{2/(1-a)}]\,L$. The equilibrium profit flow will be:

$$\Pi = ([1-a]/a]a^{2/(1-a)}L \tag{4}$$

Substituting $X = A\,I$ into (2), we have: $Y = A\,I^a\,L^{1-a}$. Since GDP = Y − X, we have GDP = $A\,(L^{1-a}I^a - I)$. Given that L and I are constant, the growth rate of GDP (g) is: $g = g_A\,(= (dA/dt)\,(1/A))$.

Product variety is assumed to grow at a rate that depends on the amount R of final output that is used in research: $dA/dt = \lambda R$, where λ is a parameter that indicates the productivity of the research sector.

Free entry into the research sector implies that the present discounted value of profits from innovation cannot exceed the entry cost. Profit is the flow of revenue minus the cost (R) and the flow of revenue is the price of a blueprint $(\Pi/r)^4$ times the flow of new blueprints $(dA/dt = \lambda R)$. Thus, the zero profit condition implies $(\Pi/r)\,\lambda\,R - R = 0$. This implies the research arbitrage equation: $r = \lambda\Pi$

To close the model we need to impose the relation between the growth rate (g) and the interest rate (r) implied by the Euler equation, i.e., by the preference side of the model. As in Chapter 3, the Euler equation shows the steady state rate of growth as $g = (r - \rho)/\theta$, where r is the rate of interest, ρ is the discount rate, and $1/\theta$ is the elasticity of intertemporal substitution. Combining the research arbitrage equation with the Euler equation implies: $g = (\lambda\Pi - \rho)/\theta$ Substituting from (4) into this expression yields:

$$g = \{\lambda(1-a)/a]L\,a^{2/1-a} - \rho\}/\theta \tag{5}$$

The rate of growth is an increasing function of the productivity of research (λ) and the size of the labor force (L), and a decreasing function of the rate of time preference (ρ). The productivity of research, depending presumably on the level of human capital in a more detailed model, has a positive direct effect on the rate of expansion of product variety and thus productivity. The growth rate depends positively on profits, through the research arbitrage equation and the Euler equation, and profits depend positively on the size of the economy which through this channel affects the growth rate. The discount rate affects negatively the growth rate since it positively affects current consumption and inhibits investment in research.

[4] The blueprint entitles the monopolist in the intermediate goods sector to a flow of profit Π in perpetuity. The price that he is willing to pay for the blueprint must then be the present discounted value of future profits, discounted with the interest rate. If the monopolist was willing to pay less than that, the inventor of the blueprint would be able to find another entrepreneur willing to pay more and at the same time make a profit.

The model with economies of specialization and research spillovers

Suppose now that labor is used as an input in the research sector. Then $L = L_Y + L_R$ where L_Y is labor employed in the final goods sector and L_R is labor employed in the research sector. The main changes with respect to the previous model are the following. First, the profit flow in the intermediate goods sector depends now on L_Y (rather than L): $\Pi = ([1-a]/a)\, a^{2/(1-a)}\, L_Y$. Second, product variety now grows at a rate that depends on L_R (rather than R):

$$dA/dt = \lambda A L_R \text{ or } g_A = (1/A)\,(dA/dt) = \lambda L_R$$

There are now two sources of increasing returns: specialization or product differentiation and research spillovers in the sense that all researchers can make use of the accumulated knowledge A embodied in existing designs.

The third change is that the flow of profit in the research sector is now: (Π/r) $\lambda A L_R - w\, L_R$, where w is the wage paid in the Research and Development (R&D) sector. Setting this profit flow equal to zero yields $r = \lambda A\Pi/w$.

The equilibrium wage rate w is found by setting it equal to the marginal product of labor in the final goods sector (assuming that there is only type of labor that can work in the final sector or in the R&D sector). Since each intermediate sector produces the same constant output (I), the production function in the final goods sector implies: $Y = A\, I^a\, L_Y^{1-a}$.

Setting the wage equal to the marginal product of labor implies: $w = dY/dL_Y =$ $A\, I^a\, (1-a)\, L_Y^{-a}$ and using the expression for I ($I = a^{2/(1-a)}\, L_Y$), we have: $w = (1-a)\, a^{2/(1-a)}\, A$, which implies that the wage grows at the same rate as output and productivity.

Substituting from the expressions for Π and w into the research arbitrage equation, we get: $r = a\, \lambda\, L_Y$. Since $g = g_A = \lambda L_R = \lambda(L - L_Y)$. This implies $r = a\, (\lambda L - g)$. Substituting this expression into the Euler equation and solving for g, we get

$$g = (a\, \lambda\, L - \rho)/(a + \theta) \tag{5'}$$

As before, this expression shows the rate of growth increasing with the productivity of research (λ) and with the size of the labor force (L), and decreasing with the rate of time preference (ρ).

Figure 5.1 shows a graphical determination of the growth rate at the intersection of two linear functions. The line SS corresponds to the Euler equation showing the steady state rate of growth as a positive function of the interest rate $g = (r - \rho)/\theta$. This can be seen as a supply of saving schedule. The equation for line DD, derived from the research arbitrage equation, is $r = a$ $(\lambda L - g)$ and establishes a negative relationship between the interest rate and growth that can be interpreted as a demand for funds equation.

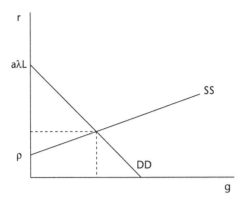

Figure 5.1 A model with economies of specialization

Policy implications

What are the welfare implications of product variety models? There are two reasons why the decentralized equilibrium is inefficient in these models. First, firms in the intermediate goods sector exert monopoly power and charge a price in excess of the marginal cost of production. This leads to an underproduction of each variety of intermediate goods. Second, the accumulation of ideas produces externalities that are not internalized in the laissez-faire economy. Innovating firms compare the private cost of innovation with the present discounted value of profits. However, they ignore the spillover on the future productivity of innovation.

Since technical change consists of horizontal innovations that do not turn previous goods obsolete, so that the entry of new firms does not reduce previously existing rents, innovation does not cause "creative destruction" as in Schumpeterian models. As a result, and given that the intertemporal knowledge spillover is not internalized, growth is always sub-optimally low in the laissez-faire equilibrium. Policies aimed at increasing research activities (e.g., through subsidies to R&D or intermediate production) are both growth- and welfare-enhancing.

Trade, integration and growth in the product variety model

Traditional trade theory has focused on static gains from trade. These gains can explain why an open economy has a higher level of income but not why it may grow faster. Endogenous growth models of an open economy address the challenge of showing why an open economy may grow faster. While there are in principle various channels through which can affect TFP (see Grossman and Helpman, 1991), the channel on which most of the literature has focused is the increase in the number of available input varieties brought about by a trade liberalization.

Product variety models feature scale effects on growth in the sense that the rate of growth of the economy depends on the size of the labor force. This has clear-cut implications for economic integration. If two economies merge, the growth rate of the single, unified economy will be larger than the two previously separate entities. Indeed, consider two identical economies with the same labor force, $L = L^*$. In isolation, each country grows at a rate given by eq. (5′). If they merge, the integrated country grows at a higher rate given by: $g = [a \lambda (L + L^*) - \rho]/(a + \theta) = (2a \lambda L - \rho)/(a + \theta)$.

Consider now the effects of trade in these models. These effects depend on whether knowledge spillovers remain localized within national borders or not and on the level of development of the two economies. In the case of local spillovers and identical economies with $L = L^*$ and $A = A^*$, where the asterisk refers to the foreign country, growth is unaffected by trade (Rivera-Batiz and Romer, 1991). The reason is that growth can only be affected by the split of the labor force between the goods and R&D sectors. In this case trade increases the productivity of workers in production and the profitability of research by the same proportion leaving the sectoral division of the labor force unaffected. Thus trade brings only static gains as a result of the increase in the variety of intermediate products available.

If initially productivity levels are different, trade leads to specialization and an increase in the growth rate (Devereux and Lapham, 1994). This is because the country with an initial advantage in productivity reduces employment in production and increases research activity which increases growth. Although trade leads to no innovation in the less advanced country, the location of innovation has no effect on the relative welfare of the two countries as final good producers in the two countries can use the same varieties of intermediates.

If knowledge spillovers cross national borders, the flow of new designs is now proportional to the world stock $(A + A^*)$ in the two countries and thus, even if the composition of the labor force remained unaffected, the productivity growth rate increases. Moreover, the larger knowledge spillover increases the productivity of the R&D sector and leads to an increase in employment in this sector which is growth enhancing. This is equivalent to an increase in λ which shifts the DD schedule upwards in Figure 5.1 leading to a higher interest rate and growth rate in both countries.

As noted by Rodriguez and Rodrik (2001), contrary to the belief that endogenous growth models have provided the link between trade and growth missing in traditional trade theory, the answer of these models to the question of whether trade promotes growth in a small open economy is ambiguous and depends on how trade specialization reallocates resources, benefiting or not sectors that generate long-term growth through externalities in research and development or expanding product variety. Examples of such models, which formalize old ideas about infant industry protection, are present in Grossman and Helpman (1991), Matsuyama (1992), Feenstra (1996), and Rodriguez and Rodrik (2001). We shall return to this subject in Chapters 9 and 14.

Criticisms and empirical assessments[5]

Product variety models, in closed and open economies alike, feature scale effects on growth. These effects have, however, unrealistic implications. Since the size of the labor force has a level effect on the rate of growth, with a growing population the rate of growth of output should itself be increasing over time. This clearly has not happened. As noted by Jones (1995), the number of R&D scientists has increased almost nine fold since 1953 while the growth rate of output and technology has not increased.

The scale effect on the economy's rate of growth is due to a key assumption in these models. This is that the rate of technological progress is a linear function of the number of workers who are devoting their time to R&D, i.e., $g_A = \lambda L_R$. There are two features that are unsatisfactory in the implicit technology production function. The first is that the *rate of growth* of technology does not depend on the *level* of technology. There are in fact two likely effects of the level of technology. One is that the invention of ideas in the past raises the productivity of researchers in the present. The discovery of calculus, the invention of the laser, and the development of integrated circuits are examples of ideas that have increased the productivity of later research. This effect has been called the "standing on the shoulders" effect.[6] This is a positive effect of the level of technology on the rate of technology creation. This would suggest a technology production function in which the rate of productivity growth is a function of L_R, λ, and the level of technology with a positive exponent: $g_A = \lambda L_R A^{\eta}$.

There is another effect of the level of technology. Perhaps the most obvious ideas are discovered first and subsequent ideas are increasingly difficult to discover. This is the "fishing out effect" according to which the fish become harder to catch over time. This is a negative effect of the level of technology on the rate of technology creation. Further, because more is known today than in the past, it takes more effort for a researcher to learn everything required to work at the cutting edge. This would suggest a production function in which the rate of productivity growth is a function of L_R, λ, and the level of technology with a negative exponent: $g_A = \lambda L_R A^{-\phi}$.

---

[5] For empirical assessments of product variety models, see Jones (1996, 2002), Aghion and Howitt (2009), Weil (2009).

[6] After Newton's famous statement that "If I have seen farther than others, it is because I was standing on the shoulders of giants" recognizing how Newton had benefited from the knowledge created by previous scientists such as Kepler.

Note that the simple technology function assumed above makes the implicit assumption that the standing on the shoulders effect and the fishing out effect cancel each other out. This makes dA/dt to be a linear function of A. As Romer (1990, p. S84) explains: "Linearity in A is what makes unbounded growth possible, and in this sense, unbounded growth is more like an assumption than a result of the model....... If A were replaced ..... by some concave function of A .... This will cause the rate of growth to slow down".

This linearity assumption has been questioned (see, in particular, Jones, 1995; and Weil, 2009, ch. 9). As already mentioned, the number of R&D scientists has multiplied several times since the 1950s while the growth rate of technology has not increased. This suggests that the fishing out effect is the dominant influence on the pace of productivity growth. This would suggest a technology production function in which the rate of productivity growth is a function of L_R, λ, and the level of technology with a negative exponent: $g_A = \lambda L_R A^{-\theta}$.

The second unsatisfactory feature of the simple technology production function is that the growth rate of technology is proportional to the number of people engaged in R&D (i.e., g_A is proportional to L_R). The assumption is that there are constant returns to labor in the technology function. There are in fact likely to be decreasing returns to labor in technology production so that doubling the number of researchers doing R&D will less than double the rate of technology creation. The reason is that duplication of effort is more likely when there are more people engaged in research. This would imply a technology function such as: $g_A = \lambda L_R^{\epsilon}$, where the exponent ϵ is a parameter between 0 and 1.

Combining the two features, the effect of the level of technology and the assumption of decreasing returns to labor in technology production, we get a technology production function of the form: $g_A = \lambda L_R^{\epsilon} A^{-\theta}$ (see Jones, 1995). One implication of this production function is that if the rate of technology growth is constant over time, as it has roughly been over the past 100 years, then the rate of technology creation depends on the rate of growth, rather than the level, of the labor force employed in the R&D sector. Indeed, taking logs and differentiating with respect to time, the equation then implies: $\epsilon \hat{L}_R = \theta g_A$, and thus $g_A = \epsilon \hat{L}_R / \theta$. In this case long-run per capita growth is proportional to the rate of population growth rather than its level. A policy implication is that incentives to research and development may affect the level of income but not its long-run rate (see Jones, 1999). Another implication of this result is that in the very long run when the population stabilizes and the share of researchers in the labor force approaches a maximum, the rate of technology creation will inevitably slow down as a consequence of the fishing out effect and the presence of decreasing returns to labor in technology production. In the short and medium term the rate of technology creation can continue unabated as those effects are offset by a continuous increase in the share of researchers in the labor force and the incorporation of new countries to the cutting edge of technology.

Product variety models can also be criticized as a formalization of Young ideas. Are these models a formalization of how the division of labor increases with the size of the market according to Young? Lavezzi (2001) argues that there are important differences between product variety models a la Romer (1987, 1990) and Young's vision. These differences include the use of an equilibrium approach against the disequilibrium approach chosen by Young, a supply oriented model in Romer versus an important role for demand in Young, and a different emphasis on fixed costs whose role was in fact played down by Young.[7] We can add that a key aspect of Young's vision is the use of machinery as a consequence of the division of labor simplifying the production process "into a succession of simpler processes, some of which, at least, lend themselves to the use of machinery". It is clear that the models presented, which omit in fact fixed capital, have no role for this process and thus miss what according to Young is the largest advantage secured by the division of labor among industries: the fuller realizing of the economies of capitalistic or "roundabout" methods of production.

3. Schumpeterian Models of Endogenous Innovation and Creative Destruction[8]

The process of economic growth under capitalism as one of "creative destruction" emphasized by Schumpeter has been formalized in Aghion and Howitt (1992, 1998), Grossman and Helpman (1991, 1991a) and Segerstrom, Anant, and Dinopoulos (1990). Here, by contrast to the product variety models, growth is generated by a sequence of quality-improving (or vertical innovations) so that the innovations that drive growth by creating new technologies also destroy the results of previous innovations by making them obsolete.

From the perspective of Schumpeterian growth theory, product variety models suffer from two main shortcomings (Aghion and Howitt, 2006). First, there is no role in these models for the notion of a technology frontier and for distance to the frontier. Gershenkron's advantage of backwardness, which has an important role in technology gap models, Nelson and Phelps

---

[7] As argued by Sandilands (2000, p. 315, cited by Lavezzi, 2001): "Young did not say that specialization is limited by the presence of fixed costs though he did say that specialization increasingly took the form of greater roundaboutness in the economy as a whole. In his theory, fixed costs and increased roundaboutness are not so much a constraint on growth as its consequence".

[8] The formalization in this section relies on Aghion and Howitt (2009).

writing and, as we shall see, Schumpeterian models, has therefore no place in product variety models. Second, there is no role in these models for exit and turnover of firms, a crucial aspect when innovation as in Schumpeterian models turns old production methods obsolete. In fact, exit of firms can only reduce GDP in the product variety model by reducing the number of varieties that determines aggregate productivity. This implication appears to contradict a number of empirical findings regarding the role of threat of entry and product market mobility in economies near the technology frontier (see Aghion, Blundell, Griffith, Howitt, and Prantl, 2004). Let's turn to describe a simple Schumpeterian model.

Technology and market structure

The economy considered has a fixed labor supply (L). There is a competitive final goods sector using labor and a single intermediate product (I) with a Cobb-Douglas production function:

$$Y = I^a (A L)^{1-a} \qquad 0 < a < 1 \qquad (6)$$

where A is a productivity variable. Production of the intermediate good uses final good as an input with a one for one technology, just as in the product variety model. Final output that is not used for intermediate good production constitutes GDP available for consumption and investment in research. GDP is thus:

$$GDP = Y - I \qquad (7)$$

The intermediate good is produced by a monopolist that maximizes profit Π, which measured in units of final good is given by: $\Pi = p I - I$, where p is the price of the intermediate good relative to the final good. This is just as in the product variety model.

How is the monopolist price determined? The monopolist price will be the marginal product of the intermediate good in the final sector. Using the production function (6), we have then: $p = dY/dI = a I^{a-1} (A L)^{1-a}$.

The monopolist chooses the quantity I that maximizes profit given by: $\Pi = a$ $(A L)^{1-a} I^a - I$ (substituting the expression for p into the expression for profit). The quantity I is thus obtained from setting $d\Pi/dI = 0$ which implies $a^2 (A L)^{1-a} I^{a-1} - 1 = 0$. Solving for I, we get

$$I = a^{2/(1-a)} A L \qquad (8)$$

and substituting into the expression for profit, equilibrium profit is: $\Pi = \pi A L$ where $\pi = (1-a) a^{(1 + a)/(1-a)}$.

Note that both I and Π are proportional to the effective labor supply AL. Substituting from (8) into (6) and (7), Y and GDP are also proportional to AL: $Y = a^{2a/(1-a)}$ A L, and:

$$GDP = a^{2a/(1-a)}(1 - a^2)A \, L \qquad (9)$$

Innovation and growth

In each period, there is one person (the "entrepreneur") who has an opportunity to attempt an innovation. If she succeeds, the productivity of the intermediate product will go from A_{t-1} up to $A_t = \gamma A_{t-1}$, where γ, reflecting the size of the innovation, is a parameter greater than 1. Otherwise, i.e. if she fails, $A_t = A_{t-1}$.

Innovation requires research. The probability η that an innovation occurs in any period t depends on the amount of the final good spent on research, R: $\eta = \phi (R^A)$, where $R^A = R/A^*$ and $A^* = \gamma A_{t-1}$ is the productivity of the new intermediate product that will result if the research succeeds. The reason why the probability of success depends inversely on A^* is that as technology advances it becomes more complex and thus harder to improve upon. There is a "fishing out effect".

Assume that the innovation function $\phi (.)$ takes the following form: $\phi (R^A) = \lambda R^{A\sigma}$, where λ reflects the productivity of research and $0 < \sigma < 1$. Then the marginal product of (productivity adjusted) research in generating innovations is positive but decreasing:

$$\phi'(R^A) = \lambda \sigma (R^A)^{\sigma-1} > 0 \qquad \text{and} \qquad \phi''(R^A) = \lambda \sigma (\sigma-1) R^{A\sigma-2} < 0$$

If the entrepreneur at t successfully innovates, she will become the intermediate monopolist in that period. The reward to a *successful* innovator is the profit Π^*_t that she will earn as a result. Since the probability of success is $\phi (R^A)$, her expected reward is: $\phi(R^A) \Pi^*$

The net benefit from research is the expected reward minus the cost of research, R: $\phi(R^A) \Pi^* - R$. The entrepreneur will choose the investment in research (R) in such a way as to maximize the net benefit. The first order condition is: $\phi'(R^A) \Pi^*/A^* - 1 = 0$, which implies the research arbitrage equation:

$$\phi'(R^A) \, \pi L = 1 \qquad (10)$$

using $\Pi = \pi$ A L. The right hand side of eq. (10) is the marginal cost of research (= 1). The left hand side is the marginal benefit of research (the incremental probability of innovation times the value of a successful innovation). Under the Cobb Douglas formulation, the corresponding values of R^A and η are: $R^A = (\sigma \lambda \pi L)^{1/(1-\sigma)}$ and $\eta = \lambda^{1/(1-\sigma)}(\sigma\pi L)^{\sigma/(1-\sigma)}$

The rate of economic growth is the proportional growth rate of GDP/L which according to (4) is the growth of A: $\gamma = (A_t - A_{t-1})/A_{t-1}$. This means that growth will be random: with probability η, $g = (\gamma A_{t-1} - A_{t-1})/A_{t-1} = \gamma - 1$, and with probability $(1-\eta)$, $g = 0$.

What will be the economy's long-run average growth rate? By the law of large numbers, the mean of the distribution will also be the economy's long-run growth rate: $g = E(g) = \eta(\gamma - 1)$. Substituting from the expression for η, we get:

$$g = \lambda^{1/(1-\sigma)}(\sigma\pi L)^{\sigma/(1-\sigma)}(\gamma - 1)$$

This expression shows that the rate of growth is an increasing function of the productivity of research (λ), the size of innovations (γ), and the size of the population (L). The model thus highlights the importance of education (which affects the productivity of research) and implies that a country that lags behind the world technology frontier has the advantage of backwardness (since γ is likely to be larger). It also features a scale effect (since growth depends on L) just as the product variety model.

Innovation and product market competition

In the previous model there is no threat of entry by potential competitors. In industrial organization theory this is called the drastic innovation case. Instead, now suppose that there is a competitive fringe of firms able to produce a "knock off" product that is perfectly substitutable for the monopolist's intermediate product but is more expensive to produce. It costs $q > 1$ units of final good to produce. Then the incumbent monopolist cannot charge more than q in equilibrium, since otherwise potential competitors would displace him. Thus we have now that the price p of the monopolist intermediate good must be less or equal than q: $p \leq q$.

The price chosen by the monopolist in the absence of potential competitors is $1/a$. Indeed, substituting $I = a^{2/(1-a)} A L$ into $p = a I^{a-1}(A L)^{1-a}$ yields $p = 1/a$. When $q > 1/a$, the limit price constraint is not binding and we have the drastic innovation case examined previously.

When $q < 1/a$, we have the non drastic innovation case. The model is modified as follows. Using $p = q$, substituting into the expression for p before and solving for I, the equilibrium quantity is now: $I = (a/q)[1/(1-a)] A L$. Note that we can use the earlier expression for p because the final goods sector being a competitive sector, the price (q now) is still equal to marginal product of the intermediate product.

The monopolist's equilibrium profit is thus: $\Pi = pI - I = \pi AL$ where $\pi = (q-1)$ $(a/q)^{1/(1-a)}$, which can be shown to be increasing in q (provided that $q < 1/a$, the non drastic innovation case).

The growth rate is the same as before: $g = \lambda^{1/(1-\sigma)} (\sigma\pi L)^{\sigma/(1-\sigma)} (\gamma - 1)$ with, however, the important difference that now π is an increasing function of q. In addition to the properties of the previous model, what are the new implications of the present one? First, growth increases with the degree of property rights protection, as measured by q, to the extent that a higher q may reflect stronger patent protection (which increases the cost of imitating the current technology). A higher q should thus lead to more intense research as it raises the profit that accrues to a successful innovator, thus leading to higher growth. Second, growth decreases with the degree of product market competition, to the extent that a lower q may reflect an increased ability of other firms to compete against an incumbent monopolist. This is an insight that goes back to Schumpeter (1942). As Schumpeter realized, well before recent endogenous growth theory, technological progress is inconsistent with a very high degree of competition in product markets. As he put it:

> The introduction of new methods of production and new commodities is hardly conceivable with perfect—and perfectly prompt—competition from the start. And this means that the bulk of what we call economic progress is incompatible with it. As a matter of fact, perfect competition is and always has been temporarily suspended whenever anything new is being introduced—automatically or by measures devised for the purpose—even in otherwise perfectly competitive conditions. (Schumpeter, 1950, pp. 104–5).

The empirical evidence on competition and innovation in developed countries does not fully confirm Schumpeter's insight. The empirical relationship across industries between innovative activity (measured by patents) and competitive market structures has the shape of an inverted U: innovation increases with competition but only up to a point beyond which more competition discourages innovative activity. Aghion and Howitt (2009) have extended Schumpeter's analysis of the effects of competition on innovation and explained the inverted U relationship arguing that these effects are ambiguous. More precisely, in addition to the negative Schumpeterian effect, there is a positive effect that results from the fact that an innovation that improves the quality of an intermediate product can reduce the potential competition of the competitive fringe of firms and thus increase the post-innovation profits of the monopolist. The higher is the competition of the fringe, the higher are the post-innovation profits and the stronger the incentive to innovation. This is the "escape from competition effect" which Aghion and Howitt argue will be more intense the closer an economy is to the technological frontier. Aghion and Howitt (2005) illustrate the operation of the two effects of competition with the industrial policies of Japan and South Korea during their industrialization period: a combination of trade protection for firms producing for the domestic market and operating with technologies behind the frontier and export incentives and targets for firms competing in the international markets and closer to the technological frontier.

Aghion and Howitt (2006) explain the inverted-U shape of the relationship between competition and innovation as follows: at high degrees of competition, they argue, an increase in competition results in a slower innovation rate as the negative Schumpeterian appropriability effect predominates. At low degrees of competition, by contrast, there is little incentive for neck-and-neck firms to innovate, so that an increase in competition results in a faster innovation rate as the overall effect of competition becomes dominated by the escape-competition effect.

Policy implications

The welfare implications of the Schumpeterian model can be derived by comparing the allocation of labor in the Schumpeterian model with that of a social planner which maximizes utility. There are three main differences. The first is that the social planner in deciding the allocation of resources will take into account that each innovation increases the productivity of future innovations (which will be made by future innovators). In the model, the innovator does not take into account this intertemporal spillover and thus will allocate too few resources to research and development. This reduces the rate of growth below the level that would prevail in the allocation of the social planner. The second difference is that the social planner maximizes utility (or total output) while the monopolist maximizes profits. Since profits are only a part of output this appropriability effect generates also too little investment in research under laissez faire.

The third difference is paradoxical. The social planner will tend to internalize the loss caused by an innovation to the incumbent monopolist. He will, that is, internalize the costs of "creative destruction". Private enterprise does not internalize these effects. This tends to generate too much investment in research under laissez faire. It is then possible, as observed by Schumpeter, that the economy's growth rate under laissez faire is excessive compared to the socially optimal growth rate!

4. A Schumpeterian Model of Capital Accumulation and Innovation

The product variety model and the Schumpeterian model, in the versions presented in this chapter, assume physical capital accumulation away. In this section, I present a Schumpeterian model that includes both endogenous capital accumulation and endogenous technological progress. As the reader will see, in addition to the factors that determine growth in the Schumpeterian model, the savings/investment rate will also be a determinant of the growth rate.

Technology and market structure

As in the one sector Schumpeterian model, final goods production is given by:

$$Y = I^a (A\,L)^{1-a} \qquad 0 < a < 1 \qquad (11)$$

The simplest way to bring in capital is to have the intermediate good be produced with capital. So assume that the final good is now storable, in the form of capital, and the intermediate good is produced with capital according to the production function: $I = K$

The monopolist price is again the marginal product of the intermediate good: $p = dY/dI = aA^{1-a}I^{a-1}$ (setting, for simplicity, $L = 1$). The monopolist cost is the rental rate of capital (R_k) times the capital stock: $R_k\,K$ or, using the production function, $R_k I$. The monopolist chooses the quantity produced I in order to maximize profit given by: $\Pi = aA^{1-a}\,I^a - R_k I$. The first order condition implies the quantity:

$$I = (a^2/R_k)^{1/(1-a)} A, \text{ which implies:} \qquad (12)$$

$$K = (a^2/R_k)^{1/(1-a)} A \qquad (12')$$

Let $k = K/AL$ be the capital stock per effective worker. Solving (12') for R_k as a function of k yields:

$$R_k = a^2 k^{a-1} \qquad (13)$$

which implies that the rental rate is a decreasing function of the capital stock per effective worker.

From (12) and (12'), we have:

$$I = A\,L\,k \qquad (14)$$

Substituting (13) and (14) into the expression for profits, we get:

$$\Pi = a(1 - a)k^a A\,L \qquad (15)$$

showing that profits are increasing in the capital stock per effective worker, k. This is because an increase in k reduces the monopolist's per unit cost of production as it reduces the rental cost R_k.

Substituting now from (14) into (11), we get the following expression for Y:

$$Y = A \, L \, k^a \tag{16}$$

which is the production function used in the neoclassical model.

Innovation and capital accumulation

As in the Schumpeterian model, there is an entrepreneur who has an opportunity to attempt an innovation. If successful, the productivity parameter goes from A_{t-1} to $A_t = \gamma A_{t-1}$ where $\gamma > 1$. The probability of success is as before: $\eta = \phi(R^A) = \lambda(R^A)^\sigma$ where $A^*_t = \gamma A_{t-1}$.

Research expenditure (R) will be chosen, as in the basic Schumpeterian model, to maximize net benefit: $\phi(R^A)\Pi^* - R$, where Π^* is the profit if she succeeds. The first order condition is: $\phi'(R^A) \, \Pi^*/A^* - 1 = 0$, which we can write using (15) as: $\phi'(R^A)a(1-a)k^a = 1$, where $\phi'(R^A) = \sigma\lambda \, R^{A\sigma-1}$ as before. This implies: $R^{A \, 1-\sigma} = \sigma \, \lambda a(1-a) \, k^a$. That is, the productivity-adjusted level of research, R^A, is an increasing function of k. This is simply because a higher k increases the monopoly profit that constitutes the reward for innovation.

As before, the productivity growth rate g_A is the frequency of innovations $\phi(R^A)$ times the size of innovations $(\gamma - 1)$. Then, productivity growth is also an increasing function of k:

$$g_A = \lambda \, R^{A\sigma}(\gamma - 1) \tag{17}$$

where R^A is increasing in k such that $(R^A)^{1-\sigma} = \sigma \, \lambda a \, (1-a)k^a$.

The dynamic equation for the capital stock is: $K_{t+1} - K_t = sY - \delta K$. Dividing by K, and using eq. (16), we get:

$$g_K = sY/K - \delta = (sALk^a/K) - \delta = (s/k^{1-a}) - \delta \tag{18}$$

Eq. (18) shows that the rate of capital accumulation is a decreasing function of k. It can be shown that the economy will converge to a steady state in which $g_A = g_K$ and capital per effective worker remains constant over time. Indeed, suppose that initially $g_K > g_A$ and the capital stock is growing faster than productivity. Capital per effective worker is growing over time. This will reduce g_K and increase g_A until both growth rates are equal. Similarly, if $g_A > g_K$ initially, capital per effective worker will be falling over time. This will reduce g_A and increase g_K until both rates are equal.

The determination of the rate of economic growth and capital per effective worker is shown in Figure 5.2 in (g, k) space at the intersection of the upward sloping line, g_A (k), given by eq. (17) and the downward sloping line, $g_K(k)$, given by eq. (18).

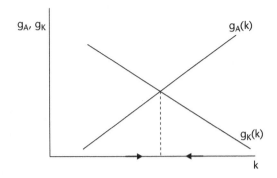

Figure 5.2 A Schumpeterian model with capital accumulation

The determinants of the growth rate in the steady state involve the productivity of research and the size of innovations, γ and λ which shift the g_A (k) line upwards, thus increasing g and reducing k. It also now includes the savings rate (s) which shifts the g_K (k) line up, increasing both g and k. Thus, the economy's steady state is determined by the key parameter of the neoclassical model (the savings/investment rate) as well as by the parameters of the Schumpeterian innovation function (γ and λ). Using eqs (17) and (18) and assuming $\delta = 0$, the expression for the steady state growth rate (g*) is:

$$g^\star = s^{a\sigma/e}\lambda^{[d+s(1-a)]/e}(\gamma-1)^{d/e}[\sigma a(1-a)]^{\sigma(1-a)/e}$$

with d = (1−a) (1−σ) and e = aσ + d, where, again, s is the investment rate, λ is the productivity of research, γ is the size of innovations, and σ is a parameter of the innovation such that $0 < \sigma < 1$.

What keeps labor productivity growing in the steady state despite the fact that there are diminishing returns to capital? This is the fact that capital accumulation tends to reduce the rental rate of capital which increases profits in the intermediate goods sector operating under monopolistic conditions. The larger profits stimulate investment spending in research and development which eventually lead to technological innovations that increase productivity A. This increase in productivity tends to offset the role of diminishing returns to capital, and keeps growth going on instead of coming to a stand still as happens in the neoclassical model (in the absence of exogenous technical progress).

It is worth noting that the model has interesting critical implications for growth decomposition exercises, i.e., for exercises that decompose the growth of output into its "sources": the changes in the capital stock, the labor force and productivity. In these exercises, total factor productivity growth and capital accumulation are treated as independent of output growth and independent of each other. This may be valid if the economy behaves like in the neoclassical model where growth equals in the steady state the exogenous rate of labor augmenting technological progress.[9] In the present model, however, productivity growth is endogenous and we cannot speak meaningfully of it as causing output growth.[10] Indeed, consider a change in the incentives to invest in research resulting from greater patent protection. This change will result in a higher steady state growth rate that we should attribute to the forces of innovation since it is in the innovation side of the economy where the change occurred. But consider now a change in the savings rate that shifts the g_K curve to the right causing again an increase in the growth rate. In this case the change should be attributed to capital accumulation since the reason for it was a change in the savings rate and not in innovation. In both cases, a growth accountant will conclude that a fraction "a" of the change in growth is due to capital accumulation (capital deepening) and a fraction (1–a) is due to the growth of TFP as implied by the Cobb-Douglas production function. However, it is clear that in one case the change was due to innovation and in the other it was due fully to capital accumulation.[11]

Criticisms and empirical assessment

New growth theory has been criticized from an evolutionary perspective as a formalization of the Schumpeterian process of creative destruction and as offering an insufficient departure from old neoclassical growth theory.[12] Perhaps the most comprehensive theoretical assessment from this perspective is Nelson (1998) who argues that some of the basic assumptions of new growth theory inhibit its ability, just as much as in old neoclassical theory, to throw light into the process of economic growth as a disequilibrium phenomenon led by firms with different capabilities that operate under Knightian, or fundamental, uncertainty rather than perfect foresight or quantifiable risk, and that is supported by a rich body of economic institutions including a system of research universities.

In their empirical assessment of the Schumpeterian model, Howitt (2000) and Howitt and Mayer-Foulkes (2005) argue that the model is consistent with two key features of the evolution of the world's income distribution (reviewed in Chapter 1): the increasing productivity and income gap between the richest and the poorest countries (the great divergence) and the narrowing of productivity differences among a number of today's industrialized countries (club

---

[9] Even in this case capital accumulation is not independent of technological progress.

[10] The exception would be when the g_A curve is horizontal so that the rate of technological progress does not respond to capital accumulation. In this case, as in the neoclassical models, innovation would be the only force determining the long-run growth rate.

[11] Another, older objection to growth decomposition exercises, is also mentioned by Aghion and Howitt (2009, ch. 5). This arises from the fact that technological progress is often embodied in new capital goods, which makes it hard to separate the influence of capital accumulation from the influence of innovation.

[12] On evolutionary theory, see, especially, Nelson and Winter (1982).

convergence). They construct a multi-country Schumpeterian model that features long-run convergence to the same growth rate in all countries engaged in R&D, and stagnation, and thus divergence, in those countries which do not invest in R & D. That is, as in the neoclassical model countries converge to parallel growth paths with the same growth rate of productivity but unlike the neoclassical model productivity growth is endogenous and convergence, resulting from innovative activity and technology transfers, is restricted to countries investing in R & D. Moreover, long-run differences in relative productivity and income levels are explained not only by incentives to accumulate capital but also by incentives to innovate.

How do Howitt and Mayer-Foulkes (2005) generate divergence between richest and poorest countries and club convergence among the high and middle-income countries? A key feature of their model makes the change in a country's productivity a function of the distance to the technological frontier (the technology gap) and a measure of absorptive capacity. Thus, just as the Nelson and Phelps model (see Chapter 4), the model features Gershenkron's "advantage of backwardness", i.e. the larger the technology gap the faster the rate of domestic productivity growth. This is so given absorptive capacity which is a function, as in the Schumpeterian models reviewed above, of the productivity of the innovation process, the incentive to innovate, the incentive to save, and the quantity or quality of education. Moreover, absorptive capacity depends on relative productivity itself as affected by geography, policies and institutions that tend to make productivity higher even if they do not affect the innovation process. This positive "absorption effect" of relative productivity on absorptive capacity makes their model different from that of Nelson and Phelps which makes absorptive capacity a function of human capital.

The reason why now absorptive capacity is itself a function of relative productivity (the ratio of domestic productivity to the frontier) is the result of a "fishing out effect" in the innovation process and a human capital externality in skill formation. Due to the first effect, the more advanced the technology the more difficult it is to innovate. That is, the level of entrepreneurial skill required to innovate at any given rate rises with the global technological frontier. At the same time, the human capital externality is a local one: the acquisition of skills is more productive in a technologically more advanced economy where there is more to learn from others. Thus, the actual level of entrepreneurial skill rises only with the domestic level of productivity. As a result absorptive capacity is a positive function of relative productivity: it rises with the absolute level domestic productivity and falls with the level of the global technology frontier. This implies a disadvantage of backwardness since absorptive capacity falls with the technology gap.

The combination of Gershenkron's advantage of backwardness and the disadvantage of backwardness implied by the positive relationship between absorptive capacity and relative productivity can generate a variant of Benhabib and Spiegel's (2005) extension of the Nelson and Phelps model. Recall that in this extension there is a threshold value of absorptive capacity (or relative productivity) below which the rate of growth of the followers with low absorptive capacity diverges as the disadvantage of backwardness dominates over the advantages. In this case, the equilibrium relationship between the productivity of the follower and that of the leader tends to zero. At the same time, above the threshold level, when the disadvantage of backwardness does not offset the advantages, the rate of growth of the follower's productivity converges to that of the technology frontier and the level of relative productivity stabilizes at a steady state level determined by the key innovation and investment parameters of the Schumpeterian model. The major difference, however, between the two models is that Howitt and Mayer-Foulkes determine endogenously the rate of progress of the technological frontier. This is the distinctive Schumpeterian feature of their model since there is nothing in the interplay of the Gershenkron backwardness advantage and the backwardness disadvantage of the "absorption effect" that can be attributed to Schumpeter's writing. And it is precisely the interplay between those two effects that allow the authors to generate a pattern of divergence between the richest and poorest countries occurring simultaneously with a process of club convergence among the more advanced countries.

In the Schumpeterian model, just as in Benhabib and Spiegel (1994 and 2005), technological advance can be generated either through the absorption and implementation of existing frontier technologies or through innovation on past technologies. Suppose now that different types of education spending lie behind implementation and innovation: university education has a bigger effect on the ability to make innovations while primary and secondary education are more important in a country's ability to implement existing frontier technologies. If the relative importance of innovation increases as a country moves closer to the technological frontier, the growth gains from investing in tertiary education will be greater the closer the country is to the technological frontier. And conversely, the farther behind a country is from the technology frontier, the more growth enhancing will be the investments in primary and secondary education. Using a fixed effects model with interaction variables, Vandenbussche, Aghion, and Meghir (2006) find support for these implications of the model's extension in the cross-country panel evidence on higher education, distance to frontier, and productivity growth.

In the next four chapters we shall explore the earlier contributions of classical development theory and discuss whether this analytical framework provides a more convincing explanation of the processes of divergence between richest and poorest countries and club convergence among the high and middle-income countries.

Part II
Classical Development Theory

6

The Lewis Model and the Labor Surplus Economy

Most of the neoclassical and endogenous growth models discussed in Chapters 2 through 5 remain within the framework of a capitalist economy with a single goods-producing sector, neglecting the coexistence of capitalist and non capitalist sectors that development economists have generally viewed as a most striking feature of "underdevelopment". I bring in now, along with the capitalist sector of the Solow model, a non-capitalist sector using "subsistence technologies". The simplest case refers to a two-sector, one-good economy, with constant returns to scale in both sectors. This case has identical properties to Arthur Lewis (1954) classic model of economic growth with "unlimited supplies of labor": a long off-steady-state transition period in which the capitalist sector faces a perfectly elastic labor supply, leading to a Solow-type steady state in which the non-capitalist sector has disappeared. I consider whether this provides a solution to the failure of the standard prediction of neoclassical models, of a falling rate of profit, to come to pass, as noticed by Arthur Lewis (1976).[1] As noted in Chapter 2, this failure is what seems to be behind the empirical shortcomings of the neoclassical model.

The chapter addresses two other major questions: (1) the conditions under which the two sectors coexist and (2) those under which this coexistence generates a more or less elastic labor supply to the capitalist sector. The assimilation of these two different issues has been a source of confusion in the past. Indeed, considerable confusion has prevailed in the development literature about the exact meaning of the very influential concept of surplus labor, its relation to the elasticity of labor supply, and its macroeconomic

---

[1] According to Lewis: "All schools of economics have tried their hand at this [what will happen to distribution], but their favourite forecast—the falling rate of profit—has not yet come to pass". (Gersovitz 1983, 452). Lewis was, of course, writing well before the appearance of endogenous growth models with non diminishing returns to capital.

ˈ

implications. In addition, I compare Lewis' type of labor surplus to other related notions and examine the factors affecting the elasticity of labor supply. This analysis highlights the role of returns to labor in the subsistence sector, the elasticity of substitution in consumption between subsistence and capitalist sector goods, and the existence of underemployment due to efficiency wage considerations in the capitalist sector.

1. The Lewis Model

There are two sectors in the economy, indicated by subscripts S and M. Sector M is a Solow-type capitalist sector. Sector S is non-capitalist in the sense that workers there receive the average product of labor. This sector produces the same (composite) good as the capitalist sector. Thus, it is one in which, to use Haavelmo's expression, workers know "different ways of doing the same thing" (Haavelmo, 1954, p. 49). The key difference between the two sectors is that the non-capitalist or subsistence sector uses a negligible amount of capital in production. As stated by Lewis (1954): "The subsistence sector is by difference all that part of the economy which is not using reproducible capital" (p. 147).

The capitalist (or modern) sector uses a constant-returns-to-scale technology. We assume, for simplicity, a Cobb-Douglas function: $M = A \, K^a \, (L_M)^{1-a}$, where M and L_M are output and employment in this sector, and K is the capital stock. In sector S, technology displays constant returns to labor, and output (S) is then given by: $S = w_S \, L_S$, where w_S is the given output per worker in the subsistence sector and L_S is the labor force employed in this sector.

Labor markets are competitive in the sense that "the wage which the expanding capitalist sector has to pay is determined by what people can earn outside that sector" (Lewis, 1954, p. 148). More precisely, the wage in the capitalist sector is determined by the wage in sector S plus a wage premium that the capitalist sector has to pay to attract workers from the subsistence sector, determined by migration costs and the higher cost of living in congested towns (Lewis, 1954, p. 150).[2]

The wage premium $(f-1)$ is constant so that, as long as the two sectors coexist, the capitalist sector pays a real wage w_M given by:[3]

$$w_M = f w_S \qquad \text{for} \quad L_S > 0 \qquad (1)$$

[2] There is also a hint in Lewis (1954) that the wage premium may be related to efficiency wage considerations (in particular to the need to reduce turnover costs in the capitalist sector).

[3] Because it is constant, the wage premium may, if one likes, be assumed equal to zero (so that f = 1) without making any significant difference to the analysis that follows.

Employment (L_M) in the capitalist sector is determined by the usual profit maximization conditions under the technology constraint. Assuming perfect competition in goods and labor markets, this implies the following demand for labor in the M sector:

$$L_M = [(1 - a)A/w_M]^{1/a}K = L_M(w_M, A, K) \qquad L_{M1} < 0, L_{M2}, L_{M3} > 0 \qquad (2)$$

where w_M is determined by the wage premium and productivity conditions in the subsistence sector (eq. 1) as long as $L_M < L$.

There is no open unemployment so that workers not employed in the capitalist sector work in the subsistence sector: $L = L_M + L_S$

Lewis labor surplus, Keynesian unemployment and the Classical subsistence wage

Figure 6.1 shows the determination of employment in the capitalist sector and, by difference from the total labor force, the amount of labor employed in the subsistence sector. When $L_M = L$, and the subsistence sector has disappeared, the real wage will be determined by the intersection of labor demand in sector M and the given overall supply of labor, as in the one sector model of a mature economy.

What are the necessary conditions for the coexistence of the two sectors? One condition is fairly obvious and we have already alluded to it: the average product of labor must be less in the subsistence sector than in the capitalist sector. Otherwise, the capitalist sector would not be able to generate a surplus; the capital using technology would not be used and the whole of the labor force would find employment in the subsistence sector. Lewis takes this condition for granted when he says: "output per head is lower in [the subsistence sector] than in the capitalist sector because it is not fructified by capital" (p. 147).

The second condition can be derived from Figure 6.1. A positive fraction of the labor force will find it worthwhile to employ itself in the subsistence sector as long as what workers can earn there is more than the marginal product of labor (adjusted for the wage premium) that would result from employing the whole of the labor force in the capitalist sector. That is, a labor surplus will exist as long as the average product of labor of the non-capitalist technology is more than the marginal product of labor (MPL) at full employment in the capitalist sector, equal to the real wage at the intersection of the labor demand curve and the vertical line at L. It is then and only then that at least some workers will be better off working in the subsistence sector rather than searching for jobs in the capitalist sector.

Since the MPL at full employment is an increasing function of the economy-wide capital-labor ratio, the coexistence of the two sectors will be characteristic

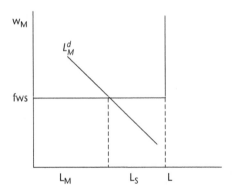

Figure 6.1 Lewis labor surplus

of capital-scarce and labor-abundant countries.[4] This is the type of economies that Lewis had in mind and for which he considered that the neoclassical model would not apply. In its determination of the real wage, the neoclassical model makes the implicit assumption that the MPL at full employment is higher than the subsistence wage. This, Lewis considered appropriate for a "mature economy" (and for "some parts of Africa and of Latin America" where "there is an acute shortage of male labour", p. 140), but not for those developing economies where a capital shortage would give rise to a "labor surplus".

It is worthwhile comparing this notion of labor surplus with two other situations in which the level of employment in the capitalist sector can be said to be demand-determined. The first is Keynesian unemployment (see Figure 6.2). While Lewis labor surplus is the result of a low level of the economy-wide capital-labor ratio, unemployment in Keynes arises from a low level of effective demand in the goods market. In Keynes, a deficiency of demand for goods keeps the real wage above the marginal product of labor at full employment and thus gives rise to an excess supply of labor. An increase in effective demand for goods that reduces the real wage—by increasing the price level, given the nominal wage—will then cause an expansion of employment *along* the labor demand curve thus reducing unemployment.

The similarity with Lewis is that, in both cases, the real wage is above the MPL at full employment in the capitalist sector. The difference is that, in Lewis, nothing can be done about it by increasing effective demand in the goods market. For employment in the capitalist sector to increase as a result of an expansion in the demand for goods, the real wage would have to fall below the wage in sector S (adjusted for the wage premium). This is prevented by

---

[4] From eq. (2), setting $L_M = L$, the marginal product of labor at full employment (MPL_F) is given by: $MPL_F = (1 - a) A k^a$, where k is the economy-wide capital-labor ratio (K/L). MPL_F is thus an increasing function of k.

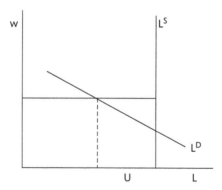

Figure 6.2 Keynesian unemployment

competition in the labor market. The only way to reduce the labor surplus is by expanding, not the aggregate demand for goods, but the capital stock: an *upward shift* in the labor demand curve rather than a movement *along* it. In modern terminology, the Lewis model refers to a situation of labor market equilibrium with a labor surplus arising from a "real rigidity". Keynes unemployment is a situation of labor market disequilibrium associated with (even if not due to) a "nominal rigidity".

The classical model refers to another distinctive situation. In both Lewis and the classical model, the capitalist sector faces a perfectly elastic supply of labor at a "subsistence wage". However, the meaning of "subsistence wage" and the reasons for the elastic supply of labor are very different. The classical model is really a one-sector model, in the sense that there is no subsistence technology being used by a non-capitalist sector à la Lewis. The labor supply for the economy as a whole is perfectly elastic in a very long-run sense. It is through the effects of the real wage on population growth and the operation of the Malthusian principle of population, that the labor supply adjusts to the demand for labor at that wage (shown as ω in Figure 6.3)

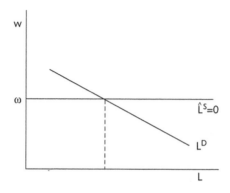

Figure 6.3 The Classical subsistence wage

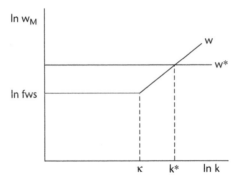

Figure 6.4 The Lewis model

which keeps population at a stationary level.[5] Rather than a subsistence sector, the classical model has an endogenous labor supply and the elastic supply of labor is a locus of stationary population.

Short-run equilibrium and capital accumulation

We now derive, as we did in Chapter 2 for the Solow model, the schedule of short-run equilibria showing the market equilibrium real wage in the capitalist sector (w_M) at different levels of the *economy-wide* capital endowment per worker (k).

As long as the two sectors coexist, i.e., in a labor surplus economy, the equation of the schedule is given by (1). The equilibrium wage w_M is independent of k and determined solely by the wage in sector S and the wage premium. The schedule of short-run equilibria in the labor surplus economy is thus a straight line, shown in Figure 6.4 as the horizontal segment of the w curve. Changes in the capital-labor ratio determine changes in the employment share of the capitalist sector but leave the real wage unaffected.[6]

When the subsistence sector disappears ($L_S = 0$), the economy becomes a "mature" one-sector economy. The equation of the w curve is now derived from the market clearing condition that the total labor supply (L) is equal to

[5] A simple formulation of the idea is to make the rate of change in the labor force ($\hat{L}$) an increasing function of the gap between the actual real wage and the subsistence wage: $\hat{L} = f(w - \omega)$ with $f' > 0$ and $f(0) = 0$.

[6] Dividing both sides of eq. (2) by L, we have: $L_M/L = ((1-a) A/w_M)^{1/a} k$. When $L_M/L < 1$, $w_M = f w_S$ and changes in k affect L_M/L leaving w_M constant. In contrast, when $L_M/L = 1$, w_M is determined by $w_M = (1-a) A k^a$ and increases in k then raise w_M.

labor demand in the capitalist sector (L_M). Substituting this condition into eq. (2) and solving for w_M, we obtain:

$$w_M = A(1 - a)k^a \qquad (3)$$

In the mature economy, the w curve slopes upwards with slope equal to "a" in (ln w_M, ln k) space (see Figure 6.4) and is thus identical to that in the Solow model. Let κ be the capital-labor ratio at the turning point between a labor surplus and a mature economy. At the turning point, the labor surplus has been absorbed but the wage remains equal to the subsistence wage plus the wage premium. Thus, the value of κ can be derived by solving (2) for k under $w_M = f\ w_S$ and $L_M = L$. This is $\kappa = [f\ w_S/(1-a)\ A]^{1/a}$. In Figure 6.1 above, this is the value of the capital-labor ratio for which the MPL at full employment in the capitalist sector is just equal to the average product of labor in the subsistence sector (plus the wage premium).

Consider now the schedule of long-run equilibria. Lewis followed the classical economists in viewing profits as the major source of capital accumulation and workers' aggregate saving as negligible. We adopt this hypothesis and assume that workers in both the capitalist and subsistence sectors consume all their earnings. The rate of capital accumulation is then: $I/K = s_\pi\ r - \delta$, where s_π is savings rate out of profits, and r and δ are the profit rate and the depreciation rate.[7] If we leave aside technical progress, so that the natural rate of growth is equal to the growth rate of the labor force (n), the steady state condition becomes: $s_\pi\ r - \delta = n$.

The profit rate as a function of the wage is derived as in Chapter 2. This is: $r = a\ A^{1/a}\ [(1-a)/w]^{(1-a)/a}$. Substituting from this profit-wage curve into the steady state condition and solving for w_M, yields the real wage ($w_M{}^*$) required to satisfy the steady state condition:

$$w_M{}^* = (1 - a)A^{1/(1-a)}[a\ s_\pi/(n + \delta)]^{a/(1-a)} \qquad (4)$$

This is the equation of the schedule of stationary capital-labor ratios. The schedule, as in the Solow model, is a straight line in (w_M, k) space, shown as the w^* line in Figure 6.4.

Depending on the values of fw_S and w^*, the w and w^* curves may not intersect. This would happen if the subsistence wage, adjusted for the wage premium, is higher than the required wage ($fw_S > w^*$). Then, the w^* line lies below the w line and, starting from any initial capital-labor ratio, population growth would outpace capital accumulation. The capitalist sector would be shrinking in relative size and the economy would tend towards a steady state

---

[7] As in Chapter 2, the rate of capital accumulation is: $I/K = (s/a)\ r - \delta$. The savings rate (s) is: $s = s_\pi\ a + s_w\ (1 - a)$, where a and $(1 - a)$ are the profit and wage shares and s_π and s_w are the savings rates out of profits and wages respectively. With $s_w = 0$, s equals $s_\pi\ a$. Substituting into the expression for the rate of accumulation yields: $I/K = s_\pi\ r - \delta$.

featuring a subsistence economy with no capitalist sector. In this case $fw_S > w_M*$ and this implies using (4): $w_S > [(1-a)/f] A^{1/(1-a)} [a s_\pi/(n + \delta)]^{a/(1-a)}$. Low values of s_π and A along with high values of w_S, f and n could generate such a path with a shrinking capitalist sector and growing "informality".

If $w* > fw_S$, the $w*$ line lies above the horizontal segment of the w curve and the steady state, as shown in Figure 6.4, is at the intersection of the two curves.[8] This is the long-run equilibrium of a Solow model with no technical progress. Starting from an initial capital-labor ratio below this steady state, capital accumulation outpaces labor force growth as the actual rate of profit is higher than required by the steady state condition. The capitalist sector then expands in relative size and the capital-labor ratio increases. Eventually, the capital-labor ratio reaches the value κ and the subsistence sector disappears. The economy then enters a mature phase with the capital-labor ratio converging towards its steady state value $k*$.

2. Transitional Dynamics and Steady State Properties

Lewis focuses on this last case when $w*$ is higher than fw_S.[9] His view of the process of economic development can thus be interpreted as a transition towards a Solow-type steady state. The transition itself, however, is rather different from that in the Solow model. Even though a Solow-type steady state is the end of the process, the introduction of a labor surplus brings a number of differences to the characteristics of the transition.

First, the growth of the capitalist sector does not proceed at diminishing rates during the transition to the steady state. Rather, it goes on at a constant rate (a function of the distance between the w and $w*$ lines) until the labor surplus disappears. This constant rate is determined by the savings rate out of profits and the productivity of the capitalist technology (relative to that of the subsistence sector). Then, in the mature phase, capital accumulation continues at a decreasing rate as in the Solow model. The reason for this difference is that during the labor surplus phase the capitalist sector faces an elastic supply of labor. This counteracts the influence of diminishing returns to capital that accounts for the falling rate of growth during the adjustment process in the Solow model.

---

[8] A third possibility is if f w_S happens to equal $w*$. Then, the initial value of k will persist over time and the two sectors coexist indefinitely.

[9] There is in his article some discussion of the factors that may bring about the fulfillment of this condition. He views technological innovations (an increase in A, which shifts the $w*$ locus upwards), rather than an increase in thriftiness (which increases s_π) as the mechanism that historically triggered the expansion of the capitalist sector. However, his analysis focuses on what happens after the initial expansion has taken place.

The Lewis model then implies that the profit rate does not tend to be higher at low-income levels compared to, say, middle-income levels as long the economy remains in the labor surplus phase. Using the production functions of the two sectors, aggregate output $(Y = S + M)$ can be written as: $Y = L_S + A K^a L_M^{1-a}$, where we set for simplicity $w_S = 1$. Substituting from the labor demand function (eq. 2) under $w_M = f w_S$ and ignoring for simplicity the wage premium (so that $f = 1$), we obtain the following expression for aggregate output: $Y = L + A^{1/a} a (1-a)^{(1-a)/a} K$, which shows that even though the technology of the capitalist sector is subject to diminishing returns to capital the Lewis aggregate "production function" during the labor surplus phase displays constant returns to capital, i.e. during this phase the Lewis model behaves like an AK model (see Chapter 2).

The constancy of the profit rate during the initial phases of the transition can considerably slow down the process of convergence to the steady state. As an example, consider an economy with no population growth, where initially the employment share of the capitalist sector is 10 percent. The rate of capital accumulation is such that employment in the capitalist sector grows at an average rate of 3 percent per year. This economy will take 78 years to absorb the whole of the labor surplus into the capitalist sector (and will, of course, take longer if the labor force was expanding). After these 78 years, the economy will not yet reach the steady state (at k^*) but only maturity (at κ).

During the labor surplus phase, the capital intensity of the whole economy rises and with it per capita income increases as well. The cause of this growth in per capita income is, however, completely different from that in the mature phase (or in the Solow model). There, output per worker rises because the capital intensity in the capitalist sector increases, making each worker in this sector more productive. There is no such increase in the capital intensity of the modern sector during the labor surplus phase. The increase in output per worker in the whole economy is due to the reallocation effects of growth, to the transfer of subsistence sector labor to the capitalist sector, which has a higher average productivity. Indeed, we can write output per worker in the whole economy (y) as a weighted average of output per worker in the two sectors (w_S and y_M respectively), with the weights being the employment shares of each sector:

$$y = w_S L_S/L + y_M L_M/L = w_S + (y_M - w_S)L_M/L \qquad (5)$$

Alternatively, using the aggregate "AK production function" derived above and dividing by L (we now let w_S and f be different from 1), yields:

$$y = w_S + c k \qquad c = (a + f - 1)[(1 - a)/w_S]^{(1-a)/a}(A/f)^{1/a} \qquad (6)$$

Eq. (6) shows average output per worker as an increasing function of the capital-labor ratio in the whole economy: a higher capital-labor ratio increases the employment share of the capitalist sector and, since output per worker is higher there than in the subsistence sector, this reallocation has the effect of increasing output per worker in the whole economy (see eq. 5). It is worth noting that these productivity gains from labor force reallocation are in practice quite important in developing, labor surplus economies. Temple and Woßmann (2006) find that these productivity increases make a sizable contribution to the growth of total factor productivity (the aggregate Solow residual) given the existence of very large productivity differentials across sectors, especially in less developed countries. They also finds that structural change also explains a significant fraction of the observed international variation in productivity growth.

Assuming constant values for w_S and f, eq. (6) implies that the growth rate of output per worker (g_y) during the labor surplus phase is: $g_y = (1 - w_S/y) g_k$, where $g_y = d\ln y/dt$ and $g_k = d\ln k/dt$ is the rate of growth of k. This equation shows g_y as an increasing function of y and g_k. For given values of n and s_π, g_k remains constant during the labor surplus phase, given the constancy of w_M and thus of the rate of profit and capital accumulation. Since y is an increasing function of k (eq. 6), it follows that the growth rate of output per worker increases during the labor surplus phase. Throughout this process, g_y goes from zero (when the employment share of the capitalist sector is so low that its contribution to output is negligible) towards the limit set by the rate of expansion of the capitalist sector. This rate, given that the condition $w^* > f\,w_S$ is fulfilled, is higher than the natural rate. Then, in the mature phase g_y declines towards the value set by the natural rate. We thus encounter the hump-shaped path of growth rates discussed in Chapters 1 and 3.

Who benefits from this growth in per capita incomes during the labor surplus phase? Clearly, with constant earnings per worker in the subsistence sector, labor incomes per capita remain constant, except for the presence of a wage premium with little, if any, welfare significance. The gains in output per worker must therefore imply an increasing profit share in total output. This rising share accounts for the increasing saving rate throughout the labor surplus phase.[10] This is the major stylized fact that Lewis wants to explain:

> The central problem in the theory of economic development is to understand the process by which a community which was previously saving and investing 4 or 5 percent of its national income or less, converts itself into an economy where voluntary saving is running at about 12 to 15 percent of national income or more.

---

[10] The savings rate is equal to the savings rate out of profits times the share of profits in total output. Since the profit share is an increasing function of the employment share of the capitalist sector, the savings rate tends to zero (when L_M tends to zero) and increases, throughout the labor surplus phase, towards the value (s_π a) which prevails when the subsistence sector has disappeared.

> This is the central problem because the central fact of economic development is rapid capital accumulation (including knowledge and skills with capital). (p. 416)

The effects of technical progress on growth and income distribution depend crucially on whether technological change takes place in the capitalist or the subsistence sector. Technical progress in the capitalist sector shifts the w* line upwards and increases profits, leaving real wages constant. At the same time, by raising the profit rate, it accelerates the rate of expansion of the capitalist sector and thus speeds up the transition. In contrast, technical progress in the subsistence sector shifts the horizontal segment of the w curve upwards and fully benefits workers. By reducing the profit rate, it hinders the expansion of the capitalist sector.[11]

3. Surplus Labor and the Elasticity of Labor Supply

We now relax some of the assumptions made in section 1 and consider a more general setting. First, we allow for diminishing returns to labor in sector S— which may be due to the presence of a fixed factor, such as land in agriculture—and consider the possibility that the marginal product of labor falls to zero at some level of employment (Lo). Thus:

$$S = L_S^{1-b} \quad 0 \le b < 1 \quad \text{for } L_S < Lo$$

$$S = So \qquad\qquad\qquad \text{for } L_S \ge Lo \qquad (7)$$

where we omit for simplicity the fixed factor. Sen (1966) has analyzed the case in which output is invariant to the number of workers. In its simplest version, households in the subsistence sector take their production and working time decisions to maximize consumption per family member. As long as work time is less than the total number of hours available for work, maximizing consumption per head implies working until hours of work have a zero marginal product. The removal of a family worker from the household will lead the other members to adjust their working time so that the marginal product of hours of work remains zero. The total output of the household will thus be invariant to the number of family workers.

On the demand side, we now allow for differences in the consumption goods produced by the two sectors (the investment good being produced by

---

[11] Lewis has an interesting discussion of the political consequences of this: "The fact that the wage level in the capitalist sector depends upon earnings in the subsistence sector is sometimes of immense political importance, since its effect is that capitalists have a direct interest in holding down the productivity of the subsistence workers. Thus, the owners of plantations have no interest in seeing knowledge of new techniques or new seeds conveyed to the peasants..." (Lewis, 1954, pp. 409–10).

the capitalist sector). We retain the assumptions that workers in both sectors do not save and that there is a constant saving propensity out of profits (s_π). Using good M as the numeraire, the value of total consumption is thus:

$$p_S\, C_S + C_M = w_S\, L_S + w_M\, L_M + (1 - s_\pi)P \qquad (8)$$

where w_S is the wage in sector S measured in terms of good M. C denotes consumption and P is total profit given by:

$$P = aM = [a/(1 - a)]w_M\, L_M \qquad (9)$$

The elasticity of substitution between M and S goods is constant (corresponding to a CES utility function). Hence:

$$C_M/C_S = B(p_S/p_M)^\eta \qquad (10)$$

where η is the elasticity of substitution.

Market equilibrium requires two conditions. In the goods market:

$$S = C_S \qquad (11)$$

In the labor market, the equilibrium condition is given as before by eq. (1), i.e., the wage in sector M is in equilibrium equal to what workers can earn in sector S (plus a wage premium). The value of the average product of labor in sector S (w_S) is now determined as:

$$w_S = p_S\, L_S^{-b} \qquad \text{for } L_S < Lo$$

$$w_S = p_S\, S_o/L_S \qquad \text{for } L_S \geq Lo \qquad (12)$$

Determinants of the labor supply elasticity

How elastic is, in this more general setting, the labor supply function to the capitalist sector? The derivation of the labor supply elasticity involves the equilibrium conditions and a number of behavioral equations of the model. The steps are presented in the Appendix where the elasticity ($e = d \ln L_M/d \ln w_M$) is shown to be:

$$e = (1 - l_M)/[b\, l_M + (\eta - 1)^{-1}] \qquad \text{for } L_S < Lo$$

$$e = (1 - l_M)/[l_M + (\eta - 1)^{-1}] \qquad \text{for } L_S \geq Lo \qquad (13)$$

where l_M is the employment share of the capitalist sector (L_M/L). Eq. (13) shows that the elasticity of substitution in consumption between S and M goods is a critical variable affecting the labor supply elasticity. In particular, for the labor supply elasticity to be positive, the elasticity of substitution in consumption must be greater than one.[12] Indeed, consider the case of unit elasticity ($\eta = 1$). The consumption shares of the two goods are then constant. The level of employment in the S sector is then independent of relative prices (p_S/p_M) and of the product wage in sector M, as is readily verified from eqs (8) to (11) using the equilibrium condition in the labor market. In this case, an increase in labor demand in sector M will increase the product wage there by exactly the amount required to keep L_S (and thus L_M) constant. The labor supply to sector M is then as inelastic as in a one-sector economy. Eq. (13) also shows the labor supply elasticity as a decreasing function of the employment share of the modern sector (and thus increasing with the employment share of sector S). Indeed, a higher employment share of sector M implies that the same increase in L_M leads to a larger proportional reduction of employment in the subsistence sector. The equilibrium product wage then increases by a larger amount.

We can now address the question of under what conditions the capitalist sector will face a perfectly elastic supply of labor or, as Lewis puts it, there will be "unlimited labor available at a constant real wage". Besides the existence of a subsistence sector ($l_M < 1$), the expression in (13) makes clear that for e to tend to infinity the denominator in the expression must be zero. For this, two conditions are required.

The first condition is an infinite elasticity of substitution in consumption. That is, the goods produced by the two sectors must be perfect substitutes or, what comes to the same, the two sectors must produce the same good. This is one of the assumptions made in section 1. For suppose that the two sectors produce different goods: food is grown in the subsistence sector while the capitalist sector produces textiles. Reallocating labor from the subsistence to the capitalist sector will reduce the output of food and increase the output of textiles thus generating an excess demand for food and an excess supply of textiles at the original relative prices. The terms of trade will move in favor of the food-producing sector, thus raising the subsistence wage (and the capitalist sector wage) in terms of textiles. The capitalist sector will thus face an upward sloping supply curve of labor. The required shift in the terms of trade depends on how close substitutes the two goods are. It is only when the two goods are perfect substitutes that no change in the subsistence wage will be required (provided the second condition below is fulfilled). Then, the excess demand for the goods produced by the subsistence sector is offset by the extra output generated in the capitalist sector, so that no shift in "relative prices" between the two sectors is needed.

---

[12] Eq. (13) can be written as: $e = (\eta - 1)/(1 + (1 - b + b\,\eta)\,L_M/L_S)$. Since $b \leq 1$ and $\eta \geq 0$, the denominator of this expression is always positive. For the numerator, and thus for e, to be positive, η must be greater than 1.

The second condition is that $b = 0$. This is the assumption of constant returns to labor in the subsistence sector that was also made in section 1. With diminishing returns to labor in the subsistence sector ($b > 0$), the average product of labor in sector S, and thus the wage in this sector, will increase as labor is withdrawn from this sector. Labor would then be available to the capitalist sector at an increasing real wage, even if the two sectors produce the same good.

How much of Lewis' model survives when the conditions for a perfectly elastic supply of labor are not fulfilled, i.e., when we move to a two-good economy? As we have seen, a key reason why the subsistence sector is a reserve of surplus labor for the modern sector (in the sense that it provides a perfectly elastic supply of labor) is that it competes in the goods market with the modern sector by producing the same good. The elasticity of labor supply is infinite because the elasticity of substitution is infinite. More generally, how much a sector has to raise wages to attract additional workers from other sectors depends on how many workers are displaced by the increase in production in that sector, and this depends on how substitutable the goods produced are. Thus, the extent to which the non-capitalist sector provides an elastic supply of labor to the modern one depends on the extent to which it competes with it in the goods market by producing more or less close substitutes.

Consider the case in which the subsistence sector produces goods with a price elastic demand and the elasticity of substitution in consumption is greater than unity. How does Lewis' story change when we adopt this broader notion of labor surplus?[13]

Using (2) and (13), the slope of the w curve in ($\ln w_M$, $\ln k$) space can be written as:

$$d\ln w_M / d\ln k = 1/(e + 1/a) \qquad (14)$$

which shows that the higher e is, the flatter the w curve. As already indicated, when $\eta > 1$, the labor supply elasticity is positive. This guarantees that the employment share of the subsistence sector and, thus, the elasticity of labor supply are decreasing functions of the economy-wide capital-labor ratio.[14] The slope of the w curve increases with the capital-labor ratio and, using (13) and (14), we have:

---

[13] If the elasticity of substitution in consumption is unity or less little remains of the Lewis model unless additional assumptions are introduced (more on this below). In what follows, we shall focus on the case $b < 1$ and neglect population growth. The analysis would proceed analogously in the case of a growing labor force if eq. (7) was reformulated to avoid pure scale effects, so that $S = L(L_S/L)^{-b}$. We return later to the role of returns to labor in sector S.

[14] From (13) and (14) we have: $d\ln l_M/d\ln k = e/(e + 1/a)$. A positive e guarantees that l_M is an increasing function of k.

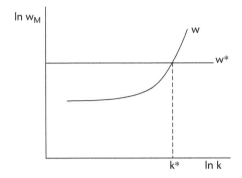

Figure 6.5 A two good-two sector model with price elastic demands

$$\text{dln } w_M / \text{dln } k \longrightarrow a/[a(\eta - 1) + 1] \qquad \text{for } l_M, k \longrightarrow 0 \text{ and } e \longrightarrow \eta - 1$$

$$\text{dln } w_M / \text{dln } k \longrightarrow a \qquad \text{for } l_M \longrightarrow 1, k \longrightarrow \infty \text{ and } e \longrightarrow 0$$

Thus, the slope of the w curve increases tending towards the value "a" of the mature phase in the Lewis model. Although the curve is steeper now at low levels of k than in the Lewis model, it is flatter than before at high levels of k. This is because the elasticity of labor supply always remains positive no matter how large k is. Rather than a sharp turning point from the labor surplus phase to maturity, we now have, as shown in Figure 6.5, an increasing product wage, rising gently first and more steeply later as the capital-labor ratio increases. The subsistence sector, although shrinking in size as k increases, never disappears (the production technology in sector S implies that productivity tends to infinity when employment tends to zero). Therefore, the steady state features now the coexistence of the two sectors.

The labor supply elasticity and the role of returns to labor

The role of returns to labor in the subsistence sector deserves further attention. There are several notions of surplus labor in the development literature. We will focus in this section on two of them. One notion, present in Lewis' article, refers to a perfectly elastic labor supply, as labor available at a constant real wage (equal to the subsistence sector wage plus a constant wage premium). In this case, the labor surplus is the whole labor force in the subsistence sector, in the sense that the labor supply to the capitalist sector remains perfectly elastic until this sector has absorbed the whole of the labor force in the subsistence sector. The required conditions—constant returns to labor in the subsistence sector and an infinite elasticity of substitution in consumption—are those that yield the properties of Lewis' model: the constancy of the real wage, the effects of technical progress, and the trends in income distribution.

A second notion refers to a situation in which labor is so abundant that, given the technology and other factor supplies available to the subsistence sector, the marginal product of labor in this sector is equal to zero. In these conditions, a higher level of employment in the capitalist sector will not affect the level of output in the subsistence sector. In this case, the labor surplus is only that fraction of the labor force that, when withdrawn from the subsistence sector, would make the marginal product of labor positive.[15]

There has been a tendency to assimilate these two notions or, what is perhaps worse, to define surplus labor with reference to both notions simultaneously. According to Little (1982, p. 87) for example: "In the post war literature, Surplus labor must be taken to mean that, at the prevailing wage, more labor can be taken on in modern sectors of the economy without raising the wage, and without loss of output in the traditional sectors". Yet these are quite different notions that need to be clearly distinguished.[16] As our previous analysis makes clear a zero marginal product of labor is neither a necessary nor a sufficient condition for a perfectly elastic labor supply.[17] That output in the subsistence sector may remain constant as employment in the capitalist sector increases does not prevent the average product of labor in that sector from rising. In fact, a zero MPL guarantees that the average product of labor will increase, since a smaller number of workers will now share the same output in the subsistence sector. Moreover, a comparison of the two expressions in (13) makes clear that the labor supply elasticity when the MPL is positive is larger than when it is zero, as long as the average product of labor in the subsistence sector determines the supply price of labor to the capitalist sector. In other words, the existence of surplus labor, in the traditional sense that the marginal product of labor in the subsistence sector is zero, makes the labor supply to the modern sector less, not more, elastic. This should not be surprising. A zero MPL implies that the average product of labor in the subsistence sector

---

[15] A related, but not identical, notion is that surplus labor is the fraction of the labor force which when withdrawn would make the marginal product of labor equal to that in the capitalist sector: in this case, surplus labor exists until the two sectors' MPL are equal and therefore no output gain can be obtained by reallocating the labor force between sectors. This seems to be the sense in which Fei and Ranis (1964) use the concept.

[16] Lewis himself seems ambiguous regarding the notion of labor surplus being used. This ambiguity, however, largely disappears once we recognize that there are in fact two different models in his article. They have sometimes been characterized as the model without trade between the two sectors and the model with trade between the two sectors (see Lewis, 1972; Leeson, 1979). Our analysis suggests that a better characterization would be a one good—two sector model and a two good—two sector model.

[17] Even if, as we shall see below, it may imply something similar if one adds some additional but rather arbitrary assumptions about the determination of the subsistence wage.

is: $APL_S = S_0/L_S$. The elasticity of the APL_S, with respect to an employment fall in sector S, is then: $dlnAPL_S/-dlnL_S = 1$. While, if the MPL is positive, the APL_S is L_S^{-b}, which implies: $dlnAPL_S/-dlnL_S = b < 1$. It follows that, in the face of a small reduction in L_S (a small increase in L_M), the proportionate increase in the average product of labor is greater when the marginal product of labor is zero. The subsistence wage, and thus the modern sector wage, rises by more and this means a less elastic labor supply.

A brief digression is worthwhile here to discuss Fei and Ranis (1964), the major attempt to reconcile the notion of a perfectly elastic supply of labor with a zero MPL in the non-capitalist sector. These authors considered an economy in which the agricultural production function is such that, given the endowment of land, the marginal product of labor becomes zero at a certain level of employment (La*). With an available labor La greater than La* there is surplus labor, not in the sense of Lewis, but in the sense that withdrawing a fraction (La − La*) of the labor force from agriculture leaves agricultural output unaffected. In this situation, competition among workers would tend to generate a zero wage, equal to the marginal product of labor in agriculture. At the same time, some food output would remain unsold if it is larger than landlords' demand for food (i.e., demand at the saturation level). Fei and Ranis conclude that, in these conditions, the agricultural wage will be institutionally determined at a level higher than the MPL in agriculture. This institutional wage can be seen as the outcome of a non-competitive market allocation based on social consensus.

Less convincingly, Fei and Ranis then argue that this institutional wage is perpetuated over time by convention and social consensus as long as there is surplus labor in agriculture. As they put it: "as long as surplus labor continues to exist in the agricultural sector, there is no reason to assume that this social consensus changes significantly" (Fei and Ranis, 1964, p. 22). Given a constant institutional wage in terms of food and a MPL equal to zero in agriculture, the labor supply to the industrial capitalist sector is perfectly elastic during what Fei and Ranis call the labor surplus phase of economic development.

As an attempt to reconcile the notion of a perfectly elastic supply of labor to the capitalist industrial sector with a zero marginal product of labor in agriculture, the Fei and Ranis model has a number of shortcomings. The key to this attempt is the introduction of an "institutional wage" which de-links the supply price of labor to the modern sector from the current productivity conditions in agriculture. The meaning of this "institutional wage" is, however, far from clear. The wage is 'institutional' in the sense that it is not the outcome of a competitive market allocation. Yet it is not 'institutional' in the sense of being determined by convention: the wage stands in a definite relationship to demographic and technological factors. If current productivity conditions in agriculture were critical initially, why do they become unimportant later? In other words, why shouldn't the social consensus—on which the institutional wage is built—change significantly as the average product of labor in agriculture changes with the reallocation of the labor force towards the industrial sector?[18]

It is worth noting that some early development theorists were well aware that a zero marginal product of labor in the subsistence sector does not provide a perfectly elastic labor supply to the modern sector. Nurkse (1953), for example, viewed the existence of a zero marginal product of labor as concealing a hidden saving potential that, in principle, allows for an increase in investment without having to reduce consumption.[19] He argued then that all sorts of difficulties were likely to be faced in the practical application of that proposition (p. 38). Thinking of labor surplus as rural underemployment, he argued that: "Everything depends on the mobilization of the concealed saving potential in the shape of the food surplus that becomes available to the productive peasants when their unproductive dependents go away" (pp. 38–9) and which results, we may add, from the increase in the average product of labor in agriculture. Given that "the peasants are not likely to save the surplus voluntarily since they live so close to subsistence level" (p. 43), the mobilization of the saving potential will be incomplete, short of drastic measures by the State[20] or of "a widespread and radical improvement in farming techniques, accompanying the removal of the surplus farm labour, so that total farm output might be substantially increased and not merely held constant" (p. 43).

4. Efficiency Wages and Kaldorian Underemployment

A more promising approach than that of Fei and Ranis to free the Lewis model from some of its restrictive assumptions is to combine the extended Lewis model of section 2 to bring in efficiency wage considerations. Thus, we shall assume that in the capitalist sector the real wage paid by firms affects labor productivity through its influence on nutrition or health. This hypothesis—the efficiency wage hypothesis—goes back to Leibenstein's writing on

---

[18] The analytical source of these difficulties seems to be that in their 1964 book, Fei and Ranis are not fully conscious that they are determining the wage from the equilibrium condition in the food market (as they clearly do in the mathematical appendix to their 1961 article). Remaining consistent with this procedure does not, however, solve all the problems since, as soon as an industrial sector emerges, this determination of the agricultural wage leaves the terms of trade between agriculture and industry undetermined.

[19] He distinguished this situation from one of Keynesian unemployment in which both investment and consumption can expand simultaneously and from the classical situation in which in order to increase investment, consumption must necessarily be reduced.

[20] Nurkse gives the examples of Japan's "stiff land tax" in the 19th century and Soviet Union's system of collective farms as responses to the problem of mobilizing the savings potential.

economic backwardness (Leibenstein, 1957), and has been discussed, in the development literature, by Mazumdar (1959) and Stiglitz (1976) among others.

Technology in the modern sector is now described by:

$$M = K^a(EL_M)^{1-a} \qquad (15)$$

where E is an effort function of the form:

$$E = E(w_M/p) \qquad E' > 0; E'' < 0; \quad E(\omega) = 0 \qquad (16)$$

(w_M/p) is the real *consumption wage* in the M sector and ω is the minimum wage above which there is a positive effort from workers. The consumption wage, rather than the product wage (w_M/p_M), is of course the one affecting the services a worker renders whether the channel is nutrition and health or involves other possible influences on a worker's effort. Moreover, we assume that effort increases with w_M/p according to (16) as long as the real consumption wage is higher than the average product of labor in the subsistence sector plus the wage premium (fw_S/p). Otherwise, the wage in the M sector is determined by fw_S.

Firms treat prices as given and maximize profits over w_M and L_M subject to (15), (16), and $w_M > f\, w_S$. The first order conditions of this maximization program imply the "Solow condition" that the wage elasticity of effort is equal to unity (Solow, 1979):

$$E'(w_M/p)(w_M/p)/E(w_M/p) = 1 \qquad (17)$$

Solving (17) for (w_M/p) yields the equilibrium value of the "efficiency wage" (the real consumption wage that maximizes profits) as a function only of the parameters of the productivity (or effort) function E. Consider, for example, an effort function of the form:

$$E = (w_M/p - \omega)^d \qquad d < 1 \qquad \text{for } w_M/p > \omega$$

$$\text{and } 0 \text{ otherwise}$$

Using (17) and solving explicitly for the efficiency wage yields:

$$w_M/p = \omega/(1 - d) \qquad (18)$$

Assume that workers' utility function is of the Cobb-Douglas form: $U = C_S^a\, C_M^{1-a}$, with a unit elasticity of substitution in consumption. This specification has the advantage of making it possible to derive an exact measure of the real consumption wage. The corresponding price index (p) is:

$$p = p_S^a p_M^{1-a} \qquad (19)$$

Combining (18) and (19), we can also solve for the efficiency product wage:

$$w_M/p_M = (p_S/p_M)^a \omega/(1-d) \tag{20}$$

which shows the efficiency product wage as an increasing function of the efficiency consumption wage, $\omega/(1-d)$, and of the terms of trade between the subsistence and modern sectors (p_S/p_M). It is worth noting that the efficiency product wage increases with the expenditure share of subsistence goods (a).

Earnings in the subsistence sector are determined, as before (eq. 12), by the value of the average product of labor: $w_S = p_S L_S^{-b}$, where L_S is equal to the difference between the total labor force and employment in the modern sector. Clearly, in this model the market clearing condition, $f\, w_S = w_M$, will in general not be fulfilled. The reason is that when subsistence earnings, adjusted for the wage premium ($f\, w_S$), are below modern sector wages as determined by (20), competition among workers will not lead to lower wages in the modern sector. It is not profitable for firms to undertake such wage reductions. Wage determination is then compatible with the existence of an excess supply of labor to the modern sector. Even though all workers find employment in one of the two sectors, there is an excess supply of labor in the sense that the earnings' differential between the modern and subsistence sectors is larger than the wage premium required to lure workers out of the subsistence sector.[21]

How elastic is the labor supply to the modern sector in the presence of this excess supply of labor? It is clear from (20) that the answer depends exclusively on how much the terms of trade (p_S/p_M) change as employment in sector M changes. We can find the terms of trade as a function of L_M by combining the goods market equilibrium eqs (8) and (11) and the consumption demand functions (eq. 10, when $\eta = 1$). This yields:

$$p_S/p_M = (1/B)(w_M/p_M)(L_M/L_S^{1-b})(1-s_\pi a)/(1-a) \tag{21}$$

where $1/B$ is now equal to $a/(1-a)$. Eq. (21) shows the terms of trade for the subsistence sector increasing with L_M/L_S. An increase in L_M (which reduces L_S) creates excess demand for S goods and the relative price of S goods has to increase to clear the goods market.

Using (20) and (21) to eliminate (p_S/p_M) and taking logs, total differentiation yields, after some manipulation, the labor supply elasticity (dlnL_M/dlnw_M): $e = (1-a)/a\,[1 + (1-b)\,L_M/L_S]$. The elasticity of labor supply is a decreasing function of the expenditure share of subsistence sector goods and of the employment share of the modern sector. An increase in these shares

---

[21] $f\, w_S < w_M$ implies that $(w_M - w_S)/w_S > f-1$, i.e., the earnings differential is higher than the wage premium and there are no mechanisms to bring them into equality.

turns the terms of trade in favor of the subsistence sector and, even though the real consumption wage is unaffected, the product wage increases.

There are two interesting differences with the labor supply elasticity derived in the previous section. First, a positive value for the labor supply elasticity no longer depends on the elasticity of substitution in consumption being more than unity (the elasticity has been derived on the assumption of a unit elasticity of substitution). Second, returns to labor in the subsistence sector now affect the labor supply elasticity in a completely different way, and one that conforms to conventional wisdom. Indeed, the labor supply elasticity now increases with parameter "b". This means that the elasticity is at its maximum when the marginal product of labor is zero, or b = 1, and at its minimum level when b = 0 (constant returns to labor). There is here a striking contrast with the model in the previous section. The source of the difference is the nature of the labor surplus. The increase in the average product of labor in the subsistence sector—which results from an increase in employment in the modern sector—now has no effect on the modern sector consumption wage (eq. 18 shows the real consumption wage determined only by the parameters of the productivity function). The efficiency product wage rises, but only because the terms of trade turn against the modern sector. This terms of trade effect is at its minimum when the marginal product of labor is zero, precisely because there is no output loss in the subsistence sector as a result of the increase in employment in the modern sector. The labor supply elasticity is thus highest when the MPL in sector S is zero.

It is worth noting that if productivity in the subsistence sector was also affected by workers' earnings there, a reasonable assumption in the context of a nutrition-based efficiency wage model, the shift in the terms of trade will have a positive productivity effect on sector S that tends to make the labor supply more elastic. Indeed, this productivity effect moderates the shift in the terms of trade required to clear the goods market, as employment in the modern sector increases, thus making the increase in the product wage that the modern sector has to pay smaller.[22] This is an additional reason why, in the presence of efficiency wages, a zero MPL in sector S is more likely to be associated with a large elasticity of labor supply. For such situations are typically associated with labor abundance and widespread poverty in the subsistence sector.

In the presence of efficiency wages, a labor surplus can develop in the subsistence sector that provides an elastic labor supply to the modern sector. This labor surplus is quite different from the conventional type, since the

---

[22] Formally, if production conditions in sector S are given by: $S = (F\ L_S)^{1-b}$ where F is a productivity function of the form $F = (w_S/p)^\phi$, output per worker in sector S is given by: $S/L_S = (w_S/p)^{\phi(1-b)} L_S^{-b}$, which increases with L_M for two reasons: 1) the fall in L_S raises productivity due to the presence of diminishing returns to labor in S; 2) as the terms of trade shift in favor of sector S, F increases.

marginal product of labor in the S sector need not be zero, as well as from the Lewis variety, because now the labor market does not clear. We may refer to it as Kaldorian underemployment since the distinctive feature of Kaldor's definition of labor surplus is its emphasis on a labor market in disequilibrium:

> The best definition I could suggest for the existence of "labor surplus" ... is one which is analogous to Keynes' definition of "involuntary unemployment": a situation of "labor surplus" exists when a faster rate of increase in the demand for labor in the high productivity sectors induces a faster rate of labor transference even when it is attended by *a reduction, and not an increase, in the earnings differential between the different sectors.* (Kaldor, 1968, p. 386, italics in original)[23]

A reduction of the earnings differential (w_M/w_S), as the employment share of the modern sector increases, is precisely what happens when the modern sector faces an excess supply of labor. Combining eqs (20) and the expression for the value of the average product of labor in sector S yields: $w_S/w_M = (p_S/p_M)^{1-a} L_S^{-b} (1-d)/\omega$. Using (21) to eliminate (p_S/p_M) and taking logs, total differentiation yields:

$$d\ln(w_S/w_M) = (1 + L_M/L_S)d\ln L_M \qquad (22)$$

which shows that increases in modern sector employment tend to narrow the earnings differential, the impact being greater the larger the employment share of the modern sector.

As the employment share of the modern sector increases throughout the transition to a steady state, the earnings differential will eventually narrow to the point where it equals the wage premium ($f-1$). The market clearing condition ($fw_S = w_M$) is then reestablished. With further increases in the employment share of the modern sector, eq. (20) no longer applies and is replaced by the market clearing condition (eq. 1). The elasticity of labor supply is then determined, as in section 2, by the elasticity of substitution in consumption. Since this elasticity is one in the present model, the corresponding labor supply elasticity is zero (see eq. 13 when $\eta = 1$). The earnings differential is now determined by the wage premium and no longer shrinks as the employment share of the modern sector increases. Kaldor refers to this situation as "economic maturity" defined as a state of affairs where real income per capita has reached broadly the same level in the different sectors of the economy (Kaldor, 1967, p. 8). This notion of maturity is different from that of the Lewis model. Its defining characteristic is the disappearance of an earnings differential among sectors (up to a wage premium with no welfare

---

[23] Although analogous to Keynesian unemployment in the sense that there is an excess supply of labor, this type of underemployment, just like Lewis labor surplus, is completely resilient to changes in the aggregate demand for goods.

significance). In the Lewis model, this condition always holds and the defining characteristic of the mature economy is instead the disappearance of the subsistence sector.

The Kaldorian notion of underemployment is also different from, although not necessarily inconsistent with, the type of unemployment analyzed by modern theories of efficiency wages.[24] In these theories, the wage *relative* to some fallback position plays a prominent role, along with the given parameters of the effort function, in determining work effort, unlike our specification which neglects the influence on effort of factors other than the *absolute* level of the real consumption wage. This raises the question of whether the conclusion that the earnings differential falls as employment in the modern sector increases, survives when we bring the cost of job loss, or more generally wage relativities, into the determination of the efficiency wage. To address this question, suppose that the minimum wage (ω) in the effort function increases with the real consumption wage in the S sector (w_S/p): the higher this wage, which represents the earnings that workers in sector M will obtain if they lose their job, the higher is ω and thus the efficiency wage that firms in sector M have to pay. Let ψ be the elasticity of ω with respect to w_S/p, such that: $\omega = (w_S/p)^\psi$. Following a procedure similar to that followed in order to derive (22), and noting that ω is no longer exogenous, we have:

$$d\ln(w_S/w_M) = (1 - \psi)(1 + L_M/L_S) \quad d\ln L_M \qquad (23)$$

Eq. (23) shows that the wage differential will narrow with an increase in modern sector employment provided that ψ is less than unity. A unit elasticity represents the extreme case in which all that matters is the wage relative to the fallback position (so that a 50 percent reduction in the fallback position (w_S/p) implies a 50 percent reduction in the efficiency wage). This case is clearly inconsistent with Kaldor's definition of labor surplus, since it implies that the wage differential is independent of the employment share of the modern sector. The other extreme case is a zero elasticity in which all that matters is the absolute wage. This is in the tradition of early theories of efficiency wages and is the case examined in this section. Note that for $\psi = 0$, eq. (23) indeed simplifies to eq. (22). It is interesting that the middle ground in between these two extreme cases—when $0 < \psi < 1$ and work effort depends on both the absolute level of the wage and the fallback position—also fits into Kaldor's notion of labor surplus: the wage differential narrows when modern sector employment increases although less than when $\psi = 1$.

---

[24] See, in particular, Akerlof and Yellen (1985, 1986) and Bowles (1985).

Appendix

Derivation of the Labor Supply Elasticity in Section 2

Substituting from eq. (12) into the labor market equilibrium condition, and dividing by p_M, yields:

$$w_M/p_M = f L_S^{-b} p_S/p_M \qquad \text{for } L_S < L_o$$
$$w_M/p_M = f S_o L_S^{-1} p_S/p_M \quad \text{for } L_S \geq L_o \tag{A.1}$$

Substituting from (10) into (A.1):

$$w_M/p_M = f(1/BC_M/C_S)^{1/\eta} L_S^{-b} \qquad \text{for } L_S < Lo \tag{A.2}$$
$$w_M/p_M = f(1/BC_M/C_S)^{1/\eta} S_o/L_S^{-b} \quad \text{for } L_S \geq Lo$$

Substituting from (9) into (8) and using (7), (11) and (12):

$$C_M/C_S = [(1 - s_\pi a)/(1 - a)](w_M/p_M)(L_M/L_S^{1-b}) \quad \text{for } L_S < Lo \tag{A.3}$$
$$C_M/C_S = [(1 - s_\pi a)/(1 - a)](w_M/p_M)(L_M/So) \qquad \text{for } L_S \geq Lo$$

Substituting from (A.3) into (A.2), we obtain w_M/p_M as a function of L_M and L_S. Taking logs, total differentiation yields, after some manipulation:

$$d\ln L_M/d\ln(w_M/p_M) = (L_S/L)/(1/(\eta - 1)) + b(1 - L_S/L) \qquad \text{for } L_S < Lo$$
$$d\ln L_M/d\ln(w_M/p_M) = (L_S/L)/(1/(\eta - 1)) + (1 - L_S/L) \qquad \text{for } L_S \geq Lo \tag{A.4}$$

7

Increasing Returns, External Economies, and Multiple Equilibria

With the introduction of a labor surplus and an elastic labor supply, Lewis took an important step away from the neoclassical model of a "mature economy". This was a major departure but it was the only one. Implicitly or explicitly, Lewis assumes a constant-returns-to-scale technology and perfect competition in the capitalist sector together with exogenous technical progress. Other contributors to the theory of economic development in the 1940s and 1950s, Rosenstein-Rodan and Nurkse in particular, took more radical steps and considered the implications of increasing returns to scale in the technology of the capitalist sector. This chapter begins with recalling first the main sources of aggregate increasing returns to scale in the early development economics literature (external and internal to the firm). We then focus on the case of technological external economies arising from workers' training or learning-by-doing. Combined with labor surplus, the presence of aggregate increasing returns raises the possibility of multiple equilibria including a Solow-type mature economy equilibrium and a critical level of investments below which there is a poverty trap. A final section examines the evolution of the distribution of income in a model with increasing returns.

The source of aggregate increasing returns to scale may be external or internal to the firms operating in the modern sector. In the first case, on which this chapter focuses, even if each firm operates individually with a constant-returns-to-scale technology, returns to scale may increase at the sector or economy-wide level if the firms' activities collectively affect the production conditions of a large number of firms. When these external effects are positive the aggregate production function (at the industry or economy level) may display increasing returns to scale. In Rosenstein-Rodan (1943, 1984), these effects arise from activities such as industrial training. A related example, formalized by Arrow (1962), is learning by doing, which increases the stock of experience and "know-how" as a by-product of production activities. In both cases, the expansion of the economy increases the pool of trained workers and skills on which each firm can rely. This raises the productivity with which modern technologies can be applied to production, so that even if the costs of an individual firm do not fall with its own expansion, the firm's costs fall with the expansion of its industry or the economy as a whole. Nurkse suggests another source of external effects when he mentions that the productivity of modern technology depends on the quality of management (or as he puts it, "the qualities of enterprise and initiative") and that the supply of managers and their quality will tend to increase with the expansion of the capitalist sector (Nurkse, 1953, p. 10).[1]

Whether external or internal to the firm (as we shall see in the next chapter), increasing returns are associated with externalities—divergences between social and private costs and benefits. Drawing on a distinction first introduced by Viner (1931) and later developed by Meade (1952), Scitovsky (1954) distinguished between technological and pecuniary externalities. Following Meade (1952), he defined the former as those external economies arising from direct interdependence among producers, a property of the production function.[2] For example, the economies resulting from industrial training or learning by doing, discussed in this chapter, accrue to a firm directly with the growth of an industry or the whole industrial system. When the firm's production function displays constant returns to scale, it is these effects, external to the firm, that cause aggregate returns to scale to increase and, at the same time, cause a divergence between social and private costs and benefits. In the case of industrial training for instance, this divergence arises from the incomplete appropriability of the social returns from this activity (see Rosenstein-Rodan 1943, 1984).

Whether external to the firm or as a result of plant-level economies of large-scale production, many early contributors to development theory viewed increasing returns to scale as characteristic of modern technology. In this chapter we focus on the analytically simpler case of technological externalities as the source of increasing returns and look at the implications of this assumption when combined with the assumption of surplus labor. The next chapter considers increasing returns arising from internal economies and giving rise to pecuniary externalities.

---

[1] Nurkse's suggested external effects are an example of social interactions, associated with the expansion of the capitalist sector, leading to changes in attitudes and motivation. These, together with the effects of social interactions on technological diffusion and innovation, are sometimes described as dynamic technological externalities (see Stewart and Ghani, 1992).

[2] The beekeeper—orchard example, provided by Meade, illustrates this direct interaction between producers. The laundry-factory example and many other environmental effects illustrate cases of negative technological externalities.

1. Technological Externalities, Increasing Returns to Scale and Surplus Labor

In the economy considered, increasing returns to scale are associated with industrial training à la Rodan or learning by doing à la Arrow, and are external to the firm. This allows us to skip, at this stage, issues of market structure and imperfect competition that will appear in the next chapter when we deal with internal economies of scale.

A Lewis-Rosenstein-Rodan model

Technological external effects are combined with the presence of surplus labor à la Lewis.[3] Consider an economy with two sectors (S and M) which produce the same good (or basket of goods). As in Lewis, sector S uses traditional production techniques that are labor-intensive (or, more generally, with low-productivity owing to the limited use of capital). The other sector (M) uses a capital-intensive technology subject to increasing returns to scale as in Rosenstein-Rodan. The production functions are:

$$S = L_S \tag{1}$$

$$M = (\tilde{K})^{\mu} K^a L_M^{1-a} \qquad \mu > 0, \quad a + \mu < 1 \tag{2}$$

where S and M are the levels of production in the two sectors, L_S and L_M are the labor inputs in each sector, K is the capital stock and $(K\sim)^{\mu}$ reflects the existence of technological externalities associated with the capital stock accumulated in the past. I have chosen units so that the average product of labor in sector S is 1. A positive value of parameter μ guarantees that the capitalist technology exhibits increasing returns to scale. The restriction $a + \mu < 1$ implies the assumption of diminishing returns to capital in the production function of the capital-intensive sector.

Note that besides being external to the firm, increasing returns to scale have two features: 1) they arise from the stock of experience, collectively generated and available to firms, and are a function of cumulative output; 2) they are assumed to be specific to the capitalist sector to emphasize the role of social interaction in the learning process. In equilibrium, the average capital stock will be equal to the capital stock of the representative firm, that is $K\sim = K$. This specification is virtually identical to a model of learning by doing with the

---

[3] An alternative presentation would blend increasing returns to scale, associated to technological externalities, with the type of Kaldorian underemployment analyzed in Chapter 6. See Ros (2000, ch. 4) for such a model.

capital stock as a proxy for cumulative output.[4] Alternative specifications would make the state of technology a function of the capital stock per head—in which case technology would not display pure scale effects—as in Kaldor's (1957) "technical progress function" (see Chapter 11) or Romer's (1986) specification of a different type of external effects (see Chapter 2).

Let us also assume that both sectors operate in competitive conditions. The assumption that the capitalist sector is profit-maximizing generates the following labor demand function:

$$L_M = [(1 - a)K^\mu / w_M]^{1/a} K \tag{3}$$

In addition, assuming that workers who do not find employment in the capitalist sector are employed in the traditional sector and that wages in the two sectors are equal owing to labor market competition, we have:

$$L = L_S + L_M \tag{4}$$

$$w_M = 1 \tag{5}$$

where L is the total labor force and w_M is the wage in sector M. Since I have chosen units so that $w_S = 1$ and $w_S = w_M$, we have $w_M = 1$.

When the subsistence sector has disappeared, the wage in the capitalist sector clears the labor market with an inelastic labor supply and is thus the solution to eq. 3 with $L_M = L$. This is:

$$w_M = [(1 - a)L^{-a}]K^{a + \mu} \tag{6}$$

2. Multiple Equilibria, the Paradox of Underdevelopment, and Transitional Dynamics

It will again be convenient to present the model with the now familiar real wage diagram in $(\ln w_M, \ln K)$ space. The w curve, the schedule of short-run equilibria, has just been derived. This is given by a horizontal segment ($w_M = 1$ as shown by eq. 5) as long as the two sectors coexist and an upward sloping line with slope equal to $a + \mu$, in the mature phase. This w line is thus identical to that in the Lewis model except for the presence of the increasing returns parameter which increases the slope of the line in the mature phase given the external productivity effects of capital accumulation.

---

[4] Arrow's (1962) original model of learning by doing makes productivity a function of cumulative gross investment.

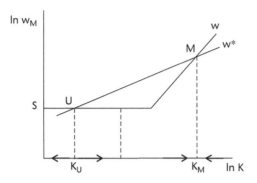

Figure 7.1 A Lewis-Rosenstein-Rodan model

A major change, with respect to most previous models, can be seen in the schedule of stationary capital stocks or long-run equilibrium (the w* curve).[5] Using the production function, the profit-wage curve is now: $r = a\,K^{\mu/a}\,[(1-a)/w_M]^{(1-a)/a}$. Substituting into the steady state condition, $s_\pi\,r = \delta$, and solving for the real product wage yields the equation of the w* curve:

$$w_M^* = (1 - a)(as_\pi/\delta)^{a/1-a}K^\mu/(1 - a)$$

The required wage is no longer independent of the capital stock. As in Romer (1986) and the AK model, it is now an increasing function of K, so that the w* curve in (w_M, K) space is a positively sloped curve (see Figure 7.1). This is due to the (external) productivity effects of increases in the capital stock. Since the profit rate depends on the real wage and productivity, which in turn depends on the capital stock, the same rate of profit and, thus, the same rate of capital accumulation can now be generated at low levels of wages and capital stock and at higher levels of wages and capital stock. There is no longer a unique value of the real wage that can generate the steady state rate of accumulation. There is now a locus of (w, K) combinations that generate this equilibrium rate of accumulation.

The novel feature of the model is that it generates multiple equilibria. Given that the capital stock increases when the economy is below the w* line and contracts when it is above, these equilibria, when they exist, must be as follows: 1) A locally stable non-capitalist steady state at point S with per capita incomes and wages at subsistence sector levels; 2) A locally stable steady state at point M with high real wages and high capital intensity corresponding to K_M; 3) An unstable equilibrium at point U with capital stock K_U. Depending on initial conditions, the economy moves away from this equilibrium towards either the high-level or low-level stable equilibria.

---

[5] We continue to neglect, for simplicity, labor force growth.

To better understand why the intersection at U is unstable (and thus why the other two equilibria are stable), consider an initial capital stock below K_U in Figure 7.1. At this low level of the capital stock, the market-clearing wage (on the w curve) is higher than the real wage required to generate the steady state rate of accumulation (on the w* curve). The rate of accumulation is thus less than depreciation and the capitalist sector shrinks over time in size. The economy's capital intensity declines, thus moving away from K_U and towards the subsistence (or non-capitalist) economy at point S. Similarly, consider an initial value of K just above K_U. The market-clearing wage is now lower than the required wage. The rate of capital accumulation is thus higher than its steady state value. The capital intensity of the economy rises over time, increasing the capital stock further away from K_U and towards the steady state at K_M. Above K_M, the wage is again higher than required and the lower profit rate will reduce the rate of capital accumulation, until the economy is back to the stable equilibrium at M.

There is a development trap below the low K intersection at K_U. The low level stable equilibrium at S is a trap in the sense that it is only a locally stable equilibrium and a sufficiently large departure from it will trigger a self-sustained process of expansion towards the high level equilibrium. The local stability arises from the fact that, below K_U, the elastic supply of labor and increasing returns interact negatively to hinder the expansion of the capitalist sector: the elastic labor supply sets a floor to the real wages that the capitalist sector has to pay and, together with the initial conditions of low productivity this prevents the profitable use of capital intensive technologies with increasing returns. These interactions can be described as a vicious circle between the inducement to invest and the scale of the capitalist sector. The inducement to invest is weak because the scale of the capitalist sector and thus the level of productivity (as determined by K), are small. The size of the sector and productivity remain small because the inducement to invest is weak (profitability is low).

Above the low-level intersection there is, in contrast, a virtuous circle between productivity increases and the inducement to invest. In this case, the interactions between increasing returns to scale and an elastic supply of labor become positive and counteract the influence of diminishing returns to capital. The reason is that the presence of increasing returns to scale strengthens the productivity effects of capital accumulation while, at the same time, the elastic supply of labor weakens the effects of capital accumulation on the real wage. Growth can then go on with an increasing rate of return on capital during the surplus labor phase of the development process. This virtuous circle is followed by a process of convergence to the high level equilibrium in which labor surpluses have been absorbed into the capitalist sector and the economy, with a large capital endowment, is able to generate high real wages. This high equilibrium is the final stage of the transition phase towards a mature economy in which the rate of growth would depend exclusively, as in the Solow equilibrium path, on technical progress and labor force growth.

Increasing returns to capital during the surplus labor phase of the transition can also be seen if we look at aggregate production function:[6]

$$Y = L + a \, (1 - a)^{(1-a)/a} \, K^{1 + \mu/a} \tag{7}$$

Eq. (7) shows that even though the capitalist sector's technology is subject to diminishing returns to capital ($a + \mu < 1$), the aggregate production function shows increasing returns to capital ($1 + \mu/a > 1$).[7] This is so, of course, provided that the two sectors coexist (since eq. (7) is derived from the assumption $w_S = w_M = 1$). Otherwise, if the traditional sector disappears, the aggregate production function is the same as that of the capital-intensive sector.

The unstable intersection, in between the vicious and virtuous circles, has to be associated with Rosenstein-Rodan's writing. For it corresponds, indeed, to that critical mass of investment that generates the externalities and scale economies required for a big push towards sustained economic development. This critical mass of investment, corresponding to K_U, need not be spontaneously achieved and may require policy action. As Rosenstein-Rodan stated it: "There is a minimum level of resources that must be devoted to . . . a development program if it is to have any chance for success. Launching a country into self-sustaining growth is a little like getting an airplane off the ground. There is a critical ground speed which must be passed before the craft can become airborne" (Rosenstein-Rodan, 1984, p. 210).

The development trap below the low K intersection has to be distinguished from a poverty trap due to insufficient savings. In the savings trap model of Chapter 3, the rate of accumulation is low at small levels of K because low incomes, barely enough for subsistence consumption, adversely affect the savings rate. Below the low K intersection in that model, the capital stock contracts because savings, despite the high profitability of investment, fall below depreciation due to the low propensity to save. Unlike that model, in the present one both real wages *and* the rate of return to capital are low. This paradox of underdevelopment, the fact that the profit rate is low despite capital being very scarce, results from the combination of increasing returns

---

[6] Using eqs (1) and (2) total output ($Y = S + M$) can be written as $Y = L_S + K^{a + \mu} L_M^{1-a}$. Using (4) to eliminate L_S from this expression and (3) to eliminate L_M (and also using eq. (5)) gives eq. (7).

[7] It is worth noting that with constant returns to scale in the production of the capitalist sector ($\mu = 0$), the aggregate production would feature constant returns to capital, as long as the two sectors coexist, exactly as in the Lewis model and modern AK models.

to scale and surplus labor. The rate of capital accumulation (s_π r) is thus low at small levels of K because profitability (r) is low. Even though a low savings rate may aggravate the problem, it is the low profit rate, due to the small capital stock, that prevents the rate of capital accumulation from rising above depreciation. It is in this sense that the weakness of the inducement to invest, rather than the scarcity of savings, is the source of problem and explains why the initial conditions of low productivity and capital scarcity persist. This is an important difference between the two models. Unlike what happens with a savings trap, even a large degree of international capital mobility may now be insufficient to lift a poor economy out of the present type of development trap.

The presence of international capital mobility, however, modifies the model significantly. The steady state condition s_π r = δ is replaced by I/K = ψ (r – r*) = δ, where ψ is a propensity to invest and r* is a risk-adjusted international profit rate. Using the profit-wage curve, r = r (w_M, K), the equation of the w* schedule makes now the required wage a positive function of the capital stock and the propensity to invest and a negative function of the depreciation rate and the risk adjusted international profit rate. The role of the propensity to invest and the risk premium in the determination of the required wage (and thus the position of the w* schedule) opens the door to the influence of institutional factors in the determination of the long-run equilibrium real wage and, as we shall see, in the conditions for the existence of multiple equilibria. For example, a higher propensity to invest or a lower country risk premium (which lowers r*) shift the w* schedule upwards and increase the value of the high level equilibrium real wage.

The multiple equilibria generated by the model should also be distinguished from an example of multiple equilibria with a non-convex technology that first appeared in the original Solow article (see Solow, 1956, p. 71). In the Solow diagram of Figure 7.2, the curve showing gross investment per worker as

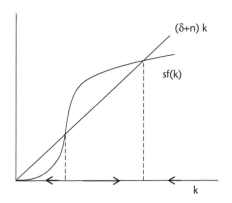

Figure 7.2 A case of multiple equilibria in Solow (1956)

a function of the capital-labor ratio has the shape of an S which may then intersect the effective depreciation line at more than one point. In this case, the technology itself of the single modern sector being considered features increasing returns *to capital* over a range of capital-labor ratios (with diminishing returns to capital at higher levels of the capital-labor ratio).[8] There is, however, little discussion of why this may be so. One exception is Sachs (2005) which argues as follows in favor of the hypothesis of increasing returns to capital at low-income levels:

> An economy with twice the capital stock per person means an economy with roads that work the year round, rather than roads that are washed out each rainy season; electrical power that is reliable twenty-four hours each day, rather than electric power that is sporadic and unpredictable; workers who are healthy and at their jobs, rather than workers who are chronically absent with disease. The likelihood is that doubling the human and physical capital stock will actually more than double the income level, at least at very low levels of capital per person. (p. 250)

The increasing marginal product of capital can generate low or medium level unstable intersections, and therefore multiple equilibria. The similarity with the present model is that in both cases profitability increases over a range of capital stocks. The key difference is that here this is not a property of the production function. The technology of the capitalist sector features diminishing returns to capital over the whole range of capital stocks and it is the interaction between increasing returns *to scale* and an elastic labor supply which generates multiple equilibria.

The conditions for multiple equilibria

What are the key assumptions that guarantee the existence of multiple equilibria in the Lewis-Rosenstein-Rodan model? The slope conditions for the existence of multiple equilibria can be derived from the geometry of Figure 7.1. For the model to generate a low level intersection, the w curve must be flatter than the w* locus at low levels of K. For this, there must be increasing returns to scale (μ must be positive). This condition is evident from Figure 7.1. Otherwise, the w* curve would be horizontal and, as in the Solow or the Lewis models, there would only be a unique equilibrium (in Lewis, a subsistence economy or a mature economy equilibrium depending on the position of the two curves). Had we assumed constant returns to scale, there would not be a critical level of the initial capital endowment below which no sustained growth is possible. With constant returns, production can be undertaken at the smallest imaginable scale without any adverse effects on

---

[8] See, for related examples, Wan (1971, ch. 2 section 2), Barro and Sala-i-Martin (1995, section 1.3.5), and Azariadis (1996).

profitability. Then, if profitability is not high enough to generate sustained growth, this will be true no matter how large the initial capital stock, and if it is high enough, this will be true regardless of how small the initial capital stock is. In Lewis' model, for example, even the smallest initial capital stock leads to self-sustained growth provided that the saving propensity out of profits is sufficiently high and modern technology sufficiently productive.[9]

For the existence of a low K intersection in the absence of increasing returns *to capital* $(a + \mu > 1)$, the labor supply must be elastic. In the present model, this is guaranteed by the perfectly elastic supply of labor assumed by Lewis. In a more general model, there must be surplus labor in the broad sense of an elastic labor supply, in order to generate a relatively flat segment of the w curve at low levels of K to make possible the low K intersection.[10] Otherwise there would only be a mature economy intersection (if it exists). This is because without a subsistence sector where workers can work if they do not find employment in the capitalist sector, the real product wage would drop enough to make the capitalist sector profitable.

While returns must increase to generate the low K intersection at U, they must not increase dramatically, if the model is to generate the high K intersection. As Figure 7.1 makes clear, for this intersection to exist, the slope of the w* line, given by $\mu/(1 - a)$, must be less than the slope of the w curve in the mature phase (given by $a + \mu$). Thus, it is necessary that: $\mu/(1 - a) < a + \mu$, which implies: $a + \mu < 1$. The increasing returns parameter (μ) must not be so high as to generate aggregate increasing returns to capital. Under such dramatically increasing returns, there would be no mature steady state. After reaching the critical value K_U, the economy would keep on growing without bounds. Even in the mature phase, the effects of capital accumulation on productivity would more than outweigh the effects of raising real wages on the profit rate. The profit rate, the rate of capital accumulation and the capital-labor ratio would go on increasing in a process of endogenous growth, similar to that in the Romer's 1986 model discussed in Chapter 2.

The existence of multiple equilibria also requires that the w and w* schedules intersect. If the wage required to generate a positive rate of capital accumulation even when the whole labor force is employed in the modern

---

[9] It is worth noting that the condition refers, indeed, to increasing returns rather than to positive technological external effects. Positive technological externalities need to be positive here *only to the extent* that they are the source of aggregate increasing returns.

[10] In the Rodan-Leibenstein model in Ros (2000), the necessary condition is that the sum of the parameter of returns to capital $(a + \mu)$ and the product of the increasing returns parameter and the labor supply elasticity $(e\,\mu)$, must be greater than one. This condition is likely to be fulfilled when the labor supply elasticity is high at low levels of K even with a small dose of increasing returns. In a model without efficiency wages, with labor market clearing and CES utility functions, the necessary condition involves a sufficiently high elasticity of substitution between the goods produced by the two sectors (see Ros and Skott, 1998).

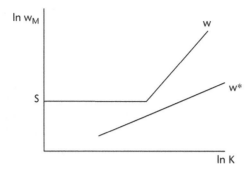

Figure 7.3 A unique subsistence economy equilibrium

sector is lower than the subsistence wage, the two schedules do not intersect and there is then a unique and stable long-run equilibrium at point S (see Figure 7.3). This case implies that the size of the labor force is so small that industrialization will never be worthwhile, given the specification of the production possibilities. One factor contributing to this possibility in an economy under international capital mobility is a high country risk premium (high r*) or a low propensity to invest (ψ) which, as we have seen before in this chapter, determine the position of the w* schedule in the case of international capital mobility.

3. Properties and Extensions of the Classical Development Model

We now turn to discuss some implications of the Lewis-Rosenstein-Rodan model. Although our main focus will be on the properties of the transition to the steady state, it is worthwhile to start by saying something about the determinants of the steady state in the high level equilibrium.

Determinants of the mature steady state

The high level equilibrium features a Solow or Lewis-type steady state. This is because in the mature phase the economy is a one-sector economy since the subsistence sector has completely disappeared. Suppose instead that the subsistence sector uses a fixed factor and labor under diminishing returns and produces a different good as in the last section of Chapter 6. This implies that the two sectors will coexist in the steady state. This feature, together with the presence of increasing returns to scale in the modern sector, has novel implications for the determinants of the steady state.

The employment share of the modern sector in the "mature phase"—in the Kaldorian sense of maturity (see Chapter 6, section 4)—remains constant during the mature phase, given our assumption of constant expenditures shares. Assuming that the high level equilibrium occurs in the mature phase, this is then the employment share of the modern sector in the high level steady state. Two features of the high level equilibrium stand out. First, the steady state is not independent of the scale of the economy. The capital-labor ratio is an increasing function of the size of the labor force in the presence of increasing returns. When extended to allow for population growth, the model implies that the steady state value of the capital-labor ratio—and of labor productivity in the modern sector—will be growing at an endogenous rate given by n $\mu/(1 - a - \mu)$ (see Ros, 2000, ch. 4).[11] With population growth, the steady state is thus characterized by a situation in which profitability is constant, employment in the modern sector grows at the same rate as the overall labor force, and the rate of capital accumulation is higher than Harrod's natural rate (equal to n in the absence of exogenous technical progress) by an amount that depends on the increasing returns parameter. The steady state growth rate of the capital stock is endogenous in the sense that it depends on technology parameters (in particular μ), but not in the sense that it is affected by the savings rate. In this, and unlike recent endogenous growth models, the present model features one of the key properties of the Solow model—the independence of the steady state growth rate from the savings rate.

A second distinguishing feature of the steady state is the presence of the employment share of the modern sector among its determinants. There are two reasons for this. First, the larger the employment share, the higher is, for a given scale, the steady state value of the capital-labor ratio and—through the (external) productivity effects of capital accumulation—the higher the steady state real wage tends to be. Second, a smaller sector S implies a higher productivity of this sector in the steady state given the presence of diminishing returns to labor in this sector. This effect has a positive influence on the real wage and disappears only under constant returns to labor in sector S which implies that productivity is independent of employment. In the present closed economy model, the long-term equilibrium employment share is largely determined by the consumption shares of the two goods, along with saving

---

[11] This feature is akin to Arrow's (1962) model of learning by doing, where the rate of per capita output growth in the steady state increases with the rate of growth of population. This implication has been often considered to be empirically questionable (see for example, Romer, 1986) and this would certainly be the case if it is taken to mean that high productivity growth rates should be observed in countries with a fast growing labor force. It is worth noting, however, that this objection seems to overlook that the implication applies only to the steady state. Moreover, in the present model with two sectors the implication applies to the growth of labor productivity in the modern sector, but not to aggregate output per capita, as discussed below.

rates and technology parameters (affecting distribution between profits and wages). In an open economy, as we shall see in Chapter 9, the employment share will primarily be affected by the pattern of specialization in international trade, as determined by resource endowment and economic policy.

How does the presence of increasing returns affect the steady state income gaps across countries? The presence of increasing returns has the effect of enlarging the steady state income gaps compared to those in the neoclassical model. Intuitively, this is because in the neighborhood of the steady state the productivity and profitability effects of increasing returns make the profit rate diminish less strongly than otherwise, and allow economies with a higher investment share to reach a higher steady state capital-labor ratio than otherwise and thus a higher level of income in the steady state. The practical answer depends on how much returns increase. If the effects of increasing returns are moderate, as suggested by the evidence on scale effects, then the picture may remain largely unaffected.[12] Table 7.1 presents estimates of the steady state income gaps in a Solow model "augmented" by technological externalities.[13] Using the augmented production function, we can adjust the steady state income gaps in the Solow model for the 5 country groups of Chapter 2 (shown in Table 2.1). The steady state values of output per worker in any given group (i) of countries relative to the steady state value in the high-income economies of group 1 can be estimated from: $\ln (y^*_i/y^*_1) = [1 + \mu/a$

Table 7.1 Actual and steady state income gaps

	Averages for country groups				
	1	2	3	4	5
Income as % of group 1 (2008)	100	50.7	22.6	8.6	2.7
Steady state income as % of group 1 (Solow model)	100	94.7	86.9	87.2	78.5
Steady state income as % of group 1 (adjusted for $\mu = 0.2$)	100	90.9	77.9	78.4	65.1
Number of countries	17	17	17	18	18

See Appendix to Chapter 1 for sources and definitions.

[12] On direct evidence on returns to scale showing the existence of moderately increasing returns to scale in a number of developing and developed countries, see Kraay and Raddatz (2007, table 4).

[13] For simplicity, I reformulate the influence of technological externalities to avoid pure scale effects. The production function is then: $Y = (\tilde{K}/L)^\mu K^a (A L)^{1-a}$. The equations of the y^A and y^{A^*} curves are given by: $y^A = k^{Aa + \mu}$ and $y^{A^*} = [s/(n + g_A \sim + \delta)]^{a/1-a} k^{A\mu/a}$. From these equations, we can solve for the steady state value of output per effective worker: $y^{A^*} = [s/(n + g_A + \delta)]^{(a + \mu)/(1-a-\mu)} = [(s/(n + g_A + \delta))^{a/1-a}]^{(1 + \mu/a(1-a-\mu))}$. This expression is very similar to the steady state value of y^A in the Solow model (see eq. 5' in Chapter 2). The difference has to do with the increasing returns parameter whose presence enhances the positive effects of savings rates and the negative effects of labor force growth on the steady state level of income. Indeed, the effect of the increasing returns parameter on the steady state level of income is identical to that of enlarging the capital share in the Solow model.

$(1-a-\mu)]$ ln $(y*_i/y*_1)_s$, where $(y*i/y*1)_s$ is the relative steady state income in the Solow model (see eq. 5' in Chapter 2).

The exercise assumes a value of $\mu = 0.2$ and, for comparative purposes, the table reproduces the steady state income gaps of the Solow model (i.e., the same model with $\mu = 0$). The exercise confirms that the presence of increasing returns has the effect of enlarging the steady state income gaps, but that a moderate dose of increasing returns does not make a dramatic difference.

On the other hand, the investment share will now tend to rise throughout the transition, as it does in the Lewis model. This has the opposite effect of narrowing steady state income gaps, as differences in the steady state investment shares are now likely to be much smaller than actual differences. The implication for the Lewis-Rosenstein Rodan model is that actual differences in income levels should largely be viewed, just as in the Solow model, as the result of differences in the relative position with respect to the steady state.

The transition to the steady state and the profitability trap

The more striking implications of the model concern the characteristics of the transition and the possibility of poverty traps. The more general implication is that the adverse effects on productivity and profitability of low capital-labor ratios will inhibit growth at low-income levels and thus weaken the tendency to convergence of neoclassical growth models. Moreover, if multiple equilibria exist, the profit rate (and the rate of accumulation) in the modern sector is no longer a monotonically decreasing function of the capital-labor ratio. From the profit-wage curve, we have $r = K^{\mu/a} [(1 - a)/w_M]^{(1-a)/a}$. Using the equation of the w curve to eliminate w_M, taking logs and differentiating with respect to ln K, we obtain: d ln r/d ln K $= \mu/a$, when $w_M = 1$, and d ln r/d ln K $= a + \mu - 1$, when $w_M = [(1 - a) L^{-a}] K^{a + \mu}$. That is, during the labor surplus phase the sign of the derivative d ln r/d ln K is positive and the profit rate is an increasing function of the capital stock while during the mature phase, when the non capitalist sector has disappeared, the sign of the derivative d ln r/d ln K is negative and the profit rate is a decreasing function of the capital stock provided that $a + \mu < 1$ (i.e. diminishing returns to capital in the production function of the capitalist sector).

As we did for the Solow model, we can write the transitional component of growth in the modern sector as s $(r - r*)$ where s here is equal to "a s_π". Let us define the rate of convergence as the ratio of this transitional component to the log difference between the steady state and the actual values of the real product wage in the modern sector. It follows then that since the profit rate follows an inverted U pattern, the rate of convergence will be low and increasing at low levels of income and relatively high and decreasing as the economy approaches the steady state.[14]

The model thus predicts, under certain conditions, a pattern of conditional divergence/convergence at low and middle-income levels, with the highest rates of accumulation occurring in the intermediate rather than in the initial stages of the transition (as predicted by the neoclassical model).[15] The key condition is for the profit rate to increase over a range of capital-labor ratios. Since, as the reader may have noticed, this condition is the same as the one for the existence of a low K intersection, and thus for a trap with low profitability, the model also suggests the possibility of divergence between high-income and low-income countries. Moreover, if technical progress is largely specific to the modern capitalist sector, the model suggests that the lowest growth rates are to be found in the poorest countries (further away from the high steady state) with negative growth rates for those countries in the poverty trap.

Allowing for international capital mobility tends to strengthen these properties of the model, as the low profit rates in the poorest countries implies that capital will flow towards the middle-income and high-income economies, while the middle-income economies will tend to receive capital from the high-income economies with lower profit rates. Suppose indeed, as we did for the neoclassical model in Chapter 3, that the rate of capital accumulation is a function of the difference between the current profit rate and a risk-adjusted, international profit rate (r^*): $I/K = \psi\,(r - r^*)$, with $\psi' > 0$ and $\psi\,(0) = 0$. Given the relationship between the profit rate and the level of the capital stock in the presence of increasing returns to scale and elastic labor supply, the rate of capital accumulation will tend to follow the same inverted U pattern of the profit rate. At sufficiently low levels of K, the profit rate will fall below r^*, as a result of the interaction between increasing returns and elastic labor supply, rather than political risk increasing the value of r^*. Unlike the savings trap of Chapter 3, international capital mobility exacerbates, rather than eliminates, the development trap at low-income levels associated to a low rate of return on capital. All this, of course, as already noted earlier, does not imply that political risk, which affects r^*, is unimportant. In fact, opening the economy to capital flows brings in political risk and the factors affecting it into the model, the determination of the high level steady state that the economy reaches and that of the level of the capital stock and income below which there is a poverty trap.

---

[14] Formally, the rate of convergence (Ω) can be written as: $\Omega = a\ s_\pi\ r^*\ (r/r^* - 1)/(\ln w^* - \ln w)$. Substituting from the profit wage curve yields: $\Omega = a\ s_\pi\ r^*\ [(K/K^*)^{\mu/a}\ (w^*/w)^{(1-a)/a} - 1]/(\ln w^* - \ln w)$.

[15] In terms of Figure 7.1, the rate of accumulation is the highest when the gap between the w^* and w curves is the largest.

4. Dynamics of Rural-Urban Disparities under Increasing Returns: A Kuznets-Myrdal Model

I close this chapter with an analysis of the dynamics of income distribution in classical development models. In Chapter 6, we looked at the implications that economic development has on income distribution in the Lewis model and highlighted two features that characterize the surplus labor phase of the transition to the steady state: the increasing share of profits and the unequal-izing effects of technical progress in the capitalist sector as productivity gains accrue to capital rather than labor. These central features, as the Lewis-Rosen-stein Rodan model in this chapter makes clear, are exacerbated by the presence of increasing returns to scale since their interaction with elastic labor supplies strengthens the increase in the share of profits during the transition. In this section, we look at another aspect of the evolution of economic disparities during the process of expansion of the capitalist sector, the evolution of urban-rural disparities that has been the focus of so many regional develop-ment models inspired by Gunnar Myrdal's pioneering contributions to devel-opment economics.

The economy considered is open to international trade and has two sectors, A and M, that face given world prices, p_A and p_M, in the international market. The agricultural sector (A) is labor-intensive and produces under diminishing returns to labor:

$$A = L_A^{1-b} \qquad\qquad b < 1, \qquad\qquad (8)$$

where we have set the fixed endowment of land equal to unity. The manufac-turing sector (M) is capital-intensive and features technological externalities which generate increasing returns to scale:

$$M = (\tilde{K})^{\mu}\, K^a L_M^{1-a} \qquad\qquad a + \mu < 1 \qquad\qquad (9)$$

where $(\tilde{K})^{\mu}$ is the external effect of the average capital stock. The inequality restriction in (9) rules out increasing returns to capital. For simplicity, we leave aside labor force growth. Agricultural workers earn the average product of labor and manufacturing workers earn the marginal product of labor. Thus, labor earnings per worker in the two sectors are:

$$w_A = L_A^{-b} \qquad\qquad (10)$$

$$w_M = (1 - a)K^{a + \mu}L_M^{-a} \qquad\qquad (11)$$

where we have chosen units such that $p_A = p_M = 1$.

The migration rate ($m = MR/LF_A$, where MR is the number of migrants and LF_A is the rural labor force including migrants and agricultural workers) is an increasing function of the urban-rural wage differential. A simple version of such a migration function is:

$$L_A/LF_A = (w_A/w_M)^{\theta} \qquad \theta > 0 \qquad (12)$$

which implies $(1 - m)^{-1/\theta} = \omega$, where $\omega = (w_M/w_A)$.

In the short run, the capital stock is given and there is no labor mobility between the two sectors. The urban labor market clears at a wage determined by the equality between the exogenously given urban labor force and labor demand in industry. The rural wage is determined by the average product of labor at the existing level of agricultural employment, which in turn is equal to the given rural labor force less the migrants.[16] The model gives us solutions for w_A, w_M, and m. From (10) and (11), we have:

$$\omega = (1 - a)K^{a + \mu}LF_A{}^b(1 - m)^b/L_M{}^a \qquad \omega = w_M/w_A \qquad (13)$$

which shows a negative relationship between the urban wage premium and the migration rate. The higher is migration the lower is employment in agriculture and the higher the average product of labor in that sector which reduces the wage differential between industry and agriculture.

From the migration function (12), we have a positive relationship between the urban wage premium and migration. A higher wage premium induces a larger migration rate:

$$\omega = 1/(1 - m)^{1/\theta} \qquad (14)$$

Eqs (13) and (14) determine simultaneously the short-run equilibrium values of the urban-rural wage differential (ω) and the migration rate (m). Figure 7.4 illustrates the short-run solution to the model. The m (ω) curve is the graph of the migration function (eq. 12): it is positively sloped since a higher urban-rural wage differential raises the migration rate. The ω (m) curve shows the market equilibrium value of the ratio of urban to rural wages at each given level of the migration rate (eq. 13). This curve is negatively sloped: a higher migration rate reduces the level of employment engaged in agricultural production and increases the average product of labor in this sector, given the presence of diminishing returns to labor. Thus, the urban wage premium narrows.

The model features unemployment in the short run (the migrants are the unemployed). This unemployment may properly be called migration-induced unemployment. It is worth noting, however, that its nature is rather different from that in the well-known Harris-Todaro model: migration is not zero when the economy is in short-run equilibrium. In fact, if there were no migration

---

[16] Because migration takes time, higher migration reduces the level of employment in agriculture in the current period without increasing the labor supply in the urban industrial sector.

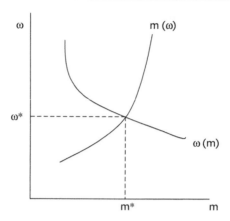

Figure 7.4 Short-run determination of migration and the urban wage premium

there would be no unemployment and no wage differential. The wage premium arises from imperfect labor mobility, rather than being exogenous as in the Harris-Todaro model.[17]

Consider the effects of changes in the capital stock and in the urban-rural composition of the labor force. An increase in the capital stock shifts the ω (m) function upwards (see eq. 13). By raising labor demand in the urban sector, it increases the urban wage premium, as well as the migration rate. This unequalizing effect of capital accumulation—in the sense that it increases urban-rural disparities—is analogous to the effect that a higher level of urban employment has on unemployment in a Harris-Todaro model, in which a higher demand for labor in the urban areas induces a higher rate of migration and unemployment.[18] As shown by eq. (11) the strength of this effect depends here positively on the degree to which returns to scale increase in the industrial sector.

An increase in the urban labor supply relative to the rural labor force shifts the ω (m) curve downwards and reduces migration and the urban wage premium (see eq. 13). Urbanization, understood as an increase in the urban labor force and a reduction in the rural labor force, has an equalizing effect on urban-rural disparities. Ultimately, this is due to the presence of

[17] Unlike previous chapters, the short-run equilibrium does not feature the equalization of labor earnings across sectors ($w_M = w_A$). This is because migration is costly and labor mobility is imperfect. The model also differs from the Harris and Todaro model where the urban rural wage differential is exogenous and the short-run equilibrium features the equalization of the expected urban wage and the rural wage. In this model, the expected urban wage in turn is an inverse function of the urban unemployment rate as the probability of being employed falls as unemployment rises.

[18] This is not due, however, to the increase in urban employment initially raising the probability of being employed, but rather because with imperfect labor mobility, a higher urban demand for labor raises the urban wage, which leads to a higher migration rate.

diminishing returns to labor in both sectors. It is worth noting that this equalizing effect is not present in the standard Harris-Todaro model, since there the urban-rural wage differential is given. The reader may also verify that an exogenous increase in the rural labor force shifts the ω (m) curve upwards and increases the wage premium by reducing the average product of labor in agriculture. Our analysis in what follows will focus on the effects of capital accumulation and the changing composition of the labor force.

Over time, migration proceeds at a rate that increases with the urban wage premium. We assume that the accumulation of capital is increasing in the industrial profit rate. The resulting changes in the composition of the labor force and the capital stock modify the short-run equilibrium values of urban and rural wages. What is the path of urban-rural disparities as a result of these changes? Clearly, the evolution of urban-rural disparities will depend on the strength of each of the two effects described above, the unequalizing effect of capital accumulation and the equalizing effect of urbanization. As we now shall see, the balance of the two effects can be shown to depend on the urban-rural composition of the labor force.

For small values of the urban labor force, the equalizing effects of urbanization associated with the presence of diminishing returns to labor in agriculture are relatively weak. The reason is that with most of the labor force employed in agriculture, the reallocation effects of migration have a small effect on rural wages. As a result, the unequalizing effects of capital accumulation, operating through the increase in the urban wage premium, tend to dominate. This is so whether the initial urban labor force is large or small relative to the capital stock in industry. In the first case, when the urban labor force is large, the positive productivity effects of industrial employment (associated with increasing returns) translate into positive profitability effects on capital accumulation, which reinforce the growth of the urban-rural wage differential. When the urban labor force is small those profitability effects are offset by the relatively large impact of capital accumulation on urban wages. In this case, however, the increase in labor demand pulls the urban wage up to such an extent that despite the negative effect on capital accumulation, the urban wage premium increases.[19] Urbanization and capital accumulation then go hand in hand with a widening of rural-urban disparities. Because these disparities induce increasing migration rates, we have also in this phase a Todaro-type phenomenon of urbanization tending to outpace the rate of industrialization.

---

[19] It is only over an intermediate range of levels of the urban labor force (relative to the capital stock) that the urban wage premium does not increase. In this range, the labor force is sufficiently large to offset the positive profitability effects on capital accumulation but too small for the upward pressure on urban wages to generate an increase in the wage premium.

At higher levels of urbanization, the equalizing effects of migration become stronger and capital accumulation proceeds at a slower pace as the profit rate falls. The mechanisms described operate in reverse, and the equalizing effects of migration more than offset the unequalizing effects of capital accumulation. The urban-rural wage differential then tends to fall as urbanization proceeds.

Formally, suppose that the capital stock changes at a rate (I/K) which is a positive function of the differential between the domestic rate of profit (r) and an international, risk-adjusted profit rate (r*):

$$I/K = \psi(r - r^*) \tag{15}$$

where ψ is a positive parameter. In competitive equilibrium the profit rate is given by:

$$r = aL_M^{1-a}/K^{1-(a + \mu)} \tag{16}$$

Substituting from (16) into (15), we get the dynamic equation for K:

$$I/K = \psi\left(a\ L_M^{1-a}/K^{1-(a + \mu)} - r^*\right) \tag{17}$$

From (17), setting I/K = 0, we obtain a locus of (L_M, K) combinations along which the capital stock is stationary:

$$L_M = [r^*K^{1-(a + \mu)}/a]^{1/(1-a)} \tag{18}$$

Using now (13) and (14) to eliminate ω, we obtain a reduced form equation for the short-run value of the migration rate. Setting m = 0, we obtain a locus of (L_M, K) combinations along which the rural labor force (LF_A), and thus also the urban labor force, are stationary. The equation of this locus is:

$$L_M = [(1 - a)K^{a + \mu}LF_A^b]^{1/a} \tag{19}$$

Figure 7.5 shows the long-run solution of the model in $(\ln L_M, \ln K)$ space. The slope of the $\hat{K} = 0$ locus (or I/K = 0), obtained by taking logs in (18) and differentiating with respect to ln K, is a constant less than unity under the assumption of increasing returns ($\mu > 0$): d ln L_M/d ln K = $[1 - (a + \mu)]/(1 - a)$.

The slope of the locus $\hat{L}_M = 0$ is derived in a similar way from (19): d ln L_M/d ln K = $(a + \mu)/[a + b (L_M/LF_A)]$. The slope is thus larger than unity (and thus larger than the slope of the $\hat{K} = 0$ locus) when L_M is small (for $L_M = 0$, the slope is clearly more than one with $\mu > 0$) and tends to zero at high values of L_M, when LF_A tends to zero.

As shown in Figure 7.5, the model features multiple interior equilibria, one of which is a saddle point at the low K intersection, and the other is a locally stable equilibrium at the high K intersection. The downward sloping saddle path is a critical locus of (L_M, K) combinations below which the economy is in

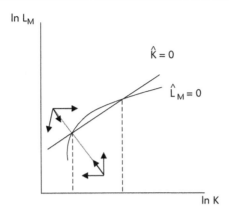

Figure 7.5 Long-run dynamics of urbanization and capital accumulation

a development trap. In this trap, capital accumulation and urbanization cannot get off the ground. Rural-urban migration is insufficient to offset the negative effects of capital accumulation on profitability. The low profit rate then leads to a contraction of the capital stock, which reduces the urban wage premium and migration. The reader may want to verify that the presence of increasing returns to scale ($\mu = 0$) is critical for the existence of the trap.

Above the saddle path, and provided that the economy is either below the $\hat{K} = 0$ schedule or above the $\hat{L}_M = 0$ locus, the path towards the high K equilibrium will feature a negative slope (d ln L_M/d ln K < 0) initially. This negative slope is a sufficient condition for the existence of an initial period in which rural-urban disparities tend to increase. Indeed, solving (13) and (14) for the urban wage premium, taking logs and differentiating with respect to ln K, we obtain:

d lnω/d ln K = {$(a + \mu)/(1 + \theta b)$] − [a + b(L_M/LF$_A$)]/(1 + b)}(d ln L_M/d ln K)

With d ln L_M/d ln K < 0, the process will feature an initial period in which d ln ω/d ln K is positive and therefore the urban wage premium rises with capital accumulation. When the slope of the actual path becomes positive, the increase in urban-rural disparities slows down and eventually is reversed as (L_M/LF$_A$) is sufficiently large to make d ln ω/d ln K negative.

The model generates under certain conditions the inverted-U shape of the Kuznets curve for the evolution of urban-rural disparities. In this framework, the critical assumptions required to generate this pattern are the following. The first is the presence of imperfect labor mobility. Otherwise, the short-run equilibrium would be characterized by a zero migration rate and the urban wage premium would not change, always being such as to generate the zero migration rate.[20] The second assumption refers to the presence of diminishing returns to labor in agriculture. Indeed, suppose that there were increasing returns in agriculture. The effect of employment growth in the modern sector would unambiguously lead to a widening of urban-rural wage differentials, as the contraction of the agricultural sector brings about a fall in its productivity and both capital accumulation and the increase in the urban labor force tend to have unequalizing effects. Interacting with increasing returns in industry, this worsening of urban-rural disparities would further accelerate the growth of the modern sector and the contraction of agriculture. In this Myrdalian cumulative process of uneven regional development, the growth acceleration phase would continue until the agricultural sector disappears. This process would be accompanied by ever worsening disparities among regions. The third assumption, although not strictly necessary, is the presence of increasing returns to scale in industry. Under these conditions, the impact of the reallo-cation towards this sector (i.e. of a faster rate of employment growth in the modern sector than in agriculture) during the early stages of the process is to increase the productivity growth differential in favor of industry. Under con-stant returns to scale in the industrial sector, there would be no tendency for capital accumulation to accelerate in the early stages and thus the tendency for the urban wage premium to increase would be more moderate. This account of the Kuznets curve is very 'Myrdalian' to the extent that the unequalizing increasing returns effects (or "backwash effects" in Myrdal) dominate at low- and middle-income levels, and the equalizing diminishing returns effects (or "spread effects") dominate at higher income levels.[21]

Is there any empirical evidence that favors our interpretation? It has often been argued that the upward sloping section of the Kuznets curve is perfectly escapable or may become a perpetual fate depending on the style of economic development.[22] Our analytical framework has a number of implications con-cerning the effects of growth on inequality that provide some support for this assertion. The implications that the model has for the effects of the style of growth on inequality can be summarized as follows. First, growth based on physical capital accumulation generates more inequality at low- and middle-income levels, by worsening the urban-rural income distribution, and less inequality at high-income levels by improving urban-rural disparities. As argued earlier, the overall impact of capital accumulation on inequality is

---

[20] In this setting, the wage premium may actually tend to fall throughout the process of urbanization to the extent that increasing migration costs raise the supply price of labor to industry.

[21] Our analysis is far, however, from giving a full account of the mechanisms envisaged by Myrdal.

[22] On the role of the pattern of growth and its influence on income distribution and poverty, see among others (Griffin, 1989). For a survey of research on the subject, see Lipton and Ravaillon (1995, section 5).

likely to vary with the level of urbanization: the worsening of the rural-urban distribution dominating at low levels of urbanization and the equalizing effects dominating at higher levels. It therefore follows that, *other things being equal,* the impact of growth on the distribution of income varies with the level of development and changes sign from low to high levels of income.

Second, balanced productivity growth between agriculture and industry generates less inequality than does industry-biased productivity growth. A higher rate of land-augmenting technical progress implies a higher rate of growth of rural wages, at each level of the urban labor force. Actual urban-rural disparities tend to be smaller. The effects on distribution of a higher rate of population growth in the rural areas will instead worsen the urban-rural income distribution as they are symmetrically opposite to those of agricultural technical progress (reducing rather than increasing the average product of labor in agriculture).

Finally, growth based on physical capital accumulation is likely to generate less equality than does skill-based growth. In its simplest version, the accumulation of skills is equivalent in its effects to labor-augmenting technical progress. As such, in a small open economy facing given relative prices, it will tend to benefit the labor-intensive sector. If agriculture is more labor-intensive than industry, this has a negative effect on the urban-rural wage differential and, therefore an equalizing effect. One should add, however, that a number of mechanisms may counteract these equalizing effects, to the extent that educational services are concentrated in the urban areas. Under these conditions, the external effects of skill acquisition are larger in the urban than in the rural sector and rural-urban migration is likely to change adversely the average level of skills in the rural areas. This redistribution of skills will prevent the growth in the skilled labor force from being uniform by augmenting the growth of skills of the urban labor force and slowing it down in the rural sector.[23]

Appendix. A stable low-level equilibrium with a small capitalist sector

In the Lewis-Rosenstein Rodan model, the low level stable equilibrium is a subsistence economy without a capitalist sector. The same applies if we relax the assumption of two sectors producing the same good and allow each sector to produce a different good with constant expenditure shares for the two goods produced (see Ros, 2000). We now

---

[23] This unequalizing influence acts in the same way as if there were increasing returns in agriculture because agricultural productivity tends to decline with the fall in the agricultural labor force. As already noted above in our reference to Myrdal, this redistribution of skills tends to prolong the phase of increasing inequality, as well as to increase the level of inequality at which the "turning point" occurs.

consider a variant of this model that generates a low level stable equilibrium with a capitalist sector. The key change is to abandon the assumption of constant expenditure shares, which follow from a Cobb-Douglas specification of the utility function, and consider instead changing expenditure shares. We do this in a simple way. Suppose that the expenditure share of the subsistence sector good (a) falls as K increases, due to a relatively high income elasticity of demand for the M sector good. At low levels of K, the high value of the expenditure share (a) will moderate the high value of the labor supply elasticity arising from the low employment share of the modern sector (a low L_M/L_S). If, for example, a tends to one when K tends to zero, the labor supply elasticity will be zero just as in the mature phase at high levels of capital stock. The slope of the w curve will thus be larger than the slope of the w* locus (provided returns to capital are non-increasing). At intermediate levels of K, the lower value of a tends to increase the labor supply elasticity. The combination of a labor surplus with an income elastic demand for M goods makes the w curve relatively flat. It is then possible that, over a range of K values, the w curve becomes flatter than the w* line, before becoming steeper again at high values of K. The w curve will thus have the shape of an inverted S as in Figure 7.A.1.[24]

The model generates a low level stable equilibrium at strictly positive values of K. What gives local stability to the low level intersection is the relatively inelastic labor supply, which exists when K is small. This low labor supply elasticity is due to the small expenditure share of M goods, which implies that the additional income generated by an expansion of the capital stock is mostly spent on S goods. This turns the terms of trade against the M sector, thus raising the product wage in this sector and preventing a self-sustained expansion of the capital stock.

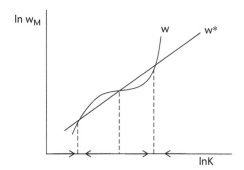

Figure 7.A.1 A low-level equilibrium with a capitalist sector

[24] The following formulation with variable expenditure shares and efficiency wages generates a shape similar to that in Figure 7.A.1. Suppose $(1-a)/a = z\, w_M{}^{\eta}$. Assuming for simplicity $b = 0$ (constant returns to labor in the S sector), the elasticity of labor supply becomes: $e = (\eta + \Delta\, (L_M/L_S)^{\partial})/(1 + L_M/L_S)$, where: $\partial = \eta/[(1-a)/a) - \eta]$, $\Delta = [w/(1-d)]^{\partial}/a\ [(1-s_{\pi}\, a)/(1-a)]^{\partial}$, and d is a parameter of the effort function (see Chapter 6). When $a = 1$, ∂ is negative and e falls as L_M increases. The slope of the w curve increases with L_M. When $(1-a)/a > \eta$, ∂ is positive and e increases over a range with L_M. The slope of the w curve falls as L_M increases. Eventually as a tends to zero, ∂ tends to zero, and e falls again as L_M increases. The slope of the w curve then increases with L_M. Two low-level equilibria with a positive capital stock (one stable and one unstable) can arise from this shape of the w curve.

8

Internal Economies, Imperfect Competition, and Pecuniary Externalities

The source of aggregate increasing returns to scale, as mentioned in Chapter 7, may be external or internal to the firm. When internal, the firm's technology is itself subject to increasing returns to scale as a result of fixed costs, area/volume relationships and technical discontinuities. The presence of these plant-level economies of scale was seen as characteristic of mass production methods in early development theory writing. Rosenstein-Rodan's (1943) dramatizes them with the example of the shoe factory which to operate profitably with modern technologies would have to employ no less than 20,000 workers. In Nurkse (1953, ch. 1) relying on Young (1928), the relative convenience of the hammer and stone technologies for Robinson Crusoe depends on the number of nails to be driven. Economies of scale due to indivisibilities and technical discontinuities are also characteristic of the provision of infrastructure (or "social overhead capital") which "require a minimum high quantum of investment which would serve, say, fifty factories but would cost far too much for one" (Rosenstein-Rodan, 1984, p. 208).

When the source of increasing returns is a property of the individual firm's production function, externalities that are not of a technological nature can also arise. These are pecuniary externalities, in which interdependence among producers takes place through the market mechanism rather than directly as in the case of technological externalities. As Scitovsky (1954, p. 300) stated it, all that is necessary for these external effects to take place is that "the profits of one producer are affected by the actions of other producers". Such external effects arise from the expansion of one firm which, operating under economies of scale, reduces the production costs for other producers (through the reduction of its own costs), or from the expansion of other producers enlarging the size of the market for the individual firms and thus reducing its production costs. As a result, and even without technological externalities, additional returns would accrue to a firm, not only with its own expansion, but also with the growth of an industry and the whole economy. Fleming (1955, p. 283) further distinguished "horizontal" from "vertical" pecuniary externalities, depending on whether interdependence takes place "horizontally" through the interrelated markets of final goods industries, or "vertically" by industries interacting as suppliers and customers.

In this chapter we turn to economies in which aggregate increasing returns originate in economies of scale at the firm level and where pecuniary externalities can arise. Combined with elastic factor supplies, economies of scale lead to pecuniary externalities and can generate multiple equilibria and the need for a "big push". In the two models to be examined, the presence of internal economies of scale forces us to abandon the assumption of perfect competition. In the first model, pecuniary externalities involve demand spillovers across final goods industries, a case of "horizontal" external economies in Fleming's terminology. In the second model, external effects involve "vertical" external economies in the spirit of Hirschman's (1958) "forward and backward linkages". The chapter also assesses empirically the role of increasing returns and elastic labor supplies in the process of capital accumulation by looking at the evidence on returns to scale, the pattern of growth rates at low, middle and high income levels, and poverty traps.

1. The Big Push Argument Based on Horizontal Pecuniary Externalities

Murphy, Shleifer, and Vishny (1989) formalized Rosenstein-Rodan's idea of the need for a big push to overcome the coordination problems arising from the existence of multiple equilibria. In this model, economies of scale arise in the production of final consumer goods and market structure is such that a single firm in each sector has access to the increasing returns technology.

Consider a multisectoral economy producing n final goods, each of which has an equal and constant share $(1/n)$ in final expenditure. There are two techniques in the production of each good: a traditional technique with constant returns to scale (cottage production) and a modern technique with increasing returns to scale (mass production). The modern technique dominates the traditional technique at high levels of output, but is less productive at low levels. Letting S and M be the output levels produced with each technique in any given sector, technology is thus described by:

$$S = L_S \qquad (1)$$

$$M = k(L_M - F) \qquad k > 1 \qquad (2)$$

with M > S when $L_M = L_S = L/n$, L being the total labor force. We choose units so that the CRS technique converts one unit of labor into one unit of output. F is a fixed labor input required to start mass production. With F > 0, the modern technique displays increasing returns to scale. Since S and M refer to the same good in each sector, L_S provides a perfectly elastic supply of labor for the production of M.

When it is in existence, atomistic producers operating under perfect competition use the traditional technique. In contrast, a single firm in each sector has access to the modern technique. This firm will charge the same price that traditional producers would, even when it becomes a monopolist. Indeed, the firm would lose all its sales if it charges more and finds it unprofitable to charge less since it faces a demand curve with a unit elasticity (given the constant share of each good in final expenditure). The modern firm has to pay a factory wage premium (w − 1), where w is the wage paid by the modern firm and the traditional wage is set equal to one.

Let Y be aggregate income (measured in traditional wage units). The monopolist profit in any given sector is equal to sales (Y/n) minus total costs, w L_M. Since the price is one (and thus M = Y/n), using (2) the monopolist profit (π) can be written as:

$$\pi = a\,(Y/n) - wF \qquad a = (1 - w/k) \qquad (3)$$

where 1 is the price he charges and w/k is his unit variable cost. It is worth noting that the difference between price and variable cost, a = (1 − w/k), must be positive for the factory to break even, whatever the level of income. This implies:

$$w < k \qquad (4)$$

i.e., the wage premium must not be so high as to offset the advantages of mass production. Still, even with (4) fulfilled, the monopolist will incur the fixed costs wF only if he expects sales (Y/n) to be high enough for the investment in mass production to be profitable.

The monopolist expected sales are a function of the fraction (η) of sectors in the economy that industrialize. Indeed, aggregate income can be expressed as the sum of income in the traditional sectors, $(1 - \eta)$ L, and wages and profits in the modern sectors, η (w L + n π). Spending per sector is then: $Y/n = \eta\,\pi + [1 + \eta$ (w−1)] L/n. Substituting into (3) and solving for π as a function of η yields:

$$\pi(\eta) = \{a[1 + \eta(w - 1)]L/n - w\,F\}/(1 - a\eta) \qquad (5)$$

What happens to profits as the fraction of sectors that industrialize increases? Differentiating (5) we can solve for the slope of the profit function:

$$d\pi/d\eta = a[(L/n)(w - 1) + \pi(\eta)]/(1 - a\eta)$$

which, as can be verified, is positive provided that condition (4) is fulfilled and the modern technique dominates the traditional technique at high levels of output.

Three configurations are then possible: a) π (0) > 0, in which case the expected profits of a monopolist investing in isolation are positive and no traditional economy equilibrium will exist; b) π (1) < 0, in which case no industrialization equilibrium will exist since profits are negative even when all firms in all sectors adopt the modern technique; c) π (0) < 0 and π (1) > 0, which implies that whether the modern technique is profitable or not depends on the fraction of sectors in the economy adopting the modern technique. This is the case shown in Figure 8.1. Then, if the fraction η of sectors that industrialize increases when profits are positive and falls when they are negative, there will be multiple equilibria at η = 0 and η = 1. A traditional economy (η = 0) with negative expected profits and an industrialization equilibrium (η = 1) with positive profits are self-sustaining and both consistent with the same parameter values.

As is easily verified: π (0) = aL/n − wF and π (1) = k (L/n − F) − wL/n. The conditions required for the existence of multiple equilibria, π (0) < 0 and π (1) > 0, thus imply:

$$F > a(L/n)/w \tag{6}$$

$$F < a(L/n) \tag{7}$$

Figure 8.2 presents a diagram by Krugman (1992) that will be helpful in analyzing the different configurations. The S and M lines in the diagram show

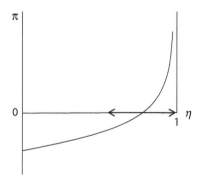

Figure 8.1 Profit expectations and multiple equilibria

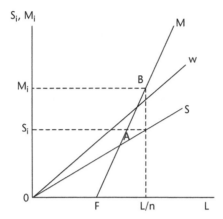

Figure 8.2 The big push model of Murphy et al. (1989)

the value of output (with a price equal to one) as a function of labor input, for each technique. These are simply the graphs of eqs (1) and (2), with (1) coinciding with the 45-degree line due to the choice of units. As drawn, the condition in (2) is met: M > S when the labor force is fully employed in mass production in each sector and labor input is L/n. The ray 0w shows total wage costs as a function of labor input when employing the modern technique. Its slope is equal to w since the traditional wage is set equal to one. The slope of the 0w ray (w) is drawn as less than the slope of the M line (k), and thus condition (4) is met.

Consider Rodan's shoe factory. An individual shoe producer adopting the modern technique will be able to sell a level of output equal to S_i by displacing previous sales by traditional producers (with a large number of goods we can ignore the increase in the demand for shoes arising from the higher wages paid to the workers employed in the shoe factory). Point A in the diagram, on the M line at the level of output Si, corresponds to the level of employment in a modern sector (the shoe factory) when it sells as much as the traditional producers would when producing at full employment. Point B, on the M line at the level of employment L/n, corresponds to production in the modern sector when it operates at full employment.

Given traditional production elsewhere (i.e., in the production of textiles, food processing, etc.), the adoption of the modern technique in the production of shoes will be profitable if point A is above the 0w ray. By merely replacing traditional producers, the shoe factory will find a large enough market to be profitable. Sales are higher than wage costs when the firm invests in isolation and the same applies to the adoption of mass production methods in other sectors. The use of modern techniques in those sectors will increase the demand for shoes, as a result of the higher wages paid and the profits generated, making it profitable for the shoe factory to increase its output to point M_i and employment to L/n (i.e., up to point B). Only an industrialization equilibrium exists with output equal to M_i in each sector. Condition (7) is met; however, condition (6) is not. This is because, given the size of the market (a function of L/n), F and w are so low that (6) is not fulfilled.

Suppose that F is so large that, not only point A, but also point B on the M line at the level of output M_i, is below the 0w ray. The modern technique is more productive than the traditional, in the sense that at high levels of output (with labor input equal to L/n) M is larger than S. Yet, given the wage premium, the potential market is not large enough to take advantage of a simultaneous application of mass production methods, let alone of the adoption of the modern technique in isolation. Condition (6) is fulfilled, but condition (7) is not. There is only a low-income equilibrium based on traditional techniques.

Between these two extremes there is a range of intermediate values of F for which both conditions are fulfilled and two equilibria exist. This is the case shown in the diagram with point B above the 0w ray and point A below. In isolation, the shoe factory is unprofitable but a simultaneous adoption of mass production methods would make a level of output at Mi profitable for all modern firms. Given F and w, the potential size of the market is large enough to make a simultaneous application of mass production methods profitable, yet insufficient to make any individual modern firm viable in isolation. Multiple equilibria exist and without a coordinated "big push" the economy may remain stuck in a traditional economy equilibrium.

There are a number of interesting differences between the present model and the one in section 1 of Chapter 7. First, the multisectoral nature of the economy is essential to generate the type of external effects that are behind the coordination problem. If a single good was produced with internal economies of scale, a need for a "big push" cannot arise. Coordination problems will only arise when capital is used in production and there are technological externalities. Thus, in an economy with a single modern firm and no external effects, the coordination problem does not exist. There would be a unique equilibrium whose nature depends on whether M is larger or smaller than S when the labor force is fully employed.

Market size also matters in a different way. In Chapter 7, cumulative output proxied by the overall capital stock matters because it makes modern technology more productive. The external effects are in the nature of technological spillovers. Here, market size matters because it makes modern techniques more profitable. It is in this sense that externalities are pecuniary. Output levels elsewhere have no technological spillovers on the shoe factory (yielding, for example, a better trained labor force). They have demand spillovers that make the same technology more profitable.

The presence of a wage premium is now essential for the multiplicity of equilibria, unlike in the model with technological externalities. This is partly due to the static nature of the model. Another reason is that pecuniary externalities are not sufficient by themselves to generate multiple equilibria. Without a wage premium, there would still be external effects but these will only operate through profits, rather than through the higher wages paid by modern firms. A positive externality would only arise if profits from the individual adoption of the modern technique are positive. Thus, if the adoption of mass production methods is unprofitable in a single sector in isolation, this will also be the case when a simultaneous adoption of modern techniques takes place, and vice versa. This can readily be seen from Figure 8.2. If w = 1, the 0w ray becomes the S line and there is no configuration in which points A and B can be on two different sides of the 0w ray. Thus, there is no conflict between individually rational behavior and collectively rational behavior. The existence of a high level equilibrium is sufficient to exclude the possibility of a low-level equilibrium because individual incentives as mediated by the market are sufficient to ensure full industrialization.[1]

2. Vertical Externalities: A Rosenstein-Rodan/Hirschman Model

We now consider an economy in which pecuniary externalities arise from the presence of increasing returns in the production of intermediate goods. The specification of technology and market structure in the sector producing intermediate goods follows Skott and Ros (1997), and features a given number of producers of such inputs operating under monopolistic competition. Multiple long-run equilibria can arise as a result of dynamic pecuniary externalities.[2] Because we focus on linkage effects between intermediate and final goods, rather than on demand spillovers across final goods sectors, we simplify and assume that only one final good is produced.[3]

Two sectors compete in the market for the final good. Traditional producers, as before, turn one unit of labor into one unit of output: $S = L_S$. Modern technology is capital intensive. Modern firms, also operating under atomistic competition and constant returns to scale, use capital (K) and intermediate goods (I) to produce output M:

---

[1] Formally, as can readily be checked, when w = 1 there are no values of F and L for which conditions (6) and (7) can be simultaneously fulfilled.

[2] Related models are the "infrastructure model" in Murphy, Shleifer, and Vishny (1989), as well as the models in Rodrik (1994) and Rodriguez-Clare (1996) with multiple equilibria in open economies (see Chapter 14).

[3] Qualitative results are unchanged if the S good is a good substitute for the M good or if there is surplus labor in sector S associated to efficiency wages in sector M.

$$M = K^a I^{1-a} \qquad\qquad 0 < a < 1, \qquad (8)$$

where I represents the input of a set of intermediate goods,

$$I = \left[\sum (1/n) I_i^\sigma \right]^{1/\sigma} \qquad\qquad 0 < \sigma < 1,$$

n being the number of intermediate goods, assumed to be given.[4] Production of these intermediate goods is subject to internal increasing returns:

$$I_i = L_i^{1+\mu} \qquad\qquad \mu > 0 \qquad (9)$$

where L_i is labor input. The I_i goods may represent a set of producer services (such as banking and insurance) and manufactured inputs, as in Rodriguez-Clare (1996), or a set of infrastructural goods (power, transport, communications, training facilities), as in Skott and Ros (1997).[5] The key difference between traditional and modern sectors is that while sector M has a "backward linkage" a la Hirschman with sector I, there are no linkages in the case of sector S.

Firms maximize profits taking input prices as parametrically given. Producers in sectors S and M also face given output prices. In sector M, the capital stock is predetermined in the short run and since producers in this sector are atomistic, a firm's future demand and supply conditions will be independent of its own short-run decisions. Hence, there are no intertemporal complications. As shown in Skott and Ros (1997), the demand function for I goods is given by:

$$I = (1 - a)^{1/a} (p_I/p_M)^{-1/a} K \qquad (10)$$

where p_I (= n p_i under symmetry) is the (minimum) cost of a bundle of intermediate goods yielding I = 1.

In sector I, producers operate under conditions of monopolistic competition and face downward sloping demand curves:

$$I_i^d = D p_i^{-\phi} \qquad\qquad \phi > 1, \qquad (11)$$

where D is a position parameter and ϕ is the price elasticity of demand facing individual producers. This elasticity is a function of σ, a, and n, and, for a large

[4] Qualitatively similar results can be derived from a Dixit-Stiglitz-Ethier type specification (used by Rodriguez-Clare, 1996).

[5] The properties of the model are also similar to those in Berthelemy and Varoudakis (1996) except for the assumption in their model of an AK technology (see Chapter 2). In Berthelemy and Varoudakis the equivalent of our I-sector is a banking system that intermediates savings. Because it operates under economies of scale, the size of this sector is critical to the productivity of the whole economy.

n, is given approximately by $1/(1-\sigma)$.[6] The inequality in (11) follows from the parameter restrictions $0 < a < 1$ and $0 < \sigma < 1$.

With a single intermediate good (n = 1), the monopoly producer of this good would clearly face an intertemporal optimization problem: the current price p_I would affect the profitability of sector M which in turn could influence capital accumulation in sector M and thereby future demand for the I-good. With multiple I-goods this intertemporal link is weakened and the decisions of an individual producer have only minor effects on the aggregate output of I and profitability in sector M. To simplify, we assume that the number of non-tradable inputs is large enough that intertemporal aspects can be ignored. From the conjectured demand function (eq. 11) and the production function (eq. 9), the optimal pricing decision for the I_i-producer is a markup over marginal cost:

$$p_i = (1 + z)\,\omega \tag{12}$$

where: $1 + z = [\emptyset/(\emptyset-1)]$ $\qquad \omega = w/(1 + \mu)\,I_i^{\mu/(1 + \mu)}$

w is the wage rate, ω is the marginal cost of labor, and z is the mark-up over marginal cost. Eqs (11) and (12), by setting $I_i = I^d{}_i$, can be solved simultaneously for p_i and I_i. Note that, unlike what happens when economies of scale arise only from the presence of fixed costs (as in the previous model), the marginal cost is not constant but falls with the scale of output.

Short-run equilibrium

To derive a short-run equilibrium, eqs (11) and (12) are combined with the input demand function in sector M (eq. 10). Assuming symmetry ($p_i = p_j$ and $I_i = I$), these three equations can be solved for I, p_I and D. We then get:

$$I = [G(1/n)(p_M/w)K^a]^{(1+\mu)/f} \tag{13}$$

where: $\qquad G = (1-a)\,(1 + \mu)\,(\emptyset - 1)/\emptyset \qquad f = a - \mu\,(1-a) > 0$

Eq. (13) describes a symmetric, short-run equilibrium solution for I. Given a conjectured value of the multiplicative constant D, the first-order conditions for profit maximization determine (p_i, I_i) as a function of D. The actual value of D depends on the pricing decisions of the firm's rivals. As shown in Skott and Ros (1997), stability requires the (empirically plausible) condition: $f > 0$.[7] It is worth noting that in this symmetric equilibrium each producer would be

---

[6] As shown in Skott and Ros (1997), the price elasticity is given by: $-\partial \ln I_i/\partial \ln p_i = 1/(1 - \sigma) - (a + \sigma - 1)/n(1-\sigma)a$

[7] The condition is realistic as it implies that economies of scale are not dramatically large.

willing to sell more goods, at the equilibrium price, if demand were forthcoming.

Consider now the labor market. Let the total work force be L. In equilibrium with $I_i = I_j$, and assuming uniform wages and absence of unemployment, we have:

$$L = L_S + L_I$$

$$\text{and} \quad L_I = \sum L_i = \sum I_i^{1/(1+\mu)} = n \, I^{1/(1+\mu)} \tag{14}$$

or, substituting from (13):

$$L_I = L_I \, (w/p_M, K) \tag{15}$$

Since $S = L_S$ and (given that there is one final good) $p_S = p_M$, $w \geq p_M$ with equality if $L_S > 0$. That is, the supply of labor to the I-sector is perfectly elastic at $w = p_M$ for $L_I < L$.

The labor demand from sector I is determined by (15). Combining this equation with the elastic labor supply at $w = p_M$ for $L_I < L$, the short-run equilibrium in the labor market implies that:

$$w = p_M \text{ and } L_I = L_I(1, K) \qquad \text{if } L_I(1, K) < L \tag{16}$$

And if $L_I (1, K) > L$, then labor market equilibrium implies $L_I = L$ and w/p_M is given by the solution to $L_I (w/p_M, K) = L$. This is:

$$w/p_M = G(1/n)^{1-f} K^a / L^f \tag{17}$$

With L_I determined, we also have the solutions for $S = L - L_I$ and $M = K^a I^{(1-a)}$. Eqs (16) and (17) define the schedule of short-run equilibria. This is shown, in log space, in Figures 8.3 (a) and 8.3 (b). As in the Lewis model, the schedule is a straight line at $w/p_M = 1$, up to the value K, at the turning point between the labor surplus phase and the mature economy, for which $L_I (1, K) = L$, and a line with positive slope equal to a, for $K > K$.

Capital accumulation and long-run equilibria

Over time, the capital stock changes. We assume a simple formulation in which investment in sector M is financed exclusively out of M sector profits.[8] The rate of capital accumulation is then equal to: $s_\pi \, r - \delta$, where s_π is the share of profits that is invested. The rate of profit is given by: $r = (p_M M - \sum p_i I_i)/p_M$

---

[8] Profits in the I-sector are thus consumed. This simplifying assumption is unnecessary in an open economy with capital mobility.

(a) $\ln (w/p_M)$

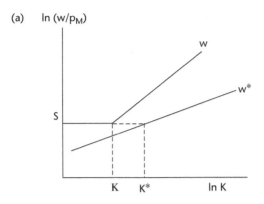

(b) $\ln (w/p_M)$

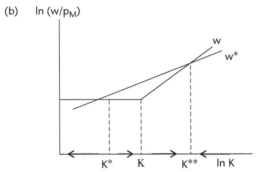

Figure 8.3 A Rodan-Hirschman model

$K = a \, (I/K)^{1-a}$ or, using the value of I as determined in short-run equilibrium (eq. 13):

$$r = a \, K^{\mu(1-a)/f}[(1/n) \, G/(w/p_M)]^{(1-f)/f} \tag{18}$$

Given the wage in terms of M goods, the profit rate increases with the capital stock. Indeed, an increase in the capital stock raises the demand for intermediate goods and reduces marginal costs in the I-sector. The fall in the relative price (p_I/p_M) of intermediate goods (for a given value of w/p_M) raises profits in sector M. It is worth noting the similarity between eq. (18) and the profit rate function in section 1 of Chapter 7. Even though there are no technological externalities, the profit rate depends positively on the capital stock, given the wage in terms of M goods. This is due to the presence of economies of scale in the I-sector and the fact that the extent to which they are exploited depends on the size of the capital stock in sector M.

The steady state condition $s_\pi r = \delta$ defines the equation of the w* schedule. Substituting from eq. (18) into this condition and solving for w/p_M yields:

$$(w/p_M)^* = (a\, s_\pi/\delta)^{f/(1-f)}(G/n)K^{\mu/1+\mu} \qquad (19)$$

which in $(\ln w/p_M, \ln K)$ space defines a line with a positive slope equal to $\mu/(1 + \mu)$. The condition $f > 0$ in (13) ensures that $a > \mu/(1 + \mu)$, i.e., the w schedule, for values of K above K, is steeper than the w* line. We then have either two intersections or no intersections between the two loci.

Figure 8.3 (a) shows the case in which the two schedules do not intersect. Here $K < K^*$, where K^* is the solution for (19) when $w = p_M$. As we have seen in Chapter 7, the subsistence wage in this case is higher than the wage required to generate a positive rate of capital accumulation even when the whole labor force is employed in the modern sector. This case implies that the size of the labor force is so small that industrialization will never be worthwhile, given the specification of the production possibilities. There is then a unique and stable long-run equilibrium with $K = 0$, $L_S = L$, $L_I = 0$.

In Figure 8.3 (b), $K > K^*$. The two loci intersect with the slope of the w schedule smaller than the slope of the w* line at the low K intersection (at K*), and vice versa for the high K intersection (at K**). It follows that there are two long-run equilibria with strictly positive values of the capital stock as well as an equilibrium with $K = 0$ and $I = 0$. It is readily seen that the equilibrium at K* is unstable, just as the equilibrium at K_U in the Lewis-Rosenstein-Rodan model of Chapter 7 (sections 1 and 2). Of the two equilibria, the low level equilibrium without an M-sector has an income per worker equal to p_M and zero profits, while the equilibrium at K** necessarily features $w > p_M$ and a positive profit rate. Thus, the real wage and the level of per capita income are unambiguously higher in the industrialized economy.

The similarity of these results to those of the model with technological externalities in Chapter 7 should not be surprising. In the economy considered, sector S provides an elastic labor supply; - or in fact, a perfectly elastic labor supply since, as in the Lewis model, this sector produces the same final good as the modern sector. Sectors M and I together use a capital-intensive technology which displays increasing returns to scale. Indeed, combining (8) and (14), the production function of this "integrated M/I sector" is given by: $M = A\, K^a\, L_I^{1-a}$ where $A = (1/n)^{(1-a)(1 + \mu)} L_I^{\mu(1-a)}$, which shows that, provided that $\mu > 0$, the productivity of this integrated sector depends on its size (the level of employment L_I).

However, unlike the model in Chapter 7, there are no technological externalities here. Multiple equilibria are associated with pecuniary externalities (even though these are not a sufficient condition, as case (a) illustrates). The presence of increasing returns to scale in the intermediate goods sector implies that production decisions in sector I, and investment decisions in sector M, have important external effects. An increase in the output of I_i affects adversely the current demand for other intermediate inputs, but reduces the price index p_I and raises both the combined input I and the profit rate in sector M. Apart from these static effects, there is a dynamic externality: higher profits in sector M lead to increased accumulation and thus to an increase in the future demand for all I-goods. On the investment side, atomistic producers of good M consider all prices given and fail to take into account the external effects of a higher capital stock on increased future demand for I-goods and a lower future price p_I.

As a result of these dynamic pecuniary externalities, an initial capital stock below the critical level (K*) leads to a cumulative contraction when all firms follow behavior that is individually rational. Because the initial capital stock is small, the demand for I-goods is low and I-goods are produced at a high cost. As a result, profitability in sector M is so low that the capital stock contracts. This further increases production costs in the I-sector and reduces profitability in sector M, moving the economy towards the low level equilibrium where sectors M and I are absent. This low level equilibrium is a trap. Rosenstein-Rodan provides an example of the coordination problem involved:

> Low wages should have been a sufficient incentive to create a textile industry in India in the post-Napoleonic era and not in Lancashire, England. Indian wages were 50 or 60 percent lower than the low wages in England...Further analysis revealed, however, that in order to build a factory one would have to build a bridge or finish a road or a railway line or later an electric power station. Each of these elements in the so-called social overhead capital requires a minimum high quantum of investment which could serve, say, fifty factories but would cost far too much for one. (Rosenstein-Rodan, 1984, p. 208)

In other words, the lack of incentives to create a textile industry in India was due to the absence of an I-sector which made textile production unprofitable despite the low existing wages. At the same time, there was no incentive for the production of I-goods given the high costs of production in the absence of demand from textile factories. This is why a coordinated effort—a big push aimed at increasing the rate of accumulation above the individually rational level, and/or at raising the supply of I-goods—becomes necessary to take the capital stock above that critical level (K*, in Figure 8.3b), at which point individual incentives as mediated by the market become sufficient to ensure industrialization.

An important difference with the Lewis-Rosenstein-Rodan model of Chapter 7 is the role of imperfect competition in sector I in the existence of equilibrium and the hold of the development trap. Indeed, the value of the capital stock at the unstable equilibrium (K*) depends on the position of the w* schedule which in turn is affected by the price elasticity of demand for I-goods (see eq. 19 and the expression for G in eq. 13). A lower elasticity reduces G and shifts the w* schedule downwards. The hold of the trap increases as K* becomes larger. Intuitively, a less competitive sector I implies higher mark-ups over marginal costs and thus a higher relative price (p_I/p_M) of intermediate inputs, which reduces the profit rate in sector M. A higher capital stock—which tends to reduce (p_I/p_M) on account of the cost reductions due to the higher demand and output of I-goods—is then required to generate the profit rate needed for a positive rate of capital accumulation.

3. Empirical Evidence on Increasing Returns and Poverty Traps

As argued in Chapters 2 to 4, the neoclassical model with its extensions (technology gaps, human capital, international capital mobility and political risk) fails to provide a satisfactory explanation of *both* differences in income levels and growth rates. The theory appears to face the following dilemma. When it views income gaps as differences in the relative position with respect to the steady state, the model, as in the simple Solow-Swan version, grossly overstates the growth rates of poor countries. This is so especially under the assumption of international capital mobility which reinforces the strong convergence properties of the model. When it interprets income differences as a result of steady state gaps, as in the Solow model augmented with human capital (Mankiw, Romer, and Weil, 1992) or in technology gap interpretations, the model fits somewhat better the observed differences in growth rates. But then, it overstates the actual differences across countries in the returns to skilled labor or relies on unreasonable differences in access to technology.

Other evidence points also to the empirical flaws of the neoclassical model. The key feature of the model—the negative relationship, conditional on other determinants, between initial output per worker and subsequent growth—is simply not statistically robust. As already noted, Levine and Renelt (1992) find that the relationship is absent in the period since the mid-1970s or when OECD countries are excluded from the sample. Estimates of quadratic growth functions presented in this chapter point in the same direction: there is no convergence, either absolute or conditional, at low-income levels.

Different problems apply to the basic endogenous growth models reviewed so far. Without further revisions and extensions, new growth theory does not pose a serious empirical challenge to the augmented neoclassical models. The empirical assessment of the theory—with its implications of excessive divergence and reliance on human-capital driven growth—prove to be rather disappointing, as discussed in Chapter 2. The theory appears to face a dilemma, which, although of a very different nature, seems no less serious than that of the neoclassical theory. This is the knife-edge problem that has been pointed out by Solow (1994). If returns to capital are increasing, the technology assumed generates infinite output in finite time. If returns to scale increase but returns to capital are diminishing, the qualitative implications are not different from those of the Solow-Swan model. This leaves the AK model as the only viable and rather fragile alternative to the neoclassical model, as it relies on there being exactly constant returns to capital.

The vision of the development process that one finds in the classical literature of development economics is consistent with stylized facts of cross-country growth performance that do not fit well with the neoclassical and the endogenous growth models reviewed so far. As we shall see in this section, the models reviewed in this and the previous chapter accommodate in particular three striking features of post-war development trends. First, the highest growth rates are found among developing countries and a number of industrial countries that were initially relatively less developed. Second, these high rates of growth are associated in many cases to a rapid process of industrialization. Third, the lowest growth rates are typically found among the low-income countries suggesting that these countries are caught in a poverty trap.

Growth acceleration at medium income levels

The conclusions reached in section 3 regarding the characteristics of the transition to the steady state and the fact that differences across countries should be viewed, as in the Solow model, as differences in the position with respect to the steady state (rather than steady state differences) imply that the classical development model not only features a pattern of *conditional* divergence followed by conditional convergence but also a pattern of *absolute* divergence/convergence. These implications find substantial empirical support in both cross-section estimates and long time series. The pattern of growth in a cross-section of countries features a hump shape with growth acceleration at middle-income levels which, as we shall see, stands the inclusion in growth regressions of other variables such as investment rate, education and political variables. Turning to the time series, the process of growth in the world economy over the last century has been characterized by absolute divergence in per capita incomes. However, over the last fifty years the dispersion of per capita incomes has considerably narrowed within the club of today's rich economies, which largely overlaps with the early industrializers. In the last five or six decades, some late industrializers, the successful East Asian economies and, for a while, a few countries in Latin America—joined the convergence club and moved rapidly towards middle- and high-income levels. A number of them, Hong Kong, Singapore, Taiwan and South Korea, had reached, by the mid 1990s, income per capita levels close to the average of OECD economies. The rest of developing countries, mostly in sub-Saharan Africa and South Asia, have barely started a process of modern economic growth and continue to lag behind the middle- and high-income economies. These patterns lend support to the transitional dynamics envisaged by development models.

The evidence from growth regressions suggests that for low-income countries the relationship between the initial level of income and subsequent growth is positive, and income levels diverge. Then, beyond a certain level of per capita income the relationship becomes negative implying convergence of income levels, even though incomes continue to rise at faster rates than in the poorest countries. This pattern of divergence/convergence is captured by a quadratic equation in which income growth rates are related to the level of initial income and the square of initial income: $g_y = a_o + a_1 y_o + a_2 y_o^2$. Provided that a_2 is negative (the condition for a maximum) and a_1 is positive (so that the maximum rate is positive), the growth rate reaches a maximum at a positive income level. If the inequalities hold, the equation also implies a threshold level of convergence, the income level at which the growth rate is equal to that in the highest income countries.

Table 8.1 summarizes a number of estimates of such quadratic equations for different periods and data sets, and also includes linear regressions of growth rates on initial income for sub-samples of high and low-income countries. The results generally support the pattern of divergence/convergence.[9] The signs of the coefficients are systematically favorable to the hypothesis and suggest that growth rates tend to reach a maximum in the intermediate income range. The linear regressions for lower income groups, except in Sarkar's pooled regressions, present coefficients which, although positive and thus indicating divergence, usually have higher standard errors than the negative coefficients for the upper income groups. This suggests that the tendency to divergence at low-income levels is more erratic than the tendency to convergence among the upper income countries. But since the positive coefficients are larger in absolute value than the negative coefficients (in all cases), this erratic pattern of divergence should not be taken as evidence for a weaker tendency for incomes to diverge. What the evidence seems to suggest is a clear lack of convergence at low and middle-income levels together with a convergence threshold that varies widely across countries within an ample income range.

The Lewis-Rosenstein-Rodan model of section 1 in Chapter 7 implies a pattern of divergence/convergence and, thus, the evidence of quadratic equations provides some support for the model. The evidence, however, is only

---

[9] Evidence in Baumol, Blackman, and Wolff (1989), Dollar (1992) and Easterly (1994), as well as that presented in Chapter 1, tends to conform to the same pattern.

Table 8.1 Growth and initial income. Regression results

Authors and period	Dependent variable	C	yo	yo^2	R2	N	Data set
Baumol and Wolff (1988) 1950–1980	ln (yt/yo) yt/yo	0.586 (4.2) 3.3 (7.7) 2.1 (5.5)	0.00038 (2.1) −0.00038 (−12.5) 0.0005 (1.3)	−9.9/10^7 (2.2)	0.07 0.30 0.03	72 17 55	Summers-Heston (1984) Upper incomegroup Lower incomegroup
Sheehey (1996)1960–1988	gy		0.0023 (2.46) −0.0006 (−2.14) 0.0028 (2.7)	−7.2/10^7 (1.93)	0.072 0.293 0.072	107 13 82	Penn WorldTable (Mark 5) Upper income Low income
Sarkar (1998)1960–93. Pooled regressions for 110 countries and various sub-periods	gy	0.57 (2.67) 5.65 (2.73)	0.0026 (4.76) −0.55$^{a/}$ (−1.89)	−0.10/10^5 (−4.25)	0.02 0.02	867 192	UN (1976)UNCTAD (1994) 24 Upper income
Easterly and Levine (1997).[3] Pooled regressions for 1960s, 1970s, and 1980s	gy	−4.28 (−3.80)	1.06$^{a/}$ (4.85) 0.09$^{a/}$ (3.74)	−0.007^a (−4.58)	0.03 0.42 0.49 0.59^b	675 41 70 67	86 Lower income World Bank Summers and Heston (1988)
Ades and Glaeser (1999). OLS regressions 1960–1985	gy	0.007 (2.25)	0.0192 (5.65)	−0.00225^c (−0.55)	0.24	99	Barro and Wolf (1989)

Notes: gy is the growth rate of per capita GDP. yt is the end of period level of per capita real GDP. yo refers to the initial level of per capita GDP. N is the number of observations. t-statistics are shown in parentheses. In the case of Sarkar (1998), numbers in parentheses are White t-statistics.

^{a} The independent variable is ln yo or (ln yo)^2

^{b} Estimated using Seemingly Unrelated Regressions: a separate regression for each period.

^{c} Eq. (4) in Table 1, which includes a number of other regressors.

suggestive. The model implies a pattern of divergence followed by convergence that is conditional on very specific determinants of the steady state, besides the required existence of multiple equilibria. Controlling for the determinants of the steady state faces a number of difficulties and for an important one—the long-run employment share of the modern sector—they are very different in an open economy setting from those considered so far. Moreover, the conditions for multiple equilibria may be met in some countries and not in others. A general specification would have to take into account a host of factors including cross-country differences in the production conditions of non-capitalist sectors and their degree of openness to international trade (both of which will affect the labor supply elasticity), as well as differences in the equilibrium employment share of the modern sector. Moreover, since the savings rate is not constant throughout the transition, investigating the behavior of the rate of convergence would involve a larger number of interactions than we have had to face in previous models. We shall look at other relevant empirical evidence in later chapters.

A second important question is how much of the inverted-U pattern of the transitory component of growth survives the inclusion of human capital variables and other likely determinants of the steady state. The question is of interest in particular because the extension by Benhabib and Spiegel (2005) of the Nelson and Phelps model, discussed in Chapter 4, predicts, just as the classical development model, a non linear relationship between growth and initial development level by postulating a threshold level of human capital below which a country's productivity grows at a rate below that of the productivity leader and a pattern of convergence prevails only above this threshold. If these predictions are correct, the pattern of divergence/convergence with growth acceleration at middle-income levels revealed by the quadratic equation should be considerably weakened if not eliminated by the inclusion of human capital among the determinants of the growth rate.

To investigate this issue, Ros (2000) included in the quadratic equation a number of variables used in Barro (1991), including in particular educational variables. The regression estimates confirmed that, after controlling for differences in investment shares, education and political risk variables, the economies of the poorest countries tended to grow more slowly than middle and high income economies and only after a threshold was there a clear process of income convergence. In the quadratic equations, the newly included variables substitute for the constant term (a_o) and therefore affect the convergence threshold $[yC = y_o^M + [a_1^2 - 4a_2(a_o - g^*)]^{1/2}/2a_2]$ with a sign that is opposite the one in the growth rate regression (provided that a_2 is negative). The regression results suggest then that higher educational achievement and higher rates of investment tend to reduce the threshold of convergence, while political risk tends to increase it. Despite the fact that the forces accounting for the non linear relationship between growth and initial income in the classical development model (increasing returns and elastic labor supply) are different from those in Benhabib and Spiegel (a large distance to the technological frontier exacerbating the difficulties of adopting the technological advances) there is in this respect a close similarity between the two models.

Other studies showing an inverted U relationship between growth and initial income and including other regressors besides the log of initial income and the square term are Easterly and Levine (1997), (see table 2), Barro (2000), and Bleaney and Nishiyama (2002). It is interesting to note that Levine and Renelt's (1992) seminal analysis of the robustness of cross country growth regressions showed that the conditional convergence result (a negative coefficient on the initial level of per capita income) is not robust over the period 1974–89 or when OECD countries are excluded (see Levine and Renelt, 1992, p. 958). This is consistent with the results of the other studies cited since the exclusion of the set of OECD countries, which largely overlaps with the set of high-income countries, leaves the country sample with (mostly) middle and low-income economies. All these results, needless to say, besides confirming the inverted U shape between growth and initial income, call again into question the "convergence result" of the empirical literature in support of the neoclassical growth model, according to which "given the human-capital variables, subsequent growth is substantially negatively related to the initial level of per capita GDP" (Barro, 1991, p. 409). The positive coefficient on initial income suggests the presence of strong forces towards divergence which are offset only at middle and high levels of income.

Industrialization and the Verdoorn law

A question, however, remains. While we have encountered the patterns of income divergence followed by convergence as an implication of the transitional dynamics of the classical development theory model, is there any evidence that these patterns obey to the mechanisms envisaged by the model?

We can start answering this question with a reference to contemporary country experiences which illustrate the empirical relevance of the transitional dynamics of the classical development theory model, such as the acceleration of growth in China over the past 30 years and in India over the past 20 years. As surplus labor is absorbed in modern industry and services and real wage increases accelerate, the presence of diminishing returns to capital will dominate and growth will eventually slow down but, for the time being, growth proceeds at extremely fast rates seemingly as a result of the interactions between elastic labor supplies and increasing returns to scale. The same applies to other growth miracles in the past which, with the exception of a few small countries with abundant natural resources, are characterized by rapid industrialization and the absorption of labor into industry from other sectors of the economy. This was the case of Japan, South Korea and Taiwan in the post war period. Going further back in time, the catching up stories of the 19th century such as that of Germany and the United States (with labor provided by immigration) are no different with respect to the key role of industrialization.

These examples point therefore towards the key role of industrialization in the acceleration of growth at intermediate development levels. Kaldor's writing, as mentioned in Chapter 1, most forcefully emphasized that the high growth rates characteristic of the transition from immaturity to maturity appear to be an attribute of the process of industrialization. In support of this view, Kaldor (1966) presented a cross country growth regression for twelve advanced countries in the period 1953–4 to 1963–4, showing a very high correlation between the rate of growth of GDP (g_Y) and the rate of growth of manufacturing production (g_M). The result of running this regression on a data set of 77 countries over the period 1970–2008 is:

$$g_Y = 1.63 + 0.42 g_M \qquad \text{(adj.) } R^2 = 0.42$$

$$(6.13) \quad (7.54)$$

t statistics in parenthesis.

In Kaldor's view, a most significant finding was that the coefficient on the rate of growth of manufacturing production (g_M) was (considerably) less than unity, as is the case with our regression, implying that "the faster the overall rate of growth, the greater is the *excess* of the rate of growth of manufacturing production over the rate of growth of the economy as a whole" (Kaldor, 1967, p. 8, italics in original). In other words, high overall growth rates are associated with fast rates of industrialization. Kaldor did not view this relationship as being, at least primarily, a demand-side phenomenon: it is not so much that high rates of GDP growth generate a high growth in manufacturing, given a high income elasticity of demand for manufactures. Causality runs primarily from manufacturing to GDP growth and more precisely from manufacturing growth to the growth rate of GDP per worker. This relationship became known as the third of Kaldor's laws (Thirlwall, 1983) and is supported by the following regression ran over our data set of 77 countries for the period 1970–2008:

$$g_y = -0.21 + 0.32 \, g_M \qquad \text{(adj.) } R^2 = 0.45$$

$$(-0.75) \quad (7.99)$$

t statistics in parenthesis.

where gy is the rate of growth of GDP per worker. For Kaldor, this relationship is the result of two mechanisms. First, the growth rate of productivity in manufacturing industries itself rises with the rate of growth of output. Second, employment growth in industry tends to increase the rate of productivity growth in other sectors. This is the consequence of diminishing returns to labor in other sectors and the absorption of surplus labor from these sectors, as well as of a faster increase in the flow of goods into consumption (which tends to increase productivity in the commerce sector) (Kaldor, 1967, p. 15).

The first mechanism is Verdoorn's law—named after Verdoorn (1949) who found a strong empirical relationship between productivity and output growth using data from a number of countries. A moment's reflection will show that for the mechanism of labor force reallocation envisaged by Kaldor to generate high rates of *overall* productivity growth, the Verdoorn relationship must be such that productivity and employment growth are positively correlated within industry. Otherwise, a high rate of manufacturing output growth will not bring about the reallocation of the labor force. This may be the reason why in his interpretation of Verdoorn's law, Kaldor laid so much emphasis on the coefficient in the regression of productivity growth on output growth (the Verdoorn coefficient) being positive *and* less than unity. For with the Verdoorn coefficient in this range of values, there will be a positive association between productivity growth and employment growth in industry.[10] In a sample of 44 countries with available information, the estimated Verdoorn relationship for 1970–2008 is:

$$g_{y_M} = 1.26 + 0.65 \ g_M \qquad \text{(adj.) } R^2 = .56$$
$$(7.49)$$

t-statistics in parentheses.

where g_{y_M} and g_M are, respectively, the rates of growth of labor productivity and production in manufacturing. The value of the Verdoorn coefficient (0.65) meant, paraphrasing Kaldor (1966), that each percentage addition to the growth of output requires a 0.35 percent increase in the growth of employment, and is associated with a 0.65 percent increase in the growth of productivity.[11]

---

[10] Let g_y, g_L and g_M be respectively the growth rates of productivity, employment and output. Substituting from $g_M = g_y + g_L$ into $g_y = c + v \ g_M$, we have $g_y = [c/(1-v)] + [v/(1-v)] \ g_L$. In order to have a positive relationship between productivity and employment growth, coefficient v must be less than unity.

[11] In contrast, the non-industrial sectors tend to feature negative relationships between productivity (g_y) and employment growth (g_L). For example, Cripps' and Tarling's (1973) pooled regressions for developed economies in the period 1950–1970 yield the following results for agriculture and mining:

Agriculture: $g_y = 2.153 - 0.919 g_L$ $\qquad R^2 = .172 \qquad N = 42$
$\qquad\qquad\qquad (.319)$
Mining: $g_y = 2.961 - 0.799 g_L$ $\qquad R^2 = .417$
$\qquad\qquad\qquad (.160)$
Standard errors are shown in parentheses.

As noted by Rowthorn (1979), Verdoorn (1949) derived the relationship between productivity and output growth from a simultaneous equation model in which the parameters of both the production function and the labor supply function affect the relationship. In the Appendix, I derive the Verdoorn coefficient (v) linking productivity and output growth from such a model, assuming a CES production function in manufacturing. The expression for the Verdoorn coefficient (v) shows that if the elasticity of factor substitution is zero or very small, then the elasticity of labor supply and the parameter of increasing returns must both be greater than zero for productivity and employment growth to be positively correlated (through a parameter $v/(1-v)$). A positive association between productivity and employment growth must reflect, in this case, that the labor supply to industry is elastic and returns to scale are increasing.[12]

The evidence on Verdoorn's law provides additional support for the view that growth acceleration at middle-income levels is based on the interaction between increasing returns and elastic labor supplies.[13] For it suggests that this is the mechanism generating the close association between overall growth rates and the rate of industrialization, and explaining why the productivity effects of industrialization are enhanced at those intermediate stages of the transition when both the demand for manufacturing products and the labor supply to industry are highly elastic.

Evidence on poverty traps

In explaining why some countries may remain stagnant at low-income levels, classical development theory emphasized the circular feedback mechanisms that keep a country poor. The original literature emphasized two processes. First, factor growth rates (of primarily capital and labor) at low-income levels are such that they perpetuate the low level of income. Malthusian or population traps certainly existed in the past and the scarcity of savings at low-income levels certainly reinforces, still today, poverty in many countries. Second, and more relevant to our world of open economies, is the type of poverty traps associated to the paradox of underdevelopment, i.e., to the fact

---

[12] For positive values of the elasticity of substitution, a positive value of the increasing returns parameter is no longer a necessary condition for $v/(1-v)$ to be positive. Yet, under constant returns to scale (i.e., with an increasing returns parameter equal to zero), a value of $v/(1-v)$ equal to unity (as implied by Kaldor's results) would require an implausibly very high elasticity of factor substitution (if the elasticity of labor supply to manufacturing is larger than unity).

[13] Including, we would argue, the weaker evidence on Verdoorn's law for cross sections of developed countries in later periods. See, on the subject, Cripps and Tarling (1973), who found a failure of Verdoorn's law in the period 1965–1970, probably as a result of a tightening of labor markets during this period in developed countries.

that poor countries tend to have low rates of return for both labor and capital which inhibit capital accumulation and perpetuate low-income levels.

This fact generates multiple equilibria associated with profitability traps. Of course, it is not necessarily the case that the profitability trap is associated exclusively with a low level of physical capital, as in the model with techno-logical externalities presented in Chapter 7, or with the lack of infrastructure and the narrowness of the domestic market, as in the models with pecuniary externalities in this chapter. Extending the models to bring other no less important determinants of development traps is essential for a fuller under-standing of underdevelopment. In Ros (2000), I presented a classical develop-ment model in which a low level of human capital may be crucial to generate a profitability trap.

Is there any evidence that any of these mechanisms is what keeps low-income countries trapped in poverty? Ros (2000, ch. 10) finds that among low-income Asian and African countries, GDP per capita growth (1960–1989) is positively correlated with initial income per capita level and negatively correlated with income inequality. The fact that the direction and significance of these effects are confined to these groups of low-income countries is con-sistent with the presence of poverty traps arising from the narrowness of the domestic market and associated to horizontal pecuniary externalities. As we shall see in Chapter 16 in greater detail, the extent of the market for manufac-tures can be negatively affected by inequality which strengthens the narrow-ness of the domestic market and inhibits the application of increasing returns technologies as in the model with horizontal pecuniary externalities in this chapter.

Graham and Temple (2006) calibrate a two-sector model with a traditional sector (agriculture) producing under diminishing returns to all its factors and a modern sector (non-agriculture) that exhibits increasing returns that are exter-nal to the firm, to generate multiple equilibria. They then use these calibra-tions to document the contribution of the differences between these multiple equilibria to cross-country income differences and find that, depending on the degree of increasing returns assumed for the non-agricultural sector, their model can account from between 15 percent and 25 per cent of the observed variation in per capita incomes across countries.

It is, however, fair to say that the large literature on poverty traps has not reached a consensus (see the survey by Azariadis and Stachurski, 2005). One of the reasons for this lack of consensus may be a common misunderstanding among those that reject the existence of poverty traps arising from increasing returns. A common view is that technology-driven poverty traps are the result of increasing returns to capital prevailing at low-income levels (see Easterly, 2006; Kraay and Raddatz, 2006). While Sachs (2005) provides a basis for this interpretation, we have seen that this is not a condition for the existence of a profitability trap at low-income levels. The condition is a combination of elastic labor supplies with a moderate dose of increasing returns to scale (rather than to capital).

Concluding comments

Much work on cross country growth regressions appears to have proceeded on the assumption that rejection of the convergence properties of the neoclassical growth model provides support for the new growth theories and vice versa. Yet this, of course, need not be the case. We have seen in this and the previous chapter that the classical literature of development economics has implications for cross-country growth performance that go quite far in overcoming the shortcomings of neoclassical models, while being free from the objections that can be raised against the endogenous growth models. The multiple equilibria models of classical development theory also seem to offer a better alternative than the extensions of the AK model that incorporate external effects of education or internal economies in financial development (King and Levine, 1993; Berthelemy and Varoudakis, 1996) to generate multiple endogenous growth equilibria with associated convergence clubs *in rates of growth*. In Berthelemy and Varoudakis (1996), for example, the real sector uses an AK technology and the financial sector operates under economies of scale and imperfect competition. These economies of scale make the productivity of the financial sector depend on the size of the real sector, while the total savings intermediated by banks and accumulated in the real sector depend on the margin of intermediation, which is affected by the size of the financial sector. In the presence of an AK technology in the real sector, these interactions generate multiple equilibria in growth rates. This type of interactions and the factors emphasized in this recent literature—financial development and education—are probably important in generating development traps and multiple equilibria. However, the assumption of constant returns to capital in the recent literature is an unnecessary straightjacket. More precisely, one can generate the more plausible multiple equilibria in *levels of income*, rather than in rates of growth, by simply replacing the empirically questionable assumption of constant returns to capital with the interactions between increasing returns to scale and elastic labor supplies.

Appendix. On Verdoorn's law

The Verdoorn law is commonly taken to imply that, in the regression of productivity growth on output growth, the regression coefficient (Verdoorn's coefficient) is positive and less than unity. After Kaldor (1966, 1967) investigated the relationship for a cross-section of developed economies, research on the subject included cross-country studies of manufacturing industries and time series for single countries (for surveys, see McCombie, 1983; Thirlwall, 1983; Bairam, 1987). The sometimes contrasting results, depending on the particular specification and estimation procedures adopted, has fueled a continuing controversy regarding the appropriate tests and specifications of the Verdoorn Law. At the source of much of this controversy are the difficulties of deriving information on returns to scale from the estimated Verdoorn coefficients.

To illustrate these difficulties, consider a common interpretation of the Verdoorn coefficient. Assume the following production function in manufacturing: $M = A K^{a + \mu} L^{1-a}$. Taking logs and differentiating with respect to time, we can decompose the growth of output (g_M) into:

$$g_M = g_A + (a + \mu)g_K + (1 - a)g_L \tag{A.1}$$

where $g_A = (d\ln A/dt)(1/A)$ and g_K and g_L refer to the growth rates of capital and labor inputs respectively. Then, assuming a constant capital-output ratio, so that $g_M = g_K$, and using $gp = g_M - g_L$, we can express the rate of growth of output per worker (gp) as:

$$gp = [g_A/(1 - a)] + [\mu/(1 - a)]g_M \tag{A.2}$$

which shows the Verdoorn coefficient, $[\mu/(1-a)]$, determined exclusively by the parameters of the production function (μ and a) and, thus, as a purely technological coefficient. A positive and less than unit Verdoorn coefficient implies $\mu > 0$ and $a + \mu < 1$, i.e., increasing returns to scale and diminishing returns to capital. With $a = 1/3$, a Verdoorn coefficient of the order of 0.5 would imply an increasing returns parameter of 1/3.

One problem with this interpretation is that eq. (A.2) holds only in the steady state, when output and the capital stock are growing at the same rate. Off the steady state, part of the productivity increases will be due to capital deepening that, in turn, will be affected by the growth in real wages and the labor supply elasticity. This will be the case as long as the elasticity of factor substitution is positive which is, of course, the case with the log linear production function assumed.

To illustrate this point, consider the Cobb-Douglas technology extended to allow for technological externalities assumed in section 1 of this chapter. As shown in Ros (2000, ch. 4) in a model with increasing returns to scale and efficiency wages, combining the labor demand function and the slope of the w curve (which depends on the labor supply function), we can express the growth of employment in sector M as a function of the growth of the capital stock:

$$g_L = [e(a + \mu)/(e\,a + 1)]g_K \tag{A.3}$$

where e is the elasticity of labor supply to sector M. Taking logs in the labor demand function and differentiating with respect to time we obtain an equation similar to (A.1) (except that now $g_A = 0$). Substituting from (A.3) and solving, as before, for the growth of output per worker as a function of output growth, we get:

$$g_p = [1/(1 + e)]g_M$$

The Verdoorn coefficient is now inversely related to the elasticity of labor supply and, in fact, turns out to be independent from the nature of returns to scale! Rather than a technological parameter, the Verdoorn coefficient is now exclusively affected by the nature of the labor supply function to sector M. An elastic, but less than perfectly elastic, labor supply can then generate a positive and less than unit Verdoorn coefficient.

It does not follow from all this that it is not possible to derive any information about returns to scale from the Verdoorn coefficient. We need, however, a more general specification to see under what conditions we may be able to do so. Consider a CES production function extended to allow for technological externalities: M = A (a Kψ + (1−a) Lψ)$^{1/\psi}$, where A = K$^\mu$ represents the external effect of the economy-wide, average capital stock, and the elasticity of factor substitution is given by σ = 1/(1- ψ). This can be written in intensive form as:

$$p = K^\mu [a\ k^\psi + (1 - a)]^{1/\psi} \qquad (A.4)$$

where p is output per worker (M/L) and k is the capital-labor ratio (K/L). After some manipulation (see Ros, 2000, p. 132), we find the expression for the Verdoorn coefficient:

$$v = d \ln p/d \ln M = (\pi\lambda + \sigma\mu)/[\pi(\lambda + e) + \sigma\mu(1 + e)], \qquad (A.5)$$

where: $\lambda = \mu\ e + \sigma(1 - \mu\ e)$

Eq. (A.5) shows that a number of variables and parameters in general affect the Verdoorn coefficient. These include the profit share π which depends on the capital-labor ratio, returns to scale (μ), and parameters of both the labor demand function (elasticity of substitution in particular) and the labor supply function (e, which depends on production conditions in the rest of the economy, the composition of employment, and the parameters of the demand functions for goods).

Eq. (A.5) is a rather complicated expression that, however, simplifies in a number of special cases. Consider, for example, the case of a unit elasticity of substitution. Setting σ = 1 in (A.5) yields: v = 1/(1 + e), which is, of course, the same expression that we obtained in the case of a Cobb-Douglas technology extended to allow for technological externalities. The reason no parameters other than the labor supply elasticity appear in the expression for v is that, with a unit elasticity of factor substitution, the wage and profit shares in output remain constant. Output per worker and the product wage then grow at the same rate, and d ln p/d ln L is equal to the inverse of the labor supply elasticity (1/e). As can be readily verified, v = ϕ /(1 + ϕ), where ϕ = d ln p/d ln L.

Consider now the case of a fixed coefficients technology. Setting σ = 0 in (A.5) yields (provided that e > 0): v = μ/(1 + μ). The Verdoorn elasticity is now a purely technology parameter, unaffected by the elasticity of labor supply. Indeed, without factor substitution the change in output per worker is completely de-linked from the change in wages. Hence, the labor supply elasticity does not appear in the determination of the Verdoorn coefficient. Moreover, without exogenous technical progress, output per worker changes only as a result of the presence of increasing returns, and the relationship between labor productivity and output growth reflects exclusively the extent of increasing returns. This, or something very similar, may be what Kaldor had in mind in his interpretation of Verdoorn's Law. For in this case, there is a strict correspondence between the existence of increasing returns to scale ($\mu > 0$) and a Verdoorn coefficient that is positive, *but* less than unity, so that indeed productivity growth and employment growth rise or fall together. It is worth noting, however, that the increasing returns parameter would have to be dramatically high ($\mu = 1$) for the Verdoorn coefficient to be of the order of Kaldor's empirical estimates (v = 1/2)

9

Openness and the Big Push: Criticisms and Extensions of Classical Development Theory

Development economics as it appeared in the 1940s and 1950s in the writings of Rosenstein-Rodan, Nurkse, Prebisch, Hirschman, Leibenstein, and others, stressed the barriers to industrialization and capital formation in underdeveloped countries. Successful development required the overcoming of various inhibiting factors, including the presence of externalities and some form of increasing returns to scale. In focusing on these problems, the classical literature of development economics generated a view of the development process in which increasing returns to scale and elastic labor supplies played key roles.

Given its conformity with a number of stylized facts, as discussed in Chapter 8, it is puzzling why early development theory drifted away from the mainstream of the economics discipline. One reason was certainly ideological. The normative implications that were derived from the initial framework became progressively unfashionable from the 1960s onwards, first in the profession and later among policy-makers (see Stiglitz, 1992). But there were also analytical reasons. Misinterpretations of the early theoretical contributions to development economics had an important role in the criticisms of classical development theory by the neoclassical counter-revolution in development economics in the 1960s and its abandonment by the mainstream.

One issue became prominent. Does the need for a big push survive in an economy that is open to international trade and capital movements? Or would openness to trade and capital movements be sufficient to overcome all poverty traps? Without exaggeration, these questions have haunted development economics since its inception. The reason is that they impinge upon the broader question of whether the analytical framework of early development theory, with its emphasis on labor surpluses, increasing returns, and imperfect competition, is at all useful and valid in the real world of open economies. Having reviewed the main contributions of the pioneers of development economics in previous chapters, it is now worthwhile to consider the criticisms and misinterpretations of classical development theory as well as the extensions of this analytical framework to the open economy.

1. Criticisms and Misinterpretations of the Big Push Argument

Elasticity pessimism?

The counter-revolution in development theory that began in the 1960s argued that except for the (rather unlikely) event of very low price and income elasticities of export demand, free trade was unambiguously good for developing countries and would obviate the need for a big push. Consider Bhagwati's interpretation of Rosenstein-Rodan's classic (1943) paper:

> The underdeveloped economy was trapped in a low level equilibrium with no effective inducement to invest: e.g., the entrepreneur investing in shoes was not sure about selling the shoes unless others invested simultaneously in textiles etc. This dilemma would, of course, disappear if the country faced constant terms of trade at which these entrepreneurs could atomistically sell what they wished. Therefore, a necessary condition for Rosenstein-Rodan's analysis and prescription is, of course, elasticity pessimism. (Bhagwati, 1985, p. 299)

Thus, in the real world of open economies, big push arguments and poverty traps were, at best, intellectual curiosities that the bright pioneers of development theory happened to be interested in when they began to think about development problems. According to this viewpoint, their mistaken "export-elasticity pessimism" had led the pioneers to focus on closed economies and to fail to notice that openness presents a solution to the problems of industrialization. Arguably, it was this line of argument, more than the difficulties of formalizing models with increasing returns and imperfect competition (as claimed by Krugman, 1992), that led to the resurgence of the perfect competition and constant-returns-to-scale paradigm. Because if, in an open economy, increasing returns do not play the crucial role that they may do in a closed economy then, contrary to the beliefs of early development theorists, little is lost by adopting the simpler assumption of constant returns.[1]

Before looking at the role that "elasticity pessimism" may have played in the early literature, it is worth noting that both Bhagwati and Stiglitz (see previous footnote) have in mind a version of the argument in which horizontal

---

[1] Stiglitz in his comment on Krugman's (1992) article makes a similar point, which, incidentally, shows the vitality of the "export pessimism" interpretation of the big push argument: "…had Rosenstein-Rodan (1943) succeeded in formalizing his ideas, I doubt that those ideas would have been more palatable. In his model the income effects associated with increasing returns leave the economy stuck in a low-level equilibrium. As Krugman points out, the problem arises from a lack of demand, but once we open the economy to international trade, this argument loses its force". (Stiglitz, 1992, p. 41). See also Romer (1993) for a similar interpretation of the big push argument.

pecuniary externalities are the source of the coordination problem. However, the defining characteristic of the big push argument, for Rosenstein-Rodan at least, is the existence of a threshold level of investments below which there is stagnation. As Rodan puts it: "Proceeding 'bit by bit' will not add up in its effects to the sum total of the single bits. A minimum quantum of investment is a necessary, though not sufficient, condition of success. This, in a nutshell, is the contention of the theory of the big push" (Rosenstein-Rodan, 1961, p. 57). A threshold level of investment is, in turn, a defining characteristic of a model with multiple equilibria. In other words, if the source of external economies is technological, the big push argument remains intact, whether the open economy faces constant terms of trade or not. The infant industry argument for protection, as we shall see in section 2, is based precisely on these type of learning-by-doing externalities. The formalization of this argument yields a "big push model" in that the combination of increasing returns and an elastic labor supply generates multiple equilibria and a development trap. As we will see later, this type of development trap is, in fact, more likely to appear in an open, than in a closed, economy. The "linkage effects" model of section 3, an open economy version of the Hirschman-Rodan model discussed in Chapter 8, illustrates how a big push problem can arise in a small open economy in the absence of technological externalities. It illustrates, in fact, that the case of technological externalities is not any different from that of pecuniary externalities arising from increasing returns in the production of non-tradable goods.

We shall return to these issues in later sections. It is now worth noting that the interpretation based on elasticity pessimism can hardly be reconciled with the original argument in the literature. One of the most influential papers, for instance, was Rosenstein-Rodan's (1943) article. After discussing the self-sufficient "Russian model" and its "several great disadvantages", Rosenstein-Rodan (1943, pp. 203–4) argues that:

> The alternative way of industrialization would fit Eastern and South-Eastern Europe into the world economy, which would preserve the advantages of an international division of labour, and would therefore in the end produce more wealth for everybody...Clearly this way of industrialization is preferable to the autarkic one.

He goes on to discuss the difficulties involved in the implementation of this process of industrialization. Primary among these difficulties, he argues, are externalities of various kinds and the presence of increasing returns to scale in many activities. At no point is it suggested that low export elasticities will be critical.[2]

---

[2] Export conditions appear at two points in the article. On p. 203 it is noted that: "International

All this is not to deny that trade pessimism prevailed at the time. Low elasticities were seen as an obstacle to higher levels of economic development in less developed countries, but elasticity pessimism applied largely to exports of primary products. In the present context, the important point is that this kind of export-elasticity pessimism does not seem to have played a significant role in the big push argument.

A demand deficiency?

The interpretation based on elasticity pessimism is not confined to the neo-classical resurgence in development economics. Similar conclusions came from more sympathetic accounts of development trap arguments that empha-sized a "lack of demand" as the source of the problem. In one version, low-level traps are linked to Keynesian effective demand problems. This interpret-ation, along with a counter-reaction to it, appears to have been widespread in the early post-war period.[3] Other, less Keynesian accounts, also led to an excessive emphasis on demand deficiencies. Basu (1984) provides a formaliza-tion of the Nurksian vicious circle, in which monopolistic firms in the modern sector of the economy face kinked demand curves for their products and an elastic supply of labor. The economy may get stuck in a demand-constrained equilibrium, in which the low real incomes associated with a low level of resource utilization hold back the expansion of modern firms. Not surpris-ingly, the vicious circle breaks down when the economy opens to

---

investment in the nineteenth century was largely self-liquidating, based on exchange of agrarian and industrial products. Nowadays liquidation can no longer be assumed to be `automatic', although the problem can be solved if it is properly planned." On p. 209, he returns to this question:

> Liquidation will have to planned—i.e. one part of the industries created in Eastern and South-Eastern Europe will have to be export industries.... The placing of these exports has to be planned and foreseen in such a way as to minimize the burden of necessary adjustment in the creditor countries. Eastern and South-Eastern Europe will most probably cease to be an exporter of cereals. It will export processed foods and light industrial articles.

> International trade in the nineteenth century functioned more or less smoothly because all countries had a high income elasticity of demand for imports. On the higher standard of living in the rich countries of the twentieth century the income elasticity of demand for imports may be lower. There may be only one good for which the income elasticity of demand is high: leisure which does not require imports of material goods. Accordingly, the rich countries may have to accept a part of their share in economic expansion in the form of more leisure.

[3] See, for example, Rao (1952) and his warnings against "a rather unintelligent application—not on Keynes's part—of what may be called Keynesian economics to the problems of the underdeveloped countries" (Rao, 1952, pp. 206–7).

international trade and modern sector firms face given terms of trade in international markets.[4]

Curiously, Krugman (1995) provides another example. After an illuminating discussion of the sources of multiple equilibria in terms of increasing returns *and* the elasticity of factor supplies, when summarizing the argument, he refers to the circular relationship between low productivity and small market size. More explicitly, he refers to "the circular relationship in which the decision to invest in large-scale production depended on the size of the market, and the size of the market depended on the decision to invest. Whatever the practical relevance of this theory, it made perfectly good logical sense" (Krugman, 1995, p. 23). In other words, the division of labor is limited by the extent of the market, and the extent of the market is constrained by the division of labor. In this view, increasing returns can become an obstacle to development at low levels of productivity, since the small size of the domestic market reduces the profitability of increasing returns technologies, with an adverse impact on the inducement to invest.

If these interpretations were fully correct, the pioneers would have had little to add to Adam Smith. Indeed, Smith explicitly noted that:

> By means of (foreign trade), the narrowness of the home market does not hinder the division of labor in any particular branch of art or manufacture from being carried to the highest perfection. By opening a more extensive market for whatever part of the produce of their labor may exceed the home consumption, it encourages them to improve its productive powers. (Smith 1776, vol. 1, p. 413)

By opening the economy, the second component of the circular relationship above breaks down, because it is no longer true that the domestic level of productivity constrains the size of the market, and the need for a big push disappears. Unfortunately, Nurkse's writing, although not Rodan's, provides some ground for this "excessively Smithian" interpretation of the argument.

What is missing in this demand-based interpretation of the big push argument? As discussed in Chapter 7, the conditions for multiple equilibria in a closed economy involve a sufficiently elastic labor supply and the presence of increasing returns to scale. Unless returns to capital increase, increasing returns to scale alone are not sufficient to generate a development trap. An elastic labor supply is essential to give local stability to the low-level equilibrium. If the labor supply was inelastic, the product wage would tend to fall until the increasing returns technologies became profitable even at low levels of the capital endowment. It is the combination of an elastic supply of labor,

---

[4] See also Taylor and Arida's (1988) survey of development theories which, based on Basu's model, brings Rosenstein-Rodan and Nurkse's contributions under the heading "Demand-driven models".

setting a floor to the wage that the modern sector has to pay, with the presence of increasing returns that produces a vicious circle. Similarly, the same interactions between increasing returns and an elastic labor supply produce a virtuous circle if a sufficiently large capital endowment has been achieved.

Fleming (1955) clearly saw that the "balanced growth doctrine", as he phrased it, does not only depend on increasing returns, and complained that the literature had insufficiently stated the assumption of elastic factor supplies:

> In order really to salvage the doctrine of external economies under examination, however, it is necessary to drop the assumption that the supply of factors of production is fixed in favour of the assumption that the supply varies positively with real factor prices ... of our authors, only Rosenstein-Rodan explicitly assumes an elastic supply of labour in his illustration of the doctrine, though Nurkse, in arguing in terms of the inducement to invest, is in effect assuming some elasticity in the supply of capital. (Fleming, 1955, p. 248)

By emphasizing the elasticity of factor supplies, Fleming early perceived what was to become a major source of misinterpretations of development trap arguments. In the next section, I will argue that the elasticity of factor supplies, which is a necessary condition for multiple equilibria, is in fact enhanced in an open economy setting.

2. Openness and Development Traps in the Presence of Technological Externalities

We have already discussed in previous chapters that international capital mobility can do little good when the source of the problem is the presence of increasing returns holding back the inducement to invest. The reason is, of course, that the development trap in this case—unlike the poverty trap that has its origins in the scarcity of domestic savings (due to a low level of income relative to subsistence consumption)—arises from a low rate of return to capital. Nurkse seems to have been fully aware of this point. He observed that capital does not flow to the poorest countries and argued that this was quite consistent with his argument: it is because these countries are in a poverty trap arising from the lack of inducement to invest that capital does not flow to them. He concluded that capital mobility was not a sufficient condition to overcome the development problem (see Nurkse, 1952, p. 574 and p. 583).

What about trade openness? Can free trade overcome the development traps that can stunt industrialization in a closed economy? The argument developed here, concisely stated, is as follows. Openness increases the elasticity of factor supplies, which in turn facilitates the existence of multiple equilibria and development traps, especially in the presence of technological externalities or of vertical pecuniary externalities involving non-tradable goods. At the same time, it also makes demand curves more elastic, thus reducing the demand spillovers arising from horizontal pecuniary externalities and, thus, the coordination problems among producers of traded goods.

An open economy model with technological externalities

Consider an economy with two sectors. Sector S produces a labor-intensive good under constant returns to scale (CRS) and without the use of capital. The other sector, M, produces a capital-intensive good under increasing returns to scale (IRS) using capital and labor. We assume here a Cobb-Douglas technology with technological externalities proportional to the size of the capital stock. The two products are substitutes in consumption with a constant elasticity of substitution greater than unity. However, only the capital-intensive good can be accumulated as capital. The equilibrium wage rate is uniform across sectors.

Consider the economy before it opens to international trade. The product wage in sector M is an increasing function of the economy-wide capital-labor ratio (k). As in the model of Chapter 6 (section 3), the w curve in this economy is upward sloping with a slope that increases with k. The profit rate in sector M is a decreasing function of the product wage and, given the IRS technology, an increasing function of the capital stock. The w* curve of this economy, showing the required value of the product wage in sector M as a function of the capital-labor ratio, is thus positively sloped. The slope is determined by the strength of the external effects of the capital stock (as in section 2 of Chapter 7).

Given the assumptions of uniform wage rates and constant returns to labor in the labor-intensive sector, and with appropriate choice of units, the product wage (w/p_M) is also the relative price ratio (p_S/p_M) between the two goods. We can therefore interpret the w curve as showing the equilibrium relative prices (p_S/p_M) that would prevail under autarky at different levels of the capital-labor endowment. This is the curve $(p_S/p_M)A$ in Figure 9.1. In a labor abundant economy (with a low k), p_S/p_M is low, i.e., the labor-intensive good is cheap and the capital-intensive good relatively expensive, while in a capital abundant economy p_S/p_M is high, because the labor intensive good becomes relatively more expensive. Under our assumptions, and given in particular that the wage in terms of good S is constant and equal to unity, the wage in terms of good M is a measure (albeit imperfect) of the real consumption wage.

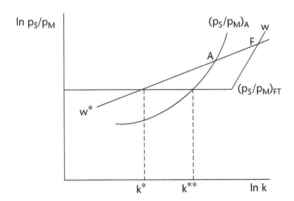

Figure 9.1 Short-run and long-run gains from trade

The gains from trade

Suppose that this economy opens up to trade and both goods are freely traded in the international market. The economy is small and a price taker for both goods. The relative prices in the international market will thus prevail in the domestic market as well, after the economy opens up to trade. These relative prices define the free trade line (p_S/p_M)FT in Figure 9.1. This line is also the w curve of the economy under free trade until the labor force in sector S is completely absorbed into sector M. Then the wage rate is de-linked from the price of good S in the international economy and the wage increases with the capital-labor ratio. The w curve of the trading economy is thus horizontal until the economy reaches complete specialization in sector M and then becomes upward sloping. The similarity to the w curve in the Lewis model should not be surprising. The assumption of constant relative prices between the two sectors plays the same role as the one good assumption in the Lewis model by making the labor supply to sector M perfectly elastic as long as the two sectors coexist.

Consider the case in which the initial capital-labor ratio is below k^{**}, the value of k at the intersection of the free trade line and the w curve under autarky. With such a capital endowment, the economy under autarky produces the labor-intensive good at a lower relative price than the rest of the world economy: below k^{**}, (p_S/p_M)A is less than (p_S/p_M)FT. When it opens up to trade, the economy is able to sell its labor intensive good at the higher relative price prevailing in the international market, i.e., in exchange for more units of the capital intensive good than it can afford to produce domestically (per unit of the labor-intensive good). This is the static (Ricardian) gain from trade: the economy can achieve, through free trade, a higher real income by exporting the good in which it has a comparative advantage and importing the good in which it has a comparative disadvantage. Measuring these benefits by its impact on real wages, it suffices to note that real wages increase to the same extent (for the reasons already indicated) as the relative price of the labor intensive good. These benefits from trade are larger the greater the discrepancy between the relative prices prevailing under autarky and internationally.

The gains from trade are unevenly distributed. Clearly, in the economy considered, all the gains accrue to labor, while capital loses. Given the higher relative price for good S, the product wage in sector M is now higher than under autarky and the profit rate, at the initial level of the capital stock, lower. As in Stolper-Samuelson (1941), the relatively abundant factor (labor in this case) benefits from the opening to trade while capital, the scarce factor, loses.[5] Exactly the opposite happens if the economy had a capital endowment above k** and labor would then be the relatively scarce factor. The economy would then have a comparative advantage in the capital-intensive good. When it opens up to trade, it would import the labor-intensive good at a lower price, real wages would fall and the rate of profit would increase in the capital-intensive industry.

Consider now the long-run effects. The story has a happy ending in this last case when the capital endowment is larger than k**. The higher profit rate stimulates capital accumulation. The capital-labor ratio continues to increase along the free trade line and, eventually, the economy will reach complete specialization in the capital-intensive industry. When this takes place, the rate of capital accumulation will still be above its steady state value (since the wage is below w*). The real wage will then increase along the w curve corresponding to a one-sector economy (the line to the right of the $(p_S/p_M)_A$ curve). In the long run, the short-term losses for labor will be reversed as the steady state value of the real wage under free trade (at point F) is above the steady state value of the wage under autarky (at point A).

What happens in the case when the capital endowment is below k**? The answer depends on whether the capital endowment is above or below k*, the capital-labor ratio at the intersection of the w* curve and the free trade line. If the capital endowment is larger than k*, the profit rate falls in the short run and capital accumulation slows down. However, the economy still remains below the w* locus. As a result, the capital-labor ratio will continue to increase with the economy eventually specializing completely in the capital-intensive good and reaching the high wage level under free trade.

---

[5] With diminishing returns to labor in sector S and labor earnings there being the average, rather than the marginal, product of labor, it is possible that both labor and capital may lose from trade. The reason is that the contraction of employment in sector M (following the opening to trade) can lead to such a fall in productivity in sector S (through, in effect, the expansion of underemployment) that, even though the product wage in sector M increases, the real consumption wage falls. The assumption of constant labor productivity in sector S (constant returns to labor) rules out this interesting and important case which here is not our main focus. For a formal analysis, see Ros (2000, Appendix to Chapter 7).

The long-run implications are quite different if the initial capital endowment is less than k*, the case of a very labor abundant economy. The wage under free trade is now above the value of w* corresponding to this level of capital endowment. As a result, the profit rate in the capital-intensive sector falls below the level that is necessary to generate a rate of capital accumulation equal to the rate of growth of the labor force. Over time, the capital stock of this economy will shrink, relative to the size of the labor force, and the economy will tend to completely specialize in the production of the labor-intensive good. Despite the disappearance of the capital-intensive industry, the economy gains from the free trade pattern of specialization: workers, at least, have a permanently higher standard of living than they had under autarky at the initial capital endowment. This is true, however, only compared to the *initial* pre-trade situation. If the economy had continued to develop under autarky, it would eventually have reached the steady state value of the wage under autarky (at the intersection of the $(p_S/p_M)_A$ and the w* curves). This wage rate, under the assumptions of Figure 9.1, is higher than the one that the economy can generate with full specialization in the labor-intensive—CRS industry.

We have here a case in which there are static gains from opening to trade, and yet free trade with specialization in the labor-intensive-CRS industry prevents in the long run the achievement of the higher wage rates that would result from a continued expansion of the capital-intensive-IRS industry. Or, more precisely, we have a case of multiple patterns of specialization under free trade, corresponding to low and high wage long-run equilibria with, in between, a critical capital endowment (k*), which is unlikely to be achieved spontaneously under a free trade regime.

Policy implications: multiple equilibria as a rationale for the infant industry argument

Can this labor-abundant economy, with a capital endowment below k*, do better than either open up to free trade or remain under autarky? It can, and this is the essence of the infant industry argument. Suppose the economy has a capital endowment (ko) and opens up to trade while protecting, with a tariff, its capital-intensive industry. As shown in Figure 9.2, the tariff modifies the international price ratio, shifting the horizontal trade line downwards from $(p_S/p_M)_{FT}$ to $(p_S/p_M (1 + t))$. This lowers the value of the capital-labor ratio below which the M sector tends to shrink (from k* to k*t in the figure). If the tariff is such as that it reduces k*$_t$ below the economy's capital-labor endowment (ko) and not so high as to reduce the product wage below its autarky level, it will put the economy in that range of k values in which labor gains from trade while allowing capital accumulation to go on. The economy will

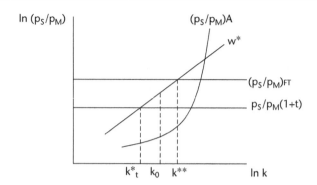

Figure 9.2 The infant industry argument

then benefit from the static gains from trade, although only partially since the wage rate in the short run will increase less than under free trade, while remaining in a position to exploit the longer term benefits of the continued expansion of its capital-intensive-IRS industry. It is worth noting that this situation provides an argument for temporary protection. When the economy has reached the capital-labor ratio k**, the capital-intensive industry can survive under free trade and, from then on, labor would gain in the long-run from a reduction in protection.

The case for policy intervention is based on the existence of multiple equilibria and the conditions for multiple equilibria are similar to those encountered in a closed economy. As already noted, the given relative prices in the international economy provide the flat segment of the w curve that is necessary for the k* intersection to exist. Together with the assumption of constant returns to labor in sector S, these given relative prices make the labor supply to sector M perfectly elastic. The existence of increasing returns in the capital-intensive industry is also a necessary condition (although not a sufficient condition as discussed below). Indeed, if technology displayed constant returns in both industries, the w* locus would be a horizontal line as shown in Figure 9.3a. We would then have two different cases:

(1) If the w* line lies below the free trade line ($(p_S/p_M)_1$ in the figure), free trade is unambiguously superior to both autarky and protection.
Then a unique free trade equilibrium with full specialization in the labor-intensive industry yields the highest possible wage rate in the long run.

(2) If the w* line lies above the free trade line, free trade cannot prevent the expansion of the capital-intensive industry. Regardless of how low the capital-labor ratio is, the product wage under free trade remains less than the required wage (w*). Even if the profit rate falls when the

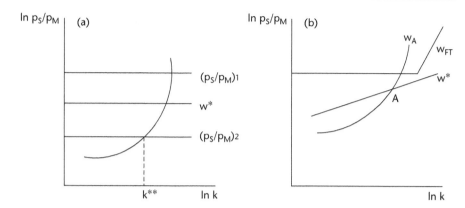

Figure 9.3 Exceptions to the infant industry argument

economy opens up to trade (if the capital endowment is below k** in Figure 9.3a), free trade allows the economy to fully reap the static gains from trade. The wage rate, during the process of expansion of the capital-intensive industry (up to k**), is higher under free trade than under either autarky or protection. There is again a unique free trade equilibrium with, in this case, full specialization in the capital-intensive industry.

The argument depends on some form of increasing returns, because this is what introduces a wedge between the private and the social costs and benefits of the development of the capital-intensive industry. It is because the industry generates external effects—in the form of, for example, learning by doing—that free market forces do not guarantee its development. Yet, the existence of technological externalities is not sufficient to warrant protection.[6] The industry must have enough potential. For suppose that the economy's savings rate is so low, or the labor force growth so high, that the highest wage it can achieve under autarky is below the wage under free trade with specialization in the labor intensive good (as shown in Figure 9.3b). It is then possible, even with full specialization in the M sector, that the survival of the capital-intensive industry would require a wage lower than can be achieved under free trade. In this case, the w* line, although upward sloping, does not intersect with the w curve under free trade. The survival of sector M would then require permanent protection. The argument for infant industry protection here breaks down because the economy does not have a long-term comparative advantage in the capital-intensive industry. This case is analogous to the

---

[6] This is the case independently of the fact that a second best argument for protection must exist. Otherwise, the optimal policy intervention is a production subsidy to the capital-intensive industry. See, on the subject, Bardhan (1970).

one in the Rodan-Hirschman model of Chapter 8 (see figure 8.3a) when the size of the labor force is so small that industrialization is not viable.

More generally, for protection to be warranted the industry should be able to meet the Mill-Bastable criterion: the present discounted value of the social costs of protection must be less than the discounted value of its social benefits. If we interpret these costs and benefits as losses and gains to labor, the Mill-Bastable criterion implies that the present discounted value of the costs, due to the lower wages during the period of protection, compared to those under free trade, must be less than the present discounted value of the gains, associated with the higher wages the economy generates once it has a comparative advantage in the capital-intensive industry. Two factors play a major role in determining these costs and benefits. First, the extent to which the economy's capital endowment is below k*, i.e., how far away the current factor endowment is from that required for the protected industry to survive under free trade. This affects critically the size of the costs of protection: in a labor abundant economy, the costs of protecting a modern aircraft industry may be much larger than the costs of protecting a less capital-intensive textile industry. A second factor is the extent to which the free trade line is below the high wage equilibrium. This determines how much of a long-term comparative advantage the economy has in the protected industry, and thus the size of the benefits from the temporary period of protection.

In our model with two goods, in which the benefits (or costs) from specialization in the IRS industry are permanent, while the losses from protection during the transition to the steady state are temporary, the conditions of the Mill-Bastable test will be fulfilled (assuming a zero social discount rate), if the long-term benefits from the expansion of the IRS industry are positive. That is, the test revolves around whether the w* line intersects twice the w curve under free trade (as in Figure 9.1) or whether there is no intersection (as in Figure 9.3b). It thus revolves around whether the conditions for the existence of multiple equilibria are fulfilled or not.

Openness, factor supply elasticity, and efficiency gains

The previous analysis illustrates the effects of trade openness on labor supply elasticity. In a closed dual economy model, an elastic labor supply will require a sufficiently high elasticity of substitution between the goods produced by the modern and the traditional sector (see Chapter 6). In an open economy this condition on the elasticity of substitution is no longer required if both goods are traded, *especially* if the economy is small and takes prices as given in the international market. With fixed terms of trade between the two goods, the expansion of the modern sector does not, as it would in a closed economy, shift the terms of trade in favor of the traditional sector. For example, in the model just discussed the modern sector faces an elastic supply of labor at a constant product wage (determined by the given terms of trade). The opening of the economy makes the terms of trade behave as if the two goods were perfect substitutes, so that the modern sector faces a perfectly elastic supply of labor as long as the two sectors coexist.[7] This is why, with the exception of the upward sloping w* curve, the model of the infant industry argument is so reminiscent of the Lewis model. In both, the w curve is a straight line as long as the two sectors coexist: in Lewis, because the two sectors produce the same good; in the infant industry model, because the two sectors produce traded goods with fixed terms of trade.

The model of the infant industry argument assumes constant returns to labor in the traditional sector (S). Suppose instead that there are diminishing returns to labor. With equalization of labor earnings in the two sectors (S and M), we have: $w_M/p_M = (p_S/p_M) L_S^{-b}$, where the labor elasticity of output in sector S is $(1 - b)$. Taking logs and differentiating, the labor supply elasticity to sector M is: $d\ln L_M/d\ln (w_M/p_M) = [1 - d\ln (p_S/p_M)/d\ln (w_M/p_M)]/b (L_M/L_S)$. In a closed economy $d\ln (p_S/p_M)$ will generally be positive (unless the elasticity of substitution between the S and M goods is infinite). In a small open economy, this term is zero, making the elasticity of labor supply higher than in the closed economy case.[8]

By making the w curve flatter at low levels of the capital stock, trade openness may generate a trap or increase the hold of the trap where it already existed. However, this argument needs to be qualified if trade brings gains (such as allocative efficiency gains) that affect the w* curve. What difference would it make to our conclusions if allocative gains were present? Suppose that the modern capital-intensive sector produces two goods, an exportable and an importable good. Alongside this sector, sector S produces a non-tradable good using labor subject to diminishing returns. With two traded goods, trade will allow the economy to obtain importable goods at lower costs. These efficiency gains are equivalent to a one time technological improvement and can be modeled as an upward shift in the multiplicative constant in the production function of sector M. An increase in this multiplicative constant, as a result of the opening to trade, shifts the w and w* loci upwards. Assuming a Cobb-Douglas production function with technological externalities, the shifts in the w and w* curves (holding K constant) are given by:

---

[7] The same applies to an open economy version of a model with efficiency wages, as long as Kaldorian underemployment exists in the traditional sector.

[8] Besides making a low K intersection more likely, the higher elasticity of labor supply has another consequence. The w curve is flatter in the open economy case. This tends to generate a higher real wage in the high level equilibrium. In this equilibrium, the M sector is larger than under autarky and wages benefit from the productivity gains associated with the expansion of the M sector, as well as from the lower cost of imported S goods.

$$dln(w_M/p_M) = [(1 - a)/(1 + ea)]dlnA \qquad (1)$$

$$dln(w_M/p_M) = dlnA \qquad (2)$$

where A is the multiplicative constant and e is the labor supply elasticity. Comparing these two expressions, it is readily seen that the shift in the w* locus (given by eq. 2) exceeds that of the w locus (given by eq. 1). The difference depends on the labor supply elasticity. The intuition behind this is simple: the profit rate is an increasing function of the state of technology, given the capital stock. A technological improvement must therefore increase the required wage by more than the market equilibrium wage. The more elastic the labor supply, the less the market equilibrium wage increases and the larger the increase in the profit rate. In fact, if the labor supply was perfectly elastic, the w curve would not shift at all (see eq. 1).

Given that the upward shift in the w* curve exceeds that of the w curve, the low K intersection in the open economy will feature a smaller capital stock than in the closed economy. Hence, the efficiency gains from trade reduce the hold of the development trap. The same argument can be made for other sources of gains arising from changes in market structure or the transmission of international external effects. However, it is interesting to note that these gains do not eliminate the low K intersection: the slopes of the loci, in (ln w_M/p_M, ln K) space, are independent of A. If the condition for multiple equilibria was fulfilled in the pre-trade situation, it will also be met after the opening to trade. All this is, incidentally, quite consistent with Rosenstein-Rodan views: "International trade undoubtedly reduces the size of the minimum push required, so that not *all* the wage-goods need be produced in the developing country, but it does not eliminate it. . . . International trade does much to reduce the danger of monopolies. It also effectively reduces the size of the minimum quantum of investment. But it does not dispense with the need for a big push" (Rodan, 1961, pp. 63 and 65).

3. Multiple Equilibria, Openness, and Pecuniary Externalities

Consider now the effects of trade openness in a model with multiple equilibria associated to pecuniary externalities. As discussed earlier, it is these effects that Bhagwati's and many other interpretations of the big push argument have in mind in their criticism of the argument. In the formalization of the big push argument by Murphy, Shleifer, and Vishny (1989) discussed in Chapter 8, demand conditions facing the monopolist in any given sector can be described by a kinked demand curve (see Basu, 1997). As shown in Figure 9.4, before the kink, demand is perfectly elastic at a price equal to the cost of production of traditional producers. After the kink, the demand curve

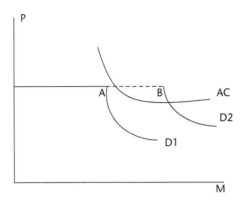

Figure 9.4 The effect of pecuniary externalities on demand and unit costs

becomes downward sloping with a unit price elasticity, given that each good has an equal share in final expenditure. As a result, marginal revenue falls to zero at the kink and beyond.

The position of the kink for, say, the shoe producer, depends on whether monopolists in other sectors invest in modern techniques. When the shoe factory considers investing in isolation, the position of the kink is determined by the volume of traditional production, since this is the volume of output that the shoe factory can expect to sell by displacing existing producers. Let this volume of output be represented by point A in Figure 9.4. In the presence of positive pecuniary externalities, the adoption of modern techniques in other sectors (textiles, for instance) has the effect of shifting the position of the kink outwards (from A to B). It is this outward shift in the position of the demand curve, arising from the actions of other producers, that creates the possibility of multiple equilibria. Given the position of the unit cost curve (AC) in Figure 9.4, it is then possible that the adoption of the modern technique would be unprofitable in isolation. On the other hand, the shoe factory would be able to recover fixed costs if modern firms were simultaneously investing in other sectors.

Suppose that this economy opens to foreign trade and faces given relative prices in the international market. As discussed earlier, Bhagwati noted that now the shoe producer will be able to sell all she wishes at given prices and the demand for her product no longer depends on the textile producer adopting the modern technique. The adoption of modern techniques in textile production still affects the domestic demand for shoes, but the domestic demand for shoes no longer constrains the profitability of modern techniques in domestic shoe production. The kink in the demand curve disappears and the demand for shoes becomes perfectly elastic at the international price.

More generally, by making demand curves more elastic, trade reduces the external effects of the modern textile producer on the shoe factory. In the example above of given relative prices in the international markets, demands become perfectly elastic and the external effects disappear altogether. This is the basis for Bhagwati's criticism. His criticism is clearly valid in the context of "horizontal pecuniary externalities" involving (in the closed economy) demand spillovers *across* final producers of (potentially) traded goods. In the open economy facing given terms of trade, the shoe factory may or may not be profitable but its profitability does not depend on other sectors adopting increasing returns technologies. It does not follow, however, that export pessimism is a condition for the existence of *pecuniary externalities* in an open economy, or even for the existence of *horizontal* pecuniary externalities in this setting.

Let us first note the fact that horizontal externalities retain a practical importance in the absence of export pessimism, unless by this we were to understand anything less than infinite elasticities of demand. The investment decision of the textile producer will still affect demand and profits in the shoe industry, unless indeed the shoe producer can sell whatever she wishes at the international price. The fact is, however, that trade in reality is not free and costless: based on the findings of Chenery et al. (1975, 1986) on medium size and large countries, Murphy, Shleifer, and Vishny (1989) emphasize the significance of domestic markets as a source of demand for domestic industry.

Consider now the following setting. Price elasticities of demand for tradable goods are infinite but each of the modern firms in the multisectoral economy of Murphy, Shleifer and Vishny uses a technique that requires non-tradable inputs produced under increasing returns (as the intermediate goods in the vertical externalities model of Chapter 8).[9] When the shoe factory invests in isolation, intermediate inputs (e.g. services or infrastructure) are produced at a high cost. These high costs may keep the unit cost of the shoe producer above the international price, even at high levels of output. The AC_1 curve in Figure 9.5 shows the unit cost of the shoe producer in this case. When firms in other sectors adopt modern techniques, the market for intermediate goods is expanded. As a result, intermediate inputs are produced at lower costs and this has the effect of reducing the unit cost for the shoe factory. The unit cost curve of the shoe producer shifts from AC_1 and AC_2 in Figure 9.5. It is then possible that the adoption of the modern technique would be unprofitable in isolation, while the shoe factory would be able to recover fixed costs if modern firms were simultaneously investing in other sectors. The possibility of multiple

---

[9] To facilitate the comparison with the previous case, we assume that the intermediate input is in the nature of a fixed cost. The price of the intermediate good is then independent of output volume in any individual sector, but falls with the number of sectors that industrialize.

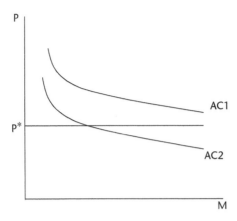

Figure 9.5 Vertical pecuniary externalities in an open economy

equilibria remains, because it is the cost curve, and not the demand curve, that shifts as a result of the actions of other producers.

Vertical pecuniary externalities can thus lead to multiple equilibria in an open economy, even if the shoe producer faces a perfectly elastic demand at the international price (p*). Chapter 15 presents a linkage effects model that also illustrates this conclusion. These examples also suggest that the transmission of vertical externalities is, in fact, more likely in an open economy than in a closed economy. The reason is, as argued earlier, that an open economy makes the labor supply more elastic and these vertical external effects require that the sector producing intermediate inputs faces an elastic labor supply.

It is somewhat ironic that early critics of the "balanced growth" implications of the presence of horizontal pecuniary externalities, based their skepticism on the view that vertical externalities were of much more practical relevance than horizontal externalities. As Fleming (1955, p. 250) argued:

> There can be little doubt but that the conditions for a 'vertical' transmission of external economies—whether forward from supplying industry to using industry, or backward from using industry to supplying industry—are much more favourable than for a 'horizontal' transmission between industries at the same stage.

He attributes the emphasis given to horizontal externalities by Rosenstein-Rodan and Nurkse to the neglect in the earlier literature (by Marshall and his commentators) of this type of externalities, at the expense of vertical external economies. He suggests that this neglect may have been due precisely to the greater practical importance of vertical pecuniary externalities than of horizontal externalities. As he puts it:

> The fact that our authors, other than Allyn Young, seem to lay more emphasis on the 'horizontal' rather than the 'vertical' variant of the balanced-growth doctrine

is probably due to the fact that the external economies underlying the former are less frequently discussed in the literature than those underlying the latter. But the 'horizontal' transmission of economies may have been neglected by Marshall and his commentators precisely because, where it exists at all, it is relatively unimportant. (Fleming, 1955, p. 250)

The relative importance of horizontal and vertical externalities impinges on the question of the relative merits of balanced vs. unbalanced growth strategies. The vertical externalities model of section 2 in Chapter 8 helps illustrating this point. The policy implication of the model is certainly not to develop simultaneously the final goods producing sectors but rather to *concentrate* resources in the capital-intensive and intermediate inputs sectors, which comes close to advocating unbalanced growth. The reason is not the same as the one advanced in Hirschman's advocacy of unbalanced growth, which was based on the scarcity of administrative and entrepreneurial capabilities in developing countries.[10] The reason, in this case (in which Hirschman's considerations do not play a role), is that multiple equilibria arise from the presence of vertical externalities. If there had been horizontal external effects between the final goods producing sectors, the policy implications would have been different and closer to a balanced growth strategy. The example then suggests that the policy implications of a big push model can either take the form of balanced or unbalanced growth, depending on the type of external effects involved. Moreover, it is interesting to note that the example points to the ambiguity of the terms "balanced" and "unbalanced" growth: a policy oriented towards shifting resources from the labor-intensive sector to the capital-intensive and intermediate inputs sectors ("unbalanced" growth) is also one aiming at the balanced development of the capital-intensive and intermediate inputs sectors.

---

[10] Hirschman's (1958) criticism of balanced growth was based mostly on feasibility considerations: "This is, of course, the major bone I have to pick with the balanced growth theory: its application requires huge amounts of precisely those abilities which we have identified as likely to be very limited in supply in underdeveloped countries" (pp. 52–3).

Part III
Aggregate Demand and Growth

10

Effective Demand and Factor Accumulation

Classical development theory, just as mainstream growth theory in its neo-classical and endogenous growth versions, has no role for aggregate demand in the growth process. Rates of factor accumulation depend on rates of return that are independent of aggregate demand or are given exogenously as in the case of labor force growth. Technological progress is exogenous, as in the neoclassical model, a by-product of capital accumulation as in endogen-ous growth or classical development models with technological externalities, or driven by such supply side factors as research and development expend-itures as in the product variety and Schumpeterian models.

All this was not the same in early mainstream growth theory. In the early years of growth theory, in the writings of Harrod (1939), Kahn (1959), and Robinson (1962), aggregate demand did have both level and growth effects. Subsequent work by heterodox growth theorists, drawing on the work of Kalecki (1971), Steindl (1952), Robinson (1962), and others, examined growth with unemployed labor and excess capacity of capital and argued that the rate of growth of the economy in the long run is affected by aggregate demand influences. I now turn to these different traditions of growth theory. Without attempting to review a vast literature, the following four chapters turn to a discussion of the links between the supply-side models of neoclassical and development theory in previous chapters and the demand-driven growth models of Keynesian and structuralist macroeconomics.[1]

This chapter and the next drop one at a time the assumptions of full employment and supply side driven technical change. This first chapter is organized as follows. The first section sets out the basic assumptions of the model and then uses this framework to address a number of issues that figured prominently in early growth theory from the 1940s to the 1960s. The second section discusses how, with given nominal wages and in the absence of labor

---

[1] For a comprehensive survey of Keynesian growth theory, see Commendatore, D'Acunto, Panico, and Pinto (2003).

supply constraints, the growth of productive capacity and aggregate demand are brought into equality through changes in the profit rate and the rate of capital accumulation, with the economy converging to a demand-constrained path. The third section removes the assumption of given nominal wages and shows how, in the absence of endogenous technical progress and migratory flows, the warranted growth rate beyond the medium run adjusts to the natural growth rate given by the exogenous growth of the labor force. However, unlike neoclassical models, the equilibrium growth path determined by the natural rate is not, in general, a full employment path.[2] As we shall see, while the economy's growth rate is *supply constrained* by the exogenous natural rate, the employment rate is *demand constrained in the long run* and there is no tendency in the economy to converge to full employment or to a unique natural rate of unemployment.

Most of our discussion of the medium and long-term interactions between factor accumulation and effective demand growth makes the assumption of a small open economy which is, in my view, the appropriate analytical framework for the typical developing economy whose growth leaves by and large unaffected the terms of trade that it faces in international markets. However, the fourth and last section of the chapter introduces the assumption of a large economy in a two-country model in order to illustrate the well known Thirlwall's law, based on Harrod's trade multiplier, according to which the pattern of trade specialization is what really matters in explaining differences among countries in the rate of growth. An appendix discusses in detail the stability of the long-run equilibrium.

1. A Small Open-economy Model: The Basic Assumptions

I shall distinguish three time periods. In the short run, as usual, nominal wages and the capital stock are taken as given. In the medium run, through the revision of expectations, the economy converges to Harrod's warranted growth rate or Joan Robinson's desired rate of accumulation with given nominal wages but a changing capital stock. In the long run, with flexible wages, the economy converges to a path in which the employment rate is stable and the warranted and natural growth rates are equal to each other.

---

[2] The adjustment to the exogenous natural rate takes place through changes in the real exchange rate and product wages. The same problem was solved in neoclassical models by assuming a flexible capital-output ratio as a result of technological substitution between capital and labor (induced by changes in factor prices) and in neo-Keynesian models by assuming a flexible savings rate that changed as a result of income redistribution at full employment between capitalists and workers (with different propensities to save) (see Sen, 1970, for a classical review).

The model is deliberately idiosyncratic. First, all the complications and negative impacts on aggregate demand and employment that wage deflation may bring about in real life are assumed away (these complications are left for Chapter 13). The small open economy considered is a price taker in international markets and a fall in nominal wages has an unambiguous positive effect on the level of employment. In fact, the only effect of wage deflation is a positive competitiveness effect on exports and overall output and employment. Yet, despite these features and the fact that nominal wages are flexible beyond the medium term, the economy does not converge to a full employment equilibrium in the long run (or to a natural rate of unemployment that is independent of effective demand). It only converges to a long-run growth path in which Harrod's warranted growth rate is equal to the natural growth rate and the unemployment rate is constant. Moreover, aggregate demand has long-run *level* effects on the employment rate when the natural growth rate is exogenous and can even have *growth* effects when the natural growth rate is endogenous.[3]

Another distinctive feature meant to simplify the analysis is that, unlike a model of a two-sector economy producing tradable goods for which the economy is a price taker in international markets and non-tradable goods produced under imperfect competition, the economy considered produces a single tradable good but firms face different competitive conditions in the domestic market and in export markets. They are price takers in export markets and can sell whatever they wish at given international prices. In contrast, in the domestic market they operate under imperfect competition, facing downward sloping demand curves with a constant price elasticity of demand. This may be the result of import barriers or, more simply, of the fact that firms (producing say *Corona* beer) face a much more price elastic demand in foreign markets than they do in their home (Mexican) market where they have a long established tradition.

Firms maximize profits equal to $P_D D + P_X X - W L$, where D is domestic sales, X is exports, W is the nominal wage, and P_D and P_X are respectively the price of domestic sales and the price of exports (equal to the international price times a constant nominal exchange rate equal to one). In maximizing profits, firms take nominal wages and the price of exports as given and are subject to two constraints. The first is the production function which we assume to be Cobb-Douglas: $Y = F(L, K) = K^a (AL)^{1-a}$, where Y is total output,

---

[3] As we shall see, two features of the economy allow aggregate demand to have these long-run effects. The first is the existence of imperfect competition in the domestic market. This, despite the fact that firms face perfectly elastic demands in foreign markets, allows domestic demand to have effects on profitability and investment and thus on future levels of employment and output. The second is the existence of imperfect wage flexibility which prevents nominal wages from continuously falling in the presence of a positive rate of unemployment.

and K and L are capital and labor inputs. The level of productivity (A) is, for the time being, taken as exogenously given and constant over time. The second constraint is a demand constraint in the domestic market given by $D = B \, (P_i/P_D)^{-\phi}$ where P_i is the individual price, in equilibrium equal to the average price of domestic sales (P_D, or domestic price for short), B is a position parameter, and ϕ is the constant price elasticity of demand.

From the first order conditions for profit maximization, the domestic price and employment are determined as:

$$P_D = (1+z)W/F'(L) \qquad 1+z = \phi/(\phi-1) \tag{1}$$

$$W/P_X = F'(L) = (1-a)A^{(1-a)}K^a \, L^{-a} \tag{2}$$

Eq. (1) shows that the domestic price is set as a mark-up (z) over marginal labor cost ($W/F'(L)$), the mark-up being determined by the price elasticity of demand facing firms in the domestic market. Because firms are price takers in export markets, they sell abroad up to the point where the price of exports is equal to the marginal cost of labor (see eq. 2). Eqs (1) and (2) imply that the ratio of the domestic price to export price is equal to the ratio of the domestic price to marginal labor cost, i.e. $P_D/P_X = (1 + z)$.

The determination of employment is derived from eq. (2) showing the equality between the marginal product of labor and the wage per unit of exports (the product wage for exporting firms). Indeed, solving (2) for L yields: $L = [A(1-a)^{(1-a)}/(W/P_X)]^{1/a} K$, which shows the level of employment determined by the capital stock, the product wage for exporting firms, and the level of productivity (A) which, by affecting the marginal labor costs of exporting firms, modifies the level of employment. This level of employment (and output) is therefore independent of domestic demand. Firms do not increase production in response to higher domestic demand (given the product wage, W/P_X). Rather, they adjust by reducing exports and increasing sales in the domestic market. The reason is that they face a perfectly elastic demand for exports. Indeed, if they increased production in response to higher domestic demand, their marginal cost would increase above the price of exports. This would induce them to reduce their exports until the marginal cost of production is again equal to the price of exports. This means that a higher domestic demand fully crowds out exports. A higher level of foreign demand, by contrast, to the extent that it increases the international price of exports has a positive effect on employment and output given the nominal wage. The same effect results from a devaluation of the nominal exchange rate since it increases the price of exports in domestic currency.

Since the price of domestic sales is higher than the marginal cost, a higher volume of domestic sales raises the average mark-up on total sales, as well as the profit rate on the given capital stock. Indeed, from the definitions of the average price of total sales (P) and the profit rate (r), we have:

$$P = (P_D D + P_X X)/Y$$

$$r = (P\ Y - W\ L)/P_I K$$

where P_I is the price of capital goods. Combining these equations and using (2) implies the following relationship between the profit rate and the share of domestic sales in output (D/Y):

$$r = [a + z\ D/Y](P_X/P_I)v \quad \text{where} \quad v = [(1 - a)A(P_X/W)]^{(1-a)/a} \tag{3}$$

where v is the output-capital ratio (Y/K). Eq. (3) shows the profit rate as an increasing function of the share of domestic sales in total output and the output-capital ratio which, given the determination of employment and output, is an increasing function of the ratio of export prices to wages (that we shall refer to as the real exchange rate).[4,5] The profit rate is thus an increasing function of domestic demand and the real exchange rate (as well as an inverse function of the ratio of capital goods prices to export prices, P_I/P_X). This means that while domestic demand does not affect output and employment in the short run, to the extent that it affects profitability and investment and, thus, the size of the capital stock in the future, it has a positive effect on future levels of employment and output.

Turning to the demand side, assume there are no savings out of wages and let s_π be the propensity to save out of profits. Consumption (C) is then determined as: $P_D\ C = W\ L + (1 - s_\pi)\ (P\ Y - W\ L)$, where we are assuming away, for simplicity, imports of consumption goods. Investment has a domestic (I_d) and an imported component (M_k). Thus: $p_I\ I = p_D\ I_d + p_M\ M_k$, where $M_k = m\ I$ so that there is a fixed amount (m < 1) of complementary imports per unit of total investment.

2. Interactions Between Profitability and Accumulation in the Medium Term

We now derive two relationships between the profit rate and the rate of accumulation such that, in a steady state, profit expectations are fulfilled. In this steady state, the rates of growth of output and the capital stock are

---

[4] Note that the profit rate exceeds its competitive equilibrium value (a $v\ P_X/P_I$) by the extent to which the mark-up is positive.

[5] The expression for v is derived from eq. (2) and the production function.

constant and, as we shall see below, equal to Robinson's "desired rate of accumulation" (Robinson, 1962).

Substituting from the imports and consumption functions into the goods market equilibrium condition and normalizing by the value of the capital stock (p_I K), we can write the equilibrium condition as the equality between savings and investment plus net exports (all normalized by the capital stock):

$$s_\pi r = (1 - m)g + x \tag{4}$$

where g is the rate of capital accumulation (I/K) and x is the export-capital ratio. We choose units such that $P_M/P_I = P_X/P_I (= 1)$. Substituting from (3) into (4), and using $D/Y = (1 - X/Y)$ and $X/Y = x K/Y$ in order to eliminate x, we get the first relationship between the profit rate and the rate of accumulation:

$$r = [1/(1 + zs_\pi)][(z + a)v + z(1 - m)g] \qquad \text{where} : v = v(A, Px/W) \tag{5}$$

Eq. (5) shows the profit rate that clears the goods market as an increasing function of the rate of accumulation. A higher rate of accumulation raises the profit rate through its effect on domestic demand, as described above. This is why higher propensities to import and to save (m and s_π), which reduce domestic demand at each level of the rate of accumulation, have according to eq. (5) a negative effect on the profit rate. The real exchange rate (P_X/W) has a positive effect on the profit rate by increasing employment and output at each given level of the capital stock, and thus the output-capital ratio.

Changes in the mark-up (z) have three different effects on the profit rate. The first operates through the level of consumption. The higher is the markup, the lower, other things being equal, is workers consumption and therefore the level of domestic demand and profits. This effect depends on the propensity to save out of profits (see the first term on the RHS of eq. 5) and is at its maximum when there is no consumption out of profits ($s_\pi = 1$), so that the fall in workers consumption is not even partially compensated by an increase in capitalists' consumption. It disappears if capitalists consume all their profits ($s_\pi = 0$) since then redistribution against wage earners has no effect on the overall level of consumption and domestic demand. The second effect is a positive effect on profits for a given output-capital ratio. Given this ratio, a higher mark up implies a higher share of profits in total income and a higher profit rate (see the second term on the RHS of eq. 5). The third effect is also a positive effect and operates as follows: a higher rate of accumulation increases the profit rate the more so the higher the mark-up. This effect is at its maximum when all capital goods are produced domestically under conditions of imperfect competition (m = 0) and disappears when all capital goods are imported (m = 1) and therefore a higher investment rate has no effects on domestic

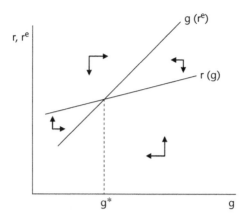

Figure 10.1 The warranted growth rate

profits. Note then that this effect is present only to the extent that investment is a component of domestic demand.[6]

The second relationship is a rate of accumulation function which makes the rate of accumulation depend on the propensity to invest (ψ) and the expected profit rate (r^e) (à la Joan Robinson, 1962), as well as a risk-adjusted international profit rate (r^*) under the assumption of international capital mobility:

$$g = \psi(r^e - r^*) \qquad \text{(which implies with } r = r^e, r = (g/\psi) + r^*) \qquad (6)$$

In a steady state, r^e = r. Figure 10.1 shows the determination of the steady state values of g and r. At the intersection of the two lines, corresponding to eqs (5) and (6), the rate of accumulation generates a profit rate that just equals the expected profit rate that induced this rate of accumulation.[7] This desired or equilibrium rate of accumulation is analogous to Harrod's warranted growth rate. For, in the present open economy context, it is such that the investment forthcoming at the equilibrium profit rate generates an addition to productive capacity such that the increase in domestic demand leaves the composition of total output between exports and domestic sales unchanged. Thus, on the warranted growth path, exports and domestic

[6] It is worth noting that there are two situations in which the profit rate is independent of the rate of accumulation. The first is when the domestic market is perfectly competitive and therefore z = 0. There is then a unique profit rate independent of the rate of capital accumulation and equal to (a v) (a horizontal line in Figure 10.1). The second is when all capital goods are imported (m = 1) and there are no effects of changes in investment on domestic sales. The profit rate is then equal to $[(z + a) \, v]/(1 + z \, s_\pi)$.

[7] In Joan Robinson's expression this is the "desired rate of accumulation", "a rate of accumulation which is generating just the expectation of profit that is required to cause it to be maintained" (Robinson, 1962, p. 130 in Sen, 1970).

demand grow at the same rate, equal to the rate of growth of productive capacity.

To the right of the r (g) line (given by eq. 5), the rate of accumulation is higher, at each level of the profit rate, than required for the domestic market to clear. Firms will thus reduce exports and increase sales in the more profitable domestic market. Thus, as shown in Figure 10.1, the profit rate increases when the economy is to the right of the r (g) line and falls when it is to the left. Above the g (r^e) line (given by eq. 6), the profit rate is higher than expected and investment decisions will be revised upwards, while below the line the rate of profit is lower than expected and the rate of accumulation decreases. As the lines are drawn in Figure 10.1 and, in the absence of labor supply constraints, the economy will converge to the stable equilibrium at the intersection of the two lines corresponding to Harrod's warranted growth rate or to the "desired rate of accumulation" in Robinson's expression. The equilibrium is stable provided that the g (r^e) line is steeper than the r (g) line, i.e. if: $(1/\psi) > z (1 - m)/(1 + z s_\pi)$.

Consider the effects of changes in key parameters. A devaluation of the real exchange rate (higher P_X/W) shifts the r (g) line up, moving the economy to a higher growth rate and a higher profit rate. The initial impact on profitability, resulting from the real devaluation, is compounded by the increase in the rate of accumulation and its positive effect on profits (operating through the higher domestic demand). Changes in domestic demand parameters, such as reductions in the propensity to save out of profits or the import coefficient, also shift the position and/or slope of the r (g) line upwards and move the economy to a new equilibrium path with a higher growth rate and a higher profitability. The difference with the effects of a real devaluation is that in the new equilibrium path, the share of exports in total demand is lower than in the case of a real devaluation but real wages are higher (since $W/P_D = (W/P_X) (P_X/P_D)$ and W/P_X falls with a devaluation). In fact when domestic demand parameters change, there is no change in real wages. The rate of profit (and accumulation) in the new equilibrium is higher precisely as a result of the change in total demand in favor of domestic sales. Changes in the mark up also affect the position of the r (g) line but the net impact depends on the relative strength of the three effects discussed earlier.

The propensity to invest and the risk premium affect the slope and/or position of the g (r^e) line. A higher propensity to invest (which may result from an increase in autonomous investment, including public investment) makes the g (r^e) line flatter and increases the equilibrium rates of profit and accumulation. An increase in the risk premium which negatively affects investment, shifts the g (r^e) to the left and reduces profitability and growth. No changes in real wages are involved here.

A comparison with Keynesian models

A similarity with early Keynesian growth models (Kaldor, 1956; Robinson, 1962) is that the mechanism which makes the profit rate depend positively on the rate of accumulation involves an increase in profit margins at an unchanged level of output in the short run. Kaldor explicitly assumes a state of full employment so that output is given at the corresponding level. In the face of a higher level of investment, the equality between investment and savings is achieved through an increase in profit margins rather than increased output. Indeed, a well-known feature of the Kaldorian model is that, with different propensities to save out of profits and wages, overall savings increase with the redistribution from wages to profits. Robinson seemingly assumes a state of full capacity with unemployment in the labor market (see on the subject Marglin, 1984; and Dutt, 1990). What makes the profit rate increase with the rate of accumulation is that the profit mark-up (not output) increases with the higher level of demand coming from investment. In our model, the mechanism is also an increase in the average profit mark-up (as an increase in investment raises domestic demand and shifts the composition of sales in favor of the more profitable domestic market) but it does not involves the assumptions of full employment (there is unemployment in the short-run equilibrium and even in the long-run equilibrium) or a binding full capacity constraint. What keeps output unaffected by domestic demand in the short run is the fact that firms have the possibility to offset a fall, say, in domestic demand by increasing exports in the face of a perfectly elastic demand in export markets.

There are also some similarities with more recent Keynesian demand-driven growth models. The stability condition derived above is similar to that present in these models. The propensity to invest out of profits (ψ), which affects (inversely) the slope of the g (r^e) line, must not be too high relative to the leakages out of the circular flow of income and expenditure which affect the slope of the r (g) line. These leakages are here determined by the propensity to save out of profits (s_π) and the import coefficient (m). Otherwise, if the stability condition is not satisfied, the "accelerator effects" of profits on investment will generate a Harrod's knife-edge instability problem. This is the case shown in Figure 10.2 in which the g (r^e) line crosses from above the r (g) line. There is then a saddle point equilibrium, the corresponding saddle path representing the (r, g) combinations below which the economy collapses and above which the economy explodes. Another possibility is that there is no intersection if the slopes happen to be the same, in which case the economy will expand indefinitely (in the absence of labor supply constraints) if the g (r^e) is above the r (g) line or contract forever in the opposite case.

Still another possibility is that of non-linearities and multiple equilibria. This is the case of Robinson's (1962) famous "banana diagram" in which the g (r^e) curve crosses from above the r (g) line at low levels of profitability, then becomes steeper at higher levels of profitability and crosses again from below, at high values of g and r, the r (g) line (see Figure 10.3). We then have a low level unstable equilibrium (below which the economy collapses) and a high level stable equilibrium similar to that in Figure 10.1.

Another similarity with Keynesian models, besides the analogous stability condition, is that when the economy is on the warranted growth path, growth is demand-led. Indeed, as we have already discussed, changes in demand parameters (s$_\pi$ and m) and in the propensity to invest (ψ) modify the position or slope of the lines and therefore the equilibrium rates of profit and accumulation.

There are, however, two important differences with recent literature on Keynesian growth theory. The first is that, unlike what happens in models

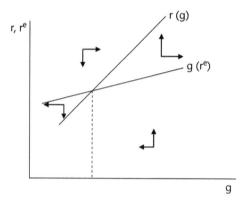

Figure 10.2 Unstable equilibrium

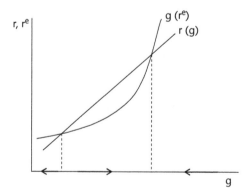

Figure 10.3 Robinson's banana diagram

that assume a technology with fixed coefficients and a variable degree of excess capacity, the steady state in this model features the desired output-capital ratio and there is no reason for firms to revise their investment decisions. The model is thus free from the objection to models in the Kalecki-Steindl tradition that in the steady state, firms' actual capacity utilization may in general not be equal to the desired degree of capacity utilization.[8] This difference is related to the fact that in the present model the level of output plays no role in the adjustment of the goods market (given the real exchange rate). This feature, however, does not prevent growth from being demand-driven. Just as in Keynesian models, an increase in the propensity to invest, a fall in the propensity to save or a fall in the import coefficient all tend to increase the steady state values of the rates of profit and accumulation. The growth effects of changes in the propensity to save and in the import coefficient are due to the assumption of imperfect competition in the domestic market. If firms faced perfectly elastic demand curves, the mark-up over marginal cost would be zero and the rates of profit and accumulation would be independent of the propensity to save and the import coefficient (s_π and m). As the reader can verify, with z = 0, the r (g) line becomes horizontal at the competitive equilibrium value of the profit rate (a v).[9]

A second difference has to do with the effects of changes in the real wage on the rate of accumulation and growth. Whether a fall in the real wage raises or reduces growth depends on the source of the real wage reduction. The real consumption wage is: $W/P_D = (W/P_X)/(1 + z)$. If the real wage falls due to an increase in the real exchange rate (P_X/W) the result is an unambiguous increase in the equilibrium growth rate as the r (g) line shifts upwards. In this case, growth is always profit-led and cannot be wage-led.[10] The reason for this difference with recent Keynesian models arises from the assumptions of a perfectly elastic export demand and a flexible capital-output ratio. Together, these assumptions imply that the fall in the product wage (W/P_X) increases employment and output, which has a positive effect on the profit rate and investment. If the fall in the real wage is due to an increase in the domestic markup over marginal cost, the effect on growth depends on whether the higher mark-up reduces or increases the profit rate. In the first case, the r (g) line shifts downwards, thus reducing the warranted growth rate. Growth is wage led. In the opposite case, the higher mark-up has a positive effect on profitability. Then the r (g) line shifts upwards and increases the equilibrium rates of profit and accumulation.

---

[8] For models in the Kalecki-Steindl tradition see Taylor (1983) and Dutt (1990).

[9] Note that while independent of the rate of accumulation, the profit rate remains a positive function of the real exchange rate.

[10] Or, in Bhaduri and Marglin's (1990) terminology, the growth regime is "exhilarationist" rather than "stagnationist".

3. Long-Run Dynamics: The Adjustment of the Warranted Growth Rate to the Natural Rate

The demand-constrained growth path of the previous section may be seen as a solution of the model for a medium run period in which we can neglect changes in nominal wages. In order to examine what happens beyond this period, we have to consider the adjustment of nominal wages and the real exchange rate that will occur as a consequence of labor market conditions.

Consider, first, the determinants of the rate of wage inflation. We adopt here a structuralist specification which makes the growth rate of nominal wages (w) depend on the rate of domestic price inflation (p) and the gap between a target or bargained real wage (ω) and the real consumption wage effectively received by workers (W/P_D):[11]

$$w = p + \lambda(\omega - W/P_D) \qquad \omega = \omega(L/N) \quad \omega' > 0 \qquad (7)$$

Further, we assume that the target real wage is an inverse function of the unemployment rate (that is, an increasing function of the employment rate, L/N). This inverse relationship is supported by empirical research on the "wage curve" which establishes a negative relationship across regions and sectors between wage levels and unemployment (see Blanchflower and Oswald, 1994 and 2005). The wage inflation equation is thus similar to a Phillips curve equation augmented by the effects of expected price inflation[12] although, as we shall see later, it does not imply a unique natural rate of unemployment independent of aggregate demand. Eq. (7) can also be interpreted as showing the dynamic behavior of the real consumption wage, $w - \pi$, as an inverse function of its level: a higher real wage (given the target wage) leads to slower growth of nominal wages in relation to domestic prices. The feedback effect on the growth of the real wage is thus negative.

Consider now the dynamic behavior of the employment rate over time. Solving (2) for the level of employment (L), taking logs and differentiating with respect to time, and then subtracting the rate of growth of the labor force (n) from both sides of the equation, we have:

$$l - n = g - (1/a)(w - p) - n \qquad g = g(W/P_D) \quad g' < 0 \qquad (8)$$

where l is the rate of growth of employment and p is the rate of change of export prices since, given the mark-up, export prices grow at the same rate as domestic prices. In eq. (8), g, the rate of capital accumulation, equal to the rate

---

[11] In addition to structuralist models of inflation, the wage equation is in line with efficiency wage models and the literature on the wage curve (see Rapetti, 2011, for further discussion).
[12] Indeed, as long as the nominal exchange rate is constant, current price inflation is nil and current inflation coincides with expected inflation.

of growth of the capital stock assuming no depreciation of capital, is determined by eqs (5) and (6) under the assumption $r = r^e$. We express this equilibrium rate of accumulation as an inverse function of the real wage. Other variables and parameters affecting the equilibrium rate of accumulation are the propensity to invest, the level of productivity, the propensity to save out of profits, the import coefficient and the mark-up. Note that since the growth of the real wage in eq. (7) is an increasing function of the employment rate, eq. (8) shows the rate of change of the employment rate $(1 - n)$ as an inverse function of its level.

Consider now the dynamic adjustments in real wages and the employment rate. Setting in eq. (7) $w = p$, we obtain the equation of a locus of $(L/N, W/P_D)$ combinations along which the real wage is stationary:

$$\lambda(\omega(L/N) - W/P_D) = 0$$

In $(L/N, W/P_D)$ space, this is an upward sloping schedule: a higher employment rate tends to raise w above p and this requires a higher real wage, which reduces w, in order to maintain stability of the real wage. Because the feedback effect of the real wage on its rate of change is negative (and thus stabilizing), the real wage falls when above the locus and increases when below it (see Figure 10.4). The position of the schedule is determined by labor market parameters (the ω (.) function) and domestic market structure (summarized in the mark-up).

Substituting from (7) into (8) and setting $l = n$, we obtain a locus of $(L/N, W/P_D)$ combinations along which the employment rate is stationary:

$$g(W/P_D) - (1/a)\lambda[\omega(L/N) - W/P_D] - n = 0 \qquad g' < 0 \qquad \omega' > 0$$

This schedule can have a negative or a positive slope. The reason is that a higher real wage has two effects on the rate of growth of employment. First, it reduces employment growth through its negative effect on the rate of accumulation. Second, it increases employment growth, via capital-labor substitution, through its negative effect on the growth of real wages. In Figure 10.4, I assume that the first effect is stronger than the second and this is why the schedule is downward sloping: the negative effect on employment growth of a higher real wage requires a lower employment rate (which by reducing wage growth increases employment growth) in order to keep the employment rate stable (see appendix for further analysis). The position of the schedule is determined by goods market and domestic demand parameters affecting the g (.) function and labor market parameters affecting the λ (.) and ω (.) functions. Because the feedback effect of the employment rate on its growth (given by $1 - n$) is stabilizing, the employment rate increases when the economy is to the right of the schedule and falls when it is to the left.

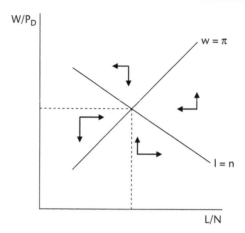

Figure 10.4 Long-term dynamic adjustments

As shown in the diagram, provided that the long-run equilibrium at the intersection of the two schedules is stable, the economy converges to a steady state in which the rate of capital accumulation is equal to Harrod's natural rate (the growth rate of the labor force, n, under our present assumptions) while the output-capital ratio, the employment rate, the real exchange rate and real wages all remain constant over time. The appendix discusses the stability conditions. Even though at first sight paradoxical, the policy implication is clear: while aggregate demand policies can increase the employment rate, and move the economy towards full employment, they cannot increase, in the absence of technical progress or endogenous labor force growth, the long-run rate of growth which is determined by the exogenous natural rate.

A comparison with neoclassical models

While the economy's growth rate is constrained, as in the neoclassical model, by an exogenous natural rate there are several important differences with that model. First, the employment rate in the long-run equilibrium need not be the corresponding to the full employment of the labor force. Why, if there is nominal wage flexibility and a positive competitiveness effect on aggregate demand from the fall in nominal wages, doesn't the labor market clear at full employment? Note that, starting from an employment rate lower than the long-run equilibrium value with a target real wage that is below the actual real wage, nominal and real wages fall until the real wage is equal to the target value. In this process, the gap between target and actual real wages shrinks due to the fall in the actual real wage (resulting from the fall in the nominal wage) and the increase in the target real wage (resulting from the increase in the employment rate as exports and employment rise). There is no reason, however, why the equality between target and actual real wages will take place at full employment.

Moreover, the long-run equilibrium employment rate in the present model is affected by aggregate demand unlike what happens in natural rate or NAIRU models in which, even though the economy does not converge to full employment, aggregate demand has no effect on the long-run employment rate. Consider, for example, an increase in the propensity to invest (or reductions in m and s_π that enter into the g (.) function). These changes, which increase domestic demand, shift the schedule of employment stability to the right and increase the long-run equilibrium values of the employment rate and the real wage. To see how this happens, consider the process of adjustment to an increase in the propensity to invest starting from a long-run equilibrium. As a result, the rate of accumulation exceeds the growth of the labor force and the employment rate increases. This brings about a rate of wage inflation above the rate of domestic price inflation and the real wage increases. The higher real wage reduces the profit rate and brings about a fall in the rate of accumulation back to the value of the natural rate. In the new long-run equilibrium the economy is again growing at the natural rate but in the process of adjustment to the new steady state the employment rate and real wages have permanently increased. The reason for this difference with natural rate models is that in the formulation of the dynamic behavior of wages adopted in eq. (7), there is not a unique employment rate (or unemployment rate) consistent with the equality between the rate of change of nominal wages and the rate of domestic price inflation. Rather, there is a locus of combinations L/N and W/P_D consistent with stable inflation and constant real wages.[13]

Changes in the supply side of the economy also have effects that are absent in the neoclassical model. Consider, for example, an increase in the rate of growth of the labor force starting from a long-run equilibrium. In a neoclassical model, a faster growth of the labor force (n) will reduce the steady state level of output per worker and will leave the employment rate unaffected. In the new steady state, the economy will be growing at the new and higher natural rate. In the present model, the economy will also converge to a higher growth rate (equal to the higher n) as a lower real wage shifts the position of the r (g) line upwards. However, in this process the employment rate will stabilize at a lower level than initially. The higher rate of growth of the labor force implies a leftward shift of the schedule of employment stability in Figure 10.4. This leads, indeed, to a lower real wage which raises the rate of

---

[13] There is, however, an interesting similarity with natural rate (or NAIRU) models. In these models the NAIRU depends on labor market parameters and competitive conditions in the goods market. In our model, the equilibrium employment rate also depends on these parameters. Changes in the target wage (for the same employment rate) or in the mark-up modify the position of both schedules and thus the equilibrium employment rate.

accumulation to the higher required level. But this in turn implies that the long-run value of the employment rate must fall.

This leads us to the final difference with neoclassical models. The growth rate in the less than full employment long-run equilibrium may be said to converge 'prematurely' to the natural rate. Indeed, the economy on its long-run path need not have a capital-labor ratio equal to that of the neoclassical steady state. Then, if the economy differs from a Solow-type steady state not only because the unemployment rate is positive but also because the capital-labor ratio is below its steady state value, the growth rate is less than the growth rate corresponding to the full employment path (before reaching the steady state). As we know from the analysis of the neoclassical model, the difference is proportional to the gap between the actual and the steady state level of income. The implication is that on the demand-constrained growth path (with $g = n$), the economy will not be converging to the Solow steady state since, for this to be case, its growth rate should be higher than "n", rather than equal to it. Convergence is prevented precisely by the effective demand constraints that keep the economy growing at a rate below the growth rate of factor accumulation models corresponding to the full employment path.

The full employment path as a special case

Consider now the case in which the growth rate, as determined by eqs (5) and (6), generates a growth of employment higher than the rate of growth of the labor force. Starting from less than full employment, the employment rate will rise over time. Suppose that eventually the economy reaches full employment before the increase in the real wage brings the rate of accumulation down into equality with the natural rate. Having reached full employment, the growth of employment will be constrained by the growth of the labor force. At the same time, the desired rate of capital accumulation will generate an excess demand for labor. The growth of labor demand can be derived from the output supply and labor demand functions and expressed as: $l = g + [1/(1-a)] \hat{v}$, where $\hat{v}$ is the rate of growth of the output-capital ratio. As a result of an increasing real wage, a falling output-capital ratio becomes the mechanism through which the equality between l and n is achieved. In this process, the profit rate and the desired rate of accumulation tend to fall with the increasing real wage. The economy may then eventually converge to a long-run steady state, in which the desired rate of accumulation generates an increase in labor demand that exactly matches the growth of labor supply.

In this special case, the properties of the model closely resemble those of a small open economy Solow-type growth model, with price flexibility and full employment. Both on and off the steady state, the economy is on a full employment path, and off the steady state, the rate of output growth is equal to the growth of the labor force plus the growth of output per worker resulting from the process of the increasing capital-labor and capital-output ratios. This last property is worth emphasizing. Just as in the Solow model, the process of capital deepening determines a growth rate that is higher than Harrod's natural rate (n, in this case).

4. The Large Economy Assumption, Thirlwall's Law and Thirlwall's Paradox

Consider now a large economy setting. The world economy is composed of two countries. For simplicity, I assume an AK technology in both the foreign and the home country.[14] Thus, production levels (Y_H and Y_F) are given as:

$$Y_H = A_H K_H \quad \text{and} \quad Y_F = A_F K_F,$$

where subscripts H and F refer to the home and foreign country respectively and A_H and A_F are given levels of productivity in the two countries. The two countries specialize in the production of two different tradable goods that differ in their income elasticities of demand. Foreigners spend a fraction a of their consumption spending on the good produced by the home country and the rest on the good produced by them. This fraction is given by:

$$\alpha = \alpha o \ Y_F^{e_F-1} P^{1-u_F} \qquad P = P_H/P_F \qquad (9)$$

Note that $e_F = u_F = 1$ implies constant expenditure shares for the two goods; $e_F < 1$ implies that demand for the home good is income inelastic; and $u_F < 1$ implies that demand for the home good is price inelastic.

The foreign good is the only investment good in the two countries. In the home country, residents spend a fraction β of their consumption spending on the foreign good and the rest on the home good. For simplicity, we assume $\beta = 1$. Trade involves then a foreign good, that is used as a consumption and an investment good in the home country, and a home good that is used as a consumption good in the foreign country.

These assumptions imply that the value of the home country's exports is given by: $P_H X_H = a \ (1-s_F) \ P_F \ Y_F$, where s_F is the savings rate in the foreign country. The value of the foreign country's exports is determined as: $P_F X_F = P_H Y_H$.

---

[14] The same results that I want to highlight would obtain in a model in which growth is demand constrained in both countries or in a model in which one country is demand constrained and the other is supply constrained (as in the North-South models of Taylor, 1981 and 1983, and Dutt, 1990 and 2003, which have a Keynes-Kalecki North and a Lewis South). The model in this section draws on Dutt (2003).

Short-run equilibrium

In the short run, capital stocks are given and markets clear through changes in the terms of trade. Trade equilibrium implies: $P_H X_H = P_F X_F$. Substituting from the export equations into this equality and solving for the terms of trade $(P = P_H/P_F)$, we get:

$$P = [a_0(1 - s_F)(A_F K_F)e_F/A_H K_H]u_F \qquad (10)$$

which shows the terms of trade as an increasing function of K_F (whose increase creates excess demand for the home good) and a decreasing function of K_H (whose increase tends to create excess supply for the home good).

The stability of the short-run equilibrium requires that $u_F > 0$. In a more general formulation the stability condition would be the Marshall-Lerner condition, which is implicitly fulfilled in our model since the price elasticity of foreign demand has been assumed equal to 1.

Long-run dynamics of accumulation and the terms of trade

In the long run, capital stocks grow according to the rates of accumulation of the two countries. Assuming that there is no depreciation of the capital stock, the rate of accumulation in the foreign country is:

$$I_F/K_F = s_F A_F \qquad (11)$$

In the home country, the rate of accumulation is:

$$I_H/K_H = s_H A_H P \qquad (12)$$

where s_H is the home country savings rate. Notice the difference with the foreign country rate of accumulation. In eq. (12), the terms of trade affect the home country rate of accumulation as the purchasing power of its savings depend on the relative price of the capital good (which is the inverse of the terms of trade P_H/P_F). In other words, in the home country savings are given by: $S_H = s_H A_H K_H$, where S_H refers to home country savings *in units of the home good*. Since investment spending in the home country is in foreign goods, home country investment will be an increasing function of the terms of trade to the extent that an increase in P increases the volume of investment goods that can be purchased with a given amount of home country savings in units of the home good: $I_H = P S_H$. Combining this equation with the expression for S_H implies eq. (12).

The long-term dynamics of growth and the terms of trade are shown in Figure 10.5. The horizontal line g_F corresponds to eq. (11) and shows g_F independent of the terms of trade. The g_H line with positive and constant

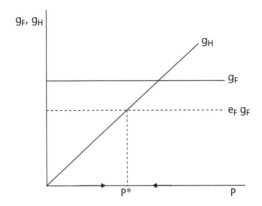

Figure 10.5 Long-run dynamics of the terms of trade and capital accumulation

slope corresponds to eq. (12). Taking logarithms in eq. (10) and differentiating with respect to time gives us the rate of change of the terms of trade:

$$(\mathrm{d}\ln P/\mathrm{d}t)(1/P) = [1/u_F][e_F g_F - g_H] \tag{13}$$

which shows that the rate of change of P depends on the gap between $e_F g_F$ and g_H. In a more general formulation with β different from 1, the change in P would depend on the difference between $e_F g_F$ and $e_H g_H$, where e_H is the income elasticity of demand of the foreign good.

Suppose now that $e_F < 1$, i.e., the home country specializes in income inelastic goods while the foreign country specializes in goods that have a unit and therefore higher income elasticity of demand. The $e_F g_F$ line is below the g_F line. The two lines, g_H and $e_F g_F$ cross at a long equilibrium with stationary terms of trade and constant rates of accumulation in the two countries. To the right of the intersection $g_H > e_F g_F$ and the terms of trade (P) fall. The reason is that since the income elasticity of demand for the foreign good is higher than that for the home good, demand for the foreign good is growing faster. As the terms of trade deteriorate for the home country, its rate of accumulation falls. This moves g_H closer to $e_F g_F$ until eventually P reaches a stationary value at P*. The opposite happens to the left of the intersection. The economies thus converge to a long-run unique and stable equilibrium with uneven development since, at this point, $g_H < g_F$, so that the home country is growing at a permanently lower rate than the foreign country.

The reason for this uneven development is that in the steady state, Thirlwall's law applies. Since e_F is the income elasticity of demand for the home country's exports (e_X) and e_H is the unit income elasticity of demand for the home country's imports (e_M), $g_H = (e_F/e_H) g_F$ implies the familiar expression for Thirlwall's law, $g_H = (e_X/e_M) g_F$. The pattern of specialization in income inelastic goods condemns the home country to a lower long-run rate of growth than the foreign country.

The steady state in the model just presented features not only Thirlwall's law, it also features what we may call Thirlwall's paradox: no matter how much the home country saves and invests, its long-run rate of growth is determined by the growth rate of the foreign country, and the income elasticities of demand for the foreign and home goods. Indeed, suppose that starting from a long-run equilibrium, home country residents increase their savings and investment rate. The g_H line becomes steeper. At the initial terms of trade, we now have $g_H > e_F g_F$. The terms of trade will then fall over time as demand for the foreign good grows faster than that for the home good, reducing again the home country's capacity for accumulation. Since in this process $e_F g_F$ does not change, the new long-run equilibrium will feature lower terms of trade for the home country and the same rate of accumulation and growth equal to $g_H = (e_F/e_H) g_F$ (see Figure 10.6). The pattern of specialization is not only an important factor for the growth of the home country; it is the only factor, together with the foreign country growth rate, that matters for growth in the long run!

The large economy assumption is crucial to Thirlwall's paradox which breaks down without it. This is a major shortcoming of the model that considerably weakens the ability to understand the constraints conditioning the growth of developing economies while exaggerating, in my view, the role of international asymmetries in the explanation of the growth performance of the typical developing economy. Note that in the extreme alternative case of exogenous terms of trade, growth is independent of the income elasticity of demand for a country's exports and, instead, domestic factors affecting the rate of capital accumulation become extremely important in the determination of long-run growth. This is true in both Keynesian open economy

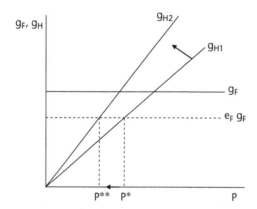

Figure 10.6 Thirlwall's paradox

growth models reviewed in this chapter and in open economy development theory models discussed in Chapter 9. It is also worth noting that the small economy assumption does not imply that the pattern of specialization is unimportant, as we have seen in detail in Chapter 9. The pattern of specialization is important but this is due to the production conditions of different goods rather than to their demand conditions.[15]

Thirlwall's law has led to an interpretation of differences in growth rates among countries as a result of the distinctive foreign demand characteristics of the goods produced and emphasizing thus differences in the patterns of trade specialization and the role of the balance of payments constraint (see, in particular, Thirlwall, 1979; Thirlwall and Hussain, 1982). The empirical evidence provided by a large literature on the subject is flawed, however, with major shortcomings. The typical empirical test of Thirlwall's law is really a test of the proposition that over the long run the balance of trade cannot be on unsustainable paths. If the large economy assumption does not hold, the test is only providing evidence that in the long-run exports and imports grow at similar rates.[16] It does not test the theoretical model behind Thirlwall's law which assumes an export function in which the growth of exports is demand determined by the income elasticity of export demand and the growth of the rest of the world. It is ironic that proponents of Thirlwall's law typically assume that the terms of trade are exogenous and constant, while our discussion suggests that, in fact, the validity of the law (for the large country case in which it can hold) depends on the possibility of an endogenous adjustment in the terms of trade. In other words, the empirical literature on Thirlwall's law does not test what we may call Thirlwall's *hypothesis*, i.e., that differences across countries in growth rates are explained by differences in the pattern of trade specialization and nothing else. I think that a proper empirical test of this hypothesis would fail. The source of this failure is a fallacy of composition in reverse. What may be true for a large group of economies, all attempting to specialize in the export of the same income-inelastic goods, need not be true for individual economies taken in isolation. In other words, trying to explain cross country differences in growth rates using Thirlwall's law is like applying a North-South model to explain individual country growth experiences.

[15] In a small economy setting, *domestic* supply and demand conditions, rather than *foreign* demand conditions, become crucial in the determination of the level of a country's exports. In fact, in this setting there is not a demand for a country's exports (and therefore an income elasticity of demand for a country's exports), say a demand for Mexican cars. What there is, rather, is a demand for cars in a market in which Mexican car producers compete.

[16] In fact, the large economy assumption is necessary but not sufficient. Consider the foreign country in the model above. It is a large economy and in long-run equilibrium we have $g_F = (e_H/e_F) g_H$. Does Thirlwall's law apply? The answer is no, for it is clear that g_F is not *determined* by g_H and the income elasticities of demand. The growth rate of the foreign country in the model is essentially determined by the propensity to save and invest in the foreign country and is independent of the terms of trade.

Appendix. Stability of the long-run equilibrium in the small open economy

This appendix presents a full analysis of the stability of the long-run equilibrium. For simplicity I assume perfect competition in the domestic market ($z = 0$ which implies $P_D = P_X = P$, the general price level).

The analysis of long-run adjustments and the resulting equilibrium involves a system of two differential equations. The first, showing the dynamic behavior of the real wage (now exactly equal to the inverse of the real exchange rate), is derived from the wage inflation equation and can be expressed in reduced form in the following equation:

$$(W/\hat{P}) = F(L/N, W/P) \qquad F_1 > 0, F_2 < 0 \tag{A1}$$

The second equation, showing the dynamic behavior of the employment rate, has the following reduced form:

$$(L/\hat{N}) = G(L/N, W/P) \qquad G_1 < 0, G_2? \tag{A2}$$

The sign restrictions on the partial derivatives follow from the analysis in the text. They imply that the locus of real wage stability, $(W/\hat{P}) = 0$, is positively sloped, while the locus of employment stability, $(L/\hat{N}) = 0$, may be positively or negatively sloped depending on whether the effect of W/P on $(L/\hat{N})$ is positive or negative. The effect of a higher W/P is to reduce wage inflation, which tends to increase the employment growth rate (making G_2 positive), but a higher W/P reduces v, the output-capital ratio (as exports and the volume of output fall), which has a negative effect on the rate of capital accumulation and the growth of employment (making G_2 negative). We have therefore to distinguish two cases: 1) $G_2 < 0$, yielding a negatively sloped $(L/\hat{N}) = 0$ locus; 2) $G_2 > 0$, yielding a positively sloped locus.

Case 1 is depicted in Figure 10.A.1 (a) which reproduces Figure 10.4 in the text. It can be shown easily that given the sign restrictions of the partial derivatives, the system has

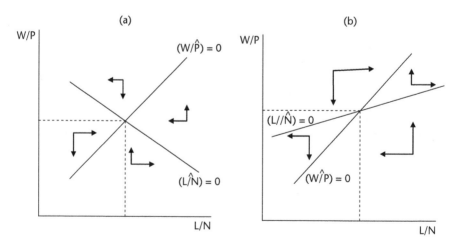

Figure 10.A.1 Long-run dynamic adjustments

a negative trace and positive determinant. The equilibrium is thus stable and the economy converges in the long run to the intersection between the two loci.

Case 2 may feature instability if G_2 is very large, i.e. if the effect of a real wage fall on wage inflation is very strong. In this case, as shown in Figure 10.A.1 (b), the slope of the $(L/\hat{N}) = 0$ locus is positive and less than the slope of the $(W/\hat{P}) = 0$ locus and the intersection is a saddle point. The instability can be explained with the example of a devaluation starting from an initial long-run equilibrium. The resulting fall in the real wage triggers a rapid process of wage inflation, so rapid that the positive effect on employment growth (via higher accumulation) resulting from the higher profitability is offset by the negative effect on employment growth arising from wage growth (and capital-labor substitution). The employment rate then falls, moving the economy away from the initial long-run equilibrium. By contrast, if G_2 is positive but relatively small so that the $(L/\hat{N}) = 0$ locus is steeper than the $(W/\hat{P}) = 0$ locus the economy converges to the long-run equilibrium with a warranted growth rate equal to the natural rate.

11

Demand-driven Technical Change, the Real Exchange Rate, and Growth

In the small open economy models discussed in the previous chapter, the employment rate is *demand constrained in the long run* and there is no tendency in the economy to converge to full employment or to a unique natural rate of unemployment. However, the economy's growth rate remains *supply constrained* in the long run by an exogenous natural rate. A reason for this is that we have not yet considered technological change. As mentioned in the previous chapter, one of the reasons why there is no role for aggregate demand in mainstream growth theory is that in this theory, technological progress is either exogenous, as in the neoclassical model, or driven by supply side factors (such as research and development expenditures) as in the product variety and Schumpeterian models.

This chapter looks at the interactions between effective demand, technical change and labor force growth by removing the assumption of an exogenous natural rate and examining the interdependence between the warranted and the natural growth rates. To this effect, I drop, one at a time, the assumptions of no technical progress, which is replaced by that of endogenous productivity growth (sections 1 and 2), and exogenous labor force growth which is replaced by an endogenous labor force growth function (section 3). A key implication of these extensions is that macroeconomic policies affecting aggregate demand have not only long-run level effects on output and employment but can also have growth effects. A final section reviews the recent empirical evidence on the level and growth effects of aggregate demand and the role of macroeconomic policies in the explanation of cross-country growth differences.

1. Effective Demand and Endogenous Technical Change: a Kaldor-Robinson Model

We shall now consider changes in productivity (A). As we did in the previous chapter, we begin with the analysis of the medium term, endogeneizing productivity growth in a simple way, i.e., assuming that Verdoorn law, as interpreted by Kaldor (1966), prevails as a result of the presence of economy-wide increasing returns to scale. I then turn to a more general formulation and discuss the long-term dynamics of the extended model.

Medium-term interactions between output and productivity growth[1]

Suppose then that productivity (A) changes over time. Note that these changes will now affect labor demand, the output-capital ratio and the rate of profit, all of which are increasing functions of A, as well as the capital-labor ratio which is a decreasing function of A (see Chapter 10, section 1). Rather than assuming exogenous changes in A as in the standard neoclassical model, suppose that the rate at which productivity increases is an increasing function of the rate of accumulation (assuming for example a production function augmented by technological externalities as in Chapter 6) and that *pari passu* with productivity, nominal and real wages increase at the same rate as productivity leaving the profit rate and the capital-output ratio constant over time. The only change with respect to the model of the previous chapter is that now the economy converges to a warranted growth path which features productivity growth and real wages growing at a constant rate which is a function of the rate of accumulation and output growth.

The representation of this model in (r, g) space is exactly the same as in Chapter 10 (see Figure 10.1). An increase in a demand parameter such as the propensity to invest will shift the g (r^e) line to the right in Figure 10.1 moving the economy to a new warranted growth path with a higher rate of capital accumulation and higher rates of growth of productivity and real wages. However, unlike the assumption made about the behavior of real wages, the rate at which nominal and real wages will grow over time will depend in fact on conditions in the labor market which we have omitted so far in the analysis. We have thus to turn to a more general formulation in order to look at the longer-term dynamics of the economy.

---

[1] I am grateful to José Antonio Ocampo for conversations on this subject.

Long-run dynamics: A Kaldor-Robinson technical progress function

We now modify the model of Chapter 10 in two directions. First, we consider a productivity growth function (or "technical progress function" in Kaldor's terminology) which is based on the contributions of Nicholas Kaldor and Joan Robinson to the theory of economic growth. In Kaldor's view (1957) productivity increases are endogenous to the process of capital accumulation per worker as a result of increasing returns to scale. Kaldor (1972) indicates three sources of increasing returns. The first are the economies of scale due to the three-dimensional nature of space.[2] The other two sources refer to two aspects of specialization: the substitution of direct for indirect labor (that is an increase in the capital/labor ratio), and learning by doing. These are directly taken from the arguments of Allyn Young and depend on the process of division of labor (see Chapter 5).[3]

For Joan Robinson, productivity growth is influenced by labor and goods market conditions. In particular, firms speed up the diffusion of new technologies in response to shortages in the labor market by adopting new technologies which reduce labor costs. For example, Robinson (1956, p. 96) argues that "[e]ven more important than speeding up discoveries is the speeding up of the rate at which innovations are diffused. When entrepreneurs find themselves in a situation where potential markets are expanding but labour hard to find, they have every motive to increase productivity".[4]

We put together these ideas by assuming the following productivity growth function:

$$g_A = \mu(g - l) + \beta(l - n) \tag{1}$$

which makes the rate of productivity growth (g_A) a function of the rate of growth of the capital labor ratio ($g - l$, a la Kaldor) and the excess of employment growth over the growth of the labor force ($l - n$, a la Robinson).

In Kaldor and Robinson views, technical change has a strong element of irreversibility. That is what Kaldor meant by "dynamic" in the expression "dynamic economies of scale" (see Kaldor 1966, p. 106; and Kaldor 1972, p. 1253). If this is the case, in eq. (1) μ ($g - l$) = 0 if $g < l$, and β ($l - n$) = 0 if $l < n$. We shall consider also the case of reversible productivity changes in which eq. (1) holds without restrictions.

---

[2] In this respect, Kaldor gives the example of a pipeline: when a stretch (of unitary length) of a pipeline is constructed, the increase in output (the liquid transported) is greater than the increase in inputs (the materials used up to build the cylinder). This example was meant to represent different types of plant-level economies of scale which directly follow from an increase in production.

[3] For contributions formalizing Kaldor's view of endogenous technical progress, see Ocampo and Taylor (1998), Rada (2007), and Ocampo, Rada, and Taylor (2009, ch. 8).

[4] For a formalization of Robinson's views, see Dutt (2006) and Dutt and Ros (2007).

A second change is that we modify the wage inflation equation as follows. We assume as before that the target real wage is determined by labor market conditions (the employment rate, L/N). But, in order to simplify the analysis and clarify the processes of adjustment, I assume that nominal wages increase beyond the rate of domestic inflation only when the target wage is above the actual real consumption wage. Otherwise, i.e., if the real consumption wage is above the target real wage, nominal wages grow exactly at the rate of price inflation (and not below it). The target real wage is then really a threshold which triggers wage inflation (above price inflation) only when the actual wage falls below it (for a similar specification, see Basu's formalization of Kalecki's model of inflation in Basu, 1997, and Chapter 12). Eq. (7) in Chapter 10 is thus replaced by:

$$w = p + \lambda(\omega - w/P_D) \quad \omega = \omega(L/N), \omega' > 0 \quad \text{for } \omega > w/P_D$$
$$w = p \qquad\qquad\qquad\qquad\qquad\qquad\qquad \text{for } \omega \leq w/P_D \tag{2}$$

I illustrate the properties of the model with the analysis of the effects of devaluation. Note first that in the absence of endogenous productivity changes a devaluation can only have short-term effects on employment and output. Consider the model of the previous chapter. In Figure 10.4 (reproduced below as Figure 11.1), an increase in P_X moves the economy to a point below the initial long-run equilibrium and into the region of increasing employment and rising wages (point A). The gains in employment are, however, short term and reversible since they are eventually offset by higher wages that make the economy converge, through oscillations, to the initial long-term equilibrium (at point E).

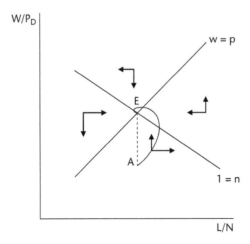

Figure 11.1 Long-term dynamic adjustments

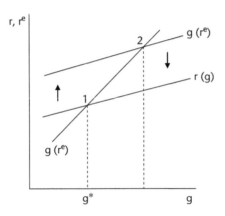

Figure 11.2 Short- and long-term effects of a real devaluation

Consider now, under the present assumptions, the effects of a devaluation starting from an initial long-term equilibrium at point 1 in Figures 11.2 and 11.3. Suppose that the initial employment rate is so low that the real wage is above the threshold wage so that nominal wages are constant (since with the given nominal exchange rate, domestic inflation is nil). Thus, the economy is on a warranted path that is also a long-term equilibrium with g = 1 and l = n. K/L and L/N are thus also constant. Since then g_A = 0, at this equilibrium the level of productivity is also constant.

Now suppose now that P_X increases as a result of a devaluation. The real wage falls and the r (g) line shifts upwards. The profit rate and the rate of accumulation increase towards a new warranted path at point 2'. Since the rate of accumulation increases, employment growth increases above the growth of the labor force. The employment rate increases but the capital labor ratio falls (as a result of the positive employment effect of the fall in the product wage). Suppose that initially nominal wages do not change because although the real consumption wage falls as a consequence of devaluation it remains above the threshold wage given the initially very low employment rate (this will be true, of course, provided that the devaluation is not so large as to reduce the real wage below the threshold). In the new warranted path, the employment rate is increasing and through its effect on productivity the r (g) line will keep on shifting up towards a still higher warranted growth rate.[5] There will come a point, at a sufficiently high employment rate, in which the threshold wage will become higher than the real consumption wage. At this point, nominal and real wages start increasing, bringing about a fall in the rates of profit and capital accumulation. Employment growth

---

[5] In the case of reversible technical changes, this requires that the initial fall in the capital-labor ratio does not offset the positive effects on productivity of the increasing employment rate.

therefore falls as a result of both the fall in the rate of capital accumulation and the positive growth of wages. This process brings employment growth back into equality with the growth of the labor force. At the point when l is again equal to n, the employment rate stops increasing. However, at this higher employment rate, nominal wages may (or may not) continue to grow. There are several possibilities.

Suppose that wages continue to grow because at the employment rate considered the target wage is above the real wage. As wages increase, employment growth falls below the growth of the labor force causing the employment rate to fall. The target wage thus falls until wage growth is again zero. If at this point the rates of capital accumulation and employment growth are lower than the rate of labor force growth, the employment rate continues to fall. With reversible productivity changes, productivity falls and it is conceivable that the resulting fall in the profit rate brings the economy back to point E. In terms of the diagram in (L/N, W/P_D) space, the shifts in the schedule of employment stability that took place are completely reversed and the economy goes back to the initial long-run equilibrium, just as in the case with no technical progress.

Another possibility is that when wage growth falls back to zero, the employment rate stabilizes at a higher level than the initial one. In this case, the economy will converge to a long-run equilibrium which features the same rates of profit and capital accumulation than the initial equilibrium (the economy goes back to point 1 in Figure 11.2) but at higher levels of productivity, the capital-labor ratio and the employment rate, all of which increased during the process of adjustment described. In terms of Figure 11.3, the higher level of productivity shifts the schedule of employment stability to the right and the economy converges to a new long-run equilibrium at point 1' with a higher employment rate and a higher real wage (since productivity and the

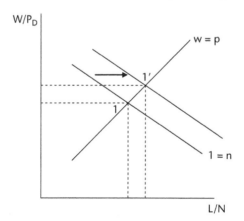

Figure 11.3 Long-term dynamic adjustment with irreversible productivity changes

capital-labor ratio are higher than their initial values, it is easily verified from the labor demand function that the product wage, W/P_X, and thus real consumption wages are higher). So, even with reversible productivity changes it is possible for the devaluation to have positive long-term effects on real wages and the employment rate. In this case, what prevents the return to the initial long-term equilibrium at point 1 is the fact that nominal wages do not fall once the threshold wage is brought back below the actual wage and therefore the capital-labor ratio (and the level of productivity) do not continue to fall.

With irreversible productivity changes, the technical changes and new technologies introduced as a result of the increase in the employment rate following the devaluation and the increase in the rates of profit and capital accumulation will unambiguously shift the schedule of employment stability to the right as a result of the increase in the level of productivity during the adjustment process. This leads the economy to a new long-run equilibrium at 1' in Figure 11.3 with a higher employment rate and higher real wages. In Figure 11.2, in (r, g) space, the r (g) line shifts back to its initial position as a result of the increase in real wages.

What if the target wage is an increasing function of the level of productivity? Suppose eq. (10) is replaced by:

$$
\begin{aligned}
&w = p + \lambda(\omega - w/P_D) \quad \omega = \omega(L/N, A), \omega_1, \omega_2 > 0, \text{ for } \omega > w/P_D \\
&w = p \qquad\qquad\qquad\qquad\qquad\qquad \text{for } \omega \le w/P_D
\end{aligned}
\tag{2'}
$$

A real devaluation can now have a long-term growth effect. In this case, wages do not stabilize as the employment rate falls and reduces the target wage. Rather, it is possible that the negative effect of wage growth on employment growth is compensated by a higher rate of capital accumulation resulting from the higher profit rate. At the same time, the negative effect of wage increases on the profit rate is compensated by the positive effect on productivity growth of the rate of accumulation being higher than employment growth (precisely because wage growth is positive). The economy then converges to a new long-term equilibrium with a rate of capital accumulation higher than the growth of employment and a positive rate of growth of wages. It is a long-term equilibrium which, compared to the initial one, features a higher rate of accumulation and faster growth of real wages, faster productivity growth and a constant employment rate. Unlike what happens in the previous cases, as productivity increases over time the target wage keeps on increasing, continually disturbing the equality with actual wages and causing the latter to grow over time. In $(L/N, W/P_D)$ space, the shifts to the right of the schedule of employment stability are accompanied by upward shifts of the schedule of wage stability which keep the employment rate constant and real wages increasing. In (r, g) space, the economy converges to a warranted path in which the rate of capital accumulation is higher than the rate of growth of

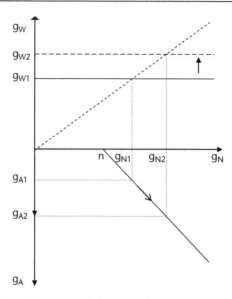

Figure 11.4 The adjustment of the natural to the warranted growth rate

the labor force and output per worker is continually increasing as a result of productivity growth equal to $g_A = \mu (g - l)$. Thus, on the long-run equilibrium path the economy no longer grows at the rate of growth of the labor force. The steady state output growth rate is no longer exogenous; it is equal to $(\mu + a)$ $g + (1 - a - \mu)$ n and that of output per worker is $(\mu + a)$ $(g - n)$, where g is the equilibrium rate of accumulation, constrained by the propensity to invest and domestic demand parameters.

How does the endogenous natural rate adjust upwards in the face of an increase in the warranted rate? The diagram in Figure 11.4 clarifies this question. Consider an initial long-run equilibrium with a warranted growth rate (g_{W1}) equal to the natural growth rate ($g_{N1} = g_{A1} + n$) given at the intersection of the g_{W1} line and the 45-degree line in the upper half of Figure 11.4. This natural growth rate is equal to the exogenous growth of the labor force (n) plus the endogenous rate of growth of labor productivity (g_{A1}), residually determined by the warranted growth rate and the rate of growth of the labor force ($g_{A1} = g_{N1} - n$).

Consider now an increase in the warranted rate as determined by a higher propensity to invest (ψ). The warranted rate increases from g_{W1} to g_{W2}. This triggers a process of faster employment growth, real wage increases followed by an acceleration of productivity growth from g_{A1} to g_{A2} and a slowdown of employment growth back to equality with the exogenously given rate of growth of the labor force (n). In the new long-run equilibrium the economy is growing at a faster natural growth rate equal to n plus the higher rate of productivity growth (g_{A2}).

2. A Comparison with Endogenous Growth Models and Classical Development Theory

When technical progress is endogenous, capital accumulation in our Kaldor-Robinson model becomes the engine of long-run growth. There is here a close affinity with classical development theory as well as with endogenous growth models which emphasize the role of capital accumulation (such as Romer, 1986, and the AK model) and a key difference with neoclassical models in which long-run growth is driven by an exogenous natural rate.

Just as in endogenous growth models such as the AK model (see Chapter 2), the natural rate is no longer independent of the warranted rate: an increase in the rate of capital accumulation brings about a higher rate of endogenous productivity growth. In the AK model, given that returns to capital are constant, this increases the natural rate by exactly the extent necessary to keep it constant at a higher level of growth, equal to the new value of the warranted rate. Something somewhat similar happens in the Kaldor-Robinson model, as discussed in the previous section. In fact, as pointed out in Chapter 2, Kaldor anticipated the endogeneity of the natural rate when he introduced the technical progress function into the neo-Keynesian model of growth and distribution.

The process by which the productivity growth rate adjusts upwards as a result of faster capital accumulation is, however, different in the Kaldor-Robinson model than in endogenous growth models. In the AK model, the upward adjustment of the productivity growth rate simply results from the assumption of constant returns to capital. In the Schumpeterian model with capital accumulation of Chapter 5 an increase in the savings/investment rate raises the rate of growth of capital per effective labor bringing down the rental rate of capital (the intermediate good) which raises profits and investment in research and development and, as a result, the rate of technological progress. In the Kaldor-Robinson model, a higher propensity to invest and the resulting increase in the rate of capital accumulation raise the rate of expansion of employment beyond the rate of growth of the labor force "speeding up of the rate at which innovations are diffused" (Robinson) while at the same time increasing real wages and bringing, as a result of wage increase, employment expansion in the steady state in line with the growth of the labor force.

At the same time, the effects of domestic demand parameters on long-run growth are very different in models where Say's law applies and in the present Keynesian framework. This can be illustrated with the role of the propensity to save. A higher propensity to save has an unambiguously positive effect on growth in endogenous growth and classical development theory models (even though this effect is diluted when we consider international capital mobility in development theory models as we have seen in Chapter 7). By contrast, the models in this and the previous chapter feature a long-run paradox of thrift.

An increase in the propensity to save in the model without technical progress, reduces the steady state values of the employment rate and the real wage. With endogenous and irreversible technical progress, an increase in the propensity to save can even reduce the long-run growth rate through its negative effect on the warranted growth rate. The distinctive role of demand means that productivity growth is endogenous in a different sense in Keynesian and in endogenous growth or development theory models. In the Kaldor-Robinson model, a faster growth of effective demand will have a positive effect on long-run productivity growth. This, of course, is not the case in endogenous growth or development theory models. Productivity growth is there endogenous but endogenous only to a rate of capital accumulation which is unaffected by effective demand.

This difference in the role of domestic demand parameters results, of course, from the absence of an automatic tendency to full employment in Keynesian models. The absence of this tendency implies that the long-run performance of the economy will depend on the extent to which, to use Swan's expression, "the authorities have read the General Theory" (Swan, 1960, p. 205, in Sen, 1970). In other words, macroeconomic policies now matter in the determination of the long-run growth rate of the economy in a way that they do not in previous models. There is therefore an important role for differences in macroeconomic policies in the explanation of cross country differences in growth. We shall return to this subject in section 4.

3. Endogenous Labor Force Growth

Suppose now that the rate of growth of the labor force responds, through immigration or emigration, to changes in the growth of labor demand. Assume, for example, that $n = n_0 + \sigma\, l$, i.e., the growth of the labor force is given by an autonomous component (n_0) and responds to the growth of labor demand through the positive parameter σ. How does this modify the model?

Consider an initial long-run equilibrium at point 1 in Figure 11.5 with $g_1 = l_1 = n_1$ and $w = p = 0$. For simplicity, assume no productivity growth. Starting from such steady state, consider the effects of an increase in the propensity to invest. The g (r^e) line in Figure 11.5 shifts to the right, moving the economy to a new medium-term equilibrium at point 2 with a higher rate of accumulation (g_2) and a higher rate of profit (r_2). This new medium-term equilibrium cannot be of course a full long-run steady state. Employment growth at point 2 (l_2) is now greater than n_1 so that the employment rate is rising, putting upward pressure on nominal and real wages and leading to a downward shift in the r (g) line that reduces the rate of accumulation. However, the adjustment to the initial position will be incomplete if, as a result of the faster growth of labor

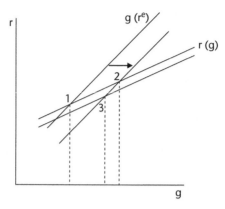

Figure 11.5 Effects of a higher propensity to invest when labor force growth is endogenous

demand, the growth rate of the labor force adjusts upwards. In this case, the new long-run equilibrium at point 3 will feature a higher rate of accumulation than at point 1. It will also feature a higher employment rate because in the process of adjustment employment grew at a faster rate than the labor force. Using the labor force growth function, the output growth rate in long-run equilibrium is again endogenous and equal to a $g + (1 - a) n_0/(1 - \sigma)$, where g is the equilibrium rate of accumulation, constrained by the propensity to invest and domestic demand parameters.

Consider the adjustment between the warranted and the natural growth rates in Figure 11.6. To compare with the previous model, suppose that productivity growth is also endogenous a la Kaldor-Robinson. Just as in the case of an exogenous rate of labor force growth, the warranted growth rate increases as a result of a higher propensity to invest raising the warranted growth rate from g_{W1} to g_{W2}. The natural growth rate increases by the same extent. However, the upward adjustment of the productivity growth rate will be less now than in the previous case given that part of the adjustment to the higher warranted rate takes place through an upward adjustment in the rate of growth of the labor force. Indeed, as a result of the higher propensity to invest and rate of capital accumulation, the line relating the natural rate and the rate of productivity growth ($g_N = n_0 + \sigma g + g^A (1 - \sigma)$) shifts outwards and moderates the increase in the productivity growth rate from g_{A1} to g_{A2}.

4. Policy Implications and Empirical Evidence

As argued in this and the previous chapter, the absence of an automatic tendency to full employment in Keynesian models opens the door for macroeconomic policies to have an important role in the long-run levels of the

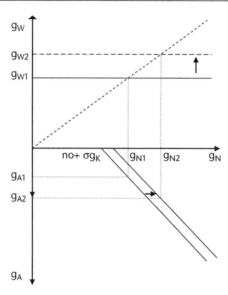

Figure 11.6 The adjustment between the natural and the warranted growth rate when labor force growth is endogenous

employment rate and even the growth rate of employment and output. Macroeconomic policies now matter in the determination of the long-run growth rate of the economy in a way that they do not in previous models. There is therefore an important role for macroeconomic policies in the explanation of cross country differences in growth. This final section briefly reviews recent developments in growth empirics that increasingly recognize the role of demand in long-term growth.

First, some recent papers emphasize the role of countercyclical fiscal policies, particularly public investment policies, in raising the long-run growth rate of the economy (see, for example, Aghion and Howitt, 2006). Related results can be found in a recent literature on the medium-term output dynamics following recessions caused by financial crises (see Boyd, Kwak, and Smith, 2005; Cerra and Saxena, 2008; IMF, 2009). The main "stylized facts" highlighted by this literature can be summarized as follows (IMF, 2009): (1) Output losses tend to be permanent following recessions triggered by banking crises, with no rebound of real output on average to the pre-crisis trend over the medium term;[6] (2) The economy tends to recover the pre-crisis medium-term growth rate in most (although not all) cases; (3) The lower output path results from permanent reductions, relative to trend, in the employment rate, the capital-labor ratio, and total factor productivity (in approximately equal

---

[6] A study of 88 banking crises from 1970 to 2002 finds that seven years after the crisis, output was nearly 10 percent below trend on average (IMF, 2009).

proportions); (4) The loss of output is especially persistent following large shocks, as suggested by the fact that the loss of short-term output is a good predictor of the medium-term outcome; (5) Economies that apply counter-cyclical fiscal and monetary policies in the short run have smaller output losses over the medium term.

There is also considerable empirical evidence on the role of differences in exchange rate policies in the explanation of cross-country growth differences. Indeed, the growth effects of real exchange rate policy have been receiving a great deal of attention in recent times after the extraordinarily high growth rates achieved by countries that have deliberately undervalued their real exchange rates (this is the case of China and, in the Latin American context and to a lesser extent, of Argentina) and the slow growth rates experienced by a large number of countries with overvalued exchange rates. This relationship has been the object of a large and increasing number of empirical studies. A recent survey of the large number of empirical studies on the subject (Rapetti, 2012) confirms the significant impact that the real exchange rate has on growth, especially in developing countries, through both undervaluation stimulating growth and especially overvaluation hurting it. This is true both in the current globalization period as well as in previous historical periods and applies to different measures of the real exchange rate (PPP- based and fundamentals-based misalignment indexes). Among a number of suggested mechanisms through which the real exchange rate influences growth, the survey concludes that the evidence favors the role of the profitability effects of the real exchange rate on capital accumulation in tradable goods sectors operating under increasing returns to scale (see Ros and Skott, 1998; Frenkel and Ros, 2006; Rodrik, 2008). This profitability or "development channel" is precisely the mechanism emphasized in our Kaldor-Robinson model of section 1.

León-Ledesma and Thirlwall (2002), for a group of OECD countries, and Libanio (2009), for a group of Latin American countries, provide further evidence on the role of aggregate demand in the growth process. These authors tested the hypothesis that the natural rate of growth is endogenously affected by the actual growth rate. They define the natural growth rate as that rate of output growth which keeps the unemployment rate constant, i.e. the natural rate is the solution to Okun's equation relating the change in unemployment ($\Delta\%U$) to the GDP growth rate (g), $\Delta\%U = a - b\,g$, setting the change in unemployment equal to zero. The main finding is that the natural rate, given by a/b, is not independent from the actual output growth rate. When the actual growth rate slows down, for example, the natural growth rate also falls, thus suggesting that the natural rate is sensitive to both supply and demand side influences.

12

Kaleckí's Dual Economy and Structuralist Growth Models

This chapter is devoted to an analysis of effective demand failures that are different from the typically Keynesian situations for which monetary and/or fiscal policies are an effective remedy. I shall address, that is, situations in which macroeconomic policies face limits that arise from a diversity of structural rigidities so that even if, in Swan's words, "the authorities have read the General Theory" they may not be able to remove demand constraints on employment and growth. Kalecki's writing on developing economies refers to such situations and provides the basic analytical framework.

The chapter is organized as follows. Section 1 discusses Kalecki's dual economy model which emphasizes the rigidity of food supply as a constraint on effective demand so that unemployment and excess capacity in a demand-constrained manufacturing sector cannot be removed due to the inelasticity of supply in the food producing sector. Section 2 introduces changes in nominal wages in Kalecki's model and illustrates how a "wage-goods constraint" can give rise to a structural type of inflation. It also reviews, using this framework, the structuralist-monetarist controversy on inflation. Sections 3 and 4 address how analogous structural rigidities underlie open economy two-gap models as well as inflation models in the structuralist tradition, contributions that are presented and discussed as open economy extensions of Kalecki's two-sector model.

1. Domestic Constraints: Kalecki's Dual Economy Model

Kalecki's view of the economic problems of developing countries is idiosyncratic. On one hand, his vision is close to that of classical development theory. Indeed, Kalecki characterizes underdevelopment in a way similar to Lewis or

Nurkse, emphasizing that in underdeveloped countries the capital stock is too small to employ the whole of the labor force:

> The crucial problem of the underdeveloped economy is different from that of the developed countries … as contrasted with developed economies [in the former the capital equipment] is not capable of absorbing all available labour, as a result of which the standard of living is very low. (Kalecki (1966 [1993]: 16)

At the same time, unlike Lewis or Nurkse who deliberately and explicitly assumed away effective demand problems, Kalecki was a theoretician of effective demand and recognized that developing economies may confront demand constraints. He recognized, however, that these problems in developing countries were different from those of developed economies and that effective demand could be subject to structural constraints that Keynesian aggregate demand management could not effectively remove.

The model

In its simplest version, Kalecki's model of the macroeconomy of less developed countries consists of a "supply-constrained" agricultural sector with flexible prices, a "demand-constrained" manufacturing sector operating under imperfect competition, and a labor market with fixed nominal wages.[1] The model generates a short-run equilibrium with open unemployment. As we shall see, the nature of unemployment is neither Keynesian—since, under some circumstances, it is not affected by changes in aggregate demand—nor classical, in the sense that it is not associated with a downward rigidity of real wages.

Let the two sectors be indicated by A and M. In the first, food output (A) is produced with labor (L_A) and a fixed amount of land (T): $A = A (L_A, T)$, with A_1, $A_2 \geq 0$. This sector operates under atomistic competition. With price taking behavior, profit maximization yields the following labor demand and output supply functions:[2]

$$L_A^d = L_A(W_A/P_A, T) \qquad L_{A1} \leq 0, L_{A2} > 0 \qquad (1)$$
$$A^s = A^s(W_A/P_A, T) \qquad A_1^s \leq 0, A_2^s > 0 \qquad (2)$$

where P_A and W_A are respectively the price and nominal wage in sector A.

Sector M produces a variety of manufacturing goods (M_i) with one producer for each good. Production of these manufactures turns one unit of labor into k units of output up to the full capacity level of output (M_i^*). Production

---

[1] See, in particular, Kalecki (1954), reprinted in Kalecki (1976).
[2] Kalecki's model is often presented with output in the agricultural sector being fixed so that the price elasticity of supply is assumed to be zero (see Taylor, 1983 and 1991; Basu, 1984). We prefer to allow for a positive elasticity of food supply and then explore the implications of this elasticity having a higher or lower value.

conditions are thus: $M_i = k L_i$, for $M_i < M_i^*$, and $M = [\sum (1/n) M_j^\sigma]^{1/\sigma}$, with $0 < \sigma < 1$, where M, as in the intermediate goods sectors of Chapter 8, represents the output of a fixed set of n manufacturing goods. The wage in manufacturing (W_M) is equal to the agricultural wage plus a wage premium ($f - 1$), so that relative wages are given by $W_M/W_A = f$.

In the goods market, manufacturing firms operate under conditions of monopolistic competition, each producer facing identical downward sloping demand curves. Profit maximization here implies that, at a symmetric equilibrium with $p_i = p_j$ and $M_i = M$, pricing decisions follow a markup rule and production is adjusted according to demand:

$$P_M = (1 + z)W_M/k \qquad 1 + z = \o/(\o - 1) \tag{3}$$

$$M = C_M + I \tag{4}$$

where P_M is the price of a bundle of manufactures yielding M = 1, z is the markup, and $\o$ is the price elasticity of demand facing individual producers. C_M and I are the consumption and investment demands for manufactures. In the labor market, firms take wages (W_M) as given and the nominal wage is assumed to remain constant for the time being. It follows that pricing decisions in sector M determine the product wage, W_M/P_M. Then, given relative wages, the agricultural wage in terms of food varies inversely with the agricultural terms of trade (P_A/P_M).

On the demand side, we treat investment as given and assume, for simplicity, that all profits are saved and all wage income is spent on food or manufacturing consumption goods. We also adopt Jorgenson's assumption (1961) of a critical level of food consumption per worker (c_A^*), below which all wage income is spent on food and beyond which all additional income is fully spent on manufactures. We limit the analysis to a situation in which agricultural wages are less than the critical level of food consumption (c_A^*). These assumptions imply that consumption of food (C_A) and manufactures (C_M) are such that:

$$P_A C_A = W_A L_A + P_A c_A^* L_M \tag{5}$$

$$P_M C_M = (W_M - P_A c_A^*)L_M \tag{6}$$

where L_M is employment in sector M.

We use a diagram from Basu (1984; for a similar formulation, see Taylor, 1983) to illustrate the short-run equilibrium of the model (see Figure 12.1). Equilibrium in the food market implies $A = C_A$. Let AS denote the agricultural surplus (food supply minus food consumption by agricultural workers). Using (1), (2), and (5), we express the market equilibrium condition as the equality between the agricultural surplus and the demand for food by industrial workers:

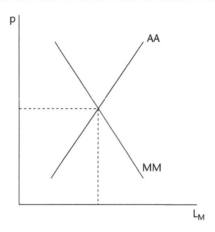

Figure 12.1 Kalecki's dual economy model

$$AS(S, p) = c_A^* L_M \tag{7}$$
$$AS(S, p) = A^s(W_A/P_A, T) - (W_A/P_A)L_A(W_A/P_A, T)$$

where $p = P_A/P_M$, and S is a position parameter that depends on land supply, technology parameters, the product wage in manufacturing and the wage premium.[3] The agricultural surplus is an increasing function of the agricultural terms of trade (p). Higher terms of trade reduce the product wage in agriculture. This raises agricultural employment and the agricultural surplus.

Eq. (7) defines a schedule of food market equilibrium in (p, L_M) space. This locus (AA in Figure 12.1, shown as a line for simplicity) slopes upwards: a higher level of employment in manufacturing raises food demand by industrial workers, which requires an increase in the terms of trade in order to generate the agricultural surplus necessary to clear the food market. The slope of the locus depends critically on the elasticity of food supply:[4] the lower this elasticity, the steeper the locus is. The special case of a fully inelastic food supply can be represented by a vertical locus.

Substituting from (6) into (4), and choosing units so that $M = L_M$, yields the following equation of a schedule of M sector equilibria:

$$L_M = I/(c_A^* p + 1 - W_M/P_M) \qquad \text{for } M < M^* \tag{8}$$

Eq. (8) shows employment in manufacturing as determined by the level of investment, times a multiplier that depends on the terms of trade and the critical level of food consumption. The equation defines a schedule (MM in

---

[3] In the Cobb-Douglas case, for example, $AS = p^{(1-b)/b} S$ and $S = [(P_M/W_M)f (1-b)]^{(1-b)/b} b T$, where $(1-b)$ is the labor share in output.
[4] In a more general formulation, it can be shown that the slope also depends on the elasticity of food demand.

Figure 12.1), which shows the effect of the terms of trade on industrial employment. The schedule slopes downwards: an increase in food prices causes a fall in workers' real incomes and consumption which, given the inelasticity of food demand, spills over to the manufacturing goods market as their consumption of manufactures declines. The lower consumption of manufactures per industrial worker reduces the multiplier and thus the level of production and employment in the M sector.[5]

Unemployment, effective demand, and the elasticity of food supply

The short-run equilibrium of the model is independent of money wages. This is readily verified from eqs (7) and (8). It is also consistent with open unemployment: there is no reason, given the level of investment, why the whole of the labor force would be fully employed. What kind of unemployment have we encountered? Can it be removed through effective demand measures such as, in particular, an increase in investment?

The answer to these questions depends on the slope of the AA schedule, which in the present setting is given by the elasticity of food supply. Consider, first, the case of a vertical AA schedule, i.e., there is a unique level of employment in sector M consistent with equilibrium in the food market. The supply of labor to the industrial sector ($L_M^s = L - L_A$, where L is the total labor force) will in this case also be vertical, since agricultural labor demand is inelastic as well. Figure 12.2 shows this configuration.

What happens if effective demand for manufactures increases as a result of a higher level of investment? Since industrial employment is demand-determined and there is unemployment and excess capacity in manufacturing, it appears that the higher level of investment should lead to an increase in industrial employment (see eq. 8). Yet, as illustrated by Figure 12.2, the higher level of investment only raises the agricultural terms of trade, without affecting industrial employment. The outward shift of the MM schedule—despite the fact that it implies a higher demand for manufactures at the initial terms of trade—leaves industrial employment and unemployment unchanged.

---

[5] If agricultural workers had a positive consumption of manufactures, the higher terms of trade, by increasing employment in agriculture, would tend to increase demand for manufactures by agricultural workers. This effect would tend to offset the decline in employment in manufacturing arising from the lower consumption of manufactures by industrial workers. It would make the schedule flatter, or even positively sloped, depending on the elasticity of food supply (and thus of agricultural labor demand) to changes in the terms of trade. More generally, the slope of the MM schedule will also depend on the price and income elasticities of food demand. The more elastic food demand is, the smaller the decline in the consumption of manufactures, since part of the decline in real wages will now fall upon food demand.

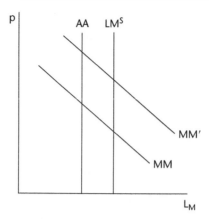

Figure 12.2 The model with an inelastic food supply

The reason why the demand for manufactures ends up being the same in both the initial and the final equilibrium is that the increase in effective demand, due to the higher level of investment, is fully offset by the fall in workers consumption of manufactures, resulting from the higher agricultural terms of trade. In fact, the terms of trade increase exactly by the extent necessary to bring effective demand back to its initial level. The result is that effective demand measures cannot cure unemployment and under-utilization of industrial capacity. As stated by Kalecki:

> The rise in investment may create a strong pressure on the available supplies of food, while at the same time it is possible to increase the production of industrial consumption goods in line with demand. It may be shown that in some instances the rigidity of food supply may lead to the under utilization of productive facilities in nonfood consumption goods. (Kalecki, 1976, p. 47)

Manufacturing employment is demand-determined, but effective demand is constrained by the availability of food supplies. Given the inelasticity of food supply, employment in manufacturing is fully determined by the position of the AA schedule.[6]

---

[6] Kalecki (1976, p. 47) goes on to state that "two factors will be involved here: a) the inelastic supply of food leading to a fall in real wages b) the benefit of food price increases accruing not to small proprietors, but to capitalists". He explains the role of this second factor as follows: "if the benefits of higher food prices accrue to landlords, merchants or money lenders, then the reduction in real wages due to the increase in food prices will not have as a counterpart an increased demand for mass consumption goods on the part of the country side; for increased profits will not be spent at all, or will be spent on luxuries". Does this mean that the result depends on the assumption that profits are not spent on M goods? The answer is no, contrary to what Kalecki suggests. A positive propensity to consume out of profits will only make the upward shift of the MM schedule larger than otherwise. The agricultural terms of trade will increase by more, since real wages in terms of food will have to fall by more to compensate for the increased consumption out of profits. But this does not change the fact that the rise in investment leaves industrial employment unaffected. The

Kalecki was well aware that the resulting unemployment is not Keynesian in its usual sense. It clearly cannot be cured through falling money wages and prices, *even if* the price declines raised aggregate demand. If, for example, a fall in money wages and prices shifted the MM schedule upwards, as a result of real balance effects or Keynes interest rate effects on investment, the result would be to change relative prices, but leave industrial employment unaffected. The ineffectiveness of aggregate demand measures is not due to "real wage rigidity", as in Lewis' labor surplus or efficiency wage models. Real wages are, up to this point in our analysis, fully flexible downwards. This type of unemployment is better described as structural. This is because it involves a maladjustment between the structure of supply and the structure of demand at full employment, together with structural rigidities on the supply side that impede the adjustment of the structure of supply in the short run. Indeed, the key assumption behind the results is the inelasticity of food supply, which in Kalecki's view is due to the agrarian conditions prevailing in many developing countries. With an elastic food supply, the AA schedule will not be vertical. The increase in the terms of trade, following the rise in investment, will then trigger a food supply response. This will allow employment and capacity utilization to increase in the industrial sector. The fall in real wages does not completely offset the effects of a higher investment on effective demand.

2. The Wage-goods Constraint, Inflation, and the Structuralist Controversy

Up to this point, we have assumed that reductions in the real wage do not trigger increases in nominal wages. Kalecki also considered real wage rigidity as a source of ineffectiveness of aggregate demand measures. In this case, even though food supply is elastic, the terms of trade at which agriculture will supply the wage goods necessary to fully employ the labor force may be so high as to trigger a continuous inflationary process. The idea is the basis of the structuralist models of inflation in the Latin American literature, and has also played a prominent role in the Indian macroeconomics literature on the "wage-goods constraint" on output and growth.[7]

Suppose then that real wages are not fully flexible downwards. Due to efficiency wage considerations or to the presence of labor unions, there is a

result depends on the inelastic agricultural supply and the inelasticity of food demand from industrial workers.

[7] Noyola (1956) and Sunkel (1958) were the seminal contributions to the Latin American structuralist approach to inflation. See also Cardoso (1981) and Taylor (1983) on structuralist models of inflation. Dutta (1988), Patnaik (1995), and Dutt (2001) provide surveys of the theory and evidence on the wage goods constraint.

minimum value of the agricultural real wage in terms of food (ω_A) that workers are willing to tolerate without asking for compensating money wage increases (or without adverse effects on labor productivity that will trigger these wage increases by employers).[8] This minimum wage is affected by labor market conditions. As in Chapter 10, we assume that this wage is an inverse function of unemployment: higher unemployment weakens unions bargaining power and increases workers tolerance to low real wages, thus reducing the minimum wage.

$$\omega_A = \omega(U) \qquad \omega' < 0 \quad \text{and} \quad U = L - L_A - L_M \tag{9}$$

This minimum real wage is a threshold: when real wages are above it, money wages remain constant, while below it, money wages increase at a rate that is an increasing function of the gap between the threshold and the actual value of the agricultural real wage ($\omega_A - W_A/P_A$).[9] Since the industrial wage premium is constant, this is also the rate of increase in industrial money wages (w). Thus:

$$w = \lambda(\omega_A - W_A/P_A) \qquad \text{for} \quad \omega_A > W_A/P_A$$
$$w = 0 \quad \text{for} \qquad\qquad \omega_A \leq W_A/P_A$$

where λ is a positive parameter. Using (1) to express L_A as a function of the terms of trade, we can substitute into (9) in order to obtain the threshold wage as a positive function of industrial employment and the terms of trade:

$$\omega A = \omega(L_M, p) \qquad \omega_1, \omega_2 > 0 \tag{10}$$

Both a higher level of industrial employment and better agricultural terms of trade (which stimulates agricultural employment) reduce unemployment and thus increase the threshold wage, ω_A. We can now derive a schedule of (p, L_M) combinations along which the actual agricultural real wage is equal to the threshold wage. Using (10) and $W_A/P_A = (W_M/P_M)/(f\,p)$, we obtain:

$$(W_M/P_M)/(fp) = \omega(L_M, p) \tag{11}$$

where the manufacturing product wage (W_M/P_M) is determined by the pricing decisions in manufacturing. How are p and L_M related along this schedule? Higher agricultural terms of trade lead to a fall in actual real wages and to a higher threshold wage (as unemployment falls with the increase in agricultural employment); in order to keep the threshold wage in line with the lower value of agricultural real wages, a fall in industrial employment is then required. Eq. (11) thus defines a downward sloping schedule in (p, L_M) space. The value of the slope depends critically on how sensitive the threshold wage

---

[8] The open economy model with real wage resistance later in this chapter (section 3) explicitly adopts an efficiency wage formulation.
[9] For similar formulations, see Cardoso (1981), Taylor (1983), Basu (1984), and Dutt (1990).

is to labor market conditions, i.e., on the ω function. If, for example, unemployment had strong negative effects on workers' bargaining strength, an increase in the terms of trade would only require a small reduction in industrial employment. The schedule would then be rather steep. The smaller the effect of unemployment on the threshold wage, the flatter is the schedule. Without such effects the locus becomes horizontal, as in Basu (1984), since there is then a unique value of the threshold wage, and thus of p, for which the actual and threshold wages are equal. It is also worth noting that changes in labor productivity as well as in Kalecki's "degree of monopoly" in manufacturing (determined by the price elasticity of individual demand curves), influence the manufacturing product wage and thus the position of the schedule.

This schedule of wage and price stability (LL) shows, for each level of industrial employment, the maximum value of the terms of trade that is consistent with stable money wages. Above the locus the terms of trade are higher than required for money wage stability. There is thus wage inflation and (given W_M/P_M and p) price inflation. The region below and bounded by the locus is, in contrast, one of money wage and price stability.

When we bring the AA and MM schedules together with the LL locus (see Figure 12.3), the terms of trade as determined by the equilibrium in the goods market may turn out to be too high to preserve price stability. For example, an increase in investment that shifts the equilibrium terms of trade from p_1 to p_2 will not only lower real wages and increase industrial employment, but will also trigger an inflationary spiral, because the terms of trade required to keep the goods market in equilibrium are inconsistent with money wage stability in the labor market. As money wages increase, industrial firms react by increasing their prices, while food prices also adjust upwards to remove excess demand for food. The rate at which money wages (and prices) increase is a function of the gap between p_2 and the terms of trade on the LL schedule, at the same level of employment.

Thus, since the agricultural surplus is elastic, effective demand policy can raise employment, but only at the cost of higher inflation. If effective demand is constrained to preserve price stability, the maximum level of employment attainable is that at the intersection of the AA and LL schedule. It is worth noting that this level of employment and the associated rate of structural unemployment do not only depend on labor market parameters. They depend also on the agricultural demand and supply conditions underlying the slope and position of the AA schedule. The "inflation barrier" here arises from the fact that the agricultural sector cannot supply the wage goods necessary to fully employ the labor force at terms of trade that preserve money wage stability in the labor market.

What is the cure for this type of inflation? This was the question debated in the monetarist-structuralist controversies of the 1950s and 1960s (see the Rio

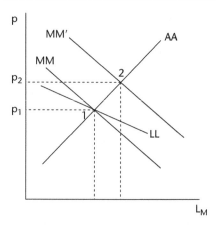

Figure 12.3 Conflict between goods market and labor market equilibrium

Conference volume edited by Baer and Kerstenetzky, 1964). Monetarists argued that, with a stable demand for money, inflation would only continue if the money supply was expanding at a faster rate than output. As for any other kind of inflation, they advocated a tight money policy that, by shifting the MM schedule downwards, would eliminate the inflationary pressures associated with a high level of employment.

Structuralists acknowledged that an accommodating monetary policy was necessary for inflation to continue (on the subject, see Olivera, 1964). However, they viewed aggregate demand measures that shift the MM locus downwards as inefficient. Employment would then fall and excess capacity would increase. Moreover, the growth of the economy would slow down, insofar as the higher excess capacity in manufacturing would discourage investment in industry and the lower terms of trade would inhibit investment in agriculture. A policy of contraction of aggregate demand did not address the key problems of low and inelastic food supplies and excess capacity in manufacturing. The control of inflation through exclusive reliance on these policies was thus likely to be ineffective in the longer run.

In this view, supply side measures oriented towards increasing food supplies are both more effective and more efficient. By shifting the AA schedule to the right, they lead to a reduction of inflation, while raising employment and capacity utilization in manufacturing. If these supply side measures require an increase of investment in agriculture, then it may be preferable to tolerate some inflation in the short run as the price to pay for dealing effectively with inflation and employment problems in the longer run. It is worth noting that in this view there is no long-run trade off between inflation and unemployment although for quite non-monetarist reasons.

In terms of our diagram, the debate can be interpreted as revolving around two issues. The first involves the elasticities of food supply and demand. A more elastic food demand makes the MM schedule turn clockwise. With sufficiently high price and income elasticities, this schedule would even slope upwards (with stability requiring that it is steeper than the AA schedule). Then, supply side measures that shift the AA schedule to the right would be less efficient than in the previous case, in the sense of not causing an increase in employment and capacity utilization. Given the elastic food demand, the reduction in the terms of trade then leads to a fall, rather than an increase, in the consumption of manufactures.

The second issue relates to the slope of the LL schedule. Suppose that the LL locus is steeper than the MM schedule, due to strong effects of unemployment on the threshold wage. As shown in Figure 12.4, the AA schedule shifting to the right will no longer reduce inflation, even though the agricultural terms of trade still will fall with the increase in food supplies. The reason is that the inflationary impact of the increase in industrial employment now offsets the deflationary effects of declining terms of trade. As the monetarist position views unemployment as determined largely by labor market parameters, rather than by agricultural demand and supply conditions, they can be considered assuming a steep LL schedule. In the extreme case of a vertical LL locus, there is only one level of industrial employment consistent with price stability. The only cure for inflation is then to reduce aggregate demand through a downward shift in the MM schedule.

Some structuralists also emphasized the role of labor market institutions in this type of inflation (see, in particular, Noyola, 1956; Sunkel, 1958). Labor market institutions matter insofar as they affect the slope and position of the LL schedule. Later structuralists have built on this insight to advocate incomes

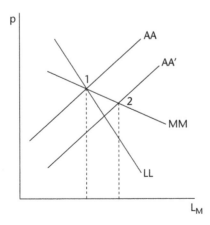

Figure 12.4 A monetarist economy

policies that, by shifting the LL schedule upwards, can reduce the short-run trade-off between inflation and unemployment.[10]

3. Foreign Exchange Constraints and Two-gap Models

The basic notion underlying two gap models is that the economy's growth may be constrained by the availability of foreign exchange as balance of payments disequilibria may not be easily corrected by exchange rate policy. This notion is analogous to Kalecki's view that the expansion of the industrial sector is constrained by the availability of food supplies. This is why two gap and open economy inflation models in the structuralist tradition can be presented in a framework that is analogous to Kalecki's two-sector model. This is the approach that we will follow here. We will look at two gap models as a Kaleckian model with two sectors (now domestic and foreign), with the key relative price being the real exchange rate, instead of the agricultural terms of trade. As we will see, the AA schedule then becomes a locus of external balance, and the MM locus becomes a schedule of goods market equilibrium.

Just as the sources of structural rigidities in Kalecki's model may be the inelasticity of supply and demand of food (a low response of quantities to relative prices), or an insufficient elasticity combined with a real wage rigidity (a low response of relative prices to changes in nominal prices), two gap models appear in two analogous versions. In one, associated with "elasticity pessimism", the source of the failure to correct balance of payments disequilibria is "limited structural flexibility" (Chenery and Strout, 1966, p. 682)—the low responses of exports and imports to changes in the real exchange rate. If primary goods dominate the export structure, and imports are mostly complements, rather than substitutes of domestic production, import and export price elasticities may be too low for the real exchange rate to significantly affect the trade balance. Given the ineffectiveness of exchange rate policy, the need to preserve external balance will constrain fiscal and monetary policies that will then be unable to increase the level of employment.

Another version of the two-gap model refers to 'real wage resistance' (see Bacha, 1984). Here, the problem is not one of low responses of quantities to relative prices (low price elasticities), but rather of a structure of relative prices being unresponsive to changes in the nominal exchange rate. If a real devaluation involves distribution effects against wage earners, there may be a minimum level of real wages (and a maximum real exchange rate), beyond which further nominal devaluations are ineffective. If this maximum real exchange

---

[10] See Ros (1993) for a review of the literature and different views on the role of conflict and coordination problems in driving wage inflation.

rate falls short of the exchange rate required to achieve external balance and full employment, macroeconomic policy will again be unable to meet these two targets simultaneously. The need to maintain external balance forces the economy into a less than full employment equilibrium. As we shall see, this version of the model can generate a type of inflation that is close in spirit to the kind envisioned by Kalecki.

Elasticity pessimism

Consider an open economy with two sectors. Sector C uses labor to produce consumer goods for domestic use and exports. Sector I uses labor and imported intermediate goods (with a fixed input-output coefficient) to produce investment goods for domestic use. Technology and market structure are similar to those assumed for manufacturing in section 1: production of both goods requires a constant input of labor per unit of output; firms take input prices as given, and operate under monopolistic competition in the goods market. Profit maximization again implies that pricing decisions follow a markup rule, while output adjusts to demand:

$$P_C = (1 + z_C)W$$

$$P_I = (1 + z_I)(W + eP^*\mu)$$

where P_C and P_I are the prices of, respectively, consumption and investment goods; W, the uniform nominal wage rate; z, the markup over unit cost; μ, the input-output coefficient for imported intermediate goods; P^*, the foreign currency price of these inputs; and e, the nominal exchange rate. We have chosen units such that the labor input-output coefficient is equal to one in both sectors.

We treat investment as given and assume for simplicity that all profits are saved and all wage income is spent on consumption goods. Exports (X) are a function of the real exchange rate (p), which we define as e P^*/P_C. These assumptions imply that output C of the consumption goods sector and the trade balance in domestic currency (T) are given by:

$$P_C C = W\,L + P_C X(p) \qquad X' \geq 0 \qquad (12)$$

$$T = P_C X(p) - eP^*\mu I \qquad (13)$$

where L is the overall level of employment (L = L_C + L_I). Using C = L_C, I = L_I, and eq. (12), we can express the equilibrium level of employment as function of I + X, times a multiplier:

$$L = [I + X(p)]/(1 - W/P_C) \qquad (14)$$

where W/P_C is determined by the pricing decisions in sector C. Using (13) and the condition of balanced trade (T = 0; we neglect for the time being capital inflows) yields:

$$I = X(p)/(\mu\, p) \tag{15}$$

Given the level of investment (I), eqs (14) and (15) can be solved for p and L, the real exchange rate and the level of employment that satisfy the goods market equilibrium and the balanced trade condition.

Assume now that the real exchange rate is available as a policy instrument and, in addition, that the government has fiscal and monetary policy instruments to influence the level of investment. We are interested in the following question: given target values for employment and the trade balance, are there values for I and p such that target values for L and T can be achieved simultaneously? More precisely, if the government wants to achieve full employment (L = L^s) and, at the same time, equilibrium in the trade balance (T = 0), how should it set its policies to meet these targets? Formally, we are looking for the level of investment and the value of the real exchange rate such that L = L^s and T = 0. This amounts to solving the model for I and p, given L = L^s and T = 0.

Swan's diagram of internal and external balance (Swan, 1955) illustrates the solution to the problem. Setting L = L^s in eq. (14) yields the schedule of internal balance, the locus of (p, I) combinations that keep the economy at full employment. A higher level of investment increases employment. With elastic responses of import and export volumes to changes in the real exchange rate, devaluation is also expansionary. The internal balance schedule will then be downward sloping, since a higher exchange rate requires a reduction in investment to keep employment at its target level.

The external balance schedule is given by eq. (15), interpreted as a locus of (p, I) combinations that preserve balanced trade. Devaluation has a positive effect on the trade balance while higher investment has a negative effect, as it increases income and imports. The external balance schedule then has a positive slope. With elastic trade responses, the values of p and I that satisfy the conditions for balanced trade and full employment will then generally exist.

Under our present assumptions, imports are inelastic given the fixed input-output coefficient for intermediate goods imports. If, in addition, exports feature low price elasticities, real devaluation will be effective only within narrow limits. There may be a value of p, beyond which the two schedules have the same slope (see Figure 12.5 where we assume, for simplicity, that the two schedules become vertical beyond p*). The internal and external balance curves do not cross: a combination of a real exchange rate and investment level that can simultaneously achieve internal and external balance does not exist. Depreciating the currency beyond p* is useless. To meet

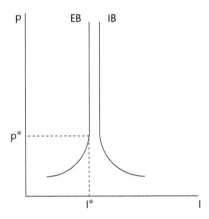

Figure 12.5 Swan's diagram with inelastic trade responses

the external balance target, fiscal and monetary policy will thus be con-strained to yield the level of investment (I^*), the maximum consistent with external balance. Given the need to meet external balance, foreign exchange revenues at $p = p^*$ operate as a constraint on aggregate demand. Macroeconomic policy is then unable to generate the full employment level of output.

Let L^* be the level of employment corresponding to I^*. The value of L^* is given by eq. (14), setting $p = P^*$ and $I = I^*$:

$$L^* = [I^* + X(p^*)]/(1 - W/P_C) \tag{16}$$

where p^* is such that $dX/dp = 0$ for $dp > 0$ and $dX/dp < 0$ for $dp < 0$, and I^* is given by the balance of payments equilibrium condition (15):

$$I^* = [X(p^*)]/(p^*\mu) \tag{17}$$

A simple extension of the model is to introduce an exogenous level of capital inflows (F). The external balance target (equilibrium in the balance of pay-ments) is now $T + F = 0$, rather than balanced trade. The maximum level of investment consistent with external balance becomes:

$$I^* = [X(p) + F]/(p\mu) \tag{17}$$

We now look at how these constrained levels of employment and investment respond to changes in exogenous variables and parameters. Consider first changes in the exogenous level of capital inflows when the economy is at less than full employment. From eq. (17'), increases in F raise I^* by $1/(p\,\mu)$:[11]

---

[11] This requires that exports are unaffected by changes in I^*. This will be the case as long as L^* is less than the total labor force.

$$dI^*/dF = 1/(p\mu) \qquad \text{for} \quad L^* < L^s$$

At some level of capital inflows, the economy reaches full employment. Further increases in F will leave L* unaffected. What happens to investment under these conditions? A larger volume of capital inflows makes foreign exchange available for an increase in imported inputs and thus in the level of investment. The transfer of labor from sector C to sector I will reduce output C and generate excess demand for goods and labor in sector C at the prevailing level of prices and wages in this sector. If prices and nominal wages increase to the same extent (there is nothing in this situation to prevent nominal wages from keeping up with increases in the cost of living), the increase in prices will lead to a real appreciation of the domestic currency.[12] Indeed, using (12), setting $L_C = L^s - I$, and solving for X (p), show that the market for C goods now clears through changes in the real exchange rate (and at levels below p*):

$$X(p) = (1 - W/P_C)L^s - I \tag{18}$$

The market clearing condition in sector C implies an inverse relationship between exports and investment: at full employment, further increases in investment can only be achieved through a real appreciation that causes a reduction in exports. This implies that part of the foreign exchange made available by the increase in F will be offset by a fall in exports. As a result, the increase in imported inputs and investment will be less than in the below full employment situation. Indeed, substituting from (18) into (17″), we find:

$$I^* = [1/(1 + \mu p)][F + (1 - W/P_C)L^s] \tag{19}$$

which shows that the multiplier effect of F on I* is now $1/(1 + \mu p)$ and thus necessarily less than before (see Figure 12.6).

The result is Chenery's theorem (Chenery and Strout, 1966): the effects of capital inflows on investment and growth—or, in Chenery's analysis, the effectiveness of foreign aid—are larger when the economy is constrained by foreign exchange (at less than full employment), than when it is constrained by savings at full employment. The difference is due to the mobilization of domestic savings, made possible by additional foreign exchange, when the economy is at less than full employment. The constrained level of investment (I*) can be seen as determined by domestic savings at the foreign exchange-determined level of employment, plus the foreign savings made available by capital inflows. When the economy is at less than full employment, additional foreign savings cause an increase in the level of output consistent with external balance (see eqs 16 and 17). This output increase leads to higher domestic

---

[12] If the government attempts to prevent the real appreciation through nominal devaluations, it will result in inflation, as discussed later.

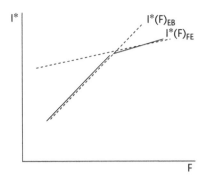

Figure 12.6 Effects of capital inflows on investment

savings and allows investment to expand to a larger extent than the additional capital inflows. This mobilization of domestic savings is absent when the economy operates at full employment.

Consider now the effects of an increase in the domestic saving rate. Given our assumptions of savings behavior, we model these effects as resulting from an increase in the "degree of monopoly" that reduces the real wage W/P_C. At less than full employment, a lower real wage reduces the level of employment while leaving investment unaffected (see eqs 16 and 17'). The additional savings at the initial level of employment simply reduce consumption demand and employment in sector C, without any other consequences.

In contrast, at full employment, the lower real wage raises I*, as shown in eq. (19). The mechanism is as follows. The fall in employment in sector C, resulting from the higher saving rate, allows the government to depreciate the currency. Since the economy was initially at full employment, the market for consumption goods was clearing at an exchange rate below p*. The real depreciation is thus effective in increasing exports. The additional foreign exchange made available by the increase in exports allows the level of investment I* to increase. In the end, the process involves a reallocation of employment from the production of domestically consumed goods to the production of investment goods and exports (which finance the additional imports of intermediate goods required by sector I).

Policies directed towards increasing domestic savings will thus have a larger impact on investment (and growth) when the economy is at full employment (under a "savings constraint") than at less than full employment (under a "foreign-exchange constraint").

Real wage resistance

We turn to the case in which, while exports and imports are elastic, real devaluation is limited by the downward inflexibility of real wages. The economy considered produces a single good that can be consumed, invested or exported. Imports consist of competing consumer goods. Local producers employ labor with diminishing returns and operate under atomistic competition. As in the efficiency wage model of Chapter 6, we assume that the real wage paid by firms affects labor productivity through its influence on nutrition and health. The production function is thus:

$$Y = (E\,L)^{1-a} \qquad\qquad 0 < a < 1 \qquad\qquad (20)$$

and the effort function E has the form:

$$E = (w/P_C - \omega)^d \qquad\qquad d < 1 \qquad\qquad (21)$$

where (W/P_C) is the real *consumption wage*, and P_C is a consumption price index derived from a Cobb-Douglas utility function of the form: $U = C_M{}^\alpha\,C_D{}^{1-\alpha}$, where C_M and C_D are respectively the quantities of imported and domestically produced consumer goods. The corresponding consumption price index is then: $P_C = (e\,P^*)^\alpha\,P_D{}^{1-\alpha}$, where P_D, P^* and e are respectively the domestic price, the price of imported consumer goods (in foreign currency) and the nominal exchange rate.

Firms treat prices as given and maximize profits over W and L, subject to the technology in (20) and the effort function (21). The first order conditions of this maximization program imply the following employment and wage decisions: $(E\,L)^d = (1{-}a)^{1/a}\,E^{1/a}\,(W/P_D)^{-1/a}$ and $W/P_D = p^\alpha\,\omega/(1{-}d)$, where $p = e\,P^*/P_D$.

Labor demand in effective units ($[E\,L]^d$) is an inverse function of the real wage per effective worker ($[W/P_D]/E$). In equilibrium all firms pay the same wage and equilibrium effort is obtained from substitution of the efficiency wage into the effort function.

The efficiency product wage is an increasing function of the real exchange rate and of ω, the minimum wage required to generate a positive effort from workers. The profit maximizing level of employment (L^d) is an inverse function of the efficiency product wage. The two equations combined imply that the profit maximizing level of employment is an inverse function of the real exchange rate:

$$L^d = L(p) \quad L' < 0 \qquad\qquad (22)$$

Setting L^d equal to the total labor force, we can solve eq. (22) for the unique value of the real exchange rate at which full employment is the profit maximizing level of employment. The horizontal IB line in Figure 12.7 shows the corresponding value of the real exchange rate.

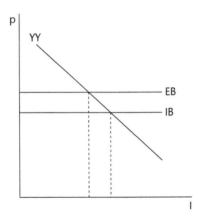

Figure 12.7 Conflict between external and internal balance

On the demand side, we treat investment as given and assume again that all profits are saved and all wage income is spent on consumption goods. Together with our Cobb-Douglas utility function, this assumption implies the following demand functions for imported and domestic consumer goods:

$$C_M = aWL/(eP^*) \tag{23}$$

$$C_D = (1 - a)WL/P_D \tag{24}$$

Exports are a positive function of the real exchange rate (p):

$$X = X(p) \quad X' > 0 \tag{25}$$

Consider now the goods market equilibrium condition. Using (20), (22), (24) and (25), the equality between output supply and aggregate demand $(Y = C_D + I + X)$ implies:

$$[E\ L(p)]^{1-a} = (1 - \alpha)L(p)p^{\alpha}[\omega/(1 - d)] + I + X(p) \tag{26}$$

Eq. (26) can be interpreted as showing the value of the real exchange rate that clears the goods market at each level of investment. From the RHS of (26), a higher level of investment raises aggregate demand and generates excess demand at the initial levels of the real exchange rate and employment. Market clearing requires an increase in aggregate supply and/or a reduction in other components of aggregate demand. The upward pressure on the price of domestic goods and the resulting real appreciation of the domestic currency achieves this. From the LHS of (26), we can see that the lower real exchange rate, through its effects on the efficiency product wage, increases output supply. In addition, the real appreciation reduces export demand and shifts the composition of consumption demand away from locally produced goods. Eventually, the goods market will clear at a higher level of employment and a lower real exchange rate.

Eq. (26) thus defines a downward sloping schedule of (p, I) combinations that keep the goods market in equilibrium (the YY schedule in Figure 12.7). Both a higher exchange rate and higher investment tend to generate excess demand for goods, and therefore the slope of this schedule is negative. Along the schedule, employment increases with the level of investment.

The levels of investment and real exchange rate consistent with goods market equilibrium and required to guarantee full employment are given at the intersection of the IB and YY lines in Figure 12.7. But is this combination feasible? Not necessarily, since the real exchange rate required for external balance may well imply an efficiency product wage that is too high to induce full employment of the labor force. Consider the external balance condition in this model. Setting the value of imports (eP* C_M) equal to the value of exports (P_D X) and using (22), (23), and (25) we obtain: $L(p) \, a \, p^a \, \omega/(1-d) = X(p)$, which can be solved for the value of the real exchange rate that is consistent with external balance, given the wage and employment decisions of firms. This value corresponds to the EB line in Figure 12.7. In the case shown by the figure, this value is higher than the exchange rate required for full employment (corresponding to the IB line). Clearly, the level of employment consistent with external balance and goods market equilibrium—at the intersection of the EB line and the YY schedule—will then be below full employment (since, as already noted, along the YY schedule employment increases with the level of investment). If the government then increases the level of investment to induce a higher level of employment, the external balance target will not be met.

The wage and employment decisions of firms, together with the external balance target, will constrain the ability of government policies to choose an exchange rate and investment level at the intersection of the EB and YY lines. The result is a less than full employment equilibrium that can neither be corrected through a nominal devaluation nor through an increase in investment. Any attempt to increase the level of employment in this way would either generate a real wage that is below the efficiency wage, with a corresponding increase in nominal wages, or the violation of the external constraint. Just as the wage-goods constraint in Kalecki's model results from the fact that the agricultural sector cannot supply the food surplus necessary to fully employ the labor force, structural unemployment here arises from a level of competitiveness that is too low to generate the real wage necessary to employ the whole of the labor force.

A higher level of employment can nevertheless be induced by other means. First, higher capital inflows, which have been ignored so far, would shift the external balance locus downwards and result in an increase in the permissible level of investment and employment. Such a shift induces an increase in employment by reducing the required real exchange rate and thus the equilibrium efficiency *product* wage. Second, an increase in productivity that reduces the efficiency product wage at each level of the real exchange rate would also move the economy closer to full employment. Finally, an import tariff can relax the foreign exchange constraint in the present setting. Under our assumptions, a higher import tariff shifts the EB line in Figure 12.7 downwards. The reason is that a tariff reduces import demand proportionately more than it increases the efficiency wage. However, this result would not hold if imports are inelastic and their price has a strong effect on prices of consumer goods.

Structural inflation in the open economy

What happens if the level of investment is higher than the level required to maintain external balance, given the labor market constraint? To answer this question, we will look at the model in (p, L) space (see Figure 12.8). Eq. (22) defines a downward sloping employment schedule (LL) in (p, L) space: a higher real exchange rate increases the efficiency product wage and reduces the profit maximizing level of employment. The goods market equilibrium locus (YY) shows the value of p that makes the volume of output forthcoming at each level of employment equal to aggregate demand. The locus is upward sloping, since a higher level of employment, which increases output, requires a higher real exchange rate in order to generate the corresponding increase in aggregate demand. The position of the YY line depends on a given level of investment. The EB line is the locus of real exchange rates and employment combinations that are consistent with equilibrium in the balance of payments. A positive price elasticity of export demand is sufficient for the external balance locus to slope upwards.[13] A real devaluation then has a positive effect on the trade balance and an increase in employment, which raises imports, is required to maintain external balance.

As drawn in Figure 12.8, the three loci do not intersect at the same point. The assumed level of investment is not consistent with the external balance and labor market constraints. To examine what will happen in this situation, we need to specify the behavior of prices, the exchange rate and nominal wages, when the economy is not in equilibrium. As in section 2, we assume that domestic prices move instantaneously to clear the goods market and that the nominal exchange rate moves instantaneously to clear the foreign exchange market. Nominal wages, in contrast, adjust sluggishly with a rate of change that is a function of the gap between real consumption wages and

---

[13] This is because, with the import price elasticity being unity, due to our Cobb-Douglas utility function, a positive export price elasticity is enough to fulfill the Marshall-Lerner condition.

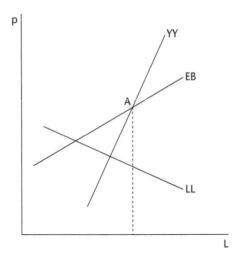

Figure 12.8 Conflict between external balance and labor market equilibrium

the efficiency consumption wage. These assumptions constrain the economy to always be at the intersection of the goods market equilibrium and external balance schedules, but allow for persistent deviations from the LL schedule. In a close analogy with the closed economy model of section 2, this schedule now shows the maximum value of the real exchange rate that is consistent with stable money wages at each level of employment. Above the locus, the real exchange rate is higher than the value required for money wage stability. In the situation depicted in Figure 12.8, the real exchange rate, as determined by equilibrium in the goods and foreign exchange markets, is too high to preserve price stability. As money wages increase, the nominal exchange rate must depreciate in order to preserve external balance, and domestic prices will then increase to maintain equilibrium in the goods market. The rate at which nominal wages (and prices) increase is a function of the gap between point A and the LL locus.[14] A reduction in investment that shifts the YY locus to the left may be an effective but (as in the analysis of section 2) not necessarily the most efficient cure for this type of inflation.

[14] For interpretations of high inflation processes along these lines, see Franco (1986), Taylor (1991), and Ros (1993).

13

Debt Traps and Growth Collapses

In the 1980s most countries in Latin America and Sub-Saharan Africa suffered economic setbacks that led to a prolonged slump. The same happened in Japan during the 1990s and may happen in Europe during the second decade of the 21st century. The main analytical issue that arises here is why the growth slowdowns persisted during such a long period of time and why macroeconomic policies were unable to overcome them.

Factor accumulation models, whether of the neoclassical, endogenous growth, or development theory varieties do not explain these severe growth slowdowns. Regardless of their relevance in earlier periods, the two-gap models reviewed in the previous chapter do not provide either a fully adequate explanation of the persistence of the slumps of the 1980s in Latin America and Japan in the 1990s. While these models may explain the ineffectiveness of macroeconomic policies, they do so under conditions at variance with the realities of these episodes. The notion that relative prices, especially the real exchange rate, have weak and unreliable effects on resource allocation cannot fully account for the problems of Latin American countries during a period that witnessed enormous changes in relative prices and substantial quantity adjustments in response to them. More generally, one could argue that the hypothesis of limited structural flexibility appears reasonable in growing economies to explain why they are not growing faster, but becomes less relevant for stagnating economies which are at the same time undergoing considerable structural adjustments. In addition, the assumption of exogenous capital flows cannot be applied to several Latin American countries during their "lost decade" when, even though the public sector remained rationed in international credit markets, the private sector, which often had most of its financial assets invested abroad, was not rationed in any meaningful sense.

The literature on three-gap models attempts to overcome these limitations and account for the economic stagnation and persistent under-utilization of resources that prevailed in Latin American economies during the 1980s.[1] This chapter discusses these contributions by extending the open economy model of capital accumulation of Chapter 10 to consider the government and private and public debts. The result is a three-gap model in which, besides foreign exchange shortages, fiscal or investment constraints originating in an over-indebtedness trap may prevent the economy from achieving a full capacity growth path. The chapter then moves to illustrating the relevance of the models for the analysis of the stabilization and adjustment problems of highly indebted countries in Latin America and their growth performance during the 1980s.

1. The Basic Analytical Framework

We extend the analytical framework presented in Chapter 10 to include a government sector and make explicit the financial flows among the private, government and foreign sectors. Table 13.1 shows the flows of funds between the sectors, together with each sector's budget constraint (column equations). The government sector (including the Central Bank) and the private sector (including domestic commercial banks) are indicated by subscripts G and P. Each of these sectors holds or issues one or more of the following financial assets: money (H), domestic government debt (B), public and private external debt (D) and international reserves (R) where, as in Chapter 10, P_X/P_I is set equal to one. X and Mk refer to (private sector) volumes of exports and imports, and G to real government spending. T, S and I refer to government disposable income, private savings and investment. These are nominal values deflated by the price of investment goods (P_I). For simplicity, we neglect interest payments on external private debt. The other symbols refer to changes in asset stocks expressed also in real values and thus to changes in real financial wealth. Since the flows of financial assets refer to changes in the real value of asset stocks, financial surpluses in the last row must also refer to

Table 13.1 Sectoral financial flows

Government	Private sector	Foreign		Total
$-\Delta H$	$+\Delta H$	0	$=$	0
$-\Delta B$	$+\Delta B$	0	$=$	0
$-\Delta D_G + \Delta R$	$-\Delta D_P$	$+\Delta D_G + \Delta D_P - \Delta R$	$=$	0
$T - (1 + z) G$	$+ S - I$	$+ r^* D_G + M_k - X$	$=$	0

[1] Contributions to this literature include Fanelli, Frenkel, and Winograd (1987), Carneiro and Werneck (1988), Bacha (1990), Taylor (1991), and Ros (1994).

changes in real financial wealth. The inflation tax and the inflationary component of domestic interest payments are therefore subtracted from both the government financial deficit and the private financial surplus.[2]

Goods market equilibrium and interactions between profitability and accumulation

In the goods market, the value of consumption is now such that:

$$P_D C = W\,L - p\,H + (1 - s_\pi)(1 - t)(PY - W\,L) + (1 - s_\pi)r_B B$$

where "t" is the tax rate on profits, r_B is the real rate of interest on domestic government debt, p is the rate of inflation (and thus, pH is the inflation tax).[3] Private disposable income now includes the interest income on private holdings of government bonds ($r_B B$) and excludes the inflation tax, which is assumed to be paid by wage earners. There are no other taxes on wages, and wage earners are assumed as in Chapter 10 to have a propensity to consume equal to one.

The goods market equilibrium condition is now:

$$P\,Y = P_D\,C + P_I\,I + P_D\,G + P_X\,X - P_M Mk$$

Normalizing by the capital stock and substituting from the consumption and import functions into the goods market equilibrium condition, we have:

$$[s_\pi + t\,(1 - s_\pi)]\,r = (1 - m)\,g + x + (1 + z)\,\theta + (1 - s_\pi)\,r_B\,b - p\,h \quad (1)$$

where "b" and "h" are the ratios of bonds and money to the capital stock, and "θ" is the ratio of government expenditures to the capital stock (G/K). The import function, as in Chapter 10, is such that there is a fixed amount (m) of complementary imports per unit of total investment. As the reader may verify, eq. (1) simplifies to eq. (4) in Chapter 10 if $b = h = t = \theta = 0$. Using now eq. (3) in Chapter 10 to eliminate x from (1), we can derive the new r (g) function, showing the profit rate that clears the goods market at each level of the rate of capital accumulation:

$$r = \Delta[(z + a)v + z(1 + z)\theta + z(1 - s_\pi)r_B b - z\,p\,h + z(1 - m)g] \quad (2)$$

where: $\Delta = 1 / [1 + z\,s_\pi + z\,t\,(1 - s_\pi)]$ and $= v\,[(1 - a)\,A\,(P_X/W)]^{(1 - a)/a}$

[2] The accounting framework is therefore in real terms in two ways: nominal income and expenditure flows are deflated and financial returns are net of inflation. Real incomes are thus defined as real expenditure plus the change in real financial wealth (see Coutts, Godley and Gudgin, 1984; Ros 1993a).

[3] Under the assumptions on price setting behavior in Chapter 10, the inflation rate is the same whether measured in terms of investment goods prices or the price of domestic sales.

Eq. (2) is similar to eq. (5) in Chapter 10, except for the positive effect on profitability of government spending (including interest payments on domestic debt) and the negative effect on profitability of the inflation tax, which affects the profit rate through its influence on domestic demand.

The presence of taxes on profits modifies the accumulation function. Thus, the rate of capital accumulation is now an increasing function of the post-tax expected rate of return:

$$g = \psi[(1 - t)r^e - r^*] \tag{3}$$

We also assume that private investment is negatively affected by inflation. One reason is that high inflation makes long-term domestic capital markets disappear, forcing firms to rely more heavily on foreign borrowing at increasing interest rates. The greater uncertainty about expected real interest rates and exchange rates, especially in the absence of indexation, favors capital flight and, to the extent that foreign assets and domestic investment are substitutes, has a negative effect on private investment. Other reasons for including the inflation rate (with negative effects) among the determinants of private investment are the resource misallocation effects of high inflation associated with the greater price variability and uncertainty about future returns as well as the premature amortization of business sector liabilities. This premature amortization results in an increase in effective financial costs and is a consequence of higher nominal interest rates in the absence of full financial indexation.[4] We introduce this and other influences of inflation on investment by making the risk adjusted international profit rate r^* an increasing function of the inflation rate: $r^* = r^*(p)$, with $r^{*\prime} > 0$.

The determination of the warranted growth rate is similar to that in Chapter 10, except for the effects of government spending, taxes and inflation. An increase in government spending increases profits by raising domestic demand and shifts the r (g) line upwards. The warranted growth rate and the profit rate increase. Higher taxes on profits reduce growth through two effects: that on the r (g) line, which shifts downwards as a result of the fall in capitalists' consumption and that on the g (r) line which shifts to the left on account of the negative effects of higher taxes on profitability. Higher inflation has adverse effects on growth and operates in a similar way to higher taxes. It shifts the g (r) line to the left by increasing r^*, and it reduces workers' consumption, thus shifting the r (g) line downwards.

---

[4] Several papers present empirical evidence from cross-country growth regressions supporting the hypothesis that high inflation has adverse (albeit non linear) effects on growth. See Barro (1995), Bruno (1995), Bruno and Easterly (1998), Ghosh and Phillips (1998), Khan and Senhadji (2001), and Burdekin et al. (2004); for a review of the literature, see Pollin and Zhu (2006).

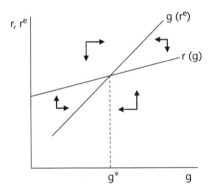

Figure 13.1 The warranted growth rate

2. Asset Markets Constraints and the Sustainable Fiscal Deficit

So far the model determines the rates of profit and capital accumulation for a *given* level of government spending. The given level of government spending, together with existing tax revenues, may, however imply an unsustainable path of debt accumulation. This is what, from the perspective of creditors, happened in Latin America in the early 1980s.[5] We are now interested in analyzing what happens after the government has become rationed in credit markets.

Thus, we shall now assume that the public sector is rationed in both foreign and domestic credit markets. Rationing takes the form of a kinked demand function for government debt on the part of domestic and foreign asset holders (see, on the subject, Ros, 1991). When $b > \tilde{b}$ or $d_G > \tilde{d}_G$ (where d_G refers to the stock of government external debt as a ratio of the capital stock), the demand for government debt becomes fully inelastic. The maximum amount of debt that the government can issue is thus equal to $g\ (\tilde{b} + \tilde{d}_G)$. Moreover, when r_B falls below r^* (plus a constant premium, λ), domestic demand for government debt becomes perfectly elastic. This forces the government to set $r_B = (1 + \lambda)\ r^*$ and to monetize the fiscal deficit whenever it is larger than the increase in the demand for government debt at the interest rates r^* and $r_B = (1 + \lambda)\ r^*$. But monetization is constrained by seignorage, beyond which international reserves would continuously fall. As a result, the amount that the government can finance by issuing money and without losing reserves is constrained by the increase in the demand for money (g h).

---

[5] The debt trap in which the economy may fall as a result is discussed in Ros (1999). Note that, in what follows, by neglecting debt dynamics we ignore the interactions between the interest payment on external debt and the current account deficit.

Let us now define the sustainable fiscal deficit as that deficit which is consistent with equilibrium in the overall balance of payments while, at the same time, keeping the stocks of base money and government debt equal to the constrained levels and, therefore, growing at the same rate as the capital stock. Thus, consider the sources of finance of the fiscal deficit (first column in Table 13.1). Set the change in international reserves equal to zero and the growth rate of domestic assets ($\Delta H/H$ and $\Delta B/B$) as well as government external debt ($\Delta D_G/D_G$) equal to the rate of capital accumulation (g). The sustainable fiscal deficit (or the asset market balance condition) is then given as:[6]

$$(1 + z)\theta - (t\,r + \pi h - r_B b - r^* d_G) = g(h + \tilde{b} + \tilde{d}_G) \qquad (4)$$

The condition expressed by eq. (4) constrains the amount of spending that the public sector can undertake. Substituting from (4) into (2) in order to eliminate $(1 + z)\,\theta$, yields:

$$r = \Omega[(z + a)v - zs_\pi r_B b - zr^* d_G + z(1 - m + h + \tilde{b} + \tilde{d}_G)g] \qquad (5)$$

where: $\Omega = 1 / (1 - t)[1 + z\,s\pi + z\,t\,(1 - s\pi)]$

Eq. (5) is the r (g) function that satisfies goods market equilibrium as well as the asset market constraints expressed in the sustainable fiscal deficit. This new r (g) line is steeper than before in (r, g) space. In addition to previous effects on profitability, faster growth now increases the constrained level of government spending which has a positive effect on the profit rate. The reason is that a higher growth rate raises the amount of debt and money that the government can issue as well as the amount of tax revenues received. This is why the tax rate now has positive effects on r, besides the negative effects operating through capitalists' consumption. It is worth noting that inflation no longer affects the position of the r (g) line. With government spending being endogenous, a higher inflation tax raises government spending by the same amount by which it reduces workers' consumption. Moreover, higher interest payments now shift the r (g) line downwards, thus reducing profitability. The reason is that higher interest payments reduce the constrained level of government spending. Finally, higher values for h,

---

[6] Derivation of (4) uses:

$$\Delta H/K = (\Delta H/H)(H/K) = (\Delta H/H)h \qquad h = H/K$$
$$\Delta B/K = (\Delta B/B)(B/K) = (\Delta B/B)b \qquad b = B/K$$
$$\text{and } \Delta D_G/K = (\Delta D_G/D_G)(D_G/K) = (\Delta D_G/D_G)d_G \qquad d_G = D_G/K$$

Eq. (4) can also be derived from the definition of the sustainable *primary* deficit. Abstracting from the external debt, the sustainable primary deficit is given by the following expression:

primary deficit $= (g + p)h + (g - r_B)b$

Adding the real interest payments on domestic debt ($r_B b$) to this sustainable primary deficit and subtracting the inflation tax ($p\,h$) yield the sustainable real fiscal deficit:

real deficit $=$ primary deficit $+ r_B b - p\,h = g(h + b)$

$\tilde{b}$, and $\tilde{d}_G$ increase the profit rate by raising seignorage and the level of government spending.

The determination of the growth rate by eqs (3) and (5) has a representation in (r, g) space similar to that in Figure 13.1 with, however, a steeper r (g) line. The adjustment dynamics is also similar although the interpretation of the adjustment off the r (g) line is slightly different. Above the r (g) line the profit rate is higher than required to clear the goods market at a level of domestic demand consistent with balance of payments equilibrium. The government will be losing reserves and forced to reduce its government spending. This brings about a fall in domestic demand, which reduces the profit rate.[7]

It is worth noting that while inflation has no effects on the position of the r (g) line, it still adversely affects growth by increasing r* and shifting the g (r) line to the left. The resulting growth rate (gi) can be said to be investment-constrained as both private capital inflows and domestic savings, due to unemployment, are below their maximum or potential levels. In contrast to two-gap models, the origin of resource under-utilization is not the lack of foreign exchange, but rather a too low level of investment. This low level of investment may arise from the asset balance constraints on government spending, or from a high inflation rate exerting depressive effects on private investment. In the first case, the closure of the model has a close affinity to the growth path in a three-gap model with a binding fiscal constraint.

There are, however, important differences between the model specification adopted here and the three-gap models. Most of the literature on three gap models (as well as on two-gap models) assumes fully exogenous capital inflows, and thus credit rationing applies to both the government and the private sectors. In our specification, private net capital inflows are endogenous as they are linked to private savings, asset demands, and private investment, through the private sector budget constraint (the second column in Table 13.1). Since the change in net foreign assets, plus the net acquisition of domestic financial assets by the private sector, must add up to its financial surplus (s_π r – g), private capital inflows are determined by:

$$\Delta d_P = g - s_\pi r + g(h + b) \tag{6}$$

where $\Delta d_P = \Delta D_P/K$. For developing countries with substantial capital flight, this endogenous determination of private capital inflows appears more appropriate than the assumption of exogenous capital inflows. The present model

---

[7] Alternatively, if the asset market constraints on government spending are always binding, the economy converges along the r (g) line to the equilibrium rates of profit and accumulation.

also differs from standard open economy models in which there is no credit rationing, and both public and private capital inflows are fully endogenous.[8]

The literature on three-gap models emphasizes the role of fiscal constraints in explaining the growth performance of highly indebted countries in the 1980s. In the framework presented above, fiscal constraints are instead endogenously determined by explicitly introducing the medium-term links between sustainable fiscal deficits, capital flight and private investment. Given the real exchange rate, as well as the parameters of the savings and trade functions, there is nothing that fiscal and monetary policy can do to increase the growth rate. Public investment, in particular, is constrained by the asset balance and external balance conditions. Beyond its endogenous value as determined by the model, increases in public investment would, if undertaken, be inconsistent with those conditions: bond-financed increases in public investment would create an unsustainable increase in domestic interest rates, while money-financed increases would generate unsustainable losses of foreign exchange reserves.[9] This modification allows us to emphasize that fiscal and current account deficits in the medium term are not exogenous, but rather simultaneously determined with private investment, capital inflows and the rate of economic growth. The "third gap" is then an investment constraint, which may or may not originate in a fiscal adjustment problem.

3. The Foreign Exchange Constraint

In addition to credit constraints on the public sector, it is possible that private capital inflows reach a maximum value, given the likelihood of credit rationing in foreign financial markets beyond a critical level of private external indebtedness. It is then clear that the accumulation function (eq. 3) will no

---

[8] The treatment of private capital inflows differs formally from the more conventional ones that specify an explicit function for net capital inflows. The demand for domestic bonds is then implicitly determined by the private sector budget constraint. Our treatment also reflects a difference in the approach itself. Foreign assets and domestic investment are here close substitutes: a fall in private investment will lead to a reduction of net capital inflows, even when interest rate differentials remain unchanged. For many developing countries, this seems more appropriate than the conventional approach for at least one reason: foreign direct investment, which is as pro-cyclical as overall private investment, is an important component of net private capital inflows.

[9] If demand for bonds was not fully inelastic, bond financed increases in public investment could be made sustainable by increasing the interest rate (and thus the stock demand for bonds "b", and bond seignorage g b). But this possibility operates within rather narrow limits. First, increases in "b" will be partly offset by reductions in "h", so that the sustainable fiscal deficit will increase by less than bond seignorage. Second, when the real interest rate exceeds the growth rate, the impact of interest payments on the fiscal deficit itself ($r_B \Delta b$) will exceed the gain in bond seignorage ($g \Delta b$), leading to a downward adjustment in public investment (rather than an increase) in order to keep equilibrium in domestic asset markets. For a fuller discussion of this subject, see Ros (1991).

longer determine the growth rate since, at the maximum value of capital inflows, investment demand is rationed and the rate of accumulation must be below the level associated with eq. (3). How are investment and growth determined in these conditions?

In this case, investment will be constrained by the level of domestic savings forthcoming at less than full employment and by the, now exogenous, level of private foreign savings. Indeed, with Δd_P equal to the maximum value of private capital inflows ($\Delta \tilde{d}_P$), eq. (6) provides the additional equation needed to determine the rate of accumulation.[10] It defines an upward sloping locus of (r, g) combinations, along which private investment demand is rationed by the availability of foreign exchange:

$$g = [1/(1 + h + b)](s_\pi r + \Delta \tilde{d}_P) \tag{7}$$

A higher profit rate raises "g", not because it makes investment more profitable, but rather because it relaxes the credit constraints on investment. The determination of the growth rate by eqs (5) and (7) has a representation similar to that in Figure 13.1. The r (g) line remains unchanged with an endogenous and constrained level of government spending. The adjustment when off this locus is the same as in the case of a fiscal constraint, with the government reducing (increasing) its expenditures whenever the profit rate is higher (lower) than on the locus at a given level of capital accumulation. The g (r) line is now given by (7) and shows the foreign exchange constrained rate of accumulation at each level of the profit rate. The economy may be assumed to always be on the g (r) line, as a higher rate of growth would imply that the foreign credit constraints on investment are being violated (or else that they are not binding, in which case the economy must be on a fiscal-investment constraint). The economy thus converges to the equilibrium rates of profit and accumulation along the g (r) line. Note also that this schedule no longer involves an expected profit rate, as in the cases examined earlier. This is because the profit rate affects investment through its effects on domestic savings, rather than through expected profitability.

The position of the g (r) schedule is affected by the savings rate out of profits and by the exogenous level of capital inflows, both of which shift the schedule to the right. An increase in private capital inflows unambiguously raises the growth and profit rates. A higher savings rate out of profits now has contradictory effects: the reduction in capitalists' consumption, which shifts the r (g)

---

[10] Alternatively, the model can be closed by using the balance of payments identity. Setting the change in international reserves equal to zero, it becomes the equilibrium condition in the foreign exchange market. Using the specification for imports and the profit rate—export ratio relationship derived in Chapter 10, we can rewrite the balance of payments equilibrium condition as:

$\Delta dp = (m - \tilde{d}_G)g + r/z(1 - t) + r^*d_G - (1 + a/z)v$

line upwards, tends to be offset by the increase in investment resulting from the outward shift in the g (r) line. This model closure has similar properties to conventional two-gap models with a binding foreign exchange constraint. A difference, however, is that the downward adjustment of the profit rate, rather than of capacity utilization, is here the equilibrating mechanism.

4. The Debt Crisis and Macroeconomic Instability in Latin America

We can summarize the analytical framework presented in previous sections by considering the determination of the medium-term equilibrium rate of accumulation in the two cases examined. Under a fiscal-investment constraint, the rate of accumulation is obtained from eqs (3) and (5) and can be shown to be positively affected by the propensity to invest (ψ) and negatively affected by domestic demand parameters (s_π and m) as well as the inflation rate (p). The effect of the real exchange rate operates directly and positively through the profit rate. As we shall see below, it can also operate by relaxing or exacerbating fiscal constraints on government spending and these effects can thus be positive or negative on the rate of accumulation. In reduced form:

$$g_I = g_I(\psi, s_\pi, m, p, P_X/W) \qquad g_{I1} > 0, g_{I2}, g_{I3}, g_{I4}, < 0, g_{I5}? \qquad (8)$$

Under a foreign exchange constraint, the rate of accumulation is obtained from eqs (5) and (7) and can be shown to be positively affected by the real exchange rate and the rationed levels of public and private capital flows and negatively affected by the import coefficient. In this case the effects of the real exchange rate on the rate of accumulation are unambiguously positive by relaxing balance of payments constraints. In reduced form:

$$g_F = g_F(P_X/W, d_G, \sim \Delta\tilde{d}_P, m) \qquad g_{F1}, g_{F2}, g_{F3}, > 0, g_{F4} < 0 \qquad (9)$$

The role of the fiscal and foreign exchange constraints may be illustrated with an analysis of the growth slump of Latin America that followed the adjustment to the debt crisis of the 1980s. The debt crisis meant an increase in the foreign interest rate and a reduction in governments' foreign credit. These shocks 'opened' a fiscal and a foreign exchange gap as the net inflows of foreign exchange were cut down in both the fiscal and balance of payments accounts. Both of these developments shifted the r (g) line downwards causing a fall in the rate of accumulation along the g (r) line, and the adjustment to them involved sharp real devaluations and fiscal contraction in all the highly indebted countries. The stabilization and adjustment difficulties that followed differed, however, between two types of economies. In the first, the country's public sector had foreign exchange revenues (e.g., oil revenues in Mexico and

Venezuela) and the real devaluations raised the real value of these foreign exchange revenues, contributing then to relax the asset balance constraints on public expenditure. In the second, the absence of such foreign exchange revenues combined with large interest payments on foreign public debt meant that the government had a negative foreign exchange balance. Public savings were thus adversely affected by real devaluations and this negative effect exacerbated the fiscal constraints on government spending. This was the case, among others, of Argentina and Brazil.

Mexico: debt crisis, inflation and investment collapse

Consider the experience of the first type of economies, which is best illustrated by Mexico's. The debt shock led to an increase in foreign interest payments by the public sector and a reduction in foreign lending to the government. To this, the decline in oil prices in 1986 further added to the reduction of the government's foreign exchange revenues by cutting oil export revenues down to a third of their value at the peak in 1983.

According to the model in section 3, the real devaluation that followed contributed unambiguously to relax the foreign exchange constraint in this case. Without it, closing the foreign exchange gap would have required even larger investment and output losses. To the positive effects of real devaluation operating through the export-capital ratio and the output-capital ratio, we can add the positive effects of a higher exchange rate on the real value of the government's foreign exchange balance. This effect acts like a change of (d_G) in eq. (5) and, indeed, it is equivalent to an increase in the (rationed) amount of additional foreign debt that the government can issue. As a result of these effects, the r (g) line shifts upwards. This tends to relax the foreign exchange constraint on the rate of accumulation. The locus of combinations showing the foreign-exchange-constrained rate of accumulation (g_F) at each level of the real exchange rate is thus upward sloping (see Figure 13.2).[11]

The real devaluation, due to its effects on the r (g) line, also tends to relax the fiscal constraint. However, the higher inflation associated with the devaluation has an adverse effect on private investment, thus causing a shift to the left of the g (r) line. At low levels of inflation, this effect may be small and the positive fiscal effects of devaluation may dominate. At high levels of inflation, the negative effects of inflation on investment may well dominate and set a limit to how much the government can offset this fall, using additional real

---

[11] The scope for shifting the foreign exchange constraint through a real exchange rate devaluation is of course a major difference to conventional two gap models. In the early elasticity-pessimism versions of these models, the locus of (growth and real exchange rates) combinations would be horizontal.

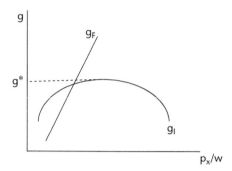

Figure 13.2 The foreign exchange and investment constraints on growth in Mexico

revenues. Note again that the positive effects on the inflation tax will not do the trick (quite independently of the likely fall in the tax base): its effects on government spending are offset (under our assumptions fully offset) by the fall in workers' consumption. Figure 13.2 illustrates the limits of real devaluation in offsetting the initial shocks over the medium term. The locus of $(g_I, PX/W)$ combinations—showing the medium-term value of the investment-constrained rate of accumulation (g_I) at each level of the real exchange rate—, takes the form of a bell-shaped curve. This shape sets a limit in the medium term to how much the government can, through real devaluations, recover the rates of growth that prevailed before the shocks.

The sharp decline of private investment in Mexico, by about 6 percentage points of GDP, is consistent with the role of the investment constraint. It followed the sharp cuts of public investment and a sharp acceleration of inflation in an economy with no financial indexation and a high degree of international capital mobility (see Ros, 1987). As a result, output growth, which in 1980 for a third consecutive year was above eight percent, was barely over one percent in 1988 (having been on average zero percent for the period 1982–8).

Large current account surpluses and a continuing capital flight accompanied the collapse of investment and the growth slowdown. Thus, a low level of potential domestic savings or a lack of foreign exchange cannot explain the sharp contraction of investment. The crucial role of the investment constraint is also confirmed by events after 1988. The 1989 debt relief agreement, the reduction of inflation following a successful heterodox stabilization program, and the decline in foreign interest rates were the major factors behind the recovery of private investment rates and capital repatriation after 1989.

Argentina and Brazil: fiscal constraints and hyperinflation

Despite its large foreign debt, the Mexican government had a foreign exchange surplus during the 1980s (largely accounted for by the public sector's oil export revenues). Under these conditions, the positive fiscal effects of real devaluations facilitated fiscal adjustment. Other highly indebted countries, such as Argentina and Brazil, with deficits in the government's foreign exchange balance, found themselves in a much more difficult position.

Consider the effectiveness of devaluation in closing the foreign-exchange gap in these deficit countries. The positive effects of devaluation on the trade balance will now tend to be offset by the increase in the real value of government's foreign exchange outlays, which shift the r (g) line downwards. As shown in Figure 13.3, if the schedule of $(g_F, P_X/W)$ combinations remains upward sloping, it will certainly be flatter than in the previous case. As a consequence, it takes larger devaluations to relax the foreign exchange constraint, while these larger devaluations have the effect of exacerbating the fiscal gap. The locus of $(g_I, P_X/W)$ combinations is now likely to be downward sloping. This is the result of the effects of inflation on private investment being added to the negative effects of devaluation on the fiscal accounts and government spending. Thus, as illustrated in Figure 13.3, the relationship between medium-term growth and the real exchange rate takes the form of an inverted V in these deficit countries.

Above the inverted V defined by the two loci of $(g, P_X/W)$ combinations—where "g" here is the minimum of g_I and g_F—the overall balance of payments is in deficit and below it is in surplus. Suppose that the economy is in the region below the foreign exchange constraint but above the fiscal constraint. The balance of payments disequilibrium has its origin in a fiscal gap, i.e., in a gap between actual government spending and its sustainable level (since the economy is above the fiscal constraint). In the absence of a fiscal adjustment that increases public savings, the resulting disequilibrium in the balance of payments will put an upward pressure on the exchange rate. Exchange rate depreciation will aggravate the fiscal gap by reducing public savings (the fiscal

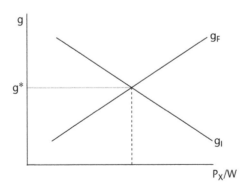

Figure 13.3 The foreign exchange and investment constraints on growth in Argentina and Brazil

constraint is downward sloping). This will in turn exacerbate the balance of payments disequilibrium and can eventually lead to hyperinflation.

These difficulties become insurmountable if the fiscal adjustment required to bring the economy back to the fiscal constraint is not socially viable. Suppose that, given foreign interest rates and the external debt-GDP ratio, the fiscal adjustment required to prevent a continuous increase in the external debt-GDP ratio is not socially viable. The foreign exchange and fiscal constraints intersect at a growth rate that is not socially feasible. In the absence of either a reduction in the value of external debt or a fall of foreign interest rates, the economy may for a prolonged period of time remain on the brink of either a debt moratorium or hyperinflation. Together with Bolivia and Peru, which also fall in the category of deficit countries, Argentina and Brazil were precisely those countries in Latin America that lived through hyperinflation episodes in the 1980s.

Regional dummies in cross-country growth regressions

A common finding in cross country growth regressions is that predicted growth rates for Latin American economies and Sub-Saharan Africa countries are higher than can be explained by factor accumulation and political variables alone.[12] Dummy variables for Latin America, for example, are systematically significant and negative, typically accounting for why growth rates there have been more than one percentage point below what would otherwise be predicted by these models. As stated by Barro (1991, p. 437): ... "the results leave unexplained a good deal of the relatively weak growth performance of countries in sub-Saharan Africa and Latin America."[13]

The significance of regional variables is likely to reflect the importance of omitted variables. Since these studies include the period of terms of trade shocks and the debt crisis of the 1980s, a reasonable hypothesis is that those shocks threw these countries into a growth path in which demand constraints prevented a full utilization of resources. Ros (2000) provides evidence supporting this interpretation, i.e., that the size and significance of these regional variables is attributable, at least partly, to the inclusion of the 1980s in the period of estimation. The exercise presented there consisted in estimating

---

[12] See, among others, Romer (1990) and Barro (1991). This finding probably no longer holds if one extends the period of analysis to the past 12 years which have witnessed rapid growth in several African and a few Latin American countries largely as a result of the boom in commodity demand coming from China and India.

[13] Barro (1997) has argued that the inclusion of the inflation rate in the growth regressions makes the Latin America dummy to become insignificant. As we shall argue later, this result is consistent with the view that the inclusion of the 1980s is critical to the significance of the dummy variables. In the case of sub-Saharan Africa, there is only one variable (the ratio of government consumption to GDP) whose omission causes the dummy to become significant.

cross-country regressions for 1960–9, 1960–75, 1960–79, and 1960–89. The variables chosen for the regressions are strictly based on Barro (1991). Two variants were estimated depending on the inclusion or not of a dummy variable for the Asian countries.[14] While the coefficients of the variables for Latin America and Africa are consistently negative and those for Asia positive (confirming previous findings), none of the dummy variables is statistically significant (at the 5 percent level) for the periods 1960–9 and 1960–75. The dummy variable for Latin America becomes significant when the 1980s are included (i.e., for the period 1960–89) and its significance for the period 1960–75 depends on the inclusion of the dummy variable for Asia. The negative coefficient of the dummy variable for Latin America increases considerably in absolute value when the 1980s are included (it nearly doubles in size from the 1960s to the period 1960–89). The dummy variable for Africa becomes significant when the late 1970s and the 1980s are included in the period of estimation (regardless of whether the dummy variable for Asia is included). This is consistent with the fact that the slump in Africa started in the mid 1970s with the negative terms of trade shocks of that decade. It is also worth noting that when the dummy variable for Asian countries is included, this variable only becomes statistically significant when the 1980s are included. This suggests that the performance of Latin America compared to Asia is unambiguously disappointing only after 1980—disappointing in the sense of being weaker than expected, given differences in other variables, such as investment and initial education levels.

In sum, the evidence on regional dummy variables provides support to the notion that demand-constrained growth paths may have prevented convergence to higher income levels in many parts of Latin America and Africa. The lack of convergence is specific to the period in which asset constraints were binding. This suggests that our interpretation may be the only reasonable one. Otherwise, why is it that economies that were converging towards higher income levels before 1980, afterwards ceased this development?

---

[14] Regressions including the square of the income term were also estimated. The main effect of including this term (which shows a consistently negative sign) was to turn the coefficient on initial income (non-squared) from negative to positive. The results are thus similar to those reported in Chapter 8.

Part IV

Deep Determinants of Comparative Development

14

Trade and Development

This chapter reviews alternative views on the role of trade openness and the pattern of trade specialization in the growth process and the tendency to convergence or divergence across countries. Section 1 discusses the approach taken by neoclassical trade theory which, unlike neoclassical growth theory, downplays the role of factor endowments and emphasizes the equalizing tendencies brought about by openness to international trade. This approach provides us with a useful benchmark, with which we can compare alternative trade and growth models. Section 2 turns to the relationship between growth and the pattern of specialization in neoclassical and new trade theory models. The analytical framework in the last case is a model with multiple equilibria in which the pattern of specialization affects the steady state level of income and/or the rate of convergence to the steady state. This provides the framework for a discussion in section 3 of development traps in the open economy and the scope and limitations of industrial policy in increasing the rate of capital accumulation. Finally, section 4 reviews the empirical evidence on the effects of trade volumes, trade openness and the pattern of specialization on incomes and growth.

1. Openness and Convergence in Neoclassical Trade Theory

In neoclassical growth models of closed economies, countries converge to different steady states, which depend on savings and population growth rates. Openness to capital flows, as we have seen in Chapter 3, reinforces the tendency of economies to converge to similar income levels. Neoclassical trade theory is far more optimistic. Even in the absence of capital mobility, a neoclassical world of trading economies will feature a tendency to convergence of factor prices across countries. Indeed, a central proposition of neoclassical trade theory is that through the international exchange of goods and the equalization of goods' prices, competition in domestic factor markets will tend to equalize factor prices among free trading economies. Real wages will not be lower in labor abundant countries because free trade—by allowing the labor abundant economy to specialize in those goods produced with labor intensive techniques—will make labor intensive techniques be used more extensively than in the previously low-income closed economy. The key questions from this perspective do no longer refer to the constraints posed by the stage of capital accumulation, but rather to what prevents this tendency to factor price equalization to take place. Is it the presence of obstacles to free trade and other sources of resource misallocation, as discussed by the recent empirical literature on convergence in open and closed economies or by earlier writing on the relationship between growth and the "outward" or "inward" orientation of trade policy regimes?[1] Or is it that the restrictive conditions on returns to scale, access to technology, and factor and product markets required for factor price equalization and convergence to operate are rarely met in practice? And if so, what are the policy implications? We look, in this chapter, for answers to these questions. Consider first how openness modifies the convergence properties of the neoclassical growth model.

Factor price equalization and convergence

Consider a Heckscher-Ohlin model with two goods produced using two factors (capital and labor) in two different countries. One good is relatively capital-intensive and the other good relatively labor-intensive. The two goods are produced under constant returns to scale and both countries have access to the same technologies. Within each country, competition in factor markets establishes uniform wage rates for labor and uniform rental rates for capital. Profit maximization under perfect competition implies the equality between factor prices and marginal products. International trade leads to the equalization of goods prices. Together, these tendencies imply that relative wages and capital rentals must obey certain relationships. Thus, the equality within each country between the product wage in each sector and the marginal product of labor in the same sector, together with the equalization of goods prices through trade, imply that the capital-labor ratio in the production of each good will be the same in both countries.

This is a striking implication: regardless of differences in the overall capital and labor endowments between the two countries, each of the two goods will be produced with the *same* capital intensity in *both* countries. The labor abundant country will of course tend to specialize in the production of the labor-intensive good and export this good to the capital-rich economy.

---

[1] See, on the older literature, Little, Scitovsky, and Scott (1970), Helleiner (1992), Edwards (1993), Ffrench-Davis and Agosin (1993).

However, as long as it produces some of the capital-intensive good, it will produce it with the same capital intensity that prevails in the capital abundant country. The value of the marginal product of its labor will be the same as in the capital-rich economy despite having a comparatively larger labor endowment. As a result, the wage rates in both countries will indeed be identical.

Factor price equalization does not imply the convergence of income or output per worker since factor quantities will still differ across countries. However, factor price equalization clearly implies a stronger tendency to convergence of incomes than is present in a closed economy framework: it is hard to imagine a world in which wages tend to be equalized internationally without income gaps being much smaller than in the absence of such a tendency. Moreover, the tendency to factor price convergence takes place independently of whether economies are in the steady state or not (in the Heckscher-Ohlin model capital is mobile across sectors but the overall capital stock is given and need not be at its steady state value).

Factor price equalization requires a number of restrictive assumptions. I highlight those which are more relevant for our purposes in this and subsequent chapters in which the tendency to factor price equalization will not take place. First, constant returns to scale, as well as both countries having access to the same technology, are essential. With increasing returns, arising for example from external effects of the overall capital endowment, the techniques used by the capital abundant country will be more productive in both sectors and real wages will accordingly be higher in the capital abundant country. Second, both goods must be produced in both countries. If the labor abundant country would fully specialize in the production of the labor-intensive good, the link between relative wages and capital intensities in the production of the capital-intensive good would be broken and factor endowments will again play a role in the determination of relative wages. Third, both factors must enter into the production of both goods.

2. Growth and the Pattern of Specialization in Neoclassical and New Trade Theory

In the previous analysis of convergence of factor prices, factor endowments are assumed given. The question we now address is: What is the relationship, if any, between the pattern of specialization and growth in neoclassical models? In textbook neoclassical theory, the pattern of specialization is uniquely determined independently of initial conditions by factor endowments. At the other extreme of the theoretical spectrum, some new trade theory models treat productivity growth as the result of learning by doing and assume away factor endowments as a determinant of comparative advantage (see for example Krugman, 1987). The pattern of specialization cannot then be determined independently of initial conditions and history. Real shocks like a temporary resource boom or monetary shocks like a temporary currency overvaluation, are then all important in its influence on the pattern of trade specialization. Industrial policy also becomes crucial in acquiring new comparative advantages independently of factor endowment. This section discusses the assumptions under which these different possibilities can arise. The discussion shows how different patterns of specialization, consistent with the same factor endowment, can have different dynamic implications in the presence of multiple equilibria.

The pattern of specialization in a neoclassical model of a small open economy

Consider a small open economy producing two tradable goods (M and S), both of which require capital and labor. Technology in these sectors is described by:

$$M = K_M{}^a LM^{1-a} \qquad S = K_S{}^b L_S{}^{1-b}$$

where $a > b$; i.e., sector M is more capital intensive than sector S. Good M is the capital good. Labor demand and the profit rate in sector S are given by:

$$L_S = L_S(w/p_S, K_S) \qquad L'_{S1<0}, L'_{S2>0} \qquad (1)$$

$$r^S = r_S(p_S/p_M, w/p_S) \qquad r'_{S1>0}, \ r'_{S2<0} \qquad (2)$$

Labor demand and the profit rate in sector M are determined as:

$$L_M = L_M(w/p_M, K_M) \qquad L'_{M1<0} \quad L'_{M2>0} \qquad (3)$$

$$r_M = r_M(w/p_M) \qquad r'_{M<0} \qquad (4)$$

Note that because by assumption M is the capital good, the profit rate in sector S is also a function of the terms of trade (p_S/p_M). In this section, we choose units such that $p_S/p_M = 1$. This implies that for the same product wage, sector M is always more capital intensive than sector S.

Equilibrium in the labor market implies a uniform wage between the two sectors, as well as the full employment of the labor force (L): $L = L_S + L_M$. The schedule of labor market equilibrium shows the equilibrium wage as an inverse function of the capital stock K_M, given the overall capital stock and the full employment assumption. Formally, its equation is obtained by substituting from the labor demand functions into the full employment condition, $L = L_S + L_M$, setting $K_S = K - K_M$. We get: $L_S (w/p_S, K - K_M) + L_M (w/p_M, K_M) = L$.

The schedule slopes downward in (w, K_M) space (see Figure 14.1) since an increase in K_M (and a fall in K_S) creates excess supply of labor as the overall demand for labor falls with capital being reallocated toward the capital intensive sector. This requires a fall in the wage to clear the labor market. Along the schedule the overall stock of capital is held constant. A change in the overall capital stock thus shifts the position of the schedule. For example, an increase in the capital stock, holding the overall labor force constant, shifts the locus upwards: a higher overall capital-labor ratio raises the market-clearing value of the wage for each given allocation of the capital stock.

Capital is mobile between sectors S and M. Capital market equilibrium requires the full employment of the aggregate capital stock (K) and equality between the profit rates in the two capital-using sectors (insofar as the two sectors coexist): $r_S (p_S/p_M, w/p_S) = r_M (w/p_M)$. In ($\ln K_M$, $\ln w$) space, the schedule of capital market equilibrium is a horizontal line (see Figure 14.1). Indeed, under our present assumptions, there is a unique value of the wage independent of the capital stock in sector M that satisfies the condition for profit rate equalization. This value depends on technological parameters and the terms of trade but not on factor endowments. A shift in the terms of trade in favor of the labor-intensive sector (sector S) increases the value of the wage required for profit rate equalization.

What happens when the economy is off the locus of capital market equilibrium? Clearly, the profit rates in the two sectors cannot be equal. If the wage is higher than its value on the schedule of capital market equilibrium, the profit rate in the capital-intensive sector is higher than in the labor-intensive sector. Capital will thus flow towards the capital-intensive sector (M). Below the schedule, the low wage implies that the profitability of the labor intensive sector is higher and capital thus flows towards sector S. With labor market equilibrium obtaining at all times, and given the negative slope of this schedule, the allocation at the intersection of the two loci is then stable (see Figure 14.1).

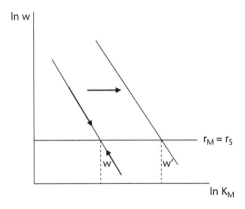

Figure 14.1 The pattern of specialization in a neoclassical model

The structure of this economy, and the associated pattern of specialization, depend on technology and the terms of trade, which affect the schedule of capital market equilibrium, as well as on factor endowments, the overall capital stock and the total labor force, both of which affect the position of the schedule of labor market equilibrium. The model thus has a clear-cut answer to the question of what determines the pattern of specialization. Given the technology, the terms of trade and the endowment of factors, there is a unique allocation of resources that satisfies the equilibrium conditions in the labor and capital markets.

The pattern of specialization under increasing returns

We now extend the model to show that, under slightly more general assumptions, the analysis of the pattern of specialization suffers from a fundamental indeterminacy that opens the door to the role of other determinants, including institutional factors and policies. This extension can be interpreted as an amended neoclassical model which allows for the presence of increasing returns in the production of non-traded inputs. Alternatively, it can be seen as a new trade theory model—such as Krugman's (1987) analysis of the Dutch disease and the "competitive consequences of Mrs. Thatcher"—which abandons the assumption of a Ricardian technology and allows for the presence of non-traded goods.[2]

The economy considered produces two tradable goods: good S (identical to that in the previous model) and good M which is now produced with capital and non traded inputs. We introduce the assumption of increasing returns to scale into the model by assuming that the non-tradable inputs are produced under internal increasing returns and monopolistic competition (just as the intermediate goods sector of Chapter 8). As shown in Chapter 8, this implies the following determination of employment in the intermediate goods sector (I) and of the profit rate in sector M:

$$L_I = L_I(w/p_M, K_M) \qquad L'_{I1 < 0}, \quad L'_{I2 > 0} \qquad (5)$$

$$r_M = r_M(K_M, w/p_M) \qquad r'_{M1 > 0} \quad r'_{M2 < 0} \qquad (6)$$

The main difference with the model of the previous section is that the profit rate in sector M is now not only an inverse function of the product wage but, given this wage, a positive function of the capital stock invested in this sector. This positive effect of the capital stock is due the presence of economies of scale in sector I. Indeed, a higher capital stock in sector M raises the demand

[2] Other related models are in Rodrik (1994), Rodriguez-Clare (1996), and Ciccone and Matsuyama (1996).

and output for I-goods; the higher scale of output implies an increase in productivity which, given the wage, reduces the relative price of intermediate goods (in terms of M-goods) and thus increases the profit rate in sector M.

How are the schedules of labor and capital market equilibrium affected? Consider, first, the schedule of labor market equilibrium. At low levels of K_M, the equilibrium wage falls as capital is reallocated towards sector M (just as in the previous model). When K_M is small, sector I is also small and produces at high costs, given the presence of economies of scale in this sector. The relative price of intermediate inputs (p_I/p_M) being very high, the K/I ratio is also very high despite K_M being small in absolute value. With a high K/I ratio, the "integrated M/I sector" is relatively capital-intensive and a reallocation of the capital stock towards sector M has the effect of generating excess supply of labor, thus reducing the market clearing wage. At high levels of K_M, when these values exist, the schedule of labor market equilibrium becomes positively sloped. The indirect employment effects of the expansion of sector M can offset the fall in labor demand in sector S. The larger scale of the I-sector has then made this sector more productive and reduced the relative price of intermediate goods, making the integrated M/I sector relatively labor-intensive. With a smaller K/I ratio, the expansion of sector M at the expense of sector S can then have the effect of generating excess demand for labor and increasing the market-clearing wage.

The condition for profit rate equalization yields, as before, the schedule of capital market equilibrium by substitution from the profit rate functions. The new feature is that the value of the wage required for profit rate equalization is no longer independent of the allocation of the capital stock. We now have a locus of (w, K_M) combinations, rather than a unique value of the wage, along which the condition of profit rate equalization is fulfilled. Formally, the slope of the schedule of capital market equilibrium in (ln w, ln K_M) space is:

$$\text{dln } w/\text{dln } K_M = [\mu(1-a)/f]/[(1-a)(1+\mu)/f - (1-b)/b]$$

The case shown in Figure 14.2 assumes b > f which implies (1–a) (1 + μ) > (1–b), i.e., the labor share of the integrated M/I sector is larger than the labor share of sector S (even though sector M is "directly" more capital intensive than sector S, in the sense that a > b). In this case, a wage increase (given K_M) reduces the profit rate in sector M more than it does in sector S. An increase in K_M (which affects positively r_M) is required to restore the equality of profit rates. This makes the slope of the schedule positive.[3]

---

[3] In the other case, we have: b < f. This implies: (1 – a) (1 + μ) < (1 – b), i.e., the labor share of the integrated M/I sector is smaller than the labor share of sector S. The slope of the schedule is then negative. The analysis of this case is similar to the one shown in Figure 14.2 (see Ros, 2000, ch. 9).

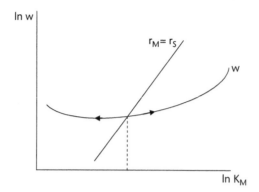

Figure 14.2 The pattern of specialization under increasing returns

In the configuration shown in Figure 14.2, the region to the right of the capital market locus ($r_M = r_S$) is one in which sector M is more profitable than sector S. This is because it is a region where K_M is relatively large, at each level of the wage, and K_M has a positive effect on the relative profitability of sector M. In this region, capital will be flowing towards sector M and thus K_M/K_S will increase. In contrast, to the left of the capital market locus r_M is lower than r_S and capital is flowing towards sector S. It then follows that the capital allocation at the intersection of the two loci is an unstable equilibrium.

We can also verify that when the two schedules intersect, this intersection is unique.[4] It follows then that if an intersection exists, there will be two stable allocations in which the whole capital stock is invested in one of the two sectors. In one allocation, the economy fully specializes in the production of good S. Since no I sector will exist, not only the capital stock but the whole labor force is also employed in sector S. We shall refer to this capital and labor allocation as the S-equilibrium. In the other allocation, the economy specializes in the production and export of good M and, since there will not be an S sector, the whole labor force is employed in sector I. We call this allocation the M-equilibrium.

In our economy, an S-equilibrium always exists whether multiple equilibria exist or not. This is due to the assumption that sector S does not use intermediate goods produced under increasing returns.[5] At low levels of K_M, the profit rate in sector M tends to zero while it remains positive in sector S no matter

---

[4] This is because the locus of the capital market equilibrium remains steeper than the locus of the labor market at high levels of K_M. Necessary and sufficient conditions are $a > b$ and $f > 0$.

[5] In Rodriguez-Clare (1996), sector S uses non-tradable inputs produced under increasing returns. We then have three configurations. First, over a range of low values of the aggregate capital stock, a unique S-equilibrium exists. Then, over a range of intermediate values of the capital stock, two stable equilibria, with specialization in S and M goods, exist. For high values of the capital stock, we have a unique M-equilibrium.

how large the capital stock is. There are thus some capital allocations, at sufficiently low levels of K_M, for which sector S is more profitable than sector M.

Since an S-equilibrium always exists, it follows that the existence of an M-equilibrium guarantees the existence of an intersection and, therefore, ensures the presence of multiple stable equilibria. An M-equilibrium, in turn, will exist if profitability in sector M, when the whole of the capital stock is allocated to this sector, is higher than that of sector S (evaluated at the market clearing wage corresponding to $L_I = L$). Consider, first, the wage in the M-equilibrium (w_M^*). From eq. (5), setting $L_I = L$ and $K_M = K$ and solving for the wage, we have:

$$w_{M^*} = G(1/n)^{1-f} p_M K^a / L^f \tag{7}$$

Substituting from (7) into (6), setting $w_M^* = w_M$ and $K_M = K$, we obtain the profit rate in the M-equilibrium (r_M^*):

$$r_{M^*} = a(L/n)^{1-f} / K^{1-a} \tag{8}$$

The profit rate in sector S evaluated at the M-equilibrium wage (r_M^s) is obtained from substitution of (7) into (2):[6]

$$r_M^s = b(p_S/p_M)^{1/b} [(1-b)n^{1-f} L^f / G\, K^a]^{(1-b)/b} \tag{9}$$

From (8) and (9), the condition for $r_M^* > r_M^s$, and thus for the existence of an M equilibrium, is:

$$K^{a-b} > K^{*a-b} = (b/a)^b (p_S/p_M)[(1-b)/G]^{1-b} n^{1-f} L^{f-b} \tag{10}$$

Condition (10) shows that the existence of multiple equilibria depends on the capital-labor endowment and the terms of trade (p_S/p_M). For an M-equilibrium to exist, the aggregate capital stock must be sufficiently large so that, when the whole of it is allocated to sector M, the price of intermediate goods is low enough to make the M sector viable. The threshold value (K^*) of the aggregate capital stock rises with the relative price ratio (p_S/p_M), which increases the profitability of sector S. It also increases with the number of firms (n) in sector I, which adversely affects the profitability of sector M. The effect of the overall labor endowment on the threshold value of K depends on the sign

---

[6] Note from eq. (9) that the profit rate in sector S, evaluated at the M-equilibrium wages, r_M^s, is an increasing function of the number of producers of I goods (n). A higher number of producers raises the unit cost of each of the I-goods and reduces the demand for labor in sector I. This has a negative effect on w_M^* and therefore tends to increase the profit rate in sector S, which does not use I goods. This negative effect on the wage is offset in the case of the profit rate in sector M, since a higher number of producers implies higher costs for sector M: r_M^* is a decreasing function of the number of producers.

of $(f - b)$, i.e., on the size of the labor share of the integrated M/I sector compared to that of sector S.[7]

When an M-equilibrium does not exist and there is a unique S-equilibrium, the economy clearly has a comparative advantage in good S and market incentives will lead the economy to specialize in sector S. However, when an M-equilibrium exists, the existence of multiple patterns of specialization consistent with the same factor endowment makes the notion of comparative advantage equivocal. This indeterminacy opens the door to the role of other factors—related to history, exogenous shocks, and policies—in the determination of the pattern of specialization. Indeed, initial conditions matter now in a way that was absent in the standard neoclassical model, since depending on the initial allocation of resources the economy will move to one or another of the two patterns of trade specialization and remain locked in that pattern. As we shall see later, temporary shocks can also be decisive and industrial policy, even if transitory, can also make a substantial difference.

We now assume that the condition for multiple equilibria is fulfilled and compare the wage and profit rates in the two stable equilibria. In an M-equilibrium, the wage and profit rate are given by eqs (7) and (8). In an S-equilibrium, we have $K_S = K$ and $L_S = L$. Using eqs (1) and (2), the S-equilibrium wage and profit rate are:

$$w_{S*} = (1 - b)p_S (K/L)^b \tag{11}$$

$$r_{S*} = b(p_S/p_M)(L/K)^{1-b} \tag{12}$$

Comparing (8) and (12) shows that for r_M* to be higher than r_S* requires:

$$K^{a-b} > K_1^{a-b} = (b/a)(p_S/p_M)n^{1-f}L^{f-b} \tag{13}$$

Comparing (10) and (13), we can establish that $K* > K_1$. The assumption of $a > b$ and the second order condition for a profit maximum among I_i producers ensure this inequality.[8] It follows that when an M-equilibrium exists $(K > K*)$, the profit rate in this equilibrium is higher than in the S-equilibrium (since K then is also higher than K_1).

---

[7] In Rodrik (1994), the level of skills affects the existence of multiple equilibria. In Rodrik's model, the sector producing non-tradable inputs under economies of scale is intensive in skilled labor. The level of skills then plays a role in the existence of multiple equilibria, along with the size of the capital stock. A higher level of skills can partly compensate for the high costs arising from a small market for I goods and thus reduce the size of the capital stock required for the existence of an M-equilibrium.

[8] For $K* > K_1$, the following condition must be fulfilled: $(1 - b)/b > [(1 - a)/a] (1 + \mu) (1 - 1/\emptyset)$. The assumption $a > b$ implies that $(1 - b)/b > (1 - a)/a$. For the second order condition for a profit maximum among I_i producers to be fulfilled, it is necessary that $(1 + \mu) (1 - 1/\emptyset) < 1$ (see Skott and Ros, 1997). Taken together, these inequalities ensure the fulfillment of the condition above.

Inspection of (7) and (11) shows that for w_M^* to be greater than w_S^* the aggregate capital stock must be such that:

$$K^{a-b} > K_2^{a-b} = (1-b)(p_S/p_M)n^{1-f} \, L^{f-b}/G \qquad (14)$$

From (10) and (14), we can establish that $K_2 > K^*$.[9] The existence of an M-equilibrium does not guarantee that the wage in the M-equilibrium is higher than in the S-equilibrium. This requires that the aggregate capital stock is larger than K_2. In this case, with $K > K_2$, and therefore K larger than K^* and K_1, an M-equilibrium will exist and feature both a profit rate and a wage rate higher than in the S-equilibrium.

Suppose that this last condition ($K > K_2$) is fulfilled and consider two economies, identical in all respects (including factor endowment, savings rates, size of the labor force), except for their pattern of specialization. One is specialized in the production and export of S goods, the other in the production of M and I goods. Since it has a higher wage rate and a higher profit rate (with the same capital endowment), the economy specializing in the production of M and I goods has a higher income per capita than the economy specializing in good S.

In the presence of multiple equilibria, does it make a difference to the growth rate of an economy whether it adopts one or the other of the two patterns of trade specialization? In the absence of international capital mobility, with identical savings rates (as well as population growth rates), it would appear according to standard neoclassical growth theory, that the economy with the lower income per capita (that specializing in sector S) should grow at a faster rate: the parameters determining the steady state value of income (savings and labor force growth) are the same as in the M-specialization and, since per capita income is lower, the economy would appear to be further away from the steady state than that with the M-specialization. Yet, it is clear that this last economy is the one that grows at the faster rate: with a higher income and the same capital stock and savings rate, its rate of capital accumulation must be higher than in the economy with the S-specialization. This higher growth rate is the result of the pattern of specialization: it is the associated allocation of the capital stock that raises the rate of capital accumulation for a given investment share (given that for the same capital stock its income level is higher).

The fact that the higher income per worker does not prevent the second economy from growing faster can be seen from a slightly different perspective. The economy specializing in M and I goods is converging to a steady state

---

[9] This requires as in the previous case: $(1-b)/b > [(1-a)/a] \, (1+\mu) \, (1-1/\emptyset)$. The fulfillment of this inequality is guaranteed by the same conditions as before (a > b, and the second order condition for a profit maximum among I_i producers).

different from that of the economy producing S goods. In this steady state, the capital-output ratio is the same in both economies since by assumption savings rates and depreciation of the capital stock are the same in both economies. Total output, however, is larger in the economy specializing in sector M. The difference is proportional to the difference in capital elasticities of output in sectors M and S.[10] This steady state income gap is the result of their different patterns of specialization which appears here thus as an additional determinant of the steady state level of income.

In the presence of international capital mobility the growth advantage is likely to be enhanced since capital will be flowing to the economy with the higher return to capital and, as we have seen, the mere existence of multiple equilibria ensures that the profit rate in the M-specialization is higher than in the S-specialization. With a higher profit rate and capital mobility, the investment share itself is likely to be higher in the M-specialization.

3. Growth Effects of Industrial Policies and Long-term Consequences of Temporary Shocks

Policy implications: the growth effects of industrial policies

Many developing countries have adopted industrial policies in an attempt to accelerate the rate of industrialization and economic growth. The results have been mixed, if we are to judge from the variety of growth performance under similar policies. This explains why the effectiveness of these policies is controversial and why widely different views coexist on whether they made a difference and, if so, whether this was positive or negative. This is the case even though observers and policymakers alike have amply documented the role of industrial policy in fostering a fast rate of industrialization in East Asia and Latin America (see, on the subject, Amsden, 1989, 2001; Moreno-Brid and Ros, 2009; Rodrik, 1994; and Wade, 1990). An important reason for this state of affairs seems to be that consensus is lacking on precisely the key issue of how and under what conditions industrial policy can significantly alter the rate of capital accumulation and growth. The analytical framework presented here may help in clarifying this question.

In models with a unique equilibrium whether of the neoclassical or new trade theory varieties, i.e., with constant returns or increasing returns to scale, the economy has a clear comparative advantage in one of the sectors in which it can specialize. Market incentives, unassisted by policy, lead the economy to

---

[10] In the presence of differences in the size of the labor force, the difference in the steady state level of income would also be proportional to the size in the labor force (due to the existence of increasing returns to scale in sector I).

specialize in the production of those traded goods in which it has a comparative advantage. It may even be argued that industrial policy can hardly improve on the market outcome. In the model with increasing returns, if a unique M equilibrium exists industrial policy is not needed in order to move the economy towards this pattern of specialization. And, if a unique S equilibrium exists a policy that succeeds in reallocating resources towards sector M will lead to a fall in the wage compared to that in the S-specialization. The profit rate is also likely to fall, especially if the aggregate capital stock is small and the costs of intermediate goods are high, as a result. With a profit rate in sector M lower than in sector S—evaluated at market wages and prices of intermediate goods—the policy-induced changes in relative prices required to make sector M viable would imply a further reduction of the wage. The M-specialization, in this case, will not feature a growth rate higher than that in the S-specialization. Ultimately, again, this is due to the fact that an M-equilibrium does not exist.

The scope for policy intervention is very different over that range of intermediate levels of the aggregate capital stock that are large enough to make a coordinated development of the M and I industries viable, yet insufficient for any individual firm to be profitable in isolation in sector M. Over this range, the economy is in a transition between different patterns of trade specialization; a transition in which old comparative advantages are being eroded, while the new ones are only slowly emerging. In this transition, as long as the low-level equilibrium exists, market incentives are unlikely to move the economy to the high growth path associated with the superior equilibrium. This is simply because the slow growth path is locally stable.

The terms of trade affect the existence of multiple patterns of specialization, alongside the size of the capital stock and the level of skills (see the condition in (8)). To illustrate the role of the terms of trade, consider an economy specialized in labor-intensive goods and suppose that, over time, the entry of new low-cost producers in the international market tends to reduce the relative price of S goods. This has the effect of generating an M-equilibrium without, at the same time, making the economy move towards this high level equilibrium. The economy is, in a sense, losing its competitiveness in S goods, without at the same time acquiring a comparative advantage in M goods. This may describe the situation of a number of semi-industrialized "sandwich economies" facing a stiff competition from new low-wage producers of labor-intensive goods while still being unable to compete with the more efficient producers of capital-intensive goods in the advanced industrial economies.[11] The economy in transition with declining terms of trade is likely to

---

[11] If we assume that good S is a primary good, the transition can be interpreted as describing the balance of payments problems and, eventually, the beginning of industrialization in resource-abundant countries facing declining terms of trade for their primary exports.

remain largely specialized in the production of the labor-intensive S-goods.[12] This is so simply because the S-specialization is a locally stable equilibrium: no individual investor in isolation will find the investment opportunities in sector M more attractive than those existing in sector S. In this transition, this economy will suffer a slowdown of its rate of growth, as a result of the decline in the relative price of S goods. As shown by eqs (2) and (12), the profit rate in this economy is an inverse function of the relative price of M goods. Insofar as the rate of accumulation depends on profitability, the decline in the relative price of S goods will adversely affect accumulation and growth. The slowdown in the accumulation of capital will in turn prolong the transition towards the capital stock necessary to make the production of M-goods spontaneously profitable. Under this "slow-growth trap", policy intervention can make a substantial difference to the growth rate in the medium term.

From the perspective of the model with increasing returns and multiple equilibria, the very high rates of economic growth achieved by industrializing late-comers in the post-war period can be seen as the result of having success-fully 'traversed' the sequence of transitions between different patterns of specialization that were faced in the road to modern industrialization, avoiding the slow growth traps characteristic of those transitions. If our analytical framework has some validity, it is hard to see how, without the policy interventions that accelerated those transitions, a market-driven devel-opment model could have produced the extremely high growth rates charac-teristic of East Asia as well as, although growth was less fast, the rapid economic development in a few Latin American countries from 1940 to the early 1980s.[13]

Long-term effects of transitory shocks

In the neoclassical model, factor endowments, technology and terms of trade determine a unique pattern of specialization. A transitory change in the terms of trade (or in the availability of natural resources in a more general model) will have transitory consequences. That is, once the terms of trade return to

---

[12] Until, that is, it eventually reaches the high levels of the capital stock that make sector M clearly profitable from the point of view of individual investors and unless the price of S-goods falls rapidly to such an extent as to eliminate the S-equilibrium.

[13] Rodrik's (1994) argument about South Korea and Taiwan fits particularly well with our framework. According to him, the distinguishing feature of these countries growth experiences was a sharp and sustained increase in their investment rates in the early 1960s. Through an array of government interventions, by subsidizing and coordinating investment decisions, government policy was successful in reallocating resources towards modern capital-intensive industries. With increasing returns in these activities, this reallocation raised the rate of return on capital and pushed the economy into a high growth path. The relatively high level of skills of the labor force in both countries was a condition for the success of industrial policy.

their original level or the newly discovered resources are exhausted, the economy will return to the original pattern of specialization.

This is no longer true in a model with multiple locally stable equilibria. Consider, for example, an economy with two equilibria (S and M) which is specialized in sector M. A temporary shock changes the terms-of-trade in favor of sector S. The locus of capital market equilibrium shifts outwards. Suppose that the shock makes the M-equilibrium disappear. Market incentives lead the economy to specialize in sector S. When later the terms of trade return to their initial level, two equilibria will again exist. However, the economy will remain locked-in the S-equilibrium since this pattern of specialization continues to exist and is a stable equilibrium. The reader will recognize here the concerns about the 'Dutch disease' if we interpret sector S as a resource-intensive sector and sector M as a manufacturing sector.[14]

The Dutch disease is an example of a transitory real shock. Similar consequences may follow from transitory monetary shocks which, in the presence of sluggish nominal wage adjustments, lead to a temporary real overvaluation of the domestic currency. This may be caused by a tight monetary policy (as in Krugman, 1987), or a trade liberalization uncompensated by a devaluation (as in Ros and Skott, 1998). Suppose, for example, that a tight monetary policy brings about a nominal appreciation of the domestic currency which, with sluggish wage adjustments, causes a real overvaluation. The price of non-traded goods relative to tradables increases causing a reduction in the profitability of sector M relative to that of sector S, which uses the non-tradable inputs less intensively. A sufficiently large shock of this type can make the M-equilibrium temporarily disappear and push the economy towards the S equilibrium. When goods and labor market equilibrium is reestablished the economy may then remain locked-in the S-equilibrium despite the fact that factor endowments, technology and the terms of trade between S and M goods have remained unchanged throughout the process of adjustment. The same mechanisms are present in Ros and Skott (1998) (see also Frenkel and Ros, 2006) which use an open economy version of the Lewis-Rosenstein-Rodan model of Chapter 7 with sluggish nominal wage adjustments to show how depending on the degree of exchange rate overvaluation following a trade liberalization the economy can deindustrialize or continue on an industrialization path. All these contributions elaborate on the profitability channel, discussed in Chapter 11, through which the real exchange rate affects long-term growth in the presence of increasing returns to scale.

---

[14] For an analogous example with a Ricardian technology and a continuum of goods, see Krugman (1987).

4. Empirical Evidence on Trade, Trade Policies, and Growth

Recent empirical research on trade and development has focused on three different questions. The first is whether an expansion of international trade generally raises output and growth. The second is whether international trade barriers inhibit or foster economic growth. The third is whether the pattern of trade specialization affects economic growth. Harrison and Rodríguez-Clare (2010) survey of nearly 200 studies of the relationships between trade volumes, trade policies and growth conclude that most studies find a positive relationship between trade volumes and growth, i.e., they give a positive answer to the first question. The second question is clearly a different question from the first for while a reduction of trade barriers may lead to an increase in trade volumes that is not the only thing that trade policies do. They may also change the pattern of specialization in international trade which, as we have seen in this chapter and Chapter 9, can have important implications for economic development.

It is thus clear that the second and third questions are the ones with growth policy implications. This question has been investigated empirically since the 1960s by means of country studies, econometric analysis of the relationship between export expansion and economic growth and cross-country growth regressions.[15] The successive surveys on the results of this empirical research reach inconclusive verdicts. Referring to the research on growth in outward versus inward oriented development experiences, Pack concluded his review of the research of the 1970s and 1980s as follows: "to date there is no clear cut confirmation of the hypothesis that countries with external orientation benefit from greater growth in technical efficiency in the component sectors of manufacturing" (Pack, 1990, p. 38). Similarly, Bhagwati, a prominent advocate of export promotion, recognized the lack of hard evidence for some of the dynamic effects claimed for outward orientation: "Although the arguments for the success of the EP [Export Promotion] strategy based on economies of scale and X-efficiency are plausible, empirical support for them is not available. The arguments on savings and innovation provide a less than compelling case for showing that EP is necessarily better on their account than IS [Import Substitution]" (Bhagwati, 1988, pp. 39–40).

Some years later, Edwards's evaluation of the literature on the relationship between exports and growth was also inconclusive: "[M]uch of the cross-country regression-based studies have been plagued by empirical and

---

[15] See Hallaert (2006) for a comprehensive history of the empirical literature on trade and growth from the OECD (Little et al., 1970) and NBER (Krueger, 1978; Bhagwati, 1978) country case studies of the 1970s to the recent literature on the role of complementary policies in processes of trade liberalization.

conceptual shortcomings. The theoretical frameworks used have been increasingly simplistic, failing to address important questions such as the exact mechanism through which export expansion affects GDP growth, and ignoring potential determinants of growth such as educational attainment. Also, many papers have been characterized by a lack of care in dealing with issues related to endogeneity and measurement errors. All of this has resulted, in many cases, in unconvincing results whose fragility has been exposed by subsequent work" (Edwards, 1993, p. 1389).

Then in the 1990s the literature on cross country growth regressions attempted to explain differences in growth rates through a number of structural, policy and geographical indicators. While in a number of specifications of these regression equations trade policy and openness variables turned out to have a positive effect on growth (such as Dollar 1992; Sachs and Warner, 1995a; Edwards, 1998), a detailed survey and critique of this evidence suggests that these results are unconvincing (Rodriguez and Rodrik, 2001). More precisely, Rodriguez and Rodrik (2001) argue that the strong results in these studies arise from misspecification and the use as measures of openness of institutional and policy variables that have an independent and detrimental effect on growth. For example, the distortion of domestic relative to international prices used by Dollar (1992) is highly sensitive to exchange rate distortions and thus to macroeconomic misalignment while the explanatory power of the openness variable constructed by Sachs and Warner (1995a) is due to inclusion of the black market currency premium, a variable conditioned by macroeconomic policy, and state monopoly on exports, which is strongly correlated with location in Africa. More recently, Harrison and Rodriguez-Clare (2010) find that, by contrast with the studies on trade volumes and growth, those focusing on the relationship between trade policies (tariffs and indices of trade restrictions) and economic growth find weak or insignificant effects.

One natural explanation of the fragility of the empirical relationship between trade policies and growth, coming out from this chapter and Chapter 9 and the literature on trade and endogenous growth, is that the effects of greater openness to international trade on growth are contingent on the pattern of specialization. That is, ultimately the reason for the fragility of the relationship is that freer trade may contribute to growth or not depending on the structure of *static* comparative advantages that an economy has at a point in time and the dynamic potential of this structure. This is also the conclusion of several models of endogenous growth in open economies which have formalized old ideas on infant industry protection showing that whether trade promotes growth or not depends on whether the forces of comparative advantage push the economy to allocate more resources to sectors with increasing returns to scale and knowledge externalities or whether they prevent the development of such activities.[16]

This leads us directly to our third question on the effects of the pattern of specialization on economic growth.[17] The available empirical evidence on this question points in the direction of an affirmative answer. For example, Ros (2000, ch. 9) finds a positive relationship between the investment share and the rate of growth of output per worker, on one hand, and manufacturing bias in trade measured by the Chenery and Syrquin index of trade orientation, on the other. Hausmann et al. (2005) show that the level of technological sophistication of a country's exports relative to its per capita income is a good predictor of a country's subsequent growth. The evidence on the effects of natural resource abundance on the pattern of specialization and growth is also relevant to this question and shall be reviewed in the next chapter. This is why future research on trade and growth is likely to be more productive if it focuses on contingent relationships as suggested by Rodriguez and Rodrik (2001) and Helpman (2004). That is, to address questions such as: Do trade restrictions operate differently in low versus high income countries? In small versus large countries? In countries with a comparative advantage in primary products versus those with comparative advantage in manufactured goods? (Rodriguez and Rodrik, 2001, p. 317).

---

[16] See, in particular, Grossman and Helpman (1991), Matsuyama (1992), and Feenstra (1996).

[17] Another direction taken by recent research to explain why the relationship between freer trade and growth is fragile is to investigate the set of conditions under which greater openness to international trade can be successful, such as the role of barriers to entry in industries, infrastructure development, and labor market flexibility (see Harrison and Rodríguez-Clare, 2010). I will come back to this subject in Chapter 17.

15

Developmental Effects of Natural Resource Abundance

One important determinant of the pattern of specialization in international trade, besides trade and industrial policies, is the natural resource endowment. How does the natural resource endowment affect economic growth? Does the abundance of natural resources promote or hinder economic development in an *open economy*? This chapter discusses the very different views that have been advanced on this issue. This includes the view that specialization in resource intensive goods can be harmful to industrialization and growth—as argued by Graham (1923), the Prebisch-Singer thesis on the terms of trade for primary commodities and the modern literature on the "Dutch disease"—and the opposite view, present in Hla Myint's (1958) "vent for surplus" approach to trade and development and the "staples thesis" of Canadian economic historians, for which exports of resource-intensive goods can turn into an engine of growth and transformation. We analyze in this chapter the key assumptions made in each of these contrasting arguments, focusing on the role of returns to scale, international factor mobility, and the domestic linkages of resource intensive sectors.

The recent literature on the subject has taken two directions. First, some of the theoretical literature has tended to emphasize the effects of natural resource abundance on growth that operate through the emergence and functioning of institutions more or less favorable to economic development rather than focusing on the direct economic mechanisms as did the earlier literature.[1] I shall leave aside these contributions, making a reference to them

---

[1] On the subject, see Gelb (1988), Ross (1999), and Auty (2001). Lane and Tornell (1996) and Tornell and Lane (1999) present models in which a natural resource boom encourages rent-seeking behavior and generates a slowdown in economic growth. Institutional characteristics and weak domestic linkages are also the basis for the distinction between "point source" natural resources—such as oil or minerals—and plantation crops with highly detrimental developmental effects and those that are "diffuse", such as livestock or agricultural goods produced by small family farms. See on the subject Perala (2002).

in Chapter 17 on institutions, and focus on the particular economic mechanisms through which natural resource abundance and primary exports may help or hurt industrialization. A second direction is that the recent empirical literature on the subject has questioned previous empirical findings that had led to the conclusion that natural resource abundance had mostly negative effects on long-term growth. In its final section, the chapter examines the empirical evidence on the developmental effects of natural resource abundance.

1. Different Income Elasticities of Demand and the Prebisch-Singer Thesis

A first difference among tradable goods refers to their income elasticity of demand. This is the key difference between primary and manufacturing goods, albeit not the only one, emphasized by the Prebisch-Singer thesis and subsequent North-South or Center-Periphery models.[2] In what ways do the income elasticities of demand in foreign trade affect the terms of trade and the growth rates of the Center specializing in manufacturing exports and the Periphery specializing in primary goods?

The Prebisch-Singer thesis in a Center-Periphery model

Let's look into this question using a model inspired by Prebisch's argument and based on the contributions by Taylor and Dutt to the literature on North-South models (see previous footnote). The model distinguishes a North that features a Keynes-Kalecki economy with excess capacity and demand constrained output and a Lewis-type Southern economy with output determined at full capacity, limited by the capital stock, a fixed real wage, and surplus labor (or, more precisely, open unemployment). In both economies, output is produced with capital and labor in fixed coefficients.

Besides this specification of production conditions, the model is similar to the two-country model presented in Chapter 10 to discuss Thirlwall's law. The central common feature is that the North, as the foreign country in Chapter 10 model, exports a good with a relatively high income elasticity of demand (a manufacture) while the home country (the South in the present model) exports an income inelastic primary good.

The long-term dynamics of growth and the terms of trade are shown in Figure 15.1 which reproduces Figure 10.8 in Chapter 10. The horizontal line

---

[2] North-South models were originally developed by Findlay (1980, 1981), Taylor (1981, 1983), and Molana and Vines (1989). In this section, I rely on Dutt (2003).

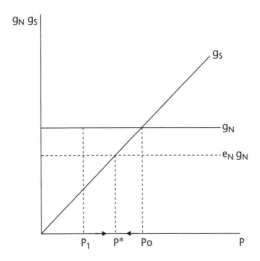

Figure 15.1 Long-run dynamics of the terms of trade and capital accumulation

g_N shows the rate of accumulation of the North as independent of the terms of trade given the assumption that the Northern good is the only one used as an investment good. The g_S line with positive and constant slope shows the rate of accumulation of the South as an increasing function of the Southern terms of trade, given the positive effect of the terms of trade on the value of Southern savings measured in terms of the capital good.

To illustrate Prebisch's argument, suppose that the South specializes in income inelastic primary goods while the North specializes in manufactures with unit income elasticity of demand. Consider an initial short-run equilibrium, with given capital stocks (K_S and K_N) and terms of trade (Po) such that the two regions grow at the same rate $g_S = g_N$. We thus have $g_S > e_N g_N$ so that P falls over time. The reason for this decline in the Southern terms of trade is that since the income elasticity of demand for the Northern good is higher than that for the Southern good, demand for the Northern good is growing faster. As the terms of trade deteriorate for the South, the South's rate of accumulation falls. This moves g_S closer to $e_N g_N$ until eventually P reaches a stationary value at P*. In this long-run equilibrium, the South will be growing at a permanently lower rate tan the North. The pattern of specialization in income inelastic primary goods condemns the South to a lower rate of growth than the North.

The model helps clarifying the assumptions necessary for the Prebisch-Singer thesis to prevail. For the terms of trade for primary goods to decline over time converging to a long-run equilibrium with unequal development, it is not enough to have an income elasticity of demand for primary goods that is less than that for manufactures. If the gap between Northern and Southern growth rates is large enough (in favor of the North), the evolution of the terms of trade will be over time favorable to the primary exporting countries of the South. To see this, consider an initial short-term equilibrium at P_1 to the left of the long-run equilibrium terms of trade (P^*), featuring a Northern growth rate well above the Southern growth rate (see Figure 15.1). The terms of trade will then move in favor of the South as the gap in growth rates more than compensates for the fact that Southern exports are less income elastic than Northern exports. In this case, the capacity for accumulation of the Periphery increases in the process of adjustment to the steady state.

Another key assumption in the Prebisch-Singer thesis (just as in Thirlwall's law as discussed in Chapter 10) is the large economy assumption. North-South models are typically two-good, two-factor and especially two-country models. In their application to particular individual countries, this is a major shortcoming as the models do not recognize that the vast majority of Southern economies (in number at least) are rather small open economies whose growth does not affect by and large the terms of trade they face in international markets.

2. The Dutch Disease and the Deindustrialization Effects of Resource Abundance

A second difference between resource intensive commodities and manufacturing goods refers to production conditions. It is worth introducing the subject with a quote from a celebrated and controversial article by Graham (1923). In this article, which is best known for having argued that increasing returns to scale could justify protection, Graham noted that:

> The principle just laid down may go far to explain why regions of slender natural resources devoted to manufactures often surpass in prosperity regions of much greater natural resources where extractive industry prevails, tho no great difference exists in native ability of their respective populations. (Graham, 1923, p. 215)

Graham illustrated his argument with a reference to the prosperous manufacturing East versus the West of the United States at the time when the latter was "almost solely devoted to extractive industry". The key assumptions behind the principle to which Graham refers are the presence of increasing returns to scale in manufacturing and the role of profits as the major source of capital accumulation, both of which are explicitly stated in his 1923 article. The mechanism involved is that, in a long-run equilibrium, a land-rich economy will have a larger natural resource-intensive sector and a smaller increasing returns industry. The negative effect on productivity of its smaller manufacturing sector can then result in lower living standards.

Graham's insight has a close affinity to Dutch disease models. Concern with the Dutch disease arises primarily from the real exchange rate effects of a natural resource boom (or of a surge in capital inflows) and the negative implications for long-term growth of the resulting contraction of industrial output, investment, and employment. These implications are negative to the extent that economic development is associated with the growth of modern tradable goods sectors operating under increasing returns to scale. The expansion of these activities generates endogenous productivity growth, within these sectors and elsewhere in the economy, due to the presence of internal economies of scale as well as positive external effects such as learning by doing externalities. In what follows I discuss the mechanisms through which a natural resource boom can lead to deindustrialization.

Real appreciation and indirect deindustrialization

Consider a small open economy with two tradable good sectors, agriculture (A) and manufacturing (M). Both sectors use labor (L) and there are two specific factors: land (T) in sector A and capital (K) in sector M. Agriculture operates under constant returns to scale and there are increasing returns to scale in manufacturing. The production functions are:

$$A = BT^b L_A^{1-b} \qquad M = (\tilde{K})\mu \ K^a L_M^{1-a}$$

where $(\tilde{K})\mu$ is the external effect of the average capital stock. Both goods are consumed and, in addition, good M can be invested. Labor is intersectorally mobile.

Along with sectors A and M, a sector S produces non-tradable consumer services by means of labor under constant returns:

$$S = L_S \tag{1}$$

A fraction (q) of the rents (R) generated in sector A is spent on non-tradables (we ignore, for simplicity, consumption of services by sector M):

$$p_s S = q \, R = q \, R(w, T, p_A) \qquad R_1 < 0, R_2, R_3 > 0 \tag{2}$$

where p_S is the price of non-tradables in terms of good M. With a uniform wage rate, and given production conditions in sector S, this price is the same as the manufacturing product wage (w). Substituting from (1) into (2) and solving for L_S:

$$L_S = (q/w) \, R(w, T, p_A) \tag{3}$$

which shows the level of employment in the non-tradable goods sector as an inverse function of the wage, and an increasing function of the land endowment and the relative price of agricultural goods. Using (3) and the full employment condition ($L = L_A + L_M + L_S$), the schedule of short-run equilibria is given by:

$$L = L_A(w, p_A, T) + L_M(w, K) + (q/w)R(w, T, p_A) \qquad (4)$$

As usual, the w curve is upward sloping in (ln w, ln K) space. A larger capital stock generates in equilibrium higher real wages through its effect on the demand for labor in manufacturing. The position of the curve depends on the natural resource endowment and relative prices. An increase in the relative price of agricultural goods or an increase in the supply of land, both shift the w curve upwards: given K, both of these factors increase the demand for labor in agriculture and services. Labor market equilibrium requires a reallocation of labor away from manufacturing and the wage in manufacturing must rise in order to make this possible. The result is as expected: a greater abundance of natural resources, *given* other factor endowments, makes the country more prosperous, if we take the real wage, as we shall in what follows, as a general indicator of living standards.

However, other factor endowments will not remain constant, at least not the capital endowment which changes over time and in the long-run equilibrium will be determined endogenously at the intersection of the w and w* schedules. Assuming a stationary labor force and no exogenous technical progress, the steady state condition simplifies to the equality between the rate of capital accumulation (I/K) and the depreciation rate of the capital stock (δ): $I/K = \delta$. Assume the rate of capital accumulation to be an increasing function of the profit rate in manufacturing. Since, given the wage, the profit rate is an increasing function of the capital stock in the presence of increasing returns to scale, the w* schedule is upward sloping as depicted in Figure 15.2.[3]

Consider now the effects of a more abundant supply of land. This, as we have seen, shifts the w curve upwards due to a higher demand for labor in sector A and a higher demand for non-tradables which results from the spending of land rents. This second effect is the *spending effect* in Corden (1984). This is a novel aspect brought in by the presence of non-tradable goods which implies that the w curve would shift upwards even if the resource-intensive sector did not use labor directly. The spending out of higher rents leads to a higher relative price of non-tradables and, thus, to a real exchange rate appreciation.[4] At the initial level of the capital stock in manufacturing, labor market equilibrium requires a reallocation of labor away from manufacturing and into services. If, in addition to being demanded by sector A, non-tradables were used as inputs into manufacturing with a

---

[3] I am assuming away, for simplicity, the possible influence of the propensity to save out of rents on the rate of accumulation. For the more general case, see Ros (2000, ch. 8).

[4] The real exchange rate is defined as the price ratio between tradable and non-tradable goods.

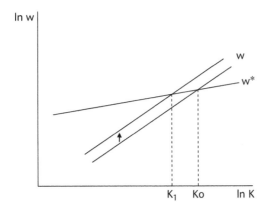

Figure 15.2 Deindustrialization effects of greater abundance of natural resources

relatively inelastic demand, the adverse effects on manufacturing output and employment would, of course, be stronger. The profitability squeeze in manufacturing slows down capital accumulation and leads to a long-run equilibrium with a smaller manufacturing sector and larger natural resource and service sectors. As a result of the adverse effects of deindustrialization on productivity, the real wage in the new long-run equilibrium is lower than initially (see Figure 15.2).

It is important to point out that the natural resource boom need not be permanent in order to cause adverse developmental effects. In the presence of multiple equilibria, as we have seen in Chapter 14, a transitory real exchange rate appreciation resulting from a temporary resource boom can shift the pattern of specialization of an economy in an irreversible way and lock in the economy permanently as an exporter of primary goods.

Intersectoral capital mobility and direct deindustrialization

Consider now the effects of a natural resource boom in the presence of intersectoral capital mobility. We leave aside non-tradables and modify the production side of the model to allow for the use of capital in the resource-intensive sector (and neglect, for simplicity, labor input in this sector). This sector is thus an extractive industry (E) using capital and land (mineral land, specific to this sector) with a Cobb-Douglas technology: $E = K_E^b T^{1-b}$. Manufacturing is identical to the earlier definition, except for the assumption that it operates under constant returns to scale. This assumption will highlight that the mechanisms involved in the contraction of manufacturing and the reduction of real wages are, in this case, independent of the presence of increasing returns. Technology in sector M is thus described by: $M = K_M^a L^{1-a}$

There are thus two specific factors: land in sector E and labor in sector M, with both sectors now using capital. With no intersectoral capital mobility, profit rates in these two sectors would generally be different since they include quasi-rents associated with the given capital stocks. Given the production functions in the two sectors, the short-run profit rates would be such that:

$$r_E K_E = [b/(1-b)] \, \theta \, T \tag{5}$$

$$r_M K_M = [a/(1-a)] w \, L \tag{6}$$

The wage rate (w) and rent per unit of land (θ) are determined by equilibrium in the labor and land markets. Hence, we have:

$$T = T^d = K_E[(1-b)p_E/\theta]^{1/b} \tag{7}$$

$$L = L^d = K_M[(1-a)/w]^{1/a} \tag{8}$$

With capital mobility, quasi-rents will tend to disappear and profit rates become equalized. In equilibrium, the amount of capital invested in sector E must yield a profit rate equal to that obtained in sector M. The common profit rate (r), and the associated composition of the capital stock, must then satisfy:

$$K = K_E + K_M \tag{9}$$

$$K_E = (b \, p_E/r)^{1-b} \, T \tag{10}$$

$$r = r_M(w) \qquad r'_M < 0 \tag{11}$$

where (10), obtained by eliminating θ from (5) and (7), expresses the relationship between capital and profit rate in sector E, and (11) shows the profit rate in manufacturing as an inverse function of the product wage.

Substituting (11) into (10) and using (9) yields the equation of a schedule of capital market equilibrium in (w, K_M) space:

$$K_M = K - [b \, p_E/r_M(w)]^{1-b} \, T \tag{12}$$

The wage rate and the capital stock invested in manufacturing are inversely related along this schedule (see Figure 15.3). A higher wage rate implies a lower profit rate in manufacturing (the labor-using sector). Restoring the equality between the two profit rates requires a reallocation of capital towards the resource-intensive sector (which reduces the profit rate there). To determine the wage rate and K_M simultaneously, we need to bring in the locus of labor market equilibrium. This is given by eq. (8), showing the usual positive relationship between the wage and the capital stock.

Consider the effects of a resource boom starting from an initial equilibrium at point A in Figure 15.3. The resource boom is caused by an increase in T or in p_E. In either of these cases, profitability in sector E rises at the initial level of

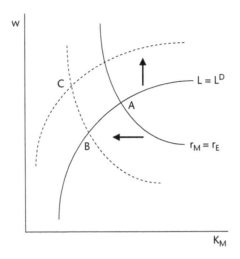

Figure 15.3 The Dutch disease with intersectoral capital mobility

the capital stock (K_E). In terms of Figure 15.3, the result is a downward shift in the capital market equilibrium locus: for each level of the wage, capital moves from the M to the E sector. The new equilibrium at B thus features a smaller capital stock in manufacturing and a lower wage. Corden (1984) labels this resource movement *direct de-industrialization*, because it is independent of the real exchange rate appreciation. Indeed, without non-tradable goods, there is no spending effect and no change in the price of tradable relative to non-tradable goods.

The reduction in real wages from A to B is not the result of a fall in manufacturing productivity under increasing returns to scale. The contraction is due to the fact that the higher profitability of sector E causes labor demand to fall following the reallocation of capital away from the labor-intensive sector. With the given labor supply, the equilibrium wage falls in order to clear the labor market.

It is easy to see that, in the presence of non-tradable goods, a second resource movement will take place that counteracts the fall in labor demand but exacerbates the contraction of manufacturing. The spending effect will increase the relative price of non-tradables and wages, causing profitability to fall in manufacturing. Capital then moves from manufacturing to the resource-intensive sector. This is *indirect de-industrialization* (see Corden and Neary, 1982; Corden, 1984). Unlike direct de-industrialization, it results from the real appreciation of the exchange rate caused by the spending effect and depends on its strength. In terms of Figure 15.3, it arises from the upward shift in the schedule of labor market equilibrium that leads to a new equilibrium at C which features a higher real wage but a capital stock in manufacturing that is even lower than at point B.

Latin America's early Import Substitution Industrialization

An interesting implication of these models is that a fall in exports of primary products may accelerate industrialization. The fall in the profitability of the primary export sector and the resulting contraction in the demand for non-tradables will cause resource movements and a real depreciation that can stimulate capital accumulation in manufacturing. Since, in the model, manu-facturing is the importables sector, its expansion will appear as a spontaneous process of import substitution. Economists and historians in Latin America have noted these mechanisms in operation during the 1930s. Then, the collapse of primary product export prices and volumes led to sharp real depreciations which, often coupled with protective tariffs, triggered the begin-ning of the so-called early phase of import substitution in light manufacturing in a number of Latin American countries.

It was this process of spontaneous import substitution that Prebisch observed in the 1930s and recommended to accelerate, through protectionist measures, in the post-war period. Paradoxically, at first sight, Prebisch should have welcomed the lower terms of trade for primary commodities, as this trend was beneficial rather than harmful to industrialization in the periphery. Upon reflection, Prebisch is quite consistent: he saw as harmful the fall in the terms of trade that was *caused* by the expansion of the supply of primary products (as noted by Bhagwati, 1985). In the face of inelastic demands for primary goods, this expansion led to a skewed distribution of the gains from trade that favored the industrial centers of the world economy (see section 1 in this chapter). This conclusion is quite consistent with the view that a reduc-tion in world demand for primary products could and would change the pattern of specialization of the periphery in favor of manufacturing activities. This is what, in a less traumatic way, a protective tariff on manufactures can achieve: by changing the (domestic) terms of trade against the resource-intensive sector, it induces an expansion of the manufacturing sector.

The raw materials export boom of the past decade in South America

The years 2000s, especially after 2003 and before the "Great Recession" of 2009, witnessed a resumption of growth in the large or medium size econ-omies of South America, led by a process of rapidly expanding exports and a medium-term improvement in the terms of trade of primary goods. Peru, a mineral exporter, led the growth table with an astonishing 20 percent annual growth in export value and a GDP growth rate of nearly 6 percent from 2000 to 2008 while other South American economies show also high export growth, respectable GDP growth rates and a favorable evolution of the terms of trade, especially in the case of Chile which recorded a sharp terms of trade improvement (see Ros, 2012). These processes are part of an acceleration of growth in the periphery of the world economy specializing in the production and export of primary goods that is closely associated to the emergence of China, a gigantic and extremely dynamic economy, as a new industrial center and formidable purchaser of agricultural products, minerals, copper, and other raw materials in the world economy. China's share in the total exports of the main South American exporters of primary goods has been rising sharply since 2000 suggesting an important role for China's growth in the expansion of South America's exports.[5]

While the dynamism of the Chinese economy and of the world demand for raw materials have had so far favorable short-term effects on the economic growth of South American countries, the medium and longer term developmental consequences of the raw materials export boom depend on its effects on real exchange rates and the profitability of the non resource intensive tradable goods sectors, that is on whether a Dutch disease is developing in the region. So far, the raw materials export boom has been accompanied by a substantial appreciation of real exchange rates in Latin America sometime after the beginning of the past decade, only briefly interrupted by the temporary depreciations that took place in 2008 an early 2009 as a consequence of the international financial crisis, the "flight to quality", and the increase in risk spreads in emerging markets. In a group of six South American primary exporters (Argentina, Brazil, Chile, Colombia, Peru, and Uruguay), real exchange rates in 2010 were, with the exception of Argentina, similar or lower than the minimum levels of the 1990s and well below (including Argentina) the average levels of 2002–8 (see Frenkel and Rapetti, 2012). This is why the primary exports boom has led to a decline in the profitability of the industrial sector: in the great majority of the six South American countries, unit labor costs in dollars tended to increase after 2002–3 in a substantial and sustained way suggesting that, at least for the labor intensive tradable goods sectors, there is an important problem of competitiveness and profitability. The result has been a generalized process of deindustrialization as the expansion of the natural resource intensive sectors appears to have had a Dutch disease effect. As shown in Table 15.1, the only countries that have not suffered from a sharp fall in the share of manufacturing in GDP are mostly those in Northern Latin America that are exporters of manufactures with the United States market as the main destination.

---

[5] China overtook the United States as Brazil's major trading partner in 2009, it is the second largest trading partner of Argentina, Colombia, and Peru, Chile's major trading partner in Asia, and the largest purchaser of Argentina's agricultural products. See Ros (2012).

Table 15.1 Latin American countries: Share of manufacturing in GDP (%), 1990–2010[a]

Country	1990	2010 [b]	Change
Uruguay	28	15	−13
Brazil	27.4[c]	15.8	−11.6
Chile	19.6	11.5	−8.1
Argentina	26.8	20.5	−6.3
Colombia	20.6	15.1	−5.5
Costa Rica	22.6	17.4	−5.2
Bolivia	18.5	13.9	−4.6
Paraguay	16.8	12.2	−4.6
Panama	9.7	6.1	−3.6
Mexico	20.8	18.1	−2.7
El Salvador	22.1	20.6	−1.5
Peru	17.8	16.6	−1.2
Venezuela	14.9	14.7	−0.2
Cuba	7.7	9.6	1.9
Honduras	16.3	18.4	2.1
Dominican Republic	18	24.1	6.1

[a] Manufacturing value added as percentage of gross value added at factor cost.
[b] 2010 or last available year.
[c] Average of 1989 and 1991.
Source: World Development Indicators.

3. The Staples Thesis, Factor Mobility, and the Positive Pecuniary Externalities of Natural Resources

The models discussed so far do not fit well with the experience of a number of resource rich countries that have achieved high levels of industrialization. The staples thesis, originally developed by Canadian economic historians, is often cited to make the point that abundance of natural resources and fast primary exports growth need not hinder industrial expansion.[6] A complementary observation is that a severe lack of natural resources may have stunted industrial development in a number of resource-poor countries.

Labor mobility and the "regions of recent settlement"

What difference does it make to the results of previous models in this chapter if we allow for the possibility of importing scarce factors? Consider a small open economy with two tradable good sectors: agriculture, using land (T) and labor under constant returns to scale, and manufacturing, using capital (K)

---

[6] On the staples thesis, see Innis (1930, 1940) and Watkins (1963) on Canada's economic development. The approach was later applied to other "regions of recent settlement", including the United States (North, 1966), Australia (McLean, 1989), and Argentina in the pre-1929 period (Diaz Alejandro, 1984; Cortés Conde, 1985). See Findlay and Lundahl (1994) for a survey of these contributions.

and labor under increasing returns to scale (associated to technological externalities). The equations for the w and w* lines are given by:

$$w = w(K, T, p_A, L) \qquad w_1, w_2, w_3 > 0, w_4 < 0$$

$$w^* = w^*(K, s_M/\delta) \qquad w^*_1, w^*_2 > 0$$

where s_M is the propensity to save out of profits and the propensity to save out of rents is set, for simplicity, equal to zero.

Suppose the rate of migration ($\hat{L}$), the only source of labor force growth, is an increasing function of the ratio between the domestic market wage (w) and the wage abroad adjusted for costs of migration (w^s):

$$\hat{L} = f(w/w^s) \qquad f' > 0 \qquad f(1) = 0$$

We also assume that foreign wages, and/or migration costs, tend to increase as the number of migrants raises the size of the labor force (L). This makes the supply price of labor (w^s) an increasing function of L:

$$w^s = w^s(L) \qquad w^{s'} \geq 0 \qquad (13)$$

with $w^{s'} = 0$ as the special case in which, with constant foreign wages and migration costs, the country faces a perfectly elastic labor supply from abroad.

Consider the solution to the model in (L, K) space. The schedule of stationary capital stocks ($\hat{K} = 0$) shows the (L, K) combinations for which the market wage is equal to the required wage. Setting w = w*, we have:

$$w(K, T, p_A, L) = w^*(K, s_M/\delta) \qquad (14)$$

The slope of this schedule is positive, if there are diminishing returns to capital. Indeed, in (w, K) space, a larger labor force shifts the w curve downwards, as the market wage falls for each given level of the capital stock. The new intersection with the w* curve will feature a higher capital stock if the w* line is flatter than the w curve. This will be the case unless technological externalities were to generate increasing returns to capital. Along the schedule, the wage increases with K since w* is a positive function of the capital stock, given the presence of increasing returns (which accounts for the positive effect of K on w*).[7] Above the locus, with a relatively high labor-capital ratio, the market wage is below the required wage and the capital stock is growing. The opposite happens below the locus.

The schedule of stationary labor force ($\hat{L} = 0$) shows the (L, K) combinations for which the market wage is equal to the supply price of labor. Setting w^s in (13) equal to w, and thus $\hat{L} = 0$, we have:

---

[7] Under constant returns, the slope of the w = w* locus is positive, but the wage does not increase with the capital stock along the locus, since w* is independent of the capital stock. In this case w* is only a function of s_M and δ.

$$w(K, T, p_A, L) = w^s(L) \tag{15}$$

The slope of this schedule is clearly positive: a higher capital stock increases the market wage (at each level of the labor force) and this requires an increase in the labor force, through migration, to bring w and ws back into equality. The smaller the labor supply response (determined by (13)), the flatter is the locus.[8] Above the locus with a relatively high labor-capital ratio, the market wage is below the supply price of labor and the labor force is falling. The opposite happens below the locus.

The two schedules divide the (L, K) space into 4 regions. At the intersection of the two schedules, the economy is in long-run equilibrium without either migration or capital accumulation taking place. Off this steady state, dynamic adjustments take place in the capital stock and the labor force. These adjustments, as indicated in Figure 15.4, are determined by the region in which the economy finds itself.

We focus, first, on the stable case in which, due to moderate labor supply elasticity, the $\hat{K} = 0$ schedule is steeper than the $\hat{L} = 0$ schedule. To illustrate the dynamic adjustment to the steady state, consider an economy at point A with an initially low capital stock and no migration taking place. The economy is thus in the high growth region (since real wages and the capital stock are below their steady state values). The capital stock expands over time. In the absence of international labor mobility and therefore of migration, the adjustment path would be along the horizontal line through A, until the economy reaches point B on the w = w* schedule. With labor mobility, adjustment will be along a path with an increasing labor force, until point C is reached. At C, the capital stock and real wages are both higher than at B (since the w* = w schedule has a positive slope and w* increases along this locus). International labor mobility thus allows the economy to reach a steady state with a larger manufacturing sector and higher real wages.

What are the effects of a greater abundance of natural resources? Comparing two economies identical in other respects, the $\hat{K} = 0$ schedule of the land-rich economy will be to the left of that of the resource-poor country (see Figure 15.5): at each level of the labor force the abundance of land reduces the steady state value of the capital stock. With labor mobility, the greater abundance of land also shifts the $\hat{L} = 0$ schedule upwards: at each level of the capital stock, it raises the market wage and, with migration, it also increases the size of the labor force. Clearly, the labor supply response is a key determinant of the shift in the $\hat{L} = 0$ schedule. With a sufficiently high labor mobility, and a correspondingly high labor supply elasticity, it is now quite possible that

---

[8] With no labor mobility and an inelastic labor supply function, the locus becomes a horizontal line in (L, K) space at the exogenously given value of the labor force.

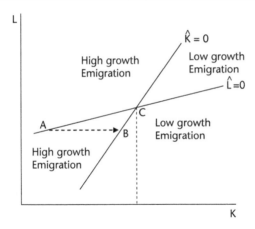

Figure 15.4 The dynamics of capital accumulation and migration under international labor mobility

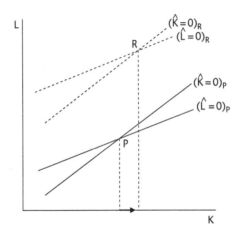

Figure 15.5 The effects of natural resources with international labor mobility

the abundance of land raises the steady state value of the capital stock and thus of real wages.

This outcome depends on the virtuous interplay between migration and increasing returns in manufacturing. Labor mobility is essential, since otherwise the new long-run equilibrium cannot feature a larger labor force, and the economy would remain stuck in a steady state with a small capital stock and relatively low real wages.[9] The presence of increasing returns is crucial, since under constant returns w* (and thus the steady state value of the wage) is independent of the capital stock.

---

[9] With no labor mobility (and a horizontal $\hat{L} = 0$ schedule), the resource abundant country would have a lower capital stock and real wage than the resource-poor country.

International capital mobility also makes a difference. Findlay and Lundahl (1994) present a Ricardo-Viner model in which capital is required to advance the land frontier. There, the condition that the rate of return on capital required to expand the arable land area is equal to the profit rate in manufacturing determines endogenously the margin of cultivation. This model presents the interesting possibility that a fall in the international interest rate or an increase in capital mobility (provided that the domestic profit rate is initially higher than abroad) will simultaneously expand the land frontier, increase manufacturing output, and raise the capital intensity of manufacturing. Although the story is not about the effects of a resource boom, it shows the possibility that a general economic expansion with rising real wages and capital deepening in the industrial sector can take place even without labor migration.

The development experience of Canada and Australia and Argentina's industrialization before 1930 can be cited as examples of how the abundance of natural resources favored the achievement of a large manufacturing sector with high real wages. The expansion of world demand for primary products and improvements in the terms of trade in the pre-1929 period, helped economic growth by attracting large inflows of immigrants and capital and "stirring up dormant resources" drawing them into economic activity for export production (see Myint, 1958; Nurkse, 1961). It is interesting that in historians' accounts of these experiences, the elasticity of factor supplies, given by the importation of scarce factors, was seen as essential to the development process (see Watkins, 1963).

Development traps in resource-scarce countries

The combination of labor mobility and increasing returns yields other interesting possibilities. As already noted, a higher labor supply elasticity makes the $\hat{L} = 0$ schedule steeper. The more returns to scale increase, the flatter is the $\hat{K} = 0$ schedule. Figure 15.6 (a) illustrates a combination of labor supply elasticity and returns to scale such that the $\hat{L} = 0$ schedule is steeper than the $\hat{K} = 0$ schedule. The intersection of the two schedules now yields a saddle-point equilibrium, as indicated by the dynamic adjustments of K and L. A developing economy with initially a small capital stock and no migration will be in a region of low growth. As the capital stock now contracts and the real wage falls, emigration will take place in the presence of a high labor supply elasticity. The reduction of the labor force prevents the restoration of profitability that would otherwise have occurred as a result of falling real wages. As in Myrdal (1957), the process is cumulative, since the capital stock continues to contract in the face of a low profit rate. The reader will recognize the situation as one in which the combination of a high labor supply elasticity

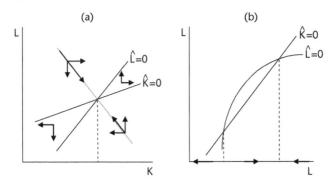

Figure 15.6 Development traps in resource-scarce economies

and increasing returns generates a profitability trap and a big push problem. The downward sloping saddle path is the locus of (L, K) combinations that need to be achieved for a process of endogenous growth to take off.

The case in Figure 15.6 (a) has the implication that an economy to the right of the saddle path will keep on growing until, presumably, it has absorbed the whole of the world's labor force. Suppose, instead, that well before this takes place, the elasticity of the labor supply falls as the size of the labor force increases. As shown in Figure 15.6 (b), the $\hat{L} = 0$ schedule then becomes increasingly flatter at high levels of L. This shape yields the possibility of multiple equilibria. The low K equilibrium is a saddle point, as in Figure 15.6 (a), while the high K intersection is a stable equilibrium, as in Figure 15.5.[10]

Consider now the effects of a greater availability of natural resources. As before, the larger land supply shifts both schedules upwards. Given that the elasticity of the labor supply falls with the size of the labor force, the shift in the $\hat{L} = 0$ schedule is larger at low levels of L. It is then possible that in the high K equilibrium, a relatively large shift of the $\hat{K} = 0$ locus at high levels of K implies that the resource-poor economy has a higher real wage and capital stock in the stable steady state. At the same time, the abundance of natural resources tends to reduce the hold of the development trap by shifting the position of the saddle path downwards. The large shift of the $\hat{L} = 0$ schedule, at low levels of L, tends to reduce the size of the capital investments and the labor force needed for industrialization to take off. As the reader can verify, similar results apply in the case of a demand expansion for primary products that increases the relative price (p_A) of the resource-intensive good in international markets. This example illustrates how the opening or expansion of trade,

---

[10] The Kuznets-Myrdal model of Chapter 7 (section 4) presents an explicit analysis of this case in the context of a two-sector open economy model with rural-urban migration.

whereby previously idle natural resources find productive employment, may be a precondition for industrialization to proceed at a rapid pace.

Linkage effects and pecuniary externalities

The staples thesis, as well as the literature on the "primary export phase" of Latin America's economic development, emphasizes also the role of linkages generated by different primary export activities. What happens when the non tradable goods sectors that benefit from the increase in the natural resource rents and its spending operate under increasing returns to scale—transport infrastructure, for example, stimulated by the expansion of the agricultural frontier—and, at the same time, the labor supply is elastic due to the presence of surplus labor in the economy or to workers migration, so that the spending effects of the natural resource boom have little effects on wages? Under these conditions, as we shall now see, the relative price of non-tradable inputs (transport costs in the example mentioned) used by manufacturing will tend to fall, rather than increase, with the expansion of the primary export sector. The development effects of natural resource abundance can then be very different from those emphasized by the Dutch disease literature.

Consider an open economy version of the Rodan-Hirschman model of Chapter 8 to make the basic point. In that model, two sectors (S and M) produce a single final good with different technologies. Alongside, a sector I, operating under increasing returns and imperfect competition, produces intermediate inputs used in the production of the capital intensive good (M). Suppose now that the capital-intensive M good and the labor-intensive S good are both traded, while the intermediate inputs, used by sector M and produced under increasing returns, are non-tradable. This time, we do not assume that the S and M sectors produce the same good. Nevertheless, the terms of trade between these two goods are determined in the international markets and are thus independent of domestic demand conditions. In addition, there is a resource-intensive sector, producing traded goods, with the same technology as sector A in section 1. A fraction (q) of the rents generated in this sector is spent on I goods. Demand for I goods thus has two components: I_M, the demand from sector M that depends, as before, on the capital stock, and I_A, the demand from sector A, that depends on agricultural rents and therefore on land endowment:

$$I = I_M + I_A = (1 - a)^{1/a}(p_I/p_M)^{-1/a} K + qR/p_I \qquad (16)$$

where: $\qquad R = R\,(w,\,T,\,p_A) \qquad R_1 < 0, \qquad R_2,\,R_3 > 0$

The price of I goods increases with the wage rate and is a decreasing function of the scale of the I sector (see eq. 12 in Chapter 8):

$$\text{pi} = (1+z)\omega \qquad (1+z)\,\phi/(\phi-1) \qquad \omega = w/(1+\mu)I_i^{\mu/(1+\mu)} \qquad (17)$$

where ϕ is the price elasticity of demand facing individual producers and μ is the increasing returns parameter in the production of I goods. The price-wage ratio is a decreasing function of the scale of the I-sector (eq. 17) and the demand for I goods increases with the capital stock and rents (eq. 16). Consequently, given the wage and the price of M goods, as determined in international markets, the relative price of I goods (p_I/p_M) is a decreasing function of K and R:

$$p_I/p_M = p_I(K, R, w/p_M) \qquad p_{I1}, p_{I2} < 0; \qquad p_{I3} > 0 \qquad (18)$$

Given the production conditions assumed in sector M (a Cobb-Douglas technology with two factors, I and K), the rate of profit can be expressed as a function of only p_I/p_M and the parameters of the production function. Since the profit rate is a decreasing function of the relative price p_I/p_M, we can express it, using (18), as:

$$r = r(K, R, w/p_M) \qquad r_1, r_2 > 0 \qquad r_3 < 0$$

As long as it exists, the labor-intensive S sector provides a perfectly elastic supply of labor at a wage (in terms of M goods) equal to the price of the S good ($w = p_S$). This flat segment of the w curve, it may be worth recalling, is not due to the assumption that the M and S sectors produce perfect substitutes (as in the closed economy model of Chapter 8). Rather, it is the consequence of the fact that both goods are traded at given international prices and that constant returns to labor prevail in sector S. The w curve of the model is thus a horizontal line for $L_S > 0$. When $L_S = 0$, the labor supply is no longer perfectly elastic and the w curve slopes upwards. Unlike what happens in the original model, the labor supply is not fully inelastic, given the presence of the A sector. Using the labor demand function in sector A, the elasticity of the labor supply to sector I can be shown to depend on the composition of the labor force and technology in sector A: $d \ln L_I/d \ln w = L_A/b\,L_I$, where w is the wage in terms of good M, the numeraire, and not the product wage in sector I. Since as K increases, L_A/L_I falls, the elasticity of labor supply falls and the w curve becomes steeper. (For simplicity, we draw in Figure 15.7 the upward sloping segment of the w curve with a constant slope).

Consider now the w* schedule. The profit rate in sector M is an inverse function of the wage (w/p_M) and increases with the capital stock. Indeed, as in the model of Chapter 8, an increase in K raises the demand for I goods and reduces marginal costs in the I-sector. The fall in the relative price (p_I/p_M) (for a given value of w/p_M) raises profits in the M sector. Thus, the required wage that is consistent with the steady state rate of capital accumulation is an increasing function of the capital stock. The new feature now is that the profit

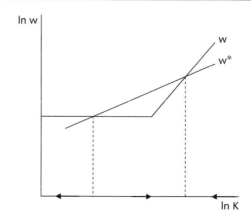

Figure 15.7 A "linkage effects" model in an open economy

rate in sector M also increases with a higher demand for I goods coming from a higher spending out of agricultural rents. The profit rate (and thus the required wage) being an increasing function of rents, the position of the w* curve depends on the abundance of land (and on the fraction of rents, q, spent on I goods).[11]

Multiple equilibria remain a possibility (as shown in the Appendix). Figure 15.7, which is identical to that of the Rodan-Hirschman and the Lewis-Rosenstein-Rodan closed economy models of Chapters 7 and 8, illustrates this case.[12] The low level stable equilibrium does not have an M sector. A small I-sector coexists with sectors A and S, but produces at such high costs that it is unprofitable to invest in sector M. In the high level stable equilibrium, there is no S sector: its labor force has been absorbed by a large sector of intermediate inputs producing at low costs for both the M and A sectors. The low K intersection shows, as usual, the size of the investments required to make the M sector viable.

Consider now the effects of a greater abundance of natural resources. The w* curve shifts upwards. This has a number of effects. First, the greater abundance of land lowers the threshold value of the capital stock required to overcome a development trap, as the resulting expansion of the I sector reduces production costs in the M sector. Second, for an economy with a capital stock larger than the threshold value but in the horizontal segment of the w curve, the induced reduction in the price of I goods increases the rates of profit and accumulation in sector M. The spending of agricultural rents has now an effect

---

[11] The presence of a resource intensive sector affects not only the position, but also the slope of the w* curve. The derivation of this slope is shown in the Appendix.

[12] If the w and w* curves do not intersect, there is a unique equilibrium without an M sector i.e., industrialization is not viable due to the small size of the labor force.

exactly opposite to a Dutch disease! This is so because the spending effect in this case is equivalent to a real depreciation since it leads to a reduction in the relative price of non-tradable I goods (and thus to an increase in the relative price of tradable goods, in particular in the relative price p_M/p_I). Third, the real wage in the high level equilibrium tends to increase even though this may be partly or completely offset by the upward shift of the w curve in the segment in which it has a positive slope. This upward shift reflects the more traditional Dutch disease effect. Note that this upward shift of the w curve does not take place at low levels of the capital stock since, for these values, the labor supply is perfectly elastic.

In sum, in the presence of linkages with an infrastructure sector subject to increasing returns to scale, the expansion of a natural resource intensive sector generates pecuniary externalities to the manufacturing industry and can thus promote industrialization. Note that the generation of these pecuniary externalities requires an elastic labor supply. In the model presented, this elastic labor supply arises from the presence of sector S. In other versions of the staple thesis, immigration of workers can play a more important role in generating the elastic labor supply.

4. Empirical Evidence on the Developmental Effects of Natural Resources

What does the empirical evidence say about these different views of the role of natural resources in development? A first observation is that natural resource abundance in the right amount and at the right time can turn an underdeveloped economy into a high income one in a short span of time. A number of countries with the highest incomes in the world owe their condition to being oil rich. This is the case of 5 countries out of the 35 countries with the highest GDP per capita in the Penn World Table (Qatar, Kuwait, Brunei, United Arab Emirates, and Trinidad and Tobago). Equatorial Guinea, thanks to oil discoveries, and Botswana, rich in diamond mines, turn out to be two of the fastest growing economies in the period 1970–2008.

A second observation is that a hundred or more years ago the abundance of natural resources clearly seemed to be a positive factor in explaining international differences in incomes per capita and even, although to a lesser extent, differences in growth rates. Resource-rich countries (such Australia, Canada, United States, and Argentina) not only had higher incomes, they were also growing faster than most resource-scarce countries, which were not growing at all at the time. According to Maddison (1982), those four countries were among the twelve countries with highest per capita incomes in 1870, with Australia far at the top of the list (with an income nearly 60 percent higher than the United Kingdom, the second country on the list). These countries were growing at relatively high rates, with the exception of Australia which, as Carlos Diaz-Alejandro (1985) once observed, "was born rich".

A third observation is that, as we move closer to today's world, increasingly intensive in capital and technology, natural resources have not only ceased to play a significant positive role, but some analysts have argued that their relationship to differences in incomes and growth is being progressively reversed. Empirical evidence and case studies lending support to an inverse relationship between natural resource abundance and growth can be found, among others, in Gelb (1988), Auty (1990, 2001), and Tornell and Lane (1999). Auty (2001) observes, for example, that, among developing countries, the median income of resource-rich countries was, in 1960, 50 percent greater than the median income of resource-poor countries. A generation later, the median income of resource-poor countries was greater than that of resource-rich countries, some of which suffered during the period veritable growth collapses. The influential papers by Sachs and Warner (1995, 2001) investigate in a cross section of countries for the period 1970–90 economic and non-economic mechanisms through which natural resource abundance affects growth, confirming a negative relationship between growth and the ratio of primary exports to GDP but finding weak evidence of links between natural resource abundance and growth operating through bureaucratic inefficiency and corruption.[13] In particular, Sachs and Warner (2001) show that natural resource intensive economies tend to have higher price levels (controlling for the relative level of income) and that this relative overvaluation of their currencies (or higher relative prices of non-tradables) had a negative effect on the contribution of manufacturing export growth to GDP growth (either because of a small share of manufacturing exports or because of slow growth of exports of manufactures). In other words, the mechanism identified by Sachs and Warner is what in the Dutch disease literature is referred to as "indirect deindustrialization" generated by natural resource abundance.

In important and influential contributions, Lederman y Maloney (see, in particular, 2007 and 2008) have carefully reviewed and criticized the previous literature. In particular, Lederman and Maloney make several criticisms of the Sachs and Warner findings. First, they argue that the negative effect of natural resource exports on growth holds only for periods containing the years between 1950 and 1989, and that this variable has a positive effect on growth (although not statistically significant) during 1820–70 and 1913–50 (see Lederman and Maloney, 2002). This, incidentally, is quite consistent with our second and third observations at the beginning of this section. Second,

---

[13] See also Gylfason, Herbertsson, and Zoega (1999), Neumayer (2004), Melhum, Moene, and Torvik (2006), and Humphreys, Sachs, and Stiglitz (2007).

they show that the negative impact of natural-resource abundance on growth is very sensitive to the use of net natural resource exports (instead of gross exports of natural resources) as the indicator of natural resource abundance and to the inclusion or exclusion of two countries (Singapore and Trinidad and Tobago). Third, the negative effects of natural resource abundance disappear when they include in the regression equation the Herfindahl index of export concentration, suggesting that the "curse" is one of concentration rather than resources (or, perhaps more precisely, that the so-called "natural resource curse" only operates when there is a high concentration of the export structure in a few resource-intensive products). Fourth, when they control for fixed effects in a panel context, the negative effect disappears suggesting that the Sachs and Warner results is being driven by the correlation of their measure of natural resource abundance with unobserved country characteristics.

The general conclusion by Lederman and Maloney is that natural resources are an asset for development that requires appropriate policies and adequate physical and human capital. According to them, evidence that this is possible is provided by the economic history of countries with great natural wealth which have been successful in development (such as Norway and, in the Latin American context, Chile). All this is quite consistent, incidentally, with the staple thesis. Other recent papers supporting this view include Bravo-Ortega and De Gregorio (2007) which, using an interactive human capital term in the regression equation relating growth to natural resource intensity, find that as the stock of human capital rises, the marginal effect of the stock of natural resources on income growth rises and becomes positive. More recently, Pineda and Rodríguez (2011) find evidence that changes in the human development index between 1970 and 2005 are positively correlated, in a cross section of Latin American countries, with the abundance of natural resources.

To conclude, after the Lederman and Maloney criticisms there is no longer a consensus or near consensus in the cross-country econometric evidence on the effects of natural resource abundance. Nevertheless, while Lederman and Maloney may have convinced us that results change depending on the sample and the empirical proxies used to represent relative resource endowments, their findings do not exclude the existence of mechanisms, such as indirect industrialization, that are present in the literature on the Dutch disease and were identified in Sachs and Warner empirical research. These findings on the deindustrialization effects of the Dutch disease are fully consistent with the overwhelming evidence on the negative effects of currency appreciation on growth reviewed in Chapter 11. Moreover, the challenge by Lederman and Maloney to previous empirical literature does not imply that natural resources cannot have negative developmental effects. What the evidence seems to suggest is that these effects exist but are highly conditional—that is, there are conditions under which natural resources may enhance growth and conditions under which they will inhibit growth. There is here a similarity with the literature on trade and development which, as discussed in Chapter 14, suggests that the effects of trade openness are contingent on the pattern of specialization. Another similarity with this literature is that it is not certain that traditional growth regressions can move forward in addressing this "conditional curse" of natural resources.

Appendix. Existence of equilibrium in the linkage effects model

Consider the determination of the slope of the w* curve in the linkage effects model. Along the w* schedule, the profit rate remains constant and this requires the relative price p_I/p_M to also remain constant. Using eq. (17), we can express the proportionate change in pI as:

$$\text{dln } p_I = \text{dln } w - [\mu/(1+\mu)] \quad \text{dln } I \tag{A.1}$$

where dln I can be expressed as: dln I = $[1/(1 + I_M/I_A)]$ dln (I_A/I_M) + dln I_M.

Using the demand functions I_A and I_M in (16), together with (A.1), and setting dln pI = 0, we can solve for the slope of the w* schedule: dln w*/dln K = $\mu/(1+\mu)$ $(1 + b \, I_A/I_M)$. The slope of the w* curve depends on the increasing returns parameter in sector I, the output elasticity of land in the agricultural production function and the composition of demand for I goods. Since this composition depends on the level of the capital stock (and, more generally, on the capital-land endowment), the slope is not constant in (ln w, ln K) space. As K increases, I_A/I_M falls (as sector I produces increasingly for the M sector) and the curve becomes steeper. At high levels of K, when I_A/I_M tends to zero, the slope tends to a constant value, $\mu/(1 + \mu)$, which is the same as in the model of Chapter 8. When K tends to zero (and sector I produces exclusively for sector A), the slope goes to zero which is also the slope of the w curve at low levels of K.

Interestingly, we now have three cases instead of the two in the model of Chapter 8. In addition to case (a), when the two schedules do not intersect, and (b), when the schedules intersect twice, it is now possible that a unique high level intersection exists. This third case arises here because, unlike the original model in Chapter 8, demand for I goods is not determined exclusively by sector M. Even if there is no sector M (K = 0) and I goods are produced at a high cost, there is a demand for them from sector A (this depends, of course, on our assumption that a given fraction of rents is spent on I goods no matter how high their price). It is then always possible, with a sufficiently low wage, or a sufficiently productive M sector, to start production of M at low levels of K and avoid the low level intersection with the w curve.

16

Inequality and Middle-income Traps

In previous chapters, we have argued that classical development economics has much to contribute to the explanation of differences across countries in income levels and growth rates. This is so especially when this analytical framework is extended to account for the role of skill acquisition and the pattern of trade specialization. However, there is one aspect of the postwar development experience that remains elusive: the economic setbacks that from time to time are suffered at middle-income levels. These setbacks cannot be attributed to economies falling into classical development traps. According to the development models discussed so far, economies should record an acceleration of growth, rather than a slowdown, at those middle-income levels. This growth acceleration is the result of virtuous interactions between elastic labor supplies and the expansion of increasing returns activities, which precisely at an intermediate range of incomes generate a maximum growth rate.

This chapter explores the links between income distribution and growth with the aim of explaining the economic setbacks and growth slowdowns suffered at low and middle-income levels. We examine first a few salient features of income distribution in developed and developing countries. Then, we review alternative hypotheses on the relationships between income distribution and the rate of income growth including the recent literature on the reverse links between inequality and growth, focusing on the specific channels through which inequality may be harmful to growth. We then bring together the different strands of the literature to show how this integration can help explain the emergence of "inequality traps" at low and medium income levels.

1. Income Distribution in Developing and Developed Countries

By and large, the societies of developing countries are more unequal than those of developed countries. Kravis (1960) and Kuznets (1963) originally

Table 16.1 Income level and inequality in 2010 (or latest available year)

Gini averages	Group 1	Group 2	Group 3	Group 4	Group 5	All countries
Average per income group	31.9 (17)	41.4 (17)	47.2 (17)	43.0 (18)	42.6 (18)	41.3 (87)
Europe	28.0 (12)	34.3 (3)				29.3 (15)
East and South Asia	50.1 (2)	36.6 (3)	40 (1)	36.6 (5)	32.5 (2)	38.3 (13)
North Africa and Mid. East		38.8 (3)	35.9 (4)	40.9 (1)		37.6 (8)
Oceania	29.4 (1)	33.5 (1)				31.5 (2)
Sub-Saharan Africa		53.9 (1)	54.7 (3)	43.0 (8)	43.9 (16)	45.1 (28)
North and South America	38.3 (2)	48.0 (6)	50.5 (9)	51.6 (4)		48.8 (21)

Gini value as percentage.
Number of countries in parentheses.
Sources: WIDER Inequality Database and World Bank, World Development Indicators, 2012. See appendix to Chapter 1.

established empirically the greater inequality found in developing countries. Table 16.1 presents data for 87 countries around 2010, aggregated into the five income levels considered in Chapter 1, and showing that the average Gini coefficients of middle- and low-income countries are systematically higher than those of high-income economies.

In a merely accounting sense, the higher inequality in poor and middle-income countries plays a minor part in explaining why the mass of their populations is poorer than their counterparts in rich countries. If their income distributions were less unequal and similar to those found in developed countries, the large differences in income per capita between these two groups of countries would imply that the mass of the populations in many, if not most, developing countries would still live in poverty. Yet, at a deeper level is there a connection between those two features, the higher inequality found in poor countries and their lower level of economic development? Why is it that we associate underdevelopment with the coexistence of the extremes of wealth and poverty? Are less developed countries poor perhaps because they are more unequal? Or are they more unequal because they are less developed? I now turn to review alternative hypotheses on the relationships between income distribution and the rate of economic growth and the empirical evidence on the different possible links.

2. The Effects of Inequality on Growth: Theoretical Arguments

The Smithian trade-off

Views on the relationship between inequality and growth were dominated for a long time by the relationships between income distribution and growth postulated by the classical political economists, Adam Smith and David Ricardo, in particular. In their vision of economic development, growth was essentially the result of physical capital accumulation. In turn, the main source of savings and investment in the economy was the reinvestment of profits by businesses. In this view, the rents of landlords tended to be spent on luxurious consumption rather than invested in expanding the stock of capital while the wages of labor were kept at a low level by Malthusian mechanisms and were just enough to provide for the subsistence consumption of workers.

All this led to clear-cut conclusions on the relationship between income distribution and growth: the higher the share of profits in total income, the higher the rate of investment and the faster the rate of growth. To the extent that profits accrue mostly to high-income groups (capital is unequally distributed), there was, as a consequence, a clear trade-off between income equality and growth. More income equality, less income inequality, would imply sacrificing growth to the extent that it leads to a lower rate of saving and investment. Jeffrey Williamson (1991) refers to this exchange as the Smithian trade-off.

The Smithian trade-off shaped the views of early development economics through the great influence of the Lewis model which adopted the basic assumptions of the classical economists, i.e. the assumption that investment in physical capital in the modern sector is the driving force of growth and the assumption that profits are the main source of saving and investment. In the Lewis model, the incomes of the traditional sector are so low that they can't be an important source of saving and the same applies to the wages of labor employed in the modern sector which are kept low in the presence of surplus labor. There is again a trade-off between equality and growth.[1]

The Smithian trade-off (as embedded in the Lewis model), together with the Kuznets curve hypothesis according to which in the development process inequality rises first and later falls, shaped development thinking in the 1950s and 1960s in the direction of neglecting income inequality issues and policies to reduce income inequalities. Indeed, if inequality is good for growth, the increasing inequalities that result from the Kuznets pattern are not only inescapable but can accelerate the transition to high levels of development. They may make the poor worse off today than otherwise but will also lift them out of poverty more rapidly. The combined message of the Kuznets hypothesis and the Smithian trade-off was: "Grow first, redistribute later".

---

[1] It is worth noting that the classical view should not be confused with that of Kaldorian and other post-Keynesian growth models. Contrary to what is often asserted in the recent literature (see, for example, Perotti, 1996, p. 175; Birdsall, Ross, and Sabot, 1995, p. 477), the functional distribution of income does not determine investment and growth in these models and higher inequality does not cause higher growth. Instead, causation runs the other way around: growth and investment are the determinants of income distribution. In Kaldor (1956), for example, income distribution is the dependent variable: higher growth leads to redistribution toward profits, precisely in order to generate endogenously the savings needed to finance the higher rate of accumulation.

The adverse effects of inequality on growth

A recent theme in the literature on endogenous growth refers to the causation from income distribution to growth.[2] This literature has antecedents among early critics of the Kuznets curve and, in particular, in old arguments about the economic efficiency gains that can arise from greater equality. Much of this recent literature, at least up to 2000, reached opposite conclusions to the classical and early development economics views and gives an affirmative answer to the question of whether inequality is harmful to growth. Other things being equal, economic development is slower in more unequal societies. Since today's less developed countries are those which have grown more slowly over the past two centuries, the implication of this view is that one reason why these countries are poorer is because they have remained more unequal.

In this literature, there is no dearth of analyses supporting the hypothesis of inequality in income or asset distribution negatively affecting growth. The posited channels through which this takes place vary widely. To facilitate the exposition, I will present the different approaches under two main headings: 1) those involving socio-political channels, along with economic mechanisms, and affecting growth through their influence on physical capital accumulation and productivity; 2) those relying essentially on economic mechanisms and affecting factor growth (capital, skills and labor) and thus the rates of capital and skill deepening.

Sociopolitical mechanisms

Suppose that the rate of physical capital accumulation is a function of the post-tax return on capital [r (1-t)] and a risk-adjusted international profit rate (r*, i.e., the post-tax profit rate abroad, adjusted for domestic political risk): $I/K = \psi$ [r (1-t)-r*]. The following approaches have in common that the link between inequality and growth involves socio-political factors affecting tax rates or political risk and, as a result, the rate of investment.

In the fiscal policy approach, income distribution affects growth via its effects on taxation and government expenditure. The key idea is that, in democratic political regimes, inequality generates pressures for redistribution: inequality lowers the income of the median voter relative to the national average and makes the middle class more likely to ally with the poor to press for redistribution. This pressure leads to distortionary taxes, such as a tax on

---

[2] For a review and synthesis of the main arguments and empirical evidence in this literature, see Bénabou (1996) and Perotti (1996). We shall look later at the post 2000 literature.

capital, which then discourages the rate of accumulation and growth.[3] Differences within this approach refer to the type of government expenditure they consider: public investment (Alesina and Rodrik, 1994), redistributive transfers from rich to poor (Persson and Tabellini, 1994), and redistribution from capital to labor (Bertola, 1993).

Empirical findings have been disappointing, on balance, for the fiscal approach. This seems to be due to two reasons. First, redistributive transfers may have a positive effect on growth by, for example, relaxing constraints on human capital investments by the poor.[4] These positive effects can then offset the negative effects of higher taxation. Second, by reducing social tensions and political instability, fiscal redistribution may have a positive effect on growth, which, again, counteracts the negative effect of higher taxation (a point made by Alesina and Perotti, 1994).

A second approach focuses on the effects of inequality on sociopolitical instability and conflict (Alesina and Perotti, 1994; Alesina et al., 1996). In this view, inequality creates strong incentives for different social groups to engage in rent seeking activities, and leads to social unrest that may make property rights insecure. The resulting uncertainty about the distribution of resources, including an increased expropriation risk, reduces the rate of accumulation and growth. Is this any different from the previous explanation, except that the emphasis is on political risk rather than a tax on capital? Bénabou (1996) points out that in these models the growth rate can be shown to be negatively related to interest groups' rent-seeking *abilities*, as well as to income disparities. This means that what really matters for insecurity and sociopolitical instability is not income inequality per se, but *inequality in the relative distribution of income and political power*. A higher income inequality accompanied by a higher inequality in political power (in the same direction) need not be detrimental to growth. What is detrimental to growth is the asymmetrical situation in which a high income inequality accompanies relative equality in political power. If, as contributors to the fiscal policy approach emphasize (see Alesina and Rodrik, 1994), the political economy mechanism of pressure for redistribution is characteristic of democratic political regimes, then these two sets of explanations come very close to one another.

---

[3] Inequality is thus harmful to growth, as it leads to a more progressive redistribution of income. The nice dialectics of this reasoning is somewhat perplexing and raises at least two related questions which, to my knowledge, are left unanswered in this approach: Why should redistributive measures take the form of taxes that discourage investment? Why can't redistributive government spending, if applied, say, to enhance human capital accumulation by the poor, be favorable to growth?

[4] Perotti (1993) finds positive, albeit insignificant, coefficients on transfers in growth regressions.

Empirical evidence in support of the importance of inequality in the *relative* distribution of income and political power comes from the fact that growth rates across Latin America are not negatively associated with inequality—unlike what happens with intercontinental differences in inequality and growth.[5] The lack of a negative relationship can be explained by the fact that some of the less inegalitarian countries in the postwar period—Argentina, Chile and Uruguay, in the Southern cone—were in that period slow growing economies while two of the fastest growing (Brazil and Mexico) were among the most inegalitarian countries. However, Brazil and Mexico did not have a higher inequality in the relative distribution of income and political power than countries in the Southern cone. Their authoritarian regimes and the weakness of their trade unions implied that their more unequal income distribution was accompanied by a higher inequality in political power in the same direction.

A third approach posits that inequality leads to polarization, which in turn undermines the consensus for policy reforms (Haggard and Webb, 1993) or the security of property and contractual rights (Keefer and Knack, 2002). While the end result is similar to that in previous approaches, the political channel here is different. Drawing on an argument by Esteban and Ray (1994), Keefer and Knack (2002) emphasize the difficulties of collective decision-making under conditions of high inequality. The consequence is that inequality reduces the stability and predictability of government decisions by making social consensus more fragile. Rodrik (1999) makes a related point when he argues that high inequality weakens the institutions of conflict management making a country more vulnerable to external shocks and growth collapses.

Potentially, this type of political channel is perhaps the most relevant in explaining cross-country differences in growth *among developing countries*. The reason is that it is less dependent upon the nature of the political regime than other political explanations. Sociopolitical approaches involving the presence of democratic institutions as crucial to the argument, seem less relevant in explaining why relatively egalitarian Korea and Taiwan grew faster than more inegalitarian Latin American economies at a time when most of these countries had authoritarian regimes.[6] Interestingly, what emerges from the empirical research on political instability and growth is a view of Asia as a region with authoritarian but stable regimes, in contrast to the much more unstable political regimes in Latin America (see Alesina et al, 1996).

---

[5] If anything, the relationship across Latin America is positive; see Fishlow (1995).

[6] It is worth noting that Clarke's (1995) comprehensive analysis of "reduced form" regressions concludes that the negative correlation between inequality and growth holds for both democracies and non-democracies. As already mentioned, empirical research on the effects of inequality operating through fiscal policy has been disappointing.

Economic mechanisms

Some potential links between income distribution and growth by-pass socio-political considerations. In the following approaches, inequality affects the rates of factor growth and/or the productivity in the use of given factor endowments. The key channels all involve essentially economic mechanisms.

A first approach emphasizes the link between income distribution and investment in education (see Loury, 1981; Galor and Zeira, 1993; Birdsall, Ross, and Sabot, 1995). Two mechanisms are involved here. The first is the existence of credit constraints that prevent the poor from undertaking the efficient amount of investment in human capital. Less income inequality then has a positive effect on human capital investment, as income redistribution relaxes budgetary constraints on the poor. In addition, there is an asset distribution effect. In the presence of diminishing returns to education, which implies that the marginal product of human capital investments by the poor is relatively high, less inequality in the distribution of human capital has a positive asset distribution effect on efficiency. A more egalitarian distribution of education implies, other things being equal, a higher productivity of a given stock of human capital.

This imperfect asset markets *cum* diminishing returns argument is similar to the old case for land reform on efficiency grounds. The main difference is that in the context of models of endogenous growth, the resulting efficiency gains can result in a permanently higher growth rate, rather than in a once and for all level effect (which, nevertheless, implies a higher growth rate in the transition to the new steady state). Several papers tend to support this channel. Williamson (1993) presents empirical evidence showing that more egalitarian societies tend to have higher enrollments in secondary education at the same average income level. Perotti's (1996) regression estimates of structural equations also suggest strong support for a positive relationship between income equality (a higher share of the middle class) and investment in human capital. Birdsall, Ross, and Sabot (1995) present evidence that less unequal societies tend to have a more egalitarian allocation of educational expenditures, including public expenditures.

A second transmission mechanism runs from inequality to fertility rates and population growth.[7] As is well known from the literature on the demographic transition, fertility rates tend to fall as incomes per capita increase. If fertility and incomes are inversely related, biological constraints must imply that the rate at which fertility increases as income falls must be decreasing. For a given average income per capita, less income inequality will tend to reduce fertility

---

[7] For models on endogenous fertility and its relationship to human capital and income distribution, see Becker, Murphy and Tamura (1990), Galor and Zang (1993), and De la Croix and Doepke (2003), among others.

rates among the poor by more than it increases fertility among the rich (if it increases them at all, given the likelihood of ratchet effects in the behavior of fertility). Fertility and population growth would then be positively influenced by inequality, for a given level of per capita income. If faster population growth reduces parental investments in their children's human capital or, more simply, the steady state value of per capita income and the transitional growth rate of income per capita (as it does in neoclassical growth models and labor surplus models with moderately increasing returns to scale), this provides another channel through which inequality adversely affects growth. Perotti (1996) shows that a larger income share of the middle class (his measure of income equality) has a strong negative effect on fertility and, through this influence, a positive effect on growth.

Finally, inequality may be harmful to growth by reducing the size of the domestic market for the increasing returns industries. In the recent literature, this mechanism is often associated with Murphy, Shleifer, and Vishny (1989a), who argue that a pre-condition for industrialization is a limited amount of inequality. In their view, income must be distributed broadly enough to materialize in higher demand for a broad range of manufactures which then can complement each other and expand together. This mechanism is often dismissed in the recent literature as lacking empirical support. This is because the argument is taken to imply the counterfactual prediction that large countries, other things being equal, should grow faster (see Knack and Keefer, 1995; Bénabou, 1996). In fact, a big push model with horizontal pecuniary externalities, as the one Murphy, Shleifer and Vishny have in mind, only suggests that inequality plays a role at low-income levels in strengthening the hold of the low-level trap (or in broadening the set of conditions under which a unique traditional economy equilibrium exists). Ros (2000) finds support for the inequality—market size—growth hypothesis in the fact that low-income Asian and African countries display the expected relationship of growth being positively affected by income and negatively affected by inequality.[8]

Beyond low-income levels, there is no reason to expect an unambiguous and systematic relationship between inequality and growth mediated by the size of the market. Earlier literature in structuralist development economics had in fact formulated alternative hypotheses on the effects of income redistribution on growth operating through these channels. Less income inequality may broaden market demand for the products of leading manufacturing sectors (and through cost reductions stimulate investment in these sectors)

---

[8] It is also worth noting that, as we shall see in greater detail below, Barro (2000) found that the coefficient of the inequality variable in a growth regression is negative and significant at low-income levels and positive and significant at high-income levels. See also Chapter 8 on the subject.

if middle- and low-income groups have a high income elasticity of demand for durable consumption goods produced under increasing returns. Alternatively, it may reduce market demand for manufactures if income elasticities of demand are higher among the rich and the upper-middle class. Furtado (1969) took the "underconsumptionist" view according to which higher inequality in income distribution, resulting from the expansion of the modern sector, limited the domestic market and discouraged the process of capital accumulation while Tavares and Serra (1971), relying on the Brazilian experience, defended an "exhilarationist" position according to which greater inequality actually expanded the market for the leading industrial sectors producing consumer durables. The resulting "unequalizing spiral" was further examined and formalized by Taylor and Bacha (1976). Lustig (1980) investigated empirically the assumptions of the alternative views regarding the size of the income elasticities of demand for consumer durables and non durables in different income groups.

Similarly, recent literature on growth and distribution in a Kalecki-Steindl tradition has developed alternative hypotheses on the effects of changes in the functional distribution of income on growth (see, on the subject, Chapter 10 and Dutt, 1984, Taylor, 1985, Bhaduri and Marglin, 1990, You, 1994). In these models growth may be wage-led—in which case the positive effects of redistribution from profits to wages on market demand and resource utilization outweigh the negative effects on profit margins—or profit-led, in which case profitability falls with the reduction in profit margins. In the first case, redistribution from wages to profits, which increases inequality, has "stagnationist" effects on growth, i.e., growth is negatively affected as a result of a reduction in demand and capacity utilization. In the second case, redistribution towards profits has "exhilarationist" effects on growth, as investment is stimulated by the higher profit margins.

To sum up, Perotti (1996) has summarized the available evidence on the specific channels through which inequality affects growth as follows. The transmission mechanisms from lower inequality to higher growth are essentially three: 1) lower fertility rates; 2) higher rates of investment of education; 3) greater political and social stability, which favors higher rates of investment. He finds no support for the idea that equality favors growth by generating fewer policy distortions as a result of fewer demands for redistribution.

3. Some More Empirical Evidence

A two by two matrix

The recent literature has produced a body of research results (largely cross country regressions) that support some (not all) of the positive links between

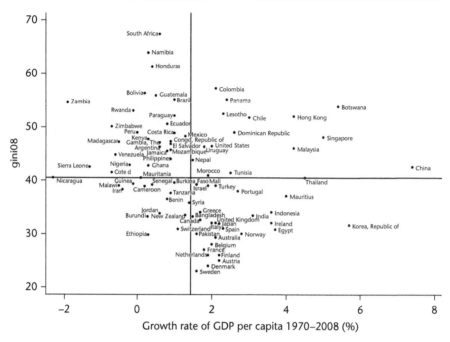

Figure 16.1 Gini coefficient and GDP per capita growth (1970–2008)
See appendix to Chapter 1 for sources and details.

equality and growth. As an introduction to this evidence, consider a two by two matrix in which countries fall into four boxes: high growth with equity, low growth with equity, low growth with high inequality, and high growth with high inequality (see Figure 16.1).

Which countries belong to which of these boxes depends on exactly where you draw the lines (the lines in the figure are the median values of the Gini and the per capita GDP growth rate) but if the figure gave a strong support to the Smithian trade-off, clearly we would find most countries clustered in the North East and South West boxes. Yet, this is clearly not the case. If there is a pattern, the opposite tends to be true: we find many relatively egalitarian high-income countries clustered with growth rates of 2 percent and above and many low growth, low-income countries in Sub-Saharan Africa and Latin America clustered together with high Gini coefficients and slow growth. Thus, if the data is to be taken as a test of the Smithian trade-off in its simplest version (i.e., of the hypothesis that inequality is necessary and sufficient for rapid growth), the hypothesis would be clearly rejected. This does not mean that the Smithian trade-off is irrelevant, especially in less simple versions. The effects of income inequality on savings and investment are not necessarily too small to deserve consideration. As already mentioned, when one looks at Latin American countries alone, there tends to be a positive relationship between inequality and growth. One possible reason is that they have followed a growth path that is intensive in physical capital, the factor emphasized in the Smithian trade-off. A second point is that the box with low inequality and slow growth is far from empty, especially if we draw the boundary of slow growth above a growth rate of 2 percent per year. High growth depends also on many other factors besides the level of inequality.

Evidence based on reduced form regressions

In addition to the papers that investigate particular channels through which inequality influences growth, empirical research on inequality and growth since the 1990s has involved adding a variable reflecting income inequality (typically a Gini coefficient of income concentration) to the independent variables determining the growth rate in a Barro-style regression. Most of these studies in the 1990s generally found a negative coefficient in the inequality variable leading most researchers to conclude that inequality has a negative effect on growth (see the survey by Benabou, 1996). These findings were taken as offering a partial explanation of the stylized fact that growth had been very fast in the relatively egalitarian East Asian countries and lower in the inegalitarian countries of Africa and Latin America.

A typical estimate of the effect of inequality on growth was that a one standard deviation decrease in inequality raises the annual growth rate of GDP per capita by 0.5 to 0.8 percentage points (Bénabou, 1996). As noted by Perotti (1996), a substantial part of the negative association between inequality and growth seems to come from interregional variation in income distribution. The addition of dummy variables for Latin America, Africa, and South-East Asia in Perotti's regressions yields the expected negative signs for the slower growing and more unequal Latin American and African regions and a positive sign for the faster growing and less unequal South-East Asia. The inclusion of these dummy variables makes the coefficient on his measure of equality fall by about 30 percent. In Fishlow (1995), the inclusion of a dummy variable for Latin America turns the coefficient on the inequality indicator to become statistically insignificant.

In the years 2000, several papers (Forbes, 2000; Barro, 2000 and 2008; Banerjee and Duflo, 2003) questioned the consensus of the 1990s. Forbes (2000) criticized previous research due to its neglect of the consequences of measurement error and omitted variable bias that could be behind the inverse relationship between inequality and growth. If a regression omits variables, such as corruption, that are positively correlated with inequality and negatively correlated with growth, the result may be to find a spurious relationship between inequality and growth. To address these problems, Forbes used a panel data model with country specific effects so as to control for omitted variables and found that the short-run relationship between inequality and growth is in fact positive. Barro (2000 and 2008) adopted a similar approach and found that the coefficient of the inequality variable in a growth regression is not significantly different from zero, but is negative and significant at low-income levels and positive and significant at high income levels. Barro interprets the result for the overall sample as indicating that inequality has different effects on growth, some positive and some negative, that tend to cancel each other in the overall sample. He attributes the negative effect of inequality on growth in low-income countries to the importance of credit constraints in those countries (which are relaxed by greater equality) in contrast to what happens in richer countries with more developed financial systems. Banerjee and Duflo (2003) criticize previous studies for their implicit assumption that the effects of inequality on growth are linear and, by relaxing this assumption, find that there are strong non-linearities in the relationship between inequality and growth so that changes in inequality (in whichever direction) reduce growth in the subsequent period. Finally, Easterly (2007) calls for focusing on the big picture and argues, using an instrumental variables approach to explain differences in levels of income (rather than growth rates), that inequality causes underdevelopment because it negatively affects both investment in education and institutional quality.

Evidence based on historical analysis

The effects emphasized by Easterly, operating through human capital and institutions, are also part of the broad historical analysis by Engerman and Sokoloff (2002) of the different development paths of the United States and Latin America in the 19th century. Engerman and Sokoloff argue that relative equality generated the conditions for growth in the former British colonies in North America. In the United States, together with a relatively high income per capita, equality in the distribution of income led to the formation of a middle class market that was essential to the development of industry, i.e., the mass production of standardized goods subject to economies of scale ("the American system of manufactures"). To the extent that the poor used to spend a smaller share of their income in manufactures and the wealthy used to spend their income on non-standardized goods, the expansion of a middle class market was critically dependent on a relatively egalitarian distribution of income. Such a distribution of income was also favorable to educational investments. Engerman and Sokoloff assert that the United States probably had the most literate population in the world by the beginning of the nineteenth century and that between 1825 and 1850, nearly every northern state that had not already done so enacted laws establishing free schools open to all children and supported by general taxes. Latin America, including the Southern cone countries with the higher levels of literacy, lagged behind by several decades. In the conditions of great inequality prevailing in Latin America, the collective-action problems associated with the establishment and funding of universal public schools were exacerbated and the wealthy, enjoying disproportionate political power and being able to procure schooling services for their own children, resisted being taxed to subsidize services to others.

Other effects of relative equality favorable to growth were those on technological innovation. For Engerman and Sokoloff, greater equality meant a general concern with extracting opportunities from innovation and this led to a patent system most favorable to the common people. Also, greater equality meant greater densities of potential users that raised the projected returns on infrastructure projects (transportation and financial intermediaries in particular). These conditions were absent in Latin America where, in addition, inequality had negative effects on the productivity of the labor force due to malnutrition, illness and lack of education as well as the higher risks of political and social upheaval leading to reduced investment.

In turn, Engerman and Sokoloff relate the degree of inequality to the composition of factor endowments (including climate, soil and density of native population, besides the abundance of land and natural resources). In Canada and Northern United States colonies, factor endowment attracted European immigrants with a relatively egalitarian distribution of human capital. It also made possible a system of family farms as the crops (grains) were not subject to economies of scale, unlike the cultivation of sugar and other highly valued crops characterized by extensive economies of scale that favored the concentration of land and the creation of slave plantations. The abundance of labor with low human capital (slaves in Brazil and West Indies and natives in Mexico and Peru) also contributed to the high inequality of income and wealth. Engerman and Sokoloff also note the role of government policies (immigration and land policies in particular) in perpetuating the factor endowment and the degree of inequality in the economy's path. Land policies in Latin America in the last quarter of the 19th century aggravated in fact the inherited high concentration.

We should note that differences in the degree of inequality are unlikely to provide a full explanation of differential paths of development. Latin America was no less unequal in the late 19th century and 20th century when economic growth finally took off. In fact several countries became more unequal, as a result of liberal economic reforms of the second half of the 19th century, than they were during the first half of that century.

An alternative approach: functional and dysfunctional inequality

We now turn to what we regard as some of the main shortcomings of the recent theoretical and empirical research on inequality and growth. A first one is that, with some exceptions already mentioned, empirical research has relied on "reduced form" regressions that do not distinguish among the specific channels through which inequality affects growth. Another shortcoming, perhaps more important, is that the recent literature fails to distinguish between different sources of inequality and their effects on growth. Our discussion so far of the determinants of income distribution suggests that different possible sources of inequality may have very different effects on growth. This type of analysis opens the door to strong non-linearities which are virtually absent in the recent literature that, in a sense, has produced one model at a time, each of them focusing on a single hypothesis.

Consider, first, two sources of inequality and the associated effects on growth. The first source depends on the composition of factor endowments and affects the structure of factor returns. For example, to the extent that physical and human capital typically tend to be more unequally distributed than labor everywhere, less developed countries (with relatively small physical and human capital endowments per capita) tend to be more unequal (especially middle-income countries) than rich countries (with abundant physical and human capital). There is a second source of inequality rooted in the distribution of factor endowments. This source is independent of factor endowments and income levels, and is associated with deviations from the "typical ownership structure" of factor endowments. Thus, a country with an abnormally high inequality in the distribution of land or capital will tend to have higher income inequality, other things being equal, than a country with a more egalitarian distribution of factor endowments.

Each of these two sources of income inequality may well have different effects on growth (both in size and sign). The effects of inequality on growth associated with the first source, the structure of factor prices for a given distribution of factor endowments, are likely to be *positive* to the extent that high factor returns on physical capital and skilled labor have positive incentive effects on the accumulation of capital and the acquisition of skills. The second component, related to the distribution of factor endowments, is the one that is most likely to have negative effects on growth through either the rates of capital accumulation and skill acquisition or the efficiency in the use of factor endowments. This is the type of effects on which the recent literature implicitly focuses.

The failure to distinguish between these two sources of inequality in the recent literature is related to the neglect of the interactions between income level and inequality (as opposed to income growth and inequality). Yet, the importance of this distinction in the estimation of the effects of inequality on growth in a *cross section of countries* should be obvious. For the sign of the effect will depend on whether international differences in income inequality are due to the first or to the second source (as well as on the strength of the two types of effects).

Ros (2000, ch. 10) attempted to empirically isolate the effects of what may be called functional and dysfunctional inequality by measuring the latter as the deviation of the Gini coefficient from the value predicted by a regression equation in which inequality is determined by the level of income per capita. The main findings were as follows. First, while the predicted Gini had a positive effect on growth in a standard reduced form growth-inequality regression, dysfunctional inequality (the difference between the actual and the predicted Gini) had negative and significant effects on growth. Second, the effects of dysfunctional inequality on factor accumulation and total factor productivity growth are both negative, the effect on the growth of total factor productivity being especially large, reflecting perhaps the adverse asset distribution effects on the efficiency of given stocks of skilled labor and physical capital. Third, the effects of "functional inequality" (measured by the predicted Gini) on factor accumulation are, by contrast, positive.

The contradictory effects that the two sources of inequality have on factor accumulation per worker, the positive effect of the predicted GIni and the negative effect of the deviation of inequality from the predicted Gini, raise further questions. Is it through population growth (and thus labor force growth), skill acquisition, or physical capital accumulation, that these effects operate? The results of regressing population growth, the investment share, and enrollments in secondary education on the Gini coefficient (circa 1965), its two components, and the initial level of GDP per capita are as follows. First, the initial level of inequality has a positive and highly significant effect on population growth, clearly confirming that more unequal societies, at similar levels of income, tend to have a higher rate of population growth. This positive effect on population growth in turn implies that inequality, on this account alone, tends to reduce the rates of factor accumulation per worker. Second, the overall effect of the Gini on the investment share is insignificant (and negative), but this hides a significant and positive incentive effect of functional inequality, associated with the predicted Gini, and an adverse effect of dysfunctional inequality, associated with the deviation of the Gini from its predicted value. The same expected signs are found in the case of enrollments in secondary education, but here both coefficients are small and far from statistically significant.

How can all these results be summarized? Our conclusions are not, in any way, radically different from Perotti's (1996) summary of the evidence cited at the end of section 2. However, we can add a number of qualifications and provisos, which would add up to the summary that follows. More unequal societies have higher rates of population growth, at any given level of income. This is reflected in lower rates of factor accumulation per capita. In addition, they have lower rates of capital accumulation (smaller investment shares at each level of income), which have its source in the amount of dysfunctional inequality, the kind of inequality rooted in a maldistribution of resources that gives no positive incentive effects in the growth process. The mechanism explaining these lower rates of investment in physical capital may be a result of unequal societies being more politically and socially unstable. However, we also found evidence consistent with inequality depressing the market demand for the goods of the increasing returns sectors and this having adverse effects on growth at low-income levels. We could not find strong evidence of inequality operating adversely on the *rates* of skill acquisition (once we control for the level of income). The large effects of dysfunctional inequality on total factor productivity growth may well be reflecting, however, the negative effects on growth of inequality in the *distribution* of human capital.

An important implication of our results is that the effects of inequality on growth (both its size and sign) are level-dependent, i.e. dependent on the level of inequality. This implication has been neglected in the recent empirical literature, which seems to suggest that more equality is always good for growth no matter how egalitarian a society already is. Yet, unless physical and human capital became as equally distributed as labor, there will be a positive amount of "efficient inequality" arising from the positive (incentive) effects of functional inequality on the rates of factor accumulation. If our previous analysis is correct, these positive effects would directly emerge in cross-country studies, if suddenly international differences in income distribution became fully associated with inequalities in the structure of factor returns. However, it would then be incorrect to conclude that equality is harmful to growth, just as it is incorrect to conclude from current cross-country studies that more equality is *always* good for growth.

Finally, it is worth highlighting the importance of the distinction between different sources of inequality for policy design. If the negative effects of inequality on growth largely come from the distribution of factor endowments, then a redistributive policy that fails to change asset distribution and acts exclusively on factor prices will be ineffective (or even counterproductive, given its incentive effects).

4. Inequality, Middle-income Traps, and Premature Maturity

How are the transitional dynamics of the classical development theory model modified by the fact that dysfunctional inequality can have negative effects on growth as discussed in this chapter? The transitional dynamics of the development models discussed in Chapters 7 and 8 are captured by a quadratic growth function of the form $g = a_o + a_1 y - a_2 y^2$, where y is the natural logarithm of income per capita, g is the growth rate of income per capita and all parameters are positive. At high-income levels the quadratic form of the growth function only holds for growth rates above the steady state rate of growth (g*). When the economy reaches g* from above, this steady state rate persists over time.

The quadratic growth function implies, as we know, that the growth rate is low at both low and high-income levels. If looked from a cross-section perspective, it implies a pattern of income divergence at low-income levels followed by convergence at middle and high-income levels. In this process, the growth rate reaches a maximum at an income level equal to: $y_o^M = a_1/2a_2$, provided that b_2 is positive (the condition for a maximum) and b_1 is positive (so that y_o is positive). The corresponding maximum growth rate is $g_M = a_o + a_1^2/4a_2$. The growth function also implies a threshold level of convergence (y_C), the income level at which the growth rate reaches from below the growth rate in the steady state (g*): $y_C = y_o^M - [a_1^2 + 4b_a(a_o - g*)]^{1/2}/2a_2$, which is less than the income level, y_o^M, at which the maximum growth rate is reached.

Suppose now that inequality negatively affects the growth rate for a given income level. The augmented growth function is now: $g = a_o + a_1 y - a_2 y^2 - G^\beta$ with $\beta > 1$, where G is an index of inequality in income distribution. The effect of inequality on growth is assumed to be nonlinear and such that, at low levels of inequality a given increase in inequality has a small effect on growth and the effect increases as inequality rises (this is what the inequality restriction on parameter β states). What are the implications of this augmented growth function? First, while the income level at which the growth rate reaches a maximum (y_o^M, equal to $a_1/2a_2$) is unaffected by the level of inequality, the maximum growth rate itself is a negative function of inequality ($g_M = a_o - G^\beta + a_1^2/4a_2$). The threshold level of convergence (y_C), i.e., the income level at which the growth rate reaches from below the growth rate in the steady state (g*) is now: $y_C = y_o^M - [a_1^2 + 4a_2(a_o - G^\beta - g*)]^{1/2}/2a_2$, which shows that an increase in inequality raises the convergence threshold or, what comes to the same, has the effect of reducing the growth rate at low-income levels.

Consider now the interactions between changes in income and changes in inequality. The analysis presented in the previous section suggests that inequality is a non linear function of the level of income per capita (as a proxy for the level of factor endowments) and a component of inequality (X, related to the distribution of factor endowments) that is assumed to be country specific and independent from the level of income per capita:

$G = b_o + b_1 y - b_2 y^2 + X$ (where all parameters are positive).[9] Consider now this equation together with the growth function. The growth function states that growth for a given level of inequality is low at both low- and high-income levels. Since inequality has adverse effects on growth, the fact that inequality is also low at low and high-income levels (as stated by the inequality equation) has the effect of smoothing out the inverted-U path of the growth rate. Indeed, taking the total derivative of the growth rate with respect to income yields: $g'(y) = g_y - ß\,G^{ß-1}\,G_y$, where: $g_y = a_1 - 2a_2\,y$, is the partial derivative of g with respect to y, and $G_y = b_1 - 2b_2\,y$, is the derivative of G with respect to y.

At low-income levels when G_y is positive, $g'(y)$ is less than g_y, i.e., the growth rate increases less with income than if inequality had no effect on the growth rate. At high-income levels when G_y is negative (and inequality tends to fall as income increases), $g'(y)$ is larger than g_y. The influence of inequality then tends to moderate the fall in the growth rate. A more striking implication is that the maximum growth rate may no longer be reached at middle-income levels. Suppose, indeed, that both the "augmented" Kuznets curve and the growth function are "well behaved", in the sense that over a range of low and middle-income levels, G_y and g_y are both positive. Even then, $g'(y)$ may become negative over this low- and middle-range of income if $ß\,G^{ß-1} > g_y/G_y$. This inequality shows that even though growth tends to accelerate, for a *given* level of inequality (g_y is positive), the growth rate may actually fall as income increases over the intermediate range of income levels.

By "inequality trap" I mean a situation in which despite g_y being positive, the inequality condition above is fulfilled and the growth rate falls at intermediate income levels as a result of the negative growth effects of high levels of inequality operating at middle-income levels. What are the conditions favoring the emergence of an inequality trap and a resulting growth slow-down at middle-income levels?[10] First, the higher the level of income inequality generated during the transition towards high-income levels, the more likely will be an inequality trap. Other things being equal, in particular the parameters of the g_y and G_y functions, this will be due to a high level of X-inequality, associated with high inequality in the ownership structure of factor endowments. Closely related to this factor, the distribution of factor

---

[9] It is worth noting that this augmented Kuznets curve equation and the growth function are both quadratic partly for the same reasons, the interactions between moderately increasing returns to scale and elastic labor supplies at low and middle-income levels. Indeed, the evolution of factor returns as income per capita changes, which is one factor accounting for the non linearity of the Kuznets curve, is behind the hump-shaped pattern of growth rates. This implies that parameters b_1 and b_2 are not independent from a_1 and a_2.

[10] The following discussion assumes $ß > 1$, which implies a nonlinear and relatively large effect of inequality on growth at high levels of inequality. With $\beta < 1$, the negative effect of inequality on growth is large at low levels of inequality and small at high levels. The fact that inequality increases in the intermediate range of incomes would in this case accentuate, rather than moderate, the inverted-U path of the growth rate.

endowments, is how adverse is the effect of inequality on growth (the size of parameter β). The more unequal is the distribution of factor endowments the larger the adverse effect of inequality on growth, since a high value of parameter β reflects a large amount of dysfunctional inequality. Thus, a high value of parameter β also increases the likelihood of "inequality traps" since with a higher β the more growth is bound to decelerate over the intermediate range of incomes in which income inequality reaches a peak.

Another factor has to do with the steepness of the Kuznets curve. A 'style' of growth based on physical capital accumulation at the expense of skill acquisition or based on industry-biased productivity growth at the expense of agricultural technical progress (with fast population growth playing a role in generating these unbalances) may imply a high value of G_y (a steep Kuznets curve) which creates conditions leading to a middle-income inequality trap.

A final factor is the response of capital and educational investments to a given increase in the rates of return on capital and education. A strong response of physical and human capital accumulation—a high value of g_y, as arguably present in the East Asian development experience—makes growth relatively elastic to the change in income per capita and thus more likely for the negative effect of inequality on growth to be offset by the positive effect of income on the growth rate. The interactions between increasing returns and the elasticity of labor supply also play a key role, with a relatively low elasticity of labor supply tending to generate a low value of g_y. It is worth noting that the condition necessary for an inequality trap ($\text{ß } G^{\text{ß}-1} > g_y/G_y$) may be fulfilled largely as a result of a relatively low g_y at middle-income levels, even though inequality is not particularly high. Such a situation can arise as a result of a premature exhaustion of labor surpluses. The resulting growth slowdown is best described, in Kaldor's (1966) terms, as "premature maturity" rather than as an "inequality trap".

Faced with a premature growth slowdown, resulting from a combination of these factors, the conditions of high inequality and slow growth will tend to be perpetuated by the adverse effect of slow growth on income distribution. It is in this sense that the situation can be described as a "trap", since the transition to higher income levels is accompanied by a protracted high level of inequality and takes place at a slow pace, or may even be interrupted by economic setbacks. Since the highest inequality tends to occur at middle-income levels, such inequality traps are likely to be characteristic of upper-low- and middle-income countries. The counterpart of these traps in egalitarian countries is, in contrast, a virtuous circle of accelerated growth and rapid equalization of incomes.

Empirical evidence in favor of our framework comes from the observation that the frequency of both growth acceleration and economic setbacks, is highest at middle-income levels. As discussed in Chapter 1, this upward and downward mobility of middle-income countries is the source of the 'twin-peaked' distribution in the world economy today, with many poor and many rich countries and relatively few countries in between.[11]

The empirical literature on political instability and growth also provides some evidence on inequality traps. Alesina et al. (1996) find that for the 1960–82 period, middle-income and inegalitarian Latin American countries had the highest frequency of major government changes and coups d'état. They also find that, according to these indicators, political instability had a negative effect on growth. Moreover, low growth tends to increase the likelihood of coups, according to Londregan and Poole (1990). All this was reflected in the significantly lower growth rates achieved by Latin America (per capita GDP growth of 2.2 percent per year) in comparison to Asian economies (3.3 percent) and developing countries in Europe (4.1 percent).

To conclude, what our analysis in this and previous chapters suggests is that the interactions between growth and inequality, along with the role of the patterns of growth and trade specialization, give rise to the relatively high upward and downward mobility of middle-income countries. The transition from middle to upper-middle and high incomes is likely to be very rapid in egalitarian countries with a manufacturing bias in their trade orientation, a rapid accumulation of skills and a high agricultural productivity growth. In countries with large economic inequality, which have a heavy primary export orientation as well as slower rates of human capital accumulation and technical progress in agriculture, the transition is much slower and protracted. As noted by Fajnzylber (1989, 1990), whose writing on the subject constitutes a pioneer's view on the role of equity in the development experiences, these are, concisely captured, some of the more salient contrasts between the transitions undertaken by the middle-income economies of East Asia and Latin America since 1960.

---

[11] As discussed in Chapter 1, Quah's (1993) work on transition probabilities estimated over the period 1962–84 finds that both upward and downward mobility is highest among middle-income economies.

17

Institutions and Development

The relationship between institutions and development is an old theme in political economy. It was, for example, a central theme for Adam Smith who in the *Wealth of Nations* writes:

> Commerce and manufactures can seldom flourish long in any state which does not enjoy a regular administration of justice, in which the people do not feel themselves secure in the possession of their property, in which the faith of contracts is not supported by law, and in which the authority of the state is not supposed to be regularly employed in enforcing the payment of debts from all those who are able to pay. Commerce and manufactures, in short, can seldom flourish in any state in which there is not a certain degree of confidence in the justice of government.[1]

The literature on this subject has thrived in recent times among development economists and economic historians. This has been due to the revitalization of the economics of growth and its application to the big questions of development economics as well as to the contributions of the new institutional economics by Douglass North and his collaborators. Indeed, in the view of the neo-institutionalists the "fundamental determinants" of development levels and rates of growth are precisely institutions, so that differences among countries in the levels of economic development are fundamentally explained by institutional differences. The recent book by Daron Acemoglu and James Robinson (2012) expresses this thesis with particular force, clarity and erudition.

The recent applied literature on institutions and development includes by now several dozens of papers. It began in the late 1980s[2] and grew exponentially in the first decade of the 2000s. Among the most influential

---

[1] Cited by Rodrik et al. (2004).

[2] Among the initial contributions are Scully (1988) and Knack and Keefer (1995). If one includes the contributions of political scientists on the relationship between political institutions and development, then the applied literature on the subject is older.

contributions are Hall and Jones (1999), Acemoglu, Johnson, and Robinson (AJR, 2001, 2002, and 2005), Easterly and Levine (2003), Rodrik et al. (2004), Glaeser et al. (2004), and Acemoglu and Robinson (2012). All these authors have in common that they take into account the contributions of neo-institutionalists like North and explore the basic hypothesis that the quality of economic and political institutions has a fundamental role in the explanation of the large per capita income gaps among countries.

AJR (2001, p. 1369) refer to North and Thomas (1973), Jones (1981), and North (1981) in order to express this basic hypothesis as follows: "Countries with better *"institutions"*, more secure property rights, and less distortionary policies will invest more in physical and human capital, and will use these factors more efficiently to achieve a greater level of income". Hall and Jones (1999) express the hypothesis stating that current international gaps in income per capita are fundamentally explained by differences across countries in social infrastructure: "The central hypothesis of this paper is that the primary, fundamental determinant of a country's long-run economic performance is its social infrastructure. By social infrastructure we mean the institutions and government policies that provide the incentives for individuals and firms in an economy". And they define a good social infrastructure as one that reduces (rather than increases) the gap between the private and social returns in the set of activities in the economy from working in a factory or invest in physical and human capital to create new ideas or transfer technologies from abroad. Moreover, a good social infrastructure is one that aligns private and social returns of activities with negative consequences for the economy and society such as theft and corruption (Hall and Jones, 1999, p. 84).

It is worth noting that, just as in Adam Smith, there are in fact two hypotheses involved here. First, there is Smith's argument in favor of protection of property rights and a good administration of justice, that is of the rule of law as a necessary condition for "commerce and manufactures to flourish". But this argument is often accompanied by another one. This is the idea that the best social infrastructure is one that gives the greatest economic freedom to individuals, the hypothesis of the invisible hand. This is what Hall and Jones mean with aligning social and private returns: that state intervention in the economy, through taxes and regulations, should be kept at a minimum so that private agents can appropriate the social returns of their economic activities to the maximum extent.[3] The following quote from Adam Smith captures the

---

[3] As they put it: "A social infrastructure favorable to high levels of output per worker provides an environment that supports productive activities and encourages capital accumulation, skill acquisition, invention, and technology transfer. Such a social infrastructure gets the prices right so that, in the language of North and Thomas [1973], individuals capture the social returns to their actions as private returns" (Hall and Jones, 1999, p. 84).

two hypotheses together: "Little else is requisite to carry a state to the highest degree of opulence from the lowest barbarism but peace, easy taxes, and a tolerable administration of justice: all the rest being brought about by the natural course of things" (Smith, cited by Azariadis and Stachurski, 2005, p. 298).

The main contributions to the applied literature on this subject evaluate one or both of these hypotheses. They take the form of cross-country regressions in which levels of per capita income or growth rates are regressed on institutional and policy variables, reflecting one or both hypotheses, in addition to other possible determinants of income levels and growth rates. In what follows, I discuss the empirical evidence that the recent applied literature on institutions and development has to offer and the theoretical basis on which it relies. I start in section 1 reviewing the first proposition (or "the rule of law hypothesis") focusing on the problems involved in measuring institutions and separating the effects of institutions on development from those of development on institutions. I then turn in section 2 to the second proposition ("the invisible hand hypothesis") on the effects of economic liberalization on growth and development and discuss the theoretical basis of the empirical models present in the literature. Section 3 then reviews some common problems with the empirical evidence offered in favor of both hypotheses and section 4 looks at the paradox of institutional convergence in Latin America over the past 3 decades coupled with a wide variety of growth performances.

1. The Rule of Law Hypothesis: The Weak and Strong Versions

In its weak version, the "rule of law hypothesis" asserts that greater enforcement of the rule of law has positive developmental effects. This is, in my view, hardly controversial. I find it hard to construct a convincing argument concluding that a higher risk of expropriation can be favorable to economic development. It should also be noted that acknowledging the role of institutions in this limited sense is not what distinguishes the new institutional economics from other strands of development and growth theory. Lewis, to take one example among the classical development theorists, gave much importance to the discussion of institutions in his book *The Theory of Economic Growth*. Moreover, whatever the view that one may take on the economic determinants of growth and the interactions among them, if growth is a function of the risk-adjusted rates of return to factor accumulation and innovation, it is clear that institutional factors will be crucial in the qualifier "risk-adjusted" and therefore in the accumulation and innovation process. In other words, in its weak version, the "rule of law hypothesis" is consistent with all growth models (including neoclassical, Keynesian, endogenous growth and classical development models) to the extent that in the open economy versions of these models with international capital mobility, the accumulation function makes political risk an important factor determining the country risk premium.

There is, however, a strong version of the hypothesis that goes well beyond the argument that strengthening the protection of property rights is favorable to economic development. The hypothesis here, as implicitly or explicitly claimed in much of the recent literature, is that the institutions protecting property rights, together with liberal economic institutions, are the fundamental determinant of economic growth, a deeper and more fundamental determinant than policies, geographical characteristics, economic structure or other possible factors affecting the rates of physical and human capital accumulation. In fact, in its strongest version, institutions are the only fundamental determinant of economic development. Acemoglu and Robinson (2012, see in particular Chapters 1 and 2) argue along these lines that the fundamental determinants are not geography, culture, or incorrect policies followed by ignorant rulers but the nature, inclusive or extractive, of political and economic institutions.

In what follows, I discuss the empirical evidence showing positive developmental effects of protection of property rights, i.e. the evidence supporting the weak version of the hypothesis. I then turn to discuss the controversies on the evidence offered to support the stronger claim that the protection of property rights is a more fundamental determinant (together with economic freedom) than other factors.

The weak version: measurement and endogeneity problems

Although the weak version of the hypothesis is hardly controversial, this does not mean that it has been empirically validated in the recent literature. Indeed, the evidence offered in its favor is not without problems. Two such problems refer to the measurement of the rule of law, through subjective indicators as an index of protection against the risk of expropriation, and to the endogeneity problem resulting from the fact that the positive correlations between development and the rule of law that have been found could reflect the effects of economic on institutional development rather than vice versa.

Institutional indicators of property rights protection or enforcement of the rule of law vary in cross-country regression studies.[4] A first source of indicators, used initially by Knack and Keefer (1995), Hall and Jones (1999), and AJR (2001), refers to survey indicators for institutional quality from the

---

[4] For a detailed discussion of institutional indicators used in cross-country studies, see Glaeser et al. (2004).

International Country Risk Guide (ICRG), constructed by Political Risk Services, a firm that specializes in providing assessments of risk to international investors and collected over the 1980s and 1990s. A second set, used by Rodrik, Subramanian, and Trebbi (2004), is an aggregated index of mostly survey assessments of government effectiveness collected by the World Bank (see for a recent version of methodology and data, Kauffman, 2010). A third set, coming from the Polity IV data set collected by political scientists (Jaggers and Marshall, 2000), aims directly to measure the limits of executive power. Perhaps the most widely used is the ICRG which rates a large number of countries according to several categories (such as government repudiation of contracts, protection against risk of expropriation, or corruption) from which a number of variants of rule of law indexes can be constructed. For example, Knack and Keefer (1995), the first paper to use the ICRG, used an index which is an average of five of the 24 categories for the years 1986–95. Subsequently, Barro (1997), Hall and Jones (1999), AJR (2001), McArthur and Sachs (2001), to mention only some of the most influential papers, have used variants of the rule of law index. All these papers claim to have found positive and significant effects of property rights protection on economic growth or the level of development.

A first problem with the use of these indicators is that they do not reflect the institutions that constrain government to preserve and protect property rights. Glaeser et al (2004) make three important points in this respect. First, they show how the subjective indexes used as indicators of institutions are in fact reflecting outcomes (policy choices by political leaders rather the constraints on them). This is why authoritarian regimes (such as Singapore or the USSR) whose leaders choose to respect property rights get scores that are as high as countries in which political constraints effectively force leaders to chose good policies. Second, the indicators are highly volatile rather than reflecting a slowly changing set of rules.[5] This contrasts with the often-quoted definition of institutions by North (1981) that emphasizes the constraints on behavior (including government behavior), rather than policy choices, and stresses the permanence of these rules and norms.[6] Third, those indicators are very weakly related with the few available measures of constitutional constraints on

---

[5] As they argue in relation to expropriation risk: "...consistent with the intellectual victory of the Washington Consensus, the data show that the average score on expropriation risk in the sample rises from 5 in 1982 to 9 (with the median of 9.5) in 1997. Whatever expropriation risk measures, it is obviously not permanent rules, procedures, or norms supplying checks and balances on the sovereign" (Glaeser et al, 2004, p. 276).

[6] In North (1981) definition, institutions are "a set of rules, compliance procedures, and moral and ethical behavioral norms designed to constrain the behavior of individuals in the interests of maximizing the wealth or utility of principals" (pp. 201–2).

government, reflecting instead subjective assessments that are themselves influenced by a country's economic performance.[7]

A second problem refers to the endogeneity of institutions. Are high development levels the result of the effects of "good institutions" on development as stressed by Adam Smith (1776) and the contemporary new institutionalism (North and Thomas, 1973; North, 1981, 1990)?[8] Or do rich countries have "good institutions" due to the dependence of institutional development on economic progress? While the basic hypothesis of the recent literature is that causality goes primarily from institutional quality to development, other social scientists have asserted that institutions and institutional quality are themselves affected by the level of economic development. For example, institutional change and the role of institutions in development was a central theme in Marx who saw, however, the direction of causality between institutions and development in a somewhat different form than Adam Smith. For Marx, the advance of productive forces was the engine of change in the social relations of production and society's superstructure, including in this superstructure all types of institutions. In the political science literature, the Lipset hypothesis makes a similar argument with respect to political institutions (see Lipset, 1960; and Alvarez et al., 2000). There are several reasons for this direction of causality. A greater wealth and stock of human capital can generate demands for institutions of higher quality such as a demand for political institutions with greater transparency and accountability (as in the Lipset hypothesis). Greater wealth can make better institutions affordable as it is costly to establish and administer institutions and the better their quality the more costly they are. Moreover, as noted by Chang (2011), economic development generates new agents of change that demand institutional changes; in the 18th century, the emerging industrial capitalists supported the development of the banking system against the opposition of landowners and, at the end of 19th and early 20th centuries, the growing power of the working class led to the emergence of the welfare state and the adoption of labor protection laws against the opposition of capitalists.

While the influence of development on institutions may have been neglected in the recent literature, as argued by Chang (2011), the most influential studies recognize that causality between institutions and economic development runs in both directions and thus that institutional quality is itself an endogenous variable.[9] The recognition of this endogeneity is precisely what

---

[7] In fact, as shown by Glaeser et al. (2004, p. 279), two of the few available measures of constitutional constraints (measures of judicial independence and constitutional review) are not correlated with income per capita.

[8] Before Smith, Montesquieu (1748) also stressed the importance of constraints on government.

[9] For example, Hall and Jones (1999, p. 99) state: "we recognize explicitly that social infrastructure is an endogenous variable. Economies are not exogenously endowed with the

motivates the adoption of an instrumental variables approach in these studies. This procedure involves using as instrument of recent institutions some indicator of the exogenous component of institutions that allows the researcher to control for the endogeneity of current institutions with respect to current income per capita. The instruments that have been used include mortality rates of Europeans in the colonies (AJR, 2001), distance from the equator (an indicator of European influence according to Hall and Jones, 1999), or the percentage of the population that speaks a European language as its primary language. All this, however, does not mean that the ways in which the empirical literature has approached the problem of endogeneity of institutions are satisfactory (for further discussion, see Glaeser et al., 2004; Przeworski, 2004; Durlauf, Johnson, and Temple, 2005; Asoni, 2008). The construction of appropriate instruments has also been questioned. Indeed, recently Albouy (2012) has raised strong doubts on the validity of AJR (2001) findings. Albouy makes two main points. First, more than half of the countries in the AJR sample were assigned mortality rates relying on conjectures, based on weak and sometimes inaccurate foundations, as to which countries have similar disease environments. Second, when the conjectured mortality rates are dropped from the sample, the relationship between expropriation risk and mortality rates weakens substantially, making the estimates of the effect of expropriation risk on income per capita unreliable.

The strong version: how fundamental are institutions?

The strong version of the rule of law hypothesis, i.e. the proposition that not only institutions matter for development but that they are the fundamental cause of long-run economic performance, is a prominent view in the controversies on the deep determinants of economic growth and development levels, i.e., on whether openness, geography, institutions, or other fundamental factors has primacy over the others. We have already alluded to the role of openness as a deep determinant in Chapter 14 and reviewed the role of particular factor endowments in Chapter 15. Chapter 18 will look at the geography versus institutions debate. Here I focus on the most influential papers that assign the primary role to institutions and comment on what may be

---

institutions and incentives that make up their economic environments, but rather social infrastructure is determined endogenously, perhaps depending itself on the level of output per worker in an economy. . . . For example, poor countries may have limited ability to collect taxes and may therefore be forced to interfere with international trade. Alternatively, one might be concerned that the experts at Political Risk Services who constructed the components of the GADP index [government antidiversion policies index] were swayed in part by knowledge of income levels."

called the policies versus institutions controversy (involving AJR and Glaeser et al., among others).

The most influential proponents of the primacy of institutions are Acemoglu, Johnson and Robinson (see AJR, 2001, 2002, as well as Acemoglu and Robinson, 2012). AJR (2001) present a theory of institutional differences among countries colonized by Europeans and their role in economic development that, together with the empirical evidence provided, led them to conclude that institutions have the fundamental role in the explanation of the enormous gaps in economic development that we observe today. The theory presented by AJR is based on the following premises. First, AJR argue that different types of colonization created different types of institutions. At one extreme, Europeans created "extractive states or institutions". These institutions did not provide much protection to private property and did not create safeguards against governmental expropriation. Their main purpose was to transfer a maximum of resources from the colony to the colonizer. Examples of this type of colonization were the Belgian colonization of the Congo or that of Burundi where the Belgians ruled indirectly through Tutsi chiefs and exploited the colony through forced labor on coffee and other cash crop plantations and compulsory food crop quotas (Easterly and Levine, 2003). Another example is the French colonization of Dahomey where it has been estimated that 50 percent of its GDP was extracted by France between 1905 and 1914 (Manning, 1982, cited by AJR, 2001). Other examples refer to the earlier colonization of Latin America (in particular of Mexico, Peru, Bolivia and Brazil) by the Spaniards and Portuguese. Coatsworth (1978), for example, has emphasized the role of Spanish colonial institutions in the backwardness and economic stagnation (compared to the United States) of Mexico during the 18th and 19th centuries. At the other end of the spectrum, Europeans emigrated and established in a number of "settler colonies", creating what historian Alfred Crosby (1986) called "Neo-Europes" and what economic historian Angus Maddison refers to as the Western offshoots (Australia, New Zealand, Canada, and the United States). The colonizers in this case replicated European institutions, with a strong emphasis on the protection of private property and safeguards against government power.

The second premise is that the type of colonization was affected by the viability of settling in the colonies. In areas that were not hospitable to European settlers because the health environment was not favorable, there were no conditions for the creation of Neo-Europes and the most likely result was the creation of an extractive state.[10] By contrast, areas that were hospitable to European settlers in the 17th, 18th, or 19th centuries ended up with

---

[10] AJR note that the Pilgrims decided to settle in the North American colonies instead of Guyana partially because of the high mortality rates in Guyana.

good institutions. The third premise is that colonial institutions persisted even after independence. Post-independence governments tended to resemble pre-independence regimes. Settler colonies tended to produce post-colonial governments that were more democratic and more devoted to defending private property rights than extractive colonies. Extractive colonies had already institutions designed to effectively extract resources, and the post-colonial elite frequently exploited the pre-existing extractive institutions rather than incur the costs of introducing better institutions.[11]

It is worth noting that the AJR thesis emphasizes the role of local conditions in the colony as they affected the viability of settling in the colony and in this way affected the nature of the institutions established. In this respect, their thesis resembles that of Engerman and Sokoloff (2002), discussed in Chapter 16, which also emphasize the role of institutions in development linking institutions to local factor endowments and inequality. These views are quite different from arguments that focus on the identity of the colonizer in order to explain the institutions that were created in the colonies. La Porta et al. (1998), for example, emphasize the importance of colonial origin (the identity of the colonizer) and the legal origin of contemporary institutions, arguing that common law countries and former British colonies have better property rights and more developed financial markets (see the recent survey by La Porta et al, 2007). Similarly, Landes (1998) and North et al. (2000) argue that former British colonies prospered relatively to former French, Spanish and Portuguese colonies due to the better economic and political institutions and the better culture that they inherited from Britain.[12]

AJR present econometric evidence in favor of the argument that institutional differences have a very important impact on economic development. They use an indicator of protection against expropriation risk, from the ICGR already mentioned, as a measure of institutional quality. Recognizing that this variable is almost surely endogenous since a country's income level influences its capacity to protect property rights, they use as an instrument (as the exogenous component of institutions caused by early colonial experience) the mortality rates of Europeans in the colonies. In this way, AJR estimate large effects of institutions on income per capita. For example, their estimates imply that an improvement of Nigeria's institutions to the level of Chile's would lead, in the long run, to multiply by 7 the income per capita of Nigeria.

---

[11] Coatsworth (1978) provides an insightful analysis of the persistence of New Spain institutions in post-independence Mexico as a major obstacle to economic development in this country during the 19th century.

[12] Earlier, Hayek (1960) had argued that British common law tradition is superior to French civil law, which was developed during the Napoleonic era in order to restrict the interference of judges with state policies (see also Lipset, 1994).

At the same time, AJR discard other interpretations of colonial experience. When they add dummies for British and French colonies, this has very little effect on the results. This and other related results lead them to conclude that the identity of the colonizer is not an important determinant of the patterns of colonization and the subsequent institutional development. They also control for legal origin, adding a dummy for French legal origin, but this has no impact on the estimates of the effects of institutions on income per capita.

Glaeser et al (2004) offer a view of economic and political development that has some features in common with the neo-institutionalist approach of AJR, such as the need for secure property rights to support investment in physical and human capital. They differ, however, from the institutionalist view that sees policies supporting physical and human capital accumulation as a result of institutional constraints on government, in that they view policies, especially in many poor countries, as the result of policy choices by often unconstrained political leaders. These authors criticize AJR arguing that their instrument, settlers' mortality, may have indeed been important in determining settlement patterns but this does not show that what is important is the institutions that the settlers imported rather than the human capital brought with them. More specifically, they argue that the results of AJR do not establish a role for institutions:

> The Europeans who settled in the New World may have brought with them not so much their institutions, but themselves, that is, their human capital. This theoretical ambiguity is consistent with the empirical evidence as well. We show that the instruments used in the literature for institutions are even more highly correlated with human capital both today and in 1900, and that, in instrumental variable specifications predicting economic growth, human capital performs better than institutions. At the purely econometric level, this evidence suggests that predictors of settlement patterns are not valid instruments for institutions. (Glaeser et al, 2004, p. 274)

They conclude that it might be more fruitful to look for policies favoring human and physical capital accumulation than for the "deep" factors explaining economic development.

In his criticism of the new institutionalism, Przeworski (2004) argues that the hypothesis of AJR (just as Engerman and Sokoloff, 2002) does not explain the enormous variation in political institutions and development trajectories that we find among former colonies with "extractive institutions". These different trajectories have led to substantial income gaps between, say, Mexico and Nicaragua and Chile and Bolivia (a ratio of 4.0 to 1 and 3.4 to 1 respectively in incomes per capita in 2011). Przeworski mentions that between 1831 and 1924 all Chilean presidents were elected for fixed periods and all but one completed their periods or died being presidents and were succeeded by a constitutionally designated successor. In Bolivia, no president completed its period during the first 125 years of independent life (and their "average life" as presidents was less than a year). We can add to this comparison the case of Mexico in which the presidency changed hands 75 times during the first 55 years of independent life from 1821 to the establishment of the dictatorship of Porfirio Díaz in 1876.

In the controversies on the role of institutions in development, some neo-institutionalists appear to have recently radicalized their position. What sets apart some neo-institutionalists such as Acemoglu and Robinson in their recent 2012 book is that in their view, among the so called deep determinants of economic development, only institutions matter while at the same time downplaying the interactions and feedback effects going from development levels to institutions. This "institutions only" view ignores the role of other important determinants, not only of such factors as geographical and cultural characteristics, but also of policies and the ideas (or economic and political ideologies) that shape these policies. To be sure, policies matter in the institutionalist view but they have no independent importance from the institutions that constrain them. In fact, policies depend on many factors, and not only on the institutional constraints facing political leaders. This seems clear, as already discussed, from the behavior of institutional indicators used in cross-country studies. Policies are, in particular, shaped by the perceptions of the elites. They are influenced by ideas of which political leaders are often slaves, as Keynes once put it. And their adoption depends also on the power that the elites have in imposing their will.

2. The Invisible Hand Hypothesis: Theoretical Aspects

The second hypothesis can be rephrased as saying that economic liberalization is always and everywhere good for growth. Before looking at the evidence, it is worth mentioning that there are at least three interrelated problems with this hypothesis.

Underdevelopment, institutions, and coordination failures

A first problem is that the invisible hand hypothesis lacks solid theoretical foundations. We know from economic theory, in particular from the contributions to the theory of general competitive equilibrium and welfare economics, that the necessary conditions for the invisible hand, i.e., free markets, to generate a unique general equilibrium that is a Pareto optimum are extremely restrictive. This raises then the question of what exactly should we understand by good institutions (favorable to growth). If, as argued by Hall and Jones (1999), these are those that reduce the gap between private and social returns to investment and productive activities then, as shown by classical

371

development theory, the best institutions are not necessarily market-oriented institutions or policies but those that involve the state in overcoming coordination failures, resulting from the existence of multiple equilibria, and promote activities with positive externalities. When poverty traps exist as a result of those failures and externalities, the existence or not of state institutions with the purpose of intervening in economic activity may be fundamental to explain why some countries develop and others don't. Abramovitz (1986)'s inclusion of industrial and financial institutions in his notion of the social capability necessary to exploit Gershenkron's advantage of backwardness and promote a process of convergence to high income levels is an example of those state institutions and their role in economic development. Przeworski (2004, p. 15) emphasizes the same point in relation to classical development theory when he says that in addition to the New Testament of North and Thomas (1973), "we also have the Old Testament, drafted by Rosenstein-Rodan (1943)...which says that institutions that matter are those that coordinate development". Bardhan (2004) makes a similar point when he states that the new institutionalism "got its institutions wrong". When market failures prevent the invisible hand from achieving a Pareto optimum, market institutions that maximize economic freedom will not be the best possible institutions for economic welfare and may be clearly insufficient for economic development. All this is not heresy from heterodox economists; it is well known by neoclassical economists in the tradition of market failures (see Chang, 2011, for further discussion).

One way of illustrating the contrast between classical development theory and the new institutionalism is by comparing the explanations of the convergence of the South of the United States that can be derived from each of the two perspectives. Acemoglu and Robinson (2012, pp. 351–52) attribute the contrast between the prosperous North and the backward South of the United States in the 19th century to the presence of extractive institutions (slavery) in the South. They note the persistence of racial segregation in the South after the abolition of slavery, an example of the perseverance of extractive institutions, and conclude that it was only in the 1950s and 1960s with the civil rights movements and the removal of segregation that the South would be able to converge institutionally and economically with the rest of the United States (Acemoglu and Robinson, 2012, p. 357). There is no doubt that the underdevelopment of the United States South in the 19th century was due, in part, to the presence of "extractive institutions" (slavery) and that the persistence of traditionalist institutions contributed to the "low level equilibrium" in which the South continued to be trapped after the abolition of slavery. As noted by William Nichols in his 1959 Presidential Address of the Southern Economics Association: "In some degree, the South has been traditional because it was poor. At the same time, it has also remained poor in part because it was traditional."[13] However, the economic convergence of the South towards the higher income levels of the rest of the United States started not in the 1950s and 1960s with the abolition of segregation. The take off of the South took place much earlier with the massive infrastructure investments of the New Deal in the 1930s which had precisely the objective of lifting the South out of a poverty trap in which the lack of infrastructure had a major role by preventing the expansion of manufacturing activities (see on the subject, Bateman, Ros, and Taylor, 2009). It was then and not earlier (with the abolition of slavery) or later (with the civil rights movement) that, despite racial segregation, the South escaped from the kind of "low level equilibrium", stressed by classical development theory, in which it had remained after the abolition of slavery in the 1860s.[14] The civil rights movement was probably much more a consequence of the economic convergence that had been taking place over the previous three decades than vice versa.

Economic liberalization, allocative efficiency, and growth

A second problem, evident for those familiar with the theorem of the second best, is that even when the external effects and market failures that prevent a decentralized economy from achieving a Pareto optimum are absent, more economic liberalization does not bring necessarily greater economic efficiency in resource allocation. The theorem of the second best of Lipsey and Lancaster states precisely that we cannot say a priori if a greater degree of liberalization of a particular market brings with it a greater efficiency in the allocation of resources unless all other markets are already completely liberalized.

It is ironic that the theorem of the second best is behind the reasoning given by orthodox economists to explain why market oriented reform in developing countries over the past few decades did not always bring the expected benefits. A remarkable example of this is when we are told that if the benefits of trade liberalization could not be fully reaped, this must be due to an excessively rigid labor market or the lack of competition in the non-tradable goods sectors.

A third problem, often overlooked in the literature on institutions and development, is that even if a more liberalized economy is more efficient in allocating resources, one cannot argue that this economy will necessarily grow at a faster rate. Greater efficiency in resource allocation does not bring

[13] Cited in Bateman, Ros, and Taylor (2009).

[14] Similarly, apartheid created a dual economy and society in South Africa, but contrary to the assertion of Acemoglu and Robinson (2012, p. 265), its abolition did not eliminate economic dualism, at least in the sense of Arthur Lewis, cited by the authors. For this, a process of capital accumulation over a long period of time will be necessary. In other words, dualism is not the product necessarily of extractive institutions (apartheid in South Africa) but of an imbalance in factor proportions (capital and labor) as discussed in Chapter 6.

necessarily faster growth. What is good for efficiency in the allocation of resources and what is good for economic growth may not coincide. What is crucial for growth is the rate of return to factor accumulation and to productivity improvements and greater allocative efficiency need not bring about such higher returns.

Two examples can help illustrate the point. The infant industry argument is about how restrictions to foreign trade, that imply static efficiency losses, can be favorable to long-term growth by promoting the development of new industries in which the economy will have in the future a comparative advantage. As discussed in Chapter 9, protection of an infant industry is favorable to growth precisely because it raises the rate of return to capital accumulation in activities where productivity grows endogenously with output and investment. Under free trade, the rate of return in these industries would be so low that these activities would not develop. Schumpeter's theory of technological innovation provides another illustration of how a high degree of competition (which is favorable to efficiency in resource allocation) can inhibit growth by slowing down technical progress. As discussed in Chapter 5, the reason here is that free competition can lower the rate of return to technological improvements. Under perfect competition, Schumpeter argued, technical progress would be absent since firms would lack the incentives for technological innovation (the appropriation of temporary monopolistic rents accruing to an innovator) and the means required to finance research and development expenditures.

3. Some Common Problems in Growth Empirics

Whether the studies test the first or the second hypothesis or both, the supporting evidence takes the form of cross-country regressions in which growth rates or levels of per capita income are regressed on institutional and policy variables together with other possible determinants of income gaps or growth rates. When the growth rate of GDP per capita is the dependent variable, the standard empirical model is generally a linear regression of growth on the initial level of GDP per capita (to investigate the hypothesis of conditional convergence) and institutional, policy and economic structure indicators. The proximate determinants of growth (in particular investment in physical and human capital) may or may not be included depending on whether the hypothesis is that the policy and institutional variables affect the efficiency with which factors of production are used or both the efficiency and the rates of factor accumulation. These regressions are often referred to as Barro regressions due to the influence of Barro's 1991 article in the *Quarterly Journal of Economics*. Their analytical foundation was provided by Mankiw,

Romer, and Weil (MRW, 1992) in a model that extends Solow's neoclassical growth model to incorporate human capital in the production function. As suggested by MRW in their original model, the term in the production function representing total factor productivity could be seen as reflecting not only the level of technology strictly speaking but also the natural resource endowment, climate, institutions, and other potential determinants of the level of technical efficiency.

The empirical evidence based on cross-country regressions has several problems. As shown by Rodriguez (2010), despite the fact that the regression equations used in the literature have an analytical foundation (the augmented neoclassical growth model), they require a set of key assumptions, the most important of which is that the logarithm of the production function is linear in the institutional, policy and structural variables. This linear specification lacks theoretical foundations: there is no reason to expect that variables as diverse as institutions, economic policies and structural characteristics have linear and separable effects on the logarithm of the production function (or, one may add, on the rates of factor accumulation in the specifications that do not include these rates among the independent variables). On the contrary, the theorem of the second best would lead us to expect that a change in a policy or institutional variable will have different effects (in size and sign) on efficiency or growth depending on its initial value and the values of other variables.

Non-linearities

Common sense and empirical observation, besides theoretical considerations, also suggest that policies and institutions have non-linear and non-separable effects. Consider, first, non-linearities. Public expenditure as a proportion of GDP is often included in cross-country growth regressions as an indicator of the economic size of government with an expected negative sign (as a bigger government implies higher taxation).[15] While it seems reasonable to expect that a reduction in public spending from, say, 80 percent to 70 percent will have a positive effect on growth, is it equally reasonable to suppose that a reduction from 10 percent to zero will have the same effect in size and sign on growth when, in such case, the economy is being deprived from the supply of the most basic public goods? Yet this is the expectation implicit in a linear specification. And if one agrees that the optimal level of public spending for

---

[15] Studies claiming to show that a large government sector negatively affects economic growth include Barro (1991), Engen and Skinner (1992), Hansson and Henrekson (1994), Gwartney, Holcombe, and Lawson (1998), and Fölster and Henrekson (2001). Some papers claim to have found a positive effect of government size on economic growth (see Ram, 1986, and Kormendi and Meguire, 1986).

growth is not zero one is accepting that the effect of public spending is non-linear and changes sign. This is in fact recognized in theoretical models. Barro (1990), for example, pointed out that the economic size of government has different and opposite effects on growth in the context of a model of endogenous growth. A larger government size requires higher taxation which reduces the growth rate through disincentive effects. At the same time, an increase in government spending raises the marginal productivity of capital which increases the growth rate. He argues that the positive effect on the marginal product of capital dominates when the government is small, and the negative effect through higher taxation dominates when the government is large. As a result, the effect of increased government spending on economic growth should be non-linear and some optimal size of government should exist.[16]

Another example of non-linearities refers to the effects of inflation on economic growth (see Chapter 13). While an increase in the rate of inflation from medium to high levels is likely to have a negative effect on growth as long-term financial contracts, essential for investment, tend to disappear and speculation becomes more profitable than productive activities, it is also likely that, at low levels of inflation, a further reduction of inflation may have no effects (or may even have negative effects) on growth. As Akerlof et al. (1996) have argued, in the presence of downward nominal rigidities in wages and prices the economic adjustment of relative prices to shocks can become sluggish under zero inflation. A moderate level of inflation provides for some real wage flexibility, which is beneficial for macroeconomic adjustments. It is worth observing that Barro (1995) finds that in samples that include countries with inflation rates of 20 percent or less the inverse relationship between inflation and growth found in other studies breaks down. Other influential papers reaching similar conclusions include Bruno (1995), Bruno and Easterly (1998), Ghosh and Phillips (1998), Khan and Senhadji (2001), and Burdekin et al. (2004).[17] All this suggests that the inflation–growth relationship is simply non linear.

The same applies to trade policy. As argued in Chapter 14, there is no compelling reason to expect that in all circumstances the level of tariffs which is optimal for economic growth is zero and if this is so then the effects of tariff levels on growth will be non linear and change sign. Consider also the effects of labor market institutions. In the context of the economic

---

[16] This common sense hypothesis is sometimes referred to as the Armey curve (see Armey, 1995). To be fair, not all cross-country growth regressions have a linear specification in the proxy for government size. Some authors also pay attention to the composition of government spending. Yavas (1998) and Heitger (2001), for example, view increases in government size resulting from increased government consumption as having an adverse effect on growth, while increases in size that arise from government investment should have positive effects on growth.

[17] For a review of the literature, see Pollin and Zhu (2006).

performance of the labor market and its adjustment to shocks, some authors argue, and have provided evidence, that both a high and a low level of centralization of wage bargaining lead to a better performance of the labor market than an intermediate level (Calmfors and Driffill, 1988). Or think about the effects of protection of intellectual property rights. As argued by Chang (2011) this is an example of an institution that in a certain dose promotes growth (as some protection of intellectual property may be absolutely necessary for growth) but can hurt growth in greater doses.

In fact, these changes in sign seem so generalized that it is hard to think about variables whose effects are strictly linear and without ambiguity positive or negative along the whole scale of values that they can assume. Thus, I don't think it essential to realize a battery of parametric and semi-parametric tests, as done by Rodriguez (2010), to reach the conclusion that the data reject not only the hypothesis of linearity but also support the view that non-linearities often lead to changes of sign in the effects of institutional and policy variables. Needless to say, to derive implications from the estimates of linear equations when the effects of independent variables are non-linear is bound to generate erroneous conclusions.

Non-separability

Almost two decades ago, Lin and Nugent (1995) concluded their survey of the literature on institutions and development saying that while there seems to be a broad consensus in the literature that secure property rights are crucial for economic growth, the effects of stronger protection of property rights are also conditional on complementary institutions or factors not always present. This is a good example of non-separability of institutional and policy variables.

The opposite assumption of separability is highly questionable, theoretically and empirically, as it excludes the existence of interactions among policies, institutions and economic structures. This goes against all that early development economics produced in terms of theory. Kenny and Williams (2011) discuss the complex interactions among policies, institutions and structure that were present in the views of early development economics and exemplify this with Gunnar Myrdal's notion of circular and cumulative causation: "More than 40 years ago, Gunnar Myrdal. . . . argued that economists concerned with economic growth need to accept not just that it may have a great number of causes, but also that these do not work in any 'linear' manner. He suggested that problems like economic growth should be examined using the concept of "circular causation" where a change in one factor would affect a number of other factors, and these changes would in turn feedback on the first factor (Myrdal, 1957, p. 16). The essence of a problem such as economic growth is that'it concerns a complex of interlocking, circular, and cumulative changes'" (Kenny and Williams, 2001, p. 14).

The assumption of separability also goes against what economic history has produced in terms of case studies and, to take an example from recent economic history, the observation of several decades of reforms in the world. In an evaluation of the results of a decade of economic reforms published by the World Bank, the role of interactions among policies, institutions and economic structure is not only recognized but plays a central role. In the words of this report:

> To sustain growth requires key functions to be fulfilled, but there is no unique combination of policies and institutions for fulfilling them . . . different polices can yield the same result, and the same policy can yield different results, depending on country institutional contexts and underlying growth strategies . . . Countries with remarkably different policy and institutional frameworks – Bangladesh, Botswana, Chile, China, Egypt, India, Lao PDR, Mauritius, Sri Lanka, Tunisia and Vietnam – have all sustained growth in GDP per capita incomes above the U.S. long-term growth rate of close to 2 percent a year. (World Bank, 2005, p. 12)

It is worthwhile noting the limitations of a commonly used approach that attempts to take into account non-linearities and non-separability by including quadratic terms and multiplicative interactions.[18] Such an approach implies accepting that growth is linear in the other variables that are included in the regression and does not take into account that the non linear effects of the variable of interest may be much more complex than what can be captured by a quadratic term or a multiplicative interaction.

Sample heterogeneity

Another problem refers to sample heterogeneity. The econometric studies assume that the relationships between growth and institutional variables (or policy variables) are the same for all countries in the sample. However, as noted by Chang (2011), if these relationships differ across countries this means, in statistical terms, that the "condition of homogeneity" is violated making parameters unstable and the results sensitive to particular samples. The policy implication is the following. If different countries have each of them a different model of growth determinants, even if these models have the same functional form, this implies that policy reforms that work in one country will not work in another country.

---

[18] One among many other examples is the quadratic term for political regime that Barro (1996) uses and which leads him to conclude that more democracy is good for growth at low levels of political freedom but starts to be adverse to growth after a moderate level of political freedom.

This is precisely the lesson that can be derived from the evidence produced by the recent literature on growth empirics. In their review of this literature, Kenny and Williams (2001) state: " ... if the evidence shows anything at all, it is that markedly different policies, and markedly different policy mixes, may be appropriate for different countries at different times" (p. 1). And later, they add: " ... the universal failure to produce robust, causally secure relations predicted by models might suggest a broader problem than statistical methodological weaknesses. The evidence appears to suggest that country growth experiences have been extremely heterogeneous, and heterogeneous in a way that is difficult to explain using any one model of economic growth" (p. 12). The problem of sample heterogeneity, together with other flaws in econometric methodology, are so serious that several authors have opted for rejecting the cross section regressions as a poor way to approach the question of economic growth and consider that detailed country case studies are far more informative and decisive as empirical evidence (see, for example, Srinivasan and Bhagwati, 1999).[19]

4. Institutional and Policy Convergence with Growth Divergence in Latin America

Institutional failures have often been blamed for the failure of policy reforms in many developing countries over the last 30 years. Have economic reforms failed to deliver fast growth because of inadequate institutions? Or have they failed for other reasons, independent of the institutional framework? Latin America's reforms and growth performance over the past 30 years constitute a natural experiment to explore the answers to these questions.

Economic and political reforms since the debt crisis

In the first decades of the postwar period, Latin America embraced a paradigm that placed a developmental state at the center of the strategy, with industrialization, which was regarded at the time as critical to increase living standards, as the major objective. Over the past 30–35 years Latin America has experienced a major overhaul in economic policies and institutions as well as in political institutions. As a result, a "great transformation" has taken place, if we may appropriate Karl Polanyi's expression for events of a different

---

[19] It is worth noting that parameter heterogeneity is not the same as non-linearity. The former assumes that the model of growth determinants is different for each country (even if the functional form is the same). The latter assumes that the model is the same for all the different countries but the effects of the variables determining growth are non linear. In practice, both problems may be very relevant and it is difficult to distinguish between the two.

scale. The major policy changes include far-reaching programs of economic reforms in different areas that gave a larger role to the private sector in the allocation of resources and greater scope to market forces and international competition, all this with the goal of entering a phase of strong export-led economic expansion. It is worth recalling what has happened.

During and after the adjustment process to the debt crisis of 1982, monetary and fiscal policies were radically transformed. In 1980, in a group of 20 Latin American countries,[20] none had an independent Central Bank. By 2012, a majority of countries (11) had an independent Central Bank (see Ros, 2012). In addition, in the largest countries (Brazil, Mexico, Chile, Colombia, and Peru) the central bank operated under an inflation-targeting regime with a floating exchange rate and price stability as its sole mandate.[21] Fiscal policy went through a similar overhaul. In 1980 no country had a balanced budget rule. By 2012, 8 countries had a balanced budget law,[22] generally a strict commitment to balance the budget every year with the exception of Chile which had a structural budget rule which allowed for fiscal deficits during recessions provided that these were compensated by budget surpluses in boom periods.

Regarding structural reforms in other areas, the early and prominent components of the reform agenda were trade liberalization and deeper integration into the world economy based on comparative advantages, as well as a broad opening to foreign direct investment (see Lora, 2001). Tariffs were sharply reduced and the tariff structure radically simplified as non-tariff barriers were largely eliminated. The median average tariff which in 1985 was 42 percent fell to 5 percent in 2010 and the highest average tariff went down from 88 percent to 11 percent (see Ros, 2012). These changes were so far-reaching that, as argued in Ocampo and Ros (2011), the objective of setting low tariffs was achieved to a much greater extent than in the classical period of primary export-led growth in the late 19th and early 20th centuries.

A wave of free trade agreements or custom unions took place with NAFTA (1994) in the North and MERCOSUR (1991) in the South being the most

---

[20] This group of 20 countries includes those Latin American countries for which information is available in the Penn World Table.

[21] Inflation targeting regimes now prevail in major Latin American countries. Chile and Colombia were the pioneers having adopted inflation targets since 1990 and 1991 respectively. Peru introduced a floating exchange rate regime in 1994 and in 2002 the central bank replaced quantitative targets for monetary aggregates with inflation targets using the interest rate as the main instrument of monetary policy. After the 1994–5 crisis, Mexico let the peso float and in 1999 moved to an inflation-targeting regime eventually adopting a target interest rate as policy instrument. Brazil also joined this group of countries in 1999 after the exchange rate crisis of the beginning of that year.

[22] These are Argentina, Brazil, Chile, Colombia, Ecuador, Mexico, Panama, and Peru. See on this subject and Central Bank independence, Jácome and Vázquez (2005), Kumar, Baldacci, and Schaechter (2009), and Ros (2012).

important initiatives. Moreover, under the leadership of Mexico and Chile, a wave of bilateral or multilateral free trade agreements was launched. All this contributed to a sharp increase in the weight of international trade in the economy. As discussed in Ros (2012), between 1985 and 2010 the share of exports and imports in GDP increased for the median country from 54.3 percent to 64.4 percent. Some spectacular increases were recorded by Argentina (from 11.5 percent to 45.1 percent), Mexico (from 28.4 percent to 58.8 percent), Costa Rica (from 56.9 percent to 100.8 percent), and Paraguay (from 47.4 percent to 105.9 percent). In turn, the relaxation of FDI regulations led to a sharp increase in the share of FDI in gross capital formation. The median country increased this share from 4 percent to 13 percent and for some countries this share rose to over 30 percent.

Trade and FDI liberalization were accompanied, in addition, by the elimination of exchange controls and domestic financial liberalization. The latter included the liberalization of interest rates, the elimination of most forms of directed credit, and the reduction and simplification of reserve requirements on bank deposits. Although it was also accepted that financial liberalization required regulation to avoid the accumulation of excessive risks in the financial system, the full acceptance of the need for regulation only came after a fair number of domestic financial crises (in particular the Tequila crisis of 1994–5).

Another component in the agenda of structural reforms was the privatization of a large set of public enterprises together with the opening to private investment of public services and utilities sectors. A general deregulation of private economic activities was also part of the agenda. The privatization process was more gradual than in the case of trade liberalization and a number of countries kept public sector banks and a number of other firms, notably in oil and infrastructure services (water and sewage more than electricity and telecommunications).

There was, finally, an agenda of at least partial liberalization of labor markets, but here political factors limited the scope of the reform proposals (Murillo et al., 2011). Even then, as many as 13 countries in our group of 20 undertook changes in labor market regulations with the aim of making the labor market more flexible (see Lora y Pagés, 1996; Vega, 2005; and Ros, 2012).

Changes in political regimes went hand in hand with economic liberalization. Following Przeworski (2004) criteria to classify a political regime as authoritarian or democratic, in 1980 there were only 4 countries (Colombia, Costa Rica, Ecuador, and Venezuela) with democratic political regimes so that 85.1 percent of the population of the 20 Latin American countries lived under authoritarian regimes. In 2009, only one country (Cuba) continued to be authoritarian, representing 2 percent of the total population.

Table 17.1 Percentile rank for Rule of Law indicator

Country	1996	2009	Change
Chile	85	87	+ 2
Uruguay	65	70	+ 5
Costa Rica	68	65	− 3
Panama	49	51	+ 2
Brazil	40	50	+ 10
Colombia	20	41	+ 21
Dominican Republic	41	48	+ 9
Mexico	30	35	+ 5
Cuba	18	35	+ 17
Argentina	55	30	− 25
Peru	30	30	0
El Salvador	20	22	+ 2
Nicaragua	35	22	− 13
Honduras	20	20	0
Paraguay	21	19	− 2
Bolivia	47	13	− 34
Guatemala	12	13	+ 1
Ecuador	36	10	− 26
Haiti	5	5	0
Venezuela	20	2	− 18

Source: Worldwide Governance Indicators (WGI). See Appendix to Chapter 1.

Along with the changes in political regimes, perceptions about the rule of law in Latin America showed a steady improvement. The information available from Worldwide Governance Indicators indicates that the percentile rank of Latin American countries improved from 1996 to 2009, with only 6 exceptions (Argentina, Bolivia, Ecuador, Nicaragua, Paraguay, and Venezuela) plus a minor fall for highly ranked Costa Rica (see Table 17.1).

Growth performance in the recent period

The economic growth performance of Latin America since the 1980s is clearly weaker than that of the previous development phase. This is true even if we leave aside the "lost decade" of the 1980s. For the period 1990–2008, the average of Latin America's per capita GDP growth rate has been 1.8 percent per year, well below the growth rate of the period 1950–80 (2.7 percent) and less than the average growth rate of the world economy. The growth performance of GDP per worker is even worse: 0.7 percent per year for 1990–2008 vs. 2.7 percent in 1950–80. This means that most of the increase in GDP per capita since 1990 has been the result of the demographic bonus resulting from the slowdown of population growth (from 2.7 percent to 1.5 percent) in the face of a still relatively fast growth of the labor force (2.6 percent per year, a rate similar to the 2.8 percent of 1950–80) (see Ros, 2009).

Table 17.2 Growth performance 1990–2008

Relative to 1950–80		Above	Below
Relative to USA average 1990–2008 (1.8%)	Above	Dominican Rep. (2.9) Peru (2.9) Chile (2.3) Uruguay (2.2)	*Panama* (2.8) *El Salvador* (2.7) *Nicaragua* (2.1)
	Below		Argentina (1.7) *Honduras* (1.5) Costa Rica (1.1) Brazil (1.0) Colombia (1.0) Guatemala (0.8) Bolivia (0.6) Mexico (0.6) *Paraguay* (–0.1) Ecuador (–0.1) Venezuela (-0.2) *Haiti* (–1.1)

In parentheses, growth rates (1990–2008) of GDP per person employed. Countries in italics are those for which GDP per person employed is not available. GDP per capita growth is shown in these cases.
Source: World Development Indicators and Maddison (2007, 2009)

Only a few countries experienced a dynamic growth of productivity at rates above 2 percent per year since 1990. As shown in Table 17.2, only 4 out of 19 countries (Dominican Republic, Peru, Chile, and Uruguay), had a better growth performance than in the period 1950–80 while at the same time having an equal or faster growth than the United States for 1990–2008. Most countries recorded growth rates below that of the US and a poorer growth performance in 1990–2008 than in 1950–80. This poor overall productivity performance is not due to the absence of new dynamic and highly productive activities; it is rather the reflection of the rising share of low-productivity informal activities, as the high-productivity sectors were unable to absorb a larger share of the labor force (Ros, 2011).

It is worth noting that, when looking across countries, there is no apparent relationship between the degree and timing of market liberalization and growth performance. The countries in the northwest box with two of the best performances are Chile, an early reformer, and the Dominican Republic, a late reformer. In addition, these two countries have two very different macroeconomic frameworks: while Chile has an independent central bank and a structural balanced budget rule, the Dominican Republic has none of this. Interestingly, all of the fast growing economies under State-led industrialization, most of which have thoroughly liberalized their economies, have now underperformed in relation to the past and world trends, with the major exceptions of the Dominican Republic and Panama. As a result of these long-term trends, the position of Latin American countries in the income per worker world table has considerably deteriorated.

Causes of slow growth: Bad governments or good governments with bad policies?

The factors explaining why some Latin American countries benefited more than others from the policy and institutional changes are to a great extent idiosyncratic (see Ros, 2012). The most important point to make in the present context is that the growth slowdown took place in the midst of institutional changes that were very positive from the perspective of the new institutional economics, including, as already emphasized, changes in the direction of so called inclusive political and economic institutions (democracy, the rule of law, and economic liberalization). The failure to accelerate growth cannot be blamed on bad governments from this perspective. Was it the result of wrong ideas and/or bad policies undertaken by good governments?

There were some common factors behind the generalized failure to accelerate growth in the region, compared to the historical performance in 1950–1980. One such factor was a wrong diagnosis of the debt crisis. The reform overhaul was rooted in many policymakers' view that the 1982 debt crisis was the unavoidable consequence of decades of trade protectionism and heavy state intervention that had marked—and in their view distorted—Latin America's development during the postwar period. Thus, this crisis, which started with the Mexican moratorium of August 1982, was taken to be a crisis of the whole post war strategy of State-led industrialization. In fact, this view was simply wrong. In countries with a large public external debt, such as Brazil and Mexico, the source of the problem was unsustainable macroeconomic policies, in particular fiscal policy, which led to a debt crisis (similar to today's fiscal crises in some European countries) when the creditor banks realized that Mexico, facing a decline in oil prices since the beginning of 1981 and higher interest rates as a result of the tight monetary policy in the United States (the Volker shock), would not be able to repay the debt. The same perceptions were then extended to the rest of Latin America. It is ironic that the diagnosis was most clearly contradicted by the problems of the Southern cone countries (Chile, Argentina and Uruguay) which had abandoned import substitution and embarked on a path of economic liberalization since the mid 1970s. These countries suffered a crisis in the early 1980s, not as a result of large fiscal deficits, but rather of increasing problems in their banking sectors and a rapid expansion of private external debt.

There was also an excessively optimistic view of the benefits of economic liberalization and the potential of structural reforms to trigger a resumption of growth. Trade liberalization, for example, was seen as a sufficient condition for export-led growth and was not accompanied by a real depreciation of the domestic currency as had been recommended by the advocates of export led

Table 17.3 Public investment and growth in Latin America

	1977–80	1982–85	1997–2000	GDP growth rate 1990–2008
Dominican Rep.	6.3	4.2	6.3	5.5
Chile	6.0	4.6	6.1	5.2
Costa Rica	8.4	6.8	5.1	4.4
Colombia	6.1	8.8	8.2	4.1
El Salvador	6.6	4.5	3.2	3.5
Mexico	9.3	7.5	2.5	3.5
Guatemala	5.9	3.9	3.0	3.4
Argentina	9.5	5.4	1.7	3.1
Ecuador	9.6	7.7	4.9	3.0
Brazil	7.8	5.9	3.4	2.6
Uruguay	6.6	5.1	3.8	2.2
Paraguay	6.7	5.8	7.8	1.9

Notes: Public investment refers to the corresponding period average as a percentage of GDP. GDP is in LCU at constant prices.
Sources: Everhart, S., and M. A. Sumlinski (2001) and Penn World Table 7.0.

growth such as Balassa and Bhagwati, as well as, in fact, Williamson's Washington Consensus Decalogue (where a competitive exchange rate was part of the 10 point program). Financial liberalization, as it was undertaken, proved a disaster leading eventually to the crisis of the liberalization experiments in the Southern cone in the early 1980s and the Mexican Tequila crisis in 1994–1995. The latter was due to the fact that the lessons from the Southern cone financial crisis of the early 1980s (that were analyzed by Frenkel, 1983, and Diaz-Alejandro, 1985a) were simply not learnt.

Another policy failure refers to public investment policy. Public investment rates in the 1980s, and along with it overall investment rates, fell in virtually all Latin American countries as a result of the fiscal adjustments that followed the debt crisis of 1982. This is the case in all the countries shown in Table 17.3 with the exception of Colombia which is precisely the country that, because it had moderate levels of external debt, suffered less from the debt crisis.[23] In some countries the lower levels of public investment persisted after the recovery of the 1990s or even continued to fall during subsequent efforts at fiscal adjustment and inflation stabilization. In other countries, very few, public investment recovered. It is striking that three of the four countries that grew fastest after 1990 (Dominican Republic, Chile, and Colombia) are precisely those in which public investment rates at the end of the 1990s were equal or higher than before the crisis. By contrast, countries where the growth slowdown was most severe (Brazil and Mexico which had grown at the highest rates from 1950

---

[23] The countries in Table 17.3 are those for which data on public investment are available over a long period of time. Data after 2000 is not available on a comparable basis.

to 1980) were those where public investment rates suffered a veritable collapse. This is clearly bad policy not a manifestation of bad institutions.

In sum, the failure of the economic policy changes of the last 3 decades in producing an acceleration of economic growth in Latin America (or even a resumption of growth at the historical rates in the pre-crisis period) is not the result of a lack of changes in economic and political institutions. These institutions have recorded far-reaching transformations as we have seen in this last section. The source of the problem has not been "bad governments" but the policies themselves, conditioned by ideas, ideologies and political constraints, undertaken by "good governments".

18

Geography, Colonialism, and Underdevelopment

The role in economic development of geographical, climatic, and ecological differences among countries has been suggested in several versions. An old one, which goes back to Machiavelli (1519) and Montesquieu (1748), is that climate has a direct effect on income through its influence on effort. In the *Wealth of Nations*, Adam Smith gave inland Africa and the interior of Asia as examples of geographically disadvantaged regions where a lack of natural access to markets resulted in slow growth.[1] Both Marshall (1910) and Toynbee (1934, vol. 1) emphasized the importance of climate in affecting work effort and productivity. Myrdal (1968), a pioneer of development economics, emphasized the effects of geography on agricultural productivity and the health of workers. Historians such as McNeill (1963) and Braudel (1972), and more recently Crosby (1986), have put Europe's geography and climate at the center of their explanations for Europe's preeminence and success in economic development. Evolutionary biologist Jared Diamond in his 1997 book "Guns, Germs and Steel" has recently contributed to a revival of interest in the role of geography in development by explaining European dominance as a result of advantages of Eurasia's East-West geographical axis in the dissemination of agricultural techniques as technological diffusion naturally works most effectively within ecological zones, along a common latitude, rather than in a North-South direction, like America's and Africa's axis, which crosses ecological zones. Among development economists, Sachs has had a major role in this revival since the late 1990s by emphasizing the role of geographical advantages and disadvantages in explaining long-run growth patterns and the current differences across countries in incomes per capita (see Gallup, Sachs, and Mellinger, 1999; Sachs 2000 and 2001).

---

[1] Cited by Darity and Davis (2005).

There is no doubt that there is a strong correlation between level of economic development and geographical location and climatic characteristics. Consider the following facts. First, as shown in Table 1.1 in Chapter 1, only 3.1 percent of the total population in the group of high-income countries (group 1) lives in tropical countries while 76.6 percent of the total population in the group with lowest incomes (group 5) is in the tropics.[2] The two rich tropical countries in group 1 are Hong Kong and Singapore and in a broader sample the rich tropical countries would include also 4 oil rich countries with small populations (Brunei, Equatorial Guinea, Oman, and Trinidad and Tobago) plus Macao and Puerto Rico. The poor non-tropical countries in group 5 are only three: Bangladesh, Lesotho and Nepal. Two other ways in which the relationship between geography and level of development can be expressed is by noting that there is a positive and strong correlation between GDP per capita and latitude (i.e., distance from the Equator). The greater the distance from the Equator, the higher GDP per capita tends to be (see Figure 18.1). Second, all the main high-income or high middle-income regions—North America,

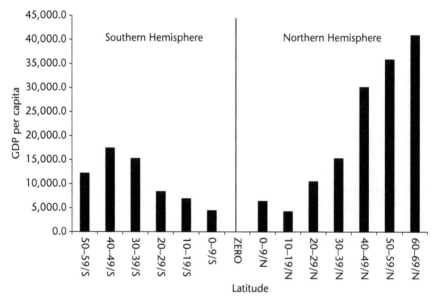

Figure 18.1 GDP per capita and latitude

Note: The sample of countries refers to the 87 countries in Chapter 1 (see Appendix to Chapter 1).
Sources: Penn World Table 7.0 for GDP per capita in 2005 dollars and Google Earth for latitude.

---

[2] Tropical countries, as mentioned in Chapter 1, are defined as those in which more than 50% of their land mass is between the tropic of Cancer and the tropic of Capricorn, i.e. between latitudes 23.5 degrees North and 23.5 degrees South.

Western Europe, North East Asia, the Southern cone of Latin Amrica and Oceania—are outside the tropics.

The question that arises is whether the strong correlation between geography and per capita income reveals the importance of geographical advantages or disadvantages in explaining the large income per capita differences among countries and if so what are the channels through which geography affects development. What has been called the "geography hypothesis" asserts that the large differences in income per capita between countries located in tropical and temperate regions are largely attributable to geographical advantages and disadvantages, to the existence of direct and strong effects going from geography to levels of development rather than to other causes. In what follows, I discuss the theoretical arguments and empirical evidence presented in favor of the geography hypothesis (sections 1 and 2) and then turn, in section 3, to review the controversy about whether geography or institutions rule in the explanation of today's large income gaps across the world. Section 4 concludes by revisiting the question of the deep determinants of economic development.

1. The Role of Geography in Economic Development: Theoretical Arguments

Sachs' argument in "Tropical underdevelopment" (Sachs, 2000) is that there are three areas in which the geographical disadvantages of the tropics have determined a substantial income gap with the temperate regions: food production, health environment, and the capacity to mobilize energy resources. The initial gap thus generated was amplified by the influence of economic, demographic and political and military forces.

Income gaps and the geographical disadvantages of the tropics

The disadvantages of the tropics in terms of levels of productivity in food production were emphasized by Myrdal (1968) and, more recently, by Sachs (2000) among others. International comparisons have found that, after controlling for differences in agricultural machinery, fertilizer inputs, and the human capital of workers, agricultural productivity in tropical countries is between a fourth and a third of the level in humid temperate zones (Weil, 2009, ch. 15). These differences in agricultural productivity among countries profoundly affect income per capita because farming continues to be the world's most important occupation. There are several possible ecological factors, identified by agronomists, biologists, and economists, which account for this low level of productivity. They have to do with soil formation and erosion, pests and parasites, the effects of outside temperature on plants, and the availability of water in conditions of high evaporation. In particular, the pattern of rainfall in the tropics is not good for farming: rain falls seasonally so torrential monsoons alternate with long dry seasons and rain tends to fall in deluges that can erode the soil. The absence of frost in the tropics has adverse effects. Tropical areas are characterized by a wealth of insect life which competes with humans in consuming food crops. This is not the case in countries where frost kills exposed organisms. Frost slows the decay of organic materials (by killing the microorganisms in the soil) and preserves the fertility of the soil. It also helps to control the types of animal diseases that place a heavy burden on tropical agriculture. Moreover, the seasonal pattern of sunlight in the temperate zones (long days in the summer and short days in the winter) is optimal for growing staple grains such as wheat and corn.

There is also good evidence that the tropics constitute a bad health environment: the incidence of disease is considerably greater in the tropics than in temperate regions. This is another way in which climate affects income, by affecting the health of people and thus its human capital. This is due to several factors: regions where the temperature never reaches freezing support a much wider selection of parasites and disease carrying insects than do temperate zones, the physical ecology supports a high level of transmission of infectious diseases, bad nutrition results from the low productivity in food production, and there are multiple interactions between malnutrition and illiteracy and lack of access to medical care. The higher incidence of diseases affects economic performance directly and indirectly: it causes a reduction of productivity due to loss of work days, reduction of physical and cognitive abilities due to chronic and acute diseases, and indirect effects operating through fertility rates, the age structure of the population, and the rate of population growth.

There are also large geographical differences in the availability of energy resources which must have had an important role in generating income gaps between tropical and temperate countries given that industrialization was stimulated initially by the availability of coal and later by that of hydrocarbons. It turns out that coal deposits are largely concentrated in temperate zones: in 2008, non-tropical countries accounted for 86.7 percent of world coal reserves (see Figure 18.2). With respect to hydrocarbons, non-tropical countries accounted for over 70 percent of global oil production and over 80 percent of global gas production in 2010.

Amplifying mechanisms of tropical underdevelopment

According to Sachs (2000), the direct effects of geography on income levels were amplified by a number of factors. A first mechanism is that while the pace of technological innovation in temperate regions was much higher than in

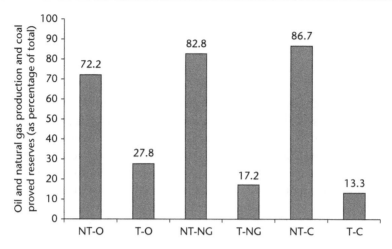

Figure 18.2 Coal reserves and oil and gas production in tropical and non-tropical countries (percentage of total), 2010

Note: NT: Non tropical countries. T: Tropical countries. O: Oil; NG: Natural gas; and C:Coal.
Sources: Oil and Natural Gas U.S. Energy Information Administration and Coal World Energy Council.

tropical zones in the 19th and 20th centuries, technological diffusion between the two regions was very limited due to the fact that key technologies are not easily transmitted between different ecological zones.

A second mechanism is that the low productivity in food production and the adverse health environment held back the demographic transition in the tropics which had the effect of widening the income gap. Low agricultural productivity slowed down urbanization making the demographic transition slower to the extent that rural areas had the highest fertility rates. The higher incidence of diseases directly slows the demographic transition since households compensate a high infant mortality rate with a high total fertility rate.

The third amplifying mechanism has to do with the fact that the economic weakness of the tropics was reflected in a geo-political weakness. Colonization frustrated long-term economic growth in the colonies through various mechanisms: the relative neglect of the provision of key public goods, especially primary education and the health of the indigenous populations, the exclusion from higher education of the colonized population, the creation of oppressive political mechanisms such as forced labor and taxes to extract resources from the local population, and the active suppression of local industry in favor of commercial crops and extractive industry.

The low relative productivity of food production in the tropics had another consequence that was noted by Arthur Lewis in his 1969 Wicksell lectures on "Tropical Trade". This is that it generates a large gap in relative wages vis à vis the temperate zones with much higher productivity in food agriculture.

As Lewis put it when explaining why the wage of a worker in the production of a tropical commercial crop (cocoa) is so much lower than the wage of a steel worker (an industrial worker) in a temperate country: "Each of these two men has the alternative of growing food. Their relative incomes are therefore determined by their relative productivities in growing food; and the relative prices of steel and cocoa are determined by these relative incomes and by productivities in steel and cocoa" (Lewis, 1969, p. 17). This is Lewis' answer to "Why does a man growing cocoa earn one tenth of the wage of a man making steel ingots?" and to "why tropical produce is so cheap". That is, the prices of tropical export agriculture tend to be relatively low given the low wages that result from the low productivity of food agriculture in the tropics. It is also the crux of Lewis argument about the long-term evolution of the terms of trade between manufactures and tropical products: as a result of faster productivity growth in the food producing sectors of industrialized countries than in tropical countries, the benefits of technical progress in manufacturing tend to be appropriated by the developed countries as wages in their industrial sectors grow faster than in tropical countries.

Indirect effects of geography through openness to trade and spillover effects

The influence of geography on development is not limited to that of climate and ecology. Geographical location affects openness to trade, with potentially beneficial effects on specialization, allocative efficiency, and the facilitation of technology transfer. Proximity to the ocean, for example, affects a country's ability to engage in international trade. Distance from the major centers of economic activity also affects a country's openness to trade as transport costs increase with distance from major centers.

A related effect of geographic location on income arises from the existence of a good deal of clustering among high-income countries. Europe is perhaps the best example. Among non-European high-income countries, there is also a good deal of clustering, such as Canada and the United States, Japan and South Korea, and Australia and New Zealand. Clustering can be explained by spillover effects if, for example, a wealthy neighbor provides market opportunities and a source of advanced technology while, by contrast, a poor neighbor is more prone to political instability and therefore is likely to be a source of refugees or military aggression (see Weil, 2009). Another possible explanation for clustering is simply that nearby countries tend to share common characteristics that may be important for growth such as climate or culture. As noted by Weil (2009), the clustering of prosperous countries may or may not represent an obstacle for development of many poor countries depending on the relative importance of the factors explaining clustering. Indeed, if clustering is largely due to spillover effects, this is a bonus for a number of developing countries near wealthy countries (such as Algeria, China, Mexico, Morocco, Tunisia, and Turkey) but bad news for most of the developing world (particularly Sub-Saharan Africa). If spillover effects do not explain clustering, the clustering itself does not represent additional bad news.

2. The Role of Geography: Empirical Evidence

The long-run growth performance of the tropical and temperate regions

Consider first the evidence on the effects of climate on economic development. Using Maddison's database, Sachs (2000) shows that in 1820 temperate and non-temperate regions had an income per capita of $794 and $543 dollars respectively (in 1990 international dollars), a ratio of less than 2 to 1. From 1820 to 1992, GDP per capita in temperate regions grew at an annual rate of 1.4 percent compared to 0.9 percent in the non-temperate regions. The difference in growth rates was such that by 1992, GDP per capita in non-temperate regions was only 25 percent of the GDP per capita of temperate regions. Moreover, the gap in growth rates and the divergence in incomes per capita have continued in the recent past. In a regression of the growth of income per capita between 1965 and 1990 on initial income per capita, education and the share of the population living in a temperate zone, Sachs (2000) found that this last variable had a positive effect on the growth rate. The size of its coefficient implies that a temperate zone economy tends to grow 1.6 percentage points faster per year that an economy in a non temperate zone (tropical, arid or a highlands climate zone) which is identical in all other respects. This means a long-run income per capita gap of the order of 2.7 to 1.

Given these facts, how can the stories of successful growth in the tropics be explained? What accounts for the outstanding growth performance of countries, such as Hong Kong, Singapore, Malaysia and Mauritius, which have been able to close the gap with the rich countries? Sachs' answer is that these countries, largely in East Asia, present two features. First, they all made great progress in public health before their economic take off. Second, they adopted policies geared to shift away from specialization in primary goods, especially tropical agriculture, and to diversify into export-oriented manufacturing. The result was that these economies were able to establish new productive activities (textiles, electronic machinery, semiconductors and electronic components) which were not adversely affected by climatic or ecological factors.

Other aspects of geographic location and their effects on income per capita

The empirical evidence supports the link between proximity to the ocean and GDP per capita. Consider the five income groups in Table1.1 of Chapter 1.

In group 1 with the highest incomes, the percentage of the total population living in landlocked countries is 2.5 percent while this percentage increases to 35.1 percent in group 5 with the lowest incomes. Austria and Switzerland are the only landlocked countries in group 1 while group 5 has 8 such countries (Burkina Faso, Burundi, Ethiopia, Lesotho, Malawi, Nepal, Rwanda, and Zimbabwe). Weil (2009) shows that GDP per capita in areas that are within 60 miles of the sea is on average twice as high as GDP per capita in areas farther inland. There is also a strong positive relationship across regions of the world between the fraction of a region's population that lives within 60 miles of an ocean or a navigable river and the region's average level of GDP per capita. This can be illustrated with a comparison between Western Europe and East Asia, on the one hand, and Sub-Saharan Africa, on the other. Western Europe and East Asia have high levels of GDP per capita and more than 60 percent of their populations have access to the sea. Sub-Saharan Africa, with a low level of GDP per capita, has only 21 percent of its population with access to the sea. Several factors account for this lack of access to the sea: a dearth of natural ports, absence of navigable rivers, concentration of the population in the interior highlands, where tropical heat is reduced, and a low ratio of coastline to land area (while Western Europe has one eight the land area of Africa, its coastline is 50 percent longer). Distance from the major centers of economic activity is another determinant of a country's international trade volumes that correlates well with differences in income per capita. Indeed, the average cost of transporting imports, expressed as a ratio of the total value of imports, is 3.6 percent for the United States, 4.9 percent for Western Europe, 9.8 percent for East Asia, 10.6 percent for Latin America, and 19.5 percent for sub-Saharan Africa. The reason is simply that transport costs increase with distance from major centers: on average, each 1,000 kilometers (600 miles) of distance from one of the most developed regions of the world (United States, Western Europe or Japan) increases transport costs by one-percentage point.

3. The Geography versus Institutions Controversy

There is by now a large literature on how important is the role of geography in economic development and, in particular, on whether it is geography or institutions, both economic and political, that play a predominant role in economic development. Another related debate is whether geography affects economic development primarily through its effects on institutions or whether it does so through other channels. The geography hypothesis, associated with Sachs and coauthors, holds that environment directly influences the quality and productivity of land, as well as the endowment of human capital and production technologies. The institutionalist view holds that the environment's main impact on economic development runs through long-lasting institutions. This is for example the argument of Hall and Jones (1999) who argue that Western Europeans have historically been associated with high quality institutions, and Western Europeans settled in climates similar to Western Europe.

Sachs and his coauthors (see in particular Gallup and Sachs, 1998; Mellinger, Sachs, and Gallup, 2000; Sachs, 2000) sparked the recent debates by offering arguments against competing hypotheses on the observed strong correlation between level of development and climatic and ecological zones, as well as other aspects of geographical location. They begin by rejecting alternative explanations of the strong correlation between level of economic development and a country's location in tropical or temperate regions. One argument is that colonization does not explain these patterns. First, tropical Africa, the poorest region in the world, was colonized only after 1870 and featured the lowest incomes per capita already in the pre-colonial period. Second, tropical countries that were not colonized do not differ in levels of economic development from tropical countries that were colonized.[3] Third, economic performance in tropical Africa did not improve with independence. In a related argument, Sachs (2000) also criticizes the interpretation by Hall and Jones (1999) of the strong correlation between latitude and income per capita that takes the effects of latitude to operate through Western influence and the creation of Western-like institutions. Sachs argues that latitude is in fact a poor measure of the degree of penetration of European institutions because many mid-latitude regions, such as Central Asia, China, Korea, and Japan, have in fact weak ties to Europe. At the same time, many equatorial regions are former European colonies, with strong ties to Europe.

AJR (2001) theory of the colonial origins of comparative development, discussed in Chapter 17, challenges Sachs' "geography hypothesis" by providing evidence against the role of geography in development. One of their empirical findings is that once the effect of institutions on economic performance is controlled for, adding latitude as an explanatory variable does not change the relationship and this variable has the wrong sign and is not significant. Another finding is that when one adds a dummy for Africa, this dummy is not significant once we control for the role of institutions. This suggests that Africa is poorer than the rest of the world due to worse institutions rather than purely geographic or cultural factors.

In a 2002 article, AJR continue their critique of the "geography hypothesis" documenting what they call "the reversal of fortune" among former European

---

[3] Sachs (2000) does not elaborate this important point. I can only think of two tropical countries that were not colonized: Ethiopia and Liberia. Both are poor countries, indeed, but perhaps too few to constitute a decisive objection to the institutionalist view.

colonies: the fact that, among these former colonies, countries or territories that were relatively rich around 1500 had become relatively poor by 1995, and vice versa, countries and territories that were relatively poor around 1500 had become relatively rich by 1995. In other words, there is a strong negative correlation between living standards in 1500 (measured by data on urbanization and population density) and living standards in 1995. For example, India, Mexico and Peru were hosts to relatively rich civilizations (the Mughals in India and the Aztecs and Incas in Mexico and Peru) as measured by their population density and urbanization, while the civilizations of North America, New Zealand and Australia were less developed. Today, the United States, Canada, New Zealand and Australia are much richer than India, Mexico or Peru. This reversal of relative incomes contradicts a simplistic view of the effects of geography on development because if geographic factors dominated development, then regions that were rich at the beginning of the 16th century should also have been rich at the end of the 20th century. Geography didn't change in between.

Sachs (2000) has attempted an explanation of the reversal of fortune that is consistent with a more sophisticated version of the "geography hypothesis" that emphasizes effects of geography that vary through time. He argues that areas that were prosperous at the beginning of the 16th century had soil and climate that were suitable for the agricultural technologies of the time, but the initial advantages of the tropics were lost with the technological developments in agriculture that favored countries with temperate climates. This explanation is rejected by AJR who argue that the reversal in the relative ranking of countries did not take place during the period of major technological progress in agriculture (before the end of the 18th century) but rather much later, during the industrial revolution, and it was related to industrialization.

What about other influences of geography that could explain the reversal of fortune? One possibility would be that certain geographic characteristics facilitate or enable industrialization. For example, industrialization requires specialization and specialization requires trade. Thus if countries differ according to their transport costs, it might be those with low transport costs that take off during the age of industrialization. AJR reject this hypothesis arguing that there is little evidence that the reversal of relative incomes was related to geographic characteristics. Many of the previously prosperous colonies that failed to industrialize include islands such as the Caribbean, or countries with natural ports such as those in Central America, India or Indonesia.

According to AJR (2002), the reversal of fortune is, in contrast, consistent with the role of institutions in development. It can be explained with an institutions based hypothesis, i.e. by the different types of institutions that were formed by the European settlers. The initially relatively poor regions were sparsely populated, which made them attractive to European settlers which once settled had an incentive to establish institutions that provided for themselves broad protection of property rights and broadly distributed political power. By contrast, in initially prosperous, densely populated areas, settlement was less attractive to Europeans which then established extractive institutions, based on both economic and political inequality. In other words, the explanation of the reversal is that European colonialism led to the development of "institutions of private property" in previously poor and scarcely populated areas while it introduced (or preserved) "extractive institutions" in previously prosperous areas with an abundant population that could be forced to work in mines or plantations or be exploited through the existing tax systems.

Another issue under debate is if the instrumental variable adopted by AJR, settlers' mortality rates, is capturing or not other effects which are linked to the impact of geography or health on development.[4] AJR (2001) examine if the settlers mortality rates are correlated with climate and other geographic characteristics by adding variables of temperature and humidity showing that including these variables has little effect on their estimates. They also investigate if the instrument they use may be capturing the general effects of diseases on development. In particular, since malaria was one of the main causes of mortality among the colonizers, the instrument used may be capturing the direct effect of malaria on economic performance (Sachs and his collaborators emphasized the importance of malaria and other diseases in the explanation of poverty in Africa). AJR find that controlling for the incidence of malaria does not make a significant difference to their estimates.

The extent to which the "reversal of fortune" really occurred has also been questioned. Using Maddison (2003) estimates, Przeworski (2004) shows that in a regression of income per capita in 2001 against income per capita in 1500, the coefficient, although not significant, is slightly positive.[5] The coefficient is also positive when we consider income per capita in 1700 and even more positive and significant when we consider 1820. Przeworski thus concludes that according to this information there was no reversal of fortune: the tropics were always poorer.

---

[4] Recall that AJR (2001) use data on the mortality rates of settlers in European colonies, as a measure of the difficulty of settling in a particular colony, and on expropriation risk at the end of the 20th century as a measure of the quality of institutions. They find that areas that were hospitable to European settlers in the 17th, 18th, or 19th centuries ended up with "good institutions" at the end of the 20th century, and those areas that were not hospitable to European settlers ended up with "bad institutions".

[5] Note that Przeworski uses GDP per capita rather than urbanization or population density, as AJR do, in order to measure the level of economic development.

There has been over time some convergence in the debate on institutions versus geography. Defenders of the geography hypothesis, such as Sachs, have moderated their position recognizing that institutional differences have an important role in the explanation of income per capita gaps among countries. For institutionalists, in turn, it is clear that geography matters through its indirect effects, i.e. as a determinant of institutions. This is very clear in the case of Engerman and Sokoloff (2002). As reviewed in Chapter 16, these economic historians relate the different economic growth trajectories in Latin America and the Caribbean as compared to the Northern United States and Canada to the different degrees of economic, social and political inequality prevailing in those two regions. These differences in inequality are in turn attributed to differences in the composition of factor endowments (including climate, soil and density of native population, besides the abundance of land and natural resources), all of which are partly conditioned by geography. The role of geography in conditioning institutions is also present, implicitly in AJR, and explicitly in Easterly and Levine (2003) for whom geography ("tropics, germs and crops") has a significant effect on the quality of institutions and, in this way, on economic development.

The scope of the debate has narrowed then to the question of whether there are direct effects of geography on income per capita, once institutional differences have been taken into account. Sachs and his coauthors argue that these direct effects exist (and think that it is absurd to argue the contrary) while AJR and Easterly and Levine argue that these effects do no exist while Rodrik, Subramanian, and Trebbi (2004) conclude that, at best, geography has weak direct effects. To wrap up, it would be surprising if the indisputably strong empirical relationship between geography and development did not reveal direct effects on income per capita of geographical advantages and disadvantages. Having said this, it is tempting to attribute a large role to geography as a fundamental, perhaps the deepest determinant of comparative development. This role should not be exaggerated. Sachs' own estimate of the long-run per capita income gap between a temperate zone economy and a non temperate zone one is of the order of 2.7 to 1, a magnitude well below that of the observed income gaps in the world economy that we need to explain. Moreover, can we be fully confident that proximity to the equator necessarily explains why countries are poor? First, as noted by Weil (2009), for every one of the channels considered as a way in which geography can affect income, we can find exceptions. For example, even though most economic activity takes place near seacoasts and in temperate climates, one of the fastest growing economies in the world is that of Botswana, a land locked country in sub Saharan Africa. The fastest growing city in the US is Las Vegas which is located in a desert, far inland. Second, one reason why tropical agriculture is less productive is that research on agricultural technologies is concentrated in developing technologies for temperate agriculture. This is an example of how different levels of development are affecting the technological constraints that can be wrongly attributed exclusively to geography. Another example has to do with the adverse health environment of the tropics. Is this really a fully exogenous factor? One reason that the tropics are so unhealthy for humans is that less money has been spent on studying tropical diseases (simply because rich countries are located in temperate climates). All this means that there is always the possibility that our explanations for the poverty of tropical countries are after the fact rationalizations. If Scandinavian countries were poor instead of being some of the most prosperous countries in the world, as Weil notes, perhaps some economists and geographers would blame their poverty on the difficulties produced by cold weather and snow, or the depressing effects of long winters.

4. Concluding Comments

In this last section I would like to comment on some trends in the recent controversies on which of the fundamental factors of comparative economic development "rules" and on the usefulness itself of the search for *the* deepest determinant.

In these recent controversies, some neo-institutionalists, as already noted in Chapter 17, have adopted an "institutions only" view that largely denies a role in development not only for geography but also for other possible determinants. An important argument, and perhaps the strongest evidence, offered to support this extreme version of the institutionalist thesis is based on natural experiments involving bordering countries or towns that share the same geography and have different institutions that have resulted in very different levels of economic development. However, the fact that, conceding the point for the sake of the argument, institutions is all that matters in explaining the comparative development of, say, North and South Korea doesn't imply that the "institutions only" view can be applied to other experiences and country comparisons. Doing so implies a non sequitur. In his review of Acemoglu and Robinson (2012), Jared Diamond puts this point as follows: "Many or most economists, including Acemoglu and Robinson, generalize from these examples of bordering countries and deduce that good institutions also explain the differences in wealth between nations that aren't neighbors and that differ greatly in their geographic environments and human populations" (Diamond, 2012). Proceeding in this way is like a geographic determinist that concludes that geography is all that matters for development from the fact that it is most important in explaining why income per capita in Nuevo Leon, a Northern Mexican state, or in the Central Federal District where Mexico City is located, is much higher (around five times) than the income per capita of Oaxaca, a Southern Mexican state which shares the same institutions.[6]

One can even go further and argue that even if we restrict ourselves to examples of bordering towns or countries, these comparisons do not always support an institutionalist explanation. Consider the case of the two Nogaleses that plays a salient role in Acemoglu and Robinson's 2012 book. According to these authors (p. 42): "The reason that Nogales, Arizona, is much richer than Nogales, Sonora, is simple; it is because of the very different institutions on the two sides of the border, which create very different incentives for the inhabitants of Nogales, Arizona, versus Nogales, Sonora". Does this case reveal something about why Mexico overall is poorer than the United States? Unlike Mexico in relation to the United States, Nogales, Sonora, is far more industrialized than Nogales, Arizona, and has a population ten times larger (over 220, 000 vs. less than 21,000 in 2010). This is, as noted by Sachs (2012), because it is one of the most industrialized towns in Mexico while Nogales, Arizona, is one of the poorest places in the United States. The gap in income per capita is probably well below 2 to 1 in favor of the American town compared with a gap of over 4 to 1 between the two countries.[7] Sachs seems to have got it right when he says that "the case of the two Nogaleses is about geography and nothing else. . . . . Nogales, Sonora, exists as an industrial city because it borders the United States and the terminus of Interstate 19. Firms invest in the city because it is an excellent location inside Mexico to serve the U.S. market, but there is no comparable reason to invest in Nogales, Arizona, since it is a lousy place inside the United States to serve the U.S. market. The upshot is that Nogales, Sonora, is highly developed compared with the rest of Mexico, whereas Nogales, Arizona, has to rely on federal and state transfers to address its poverty" (Sachs, 2012).

As we shall argue in the next chapter, the search for *the* deepest determinant of economic development is unproductive. Geographical differences may be quite important in some comparisons. Sachs (2012) is probably right in emphasizing that geographic location is most important in explaining why Bolivia, a landlocked country with much of its territory at more than 10,000 feet above sea level, has been growing more slowly in recent decades than Vietnam, a country with a vast coastline whose location in booming East Asia has made it very attractive for foreign direct investment in export oriented manufacturing plants. Institutional differences may be very important in other comparisons, such as that of North and South Korea.

---

[6] I am grateful to Emilio Ocampo for conversations on this question.

[7] The income per capita comparison between the two towns is a guess estimate considering income per capita in Nogales, Arizona and in Sonora state in Mexico.

19

Successes and Failures in Economic Development: The Keys to the Kingdom

In this chapter we go back to the stylized facts of economic development presented in Chapter 1 and review them in the light of the growth models and approaches to development studied in this book. The main themes around which the chapter is organized are highlighted in the five by five matrix presented in Table 19.1. This table classifies the 87 countries in our Chapter 1 sample according to their growth rate of GDP per worker in 1970–2008 and their initial level of GDP per worker in 1970. The table shows, first, that high income, fast growth countries are very few. For example, in the fastest growth quintile, there is only one country (Norway) that was in 1970 in the richest quintile and only four more (Finland, Ireland, Hong Kong and Singapore) that were in the second richest quintile. This clearly suggests that, at least in the contemporary world economy, high incomes and fast growth are not the same. Section 1 in this chapter develops this theme.

A second feature of the table is that low-income countries with fast growth are also very few. There are only three countries in the lowest income quintile (China, Lesotho and Mali) that are in the two highest quintiles according to growth. Most poor countries have been diverging with respect to the high-income economies. In fact, if we take the United States for comparison, all of the poor countries in the lowest income quintile, except the three mentioned above, have been diverging with respect to the United States level of income. Section 2 deals with this topic, revisiting poverty traps and growth collapses at low-income levels.

Third, the table shows that there are very few middle-income, medium-growth countries. For example, in the third quintile according to growth, there are only two countries (Colombia and Panama) that are in the second or the third quintiles according to GDP per worker. Middle-income countries are either catching up or falling behind, i.e., they tend to converge towards high income levels or tend to diverge away, falling into middle-income traps

Table 19.1 A five by five matrix: growth of GDP per worker 1970–2008

GDP per worker 1970	1	2	3	4	5
1	Norway	US, Australia, Belgium, Sweden, Austria, France, Denmark, Italy, UK	Netherlands, Switzerland, Canada, Israel, Greece	New Zealand	Venezuela
2	Finland, Ireland, Singapore, Hong Kong	Spain, Japan, Portugal, Chile		Mexico, Costa Rica, Jamaica, Argentina	Iran, South Africa, Peru, Namibia, Brazil
3	Turkey, South Korea, Malaysia, Mauritius	Uruguay, Dominican Republic, Tunisia	Colombia, Panama	El Salvador, Guatemala, Ecuador, Syria, Honduras	Nicaragua, Jordan, Bolivia
4	Egypt, Thailand, Botswana, India, Indonesia	Pakistan	Morocco, Philippines, Congo, Republic of Benin, Bangladesh, Gambia The, Nepal, Tanzania, Burkina Faso, Mozambique	Paraguay, Cameroon, Senegal	Zambia, Nigeria, Cote d'Ivoire, Mauritania, Ghana, Kenya
5	Mali, Lesotho, China			Guinea, Rwanda, Malawi, Ethiopia, Burundi	Sierra Leone, Madagascar, Zimbabwe

Source: Penn World Table 7.0. See appendix to Chapter 1.

or even recording middle-income growth collapses. The third and fourth sections look at middle-income traps and to contemporary successful development transitions. A concluding section revisits the book's explanations for the great divergence and club convergence that characterizes the trends in the world's distribution of income and comments on the fundamental determinants of economic development.

1. High Incomes and Fast Growth: Not the Same

As already noted in the introduction to this book, in his blurb of Acemoglu and Robinson (2012), Kenneth Arrow puts the answer to the question in the title of this chapter as follows: "The openness of a society, its willingness to permit creative destruction, and the rule of law appear to be decisive for economic development". Let us start by looking how well the world's wealthiest countries fit into this succinct expression of the new institutionalist position.

The highly developed countries

Consider the richest quintile (according to income per capita PPP) among the 177 countries of the Penn World Table. As noted in Chapter 15, five out of 35 countries in this quintile owe their high incomes to oil wealth combined with small populations. These countries are not models of "inclusive" economic and political institutions, to use Acemoglu and Robinson (2012) expression but, of course, it can be argued that their economies cannot be properly called developed. Their wealth depends on their good fortune in the "commodity lottery" (to use Díaz Alejandro's expression) rather than on the long and critical process of structural transformation and recurrent creative destruction that resulted in industrially and technologically advanced economies in the other high-income countries. As a result, there is little that most of the developing world can learn from them in terms of development strategy.

If we exclude the oil rich states and other countries with very small populations from the richest quintile of the Penn World table, as we did to obtain our 87-country sample, we are left with what we generally refer to as highly developed countries. The wealthiest countries include now Western European countries, the Western offshoots, as Maddison calls them (that is, the United States, Canada, Australia, and New Zealand) plus Japan and other East Asian miracles of the post war period (Singapore, Hong Kong, South Korea, and Taiwan). The hard core of this group of countries is the richest quintile of countries in our sample (see appendix to Chapter 1).

Considering this hard core of developed countries, we now get a much better fit with the institutionalist hypothesis as expressed by Arrow. Indeed, if we go back to Tables 1.1 and 1.6 in Chapter 1, we find the kind of open societies Arrow has in mind, countries with open market economies and democratic states that enforce the rule of law. The trade shares in this quintile are by far the highest in the sample, a sign of the presence of many small open economies that have become increasingly intertwined over time. Practically all of them have democratic political institutions (only 1.1 percent of this group's population lives under a non-democratic regime), and they feature the highest rule of law index (92.9 compared to 64.9 in group 2 and 31.8 in group 5). Their Gini income concentration coefficient is the lowest among the 5 sample groups, suggesting that their relatively egalitarian income distributions play a role in sustaining democracy and political stability as well as, possibly, a tolerance for creative destruction.

Having said this, it is worth noting, first, the variety of institutional arrangements that are consistent with high levels of economic development. These arrangements vary from public and free provision of health care and higher education to private provision of these services, from relatively high to moderate (albeit not low) tax burdens, from low union density in the labor market and decentralized wage bargaining to powerful unions in highly centralized wage bargaining systems, and from highly developed to less developed welfare states.

More important for the lessons we can learn from the experience of the highly developed countries is that these countries were very different from what they are today during the historical process of achieving a highly developed state, and were certainly not always guided by the rule of law and the invisible hand during this process. While they can generally be referred today as open market economies, most of them adopted industrial protection at some stage in their development process (see Chang, 2002) and had mixed economies in which the public sector provided not only basic social services and infrastructure but, through public enterprises, many other goods and services. Similarly, while the vast majority of these countries have today democratic states that enforce the rule of law, many countries in Europe and East Asia did not always have democratic political institutions. East Asian countries, in particular, adopted them relatively recently, and often after, and not before, their successful development transitions had been achieved.

The high growth countries and contemporary growth miracles

All this leads me to discuss the high growth countries and compare them to the high-income countries. Table 19.1 makes quite evident the difference between the high income and the high growth countries in the period 1970–2008. As already noted, there is only one country (Norway) which is in both the highest growth quintile for that period and the highest income quintile at the beginning of the period. Only four more countries in the highest growth quintile were in the second highest income quintile in 1970 (Finland, Ireland, Hong Kong, and Singapore). If we look again to Tables 1.6 and 1.7 in Chapter 1, we can see that the rule of law index in the fast growing countries is much lower (70.2) than in the high income countries (92.9) and is even lower than in second group of countries classified according to the growth rate. While virtually all the high-income countries have democratic political institutions only slightly more than a third of the population in the high growth countries lived in 1970 under a democratic regime. High-income countries have a small trade surplus in primary goods while fast growth countries have a large deficit, suggesting a strong manufacturing bias in their pattern of trade specialization. The group of high-income countries is the more egalitarian of the sample (with a Gini coefficient just above 30) while the high growth economies have a much higher Gini coefficient (38.1).

Taking a longer time perspective, we can identify for the whole post war period the experiences of countries with such high growth rates over an

Table 19.2 Contemporary growth miracles since 1950

	Period of high growth[a]	gGDP	GDPpC First Year[b]	GDPpC Final Year[b]	GDPpC 2008[b]
Japan	1950–73	8.7	23.7	76.6	77.9
Mexico	1950–81	6.7	25.8	39.3	29.4
Taiwan	1950–97	8.5	9.6	56.9	67.1
Hong Kong	1951–2008	7.0	22.7	101.7	101.7
Brazil	1953–80	7.8	14.5	32.1	21.5
Thailand	1958–95	7.9	5.5	18.3	18.1
Singapore	1959–2000	8.3	19.5	79.1	90.2
South Korea	1962–2000	7.7	11.1	48.3	58.9
Botswana	1965–90	12.5	3.4	18.3	25.2
Indonesia	1967–96	7.7	3.4	9.6	8.9
Malaysia	1969–97	8.1	9.7	27.2	27.5
China	1977–2008	9.8	2.0	14.8	14.8
Vietnam	1981–2008	7.0	2.7	6.3	6.3

Notes: gGDP: Rate of growth in Local Currency Units at constant prices except for those countries where the source is Maddison (Hong Kong, Taiwan and Singapore). GDPpC: GDP per capita
[a] Period in which GDP growth was 7% or more for at least 25 years or 6.5% or more for at least 30 years. Japan from 1950 to 1973 does not fit exactly with the definition but is included since its period of high growth started before 1950.
[b] As Percentage of US GDP per capita in PPP.
Sources: Penn World Table 7.0 and Maddison (<http://www.ggdc.net/MADDISON/oriindex.htm>).

extended period of time that they may be called the contemporary growth miracles. Table 19.2 presents these experiences, defining a growth miracle as the achievement of at least 7 percent annual GDP growth for more than 25 years or at least 6.5 percent annual GDP growth for more than 30 years.[1]

Leaving aside Botswana, a country with a small population and well-managed natural wealth, what all these countries have in common is that they achieved their period of fastest growth during a rapid process of industrialization (see the discussion in section 3, Chapter 8). Their most salient common feature is their pro-manufacturing bias in the pattern of trade specialization. This bias was consistent with trade regimes that combined import substitution during at least an initial period (Brazil, Malaysia, Mexico, Thailand) with varying degrees of manufacturing exports promotion (especially in South Korea, Taiwan and Singapore). Other characteristics varied across countries. The policy regimes laid greater or lesser emphasis on State-led promotion of industry going from relatively laissez faire Hong Kong to State dirigisme with mixed economies in Brazil, Korea, Mexico and Taiwan. Openness to foreign investment also varied from highly open regimes in Hong Kong and Singapore to moderately open in the Brazilian and Mexican experiences to relatively

---

[1] Spence (2012, p. 54) identifies 13 experiences of countries with an average GDP growth rate of 7 percent per year or more for at least 25 years. These countries are included in Table 19.2 with the exception of Malta and Oman that we have excluded due to their very small populations. However, the periods of the growth miracles that we identify are not the same as Spence's.

restrictive ones in South Korea and Taiwan (see Fajnzylber, 1990; Amsden, 2001; Chang, 2002). A variety of political institutions prevailed. Japan had a continuously democratic regime, periods of authoritarianism and democracy alternated in countries such as Brazil, Korea, and Taiwan, and continuously authoritarian systems (during the years of high growth) prevailed in China, Mexico, and Singapore.

A historical perspective also suggests that understanding the determinants of high income only partially overlaps with understanding high growth. Some of today´s developed countries were never fast growing economies: "Australia was born rich" as Diaz-Alejandro used to say and the United States, the technological leader, has been secularly growing at a rate (around 2 percent per year or even less in early periods of development) that pales in comparison with rates recorded by today's fast growing economies. At the same time, achieving high growth may not lead to high incomes: some of today´s low-income, fast-growing economies may not become developed in the future if they fall into a middle-income trap or suffer a growth collapse. All this means that the keys to preserve a developed economy status are not the same as the keys to achieving fast growth. The policy implication of all this is that applying the recipe, if there were a single one, to preserve a high income level may be quite inappropriate to the achievement of fast growth in a low or middle-income country. This was, in fact, a starting point of classical development theory.

2. Poverty Traps and Growth Collapses at Low-income Levels

Consider now the poorest quintile (according to income per capita PPP) among the 177 countries of the Penn World Table. In this group we have, mostly, very poor Sub-Saharan African countries (30 out of the 35 in the group) plus Haiti, the poorest country in the Western Hemisphere, and a number of South and East Asian countries (Afghanistan, Bangladesh, Nepal, and Timor-Leste).

If we limit ourselves to the low-income groups (groups 4 and 5) in our 87-country sample, for which we have information on growth performance since 1970, one striking feature in these countries is that most of them are also slow growth countries.[2] In fact, as already noted, in the poorest quintile in 1970

---

[2] The percentage of the total of low-income countries which are also slow growth countries would probably increase if more information were available in the Penn World Table. Countries such as Haiti, Afghanistan, or Nepal, which are not in the 87-country sample, would probably be in the slow growth category.

there are only 3 countries (China being the most remarkable case) which are in the fastest growth quintile. As many as 27 countries out of a total of 36 in the poorest two quintiles in 1970 are also slow growth countries in the sense that they have been diverging with respect to the United States (see Table 19.1). Twenty-two of these 27 low-income, slow growth countries are in Sub-Saharan Africa, the rest being Bangladesh, Morocco, Paraguay, Philippines and Nepal (see Table 19.1).

This fact, that the low-income groups largely overlap with the slow growth groups, clearly suggests that there must be common factors that explain both slow growth and low income and/or that there are feed-back effects from low income to slow growth, in other words that there are poverty traps. Among the possible common factors explaining and interacting with both slow growth and low income are institutional features. Most of those 27 low-income, slow growth countries were colonized by Europeans that took advantage of existing extractive institutions or created new ones. They have the lowest rule of law indexes and the highest incidence of non-democratic regimes as shown in Table 1.6 in Chapter 1. Another possible common factor refers to geographical disadvantages. Around 60 percent of the population in the two poorest quintiles lives in tropical countries (see Table 1.6 in Chapter 1). A striking feature in this group of countries refers to the high incidence of landlocked and small population countries. As already noted in Chapter 18, eight countries in the poorest quintile are landlocked although it is worth noting that one of them, Lesotho, is in the fastest growth quintile.

The feedback effects of low income on growth that can generate a poverty trap include a diversity of cannels that have been reviewed throughout this book. These encompass interactions between small market size, increasing returns to scale and high elasticity of labor supply, the feedback effects of low income on growth operating through human capital accumulation or institutional weaknesses, and the effects of geographical disadvantages exacerbating the adverse consequences of small population size or increasing returns to scale. A result of these feedback effects is the existence of a threshold level of income below which no sustained growth is possible. This threshold may result from a variety of sources including a low level of human capital determining a low "absorptive capacity" in the sense of Nelson and Phelps (1966) as in Benhabib and Spiegel (2005). Institutional factors include the absence of the rule of law in poor countries (as in Easterly's 2006 criticism of the big push) or the existence of institutions that do not permit full advantage to be taken of technology transfer (Acemoglu, Aghion, and Zilibotti, 2006). Still other possibilities are high inequality generating political instability (see Chapter 16 on the effects of inequality on the threshold level of convergence), a small market size interacting with increasing returns and geographical disadvantages, or what Abramovitz (1986) meant by a lack of "social capability" which encompasses some of these factors.[3]

3. Middle-income Traps and Growth Collapses

Not all the countries with negative or very slow growth rates have low incomes. Slow growth traps and growth collapses can also take place at middle-income levels.[4] In these experiences, countries with substantially higher incomes than the poorest countries have been diverging vis a vis the per capita incomes of the high-income economies. In some cases, they have been recording negative growth rates and thus have suffered veritable growth collapses.

As shown in Table 19.1, several countries in the intermediate income quintiles (groups 2 and 3) suffered stagnation or negative growth rates over the period 1970–2008. The Latin American cases include Argentina, Brazil, Costa Rica, Ecuador, El Salvador, Guatemala, Honduras, Mexico, Peru, plus Venezuela if we include a country from the highest income quintile. These experiences have been discussed in Chapter 13 where we saw that it was the growth collapse following the debt crisis of the 1980s which initiated their slow growth period. In other regions, similar experiences of middle-income traps or collapses include Iran, Jordan and Syria in the Middle East and South Africa and Namibia in Sub-Saharan Africa.

Most of these countries have in common high levels of inequality, a pattern of trade specialization biased towards primary goods exports,[5] and external shocks, particularly a debt crisis, as the trigger of the growth collapse. They have recurrently been used to illustrate the demand constraints on growth arising from debt traps (Chapter 13), the risks of badly managed natural resource abundance and the vulnerability to external shocks in conditions of high primary exports dependence (Chapter 14), as well as the weakness of institutions of conflict management in conditions of high inequality (Chapter 16).

---

[3] As noted in Chapter 3, Abramovitz (1986) includes as important elements of social capability a society's educational level and its political and economic institutions (including industrial and financial institutions).

[4] Divergence starting from high incomes is rare. As shown in Table 19.1, only two high-income countries in 1970 (New Zealand and Venezuela) were in the two lowest quintiles according to growth in 1970–2008. In the past, Argentina also belongs to this group of initially high-income countries and divergence away from the technological leaders. The incidence of growth collapses at high income levels may change in the future if the current European slump persists for a long period of time.

[5] This applies also to Mexico, a major oil exporter at the time the growth collapse occurred.

4. Successful Development Transitions

Some six decades ago, a number of today's high-income countries were lagging well behind the United States level of per capita income. Their experiences constitute the contemporary successful transitions to a highly developed state. The most remarkable cases are rather few. Figure 19.1 shows, for a large sample of countries, the levels of GDP per capita as a percentage of the US level in 1950 and 2008. Consider the countries with less than 50 percent of US GDP per capita in 1950 and more than 75 percent of the US income level in 2008. Some of these successful development transitions resemble the experience of a long distance runner: the growth rate was not as spectacular as in the growth miracles reviewed earlier but a high growth rate was sustained for a long period of time. Austria, Finland, and Ireland meet these conditions. They reached income levels higher than 75 percent of the US income level in 2008 starting from a per capita income less than half the United States level but not too far from it. Other long distance runners with less than 50 percent of US income in 1950 were in 2008 close to the 75 percent mark: Italy (68.1 percent), Spain (66.8 percent), Greece (65.2 percent), and Israel (60.2 percent).

Other successful transitions are more recent and even more impressive. The experiences (Hong Kong, Japan, and Singapore) belong to the growth miracles discussed earlier. In a couple of generations these countries moved from low or lower middle incomes to very high incomes (higher than the US in the case of Hong Kong). Taiwan with 68.4 percent and South Korea with 58.9 percent of United States income in 2008 are close to replicating the same experience.

It is worth noting, however, that most growth miracles have not led, at least not yet, to successful development transitions. In Brazil and Mexico, the transition stopped at middle-income levels and for the past 30 years these countries fell into a slow growth trap at rates well below those of the technological leaders. We have looked in the previous section and in Chapter 13 to the reasons for this. In other cases (Botswana, China, Indonesia, Malaysia, Thailand, Vietnam), in which the growth miracle started relatively recently from very low-income levels, the transition process is still going on at high rates but the countries are still very far from reaching a highly developed status: in 2008 they all had less than 30 percent of the US income per capita (see Table 19.2). Whether they will or not close the gap with the technological leaders is impossible to say. Will they follow the experience of Japan and Singapore? Or will they fall into a middle-income trap as Brazil and Mexico?

What is more certain is that as they approach high income levels their very fast growth processes will slow down as diminishing returns to capital set in, Gershenkron's advantages of technological backwardness progressively

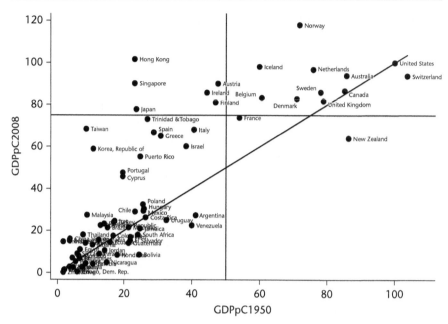

Figure 19.1 GDP per capita relative to US level in 1950 and 2008

Source: Penn World Table 7.0 and Maddison Project (<www.rug.nl/feb/onderzoek(onderzoekcentra/ggdc/index>).

disappear, or a financial crisis throws them into a demand-constrained growth path. In fact, this has started to happen. Since the Asian financial crisis of 1997–8, the GDP growth rates of Indonesia, Malaysia, and Thailand have fallen below 7 percent (2.4 percent, 4.7 percent, and 3.0 percent respectively from 1997 to 2008). The same happened to Botswana after 1990 (6.1 percent GDP growth rate from 1990 to 2008).[6]

5. Concluding Comments

One stylized fact results from the features and trends just reviewed. This is the combination of what has been called the great divergence—the widening gaps which still continue today between the world's richest and poorest countries, and club convergence—the tendency to converge towards the productivity

---

[6] It is worth noting, however, that even if growth is likely to eventually slow down, the level of output worker may well surpass that of today's technological leaders if the investment rate continues to be higher than in the leaders and even if the rate of growth of productivity converges to that of the technological leaders. In fact, today, the United States, which may be said to be the technological leader, does not have the highest output per worker among developed economies. Norway and Hong Kong do.

levels of the technological leader after some prerequisites have been fulfilled. These two features are clearly visible in Figure 19.1. The large number of initially poor countries that are below the 45-degree line (i.e., that were in 2008 even poorer relative to the United States than in 1950) speaks about the great divergence since 1950. The fact that almost all of today's developed countries are above the 45-degree line, i.e., that these initially middle-income countries have been catching up with the United States level of GDP per capita, illustrates club convergence.

There is not a single model that can explain this stylized fact and one that is clearly superior to other explanations. A classical development model featuring increasing returns to scale and surplus labor in appropriate doses to generate a poverty trap at low-income levels and a take off followed by convergence at middle-income levels may be our favorite but is indistinguishable in its implications from a variety of models that feature the "Gershenkron-Abramovitz" hypothesis, i.e. that combine a Gershenkron's advantage of backwardness together with a threshold level of income below which convergence cannot take place (see, in particular, Chapters 4 and 5). The threshold income level below which there is a poverty trap may due to a variety of factors as we have seen throughout this book and summarized in the previous section on poverty traps.

What seems clear is that the presence of increasing returns to scale is behind club convergence, as argued extensively in Chapter 8 when reviewing the evidence for the classical development model. It also seems clear that increasing returns to scale strengthens the hold of the trap and is thus behind the great divergence. As noted in Chapter 3, under constant returns to scale there are no obstacles, strictly speaking, to the adoption of the superior technologies no matter how small the amount of capital available to an individual investor. Whatever the merits of alternative explanations of poverty traps, removing the assumption of constant returns to scale and assuming increasing returns seems essential to understanding why if modern technology has shown the potential to raise living standards to first-world levels, the vast majority of the world's population lives in poverty in underdeveloped countries.

Another major topic in this book has been the role of the so-called fundamental determinants of economic development. We have already recalled in previous sections in this chapter the various roles that these determinants may have had in the great variety of contemporary development experiences. Regarding the search for *the* fundamental determinant of economic development, i.e., whether institutions. geography, openness, or some other deep determinant, "rules", it seems clear that the search itself is probably unproductive. Institutional failures may in some countries be the major factor impeding development. Clearly geography, culture or the initial endowment of human capital cannot explain why North Korea is much poorer than South

Korea. In other country comparisons, geographical disadvantages or factor endowments and the pattern of trade specialization may be much more important than institutions, as discussed in previous chapters. The developmental effects of trade policy are likely to be highly conditional on various factors including economic size and the pattern of trade specialization. The relative importance of the different determinants can also change over time for the same country. For example, geographical disadvantages, together with (rather than instead of) the lack of institutional modernization, had an important role in explaining why the Mexican economy lagged behind the United States and Western Europe before the advent of the railways in the late 19th century, but had much less importance afterwards (see on the subject, Coatsworth, 1978; and Moreno-Brid and Ros, 2009).

There seems to be a lack of recognition of this simple observation in much of the recent literature on the deep determinants of economic development. Fundamentalists on one side or another, by ignoring the role of other "deep determinants" of development and the interactions and feedback effects involved, are paradoxically led to downplay the historical reasons for development and underdevelopment. This applies paradoxically to some new institutionalist and I say "paradoxically" because the new institutionalism was originally inspired and informed by economic and political historical studies.

There is here a link with the neglect of today's developed economies history when discussing why they are developed and the resulting confusion, to which I referred to at the beginning of this chapter, between the factors that contributed to the economic process of structural transformation and the features that characterize today's advanced industrial democracies. In 1986 at the beginning of the contemporary revival of interest in growth theory and empirics, William Baumol noted and complained about the neglect of economic history in the modern economics of growth.[7] This observation continues to have relevance 27 years later. To make progress in understanding those determinants and interactions, modern development economics and growth theory need to draw much more on economic history. This implies following the original path taken by the new institutional economics and also the example set by classical development theory more than half a century ago. Perhaps it is there, in the insights of good old theory and the economic history of particular countries, where the keys to the Kingdom are to be found.

---

[7] As he put it: "For all the interest now expressed in the subject of long-run economic growth and policies ostensibly directed to its stimulation, it does not seem to be widely recognized that adequate economic analysis of such issues calls for the careful study of economic history-if only because it is there that the pertinent evidence is to be found. Economic historians have provided the necessary materials, in the form of brilliant insights, powerful analysis, as well as a surprising profusion of long- period data. Yet none of these has received the full measure of attention they deserve from members of the economics profession at large" (Baumol, 1986, p. 1072).

References

Abramovitz, M. (1952), Economics of growth, in B. F. Haley (ed.), *A Survey of Contemporary Economics*, Homewood, Ill.: Richard D. Irwin

Abramovitz, M. (1986), Catching up, forging ahead, and falling behind, *Journal of Economic History* 46: 385–406

Acemoglu, D., and J. Robinson (2012), *Why Nations Fail?*, New York: Crown Publishers

Acemoglu, D., S. Johnson, and J. Robinson (2001), The colonial origins of comparative development: An empirical investigation, *American Economic Review* 95/5: 1369–401

Acemoglu, D., S. Johnson, and J. Robinson (2002), Reversal of fortune: geography and institutions in the making of modern world income distribution, *Quarterly Journal of Economics* CXVII, November: 1231–94

Acemoglu, D., S. Johnson, and J. Robinson (2003), An African success story: Botswana, in D. Rodrik (ed.), *In Search of Prosperity: Analytical Narratives on Economic Growth*, Princeton and Oxford: Princeton University Press

Acemoglu, D., S. Johnson, and J. Robinson (2005), Institutions as a fundamental cause of long run growth, in P. Aghion and S. Durlauf (eds.), *Handbook of Economic Growth*, Amsterdam, The Netherlands: Elsevier

Ades, A., and E. Glaeser (1999), Evidence on growth, increasing returns, and the extent of the market, *Quarterly Journal of Economics* 114/3: 1025–45

Aghion, P., and P. Howitt (1992), A model of growth through creative destruction, *Econometrica* 60: 323–51

Aghion, P. and P. Howitt (1998), *Endogenous Growth Theory*, Cambridge, MA: The MIT Press

Aghion, P., and P. Howitt (2005), Growth with quality improving innovations: an integrated framework, in P. Aghion and S. Durlauf (eds.), *Handbook of Economic Growth*, Amsterdam, The Netherlands: Elsevier

Aghion, P., and P. Howitt (2006), Joseph Schumpeter lecture. Appropriate growth policy: a unifying framework, *Journal of the European Economic Association* 4/2–3: 269–314

Aghion, P., and P. Howitt (2009), *The Economics of Growth*, Cambridge, MA: MIT Press

Aghion, P., R. Blundell, R. Griffith, P. Howitt, and S. Prantl (2004), Entry and productivity growth: evidence from microlevel panel data, *Journal of the European Economic Association*, 2: 265–76

References

Agosín, M. and R. Ffrench-Davis (1993), Trade liberalization in Latin America, *CEPAL Review* 50, August: 41–50

Akerlof, G. A., and J. L. Yellen (1985), A near-rational model of the business cycle, with wage and price inertia, *Quarterly Journal of Economics* 100 (Supplement): 823–38

Akerlof, G. A., and J. L. Yellen (1986), *Efficiency Wage Models of the Labor Market*, New York: Cambridge University Press

Akerlof, G., W. Dickens, and G. Perry (1996), The macroeconomics of low inflation, *Brookings Papers on Economic Activity* 1: 1–76

Albouy, D. (2012), The colonial origins of comparative development: an investigation of the settler mortality data, NBER Working Paper Series, Working Paper 14130

Alesina, A., and R. Perotti (1994), The political economy of growth: a critical survey of the recent literature, *World Bank Economic Review* 8: 351–71

Alesina, A., and D. Rodrik (1994), Distributive politics and economic growth, *Quarterly Journal of Economics* 109: 465–90

Alesina, A., S. Ozler, N. Roubini, and P. Swagel (1996), Political instability and economic growth, *Journal of Economic Growth* 1: 193–215

Alvarez M., J. A. Cheibub, F. Limongi, and A. Przeworski (2000), *Democracy and Development: Political Institutions and Material Well-Being in the World, 1950–1990*, Cambridge: Cambridge University Press

Amsden, A. E. (1989), *Asia's Next Giant: South Korea and Late Industrialization*, New York: Oxford University Press

Amsden, A. E. (2001), *The Rise of "the Rest"*, New York: Oxford University Press

Armey, D. (1995) *The Freedom Revolution*, Washington, DC: Regnery Publishing

Arrow, K. J. (1962), The economic implications of learning by doing, *Review of Economic Studies* 29: 155–73

Asoni, A. (2008), Protection of property rights and growth as political equilibria, *Journal of Economic Surveys* 22/5: 953–87

Auty, R. (2001), *Resource Abundance and Economic Development*, Oxford: Oxford University Press

Auty, R. M. (1990), *Resource-Based Industrialization: Sowing the Oil in Eight Developing Countries*, New York: Oxford University Press

Azariadis, C. (1996), The economics of poverty traps. Part one: complete markets, *Journal of Economic Growth* 1: 449–86

Azariadis, C., and A. Drazen (1990), Threshold externalities in economic development, *Quarterly Journal of Economics*, 105: 501–26

Azariadis, C., and J. Stachurski (2005), Poverty traps, in P. Aghion and S. Durlauf (eds.), *Handbook of Economic Growth*, Amsterdam, The Netherlands: Elsevier

Bacha, E. L. (1984), Growth with limited supplies of foreign exchange: a reappraisal of the Two-Gap model, in M. Syrquin, L. Taylor, and L. Westphal (eds.), *Economic Structure and Performance*, New York: Academic Press

Bacha, E. L. (1990), A Three-Gap model of foreign transfers and the GDP growth rate in developing countries, *Journal of Development Economics* 32: 279–96

Baer, W., and I. Kerstenetzky (1964), *Inflation and Growth in Latin America*, New Haven: Yale University Press

Bairam, E. I. (1987), The Verdoorn Law, returns to scale and industrial growth: a review of the literature, *Australian Economic Papers* 26: 20–42

Banerjee, A., and E. Duflo (2003), Inequality and growth: what can the data say?, *Journal of Economic Growth* 8: 267–99

Bardhan, P. (1970), *Economic Growth, Development, and Foreign Trade: A Study in Pure Theory*, New York: Wiley Interscience

Bardhan, P. (2004), History, institutions and underdevelopment, Ms. Department of Economics. University of California, Berkeley

Barro, R. (1995), Inflation and economic growth, NBER Working Paper Series, WP no. 5326, NBER, Cambridge, MA

Barro, R. (1996), Democracy and growth, *Journal of Economic Growth* 1: 1–27

Barro, R. (1997), *Determinants of Economic Growth: A Cross-Country Empirical Study*, Cambridge, MA: MIT Press

Barro, R. (2000), Inequality and growth in a panel of countries, *Journal of Economic Growth* 5: 5–32

Barro, R., and H. Wolf (1989), Data appendix for economic growth in a cross-section of countries, NBER Working Paper No. 2

Barro, R., and J. Lee, (2010), A new data set of educational attainment in the world, 1950–2010, NBER Working Paper No. 15902

Barro, R., G. Mankiw, and X. Sala-i-Marti (1995), Capital mobility in neoclassical growth models, *American Economic Review* 85/1: 103–15

Barro, R. J. (1990), Government spending in a simple model of endogenous growth, *Journal of Political Economy* 98/5, part 2: 103–25

Barro, R. J. (1991), Economic growth in a cross section of countries, *Quarterly Journal of Economics*, 106: 407–44

Barro, R. J. (2008), Inequality and growth revisited, Asian Development Bank, Working paper Series (11)

Barro, R. J., and J. Lee (1993), International comparisons of educational attainment, *Journal of Monetary Economics* 32: 363–94

Barro, R. J., and X. Sala-i-Martin (1995), *Economic Growth*, New York: McGraw-Hill

Basu, K. (1984), *The Less Developed Economy: A Critique of Contemporary Theory*, Oxford: Basil Blackwell

Basu, K. (1997), *Analytical Development Economics: The Less Developed Economy Revisited*, Cambridge, MA: The MIT Press

Basu, S., and D. Weil (1998), Appropriate technology and growth, *Quarterly Journal of Economics* 113/4: 1025–54

Bateman, F., J. Ros, and J. Taylor (2009), Did New Deal and World War II public capital investments facilitate a "Big Push" in the American South?, *Journal of Institutional and Theoretical Economics* 165/2, 307–41

Baumol, W. J. (1986), Productivity growth, convergence and welfare: what the longrun data show, *American Economic Review* 76: 1072–86

Baumol, W. J., S. A. Blackman, and E. W. Wolff (1989), *Productivity and American Leadership: The Long View*, Cambridge, MA: The MIT Press

Baumol, W. J., and E. W. Wolff (1988), Productivity, convergence and welfare: reply, *American Economic Review* 78: 1155–59

References

Becker, G., K. Murphy, and R. Tamura (1990), Human capital, fertility and growth, *Journal of Political Economy* 98/5, Part 2: S12–37

Bénabou, R. (1996), Inequality and growth, in B. S. Bernanke and J. Rotemberg (eds.), *NBER Macroeconomics Annual* 11, Cambridge, MA: MIT Press

Benhabib, J., and M. Spiegel (2005), Technological diffusion and economic growth, in P. Aghion and S. Durlauf, *Handbook of Economic Growth*, Amsterdam, The Netherlands: Elsevier

Benhabib, J., and M. M. Spiegel (1994), The role of human capital in economic development: evidence from aggregate cross-country data, *Journal of Monetary Economics* 34: 143–73

Bernard, A. B., and C. I. Jones (1996), Technology and convergence, *Economic Journal* 106: 1037–44

Berthelemy, J. C., and A. Varoudakis (1996), Economic growth, convergence clubs, and the role of financial development, *Oxford Economic Papers* 48: 300–28

Bertola, G. (1993), Market structure and income distribution in endogenous growth models, *American Economic Review* 83: 1184–99

Bhaduri, A. (2006), Endogenous economic growth: a new approach, *Cambridge Journal of Economics* 30: 69–83

Bhaduri, A., and S. Marglin (1990), Unemployment and the real wage: the economic basis for contesting political ideologies, *Cambridge Journal of Economics* 14: 375–93

Bhagwati, J. (1978), *Foreign Trade Regimes and Economic Development: Anatomy and Consequences of Exchange Control Regimes*, Cambridge, MA: Ballinger

Bhagwati, J. (1988), Export-promoting trade strategy: issues and evidence, *World Bank Research Observer* 3: 27–57

Bhagwati, J. N. (1985), *Essays on Development Economics*, Vol. 1, Cambridge, MA: MIT Press

Birdsall, N., D. Ross, and R. Sabot (1995), Inequality and growth reconsidered: lessons from East Asia, *The World Bank Economic Review* 9: 477–508

Blanchflower, D., and A. Oswald (1994), *The Wage Curve*, Cambridge, MA: MIT Press

Blanchflower, D., and A. Oswald (2005) The wage curve reloaded, NBER Working Paper

Bleaney, M., and A. Nishiyama (2002), Explaining growth: a contest between models, *Journal of Economic Growth* 7/1: 43–56

Bowles, S. (1985), The production process in a competitive economy: Walrasian, Marxian and neo-Hobbesian models, *American Economic Review* 75: 16–36

Boyd, J., S. Kwak, and B. Smith (2005), The real output losses associated with modern banking crises, *Journal of Money, Credit and Banking* 37/6: 977–99

Braudel, F. (1972). *The Mediterranean and the Mediterranean World in the Age of Philip II*, Vol. 1, S. Reynolds, trans., New York: Harper & Row

Bravo-Ortega, C., and J. De Gregorio (2007), The relative richness of the poor? Natural resources, human capital, and economic growth, in Lederman and Maloney (eds), *Natural Resources: Neither Curse nor Destiny*, Washington, DC, and Palo Alto, CA: Stanford University Press

Bruno, M. (1995), Does inflation really lower growth?, *Finance and Development*, September, vol. 32, 35–8

Bruno, M. and W. Easterly (1998), Inflation crises and long run growth, *Journal of Monetary Economics* 41, 3–26

Burdekin, R., A. Denzau, M. Keil, T. Sitthiyot, and T. Willett (2004), When does inflation hurt economic growth? Different nonlinearities for different economies, *Journal of Macroeconomics* 26: 519–32

Calmfors, L., and Driffill, J. (1988) Bargaining structure, corporatism and macroeconomic performance, *Economic Policy* 6: 13–61

Cardoso, E. A. (1981), Food supply and inflation, *Journal of Development Economics* 8: 269–84

Carneiro, D., and R. Werneck (1988), External debt, economic growth and fiscal adjustment, Texto para Discussao No. 202, Departamento de Economia, Rio de Janeiro: PUC/Rio

Caselli, F., G. Esquivel, and F. Leffort (1996), Reopening the convergence debate: a new look at cross-country growth empirics, *Journal of Economic Growth* 1/3: 363–89

Cerra, V., and S. Saxena (2008), Growth dynamics: the myth of economic recovery, *American Economic Review* 98/1: 439–57

Chang, H-J (2002), *Kicking Away The Ladder: Development Strategy in Historical Perspective*, London: Anthem Press

Chang, H-J. (2011), Institutions and economic development: theory, policy and history, *Journal of Institutional Economics* 7/4: 473–98

Chenery, H. B., and A. M. Strout (1966), Foreign assistance and economic development, *American Economic Review* 56: 679–733

Chenery, H. B., and M. Syrquin (1975), *Patterns of Development, 1950–1970*, London: Oxford University Press

Ciccone, A., and K. Matsuyama (1996), Start up costs and pecuniary externalities as barriers to economic development, *Journal of Development Economics* 49: 33–60

Clarke, G. (1995), More evidence on income distribution and growth, *Journal of Development Economics* 47: 403–27

Coatsworth, J. (1978), Obstacles to economic growth in nineteenth-century Mexico, *American Historical Review* 83/1: 80–100

Commendatore P., D'Acunto S., Panico C., and Pinto A. (2003), Keynesian theories of growth, in N. Salvadori (ed.), *The Theories of Economic Growth: a Classical Perspective*, Aldershot: Elgar, 103–38

Corden, W. M. (1984), Booming sector and dutch disease economics: survey and consolidation, *Oxford Economic Papers* 36: 359–80

Corden, W. M., and J. P. Neary (1982), Booming sector and de-industrialisation in a small open economy, *Economic Journal* 92: 825–48

Cornes, R., and T. Sandler (1986), *The Theory of Externalities, Public Goods, and Club Goods*, Cambridge: Cambridge University Press

Cortés Conde, R. (1985), The export economy of Argentina 1880–1930, in R. Cortés Conde and S. Hunt (eds.), *The Latin American Economies: Growth and the Export Sector 1880–1930*, London and New York: Macmillan

Coutts, K., W. Godley, and G. Gudgin (1984), *Inflation Accounting of Whole Economic Systems*, Cambridge: Department of Applied Economics, University of Cambridge

References

Cripps, T. F., and R. J. Tarling (1973), *Growth in Advanced Capitalist Economies 1950–1970*, Cambridge: Cambridge University Press

Crosby, A. (1986), *Ecological Imperialism: The Biological Expansion of Europe 900–1900*, New York: Cambridge University Press

Darity, W., and L. Davis (2005), Growth, trade and uneven development, *Cambridge Journal of Economics* 29/1: 141–70

De La Croix, D., and M. Doepke (2003), Inequality and growth: why differential fertility matters, *American Economic Review* 93/4: 1091–113

De Long, B. (1988), Productivity growth, convergence and welfare: comment, *American Economic Review* 78/5: 1138–54

De Long, J. B., (1997), Cross-country variations in national economic growth rates: the role of technology, in J. Fuhrer and J. Sneddon Little (eds.), *Technology and Growth*, Boston: Federal Reserve Bank of Boston

Devereux, M., and B. Lapham (1994), The stability of economic integration and endogenous growth, *Quarterly Journal of Economics* 59: 299–305

Diamond, J. (1997) *Guns, Germs and Steel*, New York: W.W. Norton

Diamond, J. (2012), What makes countries rich and poor? *The New York Review of Books* 59/10, 7 June

Díaz-Alejandro, C. (1984), No less than one hundred years of Argentine economic history, in G. Ranis et al. (eds), *Comparative Development Perspectives*, Boulder: Westview

Diaz-Alejandro, C. (1985), Argentina, Australia and Brazil before 1929, in D. C. Platt and G. di Tella (eds.), *Argentina, Australia and Canada. Studies in Comparative Development, 1870–1965*, New York: St. Martin's Press

Diaz-Alejandro, C. (1985a), Good-bye financial repression hello financial crash, *Journal of Development Economics* 19: 1–24

Dollar, D. (1992), Outward-oriented developing economies really do grow more rapidly: evidence from 95 LDCs 1976–1985, *Economic Development and Cultural Change* 40: 523–44

Domar, E. (1957), *Essays in the Theory of Economic Growth*, London: Oxford University Press

Durlauf, S., P. Johnson, and J. Temple (2005), Growth econometrics, in P. Aghion and S. Durlauf (eds), *Handbook of Economic Growth*, Amsterdam, The Netherlands: Elsevier

Dutt, A. (2001), Demand and wage goods constraints in agriculture-industry interaction in Less Developed Economies, in A. Bose, D. Ray and A. Sarkar (eds.), *Contemporary Macroeconomics*, New Delhi: Oxford University Press, 93–127

Dutt, A. (2003), Income elasticities of imports, North-South trade and uneven development, in A. Dutt and J. Ros (eds), *Development Economics and Structuralist Macroeconomics. Essays in Honor of Lance Taylor*, Cheltenham, UK and Northapton, MA: Edward Elgar

Dutt, A. K. (1984), Stagnation, income distribution, and monopoly power, *Cambridge Journal of Economics* 8: 25–40

Dutt, A. K. (1990), *Growth, Distribution, and Uneven Development*, Cambridge: Cambridge University Press

Dutt, A. K. (2006), Aggregate demand, aggregate supply and economic growth, *International Review of Applied Economics* 20/3, July: 319–36

Dutt, A. K., and J. Ros (2007). Aggregate demand shocks and economic growth, *Structural Change and Economic Dynamics* 18(1), March: 75–99

Dutta, J. (1988), The wage-goods constraint on a developing economy: theory and evidence, *Journal of Development Economics* 28/3, May: 341–63

Easterly, W. (1994), Economic stagnation, fixed factors and policy thresholds, *Journal of Monetary Economics* 23: 525–57

Easterly, W. (2006), A Review of Jeffrey Sachs, The *End of Poverty: Economic Possibilities for Our Time*, Penguin Press: New York, 2005, *Journal of Economic Literature* 44/1, March

Easterly, W. (2007), Inequality does cause underdevelopment, *Journal of Development Economics* 84: 755–76

Easterly, W., and R. Levine (1997), Africa's growth tragedy: policies and ethnic divisions, *Quarterly Journal of Economics* CXII/4, November: 1203–50

Easterly, W., and R. Levine (2001), What have we learned from a decade of empirical research on growth? It's not factor accumulation: stylized facts and growth models, *World Bank Economic Review* 15/2: 177–219

Easterly, W., and R. Levine (2003), Tropics, germs and crops: how endowments influence economic development, *Journal of Monetary Economics* 50: 3–39

Edwards, S. (1993), Openness, trade liberalization, and growth in developing countries, *Journal of Economic Literature* 31/3: 1358–98

Edwards, S. (1998), Openness, productivity and growth: what do we really know?, *Economic Journal* 108 (March): 383–98

Engen, E., and J. Skinner (1992), Fiscal policy and economic growth, NBER Working Paper n. 4223

Engerman, S., and K. Sokoloff (2002), Factor endowments, inequality, and paths of development among New World economies, *Economia* 3/1, Fall: 41–88

Esteban, J., and D. Ray (1994), On the measurement of polarization, *Econometrica* 62: 819–51

Everhart, S., and M. A. Sumlinski (2001), Trends in private investment in developing countries: statistics for 1970–2000, Discussion Paper 44, World Bank—International Finance Corporation

Fajnzylber, F. (1989), *Industrialización en América Latina: De la "Caja Negra" al "Casillero Vacío"*, Cuadernos de la CEPAL, Santiago de Chile

Fajnzylber, F. (1990), *Unavoidable Industrial Restructuring in Latin America*, Durham and London: Duke University Press

Fanelli, J. M., R. Frenkel, and C. Winograd (1987), Argentina, *Stabilization and Adjustment Policies and Programmes, Country Study No. 12*, Helsinki: WIDER

Feenstra, R. (1996), Trade and uneven growth, *Journal of Development Economics* 49/1: 229–56

Fei, J., and G. Ranis (1961), A theory of economic development, *American Economic Review* 51: 533–65

Fei, J., and G. Ranis (1964), *Development of the Labor Surplus Economy*, Homewood, IL: Irwin

Feldman, G. A. (1928), K teorii tempov narodnogo dokhoda. *Planovoe Khoziaistvo* 11: 146–70. Discussed in E. Domar (1957), *Essays in the Theory of Economic Growth*, Oxford: Oxford University Press

Feyrer, J. (2008), Convergence by parts, *The BE Journal of Macroeconomics* 8/1, July: art. 19

Findlay, R. (1980), The terms of trade and equilibrium growth in the world economy, *American Economic Review* 70/3, June: 291–9

Findlay, R. (1981), The fundamental determinants of the terms of trade, in S. Grassman and E. Lundberg (eds.), *The World Economic Order: Past and Prospects*, New York: Saint Martin's Press

Findlay, R., and M. Lundahl (1994), Natural resources, vent for surplus, and the staples theory, in G. M. Meier (ed.), *From Classical Economics to Development Economics*, New York: St. Martin's Press

Fishlow, A. (1995), Inequality, poverty and growth: where do we stand?, in M. Bruno and B. Pleskovic (eds.), *Annual World Bank Conference on Development Economics 1995*, Supplement to The World Bank Economic Review and The World Bank Research Observer, Washington DC

Fleming, J. M. (1955), External economies and the doctrine of balanced growth, *Economic Journal* 65: 241–56

Fölster, S., and M. Henrekson (2001), Growth effects of government expenditure and taxation in rich countries, *European Economic Review* 45/8: 1501–20

Forbes, K. (2000), A reassessment of the relationship between inequality and growth, *American Economic Review* 90/4: 869–87

Franco, G. (1986), Aspects of the economics of hyperinflations: theoretical issues and historical studies of four European hyperinflations in the 1920s, Cambridge MA: Department of Economics, Harvard University (unpublished Ph.D. dissertation)

Frenkel, R. (1983) Mercado financiero, expectativas cambiarias y movimientos de capital, *El Trimestre Económico* 4/200: 2041–76

Frenkel, R., and M. Rapetti (2012), External fragility or deindustrialization: what is the main threat to Latin American countries in the 2010's? *World Economic Review* 1: 37–57

Frenkel, R., and J. Ros (2006), Unemployment and the real exchange rate in Latin America, *World Development* 34/4, April: 631–46

Furtado, C. (1969), Desarrollo y estancamiento en America Latina: un enfoque estructuralista, in A. Bianchi (ed.), *America Latina: Ensayos de Interpretación Económica*, Santiago: Ed. Universitaria

Gallup, J., and J. Sachs (1998), Geography and development, in B. Pleskovic and J. Stiglitz (eds.), *World Bank Annual Conference on Development Economics 1998*, Washington, DC: The World Bank, 127–78

Gallup, J. L., J. D. Sachs, and A. D. Mellinger (1999), Geography and economic development, *International Regional Science Review* 22/2: 179–232

Galor, O., and H. Zang (1997), Fertility, income distribution and economic growth: theory and cross country evidence, *Japan and the World Economy* 9: 197–229

Galor, O., and J. Zeira (1993), Income distribution and macroeconomics, *Review of Economic Studies* 60: 35–52

Gancia, G., and F. Zilibotti (2005), Horizontal innovation in the theory of growth and development, in P. Aghion and S. Durlauf (eds.), *Handbook of Economic Growth*, Amsterdam, The Netherlands: Elsevier

Gelb, A. H. (1988), *Windfall Gains: Blessing or Curse?*, New York: Oxford University Press

Gerschenkron, A. (1962), *Economic Backwardness in Historical Perspective*, Cambridge, MA: Harvard University Press

Gersovitz, M. (ed.) (1983), *Selected Economic Writings of W. Arthur Lewis*, New York: New York University Press

Glaeser, E.L., R. La Porta, F. Lopez-de-Silanes, and A. Shleifer (2004), Do institutions cause growth?, *Journal of Economic Growth* 9/3: 271–303

Ghosh, A. and S. Phillips (1998), Warning: inflation may be harmful to your growth, *IMF Staff Papers* 45/4: 672–86

Graham, B., and J. Temple (2006), Rich nations, poor nations: how much can multiple equilibria explain?, *Journal of Economic Growth* 11/1: 5–41

Graham, F. (1923), Some aspects of protection further considered, *Quarterly Journal of Economics* 37: 199–227

Griffin, K. (1989), *Alternative Strategies of Economic Development*, London: MacMillan

Grossman, G. M., and E. Helpman (1991), *Innovation and Growth in the Global Economy*, Cambridge, MA: MIT Press

Grossman, G. M., and E. Helpman (1991a), Quality ladders in the theory of growth, *Review of Economic Studies* 58: 43–61

Gwartney, J., R. Holcombe, and R. Lawson (1998), The scope of government and the wealth of nations, *Cato Journal* 18/2: 163–90

Gylfason, T., T. Herbertsson, and G. Zoega (1999), A mixed blessing, *Macroeconomic Dynamics* 3/2: 204–25

Haavelmo, T. (1954), *A Study in the Theory of Economic Evolution*, Amsterdam, The Netherlands: North-Holland

Haggard, S., and S. B. Webb (1993), What do we know about the political economy of economic policy reform?, *World Bank Research Observer* 8: 143–68

Hall, R., and C. Jones (1999), Why do some countries produce more output per worker than others? *Quarterly Journal of Economics* 114/1: 83–116

Hall, R. E. (1988), Intertemporal substitution in consumption, *Journal of Political Economy* 96: 339–57

Hallaert, J. J. (2006), A History of empirical literature on the relationship between trade and growth, *Mondes en développement* 3/135: 63–77

Hansson, P., and M. Henrekson (1994), A new framework for testing the effect of government spending on growth and productivity, *Public Choice* 81: 381–401

Harris, J. R., and M. Todaro (1970), Migration, unemployment and development: a two-sector analysis, *American Economic Review* 60: 126–42

Harrison, A., and A. Rodríguez-Clare (2010), Trade, foreign investment, and industrial policy for developing countries, in D. Rodrik and M. Rosenzweig (eds.), *Handbook of Development Economics*, vol. 5, Amsterdam, The Netherlands: Elsevier

Harrod, R. F. (1939), An essay on dynamic theory, *Economic Journal* 49: 14–33

Hausmann, R., J. Hwang, and D. Rodrik (2005), What you export matters, NBER Working Paper 11905

References

Hayek, F. von (1960), *The Constitution of Liberty*, Chicago: University of Chicago Press

Heitger, B. (2001), The scope of government and its impact on economic growth in OECD countries, Kiel Working Paper No. 1034. Kiel: Institute of World Economics

Helleiner, G. (1992) (ed.), *Trade Policy, Industrialization, and Development: New Perspectives*, New York: Oxford University Press

Helpman, E. (2004), *The Mystery of Economic Growth*, Cambridge, MA: Harvard University Press

Hirschman, A. (1958), *The Strategy of Economic Development*, New Haven: Yale University Press

Hirschman, A. (1977), A generalized linkage approach to development, with special reference to staples, *Economic Development and Cultural Change* 25 (Supplement): 67–98

Howitt, P. (2000), Endogenous growth and cross-country income differences, *American Economic Review* 90: 829–46

Howitt, P., and D. Mayer-Foulkes (2005), R&D, implementation, and stagnation: a Schumpeterian theory of convergence clubs, *Journal of Money, Credit and Banking* 37/1: 147–77

Humphreys, M., J. Sachs, and J. Stiglitz (2007), *Escaping the Resource Curse*, New York: Columbia University Press

Inada, K. (1963), On a two-sector model of economic growth: comments and a generalization, *Review of Economic Studies* 30: 119–27

Innis, H. A. (1930), *The Fur Trade in Canada: An Introduction to Canadian Economic History*, Toronto: University of Toronto Press

Innis, H. A. (1940), *The Cod Fisheries: The History of an International Economy*, Toronto: University of Toronto Press

International Monetary Fund (2009), *World Economic Outlook*, October, Washington, DC: IMF

Islam, N. (1995), Growth empirics: a panel data approach, *Quarterly Journal of Economics* 110: 1127–70

Jaggers, K., and M. Marshall (2000), *Polity IV Project*, College Park, MD: Center for International Development and Conflict Management, University of Maryland

Jones, E. L. (1981), *The European Miracle: Environments, Economies and Geopolitics in the History of Europe and Asia*, Cambridge: Cambridge University Press

Jones, C. (1995), R&D based models of economic growth, *Journal of Political Economy* 103: 759–84

Jones, C. (1999), Growth: with or without scale effects, *American Economic Review* 89/2: 139–44

Jones, C. (2002), *Introduction to Economic Growth. Second Edition*, New York and London: Norton

Jones, L. E., and R. E. Manuelli (1990), A convex model of equilibrium growth: theory and policy implications, *Journal of Political Economy* 98: 1008–28

Jorgenson, D. (1961), The development of a dual economy, *Economic Journal* 71: 309–34

Kahn, R. F. (1959), Exercises in the analysis of growth, *Oxford Economic Papers* 11: 143–56

Kaldor, N. (1956), Alternative theories of distribution, *Review of Economic Studies* 23: 83–100

Kaldor, N. (1957), A model of economic growth, *Economic Journal* 67: 591–624

Kaldor, N. (1966), *Causes of the Slow Rate of Economic Growth of the United Kingdom*, Cambridge: Cambridge University Press

Kaldor, N. (1967), Strategic factors in economic development, The Frank W. Pierce Memorial Lectures at Cornell University, October 1966, Cornell University, Ithaca, New York

Kaldor, N. (1968), Productivity and growth in manufacturing industry: a reply, *Economica* 35: 385–91

Kaldor, N. (1972), The irrelevance of equilibrium economics, *Economic Journal* 82/328: 1237–55

Kaldor, N. (1975), What is wrong with economic theory?, *Quarterly Journal of Economics* 89/3: 347–57

Kaldor, N., and J. A. Mirrlees (1962), A new model of economic growth, *Review of Economic Studies* 29: 174–92

Kalecki, M. (1954), El problema del financiamiento del desarrollo económico, *El Trimestre Económico* 21: 381–401

Kalecki, M. (1966 [1993]) The difference between crucial economic problems of developed and underdeveloped non-socialist economies, in J. Osiatynsky (ed.), *Collected Works of Michal Kalecki*, Vol. V, Oxford: Oxford University Press

Kalecki, M. (1971), *Selected Essays on the Dynamics of the Capitalist Economy*, Cambridge: Cambridge University Press

Kalecki, M. (1976), *Essays on Developing Economies*, Hassocks, UK: Harvester Press

Kaufmann, D., A. Kraay, and M. Mastruzzi (2010), The worldwide governance indicators: a summary of methodology, data and analytical issues, World Bank Policy Research Working Paper No. 543

Keefer, P., and S. Knack (2002), Polarization, politics and property rights: links between inequality and growth, *Public Choice* 111: 127–54

Kenny, C., and D. Williams (2001), What do we know about economic growth? Or, why don't we know very much?, *World Development* 29/1: 1–22

King, R., and S. Rebelo (1990), Public policy and economic growth: developing neoclassical implications, *Journal of Political Economy* 98: S126–S150

King, R. G., and R. Levine (1993), Finance and growth: Schumpeter might be right, *Quarterly Journal of Economics* 108: 717–37

King, R. G., and S. T. Rebelo (1993), Transitional dynamics and economic growth in the neoclassical model, *American Economic Review* 83: 908–31

Klenow, P., and A. Rodriguez Clare (1997), The neoclassical revival in growth economics: has it gone too far? in B. Bernanke and J. Rotenberg (eds.), *NBER Macroeconomics Annual 1997*, Cambridge, MA: MIT Press

Knack, S., and Keefer, P. (1995) Institutions and economic performance: cross country tests using alternative measures, *Economics and Politics* 7: 207–27

Kormendi, R., and P. Meguire (1986), Government debt, government spending, and private sector behavior: reply, *American Economic Review* 76/5: 1180–7

References

Kraay, A., and C. Raddatz (2006), Poverty traps, aid, and growth, *Journal of Development Economics* 82: 315–47

Kravis, I. (1960), International differences in the distribution of income, *Review of Economics and Statistics* 42, November: 408–16

Kristensen, T. (1974), *Development in Rich and Poor Countries,* New York: Praeger

Krueger, A. (1978), *Foreign Trade Regimes and Economic Development: Liberalization Attempts and Consequences,* Cambridge, MA: Ballinger

Krueger, A., and M. Lindahl (2001), Education for Growth: why and for whom? *Journal of Economic Literature* 39/4: 1101–36

Krugman, P. (1987) The narrow moving band, the Dutch disease, and the competitiveness consequences of Mrs. Thatcher: notes on trade in the presence of dynamic scale economies, *Journal of Development Economics* 27/1–2, October: 41–55

Krugman, P. (1992), Toward a counter-counterrevolution in development theory, in Proceedings of the World Bank Annual Conference on Development Economics, 1992

Krugman, P. (1995), *Development, Geography, and Economic Theory,* Cambridge, MA: MIT Press

Kumar, M. S., E. Baldacci, and A. Schaechter (2009), Fiscal rules—anchoring expectations for sustainable public finances, *IMF Fiscal Affairs Department,* Washington, DC: International Monetary Fund

Kuznets, S. (1955), Economic growth and income inequality, *American Economic Review* 45: 1–28

Kuznets, S. (1963), Quantitative aspects of the economic growth of nations: VIII, Distribution of income by size, *Economic Development and Cultural Change* 11/2, January: 1–80

La Porta, R., F. Lopez-de-Silanes, A. Shleifer, and R. Vishny (1997), Legal determinants of external finance, *Journal of Finance* 52/3: 1131–50

La Porta, R., F. Lopez-de-Silanes, A. Shleifer, and R. Vishny (1998), Law and finance, *Journal of Political Economy* 106/6: 1113–55

La Porta, R., F. Lopez-de-Silanes, and A. Shleifer (2007), The economic consequences of legal origins, *Journal of Economic Literature* 46/2: 285–332

Landes, D. (1998), *The Wealth and Poverty of Nations,* New York: W. W. Norton

Lane, P., and A. Tornell (1996), Power, growth, and the voracity effect, *Journal of Economic growth* 1/2, June: 213–41

Lavezzi, A. (2001), Division of labor and economic growth: from Adam Smith to Paul Romer and beyond, Pisa: University of Pisa, unpublished

Lederman, D., and W. Maloney (2002), Open questions about the link between natural resources and economic growth: Sachs and Warner revisited, Central Bank of Chile Working Papers, n. 141, February

Lederman, D., and W. Maloney (eds.) (2007), *Natural resources: Neither Curse nor Destiny,* Washington, DC: Stanford University Press

Lederman, D., and W. Maloney (2008), In search of the missing resource curse, *Economia* 9/1: 1–57

Lee, K., H. Pesaran, and R. Smith (1997), Growth and convergence in a multi-country empirical stochastic Solow model, *Journal of Applied Econometrics* 12: 357–92

Leeson, P. F. (1979), The Lewis model and development theory, *The Manchester School of Economic and Social Studies* 66, September: 196–210

Levine, R., and D. Renelt (1992), A sensitivity analysis of cross-country growth regressions, *American Economic Review* 82: 942–63

Leibenstein, H. (1957), *Economic Backwardness and Economic Growth*, New York: Wiley

Leon-Ledesma, M., and A. Thirlwall (2002), The endogeneity of the natural rate, *Cambridge Journal of Economics* 26: 441–59

Lewis, A. (1954), Economic development with unlimited supplies of labor, *The Manchester School of Economic and Social Studies* 28: 139–91

Lewis, A. (1955), *The Theory of Economic Growth*, Homewood, Ill.: Irwin

Lewis, A. (1958), Unlimited labor: further notes, *The Manchester School of Economic and Social Studies*, 32: 1–32

Lewis, A. (1969), *Aspects of Tropical Trade 1883–1965* (The Wicksell Lectures), Stockholm: Almqvist & Wicksell

Lewis, A. (1972), Reflections on unlimited labor, in L. E. di Marco (ed.), International Economics and Development (Essays in honour of Raoul Prebisch), New York: Academic Press

Lewis, A. (1976), Development and distribution, in A. Cairncross and M. Puri (eds.), *Essays in Honor of Hans Singer*, New York: Holms & Meier

Libanio, G. (2009), Aggregate demand and the endogeneity of the natural rate of growth: evidence from Latin American countries, *Cambridge Journal of Economics* 33: 967–84

Lin, J. Y., and Nugent, J. B. (1995), Institutions and economic development, in J. Behrman and T. N. Srinivasan (eds.), *Handbook of Development Economics* 3: 2301–70, Amsterdam: Elsevier

Lipset, S. M. [1960] (1981), *Political Man: The Social Bases of Politics*, Baltimore, MD: Johns Hopkins

Lipset, S. M. (1994), The social requisites of democracy revisited: 1993 presidential address, *American Sociological Review* 59/1: 1–22

Lipton, M., and M. Ravaillon (1995), Poverty and Policy, in J. Behrman and T. Srinivasan (eds.), *Handbook of Development Economics*, vol. III B, Amsterdam, The Netherlands: Elsevier

Little, I. (1982), *Economic Development: Theory, Policy and International Relations*, New York: Basic Books

Little, I., T. Scitovsky, and M. Scott (1970), *Industry and Trade in Some Developing Countries*, Oxford: Oxford University Press

Londregan, J., and K. Poole (1990), Poverty, the coup trap, and the seizure of executive power, *World Politics* 42: 151–83

Lora, E. (2001), Structural reforms in Latin America: what has been reformed and how to measure it, Inter-American Development Bank Working Paper No. 466, Washington, DC

Lora, E., and Pagés-Serra, C. (1996), La Legislación Laboral en el Proceso de Reformas Estructurales de America Latina y el Caribe, Inter-American Development Bank, Washington, DC

References

Loury, G. (1981), Intergenerational transfers and the distribution of earnings, *Econometrica* 49: 843–67

Lucas, R. E., Jr. (1988), On the mechanics of economic development, *Journal of Monetary Economics* 22: 3–42

Lucas, R. E., Jr. (1993), Making a miracle, *Econometrica* 61: 251–72

Lustig, N. (1980), Underconsumption in Latin American economic thought: some considerations, *Review of Radical Political Economics* 12: 35–43

Machiavelli, N. (1519), *Discourses on Livy*, New York: Oxford University Press

Maddison, A. (1982), *Phases of Capitalist Development*, Oxford: Oxford University Press

Maddison, A. (1991), *Dynamic Forces in Capitalist Development*, Oxford: Oxford University Press

Maddison, A. (1993), Explaining the economic performance of nations, in W. Baumol, R. Nelson, and E. Wolff (eds.), *Convergence of Productivity*, Oxford: Oxford University Press

Maddison, A. (1995), *Monitoring the World Economy*, 1820–1992, Paris: OECD

Maddison, A. (2003), *The World Economy: Historical Statistics*, Paris, OECD

Mahalanobis, P. C. (1955), The approach to operational research to planning in India, *Sankhya: The Indian Journal of Statistics* 16: 3–62

Mankiw, G., D. Romer, and D. Weil (1992), A contribution to the empirics of economic growth, *Quarterly Journal of Economics* 107: 407–37

Mankiw, G. (1995), The growth of nations, *Brookings Papers on Economic Activity* 1: 275–310

Manning, P. (1982), *Slavery, Colonialism, and Economic Growth in Dahomey, 1640–1980*, New York: Cambridge University Press

Marglin, S. (1984), *Growth, Distribution and Prices*, Cambridge, MA: Harvard University Press

Marshall, A. (1910), *Principles of Economics*. Sixth Edition, London: MacMillan and Co

Matsuyama, K. (1992). Agricultural productivity, comparative advantage, and economic growth, *Journal of Economic Theory* 58/2: 317–34

Mazumdar, D. (1959), The marginal productivity theory of wages and disguised unemployment, *Review of Economic Studies* 26: 190–7

McCombie, J. S. L. (1983), Kaldor's Law in retrospect, *Journal of Post Keynesian Economics* 5: 414–29

McLean, I. W. (1989), Growth in a small open economy: a historical view, in B. Chapman (ed.), *Australian Economic Growth*, Melbourne: Macmillan

McNeill, W. (1963) *The Rise of the West: A History of the Human Community*, Chicago: University of Chicago Press

Meade, J. E. (1952), External economies and diseconomies in a competitive situation, *Economic Journal* 62: 54–67

Mellinger, A., J. Sachs, and J. Gallup (2000), Climate, coastal proximity, and development, in G. Clark, M. Feldman, and M. Gertler (eds.), *Oxford Handbook of Economic Geography*, Oxford: Oxford University Press

Molana, H., and D. Vines (1989), North-South growth and the terms of trade: a model on Kaldorian lines, *Economic Journal* 99: 443–53

Montesquieu, C. L. Baron de (1748), *The Spirit of the Laws* (available in English from Cambridge: Cambridge University Press, 1989)

Moreno-Brid, J. C., and J. Ros (2009), *Development and Growth in the Mexican Economy: A Historical Perspective*, New York: Oxford University Press

Murillo, M., L. Ronconi, and A, Schrank (2011), Latin American labor reforms: Evaluating risk and security, in J. A. Ocampo y J. Ros (eds.), *The Oxford Handbook of Latin American Economics*, Oxford: Oxford University Press

Murphy, K., A. Shleifer, and R. Vishny (1989), Industrialization and the big push, *Journal of Political Economy* 97: 1003–26

Murphy, K., A. Shleifer, and R. Vishny (1989a), Income distribution, market size and industrialization, *Quarterly Journal of Economics* 104: 537–64

Myint, H. (1958), The classical theory of international trade and the underdeveloped countries, *Economic Journal* 68: 317–33

Myrdal, G. (1957), *Economic Theory and Underdeveloped Regions*, London: Duckworth

Myrdal, G. (1968), *Asian Drama: An Inquiry into the Poverty of Nations*, New York: Pantheon

Nelson, R. (1956), A theory of the low level equilibrium trap in underdeveloped economies, *American Economic Review* 46: 894–908

Nelson, R. (1998), The agenda for growth theory: a different point of view, *Cambridge Journal of Economics* 22/4: 497–520

Nelson, R., and E. Phelps (1966), Investment in humans, technological diffusion and economic growth, *American Economic Review* 56: 69–75

Nelson, R., and S. Winter (1982), *An Evolutionary Theory of Economic Change*, Cambridge, MA: Belknap Press of Harvard University Press

Neumayer, E. (2004), Does the "resource curse" hold for growth in genuine income as well?, *World Development* 32/10: 1627–40

North, D. (1966), *The Economic Growth of the United States, 1790–1860*, New York: W. W. Norton

North, D. C. (1981), *Structure and Change in Economic History*, New York: W. W. Norton

North, D. C. (1990) *Institutions, Institutional Change and Economic Performance*, Cambridge: Cambridge University Press

North, D. C., and Thomas, R. P. (1973), *The Rise of the Western World*, Cambridge: Cambridge University Press

North, D. C., W. Summerhill, and B. Weingast (2000), Order, disorder and economic change: Latin America vs. North America, in B. Bueno de Mesquita and H. Root (eds.), *Governing for Prosperity*, New Haven, CT: Yale University Press

Noyola, J. F. (1956), El desarrollo económico y la inflación en México y otros países latinoamericanos, *Investigación Económica* 16: 603–48

Nurkse, R. (1952), Some international aspects of the problem of economic development, *American Economic Review* 42, May: 571–83

Nurkse, R. (1953), *Problems of Capital Formation in Underdeveloped Countries*, New York: Oxford University Press

Nurkse, R. (1961), *Patterns of Trade and Development*, New York: Oxford University Press

Ocampo, J. A., and J. Ros (2011), Shifting paradigms in Latin America's economic development, in J. A. Ocampo and J. Ros (eds.), *The Oxford Handbook of Latin American Economics*, Oxford: Oxford University Press

Ocampo, J. A., and L. Taylor (1998), Trade liberalization in developing economies: modest benefits but problems with productivity growth, macro prices, and income distribution, *Economic Journal* 108: 1523–46

Ocampo, J. A., C. Rada, and L. Taylor (2009), *Growth and Policy in Developing Countries. A Structuralist Approach*, New York: Columbia University Press

Ohkawa, K., and H. Rosovsky (1973), *Japanese Economic Growth*, Stanford: Stanford University Press

Olivera, J. (1964), On structural inflation and Latin American structuralism, *Oxford Economic Papers* 16: 321–32

Pack, H. (1990), Industrialization and trade, in H. Chenery and T. Srinivasan (eds.), *Handbook of Development Economics* i: 333–80

Pack, H. (1994), Endogenous growth theory: intellectual appeal and empirical shortcomings, *The Journal of Economic Perspectives* 8: 55–72

Patnaik, P. (1995), Introduction, in P. Patnaik (ed.), *Macroeconomics*, New Delhi: Oxford University Press

Perala, M. (2002), Essays on economic development and growth, Ph.D. Dissertation, University of Notre Dame, Department of Economics

Perotti, R. (1993), Fiscal policy, income distribution and growth, Columbia University, Department of Economics, New York. Mimeo

Perotti, R. (1996), Growth, income distribution, and democracy: what the data say, *Journal of Economic Growth* 1: 149–87

Persson, T., and G. Tabellini (1994), Is inequality harmful for growth? Theory and evidence, *American Economic Review* 84: 600–21

Phelps, E. (1995), Comment on Mankiw, *Brookings Papers on Economic Activity* 1: 313–20

Pineda, J., and F. Rodríguez (2011), Curse or blessing? Natural resources and human development, in J. A. Ocampo and J. Ros (eds.), *Oxford Handbook of Latin American Economics*, Oxford: Oxford University Press

Pollin, R., and A. Zhu (2006), Inflation and economic growth: a cross-country nonlinear analysis, *Journal of Post Keynesian Economics* 28/4: 593–614

Pomeranz K. (2000), *The Great Divergence: China, Europe and the Making of the Modern World Economy*, Princeton, NJ: Princeton University Press

Prebisch, R. (1950), *The Economic Development of Latin America and its Principal Problems*, New York: United Nations

Prescott, E. (1998), Lawrence R. Klein Lecture 1997. Needed: a theory of total factor productivity, *International Economic Review* 39/3: 525–51

Pritchett, L. (1997), Divergence, big time, *Journal of Economic Perspectives* 11/3: 3–17

Pritchett, L. (2001), Where has all the education gone?, *World Bank Economic Review* 15/3: 367–93

Przeworski, A. (2004) The last instance: are institutions the primary cause of economic development, *European Journal of Sociology* 45/2: 165–88

Quah, D. T. (1993), Galton's fallacy and tests of the convergence hypothesis, *Scandinavian Journal of Economics* 95: 427–43

Rada, C. (2007), Stagnation or transformation of a dual economy through endogenous productivity growth, *Cambridge Journal of Economics* 31: 711–40

Ram, R. (1986), Government size and economic growth: a new framework and some evidence from cross-section and time series data, *American Economic Review* 76: 191–203

Ranis, G. (1995), Another look at the East Asian miracle, *The World Bank Economic Review* 9: 509–34

Rao, V. K. R. V. (1952), Investment, income and the multiplier in an underdeveloped economy, *Indian Economic Review* 1: 55–67. Reprinted in A. N. Agarwala and S. P. Singh (eds.) (1958), *The Economics of Underdevelopment*, Delhi: Oxford University Press

Rapetti, M. (2011), Macroeconomic policy coordination in a competitive real exchange rate strategy for development, Economics Department Working Paper Series, Paper No. 117, University of Massachusetts at Amherst

Rapetti, M. (2012), Real exchange levels and economic growth: some reflections on the possible channels, University of Buenos Aires, unpublished

Rebelo, S. (1991), Long run policy analysis and long run growth, *Journal of Political Economy* 99: 500–21

Reinert, E. S. (2007), *How Rich Countries got Rich . . . and Why Poor Countries Stay Poor*, London: Constable

Rivera-Batiz, L., and P. Romer (1991), International trade with endogenous technological change, *European Economic Review* 35: 971–1004

Robinson, J. (1956) *Accumulation of Capital*, London: Macmillan

Robinson, J. (1962), A model of accumulation, *Essays in the Theory of Economic Growth*, London: Macmillan, 34–59

Rodriguez, F. (2010), Does one size fit all in policy reform? Cross national evidence and its implications for Latin America, in S. Mainwaring and T. Scully (eds.), *Democratic Governance in Latin America*, Stanford: Stanford University Press

Rodríguez, F., and D. Rodrik (2001), Trade policy and economic growth: a skeptic's guide to the cross-national evidence, in B. Bernanke and K. Rogoff (eds.), *NBER Macroeconomics Annual 2000*, Cambridge, MA: National Bureau of Economic Research

Rodriguez-Clare, A. (1996), The division of labor and economic development, *Journal of Development Economics* 49: 3–32

Rodrik, D. (1994), Getting interventions right: how South Korea and Taiwan grew rich, NBER Working Paper No. 4964

Rodrik, D. (1999), Where did all the growth go? External shocks, social conflict, and growth collapses, *Journal of Economic Growth* 4/4: 385–412

Rodrik, D. (2008) The real exchange rate and economic growth, *Brookings Papers on Economic Activity* 2: 365–412

Rodrik, D., A. Subramanian, and F. Trebbi (2004), Institutions rule: the primacy of institutions over geography and integration in economic development, *Journal of Economic Growth* 9/2: 131–65

Romer, P. M. (1986), Increasing returns and long-run growth, *Journal of Political Economy* 94: 1002–37

Romer, P. (1987), Growth based on increasing returns due to specialization, *American Economic Review* 77/2: 56–62

Romer, P. M. (1990), Capital, labor and productivity, *Brookings Papers on Economic Activity*, special issue: 337–67

Romer, P. M. (1990a), Endogenous technological change, *Journal of Political Economy* 98 (part 2): 71–102

Romer, P. M. (1991), Increasing returns and new developments in the theory of growth, in W. Barnett (ed.), *Equilibrium Theory and Applications: Proceedings of the 6th International Symposium in Economic Theory and Econometrics*, Cambridge: Cambridge University Press

Romer, P. (1993), Idea gaps and object gaps in economic development, *Journal of Monetary Economics* 32: 543–73

Romer, P. M. (1994), The origins of endogenous growth, *The Journal of Economic Perspectives* 8: 3–22

Romer, P. (1995), Comment on Mankiw, *Brookings Papers on Economic Activity* 1: 275–326

Ros, J. (1987), Mexico from the oil boom to the debt crisis: an analysis of policy responses to external shocks, 1978–1985, in Rosemary Thorp and Laurence Whitehead (eds.), *Latin American Debt and the Adjustment Crisis*, Oxford: Macmillan Press

Ros, J. (1991), La movilidad del capital y la eficacia de la política con una corrida del crédito, *El Trimestre Económico* 58: 561–88 (English version (1992): Capital mobility and policy effectiveness under a credit run: the Mexican economy in the 1980s, in T. Banuri and J. Schor (eds.), *Financial Openness and National Autonomy*, New York: Oxford University Press)

Ros, J. (1993), Inflación inercial y conflicto distributivo, in J. Ros (ed.), *La Edad de Plomo del Desarrollo Latinoamericano*, México: Fondo de Cultura Económica

Ros, J. (1993a), Aspectos macroeconómicos de la estabilización heterodoxa, in J. Ros (ed.), *La Edad de Plomo del Desarrollo Latinoamericano*, México: Fondo de Cultura Económica

Ros, J. (1994), Fiscal and foreign exchange constraints on growth, in A. Dutt (ed.), *New Directions in Analytical Political Economy*, Cheltenham and Northampton, MA: Elgar

Ros, J. (2000), *Development Theory and the Economics of Growth*, Michigan: University of Michigan Press

Ros, J. (2000), Employment, structural adjustment and sustainable growth in Mexico, *Journal of Development Studies* 36/4: 100–19

Ros, J. (2012), Latin America: institutional convergence and growth divergence, UNAM, forthcoming

Ros, J. (2013), Latin America's trade and growth patterns, the China factor, and Prebisch's nightmare, *Journal of Globalization and Development*, forthcoming

Ros J., and P. Skott (1998), Dynamic effects of trade liberalization and currency overvaluation under conditions of increasing returns, *The Manchester School of Economic and Social Studies* 66, September: 4

Rosenstein-Rodan, P. (1943), Problems of industrialization in Eastern and South-Eastern Europe, *Economic Journal* 53: 202–11

Rosenstein-Rodan, P. (1961), Notes on the theory of the big push, in H. Ellis (ed.), *Economic Development for Latin America*, Proceedings of a Conference held by the IEA, New York: St. Martin's Press

Rosenstein-Rodan, P. (1984), Natura facit saltum: analysis of the disequilibrium growth process, in G. Meier and D. Seers (eds.), *Pioneers in Development*, New York: Oxford University Press

Ross, M. (1999), The political economy of the resource curse, *World Politics* 51: 297–322

Rowthorn, R. (1979), A note on Verdoorn's law, *Economic Journal* 89: 131–33

Rowthorn, R., and R. Kozul-Wright (1998), Globalization and economic convergence: an assessment, UNCTAD Discussion Papers 131 (February)

Sachs, J. (2000), Tropical Underdevelopment, CID Working Paper, December

Sachs, J. (2005), The *End of Poverty: Economic Possibilities for Our Time*, New York: Penguin Press

Sachs, J. (2012), Government, geography and growth, *Foreign Affairs* September/October

Sachs, J. D., and A. M. Warner (1995), Natural resource abundance and economic growth, National Bureau of Economic Research Working Paper No. 5398 (December)

Sachs, J. D., and A. M. Warner (1995a), Economic reform and the process of global integration, *Brookings Papers on Economic Activity* 1: 1–118

Sachs, J. D., and A. M. Warner (1997), Fundamental sources of long-run growth, *American Economic Review* 87, May: 184–8

Sachs, J. D., and A. M. Warner (2001), The curse of natural resources, *European Economic Review* 45: 827–38

Sandilands, R. (2000), Perspectives on Allyn Young in theories of endogenous growth, *Journal of the History of Economic Thought* 22: 309–28

Sarkar, P. (1998), The catching-up debate: a statistical investigation, The Helen Kellogg Institute for International Studies Working Paper No. 252 (April), University of Notre Dame

Schumpeter, J. (1942, 1950), *Capitalism, Socialism, and Democracy*. Third edition, New York: Harper and Brothers

Scitovsky, T. (1954), Two concepts of external economies, *Journal of Political Economy* 62: 143–51

Scully, G. (1988), The institutional framework and economic development, *Journal of Political Economy* 86/3: 652–62

Segerstrom, P., T. Anant, and E. Dinopoulos (1990), A Schumpeterian model of the product life cycle, *American Economic Review* 80: 1077–92

Sen, A. (1966), Peasants and dualism with or without surplus labor, *Journal of Political Economy* 74: 425–50

Sen, A. (ed.) (1970), *Growth Economics*, Middlesex: Penguin Books

Sheehey, E. J. (1996), The growing gap between rich and poor countries: a proposed explanation, *World Development* 24: 1379–84

Skott, P., and J. Ros (1997), The 'big push' in an open economy with non tradable inputs, *Journal of Post Keynesian Economics* 20: 149–62

References

Smith, A. (1976 [1776]), *An Inquiry into the Nature and Causes of the Wealth of Nations.* E. Cannan edition, New York: G. P. Putnam's Sons, 1904

Solow, R. M. (1956), A contribution to the theory of economic growth, *Quarterly Journal of Economics* 70: 65–94

Solow, R. (1979), Another possible source of wage stickiness, *Journal of Macroeconomics* 1: 79–82

Solow, R. M. (1988), *Growth Theory: An Exposition*, Oxford: Oxford University Press

Solow, R. M. (1994), Perspectives on growth theory, *The Journal of Economic Perspectives* 8: 45–54

Spence, M. (2012), *The Next Convergence. The Future of Economic Growth in a Multispeed World*, New York: Farrar, Straus and Giroux

Srinivasan, T. N. (1994), Long run growth theories and empirics: anything new? Paper presented at the Endogenous Growth and Development Conference at the International School of Economic Research, University of Siena, July 3–9, Certosa di Pontignano, Siena, Italy

Srinivasan, T. N., and J. Bhagwati (1999), Outward-orientation and development: are revisionists right?, Economic Growth Center, Yale University, Center Discussion Paper n. 806

Steindl, J. (1952), *Maturity and Stagnation in American Capitalism,* Oxford: Basil Blackwell

Stewart, F., and E. Ghani (1992), Externalities, development, and trade, in G. Helleiner (ed.), *Trade Policy, Industrialization, and Development,* New York: Oxford University Press

Stiglitz, J. (1976), The efficiency wage hypothesis, surplus labor and the distribution of labor in LDCs, *Oxford Economic Papers,* 28: 185–207

Stiglitz, J. (1992), Comment on "Toward a Counter-Counterrevolution in Development Theory" by Krugman, in *Proceedings of the World Bank Annual Conference on Development Economics, 1992,* Supplement to The World Bank Economic Review and The World Bank Research Observer, Washington, DC

Stolper, W., and P. A. Samuelson (1941), Protection and real wages, *Review of Economic Studies* 9: 58–73

Summers, R., and A. Heston (1984), Improved international comparisons of real product and its composition, 1950–1980, *Review of Income and Wealth* 30: 207–62

Summers, R., and A. Heston (1988), A new set of international comparisons of real product and price levels estimates for 130 countries, 1950–85, *Review of Income and Wealth* 34: 1–26

Sunkel, O. (1958), La inflación chilena: Un enfoque heterodoxo, *El Trimestre Económico* 25: 570–99. English translation (1960), Inflation in Chile: an unorthodox approach, *International Economic Papers* 10: 107–31

Swan, T. W. (1955), Longer-run problems of the balance of payments, in H. W. Arndt and W. M. Corden (eds.), *The Australian Economy: A Volume of Readings,* Melbourne: Cheshire Press

Swan, T. W. (1956), Economic growth and capital accumulation, *Economic Record* 66: 334–61

Swan, T. W. (1963), Growth models: of golden ages and production functions, in K. Berrill (ed.), *Economic Development with Special Reference to East Asia*, New York: Macmillan and St. Martin's Press

Syrquin, M. (1986), Productivity growth and factor reallocation, in H. Chenery, S. Robinson, and M. Syrquin (eds.), *Industrialization and Growth: A Comparative Study*, New York: Oxford University Press

Tavares, M. C., and J. Serra (1971), Más allá del estancamiento: una discusión sobre el estilo de desarrollo reciente, *El Trimestre Económico* 33: 905–50

Taylor, L. (1981), South-North trade and Southern growth: bleak prospects from a structuralist point of view, *Journal of International Economics* 11: 589–602

Taylor, L. (1983), *Structuralist Macroeconomics: Applicable Models for the Third World*, New York: Basic Books

Taylor, L. (1981), South-North trade and Southern growth: bleak prospects from a structuralist point of view, *Journal of International Economics* 11: 589–602

Taylor, L., and P. Arida (1988), Long-run income distribution and growth, in H. Chenery and T. N. Srinivisan (eds.), *Handbook of Development Economics*, vol. 1, Amsterdam, The Netherlands: Elsevier

Taylor, L, and E. L. Bacha (1976), The unequalizing spiral: a first growth model for Belindia, *Quarterly Journal of Economics* 90: 187–219

Taylor, Lance (1985), A stagnationist model of economic growth, *Cambridge Journal of Economics* 9: 383–403

Taylor, Lance (1991), *Income Distribution, Inflation and Growth: Lectures on Structuralist Macroeconomic Theory*, Cambridge, MA: MIT Press

Temple, J. (1999), The new growth evidence, *Journal of Economic Literature* 37/1: 112–56

Temple, J., and L. Wobmann (2006), Dualism and cross-country growth regressions, *Journal of Economic Growth* 11/3: 187–228

Thirlwall, A. (1979), The balance of payments constraint as an explanation of international growth rate differences, *Banca Nazionale del Lavoro* 32/128: 45–53

Thirlwall, A., and M. N. Hussain (1982), The balance of payments constraint, capital flows and growth rate differences between developing countries, *Oxford Economic Papers* 34/3: 498–510

Thirlwall, A. P. (1983), A plain man's guide to Kaldor's laws, *Journal of Post Keynesian Economics* 5: 345–58

Tornell, A., and P. Lane (1999), The voracity effect, *American Economic Review* 89/1: 22–46

Toynbee, A. (1934), *A Study of History*, Oxford: Oxford University Press

UNCTAD (1997), *Trade and Development Report*, New York and Geneva: United Nations

UNDP (several years), *Human Development Report*, New York: Oxford University Press

United Nations (1950), *The Economic Development of Latin America and its Principal Problems*, New York: United Nations

Vandenbussche, J., P. Aghion, and C. Meghir (2006), Growth, distance to frontier and composition of human capital, *Journal of Economic Growth* 11: 97–127

Vega, M. (2005), *La Reforma Laboral: Un Análisis Comparado*, Lima: ILO Regional Office for Latin America and the Caribbean

References

Verdoorn, P. J. (1949), Fattori che regolano lo sviluppo della produttivita del lavoro (Factors governing the growth of labor productivity), *L'Industria* 1: 3–10 (English translation by Thirlwall, A. P. and G. Thirlwall (1979) in *Research in Population and Economics*)

Verspagen, B. (1991), A new empirical approach to catching up or falling behind, *Structural Change and Economic Dynamics* 2/2: 359–80

Viner, J. (1931), Cost curves and supply curves, *Zeitschrift fur Nationalokonomie* 3: 23–46 (Reprinted in American Economic Association (1953), *Readings in Price Theory*, London: Allen & Unwin)

Wade, R. (1990), *Governing the Market: Economic Theory and the Role of Government in East Asian Industrialization*, Princeton, NJ: Princeton University Press

Wan, H. Y. Jr. (1971), *Economic Growth*, New York: Harcourt Brace Jovanovich

Watkins, M. H. (1963), A staple theory of economic growth, *Canadian Journal of Economics and Political Science* 29: 141–58

Weil, D. (2009), *Economic Growth*. Second edition, Boston: Pearson, Addison Wesley

Williamson, J. (1993), Human capital deepening, inequality, and demographic events along the Asia-Pacific Rim, in N. Ogawa, G.W. Jones, and J. Williamson (eds.), *Human Resources in Development along the Asia-Pacific Rim*, Singapore: Oxford University Press

Williamson, J. G. (1991), *Inequality, Poverty, and History*, Cambridge, MA: Basil Blackwell

World Bank (2005), *Economic Growth in the 1990s: Learning from a Decade of Reform*, Washington: The World Bank

Yavas, A. (1998), Does too much government investment retard economic development of a country? *Journal of Economic Studies* 25/4: 296–308

You, J.-I. (1994), Macroeconomic structure, endogenous technical and growth, *Cambridge Journal of Economics* 18: 213–33

Young, A. (1928), Increasing returns and economic progress, *Economic Journal* 38: 527–42

Young, A. (1992), A tale of two cities: factor accumulation and technical change in Hong Kong and Singapore, in O. Blanchard and S. Fischer (eds.), *NBER Macroeconomics Annual*, London and Cambridge: MIT Press, 13–54

Young, A. (1995), The tyranny of numbers: confronting the statistical realities of the East Asian growth experience, *Quarterly Journal of Economics* 110: 641–80

Index

Index